HANDBOOK ON
Communicating
and **Disseminating**
Behavioral Science

HANDBOOK ON
Communicating
and Disseminating
Behavioral Science

Melissa K. Welch-Ross
George Mason University

Lauren G. Fasig
University of Florida

SAGE Publications
Los Angeles • London • New Delhi • Singapore

For information:

Sage Publications, Inc.
2455 Teller Road
Thousand Oaks, California 91320
E-mail: order@sagepub.com

Sage Publications Ltd.
1 Oliver's Yard
55 City Road
London EC1Y 1SP
United Kingdom

Sage Publications India Pvt. Ltd.
B 1/I 1 Mohan Cooperative Industrial Area
Mathura Road, New Delhi 110 044
India

Sage Publications Asia-Pacific Pte. Ltd.
33 Pekin Street #02-01
Far East Square
Singapore 048763

Printed in the United States of America

Library of Congress Cataloging-in-Publication Data

Handbook on communicating and disseminating behavioral science/edited
by Melissa K. Welch-Ross and Lauren G. Fasig.
    p. cm.
Includes bibliographical references and index.
ISBN 978-1-4129-4030-6 (cloth: alk. paper)
ISBN 978-1-4129-4031-3 (pbk.: alk. paper)
    1. Psychology—Study and teaching. I. Welch-Ross, Melissa. II. Fasig, Lauren G.

BF77.H27 2007
300.7—dc22   2007014600

This book is printed on acid-free paper.

07   08   09   10   11   10   9   8   7   6   5   4   3   2   1

Acquiring Editor:	Cheri Dellelo
Editorial Assistant:	Lara Grambling
Production Editor:	Astrid Virding
Copy Editor:	Gillian Dickens
Typesetter:	C&M Digitals (P) Ltd.
Proofreader:	Joyce Li
Indexer:	Kathy Paparchontis
Cover Designer:	Janet Foulger
Marketing Manager:	Amberlyn Erzinger

Contents

PART V. DISSEMINATING BEHAVIORAL SCIENCE TO SERVICE PROFESSIONS

Acknowledgments

We thank the Office of Behavioral and Social Sciences Research of the National Institutes of Health and its deputy director, Deborah Olster, for funding the journalists who wrote about television news, magazines, newspapers, and national public radio for Part II. We're grateful to Sarah Brookhardt at the Association for Psychological Science, Larry Giannino at Tufts University, and Patricia Miller at the University of Georgia for giving feedback on our book proposal. We also thank Michele Garfinkle at the J. Craig Venter Institute in Rockville, Maryland, and Dan Sarewitz at the Consortium for Science, Policy & Outcomes at Arizona State University for the work and conversations that helped to shape our discussion of social technologies and science policy. We thank the authors for their patience and collegial spirit as we worked through iterations of the chapters, as well as our families, whose support made producing the book possible.

A singular felicity of induction guided all his researches and by very small means he established very grand truths. The style and manner of his publication are almost as worthy of admiration as the doctrine it contains. He has endeavoured to remove all mystery and obscurity from the subject; he has written equally for the uninitiated and for the philosopher; and he has rendered his details amusing as well as perspicuous, elegant as well as simple. Science appears in his language in a dress wonderfully decorous, the best adapted to display her native loveliness. He has in no case exhibited that false dignity, by which philosophy is kept aloof from common applications, and he has sought rather to make her a useful inmate and servant in the common habitations of man, than to preserve her merely as an object of admiration in temples and palaces.

—Sir Humphry Davy (1778–1829),
English chemist and physicist,
on Benjamin Franklin

Introduction

MELISSA K. WELCH-ROSS AND LAUREN G. FASIG

Scientists have long tried, with varied success, to explain the value of their work and to help put their findings to some use. Since the World Wars, and especially since President Johnson promoted his Great Society vision for the nation, behavioral scientists in particular have tried to use science-based innovations (knowledge, interventions, tools, and other technologies) to influence policy, to inform and persuade through mass media, and to improve vital services in society. After some turning away from the behavioral sciences in the 1980s, legislators, government agencies, service providers, advocacy groups, and private foundations increasingly seek to use the research to inform their decisions and practices. They are motivated at least in part by the wish to know whether the resources put into relieving society's problems and improving its health and well-being are producing the desired results and, if not, what more could be done. Many organizations also want to know, as do individual scientists, whether investments made in communicating science to policy makers, mass media, and others lead to taking up the science and using it in ways that benefit the public.

Despite this history and increasing demand for science-based approaches, researchers can lack realistic ideas about what communicating and disseminating science entails. They are not necessarily to be blamed. Developing the essential knowledge, skills, and perspectives—or even imparting a basic awareness of what the work involves—is not part of most behavioral science training. In fact, no entity in particular has been especially prepared for studying, planning, conducting, and evaluating the communication and dissemination of behavioral science, or for training future generations of behavioral researchers to understand or do the work. As noted by Carol Weiss, a foremost scholar on the topic, dissemination has been nobody's job.

Yet, enough has been learned so that scientists need not put their efforts together willy-nilly. Much has been published on methods of delivering science-based innovations to policy, mass media, and service professions; the barriers encountered and how they might be removed; the qualities of science that make it worthy of disseminating in the first place; advances needed to research on dissemination and communication; the challenges unique to behavioral science; and so on. But all of this scholarship is strewn through the literatures of psychology, anthropology, journalism, science communications, public health, nursing, mental health, education, business, law, philosophy, science policy, and social policy, among others. To us, it seemed time to

1

integrate some of this knowledge and insight into one volume to support those interested in knowing about and doing the work. In fact, as one reviewer of our book proposal said, it is hard to believe that the book wasn't already written.

OUR APPROACH

Our goal was not to comprehensively review all that has been offered or to include every discipline or profession that has something useful to say on the subject. Rather, we aimed for a coherent picture of what communicating and disseminating behavioral science involves—the main actors, issues, contemporary approaches, challenges, types of research, and broader conditions that influence if and how it occurs. And so we asked an interdisciplinary group of experts to describe relevant scholarship and practice and to present their informed perspectives to help readers gain insight into the complex web of ideas, concerns, activities, relationships, and environments that make up the work. Contributors include behavioral scientists from academia and government; scholars from journalism, science communication, and health policy; professional communicators from a university, scientific society, and national social issue campaign; journalists and editors from television, print, and radio; and representatives of think tanks and advocacy organizations.

Many of the topics that appear have complexities that could not possibly have been covered even in a book of this size. Some relevant disciplines—mass communications, advertising, marketing, health promotion, health communications, organization science, social marketing, program evaluation, and so on—are not discussed in detail. Only recently have diverse policy, research, and service organizations in the United States, Canada, and abroad begun to undertake the tremendous task of surveying these and other literatures and distilling principles to be applied and tested in their efforts to support various uses of scientific research. Such initiatives mark what seems to be the beginning of a new age for both communication and dissemination research and practice. We've offered therefore an appendix of related resources for readers who seek broader and more detailed information.

A FEW ANCHORING DEFINITIONS

Though readers and chapter authors may quarrel over some of them, we offer definitions of key terms, derived from our reading of the relevant literatures and from the usages of the chapter authors, to help clarify the scope of the book.

Dissemination of behavioral science refers to the spreading of innovations from science to promote widespread awareness, understanding, and use. Though often used interchangeably with *diffusion,* many now associate diffusion with passive spreading that is spontaneous, unsystematic, slow, and unreliable. Common examples are presenting research in academic journals or at conferences or issuing press releases followed only by hoping that someone "out there" is picking up the findings. Dissemination, in contrast, is becoming associated with using more active, planned methods of promoting the initial widespread use of science innovations, helping users adapt them to meet local needs, and supporting sustained use.

In practice, *science communication* refers to the particular strategies and approaches used to convey information from scientific research, as well as about how to use science-based innovations or about the scientific enterprise (for example, how science progresses toward knowledge and is administered). It ranges from large-scale social marketing campaigns that promote messages derived from science, to an advocate's use of science to influence policy makers' opinions, to the development and evaluation of museum exhibits.

The academic discipline of science communication is a broad and emerging area of scholarship. Some of its main concerns are the public's understanding of science, how science is delivered to and received by different audiences, the role of science in society, and the relationship between scientists and science communicators. Science journalism has tended to receive much attention from scholars given that it is part of mass media. The field is just beginning to describe ways of communicating science for particular audiences and purposes and the results. Most agree that the academic study of science communication could benefit from being more tightly linked to the study of communications more generally and to the practice of communicating science.

Some readers might consider dissemination to be the higher-order category, others may view communication to be the broader one, and still others may see no real difference between the two. In this book, communication is discussed mainly as being in the service of dissemination. Messages are communicated—to the public, mass media, policy makers, service providers, administrators, and so on—and ideas are exchanged to make the findings and other products of science widely available and to support their appropriate use.

Knowledge transfer, sometimes used interchangeably with *dissemination,* refers to moving knowledge, practices, and technologies within and between organizations. It includes conveying the attitudes, knowledge, and skills required for delivering and receiving these innovations to meet particular goals. Though sometimes used synonymously with *training* (e.g., guided experience, train-the-trainer programs, simulation, guided experimentation, work shadowing, paired work), in research dissemination, the term encompasses a wider range of activities, such as producing and presenting research syntheses to inform policy making and service delivery; writing plain-language summaries of research results tailored to the goals and audience; equipping professionals in law, medicine, mental health, policy, and so on to recognize research that is sound and relevant to their fields; establishing relationships with the potential users of science to better understand their needs and work settings; and developing research agendas, both basic and applied, that can work toward basic understandings and products that help solve pressing problems.

Knowledge utilization refers to using innovations from science, but it goes beyond the mere taking up of information—considering research in a policy decision, deciding to use an evidence-based mental health intervention, or producing a news report on a recent research finding. It also encompasses how the research is used and with what outcome—selecting a policy option most consistent with the research that, in turn, ends up helping the public; implementing a mental health intervention as it was intended to be delivered that, in turn, improves mental health and practical life outcomes; and news reporting that is accurate and also perceived by the audience to be informative and useful. Because promoting uptake is much easier to do and to measure than determining how the research was used to produce certain results, many experts agree that these distinctions should be made when setting goals for dissemination and developing plans to evaluate its effect.

Knowledge exchange is a relatively newer term being used to encompass both knowledge transfer and knowledge utilization. It emerged to capture the bidirectional communications between those who transfer the knowledge and those who use it and which are critical to making it more likely that innovations from science will be understood, used, and valued.

Many of the chapters discuss changes to various types of research that could advance dissemination. In these discussions, basic behavioral and social research refers to understanding the causes and conditions of psychological or social phenomena without having specific applications in mind. *Applied research* covers studies to produce new understandings for meeting a recognized need. It includes *translational research* to develop knowledge from basic science into new interventions, small- and large-scale studies to assess intervention outcomes (usually referred to as *efficacy and effectiveness studies,* respectively), and *evaluation research,* a term used mainly in policy or service settings to refer to assessing the results of a services program, policy, or communications strategy.

Any research, including basic science experiments, that intervenes to change the thoughts, behaviors, or conditions of those participating in research studies qualifies as intervention. But the type of *intervention research* most relevant to this book is that which uses scientific methods to develop and evaluate the effectiveness of practices, programs, and tools to meet the needs of particular individuals, groups, systems, or settings.

Transportability research, one type of translational research, helps prepare the interventions found to be effective under tightly controlled experiments for implementation in the broader settings, where they will actually be used. It carefully specifies the intervention components and implementation procedures along with any materials needed for delivery and training. It specifies who can deliver the intervention effectively and under which conditions. Most agree that some amount of transportability research should occur in the context of large-scale effectiveness studies before attempting broad dissemination. Innovations that are disseminated prematurely often end up not fitting people's

circumstances and needs and potentially "poison the waters" not only for a particular intervention but for the entire idea of using empirically validated information and approaches (Schoenwald & Hoagwood, 2001).

Implementation refers to the collection of actions to be taken by "front-line" users, such as clinicians and community service providers, to deliver a science-based practice or program or to use a particular tool. *Implementation research* specifies these actions and, especially in large-scale implementation studies, ideally investigates the broader conditions that affected whether implementation occurred as intended and produced the desired results. Thus, implementation research is one part of investigating transportability and so is also considered translational research.

Dissemination research investigates how to promote the widespread use of innovations from science. It identifies and evaluates approaches for encouraging awareness, understanding and uptake of innovations, and how to put the conditions in place for sustained use. Until recently, dissemination research was not a priority of the scientific enterprise and not widely regarded as scientific work. Though some studies might include a dissemination component, plans to evaluate dissemination have not been routinely solicited or made, and innovations from science, including interventions for mental health, drug use prevention, and so on, traditionally have not been developed and tested with particular dissemination objectives in mind.

TWO ORGANIZING THEMES

This book discusses many complexities involved in brokering science to diverse audiences, whether the broker is a scientist or an intermediary—a federal agency, private foundation, university public information official, think tank or advocacy organization, a technical assistance center, the mass media, or one of the growing numbers of issue networks and coalitions. The authors also give many specific suggestions about how to approach communicating and disseminating behavioral science.

These individual strands of knowledge and insight can be tied together with two main principles: One must have a strategy for dissemination, and one must understand the context in which dissemination occurs, especially if barriers are to be removed that affect whether findings from behavioral science move efficiently and effectively beyond the academic community.

Strategy

We've borrowed, and somewhat modified, a knowledge exchange framework proposed by John Lavis, a leader in the use of research in health practice and policy, to emphasize that supporting the use of behavioral research requires a strategy with five main parts (Lavis et al., 2003).

What should be transferred? What science is ready to use—what knowledge is sufficiently developed, sound, and relevant to the purpose? What messages are appropriate and consistent with the science? What interventions, tools, and other technologies are ready to deliver? Methods and mechanisms must be created to help answer these questions, and if the appropriate "what" is not being produced, solutions are needed to further develop it.

To whom should these be transferred? The possibilities tend to include the broader public or service recipients (for example, citizens, patients, and clients), service providers (such as clinicians, journalists, and attorneys), and decision makers (for example, managers and administrators in hospitals, private business, and community organizations; media journalists, producers, and

editors; and policy makers at federal, state, and local levels). The messages and materials must be sufficiently tailored in format and content, delivering the particular findings that each audience will care about given that each has its own concerns. But one initial basic step, so basic perhaps that it has often been overlooked, is to thoroughly understand the audience—its needs, roles, circumstances, knowledge, motivations, values, beliefs, ways of interpreting and processing information from science, and so on. In this way, messengers can relay better messages and plan strategies to help audiences take up the science and use it with the desired outcome.

By whom should these be transferred? The options are the individual scientist or one or more intermediaries. Issues to consider are as follows: Who has the knowledge, skills, credibility, and relationships to be a powerful messenger or an effective technician in helping others to use a particular innovation? And if any of these prerequisites is lacking, whether in the scientist or the intermediary, how might these be developed?

By what methods should transfer occur? What venues, materials, and procedures are most appropriate? Some of the options, depending on the audience and what is to be transferred, might include various methods of offering training and technical assistance, policy maker briefings, "collaboratives" that bring together all of those with a stake in an issue to plan how dissemination might be achieved and how implementation will occur, interviews with targeted or mass media, roundtable discussions, personal meetings with policy makers or program administrators, executive summaries, lists of evidence-based interventions and measures, evidence-based clinical guidelines, policy changes to encourage use of evidence-based practices, and so on.

With what effect? What is the goal of the exchange? Is it to promote awareness of a new finding or the scientific process? Is it to change attitudes about an issue or practice? Is it to modify an organizational climate, change a policy debate, or somehow affect a particular policy or journalistic practice? How should the results be evaluated? What outcomes can be measured? Which parts of the approach worked, and which did not? How can this information be used to make improvements? Despite being mentioned last, most agree that, though it rarely happens, goals for dissemination should be clearly defined from the beginning along with plans to evaluate whether the goals were achieved.

This book assumes that some degree of strategy is needed whether the dissemination is a complex, large-scale collaboration among various organizations or a more modest undertaking by an individual scientist. But before embarking on any effort to disseminate science, many scholars recommend that the scientists who participate become aware of the values, beliefs, and other preconceptions that affect the kind of research they do and their motivations for wanting to disseminate the science. Though scientists strive for the ideal of complete objectivity, in reality, they tend to align themselves, and their science, to varying degrees with particular groups and agendas. Some believe this approach enables scientists to be even more effective, though it has consequences for their ability to operate broadly as powerful messengers. And so, as suggested by one political science and communications expert, it can behoove scientists, and the science, to consider and then choose where one's attempts to communicate and disseminate science will fall on the continuum from "activist science" to "objectivist science" or, in other words, from advocate to neutral knowledge broker (Bimber, 1996).

Context

Figure 1 applies ecological systems theory, originally conceived to describe individual human development (Brofenbrenner, 1979), to understanding how forces in four nested systems—the microsystem (forces in the scientist's immediate environment), the mesosystem (interactions between two microsystem forces), the exosystem (forces affecting the micro- or mesosystems) and the macrosystem (systems making up the environment in which all the other systems operate)—interact to affect how, or if, the individual scientist contributes to the effective use of science. The model assumes bidirectional interactions among the forces within and between levels, and the element of time speaks to how change or stagnancy in the forces or in their interactions supports or thwarts attempts to disseminate behavioral research.

At the individual level, for example, scientists must be personally motivated to disseminate behavioral research. Some of the most common motivations contain varying degrees of public and self-interest:

- A personal desire to identify and help solve significant problems about which behavioral science does or could have something to offer
- A perceived professional and ethical responsibility to be good stewards of science by shepherding the effective use of research and preventing misuse and misrepresentation
- A perceived obligation to justify to society how public funds have been used by answering the following: What was bought? Who needs it? What's the point?
- A belief that greater public understanding of behavioral research leads to increased public support, funding, and the growth of the field
- A belief in the Jeffersonian ideal that creating an educated public is essential to an informed democracy and that governing bodies need access to expert advice (without supplanting the public's need to be directly informed and knowledgeable)
- A belief in the inherent value of an educated public to improving the quality of individual and collective life

But researchers can also hesitate to become involved because they fear that disseminating research might harm their reputations in the scientific community. Some believe that, being a relatively young science, most behavioral science is "not ready" for mass media, policy, or any particular purpose or that science generally is never quite ready because it is continually evolving and inherently uncertain. Researchers who support dissemination often think, quite mistakenly, that others "out there" already have been sufficiently trained to identify, understand, and use the appropriate evidence-based programs, tools, and research findings.

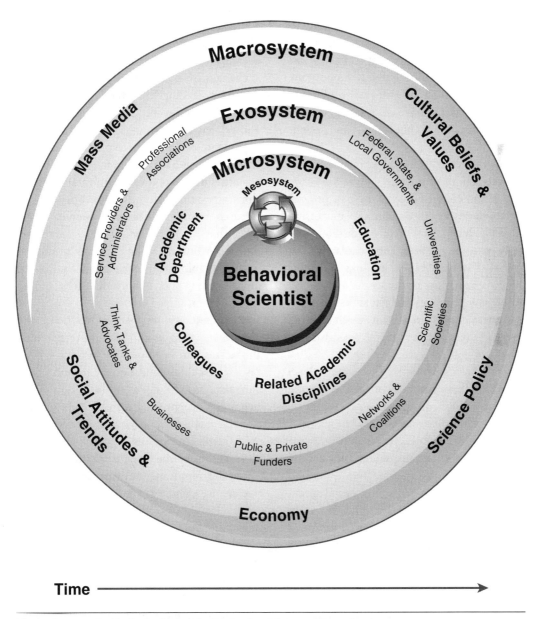

Figure 1   An Ecological Model of Behavioral Science Dissemination

SOURCE: Inspired by Fabes, Martin, Hanish, and Updegraff (2000).

Still, even the personally motivated scientists will encounter forces, many of which are presented in Figure 1, that affect whether they have the essential preparation and support to do the work. To scratch the surface:

Scientists are affected by whether the essential *graduate and postgraduate education* can be found to develop the knowledge, skills, and perspectives needed for disseminating science, whether in the form of graduate courses, postgraduate applied training, or professional development opportunities. If in the academy, scientists benefit from *academic departments* that value, tangibly support, and reward dissemination and dissemination research, as well as from colleagues, including journal editors, who understand and support the work.

Whether or not this support can be found depends on the priorities of the *university* system and culture. Despite a bit of progress and some isolated exceptions, universities generally have not perceived dissemination to be part of research and scholarship but instead view it as service that ranks last among the main university priorities. As a result, relatively few resources are available for it, and it is not part of the work on which scientists are seriously evaluated, and so scientists tend not to see it as their responsibility.

Connections among the behavioral sciences and between behavioral science and *other academic disciplines* also affect the quality of the information and other products to be disseminated, as well as the level of understanding about dissemination itself that can be achieved.

Private foundations, federal agencies, and *scientific societies* deliver or otherwise influence the resources and infrastructure available for dissemination and for research to develop the theories, methods, and measures needed to more systematically develop and test the effectiveness of various approaches. These actors also influence the availability and quality of education and training for dissemination and communication practices and research. Their interactions with university leaders help to shape the priorities and expectations for academic departments and so the direction of individual scientists.

In many ways, the heart of effective dissemination is the relationships between scientists and potential users of the science—policy makers and their staffs in local, state, and federal governments; mass media producers, editors, and journalists; decision makers in service professions; community members and organizations; and so on. Written and spoken exchanges over time build mutual credibility and trust, leading to further productive collaborations and some level of informality that allows scientists to share nuances about the research and make recommendations in which the users have greater confidence. Scientists also take away from these relationships ideas that affect the direction of their research and approaches to disseminating it, goals that often can be mutually agreed on and coordinated. The scientist's success with dissemination depends on having the ability, time, and opportunity to establish these relationships.

Businesses, professional associations, and *consumer networks* can play powerful roles. Businesses can help develop products from research, such as educational curricula. They can also have a stake in the services that behavioral science helps to provide (educational, mental health, medical services, etc.). As a result, businesses may help to spread messages from the science, persuade others about the importance of evidence-based tools and services, and provide incentives for using them. Professional associations and consumer networks can help researchers learn about the needs and concerns of certain segments of the public and can help researchers educate those who could benefit from using scientific innovations.

Federal public policy and the surrounding politics offer many opportunities for behavioral scientists, but it also places constraints on how scientists can engage in policy making, whether operating directly or indirectly through intermediaries, and how productive their attempts will be. Both federal science policy and social policy can help to drive or influence the forces at each level with a role to play in dissemination. They can also be influenced to encourage the dissemination of science-based innovations and to support the production of useful dissemination research.

Differences in *culture* between the scientific community and forces at all levels can make scientists and relevant organizations reluctant to engage with one another or lead to negative experiences and poor outcomes. Diverging goals, values, skills, motivations, attitudes, communication styles, preferred sorts of evidence, demands of the work setting, and so on must somehow be bridged. Additional challenges present themselves when the larger culture holds beliefs and values, or contains social attitudes and trends, that its members perceive to contradict scientific findings and methods or prevent them from becoming knowledgeable about science generally or about the methods and innovations of behavioral science in particular.

We return to these two themes of strategy and context in the concluding chapter to organize a discussion of the book's major themes and authors' proposals for the future.

BOOK OUTLINE

This volume has five parts. Part I, Some Conceptual and Practical Issues, begins with a selected history of behavioral science dissemination, some lessons learned from that history, and a proposal for advancing dissemination through "collaboratives." The second chapter contributed by science communication scholars describes the academic discipline and highlights contemporary themes of the research. It also points to the need for scholars, including behavioral and social scientists, to undertake programmatic research to identify effective approaches and strategies for communicating science. Chapters 3 and 4, contributed by journalism scholars, present insights from research and practice on the conditions that affect how, or whether, behavioral science gets covered in the mass media. They discuss strengths and weaknesses in behavioral science reporting, the challenges of reporting behavioral research as news given the complexities and uncertainties of science, and ways that scientists might affect the quality and amount of behavioral science coverage.

Chapter 5 uses illustrations from social psychology to explain the qualities of basic science that affect its usefulness, as well as the challenges of writing and talking about basic science to nonscientist audiences. Chapter 6 explains the barriers that universities present to dissemination and reviews recent perspectives on how the work might become better integrated into university scholarship and science.

In Part II, Understanding Mass Media Priorities and Processes, journalists and editors from television, print, and public radio explain the inner workings of news media and how they affect coverage of behavioral research. The authors explain how behavioral science tends to become part of news; describe the goals of journalists, producers, and editors; suggest opportunities for reaching members of the media and developing relationships that can affect the amount and quality of coverage; and give tips on how to present scientific research to members of the media.

Part III, Communicating With the Public, covers some of the main methods scientists use to communicate with public audiences. Chapter 11 explains from the perspective of a scientific association's communications officer some issues to consider when engaging with mass media, and it gives some of the basics of media interviews. In Chapter 12, researchers from developmental and educational psychology tell about their approach to popular speaking and writing, explain some of the challenges and rewards, and illustrate the contributions scientists can make by venturing outside the academy to learn about contemporary social issues and trends.

In Chapter 13, a leading university public communications expert explains the varied roles of public information officers, how they can support university scientists, and how scientists can build productive relationships with this critical intermediary between scientists and the media and broader public. In Chapter 14, behavioral researchers review research and share their expertise in using the Internet to promote awareness, understanding, and use of behavioral science.

Part IV, Communicating With Policy Makers, reviews scholarship, research, and practice relating to how behavioral science is delivered to and used by policy makers. In Chapter 15, a leading scholar of health policy and policy makers' use of research reviews the state of knowledge on how to make behavioral science valuable to policy makers. Chapter 16 focuses on federal public policy. It explains the critical importance of scientists' participation by illustrating how behavioral researchers have affected science policies vital to the field's interests and to public health. The chapter describes the knowledge and skills scientists should develop, opportunities to become part of policy making, and specific methods of engaging with Congress and the Executive Branch.

In Chapter 17, the director and the communications director of a large-scale, non-ideological national campaign to reduce teen pregnancy draw on their experiences working with state governments to discuss approaches to communicating research to policy makers at the state level and to

working across diverse interests to influence policy. In Chapter 18, a policy consultant and former legislative director describes the work of think tanks and advocacy organizations and how they use research to inform and affect policy.

Part V, Disseminating Behavioral Science to Service Professions, spotlights five fields: education, behavioral medicine, drug use prevention, mental health, and the military. These fields were selected to highlight contemporary approaches and themes in disseminating behavioral science and to illustrate particular challenges unique to each one. Authors cover, among other issues, the state of dissemination and dissemination research, the state of translational science, barriers typically encountered in dissemination, and suggestions for advancing dissemination research and practice.

As the outline makes clear, this book is not a "how-to" guide, though many of the chapters include "how-to" guidance. Instead, it helps to ground researchers in many of the relevant issues, practices, and research so they might get more mileage out of such "how-to" advice. "How to" has its place but, as many now realize, more than brief trainings and tutorials are needed to increase the effectiveness of the strategies and methods the field uses to communicate and disseminate science and for building a critical mass of scientists with the ability to help advance the field's approaches over time.

By the end of the volume, it should become even clearer, too, that *any* attempt at learning how to promote the awareness, understanding, and use of science, regardless of the discipline, *is* behavioral science. And so all such efforts present opportunities for behavioral researchers, no matter how basic or applied. The theories, knowledge, and tools developed in behavioral research can help all sciences thoroughly understand their audiences or potential users of the science, develop their communication strategies and approaches, create techniques and environments that support using innovations from science, and conduct evaluations to assess the quality and results of their work. One group of science policy scholars has referred to this type of work as developing the "social technologies" (Sarewitz, Foladori, Invernizzi, & Garfinkel, 2004) essential to advancing the use of innovations from science. In creating this volume, therefore, we were inspired by one fundamental idea: that discovering how best to communicate and disseminate behavioral science is itself a vital scientific enterprise, and great strides might be taken if, in some respect, it becomes every scientist's concern and ceases to be on the side of behavioral scientists' "real" jobs. We hope this book contributes to moving farther in that direction.

REFERENCES

Bimber, B. (1996). *The politics of expertise in congress: The rise and fall of the Office of Technology Assessment.* New York: SUNY Press.

Brofenbrenner, U. (1979). *The ecology of human development: Experiments by nature and design.* Cambridge, MA: Harvard University Press.

Fabes, R. A., Martin, C. L., Hanish, L. D., & Updegraff, K. A. (2000). Criteria for evaluating the significance of developmental research in the twenty-first century: Force and counterforce. *Child Development, 71*(1), 212–221.

Lavis, J. N., Robertson, D., Woodside, J. M., McLeod, C. B., Abelson, J., & the Knowledge Transfer Study Group. (2003). How can research organizations more effectively transfer knowledge to decision-makers? *The Milbank Quarterly, 81*(2), 221–248.

Sarewitz, D., Foladori, G., Invernizzi, N., & Garfinkel, M. S. (2004). Science policy in its social context. *Philosophy Today, 48*(Suppl.), 67–83.

Schoenwald, S. K., & Hoagwood, K. (2001). Effectiveness, transportability, and dissemination of interventions: What matters when? *Psychiatric Services, 52*(9), 1190–1197.

Part I

SOME CONCEPTUAL
AND PRACTICAL ISSUES

A Perspective on the History and Future of Disseminating Behavioral and Social Science

ROBERT B. MCCALL AND CHRISTINA J. GROARK

While timorous knowledge stands considering, audacious ignorance hath done the deed.

—Samuel Daniel, c. 1600

I can imagine nothing we could do that would be more relevant to human welfare, and nothing that could pose a greater challenge to the next generation of psychologists, than to discover how best to give psychology away.

—George A. Miller (1969, p. 1071)

Though not the first to promote dissemination, George A. Miller (1969), in his American Psychological Association (APA) presidential address, urged his colleagues "to give psychology away," by which he meant to disseminate the fruits of psychology's scholarly and practice endeavors to the general public, diverse practitioners, policy makers, and others who could use that information to improve human welfare. Nearly every candidate for the presidency of APA in the following two decades had a similar plank in their platform, but it was Miller's single phrase—"give psychology away"—that became the mantra for those who championed the cause of helping

AUTHORS' NOTE: This chapter was prepared with the partial support of grants to the University of Pittsburgh Office of Child Development from the Howard Heinz Endowment and the Richard King Mellon Foundation.

psychology and other social and behavioral sciences contribute to human welfare by communicating with diverse audiences.

But notice that Miller also issued a forecast that was less frequently remembered, that is, that dissemination would pose a great "challenge to the next generation of psychologists." Indeed, whereas the practice wing of psychology (mostly clinical therapists) was accustomed to directly contributing to human welfare, academic researchers were not. "Going public" was not something respectable scientists did (Goodfield, 1981). This attitude was captured in a *New Yorker* cartoon (Stevenson, 1977) portraying two dowdy scientists mulling over their relatively unproductive careers with the self-consoling justification, "One thing I'll say for us, Meyer, we never stooped to popularizing science." Miller was correct: "Giving psychology away" would be "challenging."

SOME LESSONS LEARNED AND STILL TO BE LEARNED

We've come a long way in the nearly four decades after Miller's (1969) clarion call, and this volume stands as testimony to that progress. Of course, it wasn't only Miller's admonition that created these changes; what other factors contributed to this progress?

A Selective History

To understand how far the field has come, it may help to place the contents of this volume against the backdrop of several, admittedly selected, scenes from the intellectual history of social and behavioral sciences (Groark & McCall, 2005).

From the Practical to Basic Research

Prior to the World Wars, the primary orientation of science and education was to contribute directly toward the welfare of students and society. Science was governed by the "doctrine of useful knowledge," which dictated that science would be supported if it contributed to accomplishing a societal goal (Byerly & Pielke, 1995; Smith, 1990). Correspondingly, higher education was oriented predominately toward training students for a profession or a job (Hathaway, Mulhollan, & White, 1995). Furthermore, the Morrill Act of 1862, the Hatch Act of 1887, and the Smith-Lever Act of 1914 created land-grant universities, which were to teach the practical aspects of agricultural and mechanical arts and create an "extension" of the university to disseminate such knowledge to citizens. Such dissemination was accomplished in part through substantial outreach in the form of extension offices in counties across the states from which agricultural and home economics information and technical assistance could be readily disseminated to the citizenry—in the beginning, primarily rural residents and farmers. University extensions still exist and have branched out to helping youth and urban families while continuing to be a crucial resource to the agricultural community.

However, this applied orientation changed after World War II. A "social contract" was informally adopted, which asserted that essentially all scientific knowledge was potentially useful, at least someday, implemented by someone, for some purpose (Bush, 1945; Byerly & Pielke, 1995), and thus basic science or "knowledge for knowledge's sake" emerged to head the list of academic values (Altman, 1995; Lynton, 1995; Whiting, 1968). As a result, science no longer needed to be immediately socially practical (Bush, 1945; Byerly & Pielke, 1995; England, 1982; Smith, 1990), and the U.S. government provided ample financial support for basic science in nearly all disciplines.

Psychology, in particular, perhaps more than the other social and behavioral sciences, subscribed wholeheartedly to the push for basic research. Bouncing off the philosophical and introspective approaches of its past, psychology aspired to be a truly "scientific" discipline. Consequently, chemistry and physics were invoked as models in the pursuit of discovering basic, generalizable, cause-and-effect laws that presumably govern much of human behavior. The principles of learning, for example, could be determined by studying narrow slices of behavior in highly constrained laboratory environments—rats (males only) running T mazes, pigeons pecking disks, and humans learning paired-associate words. The principles discovered in such research were presumed, at least tacitly, to be nearly universal, transcending the particulars of any situation or culture, and so there was no need to study the influences of context or the details of application. Even individual differences, such as gender, were not considered because it was assumed that most behavior by most organisms in most contexts would be similarly governed by the general behavioral principles.

To simulate chemistry and physics, the experimental method was adopted as the gold standard, especially controlled randomized experiments. The ideal results of such experiments over time would be an integrated set of theoretically derived and tested cause-and-effect principles that in turn would guide further research on the causes of behavior. And so constructing and testing theory to accumulate increasingly sophisticated knowledge, not generating answers to questions of more immediate practical concern to society, became the primary justification and rationale for conducting research.

The consequence of these postwar emphases was that almost all social and behavioral research was focused on discovering basic cause-and-effect laws through laboratory research using research methods that demanded extraordinary experimenter control over the entire process. At best, applied research was ignored; someday, application conducted by the hands of someone else would presumably follow from these highly generalizable basic principles. At worst, applied scholarship was denigrated as being less important and methodologically inferior or tainted, as well as limited to specific issues or programs and not addressing broad, general, cause-effect principles; even the study of individual differences in behavior was demeaned to be second class.

Political Threats

In the 1970s and 1980s, shortly after Miller's (1969) admonition, political criticism of the prevailing scientific value system, especially as exercised by the social and behavioral sciences, grew more vigorous. In 1975, for example, Senator William Proxmire of Wisconsin became frustrated with the federal government's financial support of what he deemed irrelevant basic research projects. He periodically bestowed a "golden fleece award" on researchers who conducted and the federal agencies that supported such scientific minutia. Proxmire's assault on what he felt was the most trivial basic research was the most visible manifestation of the pockets of political disaffection with the social contract for science, and it marked the beginning of the demise of the "golden age" of financial support for basic scientific research (Goodfield, 1981).

The political attacks came to a head in the most threatening manner when President Ronald Reagan and his director of the Office of Management and Budget, David Stockman, proposed to erase support for nearly all social and behavioral research from the federal budget. Suddenly, the entire livelihood of social and behavioral research was jeopardized, and disseminating the benefits of social and behavioral research as a means of convincing the government and the citizenry of the value of such research became necessary for the survival of the discipline. The task was made more difficult because of the emphasis on basic, theoretical research, often conducted on animals, which was perceived as less interesting and less relevant to the general public as well as to policy makers. Not surprisingly, the need for such communication continued in the years that followed as politicians periodically insisted that increasing amounts of federal research dollars be spent on achieving more directly *applied* national science and technology goals. Recently, for example, partly in response to congressional encouragement, "translational research" is being emphasized at the National Institutes of Health (NIH) to improve health and human services. Furthermore, lest scholars today chuckle in retrospect at the Reagan-Stockman annihilation attempt, attempts to politically murder social and behavior research have not stopped, most recently exemplified by Senator Kay Bailey Hutchison and others who proposed (but did not succeed) in eliminating social and behavioral sciences from the National Science Foundation (NSF) budget (e.g., Mervis, 2006).

Of all the sciences, why are the social and behavioral sciences the primary targets of political assassination? One reason is that the "soft" sciences are indeed "softer"—that is, less certain—and their methods and results are easy to criticize. Indeed, social and behavioral scientists themselves often end up contributing to the onslaught; they may be the one species in the scientific kingdom most willing to kill their own with criticism, as informally alleged by professionals at agencies such as the NIH and NSF who oversee reviews of grants from different disciplines.

Making the problem worse, most policy makers and intelligent laypersons are not equipped to debate quarks, neutrinos, and the intricacies of DNA, but the content of social and behavioral sciences seems much more commonplace, people trust their own experiences, and behavioral science loses credibility when personal experience contradicts the results of research. When research findings collide with political philosophy

(and personal values of almost any kind), research also loses. For example, the contemporary political value for abstinence as a method of preventing adolescent pregnancy trumps research demonstrating its limited effectiveness, so federal funds for abstinence programs continue to flow. Although the hard sciences are subject to the same political clashes (for example, stem cell research), it seems politically easier for all of the aforementioned reasons to threaten the social and behavioral than the biomedical sciences.

Signs of a New Era?

After years of being marginalized and threatened with extinction, suddenly social and behavioral research has become the coin of the practice and policy realms. This new value for research is reflected in the contemporary mandatory adjective of *evidence based* for nearly every viable practice and social policy. It would appear that in the past decade, the fortunes of social and behavioral science have undergone a nearly complete reversal, at least with respect to communicating research to policy makers and to professionals in various fields. What happened?

A Renewed Emphasis on Accountability

Policy makers have long desired "accountability" in the services they fund. But 20 years ago, community mental health and social services were unquestionably deemed inherently worthwhile by practitioners, and accountability consisted largely of how many people were served with what kind of services and how frequently. During the Great Society, in which a variety of new social programs were created and evaluated with randomized experiments, many of the services did not work, according to the research results. Although sometimes the evaluation rather than the program was shot dead as a result, some politicians remembered that it was not at all assured that social programs, however well intended, would actually be effective.

Consequently, as social problems, such as poverty, drug and alcohol problems, single-parent households, teen pregnancy, and violence, grew more prevalent relative to the available budget, policy makers and organizations that fund social services became more demanding that the services being provided indeed benefit the people receiving them. But they also grew more impatient with the prospect of funding a new service and having to wait 3 to 5 years or longer to find out whether the service produced the intended outcomes. The implicit reasoning therefore became the following: Let us replicate in our own locale those services that have been tried and demonstrated to be successful elsewhere, thus minimizing the risk that new services would not be effective and avoiding having to wait several years to discover this disappointing outcome. The policy and practice communities now demanded dissemination, albeit sometimes in a rather simplistic form; namely, they wanted to know which services and policies have been shown to be effective so these could be replicated elsewhere.

This new era of social and behavioral research as king presents a set of mixed blessings. On one hand, policy makers and practitioners as well as scholars should welcome the new emphasis on evidence. Presumably, the fruits of research will contribute to better programs, more efficient expenditure of funds, and improved human welfare. In addition, applied researchers are suddenly valued for what they can contribute to programs and policies ranging from school readiness to smoking cessation programs. Basic scientists also have been welcomed by policy makers and the media for a range of discoveries, from the abilities of infants to the new brain research.

On the other hand, all communities should be mindful of what they wish for. As scholars gain influence, the responsibility for providing solid, useful information in a balanced manner also increases. As evidence substantiating the effectiveness of practices and policies becomes the primary criterion for demonstrating their value, every practice and policy tends to get advertised glibly as "evidence based." This practice raises questions of what constitutes evidence and whether replicating successful programs is as reasonable a strategy as it initially appeared. In short, what should scholars be disseminating?

Replicating "Proven Programs"

The simplest expression of the evidence-based era is the tendency to replicate locally the same service program that was demonstrated elsewhere to have achieved beneficial outcomes for the participants. But this strategy of replicating "proven programs" in other domains often presents challenges for scholarship and dissemination that are frequently overlooked (Groark & McCall, 2005), specifically the following:

The "Proven Program" Must Exist

Obviously, one or more service strategies must have been tried and demonstrated with reasonable research methods to benefit participants with respect to the particular issue or social problem at hand. Such programming and evaluation evidence exists in some areas, such as the prevention of adolescent problem behavior, including school failure, risky sexual activity, substance abuse, delinquency, and violence (Weissberg & Kumpfer, 2003). But an arsenal of proven programs does not exist for most social needs.

The Service Program Is "Manualized"

Most program implementation and service procedures are not written down and packaged in sufficient detail so that others can implement the same program, and ironically, this situation is true even for service demonstration projects for which the primary intent is replicating services found to be successful. As a result, in some cases, we have evidence that the "program" is effective, but we are not certain what the "program" is.

All the Necessary Components for Success Are Identified

Even if a manual exists, does it contain instructions for creating all of the components necessary to make the replication equally effective as the initial demonstrations? The success of services often depends on elements that rarely have been systematically documented or tested, such as characteristics of the agency director and staff—their training, their motivation, their ability to form relationships with participants, and their commitment to and passion for the task, as well as the details of the procedures they follow. Service programs are known informally "not to travel well," perhaps because the initial enthusiasm of the program's creators and their skills are not duplicated when the program is implemented elsewhere with new staff. Also, procedures that worked in one locale with one staff and with a specific type of participant may not work well when these components change.

Will the Program Indeed Be "Replicated" in the New Locale?

Skilled practitioners are taught to tailor their services to the particular needs of their clients, and it is well known that even when a service program is specified in detail, it may be implemented differently across locales depending on the staff, clientele, local social and political circumstances, and other factors. Typically, such modifications are not documented or their influence evaluated, and thus they have unknown effects on the program's effectiveness.

What Constitutes Sufficient Evidence?

The most crucial and pervasive uncertainty in the evidence-based era is what constitutes evidence. Ideally, a simple set of criteria should be available that gives a grade to service programs indicating the persuasiveness of the research evidence that the program is effective. Such a scale has been offered (Biglan, Mrazek, Carnine, & Flay, 2003). It consists of a list of a few research methods in order of persuasiveness, and a program's "grade" is the rank of the method that was used in the most comprehensive research on the program. If randomized trials and replication studies support program effectiveness, this evidence would be the most persuasive. But this particular approach emphasizes some research methods (randomized trials, replication, time-series analyses) at the expense of others, and it does not take into consideration other types of information (e.g., effect size, cost-benefit ratios, or even simple costs) that are crucial to deciding whether to replicate the program. Some have offered a more comprehensive scheme based on standard principles of program evaluation (e.g., McCall, 2007).

Some Improvements

The question of what constitutes evidence is not only at the heart of deciding which programs to replicate, but it is central to deciding what information to disseminate more generally. For example, journalists often prefer to report the results of single research studies because a scholarly publication or conference presentation constitutes a "news" event. Similarly, practitioners and policy makers, who often rely on the media for research information, often latch onto the latest research or a single study that appears to meet their needs. But researchers know that "truth" tends to emerge from entire literatures of such single studies. How should such accumulated evidence be determined?

Consensus Groups

Traditionally, individual scholars review research literatures, mainly to advance science, but groups of scholars may be specifically charged with reviewing literatures on topics of great practical interest to society. The federal government (e.g., Centers for Disease Control and Prevention, 2006), the National Academy of Sciences, and some other private groups and foundations (e.g., Campbell Collaboration (C2); Cooper, 1998) have attempted to communicate social and behavioral research by adopting the biomedical practice of assembling groups of scientists to review the existing scientific literature and declare what should be done in practice. Typically, such reviews do not use a simple scheme for determining the persuasiveness of evidence (e.g., either those of Biglan et al., 2003, or McCall, 2007). Gaps routinely exist in research literatures, uncertainties abound, and often apples and oranges of evidence must be weighed requiring the expertise of experienced scholars to come to a consensus judgment. Consensus groups, in contrast to individual scholars, presumably benefit from a meeting of minds with diverse perspectives on the persuasiveness of evidence.

In its current forms, however, the consensus group approach has some limitations. The practice works best for biomedical research in which a specific disorder can be targeted, two or three therapies or drugs can be identified as being ready for evaluation, a single desired outcome can be agreed on, and double-blind randomized studies may be available to test the effectiveness of the treatments. Social and behavioral research literatures rarely meet these requirements, lessening the ability of consensus groups to prescribe specific services or courses of action. Instead, behavioral consensus groups tend to set agendas and priorities as well as guidelines for program effectiveness (e.g., Bowman, Donovan, & Burns, 2001; Hayes, Palmer, & Zaslow, 1990; Kamerman & Hayes, 1982; Shonkoff & Phillips, 2000).

For example, recent National Academy of Science reports (Bowman et al., 2001; Shonkoff & Phillips, 2000) served to raise the priority of early childhood care and education programs on the national political agenda, provided evidence that the programs can have broad short- and long-term educational and social benefits especially for low-income children and families, asserted that the quality of such programs was crucial to achieving these outcomes, and provided guidelines for improving the quality of programs—but no specific curriculum or approach was recommended, in part because the research literature was not available or did not substantiate more specific curricula or programs.

Moreover, consensus groups tend to consist solely of researchers, in keeping with the traditional unidirectional delivery of information in which scientists alone decide what scientific evidence the policy maker, practitioner, or public might need. But researchers rarely study and are likely to overlook many factors that make the dissemination of service programs effective, for example, staff commitment and matching the program to diverse clienteles. Finally, evidence is not the only criterion for social and political action. In short, at any one point in time, social and behavioral scientists alone are unlikely to have all the answers for solving a specific problem. Nevertheless, action must be taken today.

Pathways Mapping

The Pathways Mapping Initiative (PMI), developed by Lisbeth B. Schorr and colleagues (Schorr, 2003), attempts to deal with the limitations of traditional approaches to summarizing scientific research. In this structured process, a group of research scholars *plus* service professionals, policy makers, and representatives of the intended service clientele attempt to specify the processes and characteristics of programs that effectively reach a specific desired outcome.

PMI encourages the contribution of scientific knowledge as well as the reasonable judgments of best practices, professional experience, theory, and political and fiscal reality to create a comprehensive strategy for solving a specific problem. The goal is to reach broad consensus based on a preponderance of the best available scientific evidence and practice principles to forge conclusions and curb idiosyncratic opinion. Though not perfect, this broader type of consensus group at least allows meaningful multidirectional exchanges among researchers, practitioners, policy makers, and other stakeholders, with the result being a more comprehensive set of proposed actions and guidelines for program dissemination needed to produce the desired outcomes (for examples, see www.PathwaysToOutcomes.org).

In the future, such broad consensus groups could be commissioned on a range of topics and the dissemination process and outcomes evaluated. Each group could be reconvened periodically to integrate new evidence, incorporate lessons learned in attempting to implement the original plan, and consider the possible influences of new and emerging social and political circumstances.

Though communicating the reports from such broad-based consensus groups is potentially useful, it is not likely to be sufficient for changing practices and policies in communities. Even when decent information on effective services is available and communicated, localities do not always adopt those programs or avoid the ones that do not work (e.g., Ringwalt et al., 2002; Wandersman & Florin, 2003). For example, until recently, the DARE program to prevent drug abuse had been adopted in 80% of the school districts in the United States, even though research showed that it is relatively ineffective (e.g., Ennett, Tobler, Ringwalt, & Fewling, 1994; General Accounting Office, 2003). Thus, achieving consensus about the evidence and selecting evidence-based approaches is in many ways

only the beginning of dissemination, and further action must be taken to move the evidence into practice.

Technology Transfer

Supporting the appropriate and effective use of research findings and evidence-based programs can be considered one type of technology transfer. Unfortunately, the standard methods of transferring technology from the social and behavioral sciences—training and technical assistance—tend to be limited in effectiveness (Backer, David, & Soucy, 1995). These approaches typically consist of outside experts who train community professionals and staff to implement new approaches (e.g., home visiting, family support principles) and give technical assistance to agencies for creating and implementing new services.

But training alone has had only limited success. Chinman et al. (2005), in a review of training programs to prevent substance abuse, for example, concluded that whereas some training programs were helpful, the content was not always appropriate to the specific local context, and local political and regulatory circumstances often prevented incorporating the training into policy and practice. The broader literature on training alone produces a similar conclusion—training is potentially useful, but without structural supports, supervision, and other mechanisms that encourage staff to implement training in their professional activities, it has limited benefits (e.g., Morrow, Townsend, & Pickering, 1991).

Technical assistance, another primary means of transferring knowledge, frequently consists of independent professionals and sometimes university-based scientists giving direct, hands-on assistance to local providers. But such "outside" assistance is not always welcome even when provided without cost, and communities must have the financial and personnel resources to implement the assistance. Moreover, community organizations seem better able to use some forms of assistance (such as program planning, implementation, and organizational maintenance) than others (evaluation procedures, data analysis, and so on; Chinman et al., 2005).

DISSEMINATION IS MORE THAN SIMPLE COMMUNICATION

There was a tacit assumption early in the dissemination movement that if research information were communicated to the appropriate audiences, it would be translated into beneficial policies, human services, and public behavior. That is, the presumption was that if researchers would communicate their findings through the media, in legislative testimony, in articles written for practitioners, and by providing training and technical assistance to practitioners, then policy makers, practitioners, parents, and the general public would put that information into action in the form of new or improved services, policies, and personal practices. In short, all scholars needed to do was to tell relevant audiences what they knew and it would be implemented.

Reasons for Limited Effectiveness

But this operating premise was naive at best and arrogant at worst. Although communicating research and scholarly information about causes and preventive and therapeutic approaches to problems, for example, could influence policy, practice, and public behavior, usually it did not, or at least not very substantially or directly (e.g., Weiss, 1977, 1988; but see Chelimsky, 1991; Leviton & Boruch, 1983). Why was the influence of social and behavioral science communications so limited?

At least some social and behavioral scientists shied away from providing prescriptions for direct action. They might, for example, describe research detailing the most common forms of parental discipline of children, or perhaps even explain some of the consequences of those approaches, but not tell parents what they should do or how they should do it. Perhaps the data—strictly speaking—did not directly validate particular courses of action, scientists did not want to "overgeneralize" or "leap to action," and they kept looking over their shoulders to see if their scientific colleagues were watching or listening. So they left such "how-tos" to clinical and counseling psychologists as well as pediatricians, columnists, and commentators (some of whom had little or no advanced training in behavior). It was a vicious circle—many scientists viewed those who gave how-tos as having little basis for their prescriptions, scientists did not want to be perceived as being in the same category, and so researchers eschewed giving how-tos, which in turn left that task to the very people whom the scientists did not respect and perpetuated the problem.

Researchers also acted as if they failed to understand that advising practice and policy professionals is a bit different than communicating to other scientists. Scientists want the whole truth, often in nauseous detail, and nothing but the truth, including all of the qualifications, buts, and maybe nots. So scientists often equivocated when providing testimony to policy makers, for example, stating that "on the one hand research shows . . ." and "on the other hand research shows . . .," causing Bronfenbrenner (1977) to hope for "one-armed psychologists." Indeed, while scientists equivocated, waited for more compelling research, and urged that "more research needs to be done," "audacious ignorance hath done the deed." Practitioners and policy makers typically must act *today*, not when more research compels an unambiguous decision, so for them, the criterion is "the best available information today." Researchers sometimes gave that information but stopped short of saying what, according to the science available, the best course of action might be. But who is better able to interpret a murky and fragmented research literature than those who understand all of its limitations and qualifications?

The propensity of researchers to provide only descriptive "background" information had another limitation—often there was no clear intended outcome to the communication other than to impart knowledge or understanding. An hour-long special program on schizophrenia might help people recognize its characteristics, understand its origins, know that treatments are available, and have greater sympathy for those who have the disorder or who live with them. These are worthwhile consequences and are potentially measurable by those who study the effectiveness of science communications, but actions speak louder than attitudes, and the actions viewers might take are infrequent (e.g., most viewers would not directly encounter someone with schizophrenia) and varied (e.g., sympathize, recommend therapy, avoid such people). Conversely, communications campaigns that have a highly specific action goal, such as stop smoking, lose weight, or conserve energy, have been shown by communications researchers to increase the likelihood that people receiving the message would indeed change their behaviors (e.g., Warner, 1981). So communications alone can be effective if they have clear and measurable behavioral outcomes.

Another reason for the apparent ineffectiveness of simply communicating research results was a misunderstanding by scientists of the nature of the policy and practice processes they had hoped to influence. In policy making, for example, scientists sometimes assumed that if they told policy makers the most effective way to prevent or remediate a problem, the policy makers would pass legislation and approve funding to do precisely that. But even "one-armed psychologists" seemed not to influence policy very much (Chelimsky, 1991; Leviton & Boruch, 1983; Weiss, 1977, 1988). Scientists acted as if they did not understand that many factors influence the policy process besides research; policy makers did not always support the action that is most effective at achieving the intended goal because of competing criteria. Currently, for example, increasing amounts of money are being budgeted for abstinence programs to minimize adolescent pregnancy at a time when most other social programs are being cut, not because abstinence programs are very effective (research shows they are not; Alan Guttmacher Institute, 1994) but because of social, political, and religious philosophy.

Similarly, research showed that a substantial percentage of pregnancies to unwed teenagers occurred shortly after the girl first became sexually active. Adolescents were becoming sexually active at young ages, and this research result suggested that unless one gets information, services, and perhaps contraception to young people before they become sexually active, society will not prevent a substantial percentage of teenage pregnancies. But this implied course of action conflicted with the concerns of parents and policy makers, largely unsubstantiated, that such actions would only encourage sexual activity. As this example illustrates, the audience for communications—parents and policy makers, in this case—are not blank slates on which media messages are written, but they have their own values and ideas about what action should be taken. The communication message must fit those ideas, or it will be modified or negated by them. As a result, communications are likely to be more effective in telling people what to *think about* than in telling them what to *think or do* (e.g., McCombs & Shaw, 1972).

The effectiveness of communications also depends on the outcome that is expected and desired, which can differ depending on the approach to dissemination. For example, in psychological research, scholars typically want a high percentage of individuals exposed to a treatment to change their behavior, but in research on mass communications, a communication usually would be considered effective if it influenced only a small percentage of the recipients of that message in a very cost-effective way (McAlister, Puska, Koskela, Pallonen, & Maccoby, 1980; McCall, 1987). The low success rate may be because a person must first have a specific need for the message, be in a situation that matches the message, be sufficiently motivated to change his or her behavior, and have present a variety of other factors necessary before taking the recommended action. For example, even the successful mass media campaign to stop smoking was effective for only a small percentage of people, but a small percent of a large number is quite a few cases at a small cost per success.

Another reason for the limited effectiveness of simple communications is that they were largely unidirectional, sometimes irrelevant, and typically not strategically planned to effect change. Essentially, the researcher told the policy maker, practitioner, or general public (perhaps through the media) what to do with little understanding of the concerns, conditions, and needs of the audience. Researchers tended to want to communicate the results of what they had studied, rather than what the audiences needed to know something about. Since there was little contact between researchers and audience, communications were prone to being irrelevant, unrealistic, or inappropriate. For example, scientists, policy makers, practitioners, parents, and other stakeholders seldom collaborated to jointly create policies, services, and practices that were feasible, affordable, matched with local cultural and political circumstances, and a scientifically sound means of achieving the desired outcomes. Such unidirectional approaches precluded developing involvement (i.e., "buy in") by those necessary to implementing action or change, and the process often led to

the impression that academics were arrogant and, well, "academic" because their information was not very useful.

TOWARD MORE STRATEGIC AND COLLABORATIVE DISSEMINATION

The early attempts at science communication had at least two fundamental limitations—they were not very strategic, and they did not involve collaborations between the scientist and the communicator or the audience.

Strategic Dissemination

Most early attempts at science communication did not tailor the communications to specific audiences or selectively choose media formats that were likely to produce specific outcomes in specific audiences, and they were not planned systematic efforts to achieve a particular goal. Certainly, media campaigns were conducted in an organized manner to promote smoking cessation, to reduce risk factors for heart disease, and to save energy, among other purposes. But most science communications consisted of individual researchers communicating the results of their own studies through press releases and interviews with the mass media and occasionally in testimony before legislative bodies. This early stage is not surprising, given researchers' reluctance to communicate directly with the public, researchers' penchant for working alone, and the fact that few researchers had the knowledge or time to engage in a systematic dissemination effort.

But today, more researchers seem interested in dissemination. A few are willing to spend substantial amounts of time and effort at it, more are interested in directly contributing to improving people's lives through disseminating research, and there is a greater recognition that other well-established disciplines and professions know how to communicate different kinds of messages to different kinds of audiences in ways likely to produce action and change.

Collaborative Approaches

We believe that to be maximally effective and strategic in disseminating social and behavioral research, researchers' communications with practitioners, policy makers, and mass media communicators should not be unidirectional but reciprocal collaborations that help researchers select information most useful to the intended audience and ask research questions that can better meet society's practical needs and goals.

Collaborations With Practitioners and Policy Makers

One approach to creating new evidence-based programs, services, and policies is to convene a group of all relevant stakeholders (i.e., representatives of groups that have a vested interest in the service, including researchers, practitioners, policy makers, members of the intended clientele, community leaders, funders, the media) to engage in a strategic planning process. That process might use a logic model to structure the design and implementation of new services and policies (Groark & McCall, 2005, in press; see also Chapter 21, this volume). A logic model is simply a set of commonsense questions that are uncommonly asked of all relevant stakeholders that guide the groups' thinking about their goals, the services they want to provide, the rationale for why such services should achieve their stated goals (e.g., a "theory of change"), indicators and measurements of the services to be delivered and the effects they are intended to produce, and a strategy for implementation, monitoring, and evaluation.

More specifically, the W. K. Kellogg Foundation (1998, 2000) offers a workbook for constructing a generic logic model, and guides to logic models for services in specific areas, such as the Getting to Outcomes program, are also available (e.g., Chinman, Imm, & Wandersman, 2004; Fisher, Imm, Chinman, & Wandersman, 2006; http://www.RAND.org/publications/TR/TR101). Such collaborations permit each stakeholder, including the social and behavioral scholar, to contribute their knowledge and expertise to the service or policy in collaborative interaction with the other stakeholders, producing a product that is the best blend of the diverse expertise in the collaborative group. Dissemination of relevant research, practice, policy, and financial and cultural information transpires among all stakeholders continuously throughout the procedure. Though this process can be arduous, interpersonally tense, and long term, as well as require unique leadership expertise, it can produce a better service and policy outcome and one that is more likely to be sustained after its initial implementation and demonstration (Groark & McCall, in press).

A Collaborative System

Whereas the logic model is designed to develop a specific program or service, the collaborative approach can be more general. For example, Figure 1.1 shows a framework that we have developed from our own efforts to contribute to effective services for children and families. This framework requires that academics, program evaluators, service professionals, and policy makers work collaboratively to produce and refine services and policies. The collaborations could be institutionalized in the form of university, nonprofit, or public-private centers that contain all of the essential expertise.

As shown in Figure 1.1, knowledge is summarized (and generated, if needed) pertaining to the issue or problem at hand. Perhaps formal needs assessments in a community or broader geographical area are conducted. Then an innovative service program is designed by a community collaborative group using a logic model process (Groark & McCall, in press), and a demonstration project is created as the first implementation of the new service or policy. Monitoring and evaluation of the implementation, the logic-model process, and the outcomes of the new service or policy are conducted, and the information is fed back to the program for continuous program improvement and also given to funders and policy makers for making additional refinements and perhaps to justify and secure essential resources.

The process is not always conducted in this sequence. Sometimes, the policy maker initiates the project, and at other times, evaluations of existing programs suggest the need for major revisions or new services. Similarly, the feedback and influence is not typically unidirectional or sequential; each component can contribute to and influence the other at any point in the process. Notice that dissemination plays a crucial and continuing role in the process. Most traditionally, researchers might provide the theoretical rationale and empirical evidence for which kinds of programs with which characteristics are likely to achieve the intended goals. The practitioners will disseminate information about local regulations, characteristics of the local clientele for the services, and what has been tried in the local area before and how well it worked. Funders and policy makers communicate what programs and strategies are likely to be politically viable and therefore fundable. Intense communication is required between

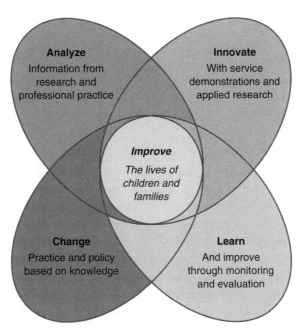

Figure 1.1   A Schematic of a Continuous Collaborative Process to Integrate Research Information Into Practice and Policy, With Dissemination a Crucial Element Throughout the Entire Process

SOURCE: Adapted from "Continuous Learning System" in *The Evaluation Exchange* by Weiss and Morrill (1998) and presented by Groark and McCall (2005). Used with permission.

practitioners and program evaluators to ensure appropriate measurements and data collection as well as interpretations of the results and appropriate modifications in the program to improve it that are stimulated by the results. These experiences may in turn stimulate researchers to design studies of new questions that have practical importance.

One such center that attempts to implement this approach is the University of Pittsburgh Office of Child Development (McCall, Green, Groark, Strauss, & Farber, 1999; McCall, Groark, & Nelkin, 2004). The Office of Child Development (OCD) employs professionals skilled in each component of this model and who could perform each of the four functions. More likely, however, OCD collaborates with other faculty, practice professionals and organizations, outside evaluators, government administrative personnel, and policy makers who perform one or more of the major functions in Figure 1.1, with OCD filling the gaps in such collaborations.

Characteristics of Successful Collaborations

Collaborations, especially among diverse individuals who have different values and performance criteria, can be challenging. Researchers tend to be trained to work independently, rather than collaboratively, for example, and group processes often tend to take more time and can be more arduous and frustrating than if a single organization or person conducted the process alone. They require compromises that can threaten the values and self-interest of participants. But they also have the potential of producing a better product or outcome, one that reflects the needs of the community and has the support of all relevant stakeholders.

Successful collaborations have several key characteristics (Groark & McCall, 2005, in press). First, there must be a shared perception of a need and therefore a common goal of the collaboration. Second, all relevant stakeholders need to be involved from the beginning, including stakeholders, whose primary role will not be implemented until later in the process so that they become involved and committed to the project. A good collaboration is one in which every member is needed and no subset of members could accomplish the goal at all or as well as the total collaboration. Third, the collaboration needs strong leadership. Although rights and responsibilities will be shared among members, a strong leader who has the respect of all members and who in turn respects all members and their diverse perspectives and roles in the collaboration is essential. Sometimes an independent leader is needed, but one who is highly committed to the process and to achieving the goal. Fourth, structure is needed, including agreement on purpose, procedures, attendance, decision rules, regular meetings, and rights and responsibilities of each member.

Revisions to the Research Enterprise

The research enterprise itself must evolve so that it will be more useful to practitioners, policy makers, and the public. Such evolution in the social and behavioral research communities should occur on at least two fronts—namely, the questions that are asked and the methodologies used to answer them.

The Questions

Several individuals and groups have called for a broader and more comprehensive applied research enterprise, which some people have called "community science" (e.g., Chinman et al., 2005). They urge applied researchers to study the process of dissemination, the creation of new service programs and policies by local communities, and the factors that contribute to service and policy success or failure.

Some (e.g., McCall, 1996) feel that the academic value system must come into greater alignment with applied scholarship to truly advance dissemination. The historical legacy of a disproportionate value for basic research and the typical narrow criteria for promotion and success in academic settings need to be broadened to include the many activities described above, including dissemination. The value system needs to embrace and reward quality scholarship in many more diverse forms and dissemination of research to many more different audiences than it does now. Writing articles in popular magazines that communicate research information aimed at parents or service professionals is a legitimate scholarly activity for faculty in journalism and social work; why not also in psychology? A faculty member who contributed knowledge of services and evaluations as a member of a community collaborative committee that designed and implemented a new service program should be credited for this activity toward academic advancement. Of course, the quality of such contributions must be high, and sometimes traditional academics counter that such activities are not as public and do not have the academic reviews for quality that peers give to journal articles and grants. But portfolio reviews by promotion committees could solve this alleged limitation if academics chose to value those activities (see Chapter 6, this volume, for more discussion about academic values and systems).

Evolution of Methodology

The research methodologies designed for discovering fundamental principles of cause and effect in behavioral science often need to be modified for applied scholarship. Some have argued (McCall & Green, 2004) that there is a disproportionate emphasis on traditional gold-standard methodology (e.g., randomized clinical trials, uniform administration of treatment, theory-guided questions, statistical treatment of data) and that many of these gold-standard methods have potentially serious limitations that are often overlooked when conducting applied research. Even some of the gold standards of program evaluation must be balanced with other approaches when applied to more modern service interventions, especially services that are tailored specifically to individual participant needs (Groark & McCall, in press). As the nature of the questions and the interventions change to fit social needs, research methodology must also change to match that evolution.

CONCLUSION

Once shunned by the scientific community, dissemination has become much more accepted in the past four decades—but it still has a long way to go. Legacies from the history of social and behavioral science persist and present lingering challenges to dissemination. Simplistic approaches of the past are not sufficient for changing professional practices, policies, or public behavior. Training and technical assistance programs, a main vehicle of disseminating science for service delivery, often are not sufficient either.

We argue that more strategic approaches are needed. Sustained and meaningful collaborations among scholars, practitioners, participants, policy makers, funders of science and services, the media, business, and other relevant stakeholders will be necessary for designing new policies, services, and practices. Not only will entering into these relationships help make the academic's knowledge more useful to practice and policy, but the academic enterprise itself, including basic science, will be enriched and become more useful because changes will occur in the questions scholars ask, in the methods they use, and the value system in which they work. This evolution will take time, and collaborations bring their own challenges, but ultimately we are more likely to improve human welfare by respecting and using our differences and working together.

REFERENCES

Alan Guttmacher Institute. (1994). *Sex and America's teenagers.* New York: Author.

Altman, I. (1995, August). *Higher education and psychology in the millennium.* Invited address by the recipient of the 1994 Distinguished Career Contributions to Education and Training in Psychology Award, American Psychological Association Annual Convention, New York.

Backer, T., David, S., & Soucy, G. (Eds.). (1995). *Reviewing the behavioral science knowledge base on technology transfer.* Washington, DC: National Institute of Drug Abuse.

Biglan, A., Mrazek, P. J., Carnine, D., & Flay, B. R. (2003). The integration of research and practice in the prevention of youth problem behaviors. *American Psychologist, 58,* 433–440.

Bowman, B. T., Donovan, M. S., & Burns, M. S. (Eds.). (2001). *Eager to learn.* Washington, DC: National Academy Press.

Bronfenbrenner, U. (1977). Toward an experimental ecology of human development. *American Psychologist, 32,* 513–531.

Bush, V. (1945). *Science: The endless frontier.* Washington, DC: Government Printing Office.

Byerly, R., Jr., & Pielke, R. A., Jr. (1995). The changing ecology of United States science. *Science, 269,* 1531–1532.

Centers for Disease Control and Prevention. (2006). *Guide to community preventive services.* Retrieved from www.thecommunityguide.org

Chelimsky, E. (1991). On the social science contribution to governmental decision-making. *Science, 254,* 226–230.

Chinman, M., Hannah, G., Wandersman, A., Ebener, P., Hunter, S. B., & Imm, P. (2005). Developing a community science research agenda for building community capacity for effective preventive interventions. *American Journal of Community Psychology, 35*(3/4), 143–157.

Chinman, M., Imm, P., & Wandersman, A. (2004). *Getting to Outcomes 2004: Promoting accountability through methods and tools for planning, implementation, and evaluation.* Santa Monica, CA: RAND Corporation. Available at http://www.rand.org/pulications/TR/TR10

Cooper, H. (1998). *Synthesizing research: A guide for literature reviews.* Thousand Oaks, CA: Sage.

England, M. (1982). *A patron for pure science: The National Science Foundation's formative years, 1945–1947.* Washington, DC: National Science Foundation.

Ennett, S. T., Tobler, N. S., Ringwalt, C. L., & Fewling, R. L. (1994). How effective is drug abuse resistance education? A meta-analysis of Project DARE outcome evaluations. *American Journal of Public Health, 84,* 1394–1401.

Fisher, D., Imm, P., Chinman, M., & Wandersman, A. (2006). *Getting to outcomes with developmental assets: Ten steps to measuring success in youth programs and communities.* Minneapolis, MN: Search Institute.

General Accounting Office. (2003, January 15). *Youth illicit drug use prevention: DARE long-term evaluations and federal efforts to identify effective programs* (GAO-03-172R). Washington, DC: Government Printing Office.

Goodfield, J. (1981). *Reflections on science and the media.* Washington, DC: American Association for the Advancement of Science.

Groark, C. J., & McCall, R. B. (2005). Integrating developmental scholarship into practice and policy. In M. H. Bornstein & M. E. Lamb (Eds.), *Developmental psychology: An advanced textbook* (5th ed., pp. 557–601). Mahwah, NJ: Lawrence Erlbaum.

Groark, C. J., & McCall, R. B. (in press). Community-based interventions and services. In M. Rutter, D. Bishop, D. Pine, et al. (Eds.), *Rutter's child and adolescent psychiatry* (5th ed.). London: Blackwell.

Hathaway, C. E., Mulhollan, P. E., & White, K. A. (1995). Metropolitan universities: Models for the twenty-first century. In D. M. Johnson & D. A. Bell (Eds.), *Metropolitan universities: An emerging model in American higher education* (pp. 5–16). Denton: University of North Texas Press.

Hayes, C. D., Palmer, J. L., & Zaslow, M. J. (Eds.). (1990). *Who cares for American children?* Washington, DC: National Academy Press.

Kamerman, S. B., & Hayes, C. D. (Eds.). (1982). *Families that work: Children in a changing world.* Washington, DC: National Academy Press.

Leviton, L. C., & Boruch, R. F. (1983). Contributions of evaluations to educational programs. *Evaluation Review, 7*(5), 563–599.

Lynton, E. A. (1995). Foreword: What is a metropolitan university? In D. M. Johnson & D. A. Bell (Eds.), *Metropolitan universities: An emerging model in American higher education* (pp. xi–xxi). Denton: University of North Texas Press.

McAlister, A., Puska, P., Koskela, K., Pallonen, U., & Maccoby, N. (1980). Mass communication and community organization for public health education. *American Psychologist, 35,* 375–379.

McCall, R. B. (1987). The media, society, and child development research. In J. D. Osofsky (Ed.), *Handbook of infant development* (2nd ed., pp. 1199–1255). New York: John Wiley.

McCall, R. B. (1996). The concept and practice of education, research, and public service in university psychology departments. *American Psychologist, 51*(4), 379–388.

McCall, R. B. (2007). *Toward more realistic evidence-based programming and policies.* Unpublished manuscript.

McCall, R. B., & Green, B. L. (2004). Beyond the methodological gold standards of behavioral research: Considerations for practice and policy. *Society for Research in Child Development Social Policy Report, 18*(2), 3–19.

McCall, R. B., Green, B. L., Groark, C. J., Strauss, M. S., & Farber, A. E. (1999). An interdisciplinary, university-community, applied developmental science partnership. *Journal of Applied Developmental Psychology, 20,* 207–226.

McCall, R. B., Groark, C. J., & Nelkin, R. (2004). Integrating developmental scholarship and society: From dissemination and accountability to evidence-based programming and policies. *Merrill-Palmer Quarterly, 50,* 326–340.

McCombs, M. E., & Shaw, D. L. (1972). The agenda-setting function of mass media. *Public Opinion Quarterly, 36,* 176–187.

Mervis, J. (2006, May 12). Behavioral and social science are under attack in the Senate. *Science, 312,* 829.

Miller, G. A. (1969). Psychology as a means of promoting human welfare. *American Psychologist, 24,* 1063–1075.

Morrow, A. L., Townsend, I. T., & Pickering, L. K. (1991). Risk of enteric infection associated with early child day care. *Pediatric Annals, 20*(8), 427–433.

Ringwalt, C. L., Ennett, S., Vincus, A., Thorne, J., Rohrbach, L. A., & Simons-Rudolph, A. (2002). The prevalence of effective substance use prevention curricula in U.S. middle schools. *Prevention Science, 3,* 257–265.

Schorr, L. B. (2003, February). *Determining "what works" in social programs and social policies: Toward a more inclusive knowledge base.* Retrieved from www.brookings.edu/views/papers/sawhill/20030226.htm

Shonkoff, J. P., & Phillips, D. A. (Eds.). (2000). *From neurons to neighborhoods.* Washington, DC: National Academy Press.

Smith, B. (1990). *American science policy since World War II.* Washington, DC: Brookings Institute.

Stevenson. (1977, October 24). "One thing I'll say. . . ." (cartoon). *New Yorker,* p. 56.

Wandersman, A., & Florin, P. (2003). Community interventions and effective prevention. *American Psychologist, 58*(6/7), 441–448.

Warner, K. E. (1981). Cigarette smoking in the 1970s: The impact of the anti-smoking campaign on consumption. *Science, 211,* 729–731.

Weiss, C. H. (1977). Introduction. In C. H. Weiss (Ed.), *Using social research in public policy making* (pp. 1–22). Lexington, MA: Lexington Books.

Weiss, C. H. (1988). Evaluation for decisions: Is anybody there: Does anybody care? *Evaluation Practice, 9*(1), 5–19.

Weiss, H. B., & Morrill, W. A. (1998). Continuous learning system. *The Evaluation Exchange, 4,* 4.

Weissberg, R. P., & Kumpfer, K. L. (Eds.). (2003). Prevention that works for children and youth. *American Psychologist, 58,* 425–490.

Whiting, A. N. (1968). A proposal for colleges of applied sciences and public service. In C. G. Dobbins & C. Lee (Eds.), *Whose goals for American higher education?* (pp. 94–97). Washington, DC: American Council on Education.

W. K. Kellogg Foundation. (1998). *W. K. Kellogg Foundation evaluation handbook.* Battle Creek, MI: Author.

W. K. Kellogg Foundation. (2000). *W. K. Kellogg Foundation logic model development guide.* Battle Creek, MI: Author.

CHAPTER 2

Science Communication Scholarship

Themes and Future Directions

MICHAEL WEIGOLD, DEBBIE TREISE, AND PAULA RAUSCH

This chapter presents an overview of recent scholarship in science communication (SC) and extends the work of earlier reviews (Grunig, 1979, 1983; Lewenstein, 1992; Weigold, 2001) to identify important themes, directions, and approaches of the discipline. We focus mainly on published works in academic science communication journals with particular attention to articles appearing from 2000 to early 2006. Our review begins by describing science communication and explaining several key assumptions behind the scholarship. Contemporary scholarship is then reviewed that has both continued themes from earlier years and developed new theoretical and methodological approaches, followed by a discussion of best practices. We conclude with a look to the future.

WHAT IS SCIENCE COMMUNICATION?

Given the complex meanings of the terms *science* and *communication,* the range of activities that *science communication* potentially refers to is very broad, and a consensus is difficult to come by (Weigold, 2001). Science communications can include mass media reports intended to inform or entertain the public, advocacy working indirectly through mass media or directly with policy makers to influence policy, press releases designed to highlight the accomplishments of organizations, activities of individual scientists giving media interviews or engaging in public discussions to inform the public or to promote their discipline, efforts of government agencies and private foundations to implement social campaigns to influence public health, museum exhibits to educate and entertain the public, and so on.

Narrow definitions of science communication restrict the term to communicating the hard sciences. Our broader working definition, however, includes not only the hard sciences such as biology, physics, chemistry, and astronomy but also the behavioral and social sciences, such as psychology and sociology, and fields of scientific application and discovery, such as agriculture and technology.

Though each has at some point been questioned, several issues and assumptions run throughout SC scholarship. We briefly summarize these next to give context to the contemporary research covered in this review (for further detail, see Weigold, 2001).

First, it is broadly accepted in the SC field that science and scientific activity are important at many levels: the individual (by helping people to improve their lives, protect their health, and increase their happiness; e.g., Burnet, 2002), the organization (science and technology are key to corporate competition and profitability and often appear in the mission statements of governing bodies), the nation (scientific advances bring national prestige and may enhance competitiveness in the global marketplace), and the world (science may help solve pressing global problems related to hunger, health, safety, global warming, and so on).

A second set of assumptions revolves around communicating science in democracies. Scholars tend to agree that understanding the beliefs and attitudes of the general public toward science is especially important in democracies because government support for scientific activity ultimately depends on the will of voters. They also assume that scientists are ultimately accountable to the public and that communicating science, whether by professional communicators or by the scientists themselves, is vital to ensuring continued support of the scientific enterprise.

Third, communicating science is thought to be difficult because the public appears to be generally "illiterate" about science and so lacks the background needed to make sense of new scientific discoveries and understand the implications for society. Indeed, surveys assessing understanding of science strongly suggest that most U.S. adults have difficulty recognizing even basic scientific facts (for example, that the moon causes tidal shifts or that it takes the Earth 24 hours to rotate). This idea that the public lacks the background required for understanding science and making sound judgments about social policy has been described as the "deficit model" of science communication. Though the deficit model has been criticized as simplistic (Rowe, Horlick-Jones, Walls, & Pidgeon, 2005; Stugis & Allum, 2004) most scholars agree that Americans generally know very little about science (Apsell, 2002), whether that knowledge is measured as grasping scientific discoveries or understanding the scientific method.

A fourth assumption, flowing from the deficit model, is that scientific illiteracy is at least partly maintained by the inadequate efforts of those responsible for communicating science in our society, in particular scientists who are poorly equipped to describe in understandable terms the meaning or importance of their work, journalists who are poorly trained to cover science, and editors and other gatekeepers who, if they cover science at all, do so using criteria that are scientifically irrelevant, such as sensationalism. Scholars also tend to question the credibility and competing roles of public information professionals, individuals whose primary function is to present the activities of science and technology organizations to nonscientific audiences that include reporters, government officials, legislative bodies, and the general public (Rogers, 1997; Weigold, 2001).

REVIEW PROCEDURE

To select relevant articles, we performed several general searches of online databases from 2000–2006 using the phrase *science communication* alone and in various combinations with *mass media, best practices, social marketing, theory, model,* and *behavior(al) science.* Databases included EBSCO Host/ Academic Search Premier, OCLC ArticleFirst (In OCLC FirstSearch), InfoTrac OneFile, and Proquest Smart Search/ABI Global Inform. Additional database searches were performed using the names of several well-known scholars in the science communication field, and their articles and books also were searched for potentially applicable content. Articles were discarded if they primarily dealt with non-science mass media (e.g., organization, workplace, family communication science studies); health, medicine, or disease (except when discussed along with general science); risk (unless risk issues were presented in the context of communicating science); broad overviews of conference coverage; political science, politics, political campaigns, or politicians; book reviews; and popular press articles or news items in scholarly journals.

Our search results showed that science communication scholarship is primarily found in the two leading journals on the topic, *Public Understanding of Science* and *Science Communication,* reinforcing the notion that the SC literature is a small but important part of communication scholarship. Research in these journals often focuses on communications about the physical sciences or biomedicine, with the behavioral and social sciences largely overlooked. The lack of attention to behavioral and social science may be the result of such scholarship not being undertaken at all, or, as we suspect, relevant studies may be published in behavioral and social science journals that do not discuss the work as being science communication per se.

In addition, SC research commonly involves investigating efforts by the mass media to inform the public about scientific topics, particularly how these outlets present specific topics, such as biotechnology, genetically modified foods, and climate change. This emphasis on mass media is not unexpected given their considerable reach and popularity. Most people are exposed to science or seek information about science via the mass media (Zehr, 2000). Though little research investigates media coverage of social science, Schmierbach (2005) suggests the few studies that have been conducted show "social science receives rougher treatment at the hands of journalists" (p. 272), with some investigation showing that it is dismissed altogether and others finding that it receives less respect than the natural sciences.

Media distain for social science may relate to the observational or naturalistic techniques often used in behavioral and social research (Schmierbach, 2005). Findings from many such studies rely on small sample sizes and are not widely generalizable, potentially making it more difficult for reporters to relate the results to their particular audiences, to find "hooks" that will draw people in, to meet the primary tests of newsworthiness, and thus to "sell" these stories to editors and other gatekeepers. In addition, the difficulty in quantifying the results of such studies may further stretch the abilities of reporters to write accurately about the issues or to express their importance, affecting the audience's ability to grasp them. In addition, general media are more prone to cover research in four scholarly journals (Kiernan, 2003), two related to medicine (*Journal of the American Medical Association* and *New England Journal of Medicine*), as well as *Science* and *Nature,* all of which widely distribute news releases; thus, research in other journals may be less apt to receive media attention. As a result, Schmierbach (2005) suggests that researchers in the "hard sciences" have "better established links with specialist news reporters" (p. 272).

Despite the concentration of science communication research on fields outside the behavioral and social sciences, a review of this literature can be instructive to behavioral and social researchers since it is likely that SC findings can provide insights about the pitfalls to be avoided as well as the successes that can be repeated in communicating behavioral research.

REVIEW FINDINGS

The Public

The deficit model places public response to science front and center. The research, however, focuses mainly on assessing what the public knows or feels, with only occasional attention to what it intends to do (Corbett, 2005) or actually does (Bord, O'Connor, & Fischer, 2000) as a result of their knowledge or feelings about science. Gregory and Miller (1998) label these broad categories of public knowledge and affect as "literacy" and "appreciation." Literacy refers to what the public learns and how they learn it, whereas appreciation refers to attitudes toward and support for science. It is often assumed that literacy and appreciation are linked and specifically that knowledge translates into appreciation (although any such relationship might just as easily work the other way). Either one or both typically are communication objectives for science outreach efforts.

Science Literacy

Jon D. Miller has led the most systematic effort to study science literacy. His two-decade-long survey research program (Miller, 2000, 2002, 2004; Miller & Kimmel, 2000; Miller, Pardo, & Niwa, 1997), sponsored by the National Science Foundation, aims to study public understanding of science and recommend what "scientifically literate citizens need" for "quality of life and economic prosperity" (Miller, 2004, p. 273).

According to Miller (2003), the attentive public for an issue, such as science or science policy, "is composed of those individuals who are very interested in a given policy area, believe themselves to be very well informed about that area, and demonstrate a pattern of continuing information acquisition" (p. 1). Operationally, Miller (2001) considers someone to be scientifically attentive if that person reports "that he or she is very interested in (and very well informed about) new scientific discoveries or new inventions and technologies and to indicate a pattern of current news and information acquisition on public policy matters" (p. 264). Miller estimates that as of 1999, there were 22 million adults, or 12% of the population, who were attentive to science and technology policy. A second group is described by Miller (1986) as science *interested*. The science-interested public consists of individuals who lack a functional understanding of science but who express interest in science information presented in mass media. About 44% of U.S. adults can be classified as science interested (Miller, 1983, 1986).

The work of Miller and others has raised important conceptual and operational issues relating to how to define and measure science literacy, and a broad consensus has not yet emerged regarding what individuals should know and how such knowledge can be measured with validity (Gregory & Miller, 1998; Pardo & Calvo, 2004). Still, Miller's definition provides a useful benchmark for evaluating public knowledge over time. Moreover, the trends Miller has observed toward increased science literacy using his definition can also be found in research showing the public's increasing knowledge of scientific concepts such as "experiments," "probability," "molecule," and "DNA," adding validity to his approach. Knowledge about science topics heavily covered in the mass media, such as global warming, is also becoming more widespread (Miller, 2004).

Contrary to some stereotypes, science literacy in the United States, as measured by surveys posing questions designed to test basic science knowledge, is at least as high as that found in Britain, France, Denmark, and the Netherlands and exceeds that in other countries, including other European nations and Japan (National Science Foundation, 2006). Where do people get information about science? Miller's data (Miller, 2004) suggest that two important contributors to science literacy are postsecondary schooling (specifically, having had a college-level science course) and informal science education resources, including use of science magazines, books, Web sites, and visits to science museums. It has long been suggested that fictional portrayals in movies, novels, television programs, games, and other media may be yet another primary source of public understanding about science and technology. Supporting data from a large number of focus groups show that the most frequently mentioned informal sources of information about genetics are documentaries, fiction films, popular television shows, science fiction, and news media (Bates, 2005).

Numerous studies have measured the impact of electronic media, such as television and radio, on public understanding of science. Most research has focused on portrayals of scientists and their research (Bates, 2005; Haynes, 2003; Jones, 2001; Jörg, 2003; Weingart, Muhl, & Pansegrau, 2003), including stereotypical scientist roles, gender-role stereotypes, and race (Flicker, 2003; Long, Boiarsky, & Thayer, 2001; Rosenstone, 2003). All suggest that public knowledge and perceptions are influenced by both positive and negative portrayals and by the information communicated whether it is accurate, inaccurate, or incomplete (Rose, 2003).

SC scholars argue that well-written science books also have a loyal audience and so can be an important medium for popularizing

science. For example, Bill Bryson's (2003) engaging attempt at science survey, *A Short History of Nearly Everything,* sold nearly 300,000 copies between the middle of 2004 and 2005. Although such sales pale in comparison to the best-selling book of the same period (a Harry Potter sequel sold more than 6 million copies), it is still a remarkable achievement for a tome with so much serious science content. Indeed, Lewenstein and Nisbet (2002) argued that science titles have an importance that goes beyond sales data, suggesting that books such as Carson's 1962 *Silent Spring* have played an important role in public debates (see Chapter 12, this volume, for more about writing popular science books).

The explosion of sophisticated and easily accessed information on the Internet has attracted the attention of SC scholars concerned with learning from the Web. For example, Macedo-Rouet, Rouet, Epstein, and Fayard (2003) contrasted standard and digital presentation formats of a series of science articles as predictors of reader understanding and satisfaction. They found that hypertext readers scored lower than print readers on comprehension of some material. Although their experiment did not involve random assignment, their conclusion that online formats don't always make learning easier seems plausible.

Still, the Web has almost limitless capacity to provide complete, balanced, and useful information from science if organized in user-friendly ways. For example, Byrne et al. (2002) evaluated the effectiveness of two university Web sites in providing information on transgenic crops. Especially given the controversial nature of the topic, they credit the sites for their ability to disseminate contemporary information quickly, globally, and in easy-to-use and easy-to-understand formats.

Similarly, Dunwoody (2001) attempted to shed light on the readers of science Web sites, Web site characteristics, and their implications for Web site efficacy by studying the

"Why Files," a science site developed at the University of Wisconsin. Surveys showed the typical visitor was a well-educated male and that most repeat visitors had at least a college degree, suggesting that users bear a strong resemblance to the demographic characteristics of Miller's attentive public, the typical Internet user, and the typical consumer of science information on TV. Based on these overlapping characteristics, Dunwoody suggested it would be difficult to determine without further research whether this site, or the Web more generally, would be useful for broadening the audience for science. In terms of presentation and usability, her analysis of Web site audit trails revealed that visitors proceeded through the Web articles much as they would through print materials. Visitors typically consumed information at the site in a linear way, going page to page and largely ignoring links to ancillary topics, a presumed benefit of Web sites. Think-aloud protocols showed that visitors often got lost in the pages and that, rather than reading content, they frequently engaged in orienting behaviors (trying to find information or return to pages previously visited).

Science Appreciation

Miller (2004) noted that a "substantial body of research from the end of World War II to the present indicates that an overwhelming majority of U.S. adults are interested in science and technology, believe that it has contributed to our standard of living, and are willing to support it with government funding" (p. 284). From 1957 to 1997, between 80% and 90% of U.S. adults agreed the world is better off due to science, although opinion surveys also suggest concerns about the effect of science on the pace of societal change and religious belief.

Although the attitudes of the public as a whole are favorable, closer examination has revealed different "clusters" of opinions about science and technology. For example, Priest

(2000, 2006) concluded that one reason for the generally favorable attitudes toward science and technology in the United States, as compared with other nations, is the existence in America of large numbers of "true believers," that is, people who believe the benefits of scientific advances generally outweigh the costs. She points out that the most common group are "utilitarians," those who believe costs and benefits should be carefully considered by experts in science. Consistent with this idea, Shanahan, Scheufele, and Lee (2001) found that more Americans support the use of biotechnology in agriculture (49%) and food production (40%) than oppose it (with about 11% expressing no opinion).

A more complicated picture of public opinion emerges for more specific science initiatives (Shaw, 2002), such as cloning, genetically modified foods, and global warming, controversies that have attracted a great deal of recent attention. Using survey data, Stamm, Clark, and Eblacas (2000) found that whereas general awareness of global warming is high, the public frequently understands little about specific causes, potential consequences, and associated policy alternatives. The researchers suggested that although mass media can contribute to public understanding of global warming, it also appears to help perpetuate inaccurate beliefs. The consequences of such inaccuracies were explored by Bord et al. (2000) by analyzing public opinions about global warming causes and solutions. The public's acceptance of accurate causes for global warming predicted the public's intention to address the problem. The authors suggested that support for global warming programs would require educating the public about the specific actions that science indicates are needed to address global warming, instead of trying to encourage concern for the environment in general.

In that vein, Krosnick, Holbrook, and Visser (2000) considered the impact of President Bill Clinton's effort to build support for the Kyoto accord to limit greenhouse gas emissions by "informing Americans of the scientific consensus that global warming was a real threat and was caused by humans" (p. 239). The researchers used two surveys, one conducted prior to the campaign and one following it, to track changes in citizen beliefs and attitudes about global warming, the degree to which the campaign engaged the public's attention to it, and the degree to which the campaign changed public attitudes and beliefs about it. Overall, public opinions, which were already largely in line with those of scientific experts, did not change significantly following the debate. However, people were affected by the news stories disseminated as a result of the campaign, with indicators showing several changes, including they had thought more about the issue and that their opinions were more certain. A greater proportion of those surveyed also cited the issue as extremely important.

The foundations for a lifetime interest in science, favorable attitudes toward science, and a desire to develop a career as a scientist are widely believed to be established during childhood and adolescence. This assumption has guided work seeking to better understand why several demographic groups are underrepresented among the ranks of scientists. For example, Breakwell and Robertson (2001) studied attitudes toward science among boys and girls ages 11 to 14 years in the United Kingdom over two time periods: 1987–1988 and 1997–1998. In both surveys, girls reported liking science less than boys, said they performed worse in science courses, were less involved in science activities after school, and had more negative overall attitudes toward science. Although both boys and girls evinced more negative attitudes toward school science in the later study, attitudes toward science in general remained constant. The authors suggested, based on the findings from eight items reflecting maternal encouragement to succeed in science and mathematics, that an important

predictor of early teenager attitudes and involvement is the perceived support of the student's mother for science.

Use of the Internet has increased, especially among teenagers, and so this venue may be valuable for disseminating information to teens that would improve both their attitudes and knowledge about science. However, maximizing the effectiveness of science Web sites targeting teens will be crucial and may require learning from commercial ventures that have reached them successfully. Weigold and Treise (2004), for example, used content analysis to compare science and nonscience Web sites for teens. They argued that nonscience commercial sites offer important lessons to science sites in how best to keep teens' attention and interest. In contrast to science-oriented sites, nonscience sites tend to be updated regularly, to be interactive, and to encourage audience-created content. The researchers augmented their content analysis with focus groups to better understand how teens use the Web to work on school projects. The results showed that, for the most part, their teachers did not encourage the students to use the Web for class projects; indeed, some viewed it as an easy way out or as a form of cheating. However, these teens said they used the Web to study for tests, to play science-related games, and to find information on topics such as solar flares, weather, and science fair projects, suggesting that the Web is an underused mechanism for helping teens to become more interested in science and scientifically literate.

Many youngsters encounter science at museums that are designed to affect public attitudes about science as much as knowledge. Thus, developing and evaluating museum exhibits continues to attract the attention of SC scholars (Henriksen & Frøyland, 2000; Persson, 2000; Tremayne & Dunwoody, 2001). For example, Heath, vom Lehn, and Osborne (2005) described novel ways that museum designers and managers are allowing visitors to interact individually with exhibits through computers. Visitors might complete a word skills test, participate in a "sex change" module that photographs the visitor as the opposite sex, and play games about controversial topics designed to encourage debate. The researchers cautioned that although new interactive exhibits may enhance involvement, it may come at the expense of the potentially beneficial social and collaborative interactions known to enhance learning at museums However, the success of such large hands-on museums, such as the Exploratorium, shows public interest in such venues (Borun, 1996; Pedretti, 2002), and so a challenge for future SC research will be to identify museum experiences that result in both learning and positive attitudes, thus maximizing their effectiveness.

The Knowledge-Attitude Link

As stated earlier, scholars often presume that science literacy translates into greater appreciation of science. Supporting this notion, Besley and Shanahan (2005) surveyed approximately 900 respondents in New York and found that support for agricultural biotech is related to respondent education, understanding of the role of the scientist, general trust, and demographic variables such as age, income, being male, and a conservative ideology.

Despite such findings, however, many questions remain regarding the literacy-appreciation (or knowledge-attitude) link, making even tentative overall conclusions about such connections impractical thus far. For example, "knowledge" measures in many studies are often quite primitive, corresponding more to awareness than to any deep understanding. It is also unclear how knowledge regarding one science, such as chemistry, may affect knowledge about other sciences, such as biology or psychology, or about science more generally. On the "effect" side,

attitude measures often vary considerably since science attitudes can include (a) very broad attitudes (science is good) or very specific ones (biotechnology is good), (b) attitudes about technologies or applications (genetically modified corn) as well as scientific processes (cloning), and (c) references to scientists in general (scientists do important work) or to specific ones (NASA scientists do important work). In addition, terms that may be indistinguishable among many members of the lay public (reproductive cloning versus therapeutic cloning and DNA cloning) have very different meanings and thus (potentially) different moral implications (National Bioethics Advisory Commission, 1999). Attitudes in the literature have been assessed with traditional evaluative terms (good-bad, positive-negative) and ones with more precise and nuanced meaning (a technology should be "encouraged" or is "morally acceptable").

Finally, science attitudes are still often measured without reference to a broader context, raising significant questions about how they might translate into specific behavior. Thus, it is easy to conclude that people have generally positive attitudes toward science. That is, would such attitudes predict support for science if considered in the context of budgetary decisions that require trade-offs among valued institutions (for example, taking dollars from education, health care, law enforcement, defense, or assistance to the needy)? Understanding these potentially complex relationships between science knowledge and science appreciation will require greater attention in future scholarship.

Media Performance

Quality of Reporting

Criticism of media coverage of science remains a consistent theme in science communication. Such analyses apply both to stories that feature science and to science reporting more generally. For example, Miller (2002) objected to newspaper reporting on the story of the first cloned human embryo in which misinformation and other problems were common. Likewise, Kua, Reder, and Grossel (2004) followed media coverage of an article on genomics published in an academic science journal and concluded that mass media reporting did not serve the basic critical function of translating scientific jargon into information that would be comprehensible to most readers. Similarly, Zehr (2000) examined how uncertainty about global warming was presented in popular press articles between 1986 and 1995 and concluded that scientific uncertainty was used to create a wedge between scientists and the lay public over the implications of global warming. Such studies suggest that negative views of media reporting on science are at least to some degree or in some cases accurate and justified.

Studies also suggest that what the public wants in science reporting differs from what the media tend to deliver. For example, Zimmerman, Bisanz, Bisanz, Klein, and Klein (2001) examined how media coverage of science information corresponded to the preferences of various audiences. After sampling the popular print media, they concluded that the primary format for reporting on science was the news brief and that the content of these briefs was compared with information considered important by scientists and desired by readers (college students) and found wanting. For example, although all of the surveyed experts indicated that it was important for news articles to discuss both the relevance of the research described and to evaluate related research, a majority of news briefs did not, and a majority of student readers did not rate these as desirable. The authors suggested that science reporting and journalism education require changes if mass media reporting is to better serve public needs for information about science.

SC scholars have attempted to identify the conditions that might lead some sciences to be reported differently from others. Cassidy (2005) examined how evolutionary psychology was covered in U.K. print media during the 1990s. She suggested that (a) coverage was closely tied to publication dates of books about the topic, (b) a greater proportion of authors in press accounts came from the ranks of science and the academy than is typical for most science topics, and (c) coverage of evolutionary psychology was more likely to be found in areas of the press not bounded as science topics, such as feature articles and columns. She reviewed several possible reasons for why evolutionary psychology is covered differently from other science topics, including the fact that it represents a relatively more accessible and easily understood topic.

Frames and Metaphors

Media performance also has been examined using approaches common in broader mass media scholarship, such as framing and metaphors. A frame is "a central organizing idea for news content that supplies a context and suggests [to audiences] what the issue is through the use of selection, emphasis, exclusion and elaboration" (Tankard, Hendrickson, Silberman, Bliss, & Ghanem, 1991, p. 11). It can have "subtle but powerful effects on the audience . . . without the audience realizing it is taking place" (Tankard, 2001, p. 97).

Media frames can vary as a function of topic (genetic applications or medicine or agriculture) and the type of source (scientists versus government officials) (Ten Eyck & Williment, 2003). With respect to nanotechnology, a recent content analysis suggested that the dominant frames relate to social effects of the science and to scientific discoveries (Stephens, 2005). Ten Eyck and Williment (2003) also conducted a sweeping content analysis of more than 2,700 articles covering genetics in two elite press vehicles (*The New York Times* and *The Washington Post*) from the 1970s through 2001. They concluded that changing media frames over the course of the study may have caused the public to be unsure about whom to trust—scientists or government officials—about larger social issues relating to science.

Scientists can be especially useful to journalists who frame stories in terms of rationality versus myth and intuition. Reporters using this frame prefer sources in positions of authority and can defer to the greater knowledge possessed by scientists. For example, Coleman and Dysart (2005) examined media frames of Kennewick Man, a 9,000-year-old skeleton, which became the subject of conflict between scientists and Native American groups. They concluded that the news stories often contrasted the "rationality" of science with the "subjective, primitive, or moral" ideology of culture (p. 7).

Reporters also commonly use ethical frames for reporting on science. In a study of genetics reporting, stories from television, National Public Radio (NPR), newspapers, newsmagazines, and newswires were analyzed for mentions of ethical dimensions or issues, defined as "duties" (i.e., faithfulness to commitments, sensitivity to human needs, sensitivity to justice and/or autonomy) and "consequences" (avoiding harm, doing good). Concerns about the negative consequences of genetic testing and especially the need to avoid doing harm were commonly mentioned; however, stories less often helped audiences to understand the underlying ethical issues.

Metaphors are another useful tool for communicating complex scientific ideas in easier-to-understand messages (Knudsen, 2005). For example, Ungar (2000) suggested that the public was better able to comprehend the ozone hole rather than climate change because it was associated with easy-to-understand metaphors. Likewise, Liakopoulos (2002) examined biotechnology metaphors in the U.K. press and suggested

that metaphors are indeed useful for popularizing complex ideas, but they also can give "highly charged" messages that may affect attitudes and beliefs as well as understanding. Väliverronen (2004) examined representations of biotechnology in the Finnish media and concluded that scientists play an important role in popularizing innovations through their own choices of metaphors and visual imagery. For example, the compelling metaphor of "medicine cows" appearing in Finnish media reports came from scientist explanations of transgenic cattle.

News Judgments and Biases

The gate-keeping function of story selection also has received scholarly attention. Nisbet and Lewenstein (2002) examined articles in *The New York Times* and *Newsweek* between 1970 and 1999 that covered biotechnology. Although biotech coverage increased over those decades in conjunction with the growth of the industry and introduction of new products, it was heavily episodic. Stories corresponded with the appearance of articles in elite science journals, political announcements, major meetings, or high-profile incidents. The authors suggested that scientists, industry, and government worked hard in their successful efforts to dominate coverage of science stories. (Perhaps not surprisingly, therefore, the reporting frequently lacked mention of controversy, and descriptions of scientific benefits outweighed mentions of risks, with the exception of coverage on recombinant DNA.)

Although many players affect the amount of science news coverage, scientists can often be a driving force. Take, for example, the highly covered story of the cloned sheep "Dolly," which was analyzed by Holliman (2004) in a content analysis from 1996 and 1997. Though level of influence varied considerably, "the public, media, scientists, and scientific institutions, and decision makers" all had a role in influencing the "production, content and reception of this coverage" (p. 125). Scientists, however, particularly those from one institute who worked methodically to insert the results of their experiments into coverage and comments, were responsible for the bulk of the coverage. Indeed, "media coverage of cloning was not just about news of assisted reproduction, but also the result of a process of assisted news reproduction" (Holliman, 2004, p. 125).

Several scholars have attempted to understand how media actors convey their stance toward the individuals and institutions of science beyond story selection. Stephens (2005) analyzed the evaluative tone of news stories about nanotechnology from a sample of domestic and international papers between 1992 and 2004 and found that articles emphasizing benefits far outnumbered those stressing risk (31.7% and 9.8%, respectively), with less than half (47.3%) showing no discernible tone, which would equate with being "balanced" from a news perspective. In biotechnology coverage, Bauer (2002) noted also that the tone varied as a function of its application. His review of coverage in the British press from the early 1970s through 1999 showed that biomedical applications during the 1990s were generally framed positively, whereas genetic food applications received more critical coverage (i.e., they were painted as more risky, less beneficial, and of greater concern). Bauer found that these press frames translated to perceptions among readers, with readers more skeptical of genetically modified foods and more positive about biomedical applications than were nonreaders.

Identifying persistent biases in how journalists and editors select science stories for coverage and how they choose to report on them is an issue of obvious importance for citizens and stakeholders alike. The possible sources of bias in news coverage are likely to be extensive, a point reinforced by Reese and Ballinger (2001), who argued for a "hierarchy of influences" (p. 641) on the media agenda, beginning at the most micro level with the personal views and roles of journalists, rising through media routines, organizations, and cultural pressures to ideology.

In this context, the term *bias* is not meant to suggest deliberate or ideological causes for media content. Indeed, Shanahan and Good (2000) found that the appearance of global warming stories in local newspapers in New York and Washington was associated with something as nonideological as changes in temperature, with warmer temperatures increasing the likelihood that climate change was covered. Some "biases" can be good for science reporting and might even be considered part of best practice. For example, Wilson (2000) examined predictors of accurate global warming coverage and found that reporters who relied on scientists as primary sources and who reported regularly on environmental issues, and so who presumably had the most technical knowledge, tended to be the most accurate. Other biases might compromise quality of reporting, however; Priest (1995) suggested the possibility that decisions about how to cover science in some controversies, including genetically engineered foods, may result from the media being "heavily subsidized" promoters of biotech.

Likewise, Cook, Robbins, and Pieri (2006) used content analysis and focus groups to examine messages about genetically modified food in Britain by evaluating coverage in two pro– and two anti–genetically modified (GM) food newspapers and gauging responses to the articles among experts and the public. The pro-GM papers tended to characterize the issues covered as primarily scientific, while the anti-GM press and many of the focus group participants considered the issue in a broader framework, linking their opposition to GM foods with issues of U.S. and British policy toward Iraq. The researchers found that coverage of the topic consistently reflected these biases through their "choice of writers and sources, in their selection and presentation of stories and in the language used" (p. 9).

Potential biases might also arise from political and religious leanings of reporters. For example, in Sachsman, Simon, and Valenti's (2002) study, only 2 of 55 environmental reporters studied—less than 4%—were registered Republicans as compared to 29% in the general public (Pew Research Center, 2004). In addition, less than 20% of reporter participants indicated that religion was "important" to them, whereas the U.S. Census Bureau (2006) data indicate that more than 80% of adults identify themselves with some religion. Whether such disparities between the political and religious orientations of environmental reporters and the U.S. public affect the quality of environmental reporting and how audiences respond to it is unclear and needs further study.

Risk Reporting

Investigations of the risks posed by scientific activities, or of the risks that science may help to ameliorate, are well represented in new scholarship (Görke & Ruhrmann, 2003; Gurabardhi, Gutteling, & Kuttschreuter, 2004). Gurabardhi et al. (2004) reviewed the risk communication literature appearing between 1988 and 2000. They suggested that the field was dominated by a relatively small number of key writers and a single important journal, *Risk Analysis*. Major and Atwood (2004) drew a sample of 840 stories about the environment from a population of 12,000 published in 93 Pennsylvania daily newspapers over a 1-year period beginning in September 1997. Their purpose was to compare stories that reported risk with those that did not. They concluded that most stories did not report risk, and overall, the newspapers did poorly at helping the public understand environmental risk. For example, although

newspapers wrote about pollution that resulted in streams being closed to fishing, the articles typically failed to discuss cancer or other risks associated with eating contaminated fish from these streams.

Risk reporting has been found to be more common in some nations than others. Rowe, Frewer, and Sjöberg (2000), for example, compared how newspapers in Sweden and the United Kingdom described risk in a 2-month period surrounding the 10-year anniversary of the Chernobyl nuclear incident. They found that reports about risk were four times more common in Sweden than in the United Kingdom. And while the Swedish and U.K. accounts were similar in reporting on the accident itself, the Swedish papers tended to broaden the focus to other nuclear hazards. Many others have noted that coverage of risk in news media tended to be alarmist and rarely involved quantitative benchmarks (Brown, Chapman, & Lupton, 1996; Greenberg, Sandman, Sachsman, & Salomone, 1989; Marino & Gerlach, 1998; Moynihan et al., 2000; Salomone, Greenberg, Sandman, & Sachsman, 1990; for a dissenting view, see Freudenburg's analyses, i.e., Freudenburg, 1988; Freudenburg, Coleman, Gonzales, & Helgeland, 1995).

Other scholars have investigated how media present scientific uncertainty, which underlies all science reporting but especially reports on risk. In his examination of popular press articles about global warming between 1986 and 1995, Zehr (2000) found several forms of uncertainty, including direct discussion about scientific uncertainty in the newspapers accounts, as well as "scientific controversy, new research, and expansion of problem domain" (p. 90). He argued that the rhetoric of uncertainty about the science was used to undermine the public's beliefs about the likelihood of global warming.

To assess how communication about health risk can affect depth of knowledge, Kahlor, Dunwoody, and Griffin (2004) examined the public's understanding of a parasite outbreak in the Milwaukee water supply and the extent and complexity of the knowledge that resulted from the media. Education level predicted the complexity of biological knowledge relating to the outbreak but did not predict understanding of where the parasite came from or how it contaminated the drinking water. People who had experience with the parasite also had more complex understandings about how it got into the water supply and how it made people sick. The findings did not show a relationship between people's depth of knowledge and their media use in this particular study (perhaps, as the authors explained, because of methodological issues). But the researchers suggested that because media are easily available and important sources of information for most people, particularly when faced with risks to personal health or safety, the ways risk information is presented in media may affect the complexity of the public's understanding about hazards.

To summarize, debates surrounding the role of the media in communicating uncertainty dates back to the beginning of risk reporting. Research continues to focus on developing new measures for assessing how well various types of mass media communicate risk and explain relevant ethical issues, as well as how coverage quells or fuels consumers' perceptions of risk.

Reporter Training

Early reviews of science journalism suggested that journalists assigned to cover science were typically inadequately trained to do so. In addition, it has been noted that reporters and editors are frequently less interested in the scientific importance of a story than in sensationalism or local angles. These assertions remain common themes in more current literature. Sachsman et al. (2002) found that only half of U.S. newspapers and less than 10% of TV news stations employed reporters who specialized in environmental issues. These specialized journalists were more likely than other journalists to have a graduate degree, but they believed they lacked sufficient knowledge about science and so tended to rely on elite papers for stories rather than peer-reviewed journals.

Other studies have examined whether research techniques influence the science that appears in the media. Schmierbach (2005) found that news reporters of social science judged quantitative studies to be more accurate and of greater news value than qualitative studies, yet a separate measure of their editors' willingness to run a story revealed no significant preferences between the two. Though the sample size was small, the study at least suggests that the reporters' feelings did not accurately reflect those of editors and other gatekeepers who actually control news content and that to better judge a study's quality and news value, reporters and editors could benefit from training that helps them to identify high-quality research, whether quantitative or qualitative, and to understand which methods are appropriate for answering which types of research questions.

Valenti and Tavana (2005) stressed the importance of continuing education programs for writers and journalists who cover science and the environment. Their article summarized outcomes from 7 years of the National Tropical Botanical Garden Environmental Journalism Fellows Program, which brings together reporters and scientists to enhance their professional relationships, which Valenti's research has shown leads to "improved reporting and increased public understanding of science" (Valenti & Tavana, 2005, p. 304). They concluded that tensions between journalists and scientists tended to dissipate, and mutual understanding increased through team efforts that provided shared familiar locales and experiences and hands-on opportunities for reporters that made it easier to understand the science.

Scientists

SC scholars often focus on scientists' presumed lack of ability or motivation to communicate effectively with the public about their work (Holmes, 2002). LaFollette (2002a), however, described how early radio (1920s through the 1940s) often featured scientists giving talks directly to audiences. Similarly, early television (1940s through the 1950s) regularly presented meaningful science programming to audiences (LaFollette, 2002b). With the increased popularity of television and the development of other entertainment genres, scientists and their work received far less attention from these mass media. Radio broadcasters, for example, eventually eliminated programs featuring scientists in favor of more polished formats believed to appeal to listeners' tastes and preferences.

Recently, SC scholars have argued that positive portrayals of scientists may be important in boosting young people's interest in science careers, especially among girls and ethnic/racial minorities, and by promoting role models (Steinke, 2004). The media could help with such presentations, but instead film portrayals tend to reinforce traditional female stereotypes, emphasizing beauty and romantic relationships over competence (Flicker, 2003; Steinke, 2005). Although some science programming has been found to counter these gender stereotypes, they fall short in breaking down others, such as in representing racial minorities in scientific careers (Long et al., 2001).

Other studies have focused on portrayals of scientists more generally and have found that both the positive and negative stereotypes in films, television programming, books, and even comics may have profound impacts on public perception. Haynes (2003), for example, suggests there are seven "master narratives" in cinematic depictions of scientists, containing a mix of good (scientist as

hero or adventurer) and bad (scientist as evil, foolish, or dangerous). In a content analysis of 222 movies, Weingart et al. (2003) concluded that activities surrounding modifying the human body and creating health threats were the primary events used in negative characterizations of scientists, and they suggested that media representations of scientists reflected ambivalence associated with new knowledge. Taking these negative depictions a step further, Haynes argued that the master narrative in Western literature was of the scientist as threatening and evil. Ambivalent portrayals of scientists are not restricted to fiction. Schnabel (2003) suggested that reporters may uncritically accept two stereotypes of scientists, that of the hero or that of a fallen angel who has turned something good (scientific knowledge) into something frightening.

Given the prevalence of scientist stereotypes, many with unflattering implications, it is not surprising that some effort has been devoted to providing the public with a more complete and accurate picture. Mitsuishi, Kato, and Nakamura (2001) described a "scientist library," which offers those with access to the CD-ROM or a Web connection a way to view the biographies and personalities of dozens of Japanese biologists. Pearson (2001) reported on the functions of U.K. Scientific Research Councils, which encourage scientists to meet with and communicate to the public. Despite good intentions, the author questioned whether the councils are working as intended and whether working to increase public understanding of science should be an obligation of all research scientists.

BEST PRACTICE

Best practice refers to those activities that separate successful and excellent programs from those less distinguished. In science communications, best practice tends to be driven by two important assumptions: The general public has little understanding of science and science communication efforts should be accountable for producing desired communication goals, just as other communications in areas such as advertising and public relations are accountable. Although the notion of best practice seems uncomplicated, it may be more complex than many assume. Next, we describe some of these complexities and relevant scholarship.

Whose practice? As this chapter attempts to make clear, the SC literature deals with many different actors, each of whom may deserve consideration in the context of best practice: scientists and their organizations, public information specialists, reporters, news media, and even the public. The study of best practice also requires attention to who is evaluating because different constituencies may value different outcomes and tactics. For example, scientists and policy makers may disagree about the importance of direct communication between scientists and the public, and journalists and public information officers may disagree about what information should be provided to news media. The SC literature is replete with such conflicts (Hartz & Chappell, 1997).

To limit the scope, we focus here on publicly funded organizations that communicate science to the public, such as museums, universities, some labs, and some federal, state, and local agencies. These collectives are frequently required to report to different publics, including taxpayers, representatives of news media, government officials, and interest groups. How might SC best practice in such organizations be evaluated?

Strategic science communications may be evaluated with the same criteria used by other organizations, such as marketers and advertisers, who also engage in targeted communication (Arens, Weigold, & Arens, 2008) and make use of persuasive and informational

message campaigns. Marketers typically organize their communication activities across several stages as determined by a marketing or advertising plan. Within each stage, communicators must make many decisions, which can be informed by experience, research, or theory. As an example, consider the initial decisions faced by a communicator whose task is to persuade audiences to consume a product or service. The communicator is faced with the task of defining the brand, distinguishing it from its competition, understanding the target audience for the brand, understanding previous communication activities used to promote the brand, and so on. Typically, as decisions are made, evaluative research activities are used to help refine tactics and avoid ineffective messages.

While SC organizations may adopt such a template, they often face communication objectives that are even more complex. The nature of the target audience may be unclear or the organization may have multiple target audiences, each of which requires different messages. Communication goals may be unclear, or an organization and its stakeholders may not agree about what those goals should be. Aspects of the communication context may hamper or hinder broader public understanding of science. (Perhaps the audience is not ready to hear the message, for example.)

These are merely some of the challenges but perhaps among the most important, and so we discuss them in more detail in the sections that follow. Though such challenges raise the bar for SC communicators, they also reinforce the need for strategic and creative thinking about communicating science.

Communication Targets

Different organizations will, of course, target different audiences. As an example, public universities represent one class of organization that considers science communication activities important to its institutional goals. Who might be their target audiences? Because universities are funded by state budgets, state legislators are a key audience. Granting agencies may also be important because many universities receive significant portions of their budgets from grants. The public at large is important, both because the public can influence legislators and because publicizing science activities may be a good way to attract talented undergraduate and graduate students. Other public audiences may be worth special attention, such as alumni who may be interested in contributing to the resources needed for studying questions of science or health.

A sophisticated understanding of one's audience is likely to increase the effectiveness of communication strategies. Take, for example, Clarke's (2003) research on the interactions between knowledge producers (scientists) and users (farmers). He observed improvements in the effectiveness of a small program in England designed to bring together agricultural scientists and farmers for discussions about agricultural innovations when the interactions changed from lectures (scientists to farmers) to interactions in the field. Although the farmers' initial response to the lecture format had been positive, they came to believe that the discussions were often too technical. Scientists, too, became dissatisfied with the lectures after coming to believe they had oversimplified science. Clarke adapted practices she observed overseas and encouraged farmers and scientists in the United Kingdom to go out into the field together to discover more opportunities for informal group communication, especially discussion about how science research related to the farmers' everyday needs and problems. This change resulted in much greater enthusiasm and mutual understanding among farmers and scientists alike.

Communication Goals

Although science organizations pursue a variety of outcomes, for most, a primary goal is persuading an organization's key publics that the science it produces merits continued funding. For example, Britain's Office of Science Technology and the Wellcome Trust (2001) found that the primary goal of SC practitioners in Great Britain was creating positive attitudes toward science activities within the sponsoring organizations. The trust pointed out that such an emphasis often poorly serves broader science literacy efforts because it is directed at narrow audiences, with few events aimed at actively engaging broad audiences. Effects on the audience, especially in the long term, are rarely assessed. The report suggests that to reach as much of the general public as possible, collaboration among science organizations may be necessary.

Audiences are not, of course, passive receivers of messages but rather seek out information they consider useful, relevant, or important (Irwin, 2001). Consistent with this active perspective, Bush, Moffatt, and Dunn (2001) consider the impact of publicly available information about air quality in the United Kingdom and how it was understood by the public. Their findings, based on 41 depth interviews, suggested that the public "critically evaluates, judges, and interprets this information in a reflexive way, on the basis of a range of social, cultural and local resources and cognitive processes," so that their knowledge is grounded in the context of everyday life and experience (p. 225). This suggests that people are not willing to merely accept facts handed down to them by local or central governments, as is often assumed in attempts to deliver messages from science. Likewise, Ten Eyck's (2005) analysis of media discourse and public opinion suggested that although audiences relied heavily on media for information about issues such as biotechnology, about which little public knowledge and experience exists, people used varied interpretive filters to evaluate the information they were given, including selectively ignoring some messages. Thus, public opinion on issues such as biotechnology does not simply reflect the coverage the topic receives in elite media, which may provide insight into the public-media link that may be helpful when attempting to communicate information from science and technology.

Communication Contexts

Communicators must also consider the context in which audiences encounter science messages. In the advertising industry, the term used to describe the "window" of opportunity for effectively reaching a target is *aperture*. Aperture refers to the context in which individuals are ready to attend to a message, think about it, and act on it (Arens et al., 2008). Consistent with such a focus, Burnet (2002) and colleagues urged communicators to broaden science communication apertures by expanding the contexts in which the public encounters science. His own efforts include bringing science to places such as supermarkets, buses, service stations, boardrooms, and pubs. In addition, he urged science communicators to emphasize the importance of science for daily life and demonstrated the critical need for evaluative research in improving communication efforts.

One important context for audiences to consider science is during the development of social and science policy and efforts to involve the public in science policy have been the focus of several scholars. Allspaw (2004), for example, considered differences between the United States and Canada in engaging the public in science policy making on xenotransplantation, noting that American and Canadian scientists diverged somewhat over conceptions of whether the public is informed enough to play a useful role. U.S. scientists,

regulators, and policy makers interviewed for the study, though critical of the particular methods used in Canada to gather public comment, agreed that the public needed to be better educated in science. Yet, "they still seemed wary of the ability of average citizens to ever fully be capable of becoming informed contributors" about complicated technologies (p. 425). This finding seems to exemplify the significant and continuing chasm that must be overcome for true public involvement in science policy to take place. Einsiedel, Jelsøe, and Breck (2001) examined a "consensus conference" approach to directly engaging citizens in science-based policy issues. At the conferences, which were held in three nations (Denmark, Canada, and Australia), a panel of 12 to 15 lay participants was established in each country to discuss controversial food biotechnology subjects and develop a consensus about the topic. This approach had a number of similar impacts across the three panels, which included increased media coverage of science policy issues that contributed to wider public debate and increased distribution of the panels' reports to government agencies for their consideration. The approach also produced similar overall concerns and regulatory proposals across the three countries, which contributed to making similar sets of policy recommendations. Thus, the authors concluded that such an approach would also work well in different contexts beyond northern Europe.

RECOMMENDATIONS FOR THE FUTURE

As this chapter shows, science communication scholarship tends to be disparate in focus, methods, and outcomes. SC studies have largely been individual ventures that often do not build on previous work. In addition, with the exception of the deficit model or studies of framing, the research frequently either lacks discussion of underlying theoretical frameworks or offers an assortment of theories and models that have not been systematically tested in sustained programs of research.

Long-term studies often focus on how various media represent specific scientific issues, such as nanoscience, genetics, climate change, and biotechnology, making cross-study comparisons difficult if not impossible. In addition, public understanding or attitudes about science have tended to be measured via surveys that seldom assess the kinds of science information people want or how they use it. Further complicating these issues is that, with the exception of health behavior campaigns, evaluation of SC endeavors has not been widely undertaken, as noted by the Research Roadmap Panel for Public Communication of Science and Technology, which said,

> The panel also was very concerned about the dearth of formative or evaluative research that underpins the vast majority of science and technology communication. . . . As a rule, this kind of evaluative framework is lacking entirely in communication programs about basic research and technology. (Borchelt, 2001, p. 200)

This 15-member panel, which convened formally eight times between 1998 and 2000, consisted of scientists, journalists, communication researchers, and science communicators appointed by the Space Sciences Laboratory of NASA's George C. Marshall Space Flight Center. Their tasks were twofold: to review science communication literature in an effort to help guide NASA's efforts to publicize its research to the public and to find effective models of science communication. The panel's efforts resulted in pilot studies in promising areas, an international conference to review best practice submissions worldwide held in 2002, and several scholarly papers and journal articles (including Borchelt, 2001; Priest, 2001; Tremayne & Dunwoody, 2001; Weigold, 2001).

This assortment of research, often focusing on specific scientific topics such as bio- and nanotechnology, global warming, and genetics, coupled with the lack of evaluation of specific efforts, suggests that a coordinated strategy for future science communication research is needed. Such a plan was developed by the Research Roadmap Panel, and its findings and recommendations still hold true.

The panel's road map is discussed more completely elsewhere (e.g., Borchelt, 2001); however, we list here the three areas it determined deserved particular attention. First, future research should identify how adult science literacy and advocacy are affected by both the quality and quantity of science communication. Second, as is the case with most forms of public communication, more knowledge is needed about the science interests of various publics and how they use the information they receive. Finally, exploration is needed into how public information officers at institutions and organizations affect the dissemination of science information, as well as into the relationships among public information officers (PIOs), scientists, and journalists.

This research road map holds for scientists across the board, whether in the natural or physical sciences or the behavioral and social sciences. The very nature of the work that behavioral and social scientists do places them in a position to make significant contributions in these areas because in essence, they require studies of human knowledge, learning, attitudes, and behavior in the context of communicating science We hope to see increased discussion and research by scientists in these fields especially related to their own efforts to communicate their work to the public. The Research Roadmap Panel pointed out, "Communication often remains an afterthought, a by-product of scientific endeavor somehow removed from the scientific process itself" (Borchelt, 2001, p. 200). Multidisciplinary cooperation to advance understanding about science communication is needed to change that convention in the future.

REFERENCES

Allspaw, K. M. (2004). Engaging the public in the regulation of xenotransplantation: Would the Canadian model of public consultation be effective in the US? [Electronic version]. *Public Understanding of Science, 13,* 417–428.

Apsell, P. (2002). Keynote address: Sex, lies, and science television. [Electronic version]. Retrieved from http://www.nist.gov/public_affairs/bestpractices/Apsell.htm

Arens, W. F., Weigold, M. F., & Arens, C. (2008). *Contemporary advertising.* Burr Ridge, IL: McGraw-Hill/Irwin.

Bates, B. R. (2005). Public culture and public understanding of genetics: A focus group study [Electronic version]. *Public Understanding of Science 14,* 47–65.

Bauer, M. W. (2002). Controversial medical and agri-food biotechnology: A cultivation analysis [Electronic version]. *Public Understanding of Science 11,* 93–111.

Besley, J. C., & Shanahan, J. (2005). Media Attention and Exposure in Relation to Support for Agricultural Biotechnology [Electronic version]. *Science Communication, 26,* 347–367.

Borchelt, R. E. (2001). Communicating the future: Report of the Research Roadmap Panel for Public Communication of Science and Technology in the Twenty-First Century. *Science Communication, 23,* 194–211.

Bord, R. J., O'Connor, R. E., & Fischer, A. (2000). In what sense does the public need to understand global climate change? [Electronic version]. *Public Understanding of Science, 9,* 205–218.

Borun, M. (1996). Families are learning in science museums. *Curator, 39,* 123–138.

Breakwell, G. M., & Robertson, T. (2001). The gender gap in science attitudes, parental and peer influences: Changes between 1987–88 and 1997–98 [Electronic version]. *Public Understanding of Science, 10,* 71–82.

Brown, J., Chapman, S., & Lupton, D. (1996). Infinitesimal risk as public health crisis: News media coverage of a doctor-patient HIV contact tracing investigation. *Social Science and Medicine, 43,* 1685–1695.

Bryson, B. (2003). *A short history of nearly everything.* New York: Broadway Books.

Burnet, F. (2002). Graphic science: New venues for science communication [Electronic version]. Retrieved from http://www.nist.gov/public_affairs/bestpractices/Broadening_the_Audience_Panel.htm

Bush, J., Moffatt, S., & Dunn, C. E. (2001). Keeping the public informed? Public negotiation of air quality information [Electronic version]. *Public Understanding of Science, 10,* 213–229.

Byrne, P. F., Namuth, D. M., Harrington, J., Ward, S. M., Lee, D. J., & Hain, P. (2002). Increasing public understanding of transgenic crops through the World Wide Web [Electronic version]. *Public Understanding of Science, 11,* 293–304.

Carson, R. (1962). *Silent spring.* London: Penguin.

Cassidy, A. (2005). Popular evolutionary psychology in the UK: An unusual case of science in the media? [Electronic version]. *Public Understanding of Science, 14,* 115–141.

Clarke, B. (2003). Report: Farmers and scientists: A case study in facilitating communication. *Science Communication, 25,* 198–203.

Coleman, C.-L., & Dysart, E. V. (2005). Framing of Kennewick man against the backdrop of a scientific and cultural controversy [Electronic version]. *Science Communication, 27,* 3–26.

Cook, G., Robbins, P. T., & Pieri, E. (2006). "Words of mass destruction": British newspaper coverage of the genetically modified food debate, expert and non-expert reactions [Electronic version]. *Public Understanding of Science, 15,* 5–29.

Corbett, J. B. (2005). Altruism, self-interest, and the reasonable person model of environmentally responsible behavior [Electronic version]. *Science Communication, 26,* 368–389.

Dunwoody, S. (2001). Studying users of the why files [Electronic version]. *Science Communication, 22*(3), 274–282.

Einsiedel, E. F., Jelsøe, E. F., & Breck, T. (2001). Publics at the technology table: The consensus conference in Denmark, Canada, and Australia [Electronic version]. *Public Understanding of Science, 10,* 83–98.

Flicker, E. (2003). Between brains and breasts—Women scientists in fiction film: On the marginalization and sexualization of scientific competence [Electronic version]. *Public Understanding of Science, 12,* 307–318.

Freudenburg, W. R. (1988). Perceived risk, real risk: Social science and the art of probabilistic risk assessment. *Science, 7,* 44–49.

Freudenburg, W. R., Coleman, C., Gonzales, J., & Helgeland, C. (1995). Media coverage of hazard events: Analyzing the assumptions. *Risk Analysis, 16,* 31–42.

Görke, A., & Ruhrmann, G. (2003). Public communication between facts and fictions: On the construction of genetic risk [Electronic version]. *Public Understanding of Science, 12,* 229–241.

Greenberg, M. R., Sandman, P. M., Sachsman, D. B., & Salomone, K. L. (1989). Network television news coverage of environmental risks. *Environment, 31,* 16–20, 40–43.

Gregory, J., & Miller, S. (1998). *Science in public: Communication, culture, and credibility.* New York: Plenum.

Grunig, J. E. (1979). Research on science communication: What is known and what needs to be known. *ACE Quarterly, 62,* 17–45.

Grunig, J. E. (1983). Communication behaviors and attitudes on environmental publics: Two studies. *Journalism Monographs, 81,* 1–47.

Gurabardhi, Z., Gutteling, J. M., & Kuttschreuter, M. (2004). The development of risk communication: An empirical analysis of the literature in the field [Electronic version]. *Science Communication, 25*(4), 323–349.

Hartz, J., & Chappell, R. (1997). *Worlds apart: How the distance between science and journalism threatens America's future.* Nashville, TN: First Amendment Center.

Haynes, R. (2003). From alchemy to artificial intelligence: Stereotypes of the scientist in Western literature [Electronic version]. *Public Understanding of Science, 12,* 243–253.

Heath, C., vom Lehn, D., & Osborne, J. (2005). Interaction and interactives: Collaboration and participation with computer-based exhibits [Electronic version]. *Public Understanding of Science, 14,* 91–101.

Henriksen, E. K., & Frøyland, M. (2000). The contribution of museums to scientific literacy: Views from audience and museum professionals [Electronic version]. *Public Understanding of Science, 9,* 393–415.

Holliman, R. (2004). Media coverage of cloning: A study of media content, production and reception [Electronic version]. *Public Understanding of Science, 13,* 107–130.

Holmes, H. (2002). Live from the field: Observing science in its natural habitat. In G. Porter (Ed.), *Communicating the future: Best practices for communication of science and technology to the public.* Washington, DC: Government Printing Office.

Irwin, A. (2001). Constructing the scientific citizen: Science and democracy in the biosciences [Electronic version]. *Public Understanding of Science, 10,* 1–18.

Jones, R. A. (2001). "Why can't you scientists leave things alone?" Science questioned in British films of the post-war period (1945–1970). *Public Understanding of Science, 10,* 365–382.

Jörg, D. (2003). The good, the bad and the ugly—Dr. Moreau goes to Hollywood [Electronic version]. *Public Understanding of Science, 12,* 297–305.

Kahlor, L., Dunwoody, S., & Griffin, R. J. (2004). Predicting knowledge complexity in the wake of an environmental risk. *Science Communication, 26*(1), 5–30.

Kiernan, V. (2003). Diffusion of news about research. *Science Communication, 25*(1), 3–13.

Knudsen, S. (2005). Communicating novel and conventional scientific metaphors: A study of the development of the metaphor of genetic code [Electronic version]. *Public Understanding of Science, 14,* 373–392.

Krosnick, J. A., Holbrook, A. L., & Visser, P. S. (2000). The impact of the fall 1997 debate about global warming on American public opinion [Electronic version]. *Public Understanding of Science, 9,* 239–260.

Kua, E., Reder, M., & Grossel, M. J. (2004). Science in the news: A study of reporting genomics [Electronic version]. *Public Understanding of Science, 13,* 309–322.

LaFollette, M. C. (2002a). A survey of science content in U.S. radio broadcasting, 1920s through 1940s: Scientists speak in their own voices [Electronic version]. *Science Communication, 24*(1), 4–33.

LaFollette, M. C. (2002b). A survey of science content in U.S. television broadcasting, 1940s through 1950s: The exploratory years [Electronic version]. *Science Communication, 24*(1), 34–71.

Lewenstein, B. V. (1992). Introduction. In B. V. Lewenstein (Ed.), *When science meets the public.* Washington, DC: American Association for the Advancement of Science.

Lewenstein, B.V., & Nisbet, M. C. (2002). Biotechnology and the American media. *Science Communication, 23*(4). 359–391.

Leydesdorff, L., & Ward, J. (2005). Science shops: A kaleidoscope of science–society collaborations in Europe. *Public Understanding of Science, 14,* 353–372.

Liakopoulos, M. (2002). Pandora's box or panacea? Using metaphors to create the public representations of biotechnology [Electronic version]. *Public Understanding of Science, 11,* 5–32.

Long, M., Boiarsky, G., & Thayer, G. (2001). Gender and racial counter-stereotypes in science education television: A content analysis [Electronic version]. *Public Understanding of Science, 10,* 255–269.

Macedo-Rouet, M., Rouet, J.-F., Epstein, I., & Fayard, P. (2003). Effects of online reading on popular science comprehension [Electronic version]. *Science Communication, 25,* 99–128.

Major, A. M., & Atwood, L. E. (2004). Environmental risks in the news: Issues, sources, problems, and values [Electronic version]. *Public Understanding of Science, 13,* 295–308.

Marino, C., & Gerlach, K. K. (1998). An analysis of breast cancer coverage in selected women's magazines, 1987–1995. *American Journal of Health Promotion, 13,* 163–170.

Miller, J. D. (1983). Scientific literacy: A conceptual and empirical review. *Daedalus, 112,* 29–48.

Miller, J. D. (1986). Reaching the attentive and interested publics for science. In S. M. Friedman, S. Dunwoody, & C. L. Rogers (Eds.), *Scientists and journalists: Reporting science as news* (pp. 55–69). New York: Free Press.

Miller, J. D. (2000). The development of civic scientific literacy in the United States. In D. Kumar & D. Chubin (Eds.), *Science, technology and society: A sourcebook on research and practice* (pp. 21–47). New York: Plenum.

Miller, J. D. (2001). Who is using the Web for science and health information? *Science Communication, 22,* 256–273.

Miller, J. D. (2002). Breaking news or broken news [Electronic version]. *Nieman Reports, 56*(3), 18–21.

Miller, J. D. (2003, February). *The conceptualization and measurement of policy leadership.* Paper presented at the annual meeting of the American Association for the Advancement of Science, Denver, CO.

Miller, J. D. (2004). Public understanding of, and attitudes toward, scientific research: What we know and what we need to know [Electronic version]. *Public Understanding of Science, 13,* 273–294.

Miller, J. D., & Kimmel, L. (2000). *Biomedical communications.* New York: Academic Press.

Miller, J. D., Pardo, R., & Niwa, F. (1997). *Public perceptions of science and technology: A comparative study of the European Union, the United States, Japan, and Canada.* Madrid, Spain: BBV Foundation.

Mitsuishi, S., Kato, K., & Nakamura, K. (2001). A new way to communicate science to the public: The creation of the Scientist Library [Electronic version]. *Public Understanding of Science, 10,* 231–241.

Moynihan, R., Bero, L., Ross-Degnan, D., Henry, D., Lee, K., Watkins, J., et al. (2000). Coverage by the news media of the benefits and risks of medications. *New England Journal of Medicine, 342,* 1645–1650.

National Bioethics Advisory Commission. (1999). *Ethical issues in human stem cell research.* Retrieved from http://www.georgetown.edu/research/nrcbl/nbac/stem cell.pdf

National Science Foundation, Division of Science Resource Statistics. (2006). *Science and engineering indicators 2006* [Electronic version]. Retrieved from http://www.nsf.gov/statistics/seind06/prsntlst.htm

Nisbet, M. C., & Lewenstein, B. V. (2002). Biotechnology and the American media: The policy process and the elite press, 1970 to 1999 [Electronic version]. *Science Communication, 23*(4), 359–391.

Office of Science and Technology and the Wellcome Trust. (2001). Science and the public: A review of science communication and public attitudes toward science in Britain [Electronic version]. *Public Understanding of Science, 10,* 315–330.

Pardo, R., & Calvo, F. (2004). The cognitive dimension of public perceptions of science: Methodological issues [Electronic version]. *Public Understanding of Science, 13,* 203–227.

Pearson, G. (2001). The participation of scientists in public understanding of science activities: The policy and practice of the U.K. Research Councils [Electronic version]. *Public Understanding of Science, 10,* 121–137

Pedretti, E. (2002). T. Kuhn meets T. Rex: Critical conversations and new directions in science centers and science museums. *Studies in Science Education, 37,* 1–41.

Persson, P. (2000). Science centers are thriving and going strong! [Electronic version]. *Public Understanding of Science, 9,* 449–460.

Pew Research Center for The People & The Press. (2004). *Democrats gain edge in party identification.* Retrieved August 8, 2006, from http://people-press.org/commentary/display.php3?analysisID=95

Priest, S. H. (1995). Information equity, public understanding of science, and the biotechnology debate. *Journal of Communication, 45,* 39–55.

Priest, S. H. (2000). U.S. public opinion divided over biotechnology? [Electronic version]. *Nature Biotechnology, 18,* 939–942.

Priest, S. H. (2001). Misplaced faith: Communication variables as predictors of encouragement for biotechnology. *Science Communication, 23,* 97–110.

Priest, S. H. (2006). The public opinion climate for gene technologies in Canada and the United States: Competing voices, contrasting frames [Electronic version]. *Public Understanding of Science, 15,* 55–71.

Reese, S. D., & Ballinger, J. (2001). The roots of a sociology of news: Remembering Mr. Gates and social control in the newsroom [Electronic version]. *Journalism & Mass Communication Quarterly, 80,* 641–658.

Rogers, C. L. (1997). Introduction. In D. Blum & M. Knudson (Eds.), *A field guide for science writers* (pp. 213–216). New York: Oxford University Press.

Rose, S. P. R. (2003). How to (or not to) communicate science. *Biochemical Society Transactions, 31,* 307–312.

Rosenstone, R. A. (2003). Comments on science in the visual media [Electronic version]. *Public Understanding of Science, 12,* 335–339.

Rowe, G., Frewer, L., & Sjöberg, L. (2000). Newspaper reporting of hazards in the UK and Sweden [Electronic version]. *Public Understanding of Science, 9,* 59–78.

Rowe, G., Horlick-Jones, T., Walls, J., & Pidgeon, N. (2005). Difficulties in evaluating public engagement initiatives: Reflections on an evaluation of the UK GM Nation? Public debate about transgenic crops [Electronic version]. *Public Understanding of Science, 14,* 331–352.

Sachsman, D., Simon, J., & Valenti, J. M. (2002). The environment reporters of New England [Electronic version]. *Science Communication, 23,* 410–441.

Salomone, K. L., Greenberg, M. R., Sandman, P. M., & Sachsman, D. B. (1990). A question of quality: How journalists and news sources evaluate coverage of environmental risk. *Journal of Communication, 40,* 117–131.

Schmierbach, M. (2005). Method matters: The influence of methodology on journalists' assessments of social science research [Electronic version]. *Science Communication, 26,* 269–287.

Schnabel, U. (2003). God's formula and devil's contribution: Science in the press [Electronic version]. *Public Understanding of Science, 12,* 255–259.

Shanahan, J., & Good, J. (2000). Heat and hot air: Influence of local temperature on journalists' coverage of global warming [Electronic version]. *Public Understanding of Science, 9,* 285–295.

Shanahan, J., Scheufele, D., & Lee, E. (2001). Attitudes about agricultural biotechnology and genetically modified organisms [Electronic version]. *Public Opinion Quarterly, 65,* 267–281.

Shaw, A. (2002). "It just goes against the grain": Public understandings of genetically modified (GM) food in the UK [Electronic version]. *Public Understanding of Science, 11,* 273– 291.

Stamm, K. R., Clark, F., & Eblacas, P. R. (2000). Mass communication and public understanding of environmental problems: The case of global warming [Electronic version]. *Public Understanding of Science, 9,* 219–237.

Steinke, J. (2004). Science in cyberspace: Science and engineering World Wide Web sites for girls [Electronic version]. *Public Understanding of Science, 13,* 7–30.

Steinke, J. (2005). Cultural representations of gender and science: Portrayals of female scientists and engineers in popular films [Electronic version]. *Science Communication, 27*(1), 27–63.

Stephens, L. F. (2005). News narratives about nano S&T in major U.S. and non-U.S. newspapers [Electronic version]. *Science Communication, 27*(2), 175–199.

Sturgis, P., & Allum, N. (2004). Science in society: Re-evaluating the deficit model of public attitudes [Electronic version]. *Public Understanding of Science, 13,* 55–74.

Tankard, J. (2001). The empirical approach to the study of media framing. In S. Reese, O Gandy, & A. Grant (Eds.), *Framing public life: Perspectives on media and our understanding of the social world* (pp. 95–106). Mahwah, NJ: Lawrence Erlbaum.

Tankard, J., Hendrickson, L., Silberman, J., Bliss, K., & Ghanem, S. (1991, August). *Media frames: Approaches to conceptualization and measurement.* Paper presented at the Association for Education in Journalism and Mass Communication, Boston.

Ten Eyck, T. A. (2005). The media and public opinion on genetics and biotechnology: Mirrors, windows, or walls? [Electronic version]. *Public Understanding of Science, 14,* 305–316.

Ten Eyck, T. A., & Williment, M. (2003). The national media and things genetic: Coverage in *The New York Times* (1971–2001) and *The Washington Post* (1977–2001) [Electronic version]. *Science Communication, 25*(2), 129–152.

Tremayne, M., & Dunwoody, S. (2001). Interactivity, information processing, and learning on the World Wide Web [Electronic version]. *Science Communication, 23*(2), 111–134.

Ungar, S. (2000). Knowledge, ignorance and the popular culture: Climate change versus the ozone hole [Electronic version]. *Public Understanding of Science, 9,* 297–312.

U.S. Census Bureau. (2006). Table 69: Self-described religious identification of adult population: 1990 and 2001. Retrieved August 8, 2006, from http://www.census .gov/compendia/statab/population/religion

Valenti, J. M., & Tavana, G. (2005). Report: Continuing science education for environmental journalists and science writers: in situ with the experts [Electronic version]. *Science Communication, 27,* 300–310.

Väliverronen, E. (2004). Stories of the "medicine cow": Representations of future promises in media discourse [Electronic version]. *Public Understanding of Science, 13,* 363–377.

Weigold, M. F. (2001). Communicating science: A review of the literature. *Science Communication, 23,* 164–193.

Weigold, M. F., & Treise, D. (2004). Attracting teen surfers to science Web sites [Electronic version]. *Public Understanding of Science, 13,* 229–248.

Weingart, P., Muhl, C., & Pansegrau, P. (2003). Of power maniacs and unethical geniuses: Science and scientists in fiction film [Electronic version]. *Public Understanding of Science, 12,* 279–287.

Wilson, K. M. (2000). Drought, debate, and uncertainty: Measuring reporters' knowledge and ignorance about climate change [Electronic version]. *Public Understanding of Science, 9,* 1–13.

Zehr, S. C. (2000). Public representations of scientific uncertainty about global climate change [Electronic version]. *Public Understanding of Science, 9,* 85–103.

Zimmerman, C., Bisanz, G. L., Bisanz, J., Klein, J. S., & Klein, P. (2001). Science at the supermarket: A comparison of what appears in the popular press, experts' advice to readers, and what students want to know [Electronic version]. *Public Understanding of Science, 10,* 37–58.

CHAPTER 3

Journalistic Practice and Coverage of the Behavioral and Social Sciences

Sharon Dunwoody

Early in 2006, a team of psychologists at the University of Amsterdam published a research article describing a novel link between information processing and decision making. Dubbed the "deliberation-without-attention" effect, the studies suggested that what appear to be quick, intuitive judgments about complex problems may actually result in better decisions than those made in the heat of intense information gathering and processing (Dijksterhuis, Bos, Nordgren, & Baaren, 2006).

Media organizations around the world turned the research into news via a timeless, global process in which journalists encounter information, recognize something worthy in it, and respond by interviewing and writing. What is remarkable about the episode, then, is not the process itself but the fact that it was applied to a piece of peer-reviewed social and behavioral science research. While journalists have always depended heavily on journals for science news, they have historically been indifferent to social and behavioral science research, making stories such as this one all too rare in the mass media.

In this chapter, I will reflect on why this particular piece of research defied the odds and became news, as well as on a set of journalistic practices that govern the selection and structure of science news generally and social and behavioral science news in particular. In the latter half of this chapter, I will dwell on one particular judgment bias that I think has a significant impact on media coverage of social and behavioral science scholarship: a tendency for journalists to fail to see social and behavioral science phenomena as amenable to systematic exploration, a failure that leads them to construct narratives that ignore issues of evidence and context.

I will employ the long, rather awkward term *social and behavioral sciences* in this chapter as it captures not only the behavioral science focus of this text but also a literature that looks more generally at media coverage of the social sciences.

THE "DELIBERATION-WITHOUT-ATTENTION" EFFECT AS NEWS

Journalists do not monitor social and behavioral science journals on a regular basis. But science journalists do attend closely to a small number of major science and medical journals, among them *Science* magazine. It was in the February 17, 2006, issue of *Science* that the decision-making article appeared.

Science attends only sparingly to the social and behavioral sciences, so most journalists who received early access to articles in the February 17 issue were not looking specifically for a good social and behavioral science piece. (As is the case with other prestigious journals, *Science* makes an issue's articles available to reporters several days in advance to give them time to interview sources for stories. Along with this access comes an embargo rule, requiring media organizations to hold their stories until the day of journal publication.) But the "deliberation-without-attention" story would have caught the attention of journalists for a number of reasons:

- Although "just" a social and behavioral science story, it was one legitimized by publication in one of the nation's top peer-reviewed journals. The rare nature of these articles in *Science* strengthens the signal that this work must be important.
- The journal made the piece even more visible to reporters both by briefly summarizing its findings in its "This Week in Science" section in the front of the journal and by generating a short news article itself, written by one of the magazine's news reporters (Miller, 2006).
- The topic of decision making and judgment had become culturally salient with the 2005 publication of Malcolm Gladwell's *Blink,* a book about the psychology of speedy decisions (Gladwell, 2005). Although "trade books" are invisible components of the environment of many Americans, the Gladwell book produced some buzz among journalists and would have been known among individuals of higher socioeconomic status, who can afford to build for themselves a rich information environment.
- The scientists' results violated our common-sense expectations, and such violations function as compelling news pegs for journalists.

We typically regard decisions buttressed by effortful information processing to be better than intuitive judgments, but this work found the latter to trump the former. In a series of studies summarized in the article, participants received information in service to both simple and complex decisions. Then the investigators varied the length of time between pondering and making a decision by introducing the laboratory equivalent of "sleeping on it." Some participants were asked to make decisions immediately after ingesting information ("conscious thinkers") while others were distracted for a period of time before making a decision ("unconscious thinkers"). The conscious thinkers made better decisions when the choices were simple, but—and here's the counterintuitive part—the unconscious thinkers were the better decision makers in complex situations.

The fact that the psychologists were at the University of Amsterdam presented interviewing hurdles that may have deterred some journalists. But the research was picked up by a number of prestigious media outlets, including *The New York Times, Discover* magazine, and *The Washington Post.* The resulting widespread publicity thus stems from a confluence of sophisticated signaling by the scientific culture in one of its top journals and topic characteristics that convinced journalists that the report would be both interesting and easily accessible to general readers. The popularized accounts not only communicated with lay audiences but probably put this study on the map among social and behavioral scientists as well, a point I will return to at the end of this chapter.

So how does a piece of social and behavioral science research find its way into the mass media? More specifically, what prompts a journalist to act, and what influences decisions regarding sources and story structure?

A relatively robust literature in the United States and elsewhere has explored dimensions of journalistic behavior (see, e.g., Berkowitz,

1997; Clayman & Heritage, 2002; Cohen & Young, 1981; Fishman, 1980; Gans, 1980; Tuchman, 1978; Tunstall, 1971), with much of modern scholarship in the United States now being captured by newer niche journals such as *Journalism Studies* and *Journalism*. The literature focusing specifically on media coverage of the social and behavioral sciences is much more modest (see, e.g., Goldstein, 1986; Haslam & Bryman, 1994; Rubinstein & Brown, 1985; Stocking & Dunwoody, 1982; Weiss & Singer, 1988). While referring the reader to these more expansive reflections on what journalists do and why they do it, I will opt here for a focus on a subset of news judgment factors that I think are particularly relevant to coverage of the social and behavioral sciences. The article about the deliberation-without-attention effects offers a good illustration of some of those factors, and I'll point out those parallels along the way. At the end of the chapter, I will offer some suggestions for enhancing the volume and quality of behavioral science stories in the media through productive interactions with journalists.

THE REACTIVE NATURE OF STORY SELECTION

Journalists feel strongly that journalism should avoid creating news and, instead, should work to reflect real-world occurrences. That "mirror" norm encourages the journalism business to follow on the heels of a process rather than try to foreshadow its twists and turns.

This reactive posture becomes apparent when researchers track back through the unfolding of major news stories. For example, after the explosion of the space shuttle *Challenger* on January 28, 1986, many journalists and scholars rummaged through years of space shuttle stories to look for accounts that may have presaged the catastrophe. Although a few reporters had indeed explored the relatively high risks of shuttle flight, most

reportage about NASA and the program remained determinedly optimistic and apparently oblivious to the risks. Journalist Gregg Easterbrook, then a national correspondent for the *Atlantic Monthly*, reflected in a panel discussion soon after the accident that "the press never covered the fundamental flaw of the shuttle program. . . . In the days when it was possible to make a change, there wasn't enough coverage at all of the fact that the shuttle was flawed as a concept from the beginning. It was too great a risk" (*Media Coverage of the Shuttle Disaster*, 1986, p. 3).

Once the explosion had occurred, coverage of the aftermath, including enterprise reporting that uncovered the likely cause of the explosion (O rings made brittle by cold weather) and laid bare a tragic trail of human decisions, won numerous awards for journalists, among them the 1987 Pulitzer Prize for National Reporting by *New York Times* reporters. But that exquisite work could only come after the explosion, not prior to it.

This reactive posture makes journalism susceptible to influence by sources. Indeed, one could argue that reactivity enables skilled sources to construct the environment within which a journalist must then operate. And, although journalists express an acute understanding of and distaste for this possibility, they also acknowledge its inevitability. When press officials at the University of Utah announced a press conference in Salt Lake City in March 1989, even journalists skeptical of cold fusion hastened there. Regardless of its potential validity, the fusion claim was going to be big news, and journalists understood that covering the announcement was part of their responsibilities.

Source influence can be much more subtle, of course, such that it goes unnoticed by reporters. For example, numerous studies have found that, while journalists are literally inundated by story ideas and reject most of the suggestions that come their way, they still behave as if those ideas constitute the universe of story possibilities. Put another way, while journalists may use proportionately *little* of the information provided to them by sources, their selection of information will still be bounded by and will be proportionately *like* the available pool. For example, in one study of the information coming across the desks of science and health writers, Dunwoody and Kalter (1991) found that the science content categories reflected in the materials retained by the journalists strongly reflected the proportions of that content in the original materials, results consonant with a number of other studies (see, e.g., Dunwoody & Shields, 1986; Gold & Simmons, 1965; Whitney & Becker, 1982). Power to construct the universe of story possibilities is great power, indeed.

Sources also play a role in determining what about a story possibility is salient. Fishman (1980) was among the first to suggest that journalists readily adopt the frames of reference of their sources, using source reactions as guides to specific story features. For example, Fishman found that journalists covering local governmental meetings tended to privilege the items that captured the attention of the officials involved and ignored those parts of the agenda that were given short shrift by these individuals.

The assimilation of source interpretations is greatly enhanced when the status of sources is high, a characteristic of many science and medical sources. Reporters will accept and employ the frames of reference of these high-status sources even when doing so will delay their work. For example, science journalists readily accept scientists' arguments that new research should be subjected to peer review before being publicly disseminated, even when it means that the journalists must delay writing about a research project for months to years.

It is this acceptance of scientists' word for quality that makes signaling via journal publication so powerful a predictor of story choice. Thus, when *Science* magazine highlighted the publication of the "deliberation-without-attention" studies in its pages, journalists responded with enthusiasm, not skepticism. Through such mechanisms, the scientific culture has a pronounced impact on media representations of science. Although many scientists profess feelings of powerlessness in the grip of a runaway journalist, the more likely victim, frankly, is the journalist. There are always exceptions, of course, but the version of reality promulgated by the media is more closely aligned with scientists' reality than with the interpretations of others (Dunwoody, 1999).

How do social and behavioral scientists fare in the story selection and structuring process relative to other scientists? Admittedly, many journalists place social and behavioral scientists lower on the status rungs than they do other types of scientists. This is changing, I think, as the quality of good social and behavioral science scholarship becomes more obvious to the culture at large. But it was not that long ago, in a study of science journalists' news choices, that I found these reporters to routinely disparage social and behavioral science work. While the journalists I studied readily wrote stories about social and behavioral science topics, acknowledging the relevance of the topics to their audiences, they openly worried about the science's quality. One journalist exiting a press conference featuring new research into the link between television content and aggressive behavior in children indicated that, although he would write the story for his newspaper, he considered the research "garbage science" (Dunwoody, 1986b, p. 72). He was offering a critique not of the specific research project being discussed in the press conference but of the "soft sciences" generally. He was not alone in his feelings at that time.

But even in today's world, where the social and behavioral science disciplines are accorded more respect than in the past, journalists cannot cover what they don't see. And they do not monitor social and behavioral science research journals. Thus, to become a part of the universe of story possibilities, journals and scientists focused on social and behavioral research must actively disseminate information, a process that I will return to at the end of the chapter.

WHAT TO DO
ABOUT TRUTH CLAIMS . . .

A major part of the normative toolkit for a working journalist is directed at managing one significant problem: Journalists cannot determine what is true.

In the course of gathering information for stories, journalists are confronted with countless truth claims, many of them contradictory. One scientist declares that his data suggest the presence of a genetic tendency toward violent behavior while others poohpooh that possibility. Respected scholars populate both sides of the debate over whether the death penalty deters would-be killers. Policy specialists duel over the effects of charter schools on learning among disadvantaged children.

Despite the fact that journalism's societal job is to provide the public with the information needed to make informed decisions about these and other issues, journalists do not declare a truth denouement, for a number of reasons. For one thing, the typical journalist has neither the training nor the time to sift through truth claims to arrive at a judgment. Many scientists use this problem as a basis for calling on journalists to be formally trained in the science they cover. But such a claim is unrealistic, as journalists cover many sciences, not just physics or just social and behavioral sciences.

A second problem with the journalist who performs triage on truth claims is that her or his readers/viewers are not prepared to accept her or his assertion that one person's truth claim may be more valid than that of another person. The official public role of a journalist in the United States is that of neutral transmitter, and any reporter who steps outside that role *as a news reporter* is open to charges of bias.

Illustrative of this is the beating *New York Times* reporter Gina Kolata has taken over the years for, among other things, her attempts to privilege the best available evidence in her stories (Marshall, 1998). For example, in the mid-1990s, Kolata reported that "the most definitive study yet of the health effects of silicone breast implants has failed to find any association between the implants and connective tissue diseases" (Kolata, 1995, p. A18), a finding that flew in the face of much anecdotal evidence at the time (for a useful summary of this controversy, see Vanderford & Smith, 1996). Kolata argued that the new data constituted the best available evidence to date in the search for a breast implant/disease link. In an article in *The Nation*, however, journalist Mark Dowie praised media coverage of the controversy that attempted to offer a balanced view and interpreted this and other Kolata stories as evidence that the journalist (and her newspaper) too readily sided with corporate views (Dowie, 1998). Experts empanelled by the Institute of Medicine some years later to look at all the breast implant/health evidence validated Kolata's weight-of-evidence judgment: Although implant ruptures and subsequent infections present a "primary safety issue," noted the panel, it could find no evidentiary basis for the claim that implants cause disease (Bondurant, Ernster, & Herdman, 1999, p. 5).

The bottom line, then, is that journalists do not possess the time, skills, or cultural permission to sift through contested claims in order to declare one "more true" than the rest. What, then, is a reporter to do? Over the decades, journalism has evolved two surrogates for validity claims, both of them equipped with advantages and debits for the journalist and his or her sources. One is objectivity; the other, a strategy called balance, calls on the reporter to offer variance in points of view. I'll look briefly at each of these.

Objectivity

If you cannot know which message is true, argues the objectivity norm, then at least accurately transmit the messages that you gather. An objective account, then, is one that faithfully captures the factual claims and opinions of a source, regardless of the validity of those claims and opinions.

On the positive side, objectivity privileges accuracy and focuses both journalist and source on that characteristic of messages. Accuracy matters very much to scientists (see, e.g., Carsten & Illman, 2002; Matas, el-Guebaly, Peterkin, Green, & Harper, 1985; Singer, 1990), and objectivity makes it a priority for journalists as well.

The disadvantages of objectivity are substantial, however. Most primally, objectivity sanctions a journalist's decision to ignore validity altogether. A story thus can communicate something that is just plain wrong and still meet the criteria for objectivity. The norm nurtures conundrums such as that highlighted in the 2005 film *Good Night and Good Luck,* the story of famous broadcaster Edward R. Murrow's decision to abandon objectivity and unmask Sen. Joe McCarthy's Communist-baiting behaviors in Congress. McCarthy's attempts to charge a variety of Americans with treason and "communist subversion" in the 1950s received copious press coverage despite journalists' strong reservations about the validity of the claims. For most journalists at the time, though, objectivity required that they transmit without judgment.

Balance

If you cannot know which message is true, argues the balance norm, then at least provide as many points of view as possible in your story. That means the truth will be in there somewhere.

The balance norm insists that reporters remain keenly aware that there can be different versions of reality, a good thing if media accounts are to have a chance of representing the complexity of belief systems. But balance in a world where objectivity prevents the journalist from making validity judgments is fraught with peril. When a reporter does seek a variety of viewpoints, the easiest way to play a neutral transmitter role is to give each of those viewpoints equal space.

The result is the "she said/he said" story, with sources often contradicting one another and leaving the reader/viewer with the feeling that "nobody knows what's true!" Journalists often make the situation worse by attempting to display the variance in expert beliefs not by sampling across the spectrum of beliefs but by capturing beliefs at the extreme tails.

The objectivity and balance norms are so strong that journalists will often obey them despite their own best judgments. An iconic study illustrating this point was conducted some years ago by communication researcher James Dearing (1995), who explored media coverage of scientific outliers such as biologist Peter Duesberg, who contends that the HIV virus is not the cause of AIDS, and cold fusion "discoverers" B. Stanley Pons and Martin Fleischmann. Consistent with the expectations of objectivity and balance norms, Dearing found newspaper coverage of these issues to be more supportive than critical of outlier claims. But tellingly, when questioned about their own beliefs about the likely validity of the claims, the journalists indicated that the outliers were probably wrong! This meant, noted Dearing, "that most of these journalists did not, at the time they were writing their articles . . . consider these mavericks to be credible" (p. 355). But the pressure to withhold judgment about what is true overrode those opinions.

Objectivity and balance are coming under increasing criticism within journalism (see, e.g., Cunningham, 2003; Mooney, 2004). But the norms are exceptionally robust and will not decay easily. In recent years, both journalists and scholars of journalism have called on reporters to adopt more of a "weight-of-evidence" approach to coverage of contested claims (see, e.g., Dunwoody, 2005; Mooney & Nisbet, 2005). Such an approach would not require journalists to assess the validity of claims themselves but, rather, to share with their audiences what the bulk of experts believes to be true at that moment.

The closest that most journalists have been willing to come to this weight-of-evidence practice is to seek the counsel of relevant experts either to provide additional voices in a story or to serve as confidential advisers to the journalists themselves as they evaluate the newsworthiness of a scientific claim. Reporters recognize this norm as advice to avoid the "one-source story," and the strategy is nicely captured in many of the stories written about the "deliberation-without-attention effect." For example, reporter Gareth Cook of *The Boston Globe* included in his account reactions to the research from two other experts, a psychologist who reflected positively on the work and a business school professor who registered skepticism (Cook, 2006).

While still far afield from a validity judgment or even from a weight-of-evidence assertion, the practice of seeking feedback from multiple experts is an important journalistic tool. Some years ago, while I was observing science writers at a large meeting, I witnessed an effort not only to seek the advice of "unbiased others" but also to share that advice among journalists who work for competing organizations. At a press conference, a social scientist argued that his analyses of a number of large survey data sets had isolated a possible genetic precursor to violent behavior. Clearly uncomfortable with the finding, science journalists streaming out of the press conference got together in the hallway and decided to contact a variety of other social scientists by phone in an effort to vet both the PI and his findings. An hour or so later, the journalists regrouped to share what they had learned. They then made individual decisions about whether to write the story or not.

Are there things that social and behavioral scientists can do to enhance the likelihood of weight-of-evidence treatment of research in their own areas? To a limited extent, the answer is yes. I will return to this at the end of the chapter.

JOURNALISTS OFTEN FRAME SOCIAL AND BEHAVIORAL SCIENCE AS . . . SOMETHING ELSE

Back in the 1980s, in what remains an important piece of baseline science communication scholarship, researchers Carol Weiss and Eleanor Singer employed funds from the Russell Sage Foundation to study coverage of the social and behavioral sciences in major U.S. media. After carefully defining what they meant by social and behavioral science—sociology, political science, economics, psychology, anthropology, criminology, demography, epidemiology, and behavioral medicine—the scholars looked for stories published in major newspapers, news magazines, and network news over the course of 5 months in 1982. They also interviewed journalists who wrote some of the stories and social scientists who were quoted in them.

One of their many findings that stood out for me and will drive this section of the chapter is the following: Journalists rarely define a social and behavioral science story as being about "science," and that failure, in turn, means that they do not apply the evidentiary standards of science to the topic. This became apparent to Weiss and Singer (1988) early in their study:

> In the course of pretesting our interviews, we talked to a number of reporters who had just written a story which we classified as social science, and we asked them if this was the first time that they had written stories about social science. Uniformly they were taken aback; some seemed to think that we were talking gibberish. In their minds the current story was not about social science at all. They were writing about crime or business or politics or education. That they were reporting the results of *research* on the topic or citing the remarks of a *social scientist* was of little consequence. It was the *topic* of the story that provided the frame of reference for their work. (pp. 55–56)

Put another way, journalists write about social and behavioral science topics all the time but rarely identify the issue or event in their sights as "scientific" and amenable to systematic exploration. The absence of such an interpretive frame has large consequences for the nature of the story, as the frame will determine the types of sources sought and the nature of the questions asked.

Let's say a journalist pitches a story to her editor about two-career couples whose work requires them to live apart. For most reporters, the topic sounds like a great lifestyle story about an increasingly familiar situation of general interest. If our journalist frames the story idea that way, the frame will lead her to seek out a few such couples through word of mouth, interview them, and write a story grounded in vivid, anecdotal materials derived from the experiences of those families.

But what if she were to define the story, initially, as one that has been the focus of research? That frame would lead her to the peer-reviewed literature to see what social scientists now "know" about the experiences of these couples. She would likely contact a couple scientists for interviews, and there is

even a chance that she would then locate couples whose situations illustrate some of the main patterns in the data with which she has become familiar. What a difference a frame makes!

Journalists' blindness to the scientific, evidentiary dimensions of social and behavioral science topics has caught the attention of an increasing number of journalists and scholars. Veteran journalist and analyst Michael Massing bemoaned the problem in an article that took issue with the press' coverage of popular culture. Major news outlets such as *The New York Times* seem suffused with stories about the new, the dramatic, off-the-wall aspects of our culture, complained Massing, but "in the process, the *Times* has neglected a critical aspect of pop culture—its effects on society" (Massing, 2006, p. 28). Survey after survey indicates that Americans indeed worry about the effects of a large range of cultural changes—entertainment, clothing choices, new electronic gadgets—on children and society at large. Notes Massing, "The journalistic questions such fare provokes seem endless, and they extend far beyond the usual ones about sex and violence into the realms of sociology, politics, and religion" (p. 30).

Similarly, mass communication researcher Michael Slater, in an analysis of media coverage of alcohol-related risks, found that journalists rarely dipped below the surface of a topic to explore the causal waters underneath. Among the health catastrophes for which alcohol serves as a major precursor, he found that only motor vehicle accidents were covered in ways that gave readers some sense of alcohol's role; coverage of other alcohol related risks, such as injuries stemming from violent crime, were handled as specific, vivid episodes that seemed to occur in a causal vacuum (Slater, Long, & Ford, 2006).

Some years ago, a California newspaper reporter realized that media coverage of violence was dominated by discrete, episodic stories that informed readers about the tragic events themselves but that failed to place the violent acts in any type of interpretive framework. Journalist Jane Stevens came to a conclusion similar to that of Weiss and Singer years earlier: A major reason for this lack of context was definitional. "I discovered that the answer lies in the way journalists report crime," noted Stevens. "We do so only from a law enforcement and criminal justice standpoint" (Stevens, 1998, p. 38). In other words, Stevens felt that the initial interpretive framework adopted by journalists covering violent crime rendered the reporters unable to "see" the epidemiology of violence and thus made them oblivious to social and behavioral science research that could help explain the occurrence of such dramatic and occasionally horrific acts.

In response to that problem, Stevens joined forces with the Berkeley Media Studies Group and the communication researchers at the University of Missouri–Columbia to examine newspaper patterns of crime reporting and then, through a variety of strategies, attempted to change reporting of violence in ways that would introduce evidentiary issues, context that could help readers develop an understanding of why such acts occur. Stevens wrote a book, *Reporting on Violence*, to provide journalists with data and ways to gather such information as the economic and psychological consequences of different types of violence, methods being developed to prevent violence, and information about how communities can implement prevention approaches (Stevens, 1997). The collaboration also designed and implemented on-site workshops at five metropolitan newspapers to introduce reporters to ways of thinking beyond the episodic, violent event. The trainers hoped to lead journalists to more evidentiary thinking about the causes and by-products of violent acts, which in turn could lead to stories that reflected more thematically on the roles of violence in society (Dorfman, Thorson, & Stevens, 2001; Thorson, Dorfman, & Stevens, 2003).

Did these efforts to transform the interpretive framework for violent press coverage from an episodic crime focus to a more thematic public health focus bear fruit? It is hard to tell. The project directors summarized journalists' reception to their workshop ideas as one of "cautious interest" (Dorfman et al., 2001, p. 417) and acknowledged that both normative and technical obstacles loomed for reporters and editors considering a more thematic, evidentiary approach to crime news. In her revised second edition of *Reporting on Violence* (available at www.bmsg.org), Stevens reflects on a small number of journalists who embraced the project material and went on to write a steady stream of contextual stories for their newspapers.

THE LEGITIMIZING EFFECT OF MEDIA VISIBILITY

Before embarking on a final section reflecting on strategies that social and behavioral scientists can employ to enhance their media visibility and improve coverage of their research, it is important to ask the following question: Why would a scientist want to go out of her or his way to interact with journalists? Historically, scientists have worried that public visibility would create more problems than perks. And for the social and behavioral scientist of 25 years ago, that worry would have been justified; scientists were often punished by their peers for "popularization" activities (Dunwoody, 1986a). But today, scientists of all kinds are becoming increasingly sophisticated popularizers, for a number of reasons:

- *Quid pro quo.* For many social and behavioral scientists, federal support of their research confers a responsibility to share results with various publics.
- *Education.* Increasing numbers of scientists are embracing the need to participate in informal science education in an effort to

increase the general level of science literacy in the United States. The National Science Foundation's renewed emphasis on the "broader impact" component of its grant proposals is illustrative.

- *Dollars.* There is plenty of anecdotal evidence on behalf of a relationship between level of public visibility and level of research resources. Systematic evidence is less obvious, but—like all humans—scientists find the vivid anecdotes compelling.

- *Legitimization.* Perhaps most important, social and behavioral scientists are beginning to understand that public visibility for their work confers a kind of cultural legitimacy that can be valuable.

As a society's primary signaling devices, the mass media make some things loom as more important than other things. Put another way, stories affect public judgments of salience even in the absence of a deeper understanding of issues. Today, for example, I encountered a major story in the "Science Times" section of *The New York Times* about recent research on the neurological costs of teenage drinking (Butler, 2006). Binge drinking is a salient issue for any university professor, but this piece stopped me in my tracks with its reflection on research detailing the extraordinary physiological cost of heavy drinking on nerve cells. Since reading it, I have been pondering how best to share the information with undergraduate students that I will encounter in my fall classes. Such is the power of media signaling.

Even more remarkable, though, is the media's ability to serve as a legitimizer *within* science. Scientists, it turns out, react to media accounts just like the rest of us. A piece of research covered by the media seems more worthy to other scientists, even those within the discipline.

A couple of studies bear this out. Both find an effect of media visibility on the number of citations to a study in the peer-reviewed literature. Phillips, Kanter, Bednarczyk, and Tastad (1991) compared citations to two groups of studies published by the *New England Journal of Medicine* (NEJM); one group had been covered by *The New York Times,* and the other group—matched on all other variables—had not. In the first year after publication, the typical research study covered by the newspaper received 73% more citations than did the *NEJM* articles not so covered.

More recently, Kiernan (2003) looked for the same pattern in a larger group of journals and media outlets and found that peer-reviewed articles that garnered media visibility earned 22% more citations in the literature than did articles that remained culturally invisible. In addition, Kiernan also found that the legitimizing effect of media visibility was not limited to stories in the *New York Times* but was influenced by coverage in a wide range of media outlets.

STRATEGIES FOR MORE EFFECTIVE MEDIA INTERACTIONS

The mass media environment is as complex as any social structure, so social and behavioral scientists pondering a foray there need to think carefully about what they want to accomplish and how best to do so. Below, I will return to three journalistic "realities" emphasized in this chapter and will offer a few tips for coping with them.

Improving the Social and Behavioral Science "Signal" in the Mass Media

The reactive nature of journalistic work and the strong likelihood that journalists do not go seeking information about social and behavioral science means that much good research will remain invisible unless scientists and their organizations take a more active role in dissemination. Two important components of this process are (1) putting information where good journalists will see it and (2) maintaining credibility in the process. I bring the second point into the discussion because, while journalists acknowledge the usefulness of sources coming to them rather than vice versa, they also react negatively to marketing efforts perceived to be "over the top." One senior science writer who got increasing numbers of calls from scientists seeking coverage of their research confided that her first question to each caller had become, "When is your grant up for renewal?" Here are some tips for improving the signal sent to journalists:

- Make publication in a high-quality, peer-reviewed journal the catalyst for the story you have to tell. For knowledgeable journalists, this publication point remains the default signal that good science is ready to be transformed into a story. Disseminating at an earlier stage is a credibility risk. This is not to say that other signals about one's research are illegitimate. Scholars present at conferences, and attending journalists may follow up. Reports from credible bodies (The National Academies comes to mind) are viewed as highly credible by reporters. But for skilled journalists, publication in a peer-reviewed setting is still considered the gold standard. Remember, journalists cannot judge the validity of what you have to say. In that situation, savvy journalists rely on the same standard as do scientists: peer review.
- Aim for publication in top journals outside your field. To land in *Science, Nature,* or the *Journal of the American Medical Association* will send a much greater signal to journalists than will publication in even the most prestigious journal in most of our disciplines.
- Call a journalist to tip her or him off to your good work only if you have established a productive relationship with that

individual. Remember, cold calls from a potential source are a bit unnerving for a reporter. He or she will immediately begin to wonder about your motive, and that does not help your cause. On the other hand, if you have worked with a reporter in the past and are selective about when and why you employ this strategy, the payoff can be substantial. A scientist on my own campus whose work was scheduled to be the cover article in an issue of *Nature* called a reporter at a major newspaper—someone he had met in a previous venue—to let her know. The resulting story unleashed a virtual avalanche of attention to his work.

- Enlist the help of your university/company's public information officers (PIOs) to prepare and disseminate a plain-English version of your research. Most of us work in organizations equipped with skilled writers who can cater to journalists' needs much better than can we scientists. You may need to signal to these individuals that you have something useful to disseminate, so don't wait for them to contact you. But once they are energized, their skills will be invaluable. Fellow chapter author Earle Holland (Chapter 13), himself a distinguished public information officer, focuses on working with university PIOs.
- Encourage your disciplinary society to become more active as an information disseminator. Remember that most of our social and behavioral science journals are virtually invisible to journalists. We can mediate that problem to some extent by developing communication strategies at an aggregate (in this case, organizational) level. Many societies now issue press releases when significant and interesting research is at the cusp of publication in their journals.
- Encourage both employers and disciplinary organizations to consider placing their press releases on such omnibus Internet sites as EurekAlert (www.eurekalert.org), an online global news service operated by the American Association for the Advancement of Science that has become a major foraging venue for journalists, who receive privileged access to the new material there.

ENHANCING THE LIKELIHOOD THAT A JOURNALIST WILL APPLY A WEIGHT-OF-EVIDENCE APPROACH TO YOUR RESEARCH

Although the strategies below will not interest the scientist who believes she or he has uncovered "truth" in her or his work, I continue to argue on behalf of encouraging reporters to think more contextually, more thematically about our research and about the uncertainties so central to exploring complex processes. Here are some ways to accomplish that in an interview:

- Regardless of whether or not the reporter asks (and she or he probably will not), share with the individual your assessment of the extent to which others in your field agree or disagree with your findings. Make it clear that opinions vary and that such variance is a natural outgrowth of scientific investigation.
- Provide the reporter with names of other credible scientists who agree with you, as well as with names of those who disagree with you. Urge the reporter to contact some of these individuals. (By the way, this tactic will do wonders for your credibility, as it emphasizes your interest in truth over advocacy of your point of view.)
- Identify outliers and recommend that the journalist avoid them. The reporter will appreciate your efforts at full disclosure and might even take your advice.
- Offer to serve as a sounding board for future questions and issues. It is important to communicate your interest in helping the reporter grapple with the larger validity issues of your field. You may be more credible in this regard if you indicate a preference for acting as a confidential source of information.

HELPING JOURNALISTS TO DEFINE BEHAVIORAL AND SOCIAL SCIENCE TOPICS AS ONES AMENABLE TO SYSTEMATIC EXPLORATION

This is perhaps the most intractable problem of all, as an initial judgment of what a story is about will drive whether a journalist contacts you in the first place! In addition, Stevens and colleagues' attempts to shift the interpretive frameworks of journalists who cover violence demonstrate how difficult it is to modify existing mental maps.

- If you are contacted in the course of a developing story, speak from an evidentiary base and make that base obvious to the reporter. At the least, this will alert the journalist to the possibility of other interpretive frameworks for her or his story.

This will be only intermittently successful, of course. I recall an instance some years ago when an editor at *The New York Times* asked me to write a column for the Sunday newspaper reflecting on the impacts of science television programming on viewers. I naively assumed that he was open to an evidentiary piece and generated a column reflecting on how little we communications scholars knew about those message effects. At that time, for example, the prevailing operational definition of "high impact" for a *NOVA* program was a large audience. No one had a clue about whether anyone learned from the programs or about the possible effects of such learning on opinions or behaviors.

The editor was flummoxed by the column. He had anticipated that I would call people in the entertainment industry, the documentary production world, and perhaps even a few superstars such as the celebrated British broadcaster Sir David Attenborough to gather their reflections on the power of their programming. "So," he said slowly and carefully, "we don't really know the effects of these programs on audiences?" "Correct!" I responded, happy to have communicated my main message so clearly. In response, he killed the piece.

- Put energy into helping future journalists and media audiences build early interpretive frames for social and behavioral issues as topics amenable to evidence. Many of us spend a significant amount of time in the classroom, and that is an ideal location for this construction effort. For example, if your university has a journalism or communication department, consider building a few bridges between your discipline and budding reporters. As a result of being invited to speak to faculty and students in a variety of science units, for example, I have become a part of a number of fruitful collaborations that provide communication training for both my journalism students and for students in an array of science disciplines, including the social and behavioral sciences.

- Infiltrate "public" venues such as the annual meeting of the American Association for the Advancement of Science (AAAS). The AAAS meeting attracts thousands of scientists and hundreds of journalists. Staging a symposium on a timely public issue and mustering speakers who can provide a significant evidentiary base will go far. Again, our more narrow disciplinary meetings will be virtually invisible to the individuals we are trying to reach.

Do these strategies actually work? The answer is probably yes, although we have little empirical proof for most of them. Although the quantity and quality of research dedicated to exploring science communication questions has proliferated in recent years (see the overview by Weigold, Treise, and Rausch in Chapter 2 of this volume), the community of

researchers remains too small to establish a thorough and empirically well-grounded picture. Still, the available scholarship on message attributes and effects is well worth scientists' time and attention. Like many sources, they waste too much time at present rediscovering patterns and reinventing strategies. Readers will find some of this information in this very volume by going to the Stocking and Sparks discussion of communicating uncertainty (Chapter 4), reflections on the Internet as a new information channel by Martland and Rothbaum (Chapter 14), and the concluding chapter by Welch-Ross and Fasig that explores research on audiences for behavioral science information.

Although I have nothing better than anecdotal data to bring to bear, I have a strong sense that media organizations are increasingly willing to see social and behavioral research as high-quality, legitimate news pegs. Society is increasingly willing to acknowledge that most—if not all—important problems that we face are overwhelmingly behavioral or social in nature. As a result, journalists are increasingly looking to social and behavioral scientists for answers. The more actively and skillfully scientists share their good work with journalists, the more quickly the legitimization of behavioral and social science scholarship will gather a head of steam.

REFERENCES

Berkowitz, D. (1997). *Social meanings of news.* Thousand Oaks, CA: Sage.

Bondurant, S., Ernster, V., & Herdman, R. (Eds.). (1999). *Safety of silicone breast implants.* Washington, DC: National Academies Press.

Butler, K. (2006, July 4). The grim neurology of teenage drinking. *The New York Times,* pp. D1, D6.

Carsten, L. D., & Illman, D. H. (2002). Perceptions of accuracy in science writing. *IEEE Transactions on Professional Communication, 45,* 153–156.

Clayman, S., & Heritage, J. (2002). *The news interview: Journalists and public figures on the air.* Cambridge, UK: Cambridge University Press.

Cohen, S., & Young, J. (Eds.). (1981). *The manufacture of news: Deviance, social problems & the mass media.* Beverly Hills, CA: Sage.

Cook, G. (2006, February 17). Thought for thinkers. *The Boston Globe,* p. A1.

Cunningham, B. (2003, July/August). Re-thinking objectivity. *Columbia Journalism Review,* pp. 24–32.

Dearing, J. W. (1995). Newspaper coverage of maverick science: Creating controversy through balancing. *Public Understanding of Science, 4,* 341–360.

Dijksterhuis, A., Bos, M. W., Nordgren, L. R., & van Baaren, R. B. (2006). On making the right choice: The deliberation-without-attention effect. *Science, 311,* 1005–1007.

Dorfman, L., Thorson, E., & Stevens, J. E. (2001). Reporting on violence: Bringing a public health perspective into the newsroom. *Health Education & Behavior, 28,* 402–419.

Dowie, M. (1998, July 6). What's wrong with *The New York Times* science reporting? *The Nation,* pp. 13–19.

Dunwoody, S. (1986a). The scientist as source. In S. M. Friedman, S. Dunwoody, & C. L. Rogers (Eds.), *Scientists and journalists: Reporting science as news* (pp. 3–16). New York: Free Press.

Dunwoody, S. (1986b). When science writers cover the social and behavioral sciences. In J. H. Goldstein (Ed.), *Reporting science: The case of aggression* (pp. 67–81). Hillsdale, NJ: Lawrence Erlbaum.

Dunwoody, S. (1999). Scientists, journalists and the meaning of uncertainty. In S. M. Friedman, S. Dunwoody, & C. L. Rogers (Eds.), *Communicating uncertainty: Media coverage of new and controversial science* (pp. 59–79). Mahwah, NJ: Lawrence Erlbaum.

Dunwoody, S. (2005). Weight-of-evidence reporting: What is it? Why use it? *Nieman Reports, 59,* 89–91.

Dunwoody, S., & Kalter, J. (1991, August). *Daily information choices among mass media science reporters.* Paper presented at the meeting of the Association for Education in Journalism and Mass Communication, Boston.

Dunwoody, S., & Shields, S. (1986). Accounting for patterns of selection of topics in statehouse reporting. *Journalism Quarterly, 63,* 488–496.

Fishman, M. (1980). *Manufacturing the news.* Austin: University of Texas Press.

Gans, H. J. (1980). *Deciding what's news: A study of* CBS Evening News, NBC Nightly News, Newsweek *and* Time. New York: Vintage.

Gladwell, M. (2005). *Blink: The power of thinking without thinking.* New York: Little, Brown.

Gold, D., & Simmons, J. L. (1965). News selection patterns among Iowa dailies. *Journalism Quarterly, 29,* 425–430.

Goldstein, J. H. (Ed.). (1986). *Reporting science: The case of aggression.* Hillsdale, NJ: Lawrence Erlbaum.

Haslam, C., & Bryman, A. (Eds.). (1994). *Social scientists meet the media.* London: Routledge.

Kiernan, V. (2003). Diffusion of news about research. *Science Communication, 25,* 3–13.

Kolata, G. (1995, June 25). New study finds no link between breast implants and illness. *The New York Times,* p. A18.

Marshall, E. (1998, May 15). The power of the front page of *The New York Times.* Science, *280,* 996–997.

Massing, M. (2006, July/August). Off course. *Columbia Journalism Review,* pp. 28–34.

Matas, M., el-Guebaly, M., Peterkin, A., Green, M., & Harper, D. (1985). Mental illness and the media: An assessment of attitudes and communication. *Canadian Journal of Psychiatry, 30,* 12–17.

Media coverage of the shuttle disaster: A critical look. (1986). Washington, DC: American Association for the Advancement of Science.

Miller, G. (2006). Tough decision? Don't sweat it. *Science, 311, 935.*

Mooney, C. (2004, November/December). Blinded by science: How "balanced" coverage lets the scientific fringe hijack reality. *Columbia Journalism Review,* pp. 26–35.

Mooney, C., & Nisbet, M. (2005, September/October). Undoing Darwin. *Columbia Journalism Review,* pp. 31–39.

Phillips, D. P., Kanter, E. J., Bednarczyk, B., & Tastad, P. L. (1991). Importance of the lay press in the transmission of medical knowledge to the scientific community. *New England Journal of Medicine, 325,* 1180–1183.

Rubinstein, E. A., & Brown, J. D. (1985). *The media, social science, and social policy for children.* Norwood, NJ: Ablex.

Singer, E. (1990). A question of accuracy: How journalists and scientists report research on hazards. *Journal of Communication, 40,* 102–116.

Slater, M. D., Long, M., & Ford, V. L. (2006). Alcohol and illegal drugs, violent crime, traffic-related and other unintended injuries in U.S. local and national news. *Journal of Studies on Alcohol, 67,* 904–910.

Stevens, J. E. (1997). *Reporting on violence: A handbook for journalists.* Berkeley, CA: Berkeley Media Studies Group.

Stevens, J. E. (1998). Integrating the public health perspective into reporting on violence. *Nieman Reports, 52,* 38–40.

Stocking, H., & Dunwoody, S. (1982). Social and social and behavioral science in the mass media: Images and evidence. In J. E. Sieber (Ed.), *The ethics of social research: Fieldwork, regulation, and publication* (pp. 171–169). New York: Springer-Verlag.

Thorson, E., Dorfman, L., & Stevens, J. (2003). Reporting crime and violence from a public health perspective. *Journal of the Institute of Justice and International Studies, 2,* 53–66.

Tuchman, G. (1978). *Making news: A study in the construction of reality.* New York: Free Press.

Tunstall, J. (1971). *Journalists at work.* London: Constable.

Vanderford, M. L., & Smith, D. H. (1996). *The silicone breast implant story.* Mahwah, NJ: Lawrence Erlbaum.

Weiss, C. H., & Singer, E. (1988). *Reporting of social science in the national media.* New York: Russell Sage Foundation.

Whitney, D. C., & Becker, L. B. (1982). "Keeping the gates" for gatekeepers: The effects of wire news. *Journalism Quarterly, 59*(1), 60–65.

CHAPTER 4

Communicating the Complexities and Uncertainties of Behavioral Science

S. HOLLY STOCKING AND JOHNNY V. SPARKS

Journalists can be gluttons for behavioral science news. On any given day, they may offer selections from a wide-ranging menu of behavioral science findings:

- Low-calorie diets are good for you.
- Children who eat dinner with their families are less likely to use drugs and alcohol.
- Yoga improves respiratory function.
- Low self-esteem at 11 predicts drug dependency at 20.
- Mild depression is often a precursor to major depression in the elderly.
- Prenatal nicotine complicates the breathing of newborns.[1]

It's a rich news feast, some of it lovingly cooked up and quite tasty and some of it cooked up as quickly as a microwave dinner and destined to give some consumers—especially scientists—indigestion.

What makes the difference between the tasty news stories and the hard-to-digest news stories for scientists is often the way journalists treat the complexities and uncertainties of their research. To the extent that journalists preserve the critical complexities and uncertainties, the meal may satisfy; to the extent that they render complex and uncertain science as simple and sure—or the science as more uncertain than it is—a good many scientists may reach for the Tums.

The significance of journalists' treatment of complex and uncertain science cannot be underestimated. It is not just a matter of how *scientists* like the news about their work. It can also be a matter of how those who are the biggest consumers of science news are able to understand and use the science they consume. Indeed, when scientific complexities and uncertainties are poorly rendered, scientific conclusions may be poorly understood by the public, and when they are poorly understood, they can lead to personal and professional decisions that are less than optimal. The stakes, for those who aspire to a society informed by the best that science has to offer, are high.

AUTHORS' NOTE: The authors would like to express their appreciation to the Ford Foundation, which helped to support the development of this chapter under the grant "Turning Sexual Science Into News: Development of a Training Approach" (2005–2006), Julia Heiman (PI).

In this chapter, we will briefly discuss the challenges of communicating scientific complexities and uncertainties to different audiences. We will review some of the more prevalent problems that surveyed scientists, scholars, and others have associated with journalistic coverage of scientific complexities and uncertainties. We will present some solutions (or best practices) based on extrapolations from existing research and informed observation. Finally, we will outline some areas for research that we hope will create more solid understandings of media coverage of scientific complexities and uncertainties. Our hope is that such understandings will make it possible for scientists and journalists to modify their practices in ways that enable members of the public and policy makers alike to make good use of behavioral science.

CHALLENGES OF COMMUNICATING TO DIFFERENT AUDIENCES

When behavioral scientists write for their colleagues, they operate according to conventions as to what is necessary for peers' understandings. They have a pretty good idea of what others in their field of expertise want and need to know about populations, measures, methods, limitations of the findings, and all the rest.

When scientists work to communicate their research findings to the public, though, the conventions as to what is necessary for the public's understanding may be less clear. For one thing, audiences are more variable; what is likely to be wanted and needed by a public that is highly attentive to science, for example, may not be wanted and needed by a less attentive audience (J. D. Miller, 1986). Moreover, much of scientists' communication to the public is mediated by journalists, who have their own conventions as to what works. Though there is considerable variation among

journalists, most are likely to be less interested in pleasing scientists than in engaging their audiences.

In journalism, complexities related to populations studied, measures taken, controls, and so forth—matters of no small significance to scientists—are likely to be omitted, simplified, or amplified in an effort to attract and keep the public's attention. From the standpoint of scientists who are accustomed to a measure of control over the communication of their findings, the challenges can seem daunting. Depending on the audience and on the claims of other sources journalists may consult, the uncertainties or limitations in the findings may be either downplayed or amplified to a degree that scientists find inaccurate or discomforting. We will discuss each of these problems in turn in this section.

Loss of Scientific Complexity and Uncertainty

For behavioral scientists who are accustomed to carefully explaining the complexities and limits of their methods and findings for other behavioral scientists to evaluate and replicate, journalistic summaries of their research can be a source of bewilderment if not absolute consternation. Indeed, when scientists have been asked to identify problems or *errors* in science news, omission of information has often been at the top of the list (Borman, 1978; Dunwoody, 1982; Singer & Endreny, 1993; Tankard & Ryan, 1974). In their book-length treatment of social science news coverage, Weiss and Singer (1988) found oversimplification of complexities a top concern for social scientists.[2] In another study, when scientists were asked what they would change in journalists' stories about their work, their most common response was to add more details. Discovery stories—those ubiquitous stories that present the findings of a new study and their significance—appear to be particularly prone to the kinds of omissions of information that scientists deem important (Broberg, 1973).

Loss of Research Methods

One of the most visible omissions across media, according to studies of science news, is research methods (Frazer, 1995; Pellechia, 1997; Schmierbach, 2005; Weiss & Singer, 1988). If research methods receive a sentence or even a paragraph in print media, that often is considered adequate, if not more than adequate. In broadcast media—where journalists typically have relatively fewer words to work with and often confine themselves to two questions: *What did you find, and why is it important?*—we might expect methods to get even shorter shrift.[3]

Even in elite print media that have their own science writers (often including social science writers), research methods can fail to make it into news accounts. Consider a *New York Times* story about new behavioral research findings on the effects of divorce on children. The relatively lengthy article got high marks from the scientist who did the study—until she saw five letters to the editor, three of which sought to counsel her on her research methods (Eisenberg, 2005; Lazarus, 2005; Petrison, 2005; Roughton, 2005; Silverman, 2005). Given what she perceived as public misunderstanding of her work, the scientist was prompted to write her own letter to the editor explaining exactly what she had done in the study (Marquardt, 2005). The original *Times* story, though otherwise "excellent" in the scientist's eyes, had said little about her research methods (Lewin, 2005, p. 13).

Failure to discuss research methods may not only bother scientists but mislead the public. Let's say a journalist covers a study that concludes television is harmful to toddlers. If the journalist fails to specify the nature of the sample studied, parents whose children do not fit the profile of

study participants or watch the same kinds of television content may be led to worry unnecessarily about the damaging effects of television on their kids.

Likewise, if news accounts cover claims about the brain-enhancing value of classical music for infants but fail to mention that the original research on which these claims are based was never tested on babies but conducted on adults (and moreover that the effects were short-lived and small), a credulous public may be led to wrongly believe that playing Mozart to their babies will make them into little Einsteins. This may appear to be a fairly benign thing, until you consider that widespread media coverage of the so-called *Mozart effect* led the governor of one state to authorize the expenditure of taxpayers' money to send recordings of Mozart home with all new mothers (Sack, 1998). During times of documented social problems and budget shortfalls, public policies based on spurious research are at the very least questionable.

On a larger scale, if methods are routinely slighted in news accounts, it may be difficult for the public to learn to distinguish between different kinds of studies—and the relative certainty they convey. As a result, the public may be led to conclude that any scientific study conveys as much certainty as another.

Obviously, this is not so. In general, experimental studies tend to carry more certainty than nonexperimental studies, and a randomized, double-blind experiment offers greater certainty than a study with a nonrandom sample. Moreover, meta-analyses, which systematically assess research findings across investigations, tend to carry more weight than single studies. If journalists fail to explain the methods that were used and the level of certainty those methods convey or, worse, fail to mention methods at all, they may lead members of the public to assume a study is a study is a study, which is, of course, grossly mistaken.

The failure of journalists to distinguish good studies from bad studies is no academic matter. In education, for example, the failure of many in the press to appreciate the difficulty of arguing causal relations from qualitative methods has led to what some scientists see as distorted coverage of debates over the best approaches to teach reading and has contributed for a long time to poor educational policy. According to these scientists (Lyon, Shaywitz, Shaywitz, & Chhabra, 2005; Reyna, 2005; Shavelson & Towne, 2005), approaches to reading instruction based on subjective impressions and weak qualitative studies have guided the decisions of many teachers and administrators in some schools for decades.

One long popular approach to teaching reading, the whole-language approach, has assumed that learning to read is as natural as learning to speak. Whole-language methods—which teach reading within natural contexts like letter writing and book writing without separating readings skills into discrete, teachable components—can be enjoyable for students and teachers alike, and they certainly have appeared to work in qualitative studies of children whose parents have prepared them well in reading fundamentals at home.

However, as large- and small-scale experiments with diverse populations have demonstrated, efforts to teach reading based on the whole-language philosophy fail miserably for children who have not learned reading fundamentals (phonemic awareness, phonics, fluency, vocabulary and comprehension strategies). This means, of course, that schools that cling to whole-language approaches for poorly prepared children are failing to provide those children with the skills they will need to finish school, get decent jobs, track finances, and take their places as fully functioning citizens in society.

The news media have begun to do a better job of reporting on this contentious issue since two national scientific consensus panels have weighed in against whole-language approaches, according to a scientist who has been at the forefront of efforts to transform education into a scientifically driven enterprise. But in his words, they initially "took any kind of research to support (whole language) claims, no matter whether it was trustworthy or not" (R. Lyon, personal communication, June 6, 2006; also see Moats, 2000).

Loss of Caveats

Like the loss of research methods, the loss of scientific caveats can be bothersome to behavioral scientists, judging from anecdotal accounts, and in point of fact, such losses are not uncommon. Weiss and Singer (1988) have documented the hardening of provisional findings as social science moves from the scientific to the popular press. Discourse analyst Jeanne Fahnestock has found that popular accounts of science exaggerate the knowledge claims and downplay the caveats and other qualifiers (Fahnestock, 1986). Studies of media coverage of the risks associated with hazards (Singer & Endreny, 1993) and studies of science documentaries (Collins, 1987; Hornig, 1990) have likewise found a tendency to minimize uncertainties in popular accounts of science. In a recent study of medical science news, too, stories rarely carried cautions about intrinsically limited research methods (Woloshin & Schwartz, 2006).

Caveats, of course, are crucial to communicating science to other scientists. Not only do they set up the conditions for the construction of knowledge gaps, which scientists may then seek to fill (Stocking & Holstein, 1993; Zehr, 1999), but they also may preempt criticism, enhance credibility, and demonstrate mastery of the process of publication, among other things (Rier, 1999). By pointing to the limitations of the research in their scientific articles, scientists can protect themselves from charges by other scientists of overreaching interpretations of their findings (Stocking &

Holstein, 1993). By offering caveats in conversations with journalists, scientists can also work to protect members of the public from overinterpreting results, with serious implications for public perceptions and actions.

To borrow an example from a social psychology textbook (Aronson, Wilson, & Akert, 2005), the media may report that the more time fathers spend with their children, the less likely they are to abuse their children; however, if they fail to caution that correlation does not necessarily mean causation and that other factors may underlie the relationship, credulous members of the public may jump to the conclusion that spending more time tending their children would be an effective intervention with dads at risk for abusing. If, in fact, the reason for this association is that fathers who already possess good parenting skills spend more time with their children, this intervention may make abuse more likely for the at-risk father who lacks such skills.

Loss of Scientific Context

Several studies of scientists' perceptions of the accuracy of science news have found particularly troublesome the loss of scientific context as science moves from the scientific literature to the popular domain. Tankard and Ryan (1974), for example, found that scientists rated continuity with prior research as one of the top problems in science news. Weiss and Singer (1988), likewise, found that social scientists cited "fragmentation, with no attempt to relate an individual story to a whole body of research," as one of their five top criticisms of media coverage of social science research (p. 130). Even some journalists have expressed concern that science stories tell but a small part of the whole scientific story (Hartz & Chappell, 1997).

Studies of news media content corroborate these perceptions. Pellechia (1997), for example, has examined science stories over

three decades and found that prior research or future studies were mentioned in fewer than 60% of the stories. Food scientists, who since 1997 have done content analyses every other year of news media coverage of nutrition, dietary choices, and food safety, have also consistently found a lack of contextual information; the 2005 study found an uptick in the use of science to buttress claims of benefit or harm, but a lot of the citations were simply *studies show, research suggests,* or *according to the research* tags that did nothing to enhance the public's sense of the overall state of the science with respect to the issues at hand (IFICF & CMPA, 2005).

Discovery stories may be especially prone to minimize context, for in many cases, they are single-source stories, and such stories, as Weiss and Singer (1988) have concluded, take on faith what the investigating scientist says and fail to present the points of view of other scientists who might present another, broader picture.

The problems for audiences with context-free stories are illuminated by a study that found that nonaggressive media content— more than aggressive content—worsened the symptoms of emotionally disturbed children (Gadow & Sprafkin, 1993). If the news media failed to put this study into a larger scientific context, a parent of an emotionally disturbed child might prematurely conclude that aggressive-laden television would actually be better for his or her children than television with nonaggressive content. In fact, this 1993 study flew in the face of a vast majority of studies (Anderson et al., 2003) on media violence and aggression, a point parents of an emotionally disturbed child surely would want to know.

Exaggerations of Scientific Unknowns and Uncertainties

Though the more common complaint from scientists is that journalists make science appear less complex and more certain than it in fact is, sometimes—as the first author has noted elsewhere (Stocking, 1999; Stocking & Holstein, 1993)—journalists make science appear more complex, or at least more uncertain, than scientists believe it to be; that is to say, the news media sometimes work in ways that exaggerate the unknowns and uncertainties of science, possibly contributing to public bafflement about the scientific enterprise.

Unexplained Flip-Flops

The very certainty of many caveat-free discovery stories in science, when followed in rapid succession by other equally certain but contradictory discovery stories, may be expected to magnify uncertainty in the public mind. Let's say, for just one example, that studies appear to suggest that children are not harmed by day care. This study is quickly followed by—or in this case with—another that appears to suggest that children are harmed. What is the public to make of such seemingly contradictory findings?

"Scientists," the first author once heard a taxi driver say when he learned of her interest in science, "can't make up their minds about anything." His remark reflected a lack of awareness that different studies, if properly understood in all their complexity, might not be contradictory at all. It may be, of course, that day care has been found to be harmful under the circumstances of some studies (when the amount of time in day care is extensive, for example, or in low-quality day care arrangements) but not under the circumstances investigated in other studies (when the amount of time is less or when the quality of day care is higher). Even if single studies are roughly comparable and the findings do appear to directly contradict one another, it does not mean that scientists don't know what they are doing; any individual scientific study is inherently uncertain,

meaning the findings of one study can contradict in the short term a study that is similar or that may even appear to be identical.

Science, it has been said, proceeds a little like a sailboat, first one way, then the other, but over time making progress in a particular direction. Without such understandings conveyed in news media accounts, scientifically illiterate members of the public, like the taxi driver, may experience a kind of cognitive whiplash that tempts them to dismiss science—and scientists—out of hand.

Controversy-Driven Exaggerations

Conflict, which has long been observed to be a staple of journalism (Burnham, 1987; Nelkin, 1995; Pellechia, 1997; Weigold, 2001), can also magnify scientific uncertainties beyond what some scientists think reasonable. This can be particularly true when journalists, in the interest of being fair or objective, attempt to balance claims that opposing sides make in a controversy, without clarifying that one side carries more scientific *weight* than another. (For further discussion of weight-of-evidence reporting, see Chapter 3, this volume).

Taking advantage of journalistic balancing practices, groups that find scientific findings threatening to their particular interests have been known to spin the inevitable holes and uncertainties of science to their own advantage. Historically, for example, the tobacco industry worked to magnify in the press the unknowns and uncertainties in the science linking tobacco and lung cancer (K. Miller, 1992). More recently, the fossil fuel industry did the same with the science of global climate change (Gelbspan, 1997), leading—at least for a time—to news stories that gave no more weight to the consensus reports of thousands of scientists around the world than to the contrarian views of a minority of scientists (Boykoff & Boykoff, 2004).

Likewise, the pork industry magnified the unknowns and uncertainties associated with research that revealed danger to the health and well-being of people who lived around industrial hog farms (Stocking & Holstein, in press); in one instance, the industry appropriated a caveat from the scientist's research, transforming it into what appeared to be an admission of guilt and using it to discredit the science (Stocking & Holstein, in press). Intelligent design advocates also magnified the gaps in Darwin's thinking on evolution (Mooney & Nisbet, 2005). The result of the actions of these "sowers of uncertainty" (Pollack, 2003, p. 13): Consensual science was rendered more uncertain than it in fact was.

In the behavioral sciences, too, interested parties to conflicts can make the science findings appear less certain—and the scientists as less capable—than they are. For example, the science of sex—an interdisciplinary enterprise including medicine, biology, physiology, psychology, sociology, and anthropology—has been frequently attacked by political, religious, and cultural conservatives as bad science and the scientists who do the research as incompetent, morally deviant, or both (Bancroft, 2004).

SOLUTIONS

Studies on solutions to the problems that have been identified are few. But this doesn't mean that solutions do not exist. Inferences drawn from existing research, coupled with our own and others' informed experience as journalists and practitioners of behavioral science, have given rise to what might be considered best practices in the public communication of the complexities and uncertainties of science. Though many of the solutions to the problems surely lie with journalists, we will concentrate in this section on those solutions over which we have come to believe

scientists, who are the primary audience for this handbook, have some control.

Solutions to Loss of Scientific Complexities and Uncertainties

Solutions to the Loss of Methods

Audience considerations appear to be one of the most important reasons that mainstream news media accounts give relatively little attention to methods. With the possible exceptions of some stories considered vital to the public interest, it is thought that the public will not tolerate the level of complexity desired by most scientists. *We're not in the education business,* many journalists will tell you; *we're in the information business* (West, 1986, cited in Weigold, 2001). This is no doubt dismaying news to behavioral scientists in the academy who would prefer journalists to act as they try to do, in their classes, teaching their students about the important complexities and uncertainties of science. But it is not as though education-minded scientists can do nothing. Although most journalists will downplay or exclude methods in their stories, some won't. Behavioral scientists who are convinced a story can't be told without complexities and uncertainties they deem important may be able to find journalists who have the time, the space, and the capacity to go beyond what is customary.

Since scientists report more satisfactory experiences with science writers than they do with general assignment reporters (Valenti, 1999), and since journalists in the main report little formal training in science (Weaver & Wilhoit, 1996), it is tempting to imagine that behavioral scientists ought to restrict their interviews to science writers. However, in their study, Weiss and Singer (1988) found that social scientists rated the stories written by beat reporters (including science reporters) as no better in completeness, accuracy, and emphasis than stories written by general assignment reporters. Indeed, the few highly rated stories in their study were produced not by science writers but by general assignment reporters who expressed a concern for satisfying the values of social science. It is hard to know why the small number of science writers in this study did not produce more highly rated social science stories, but given evidence that science writers view the social sciences as *garbage science* relative to the biological and physical sciences (see Dunwoody, 1986), it could be that science writers don't work to reflect social scientists' values or invest as much in social science stories as they do in other science news accounts. Since these findings are based on a small number of journalists and fail to offer firm guidelines for scientists, probably the best thing for a behavioral scientist to do before agreeing to an interview is to check online to find out how receptive an individual journalist is to conveying the scientific complexities and uncertainties of behavioral science studies. In looking across a reporter's stories, it is usually possible to get a sense of the level of quality of a journalist's work.

In our experience, a surprising number of reporters, even those without a science background, will be open to cultivating an understanding of research methods. Most will want to do this, not so they can actually write extensively about research methods in their stories but so they can better decide for themselves whether research findings are trustworthy enough to write about in the first place. For behavioral scientists, it may be in the vetting of stories that they can be of greatest assistance in the public communication of science. They may, for example, be able to explain to journalists the degree to which a *statistically* significant finding is of any *practical* importance. Or they may point out that the size of the *N*—a heuristic that journalists often use to determine the quality of research, according to Schmierbach

(2005)—is but one indicator of the soundness of a study. They can thus help journalists to sort the scientific wheat from the chaff. Many journalists appear to rely on particular scientists to help vet stories they cannot vet themselves, and scientists who would relish becoming a part of a journalist's *news net* (Tuchman, 1978) can perform a great public service, though behind the scenes and without the level of recognition they have been trained to accrue for themselves and their institution.

Solutions to the Loss of Caveats

Research on journalists' use of caveats, as well as the reasons for their use, is slim (Rier, 1999), offering little guidance for how to increase the likelihood that journalists will use important caveats. However, in our experience, journalists won't look favorably on extensive caveats that undermine the significance of the research. Significance is an important news value, after all, and if significance is undermined too much, so will be the journalist's story. On the other hand, an important caveat that does not appear to undermine the significance of the research, if articulated well and emphasized, may find its way into some journalistic accounts.

For the scientist, this may mean articulating ahead of time the significance of the research, along with the particular caveats that the public needs to decide whether it can use the findings. It has been our observation that when it comes to significance, most journalists, out of concern for their audiences, are going to focus on the *practical* values of the research over scientific significance, though it is also true that some journalists will be open to using, along *with* claims about practical significance, assertions about the *scientific* value of the work.

As for caveats, those most likely to be used will be those that let the audience know the value of the research for them as decision makers. So if the research is primarily of scientific interest, with little immediate practical value, it will be necessary to explain that additional studies will be needed before the practical value of the findings will become clear; if the potential practical significance of the research is high, as with research that has implications for the treatment of autistic children, it may also be necessary to explain the particular *kind* of studies that will be needed. If the research has immediate practical value, in contrast, it may be important to explain what the research does *not* tell us that someone would need to know before making a decision. For example, is there anyone to whom this finding does *not* apply? Would the study on the harmful effects of television on toddlers apply to all children or just to those who receive little in the way of alternative stimulation in their environments? Would the study on the effects of day care apply to all children or only to children in a particular kind of day care environment? And what kinds of studies would be needed to answer these questions? In our view, a caveat that arises out of this kind of thinking is likely to be more informative than the general but not very revealing *more research is needed*. The latter caveat, far from being helpful, fails to assist the public to make decisions or to improve its general understanding and appreciation of behavioral science findings. It may, in fact, be that general caveats of this nature simply lead the public to assume that the research study in question is inadequate.

Solutions to the Loss of Scientific Context

For journalists, who tend to shortchange context in news coverage of all sorts, the larger scientific context may or may not be regarded as important for the story. For behavioral scientists, however, it is likely to be regarded as critical. A single study is often

but one piece in a large scientific puzzle, and every researcher knows that a single piece in a large picture puzzle does not give you a very accurate idea of the picture on the box.

To the extent that scientists believe context is important to the public's understanding and use of their research (and it can matter most with findings that have serious practical implications and/or that are likely to add fuel to one side or another of an inflamed public controversy), it is important to explicitly state how the research fits with the larger body of scientific knowledge. Do these results confirm, extend, or contradict the bulk of prior findings? And if they contradict prevailing scientific understandings, what is the public to make of this?

Consider a study that concluded that long hours in day care can lead to more aggression in some children regardless of the quality of the care. While this particular finding cast a pall on previous studies that had concluded that high-quality care does not adversely affect children, child care experts agree that quality of care still matters. The amount of aggression observed in children who spent long hours in different day care settings was mild, and even long hours of high-quality day care was found to have the positive benefits that earlier studies had identified for children, a picture that parents need to understand as they make their decisions about their children's welfare.

Conveying such context can be tricky. It can help to think about innovative ways to do this, possibly by creating info-graphics that reflect the complexities or by listing bulleted points that journalists can insert into their stories. There is no guarantee, of course, that journalists will take the time to convey this larger context. But it is certainly the case that if you don't make the attempt to explicitly provide that context, it is much less likely to find its way into a story. It can also be useful to refer journalists to other scientists who can comment on the research and how it fits with the larger state of science in the area.

Solutions to Exaggerated Unknowns and Uncertainties

Solutions to Unexplained Flip-Flops

As we have indicated, many of the flip-flops that laypersons perceive in the news are more apparent than real. It may *appear,* for example, that the latest study on fat is a flat-out reversal of the prevailing wisdom on fat intake, when in fact it may simply be a refinement of what is already known—namely, that fat still poses dangers for health, but it is not fat per se but the type of fat—good versus bad—that matters.

One way to correct public perceptions of apparent flip-flops is to use a *transformative explanation.* A transformative explanation is an explanatory technique in which one identifies (or anticipates) a mistaken public perception, acknowledges the intuitive plausibility of the perception, explains the limitations of the plausible view, and then explains the superiority of the correct view (Rowan, 1999).

When a new study concluded that a low-fat diet does not reduce breast cancer, scientists reacted quickly to identify and acknowledge the plausibility of a conclusion that the public might draw from the latest findings—namely, that fat may now be okay. Although it is not clear that the federal agency that sponsored the research took all the other steps involved in a formal transformative explanation, it did host a press conference in which scientists said "that they hoped women would not start eating fat because of this study" (Kantrowitz & Kalb, 2006, p. 44). The scientists then explained the more complex reality and why the public should continue to consume fat judiciously (Arnett, 2006; Brody, 2006). "These studies are more complicated than a simple headline or sound

bite can convey," one official told *Newsweek* magazine, which attempted to clarify the situation for the public, "and that's an important lesson for all of us" (Kantrowitz & Kalb, 2006, p. 44). Although good fat, bad fat, and no fat were not completely explained in the news coverage of the initial study, later coverage did demonstrate a clearer recognition of the complexities of the matter.

Solutions to Controversy-Driven Exaggerations of Unknowns and Uncertainties

The solution to controversy-driven exaggerations of unknowns and uncertainties in science coverage may be more difficult to manage than the exaggerations due to apparent flip-flops. In our experience, when vocal opponents of a particular line of research magnify unknowns and uncertainties as a strategic rhetorical tool, it can be difficult for journalists to ignore such claims. Knowing this, it would appear wise for scientists to, at the very least, anticipate the claims of the opposition and prepare to defend their findings. It may help, for example, to anticipate that some journalists are likely to give equal weight to the claims of scientists and media-savvy nonscientists, as well as prepare to explicitly articulate the relative weightiness of the scientific findings. Depending on the dynamics of the controversy, it may also help, when journalists commit outright errors in their accounts, to request corrections. Alternatively, it can be useful to register a comment with a media ombudsman if there is one; the ombudsman will often circulate concerns to staff, even if he or she doesn't write anything for public consumption. In addition, it can help to write op-ed pieces or letters to the editor to set the record straight. Media relations professionals at one's institution can often be helpful, too, in preparing for and containing a controversy (see Chapter 13, this volume).

In the case of the public health researcher who studied the health effects of industrial farms, the scientist found he had no choice but to publicly counter an industry trade association when it blasted as *pseudo-science* the exploratory self-report methods he used in an epidemiological study comparing the health effects of industrial hog farms with those of other livestock farms. In this particular case, the industry also made sharp ad hominem attacks and took active steps to shut down the scientist's research (Stocking & Holstein, in press). The scientist, who never denied the exploratory nature of his findings, felt himself to have been naive about the political dynamics that can arise when science threatens entrenched interests, and he documented his experiences in a professional journal to warn other scientists who do environmental health research (Wing & Wolf, 2000). Concluding that the threatened industry was trying to intimidate him, he also granted interviews with a few journalists, who wrote explicitly about industry's aggressive attacks on his work (Stocking & Holstein, in press).

In a related vein, when critics have viciously attacked both the soundness and morality of research produced by Indiana University's Kinsey Institute for Research in Sex, Gender, and Reproduction, staff members have had to gingerly work to counter what were clearly distortions of the research record so as to not jeopardize funding. The former director of the institute, like the researcher who studied the health hazards of large-scale hog farms, documented some of the institute's travails in a publication for his peers (Bancroft, 2004). His staff prepared themselves for the inevitable media inquiries by developing and circulating in-house a line-by-line rebuttal of the opposition's criticisms. But for the most part, then and now, they have kept a low profile with respect to their opponents' charges, responding to public accusations only when necessary so as to not give the opposition a platform.

RESEARCH NEEDS

We have focused here on those problems that scientists and media scholars have identified, and we have offered solutions that we think are within the scientists' control. We believe, based on experience, that many of the solutions we have offered will be effective. But it is important to remind ourselves that these solutions are based on interpretations of a limited body of data, informed by experience. Much remains to be formally explored with respect to news media treatments of scientific complexities and uncertainties, as well as with respect to the factors that affect these treatments. We will use the rest of this chapter to outline some areas that we think offer fruitful questions for investigation. We will consider, first, studies that might be conducted on news media treatments of complexities and uncertainties, followed by suggestions for research on the roles played by journalists and scientists in those treatments; on the testing of interventions to improve media coverage; and on the effects of media coverage on audiences.

Media Treatments of Scientific Complexity and Uncertainty

Though converging empirical evidence indicates that science news often lacks research methods, context, and caveats, the research has several limitations for behavioral scientists looking for guidance into how to explain the complexities and uncertainties of their work. Most of the studies have involved content analyses of science news, broadly construed, and most of these studies have examined the content of a limited set of print media. Weiss and Singer's (1988) treatment of social science news in print and broadcast news is the rare exception, on both counts, but it is growing old and needs replication in a changing media environment. Other studies have involved surveys of scientists, only some of whom were from the behavioral sciences.

Moreover, in studies that have concluded, as Weiss and Singer (1988) did, that the news media tend to slight scientific complexities or uncertainties, there have always been science news stories that *did* give ample attention to methods, context, or caveats. Also, one recent study in the medical sciences reported that a majority of media accounts of science presented at medical science meetings at least included basic study facts, if not cautions about the limitations of the studies (Woloshin & Schwartz, 2006). These apparent departures from the dominant empirical patterns demand our attention: Who are the journalists who give more attention to the complexities and uncertainties of the sciences, especially the behavioral sciences, and how, if at all, do they differ from other journalists? And what factors might lead some reporters to give ample attention to methods, context, or caveats, while many other journalists slight them?

Given how little is known about these matters, it could be useful to conduct content analyses of a few major behavioral science news stories, supplemented by exploratory interviews with the journalists who produced the stories and possibly with other actors in the communication process. It could be useful, for example, to analyze the attention to scientific complexities and uncertainties that a diversity of media outlets (for example, print news magazines, newspapers, wire services, women's media, and online media) has given to the same widely covered behavioral science studies. Let's imagine that content analysis revealed that weekly news magazines and elite newspapers whose audiences share a similar demographic profile differed significantly from one another in their coverage of the complexities and uncertainties of the aggression and day care story; interviews with the journalists who wrote and edited these stories could help to identify some of the factors other than audience demographics that could account for the differences in coverage (characteristics of the individual journalists and their editors, for example). Subsequent research could then explore more directly the difference that these factors make to media coverage.

In one such exploratory investigation, the first author compared the coverage by major newsweeklies of findings linking heart disease to the consumption of iron; one news magazine devoted just a few paragraphs to the findings, while another devoted one page, and a third ran a lengthy cover story. The attention to claims concerning the unknowns and uncertainties of the science varied dramatically as a direct function of the amount of space given to the findings, with the stories according the least significance to the knowledge claims giving the least attention to the claims about the unknowns and uncertainties as well. The observed differences could not be accounted for by audience demographics, as the three newsmagazines appealed to similar audiences. Instead, as was discovered in interviews, the differences had most to do with variations in the individual journalists' interests in the findings (the editor on the cover story had had a recent heart attack and knew of related research). Differences in perceived constraints on the amount of space the magazines would give to emerging science also played a role (Stocking, 1996).

JOURNALISTS' POTENTIAL CONTRIBUTIONS TO THE PROBLEM

It is certainly plausible to believe that characteristics of individual journalists, including their personal relationship to the findings and their knowledge about science, could account for at least some of variations in the coverage of complexities and uncertainties.

On the presumption that journalists' knowledge of a scientific issue would affect their coverage, Wilson (2000) surveyed 249 journalists who reported on climate change and found that more than half did not know the level of scientific consensus on the issue. "Instead of correctly understanding where (and why) the scientific debate occurs, reporters were confused; they exaggerated the debate and underplayed the consensus" (Wilson, 2000). Importantly, journalists who spent the most time with scientists had more accurate knowledge of the uncertainties in the debate. Whether greater knowledge leads to more accurate treatment in actual stories, though, is not clear. It could be, for example, that even the more knowledgeable journalists will feel compelled, out of an interest in journalistic fairness, to give equal time to competing sides in the debate, regardless of the level of scientific consensus. Wilson's survey did not address the effects of knowledge on actual media content.

Though it makes intuitive sense that journalists' knowledge would affect media coverage of both uncertainties *and* complexities, Weiss and Singer (1988) found no relationship between journalists' formal training in the social sciences and their abilities to develop stories that social scientists viewed as accurate, complete, and having appropriate emphasis. Instead, they found a modest relationship between journalists' years on the job and their ability to develop such stories. It may well be that on-the-job experience provides journalists with the knowledge that they need to cover the social sciences well in scientists' eyes. But without more studies examining the direct effects of experience and knowledge on coverage of complexities, it is difficult to say.

One exploratory study suggests that, in addition to journalists' knowledge of science, journalists' perceptions of their journalistic *roles* may be a factor in media's treatment of scientific unknowns and uncertainties. The first author and a colleague analyzed news content that contained claims and counterclaims about the unknowns and uncertainties in a research study that threatened an industry's interests and also talked to the journalists who produced the content (Stocking & Holstein, in press). If a journalist saw himself as a simple *disseminator* of information (to name just one kind of role; see Weaver & Wilhoit, 1996), he was more likely to treat a threatened industry's claims about the scientific gaps and uncertainties in the research as no less deserving of space than the knowledge claims made by the scientist and so would balance the competing claims, without regard to scientific merit. If a journalist saw herself as a *popular-mobilizer* who worked hard to get the views of laypersons into the news, she was likely to give less space to industry's claims and more space to the scientific claims that bolstered laypersons' complaints about industry activities. As provocative as these findings appear to be, they too are limited in that they emerged in a study that was not designed to test for the effects of journalists' roles, and they are based on a very small sample of journalists covering one particular controversy for varying types of newspapers, all limitations that need remedying in future research (for more discussion of research options, see Stocking, 1999).

SCIENTISTS' POTENTIAL CONTRIBUTION TO THE PROBLEMS

Thus far, our discussion has tended to assume that many of the problems with media coverage of the complexities and uncertainties of science originate with journalists, but this may in fact not be the case. To the extent that scientists and scientific institutions feel competitive pressures to communicate to nonscientists to enhance their visibility among those who appropriate or dispense funding for science, they themselves may make findings appear less complex and more certain than they are and so contribute to the problems identified here. Indeed, Weiss and Singer (1988) have expressed their concerns that journalistic values, which emphasize producing good, newsworthy stories of interests to readers, may come to influence some scientists, to the detriment of traditional scientific values.

Consider a recent study on the relationship between oxytocin and trust (Kosfeld, Heinrichs, Zak, Fischbacher, & Fehr, 2005). The journal *Nature,* which published the experimental study, asked a well-known neuroscientist to write a commentary on the investigation. The scientist, who has written popular books about science, wrote an engaging piece that greatly simplified the basic research findings and exaggerated the practical implications. The online news service of *Nature* picked up this scientist's spin of the study and produced its own news account that also reduced the complexities of the science and contained few caveats. Subsequent news media coverage adopted the emphases of the commentary and online story, with the result that in the larger public domain, the complexities and uncertainties in the findings were slighted and the practicalities of future applications overplayed (Vergano, 2005; Verrengia, 2005).

A similar thing happened with the "day care causes aggression" study. One scientist made a catchy statement about the findings in a conference call with journalists. The journalists snatched it up, and until other scientists involved in the study did some fast repair work, media coverage of the complexities of the study suffered (J. Fasig, personal communication, July 25, 2006).

It is examples such as these that lead us to wonder the following: To what extent do scientists' own statements—in scientific journals, in interviews, and in news releases prepared by their institutions—fail to explain research methods or offer needed caveats or

scientific context, thereby contributing to the oversimplification and lack of provisionality of so many of their findings in the news media? We know of no studies that have explored this important question.

Of course, scientists may not contribute to just the *problems* identified here but also to the solutions. So, to what extent do scientists, in fact, engage in many of the remedies we have proposed in this chapter? To what extent, for example, do scientists work with journalists behind the scenes to help them vet scientific studies? Who serves in these *vetting* roles? In addition, to what extent do scientists take the communication of scientific complexities and uncertainties into their own hands, writing op-ed pieces and letters to the editor to combat what they see as distortions? Who takes on *truth squad* roles, requesting corrections or contacting newspaper ombudsmen when media get things wrong? What motivates individuals to take on these vetting and truth squad roles, and how, if at all, are they rewarded in their institutions and professional communities?

And most critically, to what extent do these and other practices affect journalists' treatments? Do they improve the quality of the news in scientists' eyes or in consumers' eyes? If yes, under what conditions? If not, then why not? Studies that respond to such questions could do much to guide behavioral scientists as they work with journalists to present science to those who might benefit.

INTERVENTIONS TO IMPROVE MEDIA COVERAGE

Despite the gaps and uncertainties in our empirical knowledge about news media treatments of scientific complexities and uncertainties and factors that might account for variations in treatments, some scientific organizations have moved ahead to create workshops to improve the media coverage.

Most of the workshops aimed at improving science news that we know about have been concerned with sciences other than the behavioral sciences, and most have been directed at journalists. The National Institutes of Health (NIH), for example, has conducted workshops on evidence-based medicine for health and medical writers in print and broadcast. The workshops combine lectures with hands-on exercises that offer practice in evaluating the soundness of scientific studies. Journalists are pretested on their knowledge of methods and statistics as the workshop begins, surveyed at the conclusion of the workshop, and surveyed again months later to see if what they learned remains intact. However, the effects on journalists' actual selections of studies to cover and treatment of research methods and statistics in their stories are not yet clear; the scientists who run the workshop, now a cooperative venture among NIH, Dartmouth University, and the Veterans Administration (NIH, 2006), intend in the future to supplement their follow-up surveys of workshop participants with examinations of the journalists' actual stories (S. Woloshin, personal communication, June 14, 2006).

Workshops directed at scientists, to assist them as they work with journalists to improve media coverage, have also been offered over the years and appear to be growing in popularity in response to institutional imperatives to promote public visibility of science and in response to scientists' own expressed interest in learning how to better communicate their work to journalists (Hartz & Chappell, 1997). The American Association for the Advancement of Science (AAAS) sponsored one of the most interesting such efforts, attended by the first author. This effort is particularly noteworthy because it was one in which scientists were asked to write news stories about unfamiliar science in very short order, to give them a feel for the constraints journalists operate under in their work. This session did not explicitly address the issues raised in this chapter, though a session organized for scientists very well could, requiring the scientists to decide on the spot how much in the way of research methods and context could be included in a 350-word newspaper story, as well as what caveats ought to be included for a particular audience.

Workshops that bring together equal numbers of scientists with equal numbers of journalists, to discuss public communication issues, appear to be rare. But they are not unprecedented. On the assumption that both scientists and journalists play a role in how sex research gets communicated in the press, Indiana University's Kinsey Institute along with the School of Journalism designed a workshop for equal numbers of sex researchers and journalists in 2006. The institute surveyed groups of journalists and scientists about their interactions with each other's profession and followed that up with a daylong meeting in which leading science writers and sex researchers met to hear the findings, discussed commonalities and differences in their professions, and worked toward developing a list of best practices for communicating research on this highly sensitive research topic. Similar workshops, collaboratively organized by programs in the behavioral sciences and communications, might be designed to cross-train scientists and journalists in the particular challenges of communicating scientific complexities and uncertainties to the public.

Given the public's stake in the outcomes of such workshops, it could be an exciting and useful innovation to actually involve members of the public in the discussions. Such workshops could become the basis for collaborative research by scientists and communications researchers, so as to answer the many outstanding questions about how scientific complexities and uncertainties are covered in the news, as well as the equally compelling questions as to what the public comes to understand about the complexities and uncertainties of science and the difference that understanding, if any, makes to their lives.

AUDIENCES' RESPONSES TO JOURNALISTS' TREATMENTS

How the public actually responds to news media accounts of the complexities and uncertainties of science is clearly an area ripe for research. Many scholars, including ourselves, have asserted that the tendencies to simplify science in popular discourse can affect the public's understanding and decision making; however, only a handful of scholars have begun to explore the actual relationship between the journalists' treatments and public understandings and behavior.

In research that addressed the presumed importance of scientific context, participants in a focus group read two stories—one on global warming and the other on AIDS; when asked to talk about what inhibited their understanding of the issues, one of the principle problems participants mentioned was a lack of context. Building on this work, Corbett and Durfee (2004) in a lab experiment manipulated the presence of scientific context in news stories and found that the inclusion of context significantly decreased audiences' perceptions of the uncertainty of the science. Controversy injected into a story—by the inclusion of methodological criticisms and conflicting findings from other studies—significantly increased audiences' perceived levels of uncertainty. In their conclusions, Corbett and Durfee called for additional research with particular attention to other factors that may influence public perceptions of uncertainty, including single-source stories, visuals, story structure and framing, and journalistic balancing practices that often give equal weight to scientists and nonscientists or to mainstream scientists and fringe scientists.

Research on public responses to the inclusion of *research methods* and *caveats* in news stories is also needed. In his work, Rier (1999) has suggested that there is a need to understand the circumstances under which audiences pay attention to caveats. A number of assertions have been made. Pollack (2003), for example, has suggested that scientists, when they say they don't know *everything,* can be interpreted as suggesting they don't know *anything* (Corbett & Durfee, 2004). But is this so? And when, if at all, does the public even attend to statements in news stories about what is unknown or uncertain? Answers to these questions might put scientists in a better position to know which caveats to emphasize in their interactions with journalists.

We began this chapter by spelling out our assumptions, including our view that journalists' treatments of scientific complexities and uncertainties really do matter to audiences—not only with respect to their understanding of science but also with respect to their use of science in decision making. While our assumptions have face validity, little formal evidence exists to support them. Clearly, there is work to do.

CONCLUSIONS

Anyone who has read this far has likely at some point found behavioral science news, particularly its treatment of scientific complexities and uncertainties, unappetizing fare. Perhaps, in the heat of conflict, the unknowns and uncertainties have been exaggerated, or the complexities, including research methods and context, have been tossed out like so many leftovers. Or perhaps uncertain scientific claims have, as they made their way into the news media, hardened into overly simplified claims of knowledge. Whatever the case, we have worked in this chapter toward research-based solutions that might have the effect of making behavioral science news more appetizing to those scientists who, consuming the news, have felt a little queasy.

Though we believe the suggestions we have offered to be reasonable, we would be remiss if we failed to point out that not all scientists or journalists are going to agree with our proposals. Psychologist Bennett I. Berthenthal, for one, might argue that we have been entirely too finicky, at times offering suggestions for action and research that only scientists and a few among the lay public will have the stomachs to digest.

In an article in the *American Psychologist,* Bertenthal (2002) has written,

> Overemphasis on getting the specific details straight is misguided because these details usually require a level of understanding reserved for the expert but surely not available to the novices. The key is to motivate the interest of the public by helping them to understand why and how psychological research is meaningful; focusing too intensely on specific details is likely to obfuscate and confuse rather than help. (p. 217)

Perhaps for similar reasons, a television journalist surveyed by the Kinsey Institute advised sex researchers to "keep it basic. We don't need every little detail on how you came to your findings; we just want the findings. Save the details for the actual textbooks and longer forms" (Sparks, 2006, p. 18).

If we were to take these views to heart, behavioral scientists would supply journalists with the basic ingredients when the latter are cooking up stories about their research, but that is all. To try to do much more—and to expect much more—would be only a recipe for misery.

Is this right? For many behavioral scientists and journalists, we think not, but it is hard to say. Only time—and a converging body of evidence—will tell.

NOTES

1. This sampling was taken from *The New York Times* and from the Social & Behavior Science section of *EurekAlert* on Wednesday, April 5, 2006.

2. Studies of science news usually, though not always, include news from the behavioral sciences. Weiss and Singer (1988) have written one of the few extensive treatments of social science news. Without question, it is the most thorough and systematic work on the subject to date, which is why we will make extensive use of it in this chapter.

3. Surprisingly, though, with the particular stories Weiss and Singer (1988) studied, this wasn't so. Just why is not clear, but deserving of follow-up.

REFERENCES

Anderson, C. A., Berkowitz, L., Donnerstein, E., Huesmann, L. R., Johnson, J. D., Linz, D., et al. (2003). The influence of media violence on youth. *Psychological Science, 4*(3), 81–110.

Arnett, A. (2006, February 15). Keep eating right, nutritionists say. *The Boston Globe,* p. D1.

Aronson, E., Wilson, T. D., & Akert, R. M. (2005). *Social psychology* (5th ed.). Englewood Cliffs, NJ: Prentice Hall.

Bancroft, J. (2004). Alfred C. Kinsey and the politics of sex research. *The Annual Review of Sex Research, 15,* 1–39.

Bertenthal, B. I. (2002). Challenges and opportunities in the psychological sciences. *American Psychologist, 57*(3), 215–218.

Borman, S. C. (1978). Communication accuracy in magazine science reporting. *Journalism Quarterly, 55*(2), 345–346.

Boykoff, M. T., & Boykoff, J. M. (2004). Balance as bias: Global warming and the US prestige press. *Global Environmental Change-Human and Policy Dimensions, 14*(2), 125–136.

Broberg, K. (1973). Scientists' stopping behavior as indicator of writer's skill. *Journalism Quarterly, 50,* 763–767.

Brody, J. E. (2006, March 14). Fine print sends clear message: Stay the course. *The New York Times.*

Burnham, J. (1987). *How superstition won and science lost: Popularizing science and health in the United States.* New Brunswick, NJ: Rutgers University Press.

Collins, H. M. (1987). Certainty and the public understanding of science: Science on television. *Social Studies of Science, 17*(4), 689–713.

Corbett, J. B., & Durfee, J. L. (2004). Testing public (un)certainty of science: Media representations of global warming. *Science Communication, 26*(2), 129–151.

Dunwoody, S. (1982). A question of accuracy. *IEEE Transactions on Professional Communication, PC-25,* 96–99.

Dunwoody, S. (1986). When science writers cover the social sciences. In S. M. Friedman, S. Dunwoody, & C. L. Rogers (Eds.), *Scientists and journalists: Reporting science as news* (pp. 55–69). New York: Free Press.

Eisenberg, S. (2005, November 8). Children of the "quiet" divorce [Letter to the editor]. *The New York Times,* p. 26.

Fahnestock, J. (1986). Accommodating science: The rhetorical life of scientific facts. *Written Communications, 3,* 275–296.

Frazer, E. (1995). What is the new philosophy of social science. *Oxford Review of Education, 21,* 267–283.

Gadow, K. D., & Sprafkin, J. (1993). Television "violence" and children with emotional and behavioral disorders. *Journal of Emotional and Behavioral Disorders, 1,* 54–63.

Gelbspan, R. (1997). *The heat is on.* Reading, MA: Perseus Books.

Hartz, J., & Chappell, R. (1997). *Worlds apart: How the distance between science and journalism threatens America's future.* Nashville, TN: First Amendment Center.

Hornig, S. (1990). Television's *NOVA* and the construction of scientific truth. *Critical Studies in Mass Communication, 7*(1), 11–23.

IFICF & CMPA. (2005). *Food for thought VI: Reporting of diet, nutrition, and food safety* (Vol. 2006). Washington, DC: International Food Information Council Foundation and Center for Media and Public Affairs.

Kantrowitz, B., & Kalb, C. (2006, March 13). Food news blues: Fat is bad, but good fat is good. What about fish? Wine? Nuts? A new appetite for answers has put science on a collision course with the media. *Newsweek,* p. 44.

Kosfeld, M., Heinrichs, M., Zak, P. J., Fischbacher, U., & Fehr, E. (2005). Oxytocin increases trust in humans. *Nature, 435*(7042), 673–676.

Lazarus, A. (2005, November 8). Children of the "quiet" divorce [Letter to the editor]. *The New York Times,* p. 26.

Lewin, T. (2005, November 5). Poll says even quiet divorces affect children's paths. *The New York Times,* p. 13.

Lyon, R., Shaywitz, S., Shaywitz, B., & Chhabra, V. (2005). Evidence-based reading policy in the United States: How scientific research informs instructional practices. In D. Ravitch (Ed.), *Brookings papers on educational policy* (pp. 209–250). Washington, DC: The Brookings Institute Press.

Marquardt, E. (2005, November 12). Children of the "quiet" divorce [Letter to the editor]. *The New York Times,* p. 14.

Miller, J. D. (1986). Reaching the attentive and interested publics for science. In S. M. Friedman, S. Dunwoody, & C. L. Rogers (Eds.), *Scientists and journalists: Reporting science as news* (pp. 55–69). New York: Free Press.

Miller, K. (1992). Smoking up a storm: Public relations and advertising in the construction of the cigarette problem 1953–1954. *Journalism Monographs, 136,* 1–35.

Moats, L. (2000). *Whole language lives on: The illusion of "balanced" reading instruction.* Washington, DC: The Fordham Foundation.

Mooney, C., & Nisbet, M. (2005, September/October). Undoing Darwin. *Columbia Journalism Review.*

National Institutes of Health (NIH). (2006, June 14). *Medicine in the media: The challenge of reporting on medical research.* Retrieved from http://medmediacourse.nih.gov/

Nelkin, D. (1995). *Selling science: How the press covers science and technology.* New York: W. H. Freeman.

Pellechia, M. G. (1997). Trends in science coverage: A content analysis of three US newspapers. *Public Understanding of Science, 6*(1), 49–68.

Petrison, L. (2005, November 8). Children of the "quiet" divorce [Letter to the editor]. *The New York Times,* p. 26.

Pollack, H. N. (2003). *Uncertain science . . . uncertain world.* Cambridge, UK: Cambridge University Press.

Reyna, V. (2005). The No Child Left Behind Act and scientific research: A view from Washington. In J. Carlson & J. Levin (Eds.), *The No Child Left Behind legislation: Educational research and federal funding* (pp. 1–26). Greenwich, CT: Information Age Publishing.

Rier, D. A. (1999). The versatile "caveat" section of an epidemiology paper: Managing public and private risk. *Science Communication, 21*(1), 3–37.

Roughton, R. (2005, November 8). Children of the "quiet" divorce [Letter to the editor]. *The New York Times,* p. 26.

Rowan, K. E. (1999). Effective explanation of uncertain and complex science. In S. M. Friedman, S. Dunwoody, & C. L. Rogers (Eds.), *Communicating uncertainty: Media coverage of new and uncertain science* (pp. 201–223). Mahwah, NJ: Lawrence Erlbaum.

Sack, K. (1998, January 15). Georgia governor seeks musical start for babies. *The New York Times,* p. A-12.

Schmierbach, M. (2005). Method matters—The influence of methodology on journalists' assessments of social science research. *Science Communication, 26*(3), 269–287.

Shavelson, R., & Towne, T. (Eds.). (2005). *Scientific research in education.* Washington, DC: National Academy Press.

Silverman, C. (2005, November 8). Children of the "quiet" divorce [Letter to the editor]. *The New York Times*, p. 26.

Singer, E., & Endreny, P. M. (1993). *Reporting on risk: How the mass media portray accidents, diseases, disasters, and other hazards.* New York: Russell Sage Foundation.

Sparks, J. V. (2006, June). *Preliminary report of results: Survey of journalists.* Paper presented at the conference, Turning Sex Research Into News: Sexual Science for the Public's Interest, Bloomington, IN.

Stocking, S. H. (1996, February). *How journalists deal with scientific ignorance and uncertainty.* Paper presented at the annual meeting of the American Association for the Advancement of Science, Baltimore.

Stocking, S. H. (1999). How journalists deal with scientific uncertainty. In S. M. Friedman, S. Dunwoody, & C. L. Rogers (Eds.), *Communicating uncertainty: Media coverage of new and uncertain science* (pp. 23–41). Mahwah, NJ: Lawrence Erlbaum.

Stocking, S. H., & Holstein, L. W. (1993). Constructing and reconstructing scientific ignorance—Ignorance claims in science and journalism. *Knowledge-Creation Diffusion Utilization, 15*(2), 186–210.

Stocking, S. H., & Holstein, L. W. (In press). Manufacturing doubt: Journalists' roles of the construction of ignorance in a scientific community. *Public Understanding of Science.*

Tankard, J., & Ryan, M. (1974). News source perceptions of accuracy of science coverage. *Journalism Quarterly, 51,* 219–334.

Tuchman, G. (1978). *Making news: A study in the construction of reality.* New York: Free Press.

Valenti, J. M. (1999). How well do scientists communicate to media? *Science Communication, 21*(2), 172–178.

Vergano, D. (2005, June 2). Trust via chemistry? Study says it's possible. *USA Today,* p. 8D.

Verrengia, J. B. (2005, June 2). Scientists experiment with "trust" hormone. *Associated Press Online.*

Weaver, D. H., & Wilhoit, G. C. (1996). *The American journalist in the 1990s: U.S. news people at the end of an era.* Mahwah, NJ: Lawrence Erlbaum.

Weigold, M. F. (2001). Communicating science: A review of the literature. *Science Communication, 23*(2), 164–193.

Weiss, C. H., & Singer, E. (1988). *Reporting of social science in the national media.* New York: Russell Sage Foundation.

Wilson, K. M. (2000). Drought, debate, and uncertainty: Measuring reporters' knowledge and ignorance about climate change. *Public Understanding of Science, 9*(1), 1–13.

Wing, S., & Wolf, S. (2000). Intensive livestock operations: Health and quality of life among eastern North Carolina residents. *Environmental Health Perspectives, 108*(3), 233–238.

Woloshin, S., & Schwartz, L. M. (2006). Media reporting on research presented at scientific meetings: More caution needed. *Medical Journal of Australia, 184*(11), 576–580.

Zehr, S. C. (1999). Scientists' representations of uncertainty. In S. M. Friedman, S. Dunwoody, & C. L. Rogers (Eds.), *Communicating uncertainty: Media coverage of new and uncertain science.* Mahwah, NJ: Lawrence Erlbaum.

CHAPTER 5

Communicating Basic Behavioral Science Beyond the Discipline

Reflections From Social Psychology

JOHN F. DOVIDIO AND SAMUEL L. GAERTNER

Social psychology explores the very best of human behavior, such as self-sacrifice, altruistic action, attraction, and close relationships, as well as the very worst, such as prejudice, hatred, and interpersonal and intergroup conflict and aggression. Formally defined as "the scientific study of how individuals think, feel, and behave in regard to other people and how individuals' thoughts feelings and actions are affected by other people" (Brehm, Kassin, & Fein, 2002, p. 5), social psychology addresses issues of fundamental practical importance and, as the textbooks currently emphasize, is very relevant to understanding law, business, and public policy. In addition to the insights that it offers into people's daily lives and into the functioning of social institutions, social psychology provides interventions for personal and social change that, for example, help to conserve scarce resources, promote cooperation, and reduce prejudice and discrimination.

In this chapter, we discuss ways of making basic behavioral science understandable and useful to various nonscientists from the perspective of social psychology. Specifically, we explain how conceptualizing and designing

basic research programs on psychological processes that underlie significant human problems can help both the general public and policy makers to improve the welfare of individuals and society as a whole. Though the topics covered relate to most other behavioral science disciplines, social psychology offers a particularly instructive perspective from which to consider bridging basic science and social issues because its history is marked by both a striving to meet high standards of scientific rigor and a dedication to being relevant to social problems.

We begin with a brief overview of the history of social psychology's involvement in social issues. Despite this history and the contemporary relevance of social psychology to social issues and policy, social psychology has had less impact on public policy and social institutions relative to other disciplines. Thus, we next explore some reasons why. Then, we examine three examples in which contemporary basic research has either directly or indirectly helped to shape social policy and law. We refer to these and other examples in the final section on meeting challenges to disseminating basic science. These challenges include producing basic research with qualities that potentially increase its practical value, appreciating any single discipline's larger scientific and practical context, and learning to communicate the results of basic research to relevant audiences.

SOCIAL PSYCHOLOGY AND SOCIAL ISSUES: FROM THE PAST TO THE PRESENT

Social psychology has existed as a recognized field for about a hundred years. From its very inception, science and application have been closely intertwined. Many scholars attribute the founding of the field to the pioneering works of Norman Triplett and Gustav Le Bon at the end of the 19th century (Goethals, 2003). In 1895 in the United States, Triplett began studies of how the performance of bicycle racers was influenced by the presence of others (Triplett, 1897). He found that bicycle racers worked harder and went faster when there were other riders around than when they were alone. Also in 1895 in France, Le Bon (1895/1969) published his study of group behavior and mob action. He suggested that groups develop a "collective mind" that results in behaviors that are more impulsive and less sophisticated than those of individuals.

William McDougall (1908) was among the first to analyze prosocial behavior in his pathbreaking book, *Introduction to Social Psychology*. This book helped to formalize social psychology as a discipline and led to studies of how relatives and strangers can engage in actions to improve the welfare of others. Floyd Allport's (1924) landmark volume, *Social Psychology*, firmly grounded the discipline in the scientific method but also emphasized the relevance of the field to current social issues and problems. Classic works through the 1930s examined group stereotypes (Katz & Braly, 1933) and how being part of a group shapes the way individuals perceive their worlds (Sherif, 1936). Sherif (1936), for example, found that when participants were presented with an ambiguous or confusing situation, they relied on the opinions and actions of others to shape their own views of "reality." These lines of research demonstrated the profound ways that others determine people's perceptions about what is factual.

During World War II, social psychology was used to help mobilize the nation to prepare for protracted conflict, encouraging rationing and conservation. Kurt Lewin, for example, was asked by the National Research Council to create programs to persuade women to serve rarely used animal viscera, such as sweetbreads and kidneys, to their families (Lewin, 1943; see Goethals, 2003). In 1945, the American Psychological Association acknowledged the importance of psychology for addressing social problems by incorporating the Society for the Psychological Study of Social Issues as one of its initial divisions (Division 9). After the war, social psychology offered insights into the experiences of U.S. soldiers, such as how shared threat created social bonds among soldiers that were stronger and more inclusive of people from diverse groups than the affiliations developed outside of combat (Stouffer, 1949). Then, during a period of U.S. national preoccupation with Communist influences, social psychologists illuminated key principles of persuasion to understand how Communist propaganda may operate and to inoculate people against its influence (Hovland, Lumsdaine, & Sheffield, 1949). As racial issues began to occupy more of the public consciousness, social psychologists contributed to the debate about racial integration. For example, in 1954, they provided materials that were considered by the Supreme Court in *Brown v. Board of Education,* which challenged the prevailing principle of "separate but equal." Social psychologists also outlined strategies for improving race relations to policy makers and others who were generally interested in promoting racial equality (G. Allport, 1954).

Lewin, who was a major figure in social psychology in the mid-20th century, strongly advocated connecting psychology to theory and application. He is commonly quoted as saying, "There's nothing so practical as a good theory" (Goethals, 2003). Kurt Lewin (1943) recognized the importance of developing and validating theories of social behavior that could be applied in practical ways and argued that social psychologists should appreciate how laboratory experiments and practical application can inform one another. Moreover, Lewin encouraged action research, which is research designed to motivate and influence the direction of social change.

In the following years, social psychology continued to respond to current events and social issues. Often, specific incidents were the impetus for new research. One of the clearest examples is the Kitty Genovese incident, which led to significant practical and theoretical research by Darley and Latané (1968) that rejuvenated work on prosocial behavior for decades. The incident occurred in New York City in 1964. As Kitty Genovese was returning home one evening, she was brutally attacked in the parking lot of her apartment building in three distinct episodes over 45 minutes. Thirty-eight people witnessed the attack, but none intervened or called the police.

Latané and Darley (1970) explored the psychological processes underlying this lack of responsiveness in a series of ingenious experiments. For example, in one study, participants overheard another person (actually a confederate) suffer a life-threatening epileptic seizure (Darley & Latané, 1968).

Bystanders were less likely to intervene when they could "diffuse responsibility" onto other witnesses than when they were the only witness and had to assume full responsibility for the person's welfare. This line of research offered groundbreaking insights into the psychology of the Kitty Genovese incident and subsequently to understanding a wide range of other situations, such as the conditions under which people decide to intervene in order to prevent others from driving drunk (Dovidio, Piliavin, Schroeder, & Penner, 2006).

By the 1970s, psychologists noticed a less dramatic but still significant issue. Despite the common belief both within social psychology and among the lay public that attitudes critically determine behavior, empirical evidence was accumulating to indicate that attitudes and behavior were only modestly related. Fishbein and Ajzen (1975) clarified, however, in their program of basic research that there were actually two types of attitudes—general attitudes about objects, policies, or groups (e.g., support for having a clean environment) and attitudes about performing specific behaviors toward an object, policy, or group (e.g., restricting water pollution or supporting the Sierra Club). Whereas general attitudes were weakly associated with behavior, specific attitudes were much more directly related (see also Ajzen & Fishbein, 2005). This observation formed the cornerstone of their theory of reasoned action, which eventually was developed into the more current theory of planned behavior. The Fishbein and Ajzen models have been critical in designing strategies to influence a broad range of attitudes and behaviors. For instance, principles of persuasion derived from social psychology research have been directly incorporated into advertising programs and political campaigns as well as into health promotion campaigns to promote breast-feeding and adolescents' safe-sex practices.

BARRIERS TO RECENT PUBLIC INFLUENCE

Despite the close relationship between social psychology and practical social issues, Pettigrew (1988) noted that social psychology has had much less impact in recent years on public policy and public opinion than other behavioral and social sciences, such as economics. Even though social psychology is directly relevant to understanding social issues and addressing social problems, social psychologists only rarely play prominent roles as formal or informal advisers to government leaders in the United States. Among the many possible reasons are those that derive from the methodology of psychology, the scientific method.

The scientific method has been an especially valuable approach for gaining knowledge about the world and has led to inventions and materials that are now essential parts of everyday life. The scientific method in social psychology has also produced findings that are directly useful outside the discipline. The problem of communicating behavioral science is thus not inherent in the scientific method per se but in the way it has been used and the process and results of science communicated.

Four main barriers to communicating behavioral science more broadly are (a) the emphasis on internal validity (the ability to draw cause-and-effect inferences), frequently at the expense of external validity (the ability to generalize findings beyond the conditions of the experiment); (b) the increasing fragmentation of knowledge; (c) a traditional university system that values decontextualized basic science and thus impedes progress in both theoretical understanding and practical knowledge; and (d) difficulties in communicating the findings of behavioral science that stem mainly from the use of inferential statistics unfamiliar to most of the nonscientist public, including policy makers and practitioners who seek to understand and use findings from research.

The Premium on Internal Validity

Social psychology places a premium on research that permits clear and definitive causal inferences. In pursuing internal validity, research is typically an iterative process of developing and verifying theories through a sequence of studies that hone in on the hypothesized causal relations. Thus, social psychology emphasizes a particular application of the scientific method that involves reducing complex behaviors to their basic components, abstracting the principles underlying the causes of those behaviors, and then testing these principles in a relatively sterile and controlled laboratory environment that only vaguely resembles the circumstances surrounding the social problem that stimulated the work. The process of theory development, testing, and revision is time-consuming, and each iteration often becomes increasingly distant from the "real-world" event and context that initially brought the question to the public and researcher's attention.

Fragmentation of Knowledge

One consequence of reductionism in pursuit of internal validity is the field's steadily increasing attention to micro-level, relative to macro-level, behavioral processes. Micro-level processes include physiological mechanisms such as the influence of hormone levels (e.g., amount of testosterone) on activity of certain parts of the brain (e.g., the amygdala), which can result in aggressiveness. Micro-level processes can also refer to social mechanisms, such as the ways that a person's social inhibitions and violent behaviors may be increased by the aggressive behaviors of others. In contrast, macro-level processes may link broader social conditions, such as poverty, with violence and aggression. Macro-level processes are typically more easily recognized and understood by lay audiences, and so they can be perceived by the public, including practitioners and policy makers, to be more directly relevant to social issues.

In addition, when processes are "disassembled" in basic science, they tend not to be built up again and reconnected to overriding theories or to practical situations that would facilitate application. Instead, new subdisciplines are usually spawned (e.g., social-cognitive neuroscience), which can lead to further fragmentation of knowledge and present barriers to communicating even within the discipline.

Academy Incentives

Although social issues still motivate many social psychological researchers, this motivation is not as central to social psychology as Kurt Lewin advocated. Methodological rigor and theory are valued more within the culture of science than application, and so "pure science" has enjoyed greater status (see also Pettigrew, 1988). As a consequence, the most prestigious journals in social psychology, the ones that are often weighed most heavily in decisions of tenure, promotion, and merit, place primary emphasis on the magnitude of the theoretical contribution of the work and little on issues of practical application (see Chapter 6 in this volume for further discussion). In addition, to maximize productivity during the limited pretenure probationary period, social psychology researchers commonly rely on convenience samples, mainly college students in introductory psychology courses, a practice that can raise questions about the external validity and applicability of the work.

The Statistical Challenge

One of the fundamental tools used in empirical research is statistics, which relies on probabilistic inference. For example, using sample size, average differences in the behaviors of experimental and control groups, and variability in behavior both within and between the two groups, a particular statistical technique will indicate that mean differences in the behaviors observed were either likely to be a chance occurrence ("$p > .05$," statistically nonsignificant), and so probably unreliable, or unlikely to have occurred by chance ("$p < .05$," statistically significant). Therefore, even when a study yields statistically significant effects, researchers can conclude with only 95% certainty that the observed effect is real. Given that most of the public, including policy makers and practitioners, is unfamiliar with inferential statistics, such apparently tentative conclusions of statistical analyses can undermine perceptions of what social psychologists "know."

Social psychologists also frequently neglect to put statistically significant findings into a practical perspective by failing to consider the strength, or magnitude, of study effects. Statistical significance and practical significance are not necessarily synonymous. With very large sample sizes, statistical significance may be obtained with very weak effects. Alternatively, with the relatively small samples used by social psychologists, average differences in responses to a rating scale that may appear superficially to be quite small may represent quite substantial practical effects. Some changes in the ways social psychologists report data have occurred recently—for example, reporting effect sizes along with statistical significance. Nevertheless, the field would benefit further by consistently using measures and approaches to data analysis that communicate directly how the effect sizes translate into meaningful differences in the behaviors that policy makers, practitioners, and other consumers of science care about understanding and changing.

In trying to be complete and accurate, social psychologists often tend to focus on details that may not be of primary interest or of value to lay audiences. For example, details about the size of the research sample may not be meaningful to lay audiences because they do not know how it helps them judge the trustworthiness of the conclusions being drawn. Furthermore, social psychologists often convey their conclusions in a way that undermines confidence in the results. They tend to qualify their conclusions with terms such as *likely* and *generally,* and they often focus on disagreements about specific theoretical points, all of which detracts from a broader "take-home" message of interest to general audiences. Social psychologists also repeatedly caution about "the need for further research," suggesting to nonscientists that their information is not any more reliable or useful than that from other perhaps more trusted sources, such as family anecdotes or religious doctrine. Moreover, general audiences often perceive the detailed quantitative analyses typically presented by social psychologists to be too abstract and less compelling than vivid personal stories from case studies, a common methodology in other disciplines.

Nevertheless, social psychologists *can,* under certain conditions, have substantial influence, as illustrated by the following examples in which findings from social psychology helped to affect law and social policy.

DISSEMINATING SOCIAL PSYCHOLOGY FOR LEGAL AND POLICY DECISION MAKING: THREE EXAMPLES

Some of social psychology's greatest social impact has come through contributions within the legal system and to organizational and public policy. Within the legal system, for example, social psychologists are frequently called on as expert witnesses, and psychological organizations have provided useful amicus briefs in landmark Supreme Court cases. Less obvious and dramatic, but much more typically, social psychology's influence is more indirect, first increasing the public's awareness and understanding of issues, which then helps to produce social change. We illustrate next the different types of contributions that contemporary social psychology has made to law, organizational policy, and public awareness of media influences. These examples illustrate the direct and indirect influence of social psychology on policy. We begin with the most direct case.

Social Psychology and the Supreme Court

As noted earlier, evidence from social psychology has been considered in landmark decisions by the Supreme Court involving race. In *Brown v. Board of Education* (1954), an amicus brief was offered by the Society for the Psychological Study of Social Issues, and social psychological research (e.g., the research of Clark & Clark [1947] showing that Black children preferred to play with White than Black dolls, indicating a devaluing of their racial group) was cited in the court's decision. More recently, the American Psychological Association filed an amicus brief in support of affirmative action policies in the University of Michigan cases reviewed by the Supreme Court (*Gratz v. Bollinger,* 2003; *Grutter v. Bollinger,* 2003). This brief discussed, among other psychological evidence, how Whites have racial biases that they are not fully aware of that can systematically influence how they perceive and respond to Blacks, how Blacks may become sensitive to and preoccupied with cultural stereotypes of their group in ways that adversely influence their academic performance, and how diversity in groups can promote creative problem solving and develop cross-cultural communication skills. However, the Supreme Court has also directly considered testimony by social psychologists (see Fiske, Bersoff, Borgida, Deaux, & Heilman, 1991).

The case was *Hopkins v. Price Waterhouse* (1990). Ann Hopkins, the plaintiff, had an outstanding record of accomplishment at the accounting firm of Price Waterhouse but was denied promotion to partner in the firm. Susan Fiske, a prominent social psychologist who extensively studied social cognition and stereotyping, testified as an expert witness during the District Court hearing of the case. As noted by Fiske and colleagues (Fiske et al., 1991, p. 1050), "her clients praised her, and her supporters recommended her as driven, hard working, and exacting." Although Price Waterhouse contended that Hopkins was not promoted because of interpersonal skill problems, Hopkins argued that she was denied partnership because of her gender. The American Psychological Association's amicus brief in this case emphasized the role of gender stereotyping. Testimony in the case frequently alluded to the fact that Hopkins did not conform to the traditional feminine stereotype. Fiske et al. (1991) reported, "According to some evaluators, this 'lady partner candidate' was 'macho,' she 'overcompensated for being a woman,' and she needed a 'course at charm school.' A sympathetic colleague advised that she would improve her chances if she would 'walk more femininely, talk more femininely, dress more femininely, have her hair styled, and wear jewelry'" (p. 1050; see also *Hopkins v. Price Waterhouse*, 1985, p. 1117).

As mentioned earlier, micro-level processes, such as social-cognitive processes, can have important practical consequences. Fiske's testimony in this case drew directly on social psychological research demonstrating that stereotypes operate most strongly to bias perceptions and to ultimately penalize people who deviate from these stereotypes when evaluative criteria are ambiguous. Judge Gesell, who presided over the case, ultimately ruled in favor of Hopkins. He concluded that an "employer that treats [a] woman with [an] assertive personality in a different manner than if she had been a man is guilty of sex discrimination" (*Hopkins v. Price Waterhouse*, 1985, p. 1119). Moreover, based on Fiske's testimony, he acknowledged that "a far more subtle process" than the usual discriminatory intent was operating (p. 1118).

In addition to demonstrating the direct impact that social psychology can have in the courtroom through expert testimony, this case illustrates how basic research can encourage social psychologists, and eventually the legal system and the general public, to recognize that people can have social biases that systematically affect their decisions. Specifically, the basic research on social cognition produced a deeper understanding of how stereotyping operates and its effects. Fiske's work on this topic alerted her to the possible consequences of stereotyping and enabled her to analyze the facts of *Hopkins v. Price Waterhouse* with new insight. Basic research can thus increase people's awareness of social processes in ways that can help them avert injustices.

Social Psychology and Organizational Policies on Promotion

Whereas Fiske's testimony was formal, social psychological evidence can have more informal, but still direct, influence on policy makers. For example, a number of years ago, the first author of this chapter was invited to present research and otherwise participate in a workshop sponsored by the Department of Defense on minority promotions in the military. At the time, there was a concern that Blacks who were identified as being qualified for advancement were being promoted within the officer ranks at a rate consistently lower than that for Whites (given their representations in the promotion pools) over an extended period of time. The research presentation discussed the existence of modern, subtle racial bias (aversive racism; see Dovidio & Gaertner, 2004; Gaertner & Dovidio, 1986) in which Whites are more likely to discriminate against Blacks in personnel decisions when standards are less clearly defined and bias is less easily recognized. This evidence from social psychology was consistent with the information and arguments presented by other participants in the meeting.

Within a couple of years, the Army had altered its promotion procedures. Promotion boards were given explicit instructions that Blacks under consideration for promotion were expected to be as qualified as were White candidates. Thus, if Blacks were promoted at a lower rate, then an explanation needed to be provided. According to the Army's annual Equal Opportunity Assessment Report, reframing the process to clarify promotion standards (and thus deviations from the standards) was sufficient for eliminating racial disparities as long as these guidelines remained in place.

Social Psychology and Media Violence

In addition to its direct influence, social psychology can have a profound indirect impact on policy makers by sensitizing both policy makers and the public to subtle influences on social behavior. A classic example involves the effects of media violence on aggression in children and adults. As television rapidly became the dominant form of media throughout the 1960s, a common perception among programmers and advertisers was that "violence sells." Apparently, as a consequence, violence was exaggerated on television. Violence is so common on television that by the time children turn 18, if they are average television viewers, they will witness more than 200,000 acts of violence, including 40,000 murders, on television (Huston et al., 1992). In the 1990s, 61% of television shows contained violence, no immediate punishment for violent acts was depicted in nearly 75% of the violent scenes, and the perpetrator was portrayed to be an attractive character 44% of the time (Smith & Donnerstein, 1998).

At the same time that television was growing in popularity and violence began dominating the media, social psychologists were discovering the powerful effect that models, fictional as well as real, could have on spontaneous aggressiveness and on the development of enduring orientations toward violence in both children and adults (Bandura, Ross, & Ross, 1961). This line of research soon focused on the impact of television violence. A consistent picture emerged. Violence on television increases people's perceptions of the world as dangerous. It also increases the likelihood that children, adolescents, and adults will behave aggressively, particularly when they perceive themselves to be similar to or aspire to be like the perpetrator, the violent actions on television are rewarded, or the viewer already has aggressive tendencies. More extended exposure to violence on television as children and adolescents leads viewers to become more aggressive later in life (see Anderson & Bushman, 2002a, 2002b; Anderson & Huesmann, 2003).

News of these research findings became more widespread as the work was featured in newspapers, in magazines, and on television. Partly as a consequence, public concern with violence on television grew. A 1999 CNN/ USA/Gallup Poll found that 56% of parents surveyed felt that the government should do more to regulate violence on television (Holland, 1999; http//www.cnn.com/ALL POLITICS/stories/1999/05/03.poll/). In the same survey, 65% reported that the government should do more to regulate violence on the Internet, and 58% supported more government regulation of violence in video games. By 2004, a poll by the Kaiser Family Foundation revealed that 63% of parents surveyed favored new regulations to limit the amount of violence and sex on television (CBS News, 2004). In turn, the government gave the issue close and formal attention (Congressional Public Health Summit, 2000; Senate Committee on the Judiciary, 1999). Parental protests and the consequent government scrutiny eventually led to voluntary regulation by the television industry, including the establishment of a "family hour" in prime-time television in which violent (and sexually suggestive) content would be curtailed. The industry also developed the current voluntary rating system, in which warnings of violent and sexual content are presented before television shows.

Social psychology research continues to be used in policy activities relating to media and violence. For example, Dr. Elizabeth Carll, chair of the Interactive Media Committee of the American Psychological Association, recently (March 29, 2006) testified before the Senate about the potentially harmful consequences of violent video games. Thus, research evidence from social psychology has been a critical element in educating the general public, legislators, parents, and television executives about the potential dangers of television violence, as well as about media violence more generally.

In the three examples we presented—on gender stereotyping and employment discrimination, racial bias and promotion decisions, and modeling and media violence—basic research preceded the opportunity for practical application. This research made researchers aware of how fundamental psychological processes can have unexpected negative consequences under certain condition. For instance, gender and racial stereotypes are more than descriptions of different groups; they systematically guide, often without conscious awareness, the ways people interpret information and, consequently,

make decisions. In addition, even modeling in the context of fantasy and fiction can substantially affect what people see as normal behavior. Thus, social psychological research can be particularly valuable for alerting society to impending or previously unrecognized problems, possibly helping to avoid larger problems in the future.

MEETING THE CHALLENGES OF DISSEMINATING KNOWLEDGE FROM BEHAVIORAL SCIENCE

Despite the potential of social psychology for enhancing the public's understanding of social issues and addressing social problems, its promise has not yet been significantly fulfilled. Though no simple road map exists, advances in communicating basic science may be made by (a) producing basic research with qualities that potentially make it more useful to a broad audience, (b) appreciating the discipline's larger scientific and practical context, and (c) learning how to communicate basic research beyond the profession.

Qualities of Useful Basic Science

Having an impact on public opinion and policy typically requires aligning a coherent body of scientific work that is relevant to—but not necessarily directly on—contemporary social issues and events about which social psychology theory and research can provide new insights. In the case of Darley and Latané's (1968) research on bystander intervention, scientific inquiry came directly from the circumstances surrounding the murder of Kitty Genovese. The research idea was stimulated by the incident, and the experiments themselves were designed to mimic related real-world events. In contrast, early research on modeling aggression influenced policy indirectly because it had documented general principles to explain how people learn from and imitate others. Only after this general research base had been developed was its relevance to the effects of television viewing recognized. As the result of changing social conditions that included increasing violence on television and growing public concern, this work began to gradually gravitate to the more specific issue of learning and imitating media violence.

What, then, are the qualities of basic science that give it the greatest potential for influence? The research we have described on bystander intervention, modeling and media violence, barriers to minority promotions, and the attitude-behavior relationship all shares four fundamental qualities. First, the research was programmatic; it consisted of accumulated and converging evidence as opposed to a single study. Second, the work was solidly grounded in theory. Third, the experiments were rigorously conducted, involving randomized controlled experiments and other studies that were carefully designed and executed using the most appropriate methods for answering the research question. And fourth, the experiments were designed with the knowledge and perspective the scientists had obtained through making an effort to understand the environments in which the behaviors to be explained actually occurred.

With respect to the first point, although a single study can capture media attention, such as Darley and Latané's (1968) original experiment on bystander intervention, a program of research carries more weight. The recognition that researchers earn with the public, the media, and policy makers is typically based on their *accumulated* accomplishments. Latané and Darley (1970) published an entire book describing a series of studies they had performed and presenting a model of decision steps for emergency intervention that strongly influenced a generation of social psychologists.

Second, much of the impact that social psychology has had on social issues and public policy has been because of the field's emphasis on theory development and the insights it can provide into a broad range of phenomena. To reiterate Kurt Lewin's (1943) point, "There is nothing so practical as a good theory." Research-based theories are themselves useful for making practical decisions as well as for avoiding the production of disconnected and fragmented findings that fail to reveal a coherent picture. For instance, Fiske is not known as an applied social psychologist; she is widely respected as a creative theoretician and skillful "bench scientist." Her scholarly work also embodies all of the four essential qualities outlined at the beginning of this section. It is not only theoretically based but also programmatic. She introduced a general model of when and how people rely on group membership to form impressions of others (Fiske & Neuberg, 1990), wrote extensively on social-cognitive processes in stereotyping, and conducted a series of sound experiments illustrating the conditions under which stereotyping would be more or less likely to affect people's behavior. Like the works of other scientists we have mentioned, such as Anderson, Bushman, Donnerstein, Darley and Latané, and Fishbein and Ajzen, her work came under the scrutiny of and was published by the most prestigious *academic, basic science* journals in the discipline. Although her empirical work is best described as basic research, it was regularly informed by her sensitivity to and interest in the practical consequences of stereotyping.

The third quality of science that makes it particularly useful is the essence of its approach, the scientific method. Although multiple methods are needed depending on the purpose of the research, the experiment remains the "gold standard" of the empirical process in social psychology because it allows cause-and-effect inferences. And though disciplines such as economics, political science, and sociology often use experiments to study micro-level processes, these disciplines mainly emphasize macro-level processes that cannot be directly manipulated or for which the surrounding conditions cannot be controlled. Thus, social psychology can make unique and complementary contributions to behavioral science through its primary reliance on experiments.

Finally, the potential influence of basic research findings could be increased by adhering to Lewin's (1943) guidance to intentionally connect laboratory studies of behavior to naturalistic settings and to feed the lessons learned from application back into theory development. Research on the relationship between attitudes and behavior has benefited from such field applications. At the beginning of the chapter, we discussed how Fishbein and Ajzen's (1975; Ajzen & Fishbein, 2005) insights into attitude-behavior relations not only helped to resolve an academic question about why attitudes were only weakly related to behavior but also helped guide the development of practical interventions to change behavior for personal well-being and the public good. More recent developments to the theory build on practical experiences and applied research findings about the social and individual determinants of healthful behavior, producing more elaborate models that incorporate a wider range of psychological processes for guiding the next generation of interventions. The information-motivation-behavioral skills model (Fisher, Fisher, & Harman, 2003), for example, addresses methods of targeting information to change specific attitudes, as suggested by the original work of Fishbein and Ajzen, but it also now emphasizes how using reinforcements or otherwise creating the appropriate motivation and how teaching relevant behavioral skills through training and practice can further influence behavioral intentions and, ultimately, promote healthful behavior. The model advances theory by covering more

influences and processes. In practice, the model has been applied to breast self-examination, motorcycle helmet use, and adherence to complex medical regimens (e.g., for people with AIDS), and it continues to be refined, guided by feedback about its effectiveness in clinical settings.

Advances in persuasion research also illustrate that application and theory can be mutually informative and that the tension between them can be channeled in constructive and creative ways. Robert Cialdini developed a reputation as an outstanding theoretician and researcher studying how people influence and persuade others to behave in ways they normally would not. He credits many of his ideas to the time invested in going "undercover" to work in a variety of occupations (e.g., in sales positions of various types and as a waiter) in which persuasion and social influence are critical to success (Cialdini, 2000). He talked with, listened to, and learned from people who excelled in these professions—people who knew what techniques and strategies worked but who did not necessarily know or care about the psychological explanations for why they worked. Cialdini specified these processes and tested them in controlled experiments, continually refining the ideas and principles through his program of research.

For instance, while training to be a car salesman, he learned of a technique, lowballing, in which the customer was given a price well below the amount at which the salesperson intended to sell the car in order to get the customer to commit to the purchase. Then, the offer was either rescinded, ostensibly because the sales manager voided it because the dealership would be "losing money on it" or because a "calculation error" was made and certain options were not included in the original price. After customers had committed to buying the car, they were more willing to accept the "manager's" higher price or pay more for the car with the "options" calculated into the new price. Cialdini (2000) subsequently studied the phenomenon of lowballing in the laboratory, replicating the effect and illuminating the underlying processes of the psychology of commitment. He has applied the research to field settings and communicated the findings to general audiences to help them resist manipulation.

Appreciating the Larger Scientific and Practical Context

The previous examples demonstrate the benefits of appreciating the practical contexts in which basic science might ultimately be used. Bringing academic researchers and practitioners together can produce more effective pragmatic interventions as well as influence the direction of theory development. Although familiarity with practical environments might happen informally, it may be useful to increase formal efforts to further bridge basic research and application—for example, through workshops or meetings sponsored by professional organizations to bring academic researchers and practitioners (e.g., clinicians, people who conduct antibias programs, and policy makers) together around common problems and goals.

To meet the challenge of dissemination, social psychologists also must recognize the role of social psychology in relation to other disciplines and work beyond traditional disciplinary boundaries instead of viewing their work as an isolated enterprise. Many social problems are inherently complex, making them both difficult to solve and to study. Collaborating across disciplines helps to produce more meaningful and useful research by bringing together scholarly perspectives about the influences on behavior that occur at multiple levels of analysis. For instance, racial discrimination is the result of historical events (e.g., the consequences of slavery),

economic forces (e.g., the effects of poverty), social forces (e.g., institutional racism), and psychological processes (e.g., stereotyping, prejudice, and personal discrimination). Thus, the integration of disciplinary perspectives and knowledge mirrors the complexity of human problems. It also works against the fragmentation and decontextualization of knowledge that can result from increasing specialization by assembling fragmented information into a more complete and meaningful scientific analysis, leading to a more coherent understanding of the findings from behavioral research. Multidisciplinary work may involve a single researcher who is knowledgeable about several disciplines or, as has become increasingly common, teams of scholars from different disciplines or subdisciplines. As discussed next, working across disciplinary boundaries also helps social psychologists appreciate the importance of being able to communicate effectively with those not trained in the methods and jargon of the discipline.

Communicating Beyond the Profession

Learning to present knowledge from science in understandable, useful, and engaging ways is critical to communicating effectively beyond the profession. However, the scientific community as well as each academic science discipline has a particular culture that leads to particular styles of communicating that must be overcome. Seeing the problem to be one of cultural divide leads us to provide a two-part framework derived from principles of social psychology for considering the obstacles and opportunities of disseminating scientific knowledge across cultures.

First, disseminating information beyond social psychology is essentially intergroup communication, and so naturally occurring opportunities are limited. Research on social networks amply demonstrates that whereas people regularly and freely give and accept communications within their group, communication across group lines is much rarer. Intergroup communication also requires effort, support, and skill. As a consequence, researchers need extra initiative to make their work more widely available and accessible to general audiences. Some of the most common and direct routes for disseminating knowledge beyond the profession are public talks and popular books (see Chapter 12 in this volume), press releases (Chapter 13), and Web pages and other Internet tools (Chapter 14). Of course, the initiative for communicating social psychological information can come the other way. Journalists, policy makers, and members of other professions (e.g., lawyers) frequently seek the expertise of social psychologists. (For discussions on communicating with journalists, see Chapters 3 and 4 and chapters in Part II of this volume; see also chapters in Parts IV and V on communicating with policy makers and other professionals.)

Second, academic social psychology has unique norms about communicating information that must be overcome. The classic research of Muzafer Sherif (1936), which has been repeatedly supported over the past 70 years, shows that all groups develop norms, but they may vary substantially across groups. Nevertheless, people tend to assume that others share their norms, values, and practices, which contributes to problems in communicating across group boundaries.

In social psychology, communication norms are shaped by two powerful forces: classroom teaching and academic publishing. Classroom teaching typically consists of lengthy oral communications in which the instructor leads and dictates the rules of discourse. Most often, professors speak in 50-minute lectures to a captive audience. Being clear and engaging are important teaching skills, but usually of primary importance is

communicating information, much of it detailed, technical, and factual. Written communication centers on the academic publication system, with an organization and style that conforms fairly rigidly to guidelines— for instance, the more than 400-page *Publication Manual* of the American Psychological Association (2001). Neither lectures nor research reports are effective forms of communicating with nonscientists.

A challenge of communicating behavioral science beyond the discipline is to convey the value of research using messages that are clear, crisp, and engaging while being true to the research findings and to the nature of science. In our experience, it is important to convey the "story" of the research, explaining in broad strokes how a series of studies combine to produce creative, new insights. The story opens with the problem to be solved (a mystery), foreshadows how the research speaks to the problem, and highlights the evidence that, when taken together, presents a coherent picture that helps move toward a solution (see also Cialdini, 1997).

Methods and statistical analyses are typically of secondary importance and may not be necessary for conveying the research findings and their meaning to nonscientists. More important is identifying the problem to be solved, stating in simple terms the evidence that has accumulated relevant to the problem, and explaining why the conclusions being drawn from the evidence are likely to be trustworthy. Communicating the magnitude of the effects by analyzing effect sizes accumulated across studies can help to put findings into a practical perspective, potentially avoiding overreactions to findings likely not to hold much practical value or pointing to a need for action that may not be apparent from scientists' usual presentations of inferential data. These approaches to communicating remain faithful to the nature of science. The inherently cumulative, uncertain, and continually evolving nature of the scientific enterprise can be acknowledged while the convergence of findings communicates a level of confidence in a conclusion that no single experiment can legitimately yield.

CONCLUSION

Although social psychology has concerned itself throughout its history with social issues, contemporary social psychology, like other behavioral science disciplines, heavily emphasizes "pure" science. We have argued that one virtue of this approach is that the principles derived from basic research can, under certain conditions, eventually apply to a broad range of social issues. Ultimately, however, the effective dissemination of basic science requires that researchers meet certain challenges. Some of these arise from the fundamentals of science and so are unlikely to change, such as use of the scientific method and inferential statistics. In this case, approaches to communicating with nonscientists must be strengthened. Other challenges require changes to the research enterprise itself.

First, bridging basic research and application in behavioral science requires developing in-depth knowledge of emerging social issues. This sensitivity enables basic researchers not only to direct their work in response to particular events, as Latané and Darley did to the Kitty Genovese incident, but also to anticipate emerging issues, as the work on media violence illustrated. Basic researchers can be the "canary in the coalmine," using their research to detect and avert potential social problems. Bridging basic research and application also requires conducting programmatic, theory-driven research that yields cumulative findings from experiments in which the questions and methods are informed by an understanding of the particular conditions in which behavior actually occurs.

Basic research can become more useful if the results from applied studies are used to elaborate and refine theories of behavior, and if individual disciplines, such as social psychology, make an effort to connect their work to other academic disciplines relevant to understanding and solving complex social problems. It is quite possible and especially valuable to both science and society for behavioral research to be empirically sound with strong internal validity while also having external validity. Although this balance cannot be perfectly achieved in any single study, it is feasible to work toward accumulating a converging body of knowledge that is high on both internal and external validity so that scientific integrity is not compromised for practical utility and social relevance is not sacrificed entirely for experimental control.

Finally, disseminating basic science requires learning to communicate beyond the discipline to help researchers better understand the situation surrounding the behavior to be explained and to share research findings using approaches that support nonscientists in understanding and using the results. Specifically, researchers must learn to talk in less detailed and technical ways and in more practical terms about the knowledge gained from scientific methods and inferential statistics. These communications can respect and convey the continually evolving and probabilistic nature of science in part by synthesizing across accumulated studies to state with less equivocation those findings that are relevant to the problem at hand.

Although this chapter has focused on social psychology, the fundamental issues apply to most other disciplines in behavioral science. Most disciplines struggle with the balance between internal and external validity and, for example, have the tendency to use convenience samples that allow them to meet the academy's tenure and promotion demands (e.g., developmental science often includes children from university-run preschools, and cognitive science routinely conducts research with college student participants). Thus, most behavioral disciplines could benefit from purposefully selecting samples from more theoretically meaningful and practically relevant populations. Other disciplines such as education, sociology, political science, and human geography also, for example, rely heavily on inferential statistics for data analysis and thus have similar challenges in communicating their findings. The behavioral science field as a whole will be stronger, and its impact broader and more significant, when sound theory development and the application and communication of research findings are not in tension but instead reinforce each other.

REFERENCES

Ajzen, I., & Fishbein, M. (2005). The influence of attitudes on behavior. In D. Albarracin, B. T. Johnson, & M. P. Zanna (Eds.), *The handbook of attitudes* (pp. 173–221). Mahwah, NJ: Lawrence Erlbaum.

Allport, F. H. (1924). *Social psychology.* Boston: Houghton Mifflin.

Allport, G. W. (1954). *The nature of prejudice.* Cambridge, MA: Addison-Wesley.

American Psychological Association. (2001). *Publication manual of the American Psychological Association* (5th ed.). Washington, DC: Author.

Anderson, C. A., & Bushman, B. J. (2002a). The effects of media violence on society. *Science, 295,* 2377–2378.

Anderson, C. A., & Bushman, B. J. (2002b). Human aggression. *Annual Review of Psychology, 53,* 27–51.

Anderson, C. A., & Huesmann, L. R. (2003). Human aggression: A social-cognitive view. In M. A. Hogg & J. Cooper (Eds.), *The Sage handbook of social psychology* (pp. 296–323). Thousand Oaks, CA: Sage.

Bandura, A., Ross, R., & Ross, S. (1961). Transmission of aggression through imitation of aggressive models. *Journal of Abnormal and Social Psychology, 63,* 575–582.

Brehm, S. S., Kassin, S. M., & Fein, S. (2002). *Social psychology* (5th ed.). Boston: Houghton Mifflin.

Brown v. Board of Education, 347 U.S. 483 (1954).

CBS News. (2004, September 23). *Poll: Parents want Feds to tame TV.* Retrieved May 27, 2006, from http://www.cbsnews.com/stories/2004/09/23/entertain ment/main645195.shtml

Cialdini, R. B. (1997). Professionally responsible communication with the public: Giving psychology a way. *Personality and Social Psychology Bulletin, 23,* 675–683.

Cialdini, R. B. (2000). *Influence: Science and practice* (4th ed.). New York: Morrow.

Clark, K. B., & Clark, M. P. (1947). Racial identification and preference in Negro children. In T. M. Newcomb & E. L. Hartley (Eds.), *Readings in social psychology* (pp. 602–611). New York: Holt.

Congressional Public Health Summit. (2000, July 26). *Joint statement on the impact of entertainment violence on children.* Retrieved March 23, 2006, from http://www.aap.org/advocavy/releases/jstmtevc.htm

Darley, J. M., & Latané, B. (1968). Bystander intervention in emergencies: Diffusion of responsibility. *Journal of Personality and Social Psychology, 8,* 377–383.

Dovidio, J. F., & Gaertner, S. L. (2004). Aversive racism. In M. P. Zanna (Ed.), *Advances in experimental social psychology* (Vol. 36, pp. 1–51). San Diego, CA: Academic Press.

Dovidio, J. F., Piliavin, J. A., Schroeder, D. A., & Penner, L. A. (2006). *The social psychology of prosocial behavior.* Mahwah, NJ: Lawrence Erlbaum.

Fishbein, M., & Ajzen, I. (1975). *Belief, attitude, intention, and behavior: An introduction to theory and research.* Reading, MA: Addison-Wesley.

Fisher, W. A., Fisher, J. D., & Harman, J. (2003). The information-motivation-behavioral skills model: A general social psychological approach to understanding and promoting health behavior. In J. Suls & K. Wallstin (Eds.), *Social psychological foundations of health and illness* (pp. 82–106). Malden, MA: Blackwell.

Fiske, S. T., Bersoff, D. N., Borgida, E., Deaux, K., & Heilman, M. E. (1991). Social science research on trial: Use of sex stereotyping research in Price Waterhouse v. Hopkins. *American Psychologist, 46,* 1049–1060.

Fiske, S. T., & Neuberg, S. L. (1990). A continuum of impression formation, from category-based to individuating processes: Influences of information and motivation on attention and interpretation. In M. Zanna (Ed.), *Advances in experimental social psychology* (Vol. 23, pp. 1–74). Orlando, FL: Academic Press.

Gaertner, S. L., & Dovidio, J. F. (1986). The aversive form of racism. In J. F. Dovidio & S. L. Gaertner (Eds.), *Prejudice, discrimination, and racism* (pp. 61–89). Orlando, FL: Academic Press.

Goethals, G. R. (2003). A century of social psychology: Individuals, ideas, and investigations. In M. A. Hogg & J. Cooper (Eds.), *The Sage handbook of social psychology* (pp. 3–23). Thousand Oaks, CA: Sage.

Gratz v. Bollinger, No. 02–516, 539 U.S. 244 (2003).

Grutter v. Bollinger, No. 02–241, 539 U.S. 306 (2003).

Holland, K. (1999, May 3). *Poll: Violence in the media should be regulated.* Retrieved April 26, 2006, from http//www.cnn.com/ALLPOLITICS/stories/1999/05/03.poll/

Hopkins v. Price Waterhouse, 618 F. Supp. 1109 (1985).

Hopkins v. Price Waterhouse, No. 84–3040, slip op. (D D.C. May 14, 1990) (on remand).

Hovland, C. I., Lumsdaine, A. A., & Sheffield, F. D. (1949). *Experiments on mass communication.* Princeton, NJ: Princeton University Press.

Huston, A., Donnerstein, E., Fairchild, H., Feshbach, N. D., Katz, P. A., Murray, J. P., et al. (1992). *Big world, small screen: The role of television in American society.* Lincoln: University of Nebraska Press.

Katz, D., & Braly, K. W. (1933). Racial stereotypes of 100 college students. *Journal of Abnormal and Social Psychology, 28,* 280–290.

Latané, B., & Darley, J. M. (1970). *The unresponsive bystander: Why doesn't he help?* New York: Appleton-Century-Crofts.

Le Bon, G. (1969). *The crowd: A study of the popular mind.* New York: Ballantine. (Original work published 1895)

Lewin, K. (1943). Forces behind food habits and methods for change. *Bulletin of the National Research Council, 108,* 35–65.

McDougall, W. (1908). *An introduction to social psychology.* London: Methuen.

Pettigrew, T. F. (1988). Influencing policy with social psychology. *Journal of Social Issues, 44*(2), 205–219.

Senate Committee on the Judiciary. (1999, September 14). *Children, violence, and the media: A report for parents and policy makers.* Retrieved March 23, 2006, from http://judiciary.senate.gov/mediavio.htm

Sherif, M. (1936). *The psychology of social norms.* New York: Harper.

Smith, S. L., & Donnerstein, E. (1998). Harmful effects of exposure to media violence: Learning of aggression, emotional desensitization, and fear. In R. G. Geen & E. Donnerstein (Eds.), *Human aggression: Theories, research, and implications for social policy* (pp. 167–202). New York: Academic Press.

Stouffer, S. A. (1949). *The American soldier.* Princeton, NJ: Princeton University Press.

Triplett, N. (1897). The dynamogenic factors in pacemaking and competition. *Journal of Psychology, 9,* 507–533.

CHAPTER 6

Beyond University Walls

Communicating and Disseminating Science Outside of the Academy

STACY ANN HAWKINS, DIANE F. HALPERN, AND SHERYLLE J. TAN

Social and behavioral scientists have amassed a great deal of practical and potentially useful information on a broad range of issues, including how to organize neighborhoods, improve decision making, motivate people to learn, reduce crime, and promote health, to name a few examples. Given our expertise, it would seem that every community should be clamoring to have more social and behavioral scientists active in government and service organizations and featured in local and national news. Yet, few people outside of the academy could tell you what social and behavioral scientists actually do, and even fewer see any need for our work in the community. We scholars are largely to blame for the growing irrelevance of social and behavioral science to the nonacademic world. We stay behind the walls of our universities, rarely explaining how our work applies to real-world problems or working with the community on a problem that it has identified as important.

The community, broadly and flexibly defined here to include local and national communities, such as city neighbors, the media, and local and national governments, can benefit from social and behavioral science research, but only if it is given the opportunity to participate in and learn from the science. Scholars must include the community in academic discussion by engaging in community-centered scholarship or, more specifically, community-centered research and dissemination. Though community-centered research and dissemination can certainly be theoretically based, in these projects, research questions and dissemination strategies are derived directly from community issues and questions. This includes all types of communication, whether to the general public, professional organizations, policy makers, or the media.

It is no mystery why disseminating research outside academia is not a priority for scholars, even in the social and behavioral sciences, where our research has the potential to inform public policies and help businesses and families make a wide range of better decisions. Universities give academic scientists few rewards for nonacademic dissemination in comparison to those for conducting traditional research. The savvy academic learns early what he or she must do to be professionally successful, but, as we will explain, the work that is best for one's career is often not what is best for the field as a whole or for the public. Likewise, universities typically benefit less from community-centered research and dissemination than from conducting basic science. In this chapter, we discuss these barriers to including the community in scholarship and the division between universities and the public that has resulted. Finally, we offer suggestions for creating an ongoing dialogue between academia and the community and provide examples of some of the colleges and universities taking steps toward increased community-centered research and dissemination.

PERSONAL REWARDS

You do not have to be a Skinnerian or a behaviorist to believe that people are more likely to engage in the behaviors that provide the rewards they desire (Cameron & Pierce, 1994; Woods, 1959; see also Thorndike, 1898); academics are certainly no exception. Generally speaking, rewards in higher education include promotion, pay raises, and, of course, tenure. Gaining tenure and receiving promotions are vital to a scholar's professional survival, and the criteria for both dictate much of a faculty member's work.

Time Is Not on Your Side

The pressure for new faculty members to focus on tenure-getting activities is especially strong given the limited amount of time they have to prepare for tenure review. Typically, new tenure-track faculty have 6 years to be granted tenure—although anticipating the time needed by the approval committees, candidates must be prepared for review as early as 5 years after accepting a tenure-track

position. Because the requirements for granting tenure are time-consuming, there is no time to waste. This time crunch creates a challenge for faculty interested in community-centered scholarship. Dr. Pennie Foster-Fishman, a psychologist at Michigan State University, wrote about her struggle balancing time commitments, saying,

> Those weekly visits meant a significant loss in time spent on other tasks more valued by the academy (such as writing and grant writing). While I feel that the quality and significance of the articles have been greatly enhanced by this involvement, the speed at which I could produce them was much reduced. As an untenured assistant professor, that's of great concern. (Sandmann, Foster-Fishman, Lloyd, Rauhe, & Rosaen, 2000, ¶ 30)

Dr. Foster-Fishman highlights a serious issue for junior faculty; time is a guiding factor in the activities they choose.

"The Only Thing That's Marketable"

Although specific tenure criteria differ among institutions, review committees generally consider the candidate's research productivity, teaching ability, and service contributions. These criteria, however, are not equally weighted. As Boyer (1990) writes, "Almost all colleges pay lip service to the trilogy of teaching, research, and service, but when it comes to making judgments about professional performance, the three rarely are assigned equal merit" (p. 15). This claim is confirmed by a study that asked a sample of 118 psychology department chairs to report the percentage of weight given to each of the three activities when making tenure decisions (out of 100%). The department chairs clearly rated research as the most influential factor in tenure decisions (mean importance rating was 55%), when compared to teaching (32%) and service (13%; McCaffrey, Nelles, & Byrne, 1989). Similarly, a recent qualitative study of four academic institutions pointed out the "conflicts between institutional rhetoric and the realities of reward structures, [namely] the emphasis on research to the detriment of teaching and service in promotion and tenure decisions" in colleges and universities across the country (O'Meara, 2002, p. 57).

Indeed, research is often considered "the only thing that's marketable" in the academic world (Abott & Sanders, 1991; Frank, 1995; Israel & Baird, 1988), a system Boyer (1990) refers to as "a suffocatingly restricted view of scholarship" (p. 43). In today's universities, successful scholarship is not defined by effective teaching or good service but by a strong research program. In the previously mentioned qualitative study, participant interviews revealed that successful scholarship "had become synonymous in these four different institutions with traditional research. More and more, success in tenure and/or promotion and increases in salary became closely tied with publication productivity" (O'Meara, 2002, p. 64). Indeed, this is the status quo for most American universities.

This traditional view of scholarship is also reflected in the tenure and promotion policies of colleges and universities. For example, Duke University policy makes it clear that teaching is separate from scholarship: Tenure candidates must demonstrate "excellence in the quality of the candidate's performance, especially as a teacher and as a scholar" (Duke University, n.d.). At another institution, "the nominee must be an outstanding scholar; a person who has demonstrated the capacity for imaginative and original work in his or her field and who shows promise of continuing to make significant contributions to research" (Columbia University, 2005). Here, teaching is not even mentioned; instead, successful scholarship is directly equated

with successful research. Although many colleges and universities have been consulting and providing professional expertise for nonacademic organizations for years, these activities have not been given the level of prestige that accompanies research (Lynton & Elman, 1987). "Because outreach and scholarship are viewed as different activities, junior faculty are often advised to avoid involvement with outreach until their careers are secure and their reputations as scholars established" (Michigan State University, 2000, p. 14). Considering the overall shift away from service (and toward research) in tenure and promotion reviews and in definitions of scholarship and service, the academic researcher seeking tenure is not likely to pursue community-centered research or dissemination.

Publish or Perish

Although research is the critical element in tenure decisions, designing and implementing intelligent research is not enough to support a candidate's application; successful tenure candidates must publish their research. Publication has become the hallmark of successful research and, by extension, a successful tenure candidate (Boyer, 1990; Sweeney, 2000). Psychology department heads across the country report that publication in a peer-review journal is the most important tenure-getting activity and that there is an expectation that candidates would have published *at least* 10 articles in peer-reviewed journals alone (excluding book chapters, reviews, and other abstracts) before being reviewed (McCaffrey et al., 1989).

With the tight timeline and high standards of tenure review, new scholars are wise to choose the research projects that will most quickly and sufficiently prepare them for their review. For example, by writing in the "least publishable unit," the smallest publishable analysis from a larger data set, a scholar can boost the number of his or her publications without increasing the time associated with research design and data collection (Owen, 2004). The least publishable unit articles can be quickly, and somewhat painlessly, added to an academic's curriculum vitae (CV), better preparing a candidate for tenure or promotion review. Similarly, short-term projects may be chosen over long-terms ones. Any project involving extensive data collection would not allow a new scholar enough time to publish his or her findings before tenure review—a serious concern for any pretenure professor. Furthermore, junior faculty may find themselves shying away from a cutting-edge study with a controversial approach or topic because of the potential risk of being rejected for publication by more traditional peer reviewers. Academics, then, may find themselves focusing on shorter, conservative research projects that are more likely to be accepted into peer-reviewed journals—namely, those projects that will increase their likelihood of being granted tenure or a promotion.

A critical part of the publish-or-perish mandate is the limitation on where one's work may be published so that it "counts" toward tenure. A significant consideration in tenure review is the *impact* of the journal in which a candidate publishes. Cited as "the number that's devouring science," the impact factor is a ranking given to journals based on the average number of citations each article garners (Monastersky, 2005b); journals with often-cited articles receive higher impact factor rankings. The articles cited the most, however, are not always those that make the greatest scientific advances. Often, a referenced article is one that includes a great deal of information, such as a meta-analysis or a review article. Cutting-edge research, on the other hand, may not find immediate popularity and would be less likely to yield as many citations as other, more traditional work.

Unfortunately, the unintended results of impact factors affect the pretenure scholar greatly. The impact factors of the journals in which a candidate has published are rapidly becoming a strong guideline for tenure committees' consideration. Using impact factors as indicators of candidate quality is of particular concern when a candidate's publications are either too recent to have gained wide recognition or are not in the tenure committee members' own area of expertise. In the latter case, committee members cannot make their own judgments about the quality of the research and sometimes blindly depend on the impact factor (Agrawal, 2005; Monastersky, 2005a). This reliance on *impact* can minimize the importance of studies and projects that are less popular but may end up being more influential in shaping the future of social and behavioral science. Knowing that quantity of publications in a high-impact, peer-reviewed journal will increase his or her likelihood of receiving tenure, a tenure candidate may focus his or her energy on projects that would make the cut in a high-impact journal, overlooking creative, controversial, or community-centered research projects.

Service

Within the academic system, community-centered research and dissemination are typically considered "service" (and not research or teaching). Tenure and promotion committees, however, tend to make a distinction between *university* service and *community* service, valuing the former over the latter. McCaffrey and colleagues (1989) found that university committees and professional activities (such as journal reviewing) were the primary activities psychology department chairs considered relevant to service. In rating the overall importance of university, professional, and community services, the chairs showed a strong preference for service to the university (mean rating of importance was 41%) and professional activities (44%) over community service (15%). This inequality has minimized individual and university engagement in community-centered scholarship (Lynton, 1995). The University of Vermont, for example, does not include professional *or* community service within its service requirement. Instead, service is limited to university *service* (see Kellogg Commission, 1999a).

To make matters worse, most schools do not provide any professional benefits for community-centered research and dissemination outside the scientific community. Byrne (2000) found that roughly half a sample of 94 higher education faculty from 31 institutions report that their institutions have few incentives for conducting community-centered scholarship. Academics engaging in community service, whether through consultation, applied research, or communication of important results, fight against the strong tide of the traditional academic reward system (Boyer, 1994, 1996; Jacobson, Butterill, & Goering, 2004). The minimal personal rewards associated with community-centered scholarship make it difficult for academics who want to go beyond the walls of academic institutions.

Slivers of Knowledge

It is common practice at most colleges and universities to seek outside evaluations of its faculty when they "go up" as candidates for promotions. At that time, it is not unusual for the candidate to be evaluated on his or her knowledge in the area of his or her specialization. The stated goal at many universities is that by the time a faculty member becomes a full professor, he or she will be among the most knowledgeable people in the world. If a professor is to be the world's expert, then he or she should select a very narrow area of expertise. It is far easier to

know everything (or almost everything) about a sliver of knowledge (a single play of Shakespeare's) than about a very broad area (19th-century literature). With an increasingly narrow specialization, the number of outlets for publication also decreases, as, not surprisingly, does the number of people who are interested in it. The reliance on peer review and publication in scholarly outlets often leads to a small circle of scholars who read each other's work, remain highly competitive within their area of specialization, and communicate in a specialized language that is not familiar to outsiders. For most of academia, this description represents the highest level of academic achievement.

With the "slivers" approach to knowledge, community-centered research and dissemination are difficult to conduct. Under this paradigm, a university maintains a rigid structure, reinforcing disciplinary boundaries by encouraging and rewarding scholars who have very specialized knowledge and a narrow program of research (Schon, 1987; Walshok, 1995). Community needs, however, are not easily divided into disciplines, and the public does not typically need (or benefit from) the slivered research expected of academics. Colleges today "are so inflexibly driven by disciplinary needs and concepts of excellence grounded in peer review, that we have lost sight of our institutional mission to address the contemporary multidisciplinary problems of the real world" (Kellogg Commission, 1999b, p. 20). Unfortunately, the work essential to addressing those contemporary problems fails to produce the accolades that mark a successful academic career.

UNIVERSITY REWARDS

Just as scholars conduct activities that provide personal rewards, universities encourage faculty to engage in work that benefits the university. One type of university benefit is the Carnegie Classification system, a widely known university ranking system for academic institutions across the country. Whereas baccalaureate and master's colleges are categorized by enrollment numbers and fields in which degrees are conferred, doctorate-granting universities, where most academic research is conducted, are classified differently. In the most current revision of the system, doctorate-granting universities are ranked by two indices. The first index is an aggregated combination of money spent on research, total number of research staff, and number of doctoral degrees conferred; the second is a per capita ratio of research expenses and full-time faculty (Carnegie Foundation for the Advancement of Teaching, 2005). In both cases, money spent on research is a heavily weighted indicator of the highest rated institutions.

One primary source of research funding is large grants. When a university receives a large grant, it not only enjoys the prosperity of indirect costs but also benefits by maintaining or potentially increasing its Carnegie rating. As such, it seems natural that the university would reward the faculty who get "big money" grants (Zusman, 1999). As any grant applicant knows, big money grants do not come easily. Grant applications are carefully and critically reviewed, and often a good application is not enough to make the grade. There are ways, however, to improve one's chances of receiving funding. For example, pilot studies or previous related work can help build a case that the line of proposed research will bear fruitful results. This gives reviewers (and the funders they represent) confidence in the proposed project (Ryan, 2005). Presentation of preliminary research on a grant application, much like the "least publishable unit," encourages the parceling of large-scale studies into smaller units, a difficult task for social or behavioral scientists interested in

applied research or public dissemination of research findings. In community-centered scholarship, it often is not feasible to produce the traditional pilot study.

The background of the principal investigator (PI) also plays a significant role in the grant application process. PIs who have published work in the subject area or who are considered leaders in their field are looked upon favorably. Again, an applicant's quality and credibility is based solely on a peer-review system; only peer-reviewed publications can be included in the CVs of the PI and other staff (U.S. Department of Health and Human Services [DHHS], 2004). A scholar who spent more time on community-centered research and dissemination may not be as well published or as well noted by his or her peers and so likely will be at a great disadvantage when it comes to winning grants. In this way, the activities that bring personal rewards (i.e., publication in peer-reviewed journals) can also lead to rewards for the university. In the current paradigm, though, neither the individual nor the university reward structure encourages community-centered research or dissemination.

THE GREAT DIVIDE

The personal and university reward systems of academia clearly do not support research or dissemination beyond university walls, a situation that leaves the university completely disconnected from its local, national, and international communities (Jacoby, 1987). For example, discussions about social and behavioral science research are limited almost exclusively to scholarly journals. The average person does not have access to scholarly journals, and even if he or she did, searching for appropriate articles can be overwhelming and difficult (Kellogg Commission, 1999b). Also, disciplinary and statistical jargon makes most journal articles incomprehensible to nonacademic readers. If the public, professionals, and other scholars cannot understand our work, our research has limited benefit.

The lack of communication between scientists and the public creates a constantly widening gap between the two (Caplan, 1979; Lynton, 1995; Walshok, 1995). Consequently, the public has little understanding of and appreciation for science (see Chapter 2, this volume), including social and behavioral science research. Many people fail to understand the utility of scientific research and its potential applications (Field & Powell, 2001). More generally, the public at large does not see American higher education institutions as vital research centers from which important and essential knowledge emanates to solve the problems of today's society (Boyer, 1996; Elman & Smock, 1985; Walshok, 1995).

TIMES ARE CHANGING

Despite the bleak picture for those who care about applying and disseminating social and behavioral science, times appear to be changing. The growing criticism that higher education institutions are "aloof and out of touch, arrogant and out of date" is pushing universities across the country to reflect on their structures and systems (Kellogg Commission, 1999b, p. 20). Ultimately, social and behavioral science research is not done for the sake of the research itself but to provide knowledge and information that will change the lives of families, children, the elderly, the poor, and society at large. If we want to accomplish these goals, however, we must reconsider the current personal and university reward systems.

No longer can colleges and universities wait passively for new information to disseminate via their traditional, "trickle down" mode of scholarly publication. Instead,

academic institutions, through the work of their faculties, must become active agents in ensuring that new knowledge quickly and effectively reaches those who need it. (Lynton, 1995, p. 6)

Academics are beginning to heed Lynton's (1995) call for reform. Growing discontented with the standard narrow definition of scholarship (Boyer, 1990; Halpern et al., 1998; Walshok, 1995), they are seeking opportunities to use the knowledge gained from their research to contribute to the real world. We see, for example, that academics are beginning to redefine scholarship. Boyer (1990, 1996) argues that true scholarship is seen in four overlapping areas: discovery, integration, application, and teaching. The scholarship of discovery is perhaps the one most closely aligned with research in the traditional criteria for tenure and promotion, but it also includes gaining new knowledge for the purpose of adding to the academic knowledge base as well as application to real-world situations. The scholarship of integration, then, makes sense of the knowledge gained in discovery, placing it in an appropriate context—for instance, understanding research findings within their real-world environments. In the scholarship of application, academics ask, "How can knowledge be responsibly applied to consequential problems?" (Boyer, 1990, p. 21). Finally, the scholarship of teaching is passing knowledge on to students, both in and out of the classroom, so that our knowledge is preserved and shared beyond academia (Kellogg Commission, 1999a; Sandmann, et al., 2000). Community-centered research, applied research, widespread publication of results, and directly sharing knowledge with community members are incorporated into each facet of scholarship.

A broader definition of scholarship expands service beyond university committee memberships and makes it an integral part of an academic's career. Indeed, any "work which draws upon and is the outgrowth of one's academic discipline and professional expertise is legitimately a part of the academic enterprise" and should be considered scholarship (Elman & Smock, 1985, p. 15). Some institutions are following this line of thought and redefining scholarship to be more inclusive, particularly of conducting community-centered research and communicating the results beyond the academy (see Lynton, 1995). In a survey of 729 chief academic officers at colleges across the country, 45% reported that their institutions had expanded the definition of scholarship in their mission statements and other documents (O'Meara, 2005a). Michigan State University (1993), for example, convened a Provost's Committee on University Outreach, whose resulting report strongly supported a broader understanding of scholarship, stating, "Outreach has the same potential for scholarship as the other major academic functions" (p. 71). Also, at University of North Carolina at Chapel Hill, a roundtable discussion on public outreach concluded that service to the community could (and should) transcend the typical criteria and be integrated into all three pieces of the university's mission (see Lynton, 1995, Appendix 2). At Portland State University, 79% of faculty interviewed defined scholarship more broadly than it has been traditionally (Reuter & Bauer, 2005). With a new definition of scholarship being accepted in American institutions, service is no longer always relegated to a secondary (or tertiary) position; it is becoming an important part of scholarly activity. This first step is critical for encouraging community-centered research and disseminating science outside academia because these efforts will only be undertaken if valued as scholarship (Lynton & Elman, 1987).

THE WAY FORWARD

Along with a change in the way academia conceptualizes scholarship, universities must respond to the challenges to increase community-centered research and dissemination. Considering the barriers to community-centered scholarship raised by the personal and university reward structures, we suggest four specific ways individuals and universities can bridge the divide between higher education and the greater public.

Get Engaged

One way to increase community-centered scholarship in academia is through university engagement with the community. Whereas most universities value general institutional and community service, *engagement* involves an ongoing, open two-way dialogue between the university and the community (Boyer, 1996; Jacobson et al., 2004; Kellogg Commission, 1999b, 2000; Michigan State University, 2000; Weber, 1999). As Lynton (1995) writes, "Service is not a one-way flow of information and technical assistance to external clients; instead it is a two-way communication that provides substantial opportunities for discovery and fresh insights" (p. 11). Academics serve the community by providing it with knowledge and educational opportunities. The community, in return, serves academics by providing real-world dilemmas and research questions that advance the social and behavioral sciences. In this way, *service* extends beyond university walls and into the community, becoming *engagement*.

For both research and dissemination projects, the dialogue between scientists and the community must begin at the very first stages, defining goals, research questions, or approaches to dissemination together (Kellogg Commission, 1999b). The open communication should continue throughout the entire project, as decisions are made (such as where to collect data or what medium will best communicate the results). Through this process, both community and academic needs are met, and all parties consider the project successful (Kellogg Commission, 1999b; Sandmann et al., 2000).

As social and behavioral science research is done with important contemporary questions in mind, activities that stem from mutual understanding and respect between scientists and the community have power to bring "hard data" to community issues. In fact, increased attention to community needs and collaboration with the community are two of the primary concerns of the Kellogg Commission, convened from 1996 to 2000 to address the need for reform in public and land-grant universities (Byrne, 2006; Kellogg Commission, 1999b). Although a 2000 study showed that roughly 25% of public university faculty respondents did not know whether engagement was part of their universities' mission statements or if their schools had a formal engagement plan, surveys 5 years later revealed that many universities had begun to make engagement-increasing changes to their policies and structures (Byrne, 2006). Below are a few examples of engaged institutions at the time of this book's publication:

• The University of Minnesota works in partnership with the local and national communities through its Center for Applied Research and Educational Improvement (CAREI), a collaborative organization supported by the College of Education and Human Development. CAREI conducts applied and collaborative research, as well as evaluation projects, and provides a "point of entry" to the university for local youth.

• At Michigan State University, the Institute for Public Policy and Social Research (IPPSR) focuses on the political community, providing survey research services and offering programs for undergraduate students interested in participating in Michigan government.

• Portland State University has several institutes working on collaborative, multidisciplinary work, including the Regional Research Institute for Human Services (RRI), which aims to "improve human services through applied social research" (Portland State University, n.d.). One example of RRI's many projects is the Racial and Ethnic Approaches to Community Health (REACH 2010) program, which aims to improve cardiovascular health and treatment of diabetes for African Americans in the Portland area.

• Arizona State University has built relationships with numerous local and national business, conducting research to address problems raised by these companies and providing students with real-world experience working in and with such organizations as Motorola, Wells Fargo Bank, and Bank of America.

• Ohio State University (OSU) has the Community Access to Resources and Educational Services (CARES) program in which students and staff work with the community to address local and state concerns; OSU CARES "serves as a catalyst to activate teams of university professionals to address anticipated critical issues to face Ohioans" (Ohio State University, n.d.). For example, one OSU CARES program provides information about healthy nutrition to children in Grades 2 through 8 and encourages them to apply that knowledge in making healthy choices.

Clearly, this is not an exhaustive list of engaged institutions, but it does paint a picture of how universities (and faculty) can get engaged with the community to conduct relevant research and to provide information to the greater public.

Think Outside the (Disciplinary) Box

As previously mentioned, maintaining an expertise and a research program within a specialized area can hinder community-centered scholarship. While academia is growing more fractioned, the roots of today's problems are becoming more complex and interwoven (Kellogg Commission, 1999a; Walshok, 1995). To help resolve complicated social issues, universities must take an interdisciplinary approach and increase cross-department collaboration (Kellogg Commission, 1999a; Lynton & Elman, 1987; van Ginkel, 1999). Indeed, the knowledge gained from social and behavioral science research can be most powerful when it is integrated across disciplines and applied outside the research setting, thus helping to bridge the divide between academia and the public.

The good news is that some institutions are creating mechanisms to approach multi-disciplinary problems. A survey of 31 public colleges and universities shows that nearly half of faculty respondents and more than 75% of presidents report that their institutions have systems in place to conduct inter-disciplinary community-centered research or dissemination projects (Byrne, 2000). For example, Michigan State University values multidisciplinary approaches and collaborations on community-centered scholarship, stating, "Although a multi-disciplinary or cross-disciplinary approach is not explicitly expected in every outreach project, an underlying openness to multiple inputs is expected" (Michigan State University, 2000, p. 5). Similarly, Tufts University is planning to establish at least 10 endowed chairs specifically to conduct multidisciplinary community-centered projects (Blanding, 2006).

Many universities also have institutes, centers, and organizations that conduct multidisciplinary projects. For example, the previously mentioned OSU CARES draws faculty from different disciplines to approach social problems. Also, Pennsylvania State University has a Life Science Consortium at which hundreds of scientists from various backgrounds collaborate on research and projects that relate to significant human problems. For example, one of their 2006–2011 projects examines the developmental effects of iron deficiency on the brain and behavior. Though the Life Sciences Consortium does not focus on producing social and behavioral science research, it is a place where social and behavioral scientists can collaborate with others outside their own areas of expertise, integrating the perspectives, methods, and tools from multiple disciplines. These centers are examples of thinking outside disciplinary boundaries to conduct community-centered research and disseminate important research findings outside academia.

Be Deliberate

Engagement can only work if faculty and administrators are deliberate about initiating and maintaining an open, collaborative relationship with the public. In fact, one of the Kellogg Commission's (1999b) specific recommendations to universities was to develop a detailed engagement plan. The commission argues, "A transformation of attitudes toward engagement . . . will not create itself. Planned, purposeful effort will be required to bring it into being" (Kellogg Commission, 1999b, p. 47). Likewise, the RAND Corporation, after reviewing a U.K. governmental branch to determine how to increase public dissemination, highlighted the necessity of deliberate strategies that involve the community. Community engagement plans that are targeted and specific in that they, for example, have well-defined goals and tactics suitable for reaching them have the potential to "increase the use of solid research, to inform policy, to improve service delivery, and to prevent inefficiency and inconsistency across a nation's entire research agenda" (Grant, van het Loo, Law, Anton, & Cave,

2004, p. 23). Academics pursuing community-centered scholarship must make it a priority; they cannot expect research and dissemination to automatically extend beyond the university. From identifying the research question to disseminating findings, scientists must be strategic, deliberate, and involve the community at every step.

Many of the changes toward institutional engagement can begin with the deliberate education of our future scientists. According to a survey of chief academic officers at colleges and universities across the country, the first principle of good engagement practice is to prepare graduate students to engage in and understand multiple forms of scholarship (O'Meara, 2005b). Social and behavioral science students should be taught about the importance of community-centered scholarship and the strategies to efficiently and properly conduct such research and dissemination projects (Gaff, 2005).

Future scholars need to be taught the writing and oral communication skills that enable them to communicate science effectively to both academic and nonacademic audiences. Graduate students are not currently trained to write for the public; they are taught to write in a unique scientific style specifically geared for peer-reviewed journals and books. This style of writing is often confusing and hard to read, not only to professionals and scholars outside of one's specialization but to the general public as well. Training students to speak about science is limited to preparing conference presentations for peers and perhaps lectures and discussions for undergraduate students. Few are prepared to talk about science with policy makers, professional groups, or the media. Similarly, students should be expected to engage in multidisciplinary work to prepare them for future collaborations with service organizations, professional associations, and the greater community.

Expanding students' views of scholarship and expanding their skill sets should increase academic-community engagement in the future and prepare future scientists to work with (and in) nonacademic settings. These changes, however, can only occur with deliberate teaching and guidance from social and behavioral science faculty.

Changing Mechanisms

Scientific discussions will not widen beyond academia without significant changes in the structure of higher education institutions. A transformation from a closed circle of academics to university-community collaborations requires fervent administrative support of community-centered scholarship and community engagement (Boyer, 1990; Kellogg Commission, 1999b; Walshok, 1995). For example, in a case study of the changes at Portland State University, strong leadership that considered faculty input was critical in the process of increasing engagement (Rueter & Bauer, 2005). Fortunately, many schools have added or tailored leadership positions to increase engagement, consistent with recommendations of the Kellogg Commission (Byrne, 2006).

Administrators focused on increasing engagement must make structural and systematic changes to encourage and reward community-centered scholarship (Byrne, 2000; Diamond, 2005; Grant et al., 2004; Lynton, 1995). Lynton and Elman (1987) make a clear and concise argument: "Without a substantial adaptation of the faculty reward system, all efforts at greater university outreach and expanded faculty activities will continue to be what they have been in the majority of institutions: a matter of well-intended but ineffective rhetoric" (p. 150). It is imperative that universities reward community-centered research and dissemination by their faculty. Rewarding alternative forms of scholarship will encourage faculty to think more broadly in terms of research and publishing (Kellogg Commission, 1999b; Ramaley, 2002).

Some American universities are beginning to change their tenure and promotion guidelines to recognize and reward faculty engagement. In 1997, only 6.5% of schools included service awards in their tenure and promotion policies (O'Meara, 1997). By 2005, nearly 65% had made policy changes to encourage and reward engagement and broad scholarship (O'Meara, 2005a). In another sample, 71% of schools had made changes to their tenure or promotion policies to increase faculty engagement (Byrne, 2006). The University of Illinois at Urbana-Champaign (UIUC), for example, acknowledges the role of public service in tenure decisions, citing engagement as one of the vital aspects of scholarship (University of Illinois at Urbana-Champaign, 2000). Consistent with O'Meara's (2002) conclusion that universities produce more rhetoric than action around changing reward structures, the actual weight given to engagement at UIUC is minimal; guidelines state that faculty involvement in community-centered scholarship should follow the emphasis on service within each department, leaving no push for campus-wide engagement.

Other universities have taken stronger stands in favor of community-centered scholarship. Pennsylvania State University has incorporated a measure of faculty outreach activities in its tenure and promotion processes, encouraging the "generation, transmission, application, preservation, and enhancement of knowledge between the University and external audiences" within and beyond the classroom (Kellogg Commission, 1999a, p. 39). Similarly, Rutgers University has begun to include engagement in its tenure and promotion criteria, and the institution gives merit awards to faculty working on community-centered research and dissemination (Kellogg Commission, 1999a).

One of the greatest success stories at this point is that of Portland State University, one of the only institutions emphasizing research and dissemination *outside* the university and maintaining university service as separate from community service (Rueter & Bauer, 2005; Shulock & Ketcheson, 2000; Tetreault & Ketcheson, 2002). Portland State University "seeks to foster the scholarly development of its faculty and to encourage the scholarly interaction of faculty with students and with regional, national, and international communities" (Portland State University, n.d., p. 1). In fact, the school's tenure and promotion criteria follow Boyer's (1990) definition of scholarship (i.e., discovery, integration, application, and teaching), rather than the traditional three-dimension criteria (i.e., research, teaching, and service). This effort is an example of what we hope many schools will adopt in their tenure and promotion policies. Though changing leadership administrative focus and reward structures are formidable tasks, both are essential to the concept of rewarding community-centered scholarship.

NEW UNIVERSITY BENEFITS

Although there are many benefits to universities within the current structure, institutions can benefit from supporting engaged faculty. Being linked with research that has practical applications can increase university visibility and attractiveness by bringing research findings and science to the forefront of the public. For example, media coverage of an institution increases when research findings useful to the community are reported. Such recognition not only highlights the faculty member as an expert whose work is relevant to the public; it also advertises that the institution has expertise the public can appreciate and use. This kind of recognition and publicity attracts philanthropists, legislators, funders, and potential students. Indeed, there may be no better way to publicize a university to potential students and donors than media coverage of important and influential research.

Increased engagement can also lead to additional student interest and unique opportunities for student learning. Recent graduates of Portland State University, for example, report that they are proud of the increased engagement and visibility of their alma mater (Kellogg Commission, 1999a). Students at Iowa State University are enrolling in increasing numbers in courses that include a community involvement component (Kellogg Commission, 1999a). In these classes, students have the chance to work with and for local businesses, gaining practical hands-on training and experience. Many of the organizations with whom Iowa State University has collaborated have purposely hired recent graduates because of the real-world experience the graduates received as students. Other universities, however, are missing opportunities to bring attention to the institution in this way.

The university can also benefit from faculty engagement by being recognized through the Carnegie Classification system. The classification system now includes a category for those institutions engaged with their community. This provides "another way for institutions to describe their identity and commitments with a public and nationally recognized classification" (Carnegie Foundation for the Advancement of Teaching, 2006). Institutions may receive this classification if they document that engagement is part of their "identity and culture" and that they have an "institutional commitment" to engagement and to ongoing partnerships with the greater community. The school must also show elements of engagement in its curriculum. Including community-centered research and dissemination and ongoing engagement as integral pieces of the institutional reward system can be a win-win situation for the school, the faculty member, and the public at large.

CONCLUSION

Though translating results into usable information for the government, community organizations, applied professionals, or the public at large should be considered part of any research project, social and behavioral scientists do not often prioritize this within their research plans (Grant et al., 2004). As Thomas Friedman (2005) recently wrote in his best-selling book, *The World Is Flat*, good ideas are changing today's world very quickly. Social and behavioral scientists, however, cannot contribute to changing the world if the results and conclusions of our work are not shared beyond the university. By failing to connect social and behavioral science to society in these ways, we are doing a disservice to the community and to our science. As social and behavioral scientists, we must become more responsible for the dissemination and use of our research, beyond academic discourse and peer-reviewed journals.

There are many obstacles to including the nonacademic community in social and behavioral science research and dissemination of results. Though these barriers have created a chasm between American universities and the greater public, there are steps that universities and individuals can take to increase community-centered scholarship. To bring down the university walls, we need to engage in collaborations with the community, think outside traditional disciplinary boundaries, be deliberate in planning projects and educating future scholars, and change the structure and policies of universities. As scientists studying topics with significant real-life meaning, we must begin to bridge the gap between academia and the community. Not only can social and behavioral sciences grow from applying our data and theoretical concepts, but it will make our work become more useful and valued by people in our society and around the world.

REFERENCES

Abott, D., & Sanders, G. F. (1991). On the road to tenure. *Family Relations, 40*(1), 106–109.

Agrawal, A. A. (2005, October 12). Is the impact factor having too much impact? Message posted to http://chronicle.com/colloquy/2005/10/impact/

Blanding, M. (2006, Summer). Act locally and globally. [Electronic version]. *Tufts Magazine.* Retrieved March 17, 2006, from http://www.tufts.edu/alumni/magazine/summer2006/features/cover.html

Boyer, E. L. (1990). *Scholarship reconsidered: Priorities of the professorate.* Princeton, NJ: The Carnegie Foundation for the Advancement of Teaching.

Boyer, E. L. (1994, March 9). Creating the new American college [Electronic version]. *The Chronicles of Higher Education.*

Boyer, E. L. (1996). The scholarship of engagement. *Journal of Public Service & Outreach, 1*(1), 11–20.

Byrne, J. V. (2000). *Public higher education reform: 2000: The results of a post–Kellogg Commission survey.* Retrieved May 15, 2006, from http://www.nasulgc.org/Kellogg/Kellogg2000_PostComm_survey_summary.pdf

Byrne, J. V. (2006). *Public higher education reform five years after the Kellogg Commission on the future of state and land-grant universities.* Retrieved May 15, 2006, from http://www.nasulgc.org/Kellogg/KCFiveYearReport.pdf

Cameron, J., & Pierce, W. D. (1994). Reinforcement, reward, and intrinsic motivation: A meta-analysis. *Review of Educational Research, 64*(3), 363–423.

Caplan, N. (1979). The two-communities theory and knowledge utilization. *American Behavioral Scientist, 22*(3), 459–470.

Carnegie Foundation for the Advancement of Teaching. (2005). *2005 Carnegie classifications initial release.* Retrieved March 2, 2006, from http://wwwcarnegiefoundation.org/classifications/index.asp?key=786

Carnegie Foundation for the Advancement of Teaching. (2006). *Community engagement elective classification.* Retrieved June 7, 2006, from http://www.carnegiefoundation.org/classifications/index.asp?key=1213

Columbia University. (2005). *Principles and customs governing the procedures of ad hoc committees and university-wide tenure review.* Retrieved March 6, 2006, from http://www.columbia.edu/cu/vpaa/docs/tenframe.html

Diamond, R. M. (2005). Scholarship reconsidered: Barriers to change. In K. O'Meara & R. E. Rice (Eds.), *Faculty priorities reconsidered: Rewarding multiple forms of scholarship* (pp. 56–59). San Francisco: Jossey-Bass.

Duke University. (n.d.). *The Duke University faculty handbook.* Retrieved March 6, 2006, from http://www.provost.duke.edu/pdfs/fhb/FHB.pdf

Elman, S. E., & Smock, S. M. (1985). *Professional service and faculty rewards: Toward an integrated structure.* Washington, DC: National Association of State Universities and Land-Grant Colleges.

Field, H., & Powell, P. (2001). Public understanding of science vs. public understanding of research. *Public Understanding of Science, 10*(4), 421–426.

Frank, M. J. (1995). Tenure definition document promotes wide-ranging dialogue [Electronic version]. *The University Record, 50*(21).

Friedman, T. L. (2005). *The world is flat: A brief history of the twenty-first century.* New York: Thomas Friedman.

Gaff, J. G. (2005). Preparing future faculty and multiple forms of scholarship. In K. O'Meara & R. E. Rice (Eds.), *Faculty priorities reconsidered: Rewarding multiple forms of scholarship* (pp. 66–74). San Francisco: Jossey-Bass.

Grant, J., van het Loo, M., Law, S. A., Anton, S., & Cave, J. (2004, Summer). Foot in mouth: Finding better uses for policy research. *RAND Review,* pp. 20–23.

Halpern, D. F., Smothergill, D. W., Allen, M., Baker, S., Baum, C., Best, D., et al. (1998). Scholarship in psychology: A paradigm for the twenty-first century. *American Psychologist, 53*(12), 1292–1297.

Israel, E. N., & Baird, R. J. (1988). Tenure and promotion: Changing expectations and requirements. *Journal of Industrial Teacher Education, 25*(2), 16–31.

Jacobson, N., Butterill, D., & Goering, P. (2004). Organizational factors that influence university-based researchers' engagement in knowledge transfer activities. *Science Communication, 25*(3), 246–259.

Jacoby, R. (1987). *The last intellectuals: American culture in the age of academe.* New York: Basic Books.

Kellogg Commission. (1999a). *Engaged institutions: A commitment to service: Profiles and data.* Retrieved May 10, 2006, from http://www.nasulgc.org/publications/Kellogg/ Kellogg1999_ProfilesData.pdf

Kellogg Commission. (1999b). *Returning to our roots: The engaged institution.* Retrieved May 10, 2006, from http://www.nasulgc.org/publications/Kellogg/ Kellogg1999_Engage.pdf

Kellogg Commission. (2000). *Renewing the covenant: Learning, discovery, and engagement in a new age and different world.* Retrieved May 10, 2006, from http://www.nasulgc.org/publications/Kellogg/Kellogg2000_covenant.pdf

Lynton, E. A. (1995). *Making the case for professional service.* Washington, DC: American Association for Higher Education.

Lynton, E. A., & Elman, S. E. (1987). *New priorities for the university: Meeting society's needs for applied knowledge and competent individuals.* San Francisco: Jossey-Bass.

McCaffrey, R. J., Nelles, W. B., & Byrne, D. (1989). Criteria for tenure and promotion in doctoral degree programs in psychology: Perceptions of department chairs and heads. *Bulletin of the Psychonomic Society, 27,* 77–80.

Michigan State University. (1993). *University outreach at Michigan State University: Extending knowledge to serve society: The provost's committee on university outreach.* Retrieved May 15, 2006, from http://www.msu.edu/unit/outreach/ missioncontents.html

Michigan State University. (2000). *Points of distinction: A guidebook for planning and evaluating quality outreach.* Retrieved May 29, 2006, from http://www .msu.edu/unit/outreach/pubs/pod.pdf

Monastersky, R. (2005a). Impact factors run into competition [Electronic version]. *The Chronicle of Higher Education, 52*(8).

Monastersky, R. (2005b). The number that's devouring science [Electronic version]. *The Chronicle of Higher Education, 52*(8).

Ohio State University. (n.d.). *Ohio State University CARES.* Retrieved August 19, 2006 from http://osucares.osu.edu/about.html

O'Meara, K. (1997). *Rewarding faculty professional service.* Boston: New England Resource Center for Higher Education.

O'Meara, K. (2002). Uncovering the values in faculty evaluation of service as scholarship. *The Review of Higher Education, 26*(1), 57–80.

O'Meara, K. (2005a). Effects of encouraging multiple forms of scholarship nationwide and across institutional types. In K. O'Meara & R. E. Rice (Eds.), *Faculty priorities reconsidered: Rewarding multiple forms of scholarship* (pp. 255–289). San Francisco: Jossey-Bass.

O'Meara, K. (2005b). Principles of good practice: Encouraging multiple forms of scholarship in policy and practice. In K. O'Meara & R. E. Rice (Eds.), *Faculty priorities reconsidered: Rewarding multiple forms of scholarship* (pp. 290–302). San Francisco: Jossey-Bass.

Owen, W. J. (2004). In defense of the least publishable unit [Electronic version]. *The Chronicle of Higher Education, 50*(23).

Portland State University. (n.d.). *Regional Research Institute for Human Services.* Retrieved May 5, 2006, from http://www.rri.pdx.edu/pgAboutUs.shtml

Ramaley, J. A. (2002, October 7). *Seizing the moment: Creating a changed society and university through outreach.* Keynote remarks at the 2002 Outreach Scholarship Conference: Catalyst for Change, Worthington, OH. Retrieved May 29, 2006, from http://is124.ce.psu.edu/OutreachScholarship/keynote.html

Rueter, J., & Bauer, T. (2005). Identifying and managing university assets: A campus study of Portland State University. In K. O'Meara & R. E. Rice (Eds.), *Faculty priorities reconsidered: Rewarding multiple forms of scholarship* (pp. 187–207). San Francisco: Jossey-Bass.

Ryan, L. (2005). *How to win an NIH grant—A reviewer's perspective.* Retrieved March 11, 2006, from http://statfund.cancer.gov/articles/Ryan_JSM_Aug2005 .pdf

Sandmann, L. R., Foster-Fishman, P. G., Lloyd, J., Rauhe, W., & Rosaen, C. (2000). Managing critical tensions: How to strengthen the scholarship component of outreach. *Change, 32*(1), 44–52.

Schon, D. A. (1987). *Educating the reflective practitioner.* San Francisco: Jossey-Bass.

Shulock, N. B., & Ketcheson, K. (2000). Two approaches to assessing the metropolitan university mission. *Metropolitan Universities, 10,* 63–72.

Sweeney, A. E. (2000). Should you publish in electronic journals? *Journal of Electronic Publishing, 6*(2). Retrieved February 27, 2006, from http://www .press.umich.edu/jep/06–02/sweeney.html

Tetreault, M., & Ketcheson, K. (2002). Creating a shared understanding of institutional knowledge through an electronic institutional portfolio. *Metropolitan Universities, 13,* 40–49.

Thorndike, E. L. (1898). *Animal intelligence: An experimental study of the associative processes in animals.* New York: Columbia University Press.

University of Illinois at Urbana-Champaign. (2000). *A faculty guide for relating public service to the promotion and tenure review process.* Retrieved May 5, 2006, from http://www.oc.uiuc.edu/engagement/p&tfacultyguide2000.pdf

U.S. Department of Health and Human Services (DHHS). (2004). *Public health service grant application (PHS 398).* Retrieved September 22, 2006, from http://grants.nih .gov/grants/funding/phs398/phs398.html

van Ginkel, H. J. A. (1999). Networks and strategic alliances within and between universities and with the private sector. In W. Z. Hirsch & L. E. Weber (Eds.), *Challenges facing higher education at the millennium* (pp. 85–92). Phoenix, AZ: Oryx Press.

Walshok, M. L. (1995). *Knowledge without boundaries: What America's research universities can do for the economy, the workplace, and the community.* San Francisco: Jossey-Bass.

Weber, L. E. (1999). Survey of the main challenges facing higher education at the millennium. In W. Z. Hirsch & L. E. Weber (Eds.), *Challenges facing higher education at the millennium* (pp. 3–17). Phoenix, AZ: Oryx Press.

Woods, P. J. (1959). The effects of motivation and probability of reward on two-choice learning. *Journal of Experimental Psychology, 57*(6), 380–385.

Zusman, A. (1999). Issues facing higher education in the twenty-first century. In P. G. Altbach, R. O. Berdahl, & P. J. Gumport (Eds.), *American higher education in the twenty-first century* (pp. 109–148). Baltimore: Johns Hopkins University Press.

Part II

UNDERSTANDING MASS MEDIA PRIORITIES AND PROCESSES

CHAPTER 7

Reporting on Behavioral Science

A Glimpse Inside the Television News Business

ANDREA GITOW

The television news business is an ever-changing institution that increasingly relies on experts both to provide ideas and to help viewers understand complex events and the world around them. This chapter will discuss television news format, the role of producers, the ways that behavioral science becomes part of television news, and, finally, some tips for working successfully in this venue. Though the formats of the shows discussed may be different, the points and illustrations highlighted throughout this chapter apply to all the formats. They represent the needs of the industry, as well as the current ways of thinking about news and about the presentation of behavioral research in today's press environment.

THE SHOWS

When thinking about network and cable news, it's not a "one-size-fits" all category. There are the morning shows, the network nightly newscasts, the long-format newsmagazine shows, and the cable outlets, a venue that tends to combines all three of the other formats. Each broadcast venue has its own format and, for the most part, its own needs. The morning shows are traditionally a combination of a general topic—"softer" pieces that focus largely on women's issues (e.g., what's the best way to argue with your spouse)—and series (e.g., the five ways to live a happier life). Morning shows tend to use the more traditional format of introducing a topic and then having an expert discuss it. While morning shows will always stick to the bread-and-butter story choices, such as "how to have a good relationship with your husband," the shows are also always looking both for fresh angles to the more urgent news stories and for more interesting ways to tell the softer stories beyond introducing a topic and including a question-and-answer session with an expert.

When it comes to the softer stories, shows are beginning to use what we call a "cut" piece, a 1- to 2-minute fully produced story that highlights a particular issue, such as how to be optimistic or how to beat depression. The newsmagazines do much longer, more in-depth pieces that are usually driven by a person's story that exemplifies a certain phenomenon, such as a story in which a patient with dissociative identity disorder (DID) commits a crime. The story then revolves around the question, Is the perpetrator guilty of the crime or not since his alter ego committed the crime? Or the story becomes about one victim of crime in a particular news event—for example, the shootings at Columbine. This one person, such as the man with DID or the victim at Columbine, is called a *character*. The character is used to illustrate a larger point, such as issues that arise in applying psychology to law or to a problem of violence and teens.

Newsmagazine reports now vary greatly in length. It used to be that they would be composed of three 12- to 14-minute spots, as in the *60 Minutes* format. Today, they can range from multiparters to full-hour specials on one topic. The nightly news broadcasts are also now doing more in-depth reports, moving to *character-driven* stories, often producing a 1- to 2-minute story that involves one person's tale. Still, they may do the "headline" that is a quick reading of a new finding in medical news, for example, although this practice is becoming increasingly rare.

What is becoming increasingly common, however, across all the shows is the creation of the *sidebar story*. This story is not about the facts, events, and timeline of the news story but about the issues that relate to them. The name *sidebar* comes from the newspaper in which you'll see the main story front and center and then related stories surrounding it. Research from psychology and other sciences now tend to be sidebar stories. It is very rare in today's news climate to find behavioral science *as* the news. Instead, you'll find behavioral science used as a tool to help the audience understand a news event, explain a social phenomenon, and provide context to what's happening in the world and what's being reported on. As a result, those who seek to successfully pitch behavioral science should most often view the research as relevant to the news and events in our lives as opposed to being the news story itself and try to "sell" it as such.

So what are some examples of sidebar stories? Let's take 9/11, for example. Mixed with the breaking news events of the day, network news, newsmagazine morning shows, and cable outlets did features that included "how to talk to your child about terrorism," "what's the psychology and science behind mass hysteria," and "what is PTSD and are there ways to prevent it." For Hurricane Katrina, sidebar stories included "how to make your child feel safe" and the "science of modern racism." Likewise, main news stories about Columbine were done on the shooting itself. Sidebar reports featured behavioral research on conformity, obedience to authority, and forensic psychology. A victim of the infamous school shootings in Stockton, California, in 1989 was also interviewed to examine the long-term effects of witnessing such events. Sidebar stories are now a staple of the broadcast news shows. They are as likely to appear as the main features. Simply put, sidebar stories are here to stay.

THE PRODUCERS

The job of a producer at each of these shows is tense and hectic, and he or she often has limited time to make decisions around stories. So what exactly does a producer do? Producers in the television news industry have different responsibilities than those in the movie industry, whose job focuses on money and the logistics of production. In broadcast journalism, think of the producer like a print reporter. He or she is responsible for getting the story, reporting on it, and, in many cases, writing or cowriting it. Broadcast is, however, a visual medium. As such, the producer has additional responsibilities such as envisioning what elements need to be shot, directing the camera crews in the field, screening all the footage, and sitting in on the edit. Whereas in newspaper reporting, the writer tends to work alone, in broadcast journalism, the producer works hand in hand with the correspondent or "on-air talent" whose face you see and who brings you the report.

Producers are also largely responsible for pitching stories to the show's executives. Typically, a short pitch of no more than a few paragraphs is written up and submitted by a producer to the executive producers and senior producers, who decide what is a "go" and what is rejected outright. In some cases, they may send back the pitch asking for more details or asking the producer to rethink the format of the proposed piece. The producer has very little time and space to catch the attention of the executives, so pitches must always be concise and compelling. The pitch always needs a "hook," something that ties it to current events, news of the day, an answer to a compelling question, or meaningful events in people's everyday lives.

The producers generate story ideas through a number of sources. They may look through newspapers and magazine articles as the source of story ideas. They may call on contacts they have in the field and ask what new research is out there. They may also go back over previous research and think of how it relates to the world around them. Finally, producers may also ask themselves what is of interest out in the world—are there new social or cultural trends, does something seem to be a hot topic, what's being discussed at the dinner tables and being seen on the streets? In other words, journalists work in two ways. They may either develop a story idea first and then look for relevant background and context that may lead them to behavioral science, or they may generate topics from research-based information they receive.

After a pitch is accepted, a producer typically jumps on the story right away. In a nightly newscast or morning show, he or she often has a day turnaround. He or she may pitch the story in the morning and have it on the broadcast that night or, in the case of a show such as NBC's *Today,* ABC's *Good Morning America,* or CBS's *The Early Show,*

the next morning. In-depth stories that often run 2½ minutes may take up to 1 week to produce. In a newsmagazine show, stories usually are produced within 3 months of the pitch, although the deadlines are getting more and more compressed as networks slash production budgets. Other times, however, a full hour is "crashed" in a day or two in response to breaking news, as with Hurricane Katrina, 9/11, the tsunami that hit Southeast Asia, and Columbine. In this case, almost all of the staff and up to 10 producers and associate producers may *crash* an hour at the same time. Some producers are responsible for writing the piece, others for getting interviews, and others for sitting in the edit room "cutting" the story.

A common thread across all reporting is that producers must have good contacts with science experts to both pitch stories and to get good interviews. He or she works hard to cultivate these relationships and is always on the lookout for new contacts. Many producers also have specific "beats" and so specialize in particular areas of news coverage. Whereas a few shows do have general medical correspondents and producers (which, by the way, is always a good place for you to start making contacts), many shows have producers work on certain "types" of stories. Usually, producers will report on breaking news, though others tend to do "softer," longer format stories. Producers develop an expertise—for example, in medical stories or in mental health spots—and then typically stick to doing the kinds of stories they know and do best.

Many shows also have story editors. Their job is to chart out the editorial flow of the broadcasts. They also have a lot to do with story selection, story choice, future directions of the show, and so on. They typically think of the big picture regarding their shows, including multipart shows that air over a number of nights or hour-long documentaries. Story editors rely on the pitches of the producers and also are responsible for generating story ideas themselves.

You should feel free to contact producers and story editors directly. Don't be shy about it. Call a show and ask for the name of a producer who may cover psychology stories or who may have a medical beat. See if you can get a phone number or e-mail address and contact them directly to introduce yourself and explain what the science has to offer. Producers are always looking for new material and new content. So, for example, if you are watching a newsmagazine show and you like a story in particular, get the name of that producer. Newsmagazines always put the name of the producer at the start and end of the show. Present your ideas and your work and why you believe it should be of interest to the show. If you're having a hard time reaching a producer directly, you should also feel free to contact the show's story editor. You may also want to call both and tell the story editor you've been speaking with a specific producer and ask if you should speak with anyone else.

ANGLES THAT CAN MAKE BEHAVIORAL SCIENCE USEFUL TO LONGER FORMAT TELEVISION NEWS

As you'll recall, it's the exception rather than the rule to have behavioral science findings reported *as* the news story. It used to be that traditional broadcast news would report on actual findings. It's the old standby where we see the television anchor behind the desk saying, "Today, a report in blank blank journal found that. . . ." But in today's ever competitive marketplace, news divisions are racing to create new and highly stylized reports that come across as stories, more than findings per se. So what exactly does this kind of news story look like? Here are some examples of how behavioral science findings were turned into big news stories.

Case Study 1

A number of years ago, a 27-year-old mother of two named Deletha Word was beaten on a bridge in Detroit in full view of more than 50 stopped motorists. No one, not one person, stopped to help her or even to call 911. Horrific, yes, but a national news story, no. That was until the team at *Dateline* and I decided to try to understand what exactly happened on that bridge that day. How could it be that not one single person did anything to help? What social dynamic was at play? Did other examples of such a phenomenon exist in the news historically (in this case, there was the famous Kitty Genovese story)? Was there a way we could reach out to the audience and help them answer the question, "How could this have happened, and would I have done the same thing if I was on that bridge today?" In no time, we found John Darley and Bib Latané's (1968) famous work on the bystander effect. It was a perfect example of how behavioral science could help us to understand what's happening in the news. We knew instantly that reporting on this research would help us provide context to this tragic news event and, in the process, help people better understand themselves. We knew we could get a thought-provoking piece that would extend beyond the news details and into the realm of deconstructing a social phenomenon that affected all our viewers. In this instance, everyone could put themselves in the place of both Deletha Word and the bystanders. Everyone could ask himself or herself, "What would I do?"

Case Study 2

Who can forget the horrific images—Iraqi prisoners being threatened by guard dogs and forced to wear black hoods over their heads and stand on boxes for hours on end. Events in Abu Ghraib prison in Iraq shamed the nation and raised the question, How could have such brutality have happened? There were countless solid news stories on the U.S. network and on cable stations, but the reports rarely went beyond the details of events. That's where behavioral science came in. Again, the question became, How do you explain such events, and how can people understand them? *Dateline*'s executive producer and I decided to do a special report answering such questions. To find help, we turned to a groundbreaking study conducted more than 25 years ago by Dr. Philip Zimbardo (Haney, Banks, & Zimbardo, 1973; Zimbardo, 1975), which shows what happens when some people are given great power and others are deemed powerless; this went a long way toward explaining the horrible events at Abu Ghraib prison.

Case Study 3

I remember reading a story about a young 13-year-old honor student in Florida who followed two friends into someone's house and watched as they committed a heinous murder. Under the felony murder rule, he was convicted of murder and sentenced to life in prison. I couldn't help but wonder, How could a relatively good kid blindly follow others, what kind of peer pressure existed, how strong are those forces, and just how far would people go? We had the noted social psychologist Anthony Pratkanis replicate the famous Asch conformity experiment (Asch, 1955, 1956), and with the consent of Stanley Milgram's wife, *Dateline* was able to air the famous footage of the Milgram obedience study (Milgram, 1963). Again, the broadcast report went beyond the news events and into the realm of behavioral science to answer such questions.

Case Study 4

More recently, a news story reported that a politician had undermined a colleague of his for no apparent reason. It turns out the person wasn't just a colleague but his best friend for more than 30 years. The NBC news team wanted to help viewers understand how a friend could betray a friend for little personal gain. We joined together with a researcher who spent his career studying envy.

Case Study 5

Twenty years ago, a man confessed to a crime he did not commit. He said he was coerced into confessing. The jury did not believe him and sentenced him to life in prison. Through years of diligent work and with the help of the Innocence project, he was finally released from jail after the real murderer was discovered with the help of DNA. ABC News *Primetime Live* wondered how this could have happened and sought scientific experts on false confessions.

HOW BEHAVIORAL SCIENCE EXPERTISE GETS USED

So now that we had the stories, we needed to think about format. And this is where the experts play an enormous role. The expert is an essential partner to the producer in a number of ways. The first and most important is that, if at all possible, the expert helps the producers replicate the experiment and *demonstrate the phenomena* so that viewers can see the results as they're happening. Nothing, no words or fancy explanation, will have more impact on a viewer than seeing a phenomenon unfold in front of his or her eyes. When no footage of the experiment exists, the producer and expert work hand in hand to set up a sample of the expert's experiment. It must be run according to the rules of the experiment, not reenacted to get the desired results or even the results that existed in the original experiments. That means that a smaller sample of participants completes the procedure, this time with the broadcaster's hidden cameras rolling. (By the way, informed consent to broadcast the footage is always obtained from participants after the experiment.)

The behavioral scientist is also a critical partner in setting the context for the piece. Here's where the interview comes in. Producers will have the expert do a sit-down interview with the correspondent that helps viewers understand how the experiment works, what the findings are, and what they mean. Throughout the piece, the interview will be woven together with the visuals that include video of the experiment, interviews with the "characters," and the correspondent's narration, which helps to give essential facts about the research and put the findings into context.

Now, let's go back to our case studies to see how the stories unfolded and how *Dateline* and other news outlets worked with the psychology experts.

Case Study 1

For this story, we began with reporting on the news event. We outlined the terrible events that happened on the bridge that day, interviewed Deletha's family, and even spoke with many of those bystanders who stood by and did nothing. We then had our hidden cameras rolling as John Darley replicated his famous experiment. In this case, individual Yale students believed they were participating in a study on learning in which they had to "focus" on a tape that would be playing. Half of the subjects were alone in the room, and the other half had two other students in the room with them. On their way into the room, they passed a workman on a ladder. Unbeknownst to them, he was instructed to fall off the ladder about 2 minutes into the experiment and moan and scream for help. Also unbeknownst to the subjects, the two other students in the room were confederates who were instructed to look up when the

workman fell off the ladder but not to react. What happened? When a student was alone in the room, he or she reacted 85% of the time, getting up and running out to find the "stricken" workman. But when the confederates were in the room, only 20% helped. We then interviewed John Darley, who explained about "diffusion of responsibility" and helped the viewer understand what just happened. We also interviewed the students who had participated in the study.

Case Study 2

This story, like the Deletha Word report, began with the news events. We then asked, How can something like this happen? In this instance, Dr. Zimbardo had actually filmed his study 25 years ago, and so we were able to show clips from the study, together with his current commentary. He walked us through the study in an interview and related it to a number of present-day events.

Case Study 3

As with the other stories, we began our report with details of the crime and backed into the science of the story. We replicated the Asch conformity experiment with new subjects and got surprisingly similar results all these years later. Students, to this day, will give an answer they know to be wrong just to go along with the group consensus. What's more, we aired the Milgram shock machine experiment to show the forces behind obedience. An interview with noted social psychologist Dr. Pratkanis was used throughout the story, and once again, science and psychology led to a greater understanding of the world around us.

Case Study 4

The NBC news team profiled the political events in the news and interviewed the victim of the sabotage, as always beginning our story with the details of the case. We then asked the researcher to replicate a behavioral experiment in which students who knew each other would play the game password. A student had the opportunity to give his or her partner (usually a friend) hard clues or easy clues to help him or her guess the word in play. The researcher found that when a friend was doing well, his or her partner would choose to give him or her a hard word, making it more difficult to guess. The better a person did, the harder the clue he or she was given by the friend. The conclusion was that envy was at play and, when given the choice, led to sabotage.

Case Study 5

ABC News found Dr. Kassan and asked him to help illustrate how people could confess to a crime they didn't commit. They presented the case of the man jailed, and they interviewed him and asked him why he confessed when he knew he didn't commit the crime. They then included in the segment an example of how everyday people can make false confessions. They did so with students in a university lab setting. Students were told by the researcher that they were going to perform a typing test. Each student did so and afterwards was told that he or she had broken the keyboard. The researcher then exerted pressure on the student by saying it would be easier if the student just told the truth. What happened? A majority of the students ended up confessing to the crime and saying they indeed broke the keyboard, when they knew full well that they had not.

Tips

Now that you know how behavioral science tends to get used, let's turn to tips for thinking about how to present your own research to producers and how to choose among television formats.

Decide how your work relates to the news and to current issues and events. In other words, what are the potential real-life applications of your work? To help when pitching, try to find a news story that connects to it and even search news outlets such as cable, newspapers, and magazines to stimulate your thinking. It is ultimately the job of the producer to find the right "real-life" story to match the behavioral science, but providing your own examples may help "sell" your pitch. Also, don't be afraid to try pitching to morning shows as well. Remember, even though their reports are usually topic driven, they are interested in stories that are told in "outside-the-box " ways, for example, creating mini-experiments that showcase honesty as a topic.

Don't worry if your study is not a "classic" psychology experiment such as Asch's conformity experiment or Milgram's obedience study. Today's behavioral work helps explain the world around us and so is of interest to broadcasters. Also, don't assume that shows are only looking for the research to be done within the "classic" experimental paradigm. Frankly, they just want to showcase an interesting study that helps explain a phenomenon. If your work is a more modern twist on these experiments, using a more nuanced approach to the research question and more up-to-date methodology, perhaps even enhancing the applicability of the results, so much the better.

Film your studies, film your work. If you're running experiments, try to film them with hidden cameras if needed. It's critical to be able to give footage to producers either so they can use it "as is" in the piece or so that they can get a sense of what the visuals will look like. I know it's difficult if not impossible to get the quality of footage a broadcaster may get, but allowing a producer to get a "glimpse" of the work you do will go a long way toward getting your work on the air.

When it comes to choosing among the television formats, think about what kind of news story can be attached. If a long news story is feasible, you'll want to think about a newsmagazine show. Think back to the case studies cited earlier. All of them involve cases that are complex and can sustain a good 10 minutes of television. If your research is more topic driven, such as emotional spending (spending money on items to lessen anxiety or cope with depression, for example), the importance of honesty in a marriage, five ways to control anger, or the 10 keys to happiness, you should consider a morning television format. These types of stories could not sustain a long format segment but are ideal ideas and concepts for a morning program.

THE ATTITUDES, KNOWLEDGE, AND SKILLS THAT MAKE RESEARCHERS HELPFUL RESOURCES

For the most part, a behavioral scientist appears on the news in one of two ways. As mentioned earlier, one classic example is what we call the "old school interview"—the news anchor, whether live or taped, reports on a certain story, and then he or she comes back and the expert sits in the studio for an "on-air" interview. A few questions are tossed back and forth, and the segment ends. Though these interviews are often informative, they are beginning to represent a bygone era of TV news and style.

Today, journalists, especially from morning and newsmagazine shows, are beginning to look for experts who can help generate story ideas as well as pitch and craft a story. An expert is often encouraged to come up with what would make a good story and suggestions for story content. They're also, when relevant, often asked to replicate their studies and provide a client or study subject that may be dealing or involved with the topic being covered.

Whether you are tapped for a short interview or whether your work becomes the focus of a piece, producers are always looking for experts who can speak clearly and concisely about a topic. You'll want to define your audience, decide what about the research is important to communicate and why, and then select an approach for communicating your message to them. There is no question that news is a reductionist medium. There just isn't enough time in a single broadcast to get into the complexities of the findings, no matter how much a journalist and researcher may want to do so. A good journalist will work hard to understand the science, but the findings still must be summarized and the main points hit. Journalists, for the most part, do want to understand the nuances of the research, and giving them background information can help inform their reporting.

But the bottom line is that you will need to make crisp, quick points that, among other things, requires presenting statistics and facts in ways that people can understand. Always, always remember, for example, that abstract talk of participants who score above the mean on factors of aggression or depression is meaningless to most people. They simply won't understand what you are saying. Say instead: those who are more depressed or aggressive than most people. I always remind experts that giving a talk at a conference or presenting a paper differs enormously from talking about your research on television and, believe it or not, can even be more difficult. The tip I always give is to explain the research in the interview as if you were at a dinner party. Assume your audience has no knowledge of science and statistics. Would you explain your research to your colleague the same way you would to your grandmother? Not unless your grandmother was also a researcher.

It also helps to think about the "story" of your research and your expertise and to generate a headline about it in 10 words or less. Also think of the four main points you want to get across and craft them in accessible language. These are always good starting points. And, as I mentioned earlier, a researcher is most helpful when he or she thinks about ways to frame the science in terms of real people and daily life. People viewing these programs want to know, "What does this mean for me?" "How does it affect my daily life?" "What examples from my own experience does this research relate to?" Helping audiences explore these questions is crucial. Many researchers are not able to answer, "What does your work mean and why?" or "What are the real-life applications of your work?" So, when speaking on air and when speaking with producers, always prepare by thinking about these questions. It is possible to give this perspective without overreaching and going beyond the actual research findings, which is almost always a concern of scientists. For example, statements such as "my work helps people understand why someone when given power may act in ways they may never ordinarily," "my work helps us understand why so many people feel unhappy with everyday life despite having all the material goods they want," or "my work helps people understand how they may act when under pressure from others to conform" clearly communicate the scope of the research.

You must also be firm in your answers. Don't equivocate. You want to make declarative statements. Though the tendency in science is to offer every possible qualification to an answer, this approach backfires on you in television. It leaves the viewer feeling confused and, in a worst case, can lead to misunderstandings. You can, of course, say things such as, "There are always exceptions but in most cases . . ." or "For the most part you'll find. . . ." But you have to be very careful not to backpedal or overqualify an answer. It muddies the water too much, and the equivocation will most likely undermine

your message. You have to trust that the journalist will put your words in a context and will help viewers better understand the topic at hand. Of course, you can help ensure this outcome by taking it upon yourself to help the journalist understand the topic and the context.

A good journalist will also be looking for specialists. Gone largely are the days in television when one expert would speak on all topics related to psychology and science. Now we seek experts who can speak about one issue such as violence, relationships, trauma, or even happiness. We care about credentials showing that the expert has the specialized background needed to speak on a subject with credibility and authority. Introductions of researchers now include their backgrounds: "Dr. X has spent the past 15 years studying . . ." or "Dr. Y is a noted expert on forensic psychology and has published over 15 papers on the topic." Please don't misunderstand the meaning of the word *specialist,* however. Scientists need to be able to integrate lines of research inquiry. They'll be asked to situate not only their latest findings but also their entire body of work and the accumulated knowledge relevant to it into a broader context in order for the science to be useful to the public.

When speaking with producers, always make clear the subjects you feel comfortable discussing and provide a list of topics you can address. And remember, no good journalist will ask you to speak outside your comfort zone. Also, as you recall, producers have their list of contacts and tend to go back to the same experts over and over again. In addition to relying on these experts themselves, producers also want viewers to become familiar with certain experts and begin to trust them. We have found that viewers form relationships with experts as much as they do with on-air talent. If you can make contact with the producer and share your expertise using a style that proves you can "talk" about the topic in a clear and useful way, chances are you will become one of the "go-to" people on the roster.

Though it may be frustrating at times to have the work boiled down to its essentials, it can be better for the public to get some critical information rather than no information at all. You can always ask producers to put links on their broadcast's Web sites that will allow viewers to get more information.

CONCLUSION

It can be difficult to think about how to develop new skills and become comfortable engaging with journalists. I suggest that anyone with this interest try creating a panel discussion in which a group of researchers gets together and invites a journalist whose work they respect. The panel can include a role-playing element and hands-on experience in which a researcher gets 5 minutes to "pitch" a story to the journalist. The journalist can provide feedback during the session. What about the pitch worked? What did not? Researchers can learn through their own experience and through watching others. When creating the panels, think about approaching the American Psychological Association and requesting such a panel. I was invited to such a discussion a number of years back. The panel had guests from broadcast, newspaper, and radio. It was a comprehensive training that benefited both the psychologists and the journalists.

Fellowships are also available in psychology and the media from scientific organizations. I hosted a psychologist through one program that connected a psychologist with a journalist for training. I suggest looking into this type of fellowship and then contacting a story editor or a journalist who produces psychology-oriented shows for sponsorship. The networks likely will be interested because it provides them with an "idea" person for no cost, and it benefits the researcher because it gives an "inside" look at the workings of the media.

Science coverage in TV news is only going to grow and become more relevant to the public. People are trying to understand their own motivations, to discover ways to cope with an ever-changing environment, and to know what to expect in the future. Building relationships between the behavioral scientist and the television journalist will go a long way toward improving public access to science-based information to help answer these questions.

REFERENCES

Asch, S. E. (1955). Opinions and social pressure. *Scientific American, 193,* 31–35.

Asch, S. E. (1956). Studies of independence and conformity: A minority of one against a unanimous majority. *Psychological Monographs, 70*(No. 416).

Darley, J. M., & Latané, B. (1968). Bystander intervention in emergencies: Diffusion of responsibility. *Journal of Personality and Social Psychology, 8,* 377–383.

Haney, C., Banks, W. C., & Zimbardo, P. G. (1973). Interpersonal dynamics in a simulated prison. *International Journal of Criminology and Penology, 1,* 69–97.

Milgram, S. (1963). Behavioral study of obedience. *Journal of Abnormal and Social Psychology, 67,* 371–378.

Zimbardo, P. G. (1975). On transforming experimental research into advocacy for social change. In M. Deutsch & H. Hornstein (Eds.), *Applying social psychology: Implications for research, practice, and training* (pp. 33–66). Hillsdale, NJ: Lawrence Erlbaum.

CHAPTER 8

National Public Radio

RACHEL JONES

Whenever I make presentations to researchers, foundations, or advocacy groups, I try to impart an important piece of newsroom insider information that I hope they'll take to heart. Without exception, the disclosure causes a ripple of concern, discouragement, and frustration throughout the audience.

Here goes: As a reporter, I'm less focused on communicating important issues to the general public than I am on convincing editors to let me do stories. That revelation disappoints because it sounds like we journalists are neglecting the public service aspect of journalism and merely jockeying for a gold star from an editor. For someone who became a journalist primarily to help save the world, this used to be very frustrating for *me*.

After all, I had spent years reading stacks of studies and reports, attending myriad conferences and briefings, and had scores of telephone conversations with the best and brightest researchers. I believed my grasp of social policy, child health and development, and racial disparities in health care was solid. So during meetings with editors about potential stories on these topics, I've often wanted to scream, "What part of the term *vitally important issue* do you NOT understand???"

You'll notice I used the past tense in that last sentence. As they say, advancing years bring great wisdom and insight—and the ability to determine which battles are worth fighting and which are pointless. I have accepted the fact that in the fast-paced newsrooms of America today, a reporter has about 30 seconds to convince an editor that a particular story or issue deserves precious airtime or newsprint. Now, that works just fine for reporters who cover, say, the Iraq War, immigration, or the latest indiscretion on Capitol Hill. But what happens if you're trying to convince an editor that parents need to know about this new research on child development? What happens when your editor's eyes glaze over, and you can almost hear his or her brain slam shut after your first few words?

Well, for me, that cloud has had a silver lining. The issues I'm most passionate about frequently involve some aspect of behavioral science, and I've been willing to jump into the breach over and over to get these stories in print or on the air. Why do minorities participate in clinical trials less often than Whites? What makes some teenagers engage in risky sexual behavior? Why are some children more aggressive in their earliest years of life? These types of questions are inherently interesting to me. But the nexus between an issue researchers spend decades studying and one news organizations consider worthy of coverage can be boiled down to a few simple questions.

"How does this affect real people? Does it happen only in one community or state, or is it a national trend? Is there a solution, and if not, will we wind up doing exactly what most of the general public hates about journalism . . . hyping events or research findings just to grab higher ratings?"

In other words, "What's the point?" You'd think the answer to that question is easy, but as the character Sportin' Life sang in *Porgy and Bess,* it ain't necessarily so. That's because too often, researchers don't realize that in newsrooms today, concise clarity trumps nuanced detail every time.

During my 20-year journalism career, some of my best stories have been aired or published after I was able to establish a slightly less than formal relationship with researchers. That means I was able to get them to talk to me not as though they were standing at a lectern or presenting their newest study at a conference. That kind of jargon-free interaction is the *only* way I'm able to tackle the broad range of information I'm regularly confronted with. Most people would be amazed by the piles of studies, stacks of press releases, and trunk loads of data news organizations receive on a daily basis. The harsh truth is that most of this information collects dust on our desks or gets quickly deleted from our e-mail queues. But a researcher or organization moves to the front of the pack if they understand that the best way to spark newsroom interest is by distilling copious research to one cogent, succinct concept.

Also, think context. One of the many great strengths of National Public Radio's (NPR's) Science Desk is its ability to swiftly provide the kind of information that helps listeners understand more about the headlines in the scientific world. Whether it's a natural disaster, a glitch in NASA's shuttle program, the discovery of a new species, or an amazing medical advance, Science Desk reporters know how to transform a seemingly complex topic into a listener-friendly format.

The primary sources for NPR's behavioral science stories are major research journals. Editors and reporters monitor them on a weekly and monthly basis and hash out story themes during regular desk meetings or informal conversations. Also, many colleges, universities, and research centers are savvy enough to forge their own connections with staffers. Any time a story related to research they're working on airs, the reporter often gets a call from a media relations officer, alerting him or her to similar research coming from the organization. And NPR reporters make frequent appearances at conferences, seminars, and other events related to their coverage. I've been approached many times at those events by researchers introducing themselves and gauging my interest in research they're working on.

That's one terrific way to leap the barrier between the reporter's crowded brain and hordes of e-mailed press releases and 100-page reports that land on our desk each week. That personal contact makes a big difference when we're considering what stories to add to our lists. The scientist who makes that contact should be prepared to quickly explain the importance of his or her research and how it advances an issue beyond what we already know.

This kind of "sales pitch" is probably making some of you wince. You've devoted your entire careers to amassing a body of work that you believe can change public policy, encourage people to change negative behaviors, and, like most journalists believe, "save the world." Then some crass reporter from CNN or your local newspaper (or NPR) comes along and barks, "What's the headline?" Trust me, it's just as annoying for us as it is for you.

But when it comes to behavioral science, that approach has helped me not only in "negotiations" with editors but, even more important, in the writing of stories and scripts. When reporters ask what appear to be a lot of really dumb questions, they're not just unqualified hacks wasting your precious time and insight. When a reporter asks you, "Explain this to me as if I was your next-door neighbor" or "Why would this research matter to ANYONE?" don't take offense. There may be plenty of time down the road to dazzle them with the complexities of your study, but even when there's no intense deadline pressure, a reporter is focused on one thing—getting a go-ahead signal from an editor.

In a journalism world where space for news is being chipped away by the demand for more advertising and where wars, natural disasters, and political folly will always get the most coverage, it's important to remember that the journalist is battling more than just deadlines. At NPR, which many people regard as one of the last bastions of thorough, thoughtful coverage, show editors are often forced to find a 3-, 4-, or 5-minute piece to plug a hole. The show must go on, and that often means that nuance gets sacrificed. When on deadline, a reporter has to settle for one or two authoritative voices on a particular issue and may come across as less informed than he or she should be. Sometimes, a reporter has just 10 minutes of studio time for a telephone interview; that could turn what the researcher hopes will be a careful consideration of the research into a barrage of rapid-fire questions intended to produce short, "sound-bite" ready answers. This scenario can be frustrating to the researcher who's had little interaction with the media.

It can also lead to one of the most dreaded four-letter words in the world of journalism: *hype.* Even with the best of intentions from reporters, hype happens. The most immutable thing about newsrooms is that if an issue contains a drop of contention, some sort of heated debate, or even just elicits a spirited disagreement from someone who's willing to talk about it on the record, *that's* what the editor will want to focus on.

Think back to 2001, when the first phase of National Institute for Child Health and Human Development research about the effects of day care was released to the general public. In newsrooms everywhere, reporters intently scanned the press releases, trying to craft their strategies. They were looking for a "hook" that would pass muster with the guys and gals in the glass-walled offices. Many of us considered different scenarios.

"Boss, I'd like to do a story about how important good day care is for child development. There's a new study out from Harvard that analyzes the effects."

"Not interested."

"Okay, how about if the study concludes that some kids have problems in day care, but the overwhelming majority of kids do just fine?"

"That's not news."

"Fine. Then how about a story that says day care turns kids into snarling, ungovernable monsters?"

"BINGO!!! How much space do you need for that one?"

That really isn't too much of an exaggeration. And it's a perfect example of what I try to convey to audiences, because it really illustrates a critical need for better communication between journalists and researchers.

When those early day care findings were released, you couldn't open a newspaper or magazine, or flip past a news program, without seeing headlines like, "Day Care Demons" or "Pre-School Turns Babes Into Bullies." As a reporter on NPR's Science Desk at the time, I knew our bar was set a lot higher. I also recognized that press releases and summaries about the research warned against interpreting the results too broadly. All sorts of factors were involved, including the socioeconomic background of kids, the type of day care setting, and so on.

NPR has strict guidelines for assessing whether research is newsworthy. First and foremost, it often has to have appeared in a peer-reviewed journal and stem from a creditable university or research organization. Also, we consider things such as the following: How many people were involved? Was the research based in one city, or was it a national study? Was the research longitudinal or cross-sectional? Were participants from a range of racial and socioeconomic groups? Did the researchers consider multiple data points?

Those issues were examined with the day care study, and they all passed the test. Then, my editor and I discussed how, or even *if*, we should follow the lead of other news organizations and crank out our own "Terror Tyke" story. She wanted to make sure I understood the nuances of the research, to determine whether the over-the-top coverage was even remotely accurate. When I was able to comprehend and explain what was being left out of the coverage, we decided to take a pass.

Now, if I had been working for a daily newspaper or wire service, that probably wouldn't have happened. No matter how muddled or unfinished the research was, I would have been asked to develop a story that was long enough to fill a hole in today's edition—in part because everybody *else* was doing a story. But NPR's decision was vindicated 2 years later, when the final version of the study was formally released. During those 2 years, I had kept in contact with one of the study's researchers, Harvard's Kathleen McCartney. She was more than willing to help me understand how the research was evolving. So when I interviewed her about the formal release of the study, my story had a decidedly different angle than most of the earlier coverage.

BOB EDWARDS (host): Two years ago, a government-funded child care study suggested that when children spend long hours in child care, they were more likely to become aggressive and disobedient. That study is being published formally this week in the journal *Child Development*, and researchers say the results are more complex than originally portrayed, NPR's Rachel Jones reports.

RACHEL JONES (reporting): On a Thursday morning in 2001, Kathleen McCartney awoke in a Minneapolis hotel room to discover that the new research she would be presenting that afternoon, linking time spent in child care with aggressive behavior, already had appeared in *USA Today*. McCartney, who's a Harvard University researcher, says that was just the beginning.

KATHLEEN McCARTNEY (Harvard University): Later that afternoon, when we made our presentation, there were television cameras in our faces and—so I think the investigators were not as prepared for the media onslaught as we could have been.

JONES: For weeks afterwards, stories about the National Institute of Child Health and Human Development study of more than a thousand American children featured headlines like "Fear and Loathing at the Day Care Center" and "Raising a Wild Child." McCartney says that was a low point for child development researchers.

McCARTNEY: It was a frustrating time for me and, I think, for several of my colleagues because the first round of stories really exaggerated the bad news aspects of these findings.

JONES: That "bad-news" focus centered around the finding that behaviors like bullying, disobedience, and outright defiance were three times more prevalent for children who spent 30 hours or more each week in any kind of day care. The finding seemed to suggest that the more day care children had, the worse they behaved. But with today's formal release of the NICHD study, researchers emphasize that conclusion was too simplistic. For example, study coordinator Sara Friedman says early reports failed to note that even in the group of children who spent the most time in day care, just 17 percent exhibited problems.

SARAH FRIEDMAN: It's only a minority that had elevated levels of behavior problems as rated by their mothers and teachers.

JONES: The vast majority of kids were acting just fine for their age group. And Friedman says researchers don't know if the children's misbehavior had biological roots, like lack of sleep. They point to other important factors, including things like gender and individual temperament, or the quality of the child care setting, that could influence behavior in a good or bad way.

Finally, early news coverage missed yet another important aspect of the study, Friedman says.

FRIEDMAN: A stronger predictor than the hours of care is the sensitivity of the mother. That is, the more sensitive the mother is to her child, the less likely the child is to be rated as having behavior problems.

That story was only 3 minutes and 37 seconds long, but it did more to clarify the ongoing debate about the research than most of the earlier coverage combined. It reported the results in a way that carefully explained why this kind of research is too complex to be presented so narrowly. By focusing on just one finding, and especially by emphasizing it because it's negative, journalists do a grave disservice to their listeners, readers, and viewers.

Often on NPR's Science Desk, the decision to air a story is not based on how "sexy" or controversial the topic is but on how solid the research is and how our coverage can advance the public's understanding of an issue. And the best way for a reporter to understand an issue is for the researcher to explain it in a way that resonates not just with other researchers but with the reader, viewer, or listener.

But that requires a level of trust that some researchers won't grant to a mere voice on the other end of a phone line. Though many of you may disagree, I've found that far too many researchers are unwilling to even consider discussing their work on anything other than a formal level. They can spend hours explaining study design or the history of a certain type of research, but too often, they describe their latest work to me as if I had the same PhD they earned.

But I don't let them get away with it, because of what I learned about reporting as a Science Desk reporter for NPR. When I think about it, I was incredibly lucky to have had that experience. The experience almost amounted to earning a minor degree in the art of communicating complicated research. I learned new things every day, not just from my own reporting but from the incredibly smart, talented colleagues I worked with. The experience taught me that even the most complex, scientifically rigorous research can be made accessible to the general public.

Here's an example from Michelle Trudeau, who reports many stories about child mental health and development. Whenever I hear her work, it amazes me how she's always able to distill incredibly complex information in such a breezy, human way. Here's part of a story she produced on cognitive behavioral therapy:

MELISSA BLOCK: It's estimated that one of every 20 adolescents suffers from clinical depression, and when depression begins during the teenage years, the risks are significant. Episodes can recur and interrupt important learning and development, and suicide is a significant risk. So experts say it's imperative to identify and treat young people quickly and effectively. The drug Prozac is the only antidepressant approved for children and teens, and there's one type of psychotherapy that's been effective in alleviating depression in young people. It's called cognitive behavioral therapy, or CBT. NPR's Michelle Trudeau has this conclusion of our series on cognitive therapy.

MICHELLE TRUDEAU (reporting): Research psychologist Joan Asarnow sits opposite a teenage patient with depression, whom we'll call Patty, in a small office at UCLA. They are in the middle of Patty's cognitive behavioral therapy session.

DR. JOAN ASARNOW (UCLA): And what kinds of thoughts do you think are typical of you when you're under stress?

"PATTY": I think when I'm under stress, thoughts are typical of me that just, "When's it going to stop." I just want to be free from it, and I begin to feel so just bad and blue that my thoughts turn into just sounding like some really sad, stupid song that some bad band would sing.

TRUDEAU: A large notebook is on the table between Patty and Dr. Asarnow. This is a cognitive behavioral therapy manual. Therapists trained in CBT follow a manual in treating depressed patients. In it are detailed the two major components of CBT: changing ways of thinking and changing ways of behaving that can help mitigate depression. Psychiatrist Aaron Beck, considered the father of CBT, explains.

DR. AARON BECK: Cognitive therapy consists of focusing on the negative thinking that a depressed person has and getting the patient to realize and recognize the distortions of their thinking.

TRUDEAU: The focus of CBT, Beck adds, is on the present, not on a patient's past or unconscious, like in many other talk therapies. Patty in her therapy focuses on the here and now of just having flunked a math quiz.

ASARNOW: And what kinds of thoughts did you have when you failed the math quiz?

"PATTY": "I'm not smart enough to do anything." Another thought was, "Again?" like I'm a failure.

TRUDEAU: Beck calls these types of habitual negative beliefs automatic thoughts, common to people with depression. These thoughts come so fast that the patient isn't even aware of what's at work.

BECK: But what's interesting about the automatic thought is that people tend to accept them at their face value, and they don't look for alternative explanations or for what evidence is behind them.

There is so much that's terrific about the way Trudeau crafted this story. First, the introduction does a great job of preparing listeners to hear about an effective treatment for depression in young people. It introduces data and the potential risks of untreated depression for that group. It signals the main topic in a simple, straightforward way—"So experts say it's imperative to identify and treat young people quickly and effectively." Most important, Trudeau doesn't begin her story with comments from the expert. She knows instinctively that the best way to convey information about depression in young people is to have a young person talk about it.

Who's the potential audience for this story? Concerned parents, struggling young people or those with friends they're worried about, practitioners who work with young people—the range is broad. But if the story had opened with Dr. Beck expounding on the roots of CBT, droves of listeners might have switched stations.

People like to be talked *to*. Not talked *at*. They like to hear stories about people and places they've never been or seen. They like to hear information that they never would have sought out on their own but that makes them feel just a bit smarter than they were before they heard it. And they want to hear or read it in a very accessible format. They want to walk away feeling what they've learned is relevant, even if it doesn't apply to their own lives. Moving from print journalism to broadcast has really helped me understand that in crucial ways. My goal in producing stories about complex research is to be able to figuratively ask listeners to pull up a chair and listen to what I just learned.

My colleague Brenda Wilson does that on a regular basis. Her reporting on HIV/AIDS in Africa is outstanding, largely because she paints such vivid pictures with her words, you feel as if you're standing beside her while she reports.

For example, here's an excerpt from her story about how some people place their faith in the teachings of church when it comes to dealing with the specter of HIV/AIDS.

Brenda's choice of story structure perfectly illustrates another crucial point researchers *must* confront. Sometimes, a powerful analogy swiftly removes the mental fog for journalists who are regularly pressured to be authoritative about unfamiliar topics. It helps us understand complex research much more quickly. That, in turn, helps us in the process of getting editors to understand why our news organization should be reporting on a particular issue.

BRENDA WILSON (reporting): Father Joseph Archetti is a gruff man with a sunny disposition, thick, steely gray curls, a broad grin, and a strong chin set atop a short, stocky frame. He came to Uganda 42 years ago just as the country was becoming independent. He says one story that seldom gets more than a line or two in the history books is emblematic of the people the first Catholic missionaries found here.

FATHER JOSEPH ARCHETTI (Church of Our Lady of Africa): In 1886, we had 22 Catholic martyrs who we burned alive because they didn't want to renounce their religion. Out of these 22 martyrs, five of them were baptized one week before. They knew very little about Christianity. The youngest of them is 14 years old. Now it is not easy to imagine these young boys to be burned alive as they did.

WILSON: It is the same strength and conviction, he says, that is needed to save Ugandans from AIDS. But it's going to be a struggle. HIV rates may be going down in Uganda, but he's not so sure about Mbuya Parish, where he took over the Church of Our Lady of Africa six years ago.

ARCHETTI: Of course, we visit our Christians house by house, but we did not realize the dimension of this pandemic is so great. So in January last year, I made available the premises of the church for this site, four to five rooms. And we started the clinic with 14 patients, and now there are 750.

WILSON: With so many being sick, he decided something had to be done to prevent the disease, starting with the young. But he wasn't buying the government's ABC prevention strategy, which he thinks sends a mixed message.

ARCHETTI: When you talk about AIDS and you say, "Abstinence, faithfulness. OK, if you can't, condoms"— you give a shortcut, but you don't solve the problem. When you appeal to the inner energy of people, even the youth, when they know the truth and when you help them understand the value of life, they are able to take the right decision.

WILSON: When you meet the young people, some of whom volunteer in the clinic Father Joseph started, you realize that more than just the precepts of the church go into making those decisions.

OLIVIA BERRIER: I'm saving myself until marriage now. It is (unintelligible) go now to anybody.

WILSON: 2001 was about the time that 28-year-old Olivia Berrier started volunteering at Reach Out, the parish clinic, after her elder sister became sick.

BERRIER: She wasn't all that sick for a long time because she felt sick for only one and a half month. Then she passed away.

WILSON: You get the feeling that that experience, as much as the church's teachings, informed her decision to save herself for marriage.

BERRIER: The way I see people suffering with that disease, actually it's something very hard to cope with.

WILSON: Do you have a boyfriend?

BERRIER: Actually, ever since I started Reach Out, I've stopped that business of having boyfriends because I fear a lot that maybe if I go out with him, maybe he might also be moving out with other girls. So I stopped going out with him.

WILSON: Olivia Berrier says not all of the young women in Mbuya Parish have been persuaded by the father's teachings.

BERRIER: Some listen, but some don't. Sometimes they say, "Maybe because he's a priest, he might be deceiving us, or he might be stopping us from enjoying ourselves."

This style of reporting and writing transmits ideas in ways more potent than a million lectures or a few hours at an official briefing ever could. It's real, it's human, and it vividly illustrates the consequences of a set of belief systems.

When Father Joseph Archetti discussed the history of the 22 Catholic martyrs, Brenda realized it was a natural way to evoke a mental picture of how powerful belief systems are and what impact they can have on behavior. She might have chosen to frame the story by illustrating how young women are at the epicenter of the HIV/AIDS crisis in Uganda, and yet they are still suspicious of attempts to push abstinence. The passage where Olivia Berrier says that some of the young women believed Father Joseph might be deceiving them or stopping them from enjoying themselves does a great job of highlighting the challenges of influencing human behavior.

But by starting with the Catholic martyr analogy, Brenda prepares the listener for a thoughtful exploration of how deeply rooted belief systems are. That powerful imagery signals the challenge of attempting behavioral change. But it also helps the reporter craft a central thesis about a story. That gives us lots of courage when we're pitching our story ideas to editors.

Actually, I hate using the work "pitch" when I describe my communications with editors because it's too often linked to the field of public relations. It makes me feel like a salesman, and that's the last thing on earth I'd be qualified for.

And yet, I walk up to strangers every day and ask them the most personal questions . . . often during some of the most stressful times of their lives. I'm "selling" myself to them, asking them to trust that I will interpret that information truthfully. I consider earning the trust of my sources one of the most critically important aspects of my job as a journalist.

Personally, I think NPR does the best job of reporting on behavioral science issues of any media organization in the country. That's partly due to the power of radio, of hearing the voices of families struggling with behavioral problems or a researcher who's stumped by a study outcome. I call it "3-D" print journalism. You can type up a father's deep concern over his son's hyperactivity in the newspaper, but you can hear the frustration in his voice on the radio. You can read about an African woman's attempt to protect herself from HIV, but hearing her story makes it human.

And that's really what this chapter boils down to—helping journalists make your research human. Researchers can start by making themselves human. You have to be able to "sell" journalists on why your work is important and then help us sell it to our editors as efficiently as possible. Most reporters on NPR's Science Desk have received the kind of training that makes them infinitely more approachable about difficult research topics. Editors often encourage reporters to take advantage of seminars and conferences that could expand their knowledge base. Quite a few staffers have attended research conferences, not to produce stories but to learn more about topics. Reporters are frequently awarded fellowships such as the Roslyn Carter Mental Health Reporting Fellowship and the Kaiser Family Fellowships in Health Journalism. In 2000, I was one of the first groups of journalists awarded the Knight/CDC Journalism Fellowship. I've given speeches at meetings and conferences that work on children's issues. And at every one of those gatherings, people introduce themselves, often to tell me about research they're developing or to give me tips on other important work being done.

More researchers should follow suit and stop regarding journalists as the enemy. Most of us really want to interpret your research accurately, despite the constant challenges we face. Sometimes, we may be holding our noses and jumping off the deep end of a murky pool of information. And we'll be jumping into a different one tomorrow.

But if we work together, we may just find ourselves on the same path, toward a public that is more enlightened and informed about behavioral science than ever before.

CHAPTER 9

Newspapers

Tom Siegfried

Scientists who routinely comprehend complicated phenomena and discern deep secrets of the physical and biological world often seem mystified by the media. Newsrooms seem like the brain before the days of PET and fMRI scans—events occur and news emerges, but the process of selecting information and preparing it for presentation is hidden from the outside world's view. And that leads scientists to wonder how behavioral science (or anything else, for that matter) gets into the news.

The glib response, typically from journalists cultivating the media mystique, is that to get into the news, something has to be newsworthy. But behind that simplicity are some semi-tangible criteria, mixed with some individual quirks and institutional pressures that offer some insights into what goes on inside the media black box. It is possible to understand the inner workings of newspapers, and with that understanding comes enhanced prospects for communicating behavioral science effectively.

WHAT MAKES NEWS

The newsworthiness of behavioral science is judged by the same three primary criteria as everything else: Is it new? Is it important?

Is it interesting? The stronger the affirmative response to each of these questions, the more likely that an event, say, or discovery or report will be judged worthy of coverage by reporters and editors. Rating high on all three of these points is ideal, but two out of three often will be sufficient. So, if a new finding is very interesting, it will likely rate a story even if it's not of earthshaking importance. Similarly, some topic may not offer any new information, but if it is sufficiently interesting and important (perhaps in the context of current events), reporters and editors may still deem it worth reporting.

In such cases, though, newspapers invariably impose the need to identify some element of currency—known as a "news peg"—that justifies publishing the story. Consequently, some stories without any real news will appear in conjunction with a significant upcoming event—an anniversary, or a Supreme Court decision, or a celebrity hospitalization, or the release of a new movie (the film *Kinsey* inspired a lengthy piece on his research in the *Los Angeles Times*). Publication of a new book, *What's Wrong With the Rorschach?*, led the *Times* to do an in-depth analysis of controversy surrounding the Rorschach test. Such news pegs confer immediate salience on a topic that could in principle be written about at any time.

Judgments about what is new, interesting, and important are made from the viewpoints of reporters and editors. Scientists often speak, for example, as though any finding in the past 5 years is "new" (and, from a historical perspective, that's correct). But to a newspaper editor, "new" means today or maybe yesterday, particularly in the news sections of the paper. (For feature sections, the definition of new is not quite so rigid.) In the minds of many reporters, "new" means "not reported in the general news media yet." If a paper appears in an obscure scientific journal but no newspaper reports it, most journalists will consider it to remain fair game for a story.

In deciding what is interesting and important, news editors and reporters are primarily concerned with the public's perceptions, not the scientific community's. Reporters and editors certainly care whether scientists within a field of study consider a new finding to be significant. But the reporter must also be able to articulate why the finding would matter to the general reader. Likewise, judgments about whether a study is interesting must be made through a general reader's eyes. (Or at least through the eyes of an editor's imaginary "average reader." Journalists form opinions about reader interests through interactions with their audience, mostly from personal communication such as phone calls and e-mail and sometimes even from survey research, but there is no guarantee that an editor's assessment of the public's interests is always accurate.)

ARTICLE ANATOMY

The intense pressure to produce stories that interest readers often dictates a news reporter's approach to a story and the level of detail he or she decides to include. The best newspaper stories contain some common elements that are generally considered necessary for effectively communicating to the paper's audience. These elements typically include a lede (journalistic spelling for "lead"), a main point (sometimes combined with the lede), and passages establishing the significance of the story and presenting explanatory details.

The lede is an opening sentence (or sometimes an opening paragraph) that conveys the essence of the story and attracts the reader's attention. Sometimes referred to as the "angle," the lede is designed to hook a reader into wanting to read more and find out the details.

Daily news stories often try to compress the interesting, important, and new elements into a single "lede" sentence that summarizes the information to follow—this approach to news writing is the "inverted pyramid" in which "who, what, when, where, why, and how" are all crammed together at a story's outset and details follow in descending order of importance. Wire services often still use it because individual newspapers may run only a few paragraphs of a much longer story. But depending on the newspaper, local writers have much more flexibility in their approach to writing than they used to, and some writers will focus first on an interesting local angle before weaving other key facts into a narrative.

A daily news story lede is usually (or should be) direct and to the point; a feature story lede may be more elaborate and merely suggestive of what is to follow, focusing on an aspect of the topic that has wide appeal (the angle) before narrowing into the main point. Here's an example of a typical lede from a daily news story, based on a report published in the *American Journal of Public Health*:

More than two-thirds of American Indians are exposed to some type of trauma during their lives, a higher rate than seen in most other Americans, new research reports.

Another example, from a story reporting research published in the *Journal of Personality and Social Psychology:*

> Shared moral values are less important than compatible personalities as a recipe for a good marriage, according to a study released on Sunday.

Note that in both cases, the main result of a study is stated without embellishment.

In some daily news stories, and almost always in features, the lede is constructed around an interesting angle, and the main point follows. Often this angle is presented in the form of a brief anecdote, such as this one that appeared in the *Chicago Tribune.*

> On a mission just south of Baghdad over the winter, a young soldier jumped into the gunner's turret of an armored Humvee and took control of the menacing .50-caliber machine gun. She was 19 years old, weighed barely 100 pounds and had a blond ponytail hanging out from under her Kevlar helmet. . . .

In this case, after hooking the reader with the anecdote, the writer added a little context and then spelled out the point: "But today, two years after the start of an Iraq War in which . . . women were tasked to fill lethal combat roles more routinely than in any conflict in U.S. history, the nation may be just beginning to see and feel the effects of such service."

Note that the "news peg" for this story was the 2-year anniversary of the beginning of the Iraq War.

Following the paragraph stating what the story is all about, writers typically try to hammer home its significance (in other words, "sell the story"). In the women at war example, the significance was subsequently established by noting that thousands of women return from the war emotionally damaged, with higher rates of posttraumatic stress disorder than seen in male soldiers. Sometimes the statement of significance takes the form of a simple explanatory sentence. In a story on obesity, for example, the article might say "if this theory of obesity is right, current policies to persuade people to lose weight are doomed to failure." In other cases, the significance might be established with facts, figures, or quotes from experts testifying to the importance of the subject at hand. (A vivid quote at this point in the story is a virtual requirement.)

Good stories present compelling openings, and the best go on to explain the science behind the story, elucidating the scientific underpinnings of the issue under discussion. In straight news stories, this science may be compressed to a single sentence, whereas in a long feature, it may go on for several paragraphs. If an issue is contentious (which itself is one of the reasons why a story might be written), the reporter also has an obligation to mention and explore the controversies. Though it doesn't always happen, the reporter ideally attempts to unearth some of the evidence that relates to these controversial issues, rather than merely relying on conflicting statements from competing researchers or advocates. Good stories should leave readers well informed, not merely entertained.

COVERING BEHAVIORAL SCIENCES

Behavioral science turns up in newspapers in many places and forms. The caliber of the science reporting varies widely, of course, ranging from quoting an uninformed deputy sheriff's philosophy of human nature to a science writer's in-depth analysis of brain imaging studies by social cognitive neuroscientists.

While behavioral science can show up in some way or another in many parts of the paper, it most often appears in a few specific story forms. One general category is the daily news story, typically from a new study reported in a journal, presented at a meeting, or contained in a report released by some prominent government agency or other organization. Another general category, the feature article, often appears in a lifestyles section. Many lifestyle features deal with behavior-related matters, such as stress in the workplace or road rage or gang violence. But lifestyle features are often not science based and may offer little of research-based substance. Meatier features are sometimes written by science writers, who may be reporting on new research trends or addressing the science behind current topics in the news.

Whatever the type of story, the approach to writing it usually rests fully in the hands of a reporter, albeit a reporter who has to please an editor who may impose constraints of how much science the reporter can delve into. But all reporters are not equivalent; they range from mystified novices to knowledgeable veterans. Every reporter also has idiosyncrasies that may color his or her approach. Some reporters abhor numbers, for instance, and prefer to frame research issues with human-interest anecdotes. Other reporters like to present a story by emphasizing aspects of conflict or controversy.

Whether a reporter works for a newspaper or for a wire service also affects the approach. Except for the largest papers, reporters usually must find some locally relevant aspect of a story (the research was done at a local university, or perhaps there are local examples of a national phenomenon). Wire service reporters write for a national or regional audience and so seek common ground across localities.

But whether local or wire, reporters who write about behavioral science can generally be classified into three categories: general assignments (GA) reporters, feature writers, and specialized (usually science) writers. GA writers typically cover spot news responding to the day's events. A shooting at a school may elicit a story seeking an expert's opinion on behavioral science issues, such as the motivations of the shooters or the emotional response of victims and observers.

GA writers are by definition nonspecialists, and they consequently may know very little about the subjects they write about. Good GA reporters therefore endeavor to find experts to interview, but that is often easier said than done. Many times the "experts" happen to be not the best people in their field but the most immediately accessible to a reporter working on a tight deadline. (So, it is very important for behavioral scientists who ARE top experts to respond quickly to media requests for comment.)

Feature writers also typically write stories assigned to them on the basis of events or trends, but they usually have more time to work on them. They can make more calls and do more background research to become familiar with a topic. Feature writers often care more about the human interest element of stories than about the science, though. And, sometimes even more so than other reporters, they want to present whatever science they include in a clear, comprehensible, and uncomplicated way. The behavioral scientist can help by being aware of the writer's particular needs and especially by guiding the writer away from faulty premises or conclusions, which can be achieved without trying to impart a comprehensive understanding of all the scientific nuances and complications.

Specialized science writers are the behavioral scientist's best friends. Science writers are also often enlisted to write features on topics already in the news, but they tend to be more systematic about seeking and evaluating new research for possible coverage than are feature writers and GA reporters. Science writers want to know the latest relevant research findings, the major unanswered scientific questions, and what science has to say about the behavioral issues in the news. They want to understand the science, at least at a level sufficiently deep to avoid inaccuracies and misrepresentations.

Keep in mind, though, that even sophisticated science writers must communicate their findings to a general audience in a friendly and engaging manner. Writing for the newspaper format and audience requires omitting many details and subtleties that a behavioral scientist might regard as essential. When communicating with science writers, behavioral scientists should highlight which points really are vital to the public's understanding and which ones are inside psychological baseball.

SCIENCE WRITERS
AND THEIR METHODS

A science writer's approach to covering behavioral science will differ from person to person and from paper to paper. A few science reporters, at the largest papers, specialize in behavioral science. More likely the science writer will be responsible for covering a wide range of sciences—physical sciences or life sciences in general, or in some cases, all that plus environment, health, and medicine. So, even a science writer may not be deeply familiar with any particular realm of behavioral science research.

Science writers rely on many avenues of information for story ideas. Some will regularly attend scientific meetings relevant to their areas of responsibility. Behavioral science specialists might cover the annual meetings of the American Psychological Association, the American Psychiatric Association, or other organizations. And many science reporters attend the annual meeting of the American Association for the Advancement of Science, which always includes some behavioral science sessions on its program.

There was a time when meeting coverage was the normal source for most science

journalism, but nowadays the predominant sources of science news are the weekly menu of offerings from various scientific journals. A couple decades ago, very few journals made much of an effort to promote their contents to science journalists. It used to be that *Science* and *Nature* dominated science news, with the *Journal of the American Medical Association* and the *New England Journal of Medicine* contributing the majority of medicine-related coverage. But today dozens of journals make their content available in advance of publication, under embargo until the publication date, to registered science reporters.

Among the most prominent, in addition to *Science* and *Nature*, are the *Proceedings of the National Academy of Sciences*, the various journals of the *Public Library of Science*, and various offshoots from *Nature*, such as *Nature Neuroscience*. Elsevier sends regular notices of papers thought to be newsworthy from its vast array of journals available online through Science Direct. Many other journals have some level of advance alert system for interested journalists.

Typically, a journal offers reporters, via e-mail or a Web site, a complete list of an upcoming issue's table of contents (sometimes with a "tip sheet" highlighting the most newsworthy items), usually about a week in advance of publication. Journalists who agree to respect the embargo can then download copies of the papers in which they have interest. This embargo system gives reporters time to contact the researchers and other experts so that a story can be ready for a release time that corresponds with the journal's publication schedule.

In principle, the embargo system avoids the rushed and possibly, therefore, inept reporting that might occur if a paper were simply made available for immediate release. But the embargo system also has problems, principally because of the draconian policies that some journals have toward paper authors. Researchers are often required to sign vows of silence, promising not to reveal their findings to the media in advance of the paper's publication (except to reporters who agree to adhere to the embargo time). Such gag orders sometimes limit the ability of scientists even to report their findings at scientific meetings, and impair the ability of reporters to write in-depth features about ongoing research.

Although journals provide reporters with a steady (and sometimes overwhelming) stream of story possibilities, limits of time, space, and resources allow only a tiny fraction of the articles made available to be actually covered by any reporter.

A second major source of news alerts comes to reporters in the form of individual news releases, often prepared by the researcher's home institution, or sometimes by a scientific society or association or journal. Releases and many of the advance journal notices share a common Internet portal known as EurekAlert (www.eurkealert.org). Releases are also made widely available by another Internet-based service known as Newswise (www.newswise.com). These services list a substantial number of behavioral science–related news releases at any one time, though the number varies. Here is just a partial list of release headlines from a typical day's menu on EurekAlert's "social and behavior" science news category:

Nearly half of elementary school teachers admit to bullying (from the *International Journal of Social Psychiatry*).

Trailer park residents face multiple challenges (from the *Georgetown Journal of Poverty Law and Policy*).

Research reinforces findings that Chinese exercises benefit older adults (from the *North American Research Conference on Complementary & Integrative Medicine*).

Violence from male partners associated with serious health threats to pregnant women and newborns (from the *American Journal of Obstetrics and Gynecology*).

Penn State professor looks at gender roles, pre-wedding rituals in new book (from Penn State University).

Avoiding house dust mites and changing diet proves ineffective (from the *Journal of Allergy and Clinical Immunology*).

Smoking and obesity may increase the risk of erectile dysfunction (from the *Journal of Urology*).

'Big Brother' eyes encourage honesty, study shows (from *Biology Letters*).

All work and no play: New study shows that, in the long run, virtue is regretted more than vice (from the *Journal of Consumer Research*).

Many of these news releases are produced by a sometimes neglected but very important link in the chain of science communication—the public information officer, or PIO. Most major research universities have one or more public information officers devoted to the sciences. Though sometimes underappreciated, PIOs are actually key players in communicating research from the lab to the general public. They produce news releases, field queries from media, and often attend conferences where they mix with reporters and learn about reporters' interests and needs.

The best science PIOs are widely respected and appreciated by science journalists. For that reason, researchers who want their work to be covered should cultivate close relationships with the public information officer. Good ones will let scientists know whether their work is truly newsworthy and, if it is, will know how to communicate it to journalists. Sometimes that communication will take the form of a news release, widely distributed. Or sometimes, the PIO will just pass word along to a journalist who is likely to be interested in the particular research field. Keep in mind, though, that the science PIO will lose his or her credibility with the media if pressured to promote research that is not truly newsworthy. The wise scientist will heed the counsel of science PIOs about which findings are worth trying to communicate and what reasonable expectations for coverage should be. (See Chapter 13 in this volume for additional details about public information officers.)

OTHER MEDIA

PIOs should also offer advice on whether newspapers are an appropriate medium for presenting new research. Typically, releases are sent out to all media, and the various media select on the basis of their own considerations. For the most part, news values are pretty similar from medium to medium. What's new, interesting, and important for a newspaper writer is also likely to be new, interesting, and important for TV, radio, or online reporters as well. But different media are not always alike in how they evaluate and report new research.

TV news, for instance, is much more image driven than newspaper stories, although photos or graphic illustrations are considerably more important in newspapers today than they used to be. For TV, stories are often built around compelling video footage. Radio, in a similar way, is driven by sound (or by talking and controversy), so stories offering those elements get much more consideration than a newspaper writer would give. Online writers are cognizant of all these considerations, given that their work is presented on a multimedia platform. Visuals from photos and graphics to video clips and sound files are all part of the online package

and are elements that the newspaper writer usually doesn't have to worry about in deciding whether to report a piece of research or how to approach it.

Different media will also offer different proportions of human interest, feature-type stories, lightweight fun stories, or superficial controversies as opposed to stories with depth, context, and analysis. Print usually permits more subtlety and detail than TV or radio, so some behavioral science stories are best suited for the kind of depth that print can sometimes offer. This advantage for newspapers has diminished in recent years, though, as newspaper editors have demanded shorter stories and as the Internet has provided space unlimited by paper costs.

BEING A SOURCE

Journal tip sheets and news releases are the typical vehicles of communicating behavioral science news to journalists and, if the topic is deemed newsworthy, they usually lead to further interaction between scientists and journalists, mostly in one-on-one interviews or news conferences.

After a reporter determines that a story should be written (or is so instructed by an editor), the next step is generally to interview relevant scientists. The journal paper or a news release is no substitute for direct questioning. Good reporters will want to talk with scientists directly involved in the work, as well as with "outside experts," scientists not involved in the work but knowledgeable enough to comment on its meaning and importance. (Stories without outside comment risk being regarded as naively accepting a scientist's results at face value without validation from a disinterested source.)

If you are publishing results that may be newsworthy, you should be prepared for the eventuality of an interview. Be ready to talk when a reporter calls. Typically the reporter's time to interview people and then write the story will be very short, possibly less than a day, sometimes only an hour or two. (Even when reporters get a week's notice of an upcoming paper, they are usually busy working on other stories. It is often not until the day before publication that they can turn their attention to any given daily story.) A reporter working on a feature may have the luxury of scheduling a convenient interview time, but scientists with an important paper worthy of a daily story should be prepared to talk on the spot. Sometimes, when the story is first publicized in a news release, the paper may not yet be available—so you should have a copy ready to send to the reporter by fax or, ideally, a pdf by e-mail.

In telephone interviews, it's essential to talk slowly and clearly, using plain English but colorful language so the reporter will be able to quote you directly. You have to communicate in words that an average reader will understand, even if the reporter is very knowledgeable. (As one reporter likes to say, use "cocktail party" language.) Of course, what you say should still be accurate, and if a reporter asks technical questions, you should reply with the level of nuance and depth needed to make sure that the reporter understands.

Along these lines, scientists should keep in mind the distinction between informing and educating. Many scientists regard the media as a tool for "educating" the public about science, but most journalists consider this idea anathema. There's no worse criticism of a newspaper article than to say it reads like a textbook. Science writers also do not regard their role as educating, but as informing. They particularly do not engage in efforts to expand their readers' vocabularies. Newspaper writers want to explain science by relating it to things that the reading audience is already familiar with, using the vocabulary that readers already have. Scientists hoping to communicate via journalists should keep that principle

in mind—speak in plain English and try to come up with useful analogies. The plain English rule applies with even more force to presentations before a group of journalists. While phone interviews are the norm for covering new findings appearing in journals, press (or news) conferences are a common way of presenting findings to the reporters at scientific meetings. Some reporters may attend the technical sessions at a meeting as well, but typically they get the meeting's top news from press briefings. So when speaking at a press conference, you should not assume that reporters have, or will, attend your actual talk.

Often, more than one scientist is scheduled to present at a news conference session. Sometimes, the presenters will be a team of collaborators; sometimes different researchers working on a similar topic. In any case, a presenter at a news conference typically gets 5 to 10 minutes to present the new results and then takes questions from the reporters. For this system to work well, a good initial presentation is essential.

The best presentations begin with a clear and direct statement of just what the important result is, as succinctly as it can be stated. (In other words, put the news first!) Next, it's important to explain why that result is important. Only then should the presenter start talking about the methodology or about the background behind the research. (Many scientists make the mistake of beginning with the background and methods as if presenting new findings to colleagues. Reporters generally hate that because they have no idea what the meaning or importance of the background is unless they know in advance where it is leading.) After the background has been (briefly) presented, end by summing up the results and highlighting their importance once again.

It's often helpful at news conferences to use visual aids—but they must be clear, simple, and designed to illustrate only one point at a time. It's OK to present one technical slide showing data (and error bars) or other such graphics that establish the evidence for the finding being claimed. But for explaining the methods or illustrating the importance of the results, it's a good idea to design a simplified slide or two specifically for the news conference presentation.

Whether in an interview or at a news conference, have additional sources of information available for reporters. Links to relevant Web pages are always useful. It sometimes helps to make previous papers available if they give useful background or context for the new work. It's also a good idea to be prepared to offer names of other experts in the field who would be able to give reporters outside comment. Newspapers also appreciate the availability of photos or graphics that will help illustrate the story.

All of the considerations mentioned to this point have applied to scientists reporting new work. But often reporters will call out of the blue about a story they are working on. Sometimes they will be seeking comment on other new work, sometimes they will be seeking comment on some topic in the news or some feature article they are writing.

Generally, these sorts of inquiries fall into two categories: seeking expert information on a specific question or seeking "big picture" guidance about a general topic, such as a perspective on how some new result fits into the general state of knowledge in a field. In either case, scientists should be honest with reporters about their ability to answer authoritatively. Scientists not familiar with a particular result or issue should refer the reporter to an appropriate expert. And scientists offering grand overviews of a field of research should clarify whether their perspective is widely shared or a minority view.

LOOKING TO THE FUTURE

Better communication between scientists and journalists is the key to improving the quality of behavioral science coverage in newspapers. Scientists who choose to respond to media inquiries and who also observe the principles discussed in this chapter establish credibility with journalists by becoming valued and trusted sources, regarding both their own work and the work of others in their field. These relationships are an important part of improving the overall flow of communication between scientists and the media.

To help foster such relationships as well as promote greater understanding of behavioral research, behavioral science organizations may also want to consider sponsoring workshops for increasing journalists' knowledge and awareness of behavioral science and related issues. Such venues could increase the quality of behavioral science coverage as well as the quantity, which tends to be the more difficult problem to solve. The Knight Science Journalism Center at MIT, for instance, offers occasional "boot camps" for reporters on certain scientific areas. Similar events, if sustained over time, could be helpful for reporters covering behavioral science.

To further increase the quantity of coverage, psychological and other behavioral science societies should be sure that reporters are alerted to upcoming research reports. Journals should also make their content, including full text of articles, easily available to reporters.

The institutional, economic, and logistic pressures on newspaper journalists will always limit the extent to which behavioral science (or any science) can be successfully covered. For example, in recent years, newspapers have, in the face of economic pressures, cut back on their reporting staffs, and in many cases science reporting has been curtailed. But by understanding the journalistic process and journalists' needs, cultivating productive relationships, and supporting greater awareness and understanding of behavioral research, scientists can go a long way toward improving behavioral science coverage.

CHAPTER 10

Magazines

Sally Lehrman

"'Slutty' behavior is good for the species," I once wrote, and I'll never hear the end of it. The article that contained this sentence explored recent anthropological research that contradicted the much-touted and supposedly "hardwired" evolutionary bargain of female fidelity for food. I had sold the story to an online outlet called Alternet because my regular editor thought it was "counterintuitive" and had refused to run it.

The story described a new wave of research on the evolutionary drives behind sexuality and parenting. From an anthropological perspective, I had learned, female promiscuity—combined with emotional fidelity—binds communities closer together and improves the gene pool.

Feminists loved the story. Conservatives didn't. One of my critics noted a "gleeful" tone and sternly pointed out that civilization depends on mastering impulses and, he said, in a rather odd extension, staying in school. A few men inquired as to my availability, and years later, the story is still making the rounds online.

SCIENCE, SOCIETY, AND SELF

The problem with writing about behavioral science is that everyone has an opinion, and usually it's strong. Journalists navigate very tricky territory here, from sketchy claims to hardened social belief systems.

The news never exists in isolation. Journalists, of course, apply events and information through the prism of personal experience and knowledge. Our sources have their own perspectives and goals, and our audiences take up whatever they read, see, or hear and interpret it through the framework of their own lives. All news works this way, but behavioral science is one area that touches everyone closely. It tells us about ourselves.

Behavioral science can teach us how to get along with each other better and live more satisfied lives. It can guide social policy and give us information to help us make our institutions more effectively serve community goals. Progressives, conservatives, Wiccans, and faith healers all have a stake. As journalists and as scientists, it behooves us to keep this in mind. We write out of and into a powerful social context.

Social context enters into the research itself: how and why it took place, the institutional culture in which it was performed, how it was interpreted and reported, and the reception it received in its own field. Once the research has been completed, journalists don't just serve as megaphones or transcribers—we add our own context. We digest the information, interpret it, explain it, put it in the context of current events or issues, and do our best to show why people should care. We choose how to give news developments form and meaning. Will we approach our story as breaking news, analysis, a societal trend piece, or a human interest article? Finally, the audience contributes its own context: personal experience layered with educational, cultural, and political background, to name just a few influences.

WHAT JOURNALISTS DO

In the female promiscuity story, I wasn't trying to make a case for women to go out and find an ongoing succession of partners. Honestly, though, I found the research interesting because it poked holes in lessons about gender roles that fuel popular wisdom. I've noticed these ideas take on authority without evidence in places like textbooks on evolutionary psychology. As a journalist, I'm attracted to research that makes us rethink some of the assumptions we humans make about each other.

I'll admit I had some fun with the story. I did engage in a little word play. But I stuck to the science, spent hours interviewing sources, and carefully checked everyone's credentials. As a science writer, it's my job to surprise, to engage, to teach people a little about themselves and the world around them. I challenge assumptions, both within science and about it, and apply my investigative and business reporting skills to the territory I cover.

Fundamentally, it's my mission to teach my audiences about scientific research and to show them how it affects their lives. I want to help them develop an educated voice as voters and as decision makers within their families and communities. When behavioral science feeds public policy in areas such as schools, health care, or criminal justice, I want people to feel empowered to think, question, and have their own say. Like a lot

of other journalists, I have big ambitions for my work.

In its ethics policy, the Society of Professional Journalists tells its members, "Seek truth and report it." But not any old truth. Truth that serves democracy, that alerts the public to injustice and to wrongdoing; to key social issues that require debate. The Society might even sound a little pompous, in fact, as it describes the underpinnings of a journalist's duty: "Public enlightenment is the forerunner of justice and the foundation of democracy."

"Journalists should be honest, fair and courageous in gathering, reporting and interpreting information," the policy says. We should strive toward accuracy, avoid conflicts of interest, and be accountable to our audiences, sources, and each other.

Most of us really do believe this, and I think it's fair to say that many—maybe even most—journalists have been drawn to the field by high ideals about our role in social discourse and democratic society. It's certainly not the money, respect, or fame that lures us: Most journalists earn less than a business administration major right out of college. Pay is a median $43,588 a year for men and another $6,000 less than that for women (Weaver, Beam, Brownlee, Voakes, & Wilhoit, 2003). As for respect, only 39% of the public trusts us to tell the truth, one recent Harris Poll calculated (The Harris Poll #61, 2006). (They trust scientists roughly twice as much.) We're pretty far down on the list of prestigious jobs, too.

Despite how others may view us, we think big and we pride ourselves on professional integrity. Of course, we face a number of mundane realities, too. We work under very tight time constraints. Whatever the medium, we never have quite enough space or time to explain anything thoroughly. Even if we cover a specialty beat like science, most of us aren't experts, and we must scramble to keep up with challenging new material.

WHAT MAKES
MAGAZINES DIFFERENT

Most magazine writers are freelancers, not staff writers. That means we have no job security and no benefits. To editors, we're only as good as our last story. That also means it's a reasonable guess that we feel passionately about our work. Otherwise, why do it? And most of us have survived in the business only because we make the effort to do a great job on every single piece.

Newspapers, television, and many online outlets go for the general reader, focusing on breaking news or health and science stories that cut across a wide swath of the population. Magazines tend to be more specialized. Newsweeklies, science specialty magazines, and trade journals all serve different core audiences, each with their own level of interest and background knowledge. Writers can assume a basic science vocabulary in *Nature* or *Scientific American,* for instance, although not necessarily knowledge about a particular field such as genetics or physics.

When we shift to a magazine such as *Health* or *Alternative Medicine,* our language adjusts, too. General consumer magazines like these or, say, *Details, Redbook,* or *Parenting* tackle some of the same subjects, but they try to be inviting and comfortable for readers who might even be a little fearful of science. Reading them should be like visiting a friend's house—you will find familiar topics as well as a recognizable tone and approach in every story. Articles about behavioral science often will tell a story, making points about new discoveries through the window of someone's personal experience. These magazines look at behavioral science through their own distinct frame of gender, home, or lifestyle and try to be helpful to readers. Many pieces include a section with strategies and tips that readers can apply to their own lives.

When we try to bring science down to a practical level, of course, there's plenty of opportunity to go wrong. Suddenly, theories about behavior or studies that suggest one thing or another become recipes for a better life. Consider one of my specialty areas within science, sexuality.

CASE STUDY: ADVICE INSTEAD OF INFORMATION

Soon after Pfizer won approval for its erection-prompting Viagra in 1998, the New York company began promoting the drug as useful to women. Suddenly magazines were writing enthusiastically and helpfully about "female sexual dysfunction" and how easily it could be treated—with drugs, lotions, and devices. They quoted a figure put forward by Pfizer and extracted from the National Health and Social Life Survey (Laumann, Paik, & Rosen, 1999): 43% of women have some form of this newly identified disorder, they warned. They guided women to their doctors and pharmacists for relief. But in 2001, the results of the first large study on Viagra for women came out—it was no better than a placebo (Basson, McInnes, Smith, Hodgson, & Koppiker, 2002). After more research with about 3,000 women in all, Pfizer decided not to apply for regulatory approval to sell it for "female sexual arousal disorder" (Mayor, 2004). But by that time, millions of women had discovered they had a "condition" that now even drugs couldn't treat.

If journalists had been a little more skeptical, they might have gone back to that original 1999 report in the *Journal of the American Medical Association* and checked the numbers. Here's what the survey said: 22% of women had low sexual desire, 14% had arousal problems, and 7% had pain. Even with the most generous interpretation, then, a drug like this might help between 14% and 36% of women—not almost half. Furthermore, if they'd checked the original study, journalists might have read one of its primary conclusions, which pinpointed two root causes of low sexual desire and response: social status—among ethnic minority groups, for instance—and sexual trauma. "Sexual dysfunction is highly associated with negative experiences in sexual relationships and overall well-being," the authors wrote.

Their words didn't exactly point to a plumbing problem that a vasodilator can easily fix. But advice on drugs and potions takes less space and is more immediately satisfying to readers than, say, an analysis of risk factors such as unwanted sexual contact at a young age or perhaps an essay on the ways in which a deteriorating social position, economic discrimination, and stress harm sexual desire.

Stories about "female sexual dysfunction" still appear regularly in women's magazines today, along with tips about herbs and testosterone patches. The National Health and Social Life report almost always is cited, although usually without sufficient attribution that a reader could look it up. And unfortunately, along with the predictable advice, sexual stereotypes usually prevail. In explaining why Viagra works for men but not for women, *Prevention* advises, "Face it, we're complicated" ("Satisfaction Guaranteed," 2004).

The Red Sports Car Effect

My own protestations aside, it's hard for anyone to write about something like sex without the personal creeping in. When I wrote one article that challenged the idea of female sexual dysfunction as a medical condition that needed treatment, my editor still kept insisting that I include resource information—on drugs, devices, and psychological techniques. When I wrote the piece on female promiscuity, a different editor simply couldn't conceive of the possibility. Journalists can't help but evaluate news not just from the context of our newsrooms and the publications

we write for but also from within the experience of our own lives. In *The San Francisco Examiner* newsroom, we used to call this the "red sports car" phenomenon. If an editor bought a red sports car or wanted to, suddenly red sports cars—their cost, safety, the trend of middle-aged men buying them—became big news.

The prism through which we see the world starts with personal experience, then extends beyond. While journalists do our best to be objective when we cover the news, the stories of our own lives point us to certain interpretations and understandings. Media expert Dori Maynard (www.maynardije.org), chief executive of the Maynard Institute for Journalism Education, calls these "fault lines." Five primary aspects of experience influence our perceptions of the world the most, she says: They are race, class, generation, geography, and generation. Other analysts include religious ideology in the mix.

If you're a White journalist, for instance, you simply may not think to ask questions about racial bias built into bank lending or educational opportunities. If you're a man, you may not notice when a room full of dignitaries includes no women. If you grew up in a rural area, you may have a different sense of the meaning of "neighbor" than someone who grew up in a big city. These fault lines influence the ways we interpret news events and whom we ask for opinions and perspective. Experimental social psychologists have documented unconscious bias in the way we interpret faces or whether someone is carrying a tool or a weapon. We can expect these spontaneous reactions to play a role in the reporting process, too. Unless we make an effort to fill the gaps in our vision and understanding, we skew the stories we tell and often bias the news toward people like ourselves.

As a result of this tendency and the White, male composition of most newsroom staffs, researchers who study mainstream media detect what they call "White news" (Entman & Rojecki, 2000; Heider, 2000). By that term, they mean that news coverage tends to interpret events and ideas from the perspective of White people—who make up 78% of television news staffs across the United States, 87% of newspaper workers, and an even bigger proportion of those who work in radio and magazines. Their ideas find support within a larger social phenomenon apparently shared by all ethnic groups, in which the category "American" is synonymous with being White (Devos & Banaji, 2005). Furthermore, based on newsroom numbers and other content analyses, we also could easily call journalism "straight news," "people without disabilities news," or "male news."

WHEN STEREOTYPES BECOME "FACT"

Behavioral science offers ample room for journalists' perceptions of ourselves and of others to creep in and color the story. In particular, evolutionary psychology and behavioral genetics provide fertile ground for inserting into news reporting not just our own experience—but the social stereotypes we grew up with.

These emerged in full force when genetic epidemiologist Rod Lea presented unpublished findings that Maori men—descendants of the Polynesian peoples who first settled New Zealand—were twice as likely to carry a "warrior" gene than other people (Lea, 2006). News organizations dutifully repeated the claim, along with Lea's interpretation of the gene's importance to behavior. "This means that they are going to be more aggressive and violent," Lea pointed out in an early interview with the Australian Associated Press (Australian Associated Press, 2006), and suggested "links with criminality among Maori people." He went on to explain that "the same gene was linked to high rates of

alcoholism and smoking among Maori," making them more likely to binge drink, the article said. Most stories included Lea's additional comment that nongenetic factors may also be at play, but placed this thought toward the end.

Journalists didn't appear to have probed Lea's conclusions or their basis. But they did add what they considered relevant context. Several described the overrepresentation of Maoris in violence statistics. One online publication, News-Medical.Net, went on to detail the recent deaths of two 3-month-old Maori infants earlier that year due to severe head injuries, also noting that the twins' family had refused to cooperate with the police (Medical Research News, 2006). Only later in that story did the author quote antiviolence agencies pointing out that the problem of family violence, in their view, wasn't limited to one ethnic group in New Zealand.

The context journalists generally chose almost seemed to "prove" that this gene did indeed explain criminal activity or violence within the Maori group. Referring to violence statistics does seem logical. But reporters covering this story completely overlooked other background that might have helped their audiences interpret Lea's claims. The association between violence and poverty and lack of opportunity is well documented. Journalists might have reported the high level of unemployment, poverty, health inequities, and lack of educational opportunities among the Maori. They might have pointed to documented studies on the discrimination and structural bias Maori people face at work, which in turn can influence individual behavior and how it is perceived.

Reporters failed to mention a study of nearly 7,000 patients in *The Lancet* that identified "powerful evidence of sub-optimum care" in hospitals for Maoris in comparison with other groups (Davis et al., 2006). They skipped over another *Lancet* report that concluded deprivation and both interpersonal and institutional racism—in health care, work, and housing—were contributing to health losses among Maori and health inequalities (Harris et al., 2006). They missed yet another analysis that examined Maori mortality rates, which are double the rest of the population. Its authors wondered whether socioeconomic position might account for as much as half of the excess (Blakely, Fawcett, Hunt, & Wilson, 2006).

Armed with this social context, reporters might have asked better questions about the ready interpretation of this gene as causative of a particular behavior among Maori people as a group. Knowing more about the social context in which Maori people live also would have helped audiences interpret the geneticist's claims about any so-called natural inclination toward violence.

Leaping to Conclusions

Why did journalists flock to examples of Maori violence? Why were they so quick to assume that any type of behavior could be the manifestation of a shared, innate trait within that group? Some social psychologists have found that we all have a tendency to attribute bad behavior to a permanent trait, rather than a temporary failure, when we perceive our subject as belonging to a different group than our own.

Perhaps this phenomenon was at work when, plowing ahead with this line of thinking, NewstalkZB insisted on taking the scientist's claims at face value, then went much further. The interview started off well as Hector Matthews, the executive director of Maori and Pacific health for the district Health Board, explained that correlation is not the same as causation:

> One gene . . . more common in Maori men than others doesn't necessarily (support) the lots of long bows that people are drawing, for example, towards crime.

But Ali Jones, host of the show, pressed him:

> I would have to agree with you on that, however, you can't dismiss that there could be a link, can you?

Matthews tried again:

> One other thing that is frustrating about this . . . and it often comes up with Maori issues, is that people correlate something and then they immediately go to cause. Correlation frequently doesn't mean cause . . . just because all murderers (in Australia) are Australian doesn't mean being Australian causes people to murder.

But Jones brushed this science lesson aside. She seemed intent on the idea that the research showed that racial stereotypes have a basis in fact:

> You only these days have to say the word "Jew," and already there's a connotation, or I feel, I'm being racist (*laughter*). Now that's my problem. But the point is too that Jews have been linked with good business sense, for example, being very big in the diamond and gold world particularly in New York. But that is sometimes turned into a negative, but as you've just said there are huge positives related to those sorts of racial links, if you like. (Jones, 2006)

In order to add the most interesting and illuminating context of all, journalists may instead have found it useful to look back into the history of scientific claims about "criminality." Mary Gibson, historian at John Jay College of Criminal Justice, details the physician Cesare Lombroso's powerful influence on ideas about the causes of crime in her book, *Born to Crime: Cesare Lombroso and the Origins of Biological Criminality* (Gibson, 2002). In 1876, the "father of criminology" laid out the ways in which Darwin's theories explained "the criminal man." As

Gibson's publisher describes Lombroso's theory: "Most lawbreakers were throwbacks to a more primitive level of human evolution—identifiable by their physical traits such as small heads, flat noses, large ears and the like. These 'born criminals' could not escape their biological destiny."

This hundred-year-old view of criminality as a biological inheritance might have shed light both on Lea's claims and journalists' own ease in accepting them. Lombroso used measures on physical features from skull size to cheekbone development to demonstrate the biological foundation of criminal behavior, adding that the abnormalities found in the criminal cranium called to mind "the black American and Mongol races, and above all, prehistoric man much more than white races" (Lombroso, 1876/2006). Gibson (2002) shows how prejudice and political passion underpinned "scientific" findings at the time about links between biology, psychology, and morality. "Lombroso never differentiated between correlation and causation," Gibson points out. "Criminal anthropology," she writes, "tended simply to give supposedly scientific support for popular prejudices" (p. 29). While these ideas eventually were refuted as a science, they held on in popular thinking and could be seen as making a comeback in claims such as Lea's.

The day after he described his findings, Lea denied suggesting that the gene in question was associated with criminality. In a radio interview, he qualified his earlier statements and said that behavioral traits were extremely complex and that the influence of the gene could be small. But Lea's later caution received far less attention. The "violence gene" story had already taken off.

Getting Some Distance

Most journalists avoid reporting on stories that affect our own personal lives because we know we come to them with a bias. Magazines do allow more leniency in this area, and editors often don't object to personal anecdotes. The writer, however, must remain balanced and objective in the article overall. The Society of Professional Journalists addresses this principle in its ethics policy by stating, "Act independently," then detailing, "Avoid conflicts of interest, real or perceived." But we rarely think how this concept might apply to our position in society—again, usually as White members of the upper-middle class who enjoy steady jobs and socialize with other people of comparable means. In stories about behavioral science, journalists must learn to separate both ourselves and our social assumptions from the information we are gathering.

Like any other story, there are many good ways to guard against blunders in reporting. These are the same protections we use to guard accuracy and fairness when interpreting claims by public officials, government bureaucrats, corporate executives, and everyone else. For one, we can educate ourselves about the historical context of the claims being made. We can keep up with behavioral research as it develops so we can evaluate new discoveries within the context of the science itself. We can remind ourselves to be skeptical and to consider the conflicts of interest our sources bring to the story, as well as the prisms through which they see the world. We can take into account the social assumptions that may have been built into the science or into its interpretation. And, just as we would never rely on one person to tell us what happened in a fire, a car accident, or the firing of a local official, we can rely on more than one source.

Scientists can help by pointing journalists to alternate interpretations of research findings and by sharing the trends and historical foundations within their own disciplines. When a colleague seems to be stretching too far, they can add a note of caution and provide thought-provoking critique. They can spend time going over the details, knowing they will give the journalist important context even if they never make it into print.

Looking for "Balance" Instead

Good sourcing is a way of ensuring "balance," a foundational concept in journalism. When journalists think about this practice, we often describe it as "getting all sides" of the story. This may not be the most useful frame to use for covering science. Many journalists covering the "warrior gene" story, for instance, went straight to what they considered the other side. They asked the opinion of Maori Party leaders, who predictably "panned his claims" and "reacted furiously." At least one story quoted a prominent Maori decrying the stereotypes involved. (Then the reporter inserted himself in the piece, adding, "However if the theory could be backed up with solid evidence then it might be worth a closer look.")

This sort of "he said, she said" back-and-forth does little to advance our audience's understanding of the news, its importance, or its implications. If we want to inform the public, we're not really after the opposition or a reaction on the street. In science coverage, we can think of "balance" as an important way of creating context. Instead of pro and con arguments, then, or quotes from opposing interest groups, "balance" means putting research into the context of its own field. We can look for reasonable alternate explanations for a study's findings and experts who can help us unravel the context in which scientists came up with the interpretations they did.

More often than not, the best people to offer this particular type of help are not those who were the subject of the study. As those most directly affected, they certainly have an interesting and important connection to the science. They can shed light on the research choices made by scientists, the manner in which a study was performed, and its meaning to their own lives. In the case above, the Maori offered important information about their cultural history, the value they did or didn't see in this type of study, and about social stratification in New Zealand. But journalists need to go further.

By exploring the science itself, we can convey the nature of discovery and help our audiences interpret new findings within this context. And when scientists disagree, as they often do, we can push behind the "sides" to the research itself. Coverage on science controversies tends to pit one field against another, such as biology against sociology, or "hard" science versus "soft" science. This doesn't advance anyone's understanding of the topic. Instead, we can probe the data underlying various interpretations, make uncertainties clear, explore what's missing, and dissect the assumptions behind interpretations.

Scientists can assist by refusing to allow journalists to push them out on a social or scientific limb when describing their work. Rather than stretching beyond the data into implications with little foundation, they can point out the questions that remain to be answered. Researchers can draw interest to the science itself, debate within the field, and competing ideas about where the data lead.

"CHECK IT OUT"

Lots of journalists complain that they don't have time to read original research or that they wouldn't understand it anyway. But that's as bad as admitting that your report on the latest crackdown on crime was based solely on a City Hall press release. It's as embarrassing as a story about a company's hot new product based entirely on one interview with a public relations officer or even the CEO. A cleverly worded press release can trap even smart science journalists who do thorough interviews. Several who were covering stem cell research found this out in September 2006. They trumpeted the news that scientists had discovered and demonstrated a means for creating embryonic stem cells without harming an embryo. Trouble was, the "breakthrough" they were describing required destroying all 16 embryos involved.

Press releases from both the company and the science journal involved neatly sidestepped this fact. But the experiment's methodology was clearly written in the text for anyone to read (Klimanskaya, Chung, Becker, Lu, & Lanza, 2006). While the report did demonstrate proof of concept, it didn't quite achieve all that was credited to it. Both scientists and journalists need to remember that science, like any other field, isn't immune to hyperbole and that scientists have a stake in the presentation of their work. So journalists always need to check the facts. Just like j-school professors like to tell their students, "If your mother says she loves you, check it out."

Though it would be great if every journalist could become a brilliant statistician in order to carefully analyze scientific reports, that's just not in the cards. And behavioral research presents special challenges in this area since so many other possible causes of a particular finding often have to be ruled out. First of all, journalists can ask for and review the written documentation of the science in a peer-reviewed journal. We can read the context for the study, which is typically laid out at the beginning. We can review the discussion at the end, where researchers tend to list the questions they feel still need to be answered and the problems they encountered while doing the study or interpreting the results. We can read the results and methodology, and check the figures and tables to make sure the claims match the data. Who funded the study? Did that organization have a stake in the outcome? How big was the study or its sample size? How representative was the population enrolled? What did the study really measure and how? What didn't it measure that it might seem to? Did the report appear in a peer-reviewed journal?

We can learn a bit about research statistics and design: Does the study meet the statistically significant threshold? (Check the p value.) Does the report instead say the data were "nearly significant"? Hmmm. What was the standard deviation or the overall distribution of the data? Was the magnitude of the finding (effect size) of likely practical importance? Was the study a randomized experiment? Did the study use methods to help control for other variables that may have influenced the results? Even if we don't fully understand how to interpret the mathematical assumptions built into a study, understanding some basic terms and their importance in interpreting results can help us ask the right questions. We can ask what's missing, what remains troubling or unclear, what assumptions were built into the research, and what controversies surround it still.

BETTER COMMUNICATION

News reporting relies on building relationships of trust, and science journalism for magazines is no exception. In order to make sure we have access to information in a timely fashion and can report it accurately, we need to build a network of contacts we can rely on. Journalists of all stripes often form an informal "advisory board" on subjects we cover regularly: They might include a geneticist or statistician who likes to poke holes in studies; an ethicist, lawyer, or sociologist who can give us a sense of the societal context; and someone from an affected group—perhaps an advocacy organization. Like other reporters, I don't show my copy to scientists before publication. But I might run a metaphor by them or check to make sure a technical description is correct. This type of exchange can be extremely helpful. Sometimes I find I have missed some nuance that is important.

Magazine writers have the opportunity to develop an expertise in a few areas of interest. We can linger on a topic and follow sources over time to get a better sense of both the power and the limitations of their work. We can try to keep up with the areas we generally cover, even when a story isn't breaking. Not only does this help us spot stories early and give us an edge in developing new ideas, but it also gives us the grounding needed when time is short. Even when we're working on a specific story, not every interview or conversation will end up in the piece, and this can be discouraging to the researcher. But every discussion creates essential context for the story at hand and for all the reporting that we will continue to do in that field. Together we are building a contextual framework that can ensure accuracy and clarity over the long run.

A careful approach to science reporting requires time and patience on the part of sources, not just the journalist involved. I often meet scientists who feel resigned that their work will be misinterpreted or portrayed in the wrong light. But what's the point of science that does nothing to inform people about themselves or the life issues they face? The public does want to know what sort of behavioral science is under way and what information is emerging. Most Americans (including scientists in many fields and health care professionals) learn about health and science from the mass media. News coverage stimulates excitement about research and its potential, makes the results available to society, and prepares the public for discussions about

public policy that may ensue. Magazine coverage is a crucial conduit because of the depth and length of stories, combined with their huge readership—2.3 million alone for O: the Oprah magazine, for instance.

But scientists must keep in mind our purpose: Journalism is neither publicity nor transcription. Our purpose is to shine a light on important new work and to explore its meaning for our readers. The scope and shape of our approach may not fit exactly with the ideals and intentions of our subjects—the scientists themselves, that is. Furthermore, sometimes language gets in the way. When I attended a conference of neuroscientists, psychologists, and theologians several years ago, they could barely communicate their ideas about the workings of the brain to one another. A term in one discipline might mean something completely different in another. Journalists face the same challenge. Science journalism is a form of cross-disciplinary communication, which always requires a reexamination of the language involved. We must find terms and explanations that are accurate but still meaningful to people from other walks of life.

Recently, in an academic meeting that involved social scientists, geneticists, and me, one researcher said he had been advised by his university media relations people to "dumb down" his research for journalists. I told him I couldn't think of worse advice. Besides being insulting to reporters, that approach is more likely than any other to result in oversimplification and mischaracterization of research.

At the core, we journalists do believe it is our responsibility to get information right. And so we beg the patience of researchers to spend some time going over their methodology, explaining their statistical methods, and clarifying just what they feel can and can't be inferred from the results. This detail is quite unlikely to end up in a magazine article. But it is essential to good communication and its likely outcome: accuracy.

REFERENCES

Australian Associated Press. (2006, August 8). "Warrior gene" blamed for Maori violence. *The Australian.*

Basson, R., McInnes, R., Smith, M. D., Hodgson, G., & Koppiker, N. (2002). Efficacy and safety of sildenafil citrate in women with sexual dysfunction associated with female sexual arousal disorder. *Journal of Women's Health and Gender-Based Medicine, 11*(4), 367–377.

Blakely, T., Fawcett, J., Hunt, D., & Wilson, N. (2006). What is the contribution of smoking and socioeconomic position to ethnic inequalities in mortality in New Zealand? *The Lancet, 368*(9529), 44–52.

Davis, P., Lay-Yee, R., Dyall, L., Briant, R., Sporle, A., Brunt, D., et al. (2006). Quality of hospital care for Maori patients in New Zealand: Retrospective cross-sectional assessment. *The Lancet, 367*(9526), 1920–1925.

Devos, T., & Banaji, M. R. (2005). American = White? *Journal of Personality and Social Psychology, 88,* 447–466.

Gibson, M. (2002). *Born to crime: Cesare Lombroso and the origins of biological criminality.* New York: Praeger.

Entman, R., & Rojecki, A. (2000). *The Black image in the White mind: Media and race in America.* Chicago: University of Chicago Press.

Harris, R., Tobias, M., Jeffreys, M., Waldegrave, K., Karlsen, S., & Nazroo, J. (2006). Effects of self-reported racial discrimination and deprivation on Maori health and inequalities in New Zealand: Cross-sectional study. *The Lancet, 367*(9527), 2005–2009.

The Harris Poll #61. (2006). Doctors and teachers most trusted among 22 occupations and professions: Fewer adults trust the president to tell the truth. In *The Harris Poll©.* Rochester, NY: Harris Interactive, Inc.

Heider, D. (2000). *White news: Why local news programs don't cover people of color.* Mahwah, NJ: Lawrence Erlbaum.

Jones, A. (Talk show host). (2006, August). *Health expert on Maori warrior gene* [Radio broadcast]. Christchurch, New Zealand: Newstalk ZB, 89.4.

Klimanskaya, I., Chung, Y., Becker, S., Lu, S.-J., & Lanza, R. (2006). Human embryonic stem cell lines derived from single blastomeres. *Nature, 444*(7118), 481–485.

Laumann, E. O., Paik, A., & Rosen, R. C. (1999). Sexual dysfunction in the United States: Prevalence and predictors. *Journal of the American Medical Association, 281*(6), 537–544.

Lea, R. (2006, August). *Tracking the evolutionary history of the warrior gene across the South Pacific: Implications for genetic epidemiology of behavioral disorders.* Paper presented at the 11th International Congress of Human Genetics, Brisbane, Australia.

Lombroso, C. (2006). *Criminal man.* Durham, NC: Duke University Press. (Original work published 1876)

Mayor, S. (2004). Pfizer will not apply for a licence for sildenafil for women. *British Medical Journal, 328*(7439), 542.

Medical Research News. (2006, August 9). Warrior gene theory sparks debate and highlights domestic violence in New Zealand. *News-Medical.Net.*

Satisfaction guaranteed. (2004). *Prevention, 56,* 152–187.

Weaver, D., Beam, R., Brownlee, B., Voakes, P., & Wilhoit, G. C. (2003, April 10). *Median income climbs to nearly $43,600.* Retrieved December 15, 2005, from http://www.poynter.org/content/content_view.asp?id=28805

Part III

COMMUNICATING WITH THE PUBLIC

CHAPTER 11

Making the News Interview a Success for You and the Reporter

Rhea K. Farberman

For behavioral researchers and other scientists, media reporting of news and current events offers a credible, far-reaching, and inexpensive way to educate large numbers of Americans about their research findings. For the news media, psychologists and other scientists are expert sources that can help answer the "why" of news events, human behavior, and social trends and can add interest, credibility, and a fresh or unique angle to the news. But often the relationship is a tenuous one.

WHEN JOURNALISM MEETS BEHAVIORAL SCIENCE

When journalism meets science—psychological or any other—two very different worlds are coming together. Communications strategist Richard Levick submits, "Truth for a lawyer is precedent, for a doctor it's fact, for a scientist it's proof, for a journalist it is what they know at deadline" (Levick & Smith, 2005, p. 212). But the foundation of behavioral science is the careful conducting of research over time. A fundamental force in journalism is the clock or, too often, the stopwatch; it's a continuous rush to meet deadlines and beat the competition. These two

very different realities, created in part by reporters unfamiliar with science jargon and methods and by differing expectations for the interview, the story, and its headline, produce a situation ripe for miscommunication.

If there's so much room for misunderstanding when scientists interact with the news media, why do it at all? Because public appreciation of the value of behavioral science is likely critical to increasing research funding and for supporting the broad application of research findings to daily living. The media are science's best conduit to the public. The challenge is for the scientist to learn the skills and techniques necessary to meet the media on a level playing field and to use the media to deliver accurate science information in language the public can understand.

Is staying away from the media by declining interview requests a viable alternative? "No," say news and public affairs professionals. Simply put, if you want your research accurately represented to and through the news media, you need to talk to reporters. The problem with not talking to the news media is that other people will, and those sources will likely not understand your research as well as you do and will probably not cast you and your research, university, and profession as you would.

Over 20 years ago, TV news elder states-men David Brinkley noted that when a gov-ernment or industry spokesperson "deals with television, it is not us they are dealing with. They are dealing with the American people through us. They give clear, short answers because they are more effective when they are delivered by us to the American people" (Rafe & Pfister, 1983, p. 56).

In the age of 24-hour all-news cable outlets, news blogs, and satellite radio, the news media's ability to be the conduit through which organizations speak to the American public is larger and even more powerful today.

Most scientists agree that it is important for the many science disciplines to build and maintain ongoing relationships with the news media. But most would also agree that media relations can be a double-edged sword. In short, if you don't know what you're doing, you can get hurt.

WHAT MAKES NEWS?

Understanding what is considered news by the gatekeepers of the news process (reporters, editors, and producers) is a key factor in successful media relations. (See Chapter 9, this volume, for a discussion of newsworthiness.) What's important to realize is that many of the decisions made during the process by which an event becomes news are subjective. Though most editors and producers will tell you that they make decisions about what gets in the paper or on the air based on objective cri-teria such as timeliness, uniqueness, signifi-cance, impact on the community, proximity to the audience, drama, and the availability of good visuals, their personal views of the world also can enter into the decision-making process (see Chapter 10, this vol-ume, for a related discussion).

WHAT ARE THE HURDLES TO HAVING POSITIVE INTERACTIONS WITH NEWS MEDIA?

Although the news media offer opportunities for behavioral science, they also present problems. Beyond managing language barri-ers, the scientist and the reporter must step outside of their familiar worlds to communi-cate with those from a foreign professional culture. Examples of the problems scientists must cope with are (1) the uninformed or misinformed reporter, (2) time constraints, (3) understanding the journalist's profes-sional process, and (4) fitting complex research into a sound bite.

The Uninformed or Misinformed Reporter. Typically, the reporter assigned to do a story with psychological implications has a limited understanding of psychology and behavioral science. The exception would be a large media outlet with the resources to assign an experi-enced writer to the psychology or behavioral science beat. Only a few national outlets such as *The New York Times* have such a reporter. What is more likely is that the reporter who calls you for comment or explanation of a new piece of research or a news event is a gen-eralist, called a general assignment reporter in the industry.

An investment of time and patience is required when dealing with the inexperi-enced reporter, but that investment is critical to the quality and accuracy of the final story.

A good piece of advice to the news source—the interviewee—is to approach the reporter as one would approach a student. Think of the interview as a teaching opportunity and, as such, communicate to the student (the reporter) in language he or she can under-stand. Personalize examples to illustrate abstract concepts, avoid all jargon, and define basic terms in ways that relate to the reporter's experience.

Providing reporters with background information also helps reports prepare to cover your research and for your subsequent interview. The Foundation for American Communications (1990) *Media Resource Guide* has the following to say about the importance of providing background material to reporters:

> The key to background information is an understanding that the craft of news reporting is very much a story-to-story, day-to-day profession. Unless you are blessed with a reporter covering you regularly, odds are that any reporter covering a story involving you may not know very much about you, the story, and what happened before the reporter was assigned to your story. The protection you need in that situation also happens to be an effective way of providing service to the reporter. Who knows more about you than you do? By compiling basic information, you can make the reporter's job easier. (p. 56)

In other words, by taking the time to educate the reporter and provide him or her with all appropriate background material, you are making an investment in more thorough, more accurate reporting.

Time Constraints. What drives the news media? Time, the quest for accuracy and fairness, and competition with other outlets—but mostly time. Reporters writing for daily newspapers typically receive a story assignment in the morning and face a deadline that afternoon. In this time, the reporter must quickly become educated about the issue, ascertain the facts, and get quotes from the people involved or other knowledgeable experts usually to achieve balance between both sides of a story (see Chapters 3 and 4 in this volume for discussions of balance in reporting). All this work has to be done in anywhere from 4 to 6 hours. Often the news

source who returns the reporter's call most promptly or who is most helpful to the reporter's understanding of the issues involved is the person who gets quoted or has the most effect on the story.

Radio and Web journalists face even tighter deadlines, as radio tries to provide listeners with something that newspapers cannot: hourly or even more frequent updates on the news. Often a radio station will want to interview a news source immediately or certainly within the next few hours.

Television deadlines range somewhere between the immediate need of radio and the "this afternoon" deadlines of print reporters. Deadlines vary in television according to the format of the show. Daily morning or afternoon broadcasts will want to do interviews the same day or at times do live interviews during the broadcast. Other types of television news, such as weekly magazines, have longer lead times, and reporters typically work on a show segment 4 to 6 weeks in advance of its airing.

TV news has an added dimension. Whereas the majority of interviews for print and radio journalists are done over the phone, television reporters want to go to the news source's office or to some other appropriate setting to do the interview (and get "pictures" to go along with the story). The TV reporter has to leave the studio and get videotape; that adds time and pressure to the news-gathering process.

The need for speed doesn't always allow the media to find the best fit between the news source and the story. It also doesn't always allow the reporter time to do the necessary homework for getting grounded in a topic before conducting an interview. Such situations put both the news outlet and the news source at risk of producing a story or a quote that is incorrect, out of context, or incomplete. The news organization cannot do much to change the nature of the news-gathering process and the news cycle. They certainly cannot add hours to the day. News sources can, however, take a few steps to try to be as efficient and effective as possible despite the media's time pressures. Additionally, the advent of Web-based instantaneous news reporting has removed the traditional editor (fact-checking) function from the news-reporting process, thereby putting even more onus on the news source to help the reporter understand the issue during the initial interview so he or she so can report about it with accuracy.

Understanding the Professional Process. Both journalists and researchers start their work with a potentially interesting question. Scientists ask questions in the form of precise hypotheses and then seek to isolate the conditions under which narrowly defined variables cause or influence a particular, well-defined behavior. Journalists usually start with a much broader question and seek a practical answer that provides new solutions to problems or information that is otherwise interesting and relevant to most people. Many researchers feel that the answer is always incomplete, even after a career spent asking the question. Although deadlines vary and some reporters stick to reporting on a topic of research for years, reporters mainly seek to gather the information that is as complete as it can be by deadline, close out the question, and move on.

Both fields have their own terminology, communication styles, and culture. Science is usually depersonalized and discussed in terms of theoretical concepts and applicability to specific subpopulations. The news often includes personal stories and seeks to appeal to broader society. The time constraints already discussed create a much more fast-paced environment for journalists than researchers typically experience in most academic settings. These differences can contribute to confusion and miscommunication about even the most basic concepts.

FITTING COMPLEX RESEARCH INTO A SOUND BITE

The average news sound bite today is under 10 seconds. But research is complex, and there are limitations as to how the result should be interpreted and applied. Caveats are important. Simply put, what the researcher sees in his or her research results—one piece of the overall research puzzle that can only be applied within the limits of this particular study—is different from what the reporter wants to find in a research study: the all encompassing headline (see Chapter 4, this volume, for a discussion of caveats).

The challenge for the news source, the researcher, is how to translate the research into a meaningful sound bite, especially when preparing for interviews with the electronic media of radio and television, which often emphasize speed and brevity above in-depth reporting.

One valuable strategy is to ask oneself simple questions about the research study. Why did I conduct this study? Why did I think it was important? What hypothesis did I set out to test? What were the most important things I learned that weren't known before? How might the results of this study be put to practical use in the future? What other studies will be needed, or what other conditions might need to change, before those applications can occur? Brief but descriptive answers to these questions create a sound bite that is simple without being simplistic.

Consider also the media outlet you are being interviewed by. The type of interview you would do with your community newspaper is different from the one you would do with National Public Radio and different again from the one you would do with a network evening magazine like ABC's *20/20*. A program's audience and format will affect both the way you prepare for the interview as well as the type of background information you share with the reporter. For example, if you are going to be interviewed by a reporter who specializes in science reporting and is working on a feature story, you will have the opportunity to speak in greater depth about your research. At the other end of the spectrum is a spot news report for local or national radio. These news spots cover a story in 60 seconds. A brief sound bite that captures the essence of your research succinctly and in plain English will be needed (chapters in Part II of this volume discuss these differences).

Talking about your research succinctly and in language that laypeople can understand is a critical skill whether you are reacting to a request to be interviewed or want to interest journalists in covering your research. E-mail is a particularly useful tool for the latter, but regardless of the circumstances under which you are talking to a reporter—proactively or reactively—being able to tell the reporter why your research is significant in brief and understandable terms is paramount.

HOW TO LEVEL
THE PLAYING FIELD

If you talk to researchers who have been interviewed, you'll hear stories from many of them about their research being misrepresented. Thorough interview preparation is one of the best ways to avoid the negative experiences that your colleagues might have had.

THE PREINTERVIEW PHASE

From the interviewee's perspective, one of the most important milestones of the interview process is the "interview before the interview." This preinterview is typically the first contact the news source will have with the reporter or producer. It is also the one point in the interview process when the news source gets to ask the questions. Although most reporters will want to speak to you via telephone or in person for the actual interview, e-mail messaging with the reporter or producer can help you glean useful information at this stage.

Here are some of the questions you will want to ask when deciding whether to participate.

If you're unfamiliar with the news outlet or reporter that is calling, you might ask the following: What is the outlet's format (newspaper, magazine, radio, TV spot news, TV magazine news, or other)? This information will help you prepare the right length and depth of message points for the interview. If the reporter is from a broadcast format, will the interview be live or on tape? Obviously, only the taped interviewed will be edited. How many guests are typically included in broadcast? The number will help determine how much airtime you will receive and how long your message points can be. How long are the typical stories? The answer sets limits on the number of message points to include. What type of audience does the outlet have? How much it tends to understand about the science affects how much educating you should do. To decide the tone and style of your message points, ask the following: What were some of the reasons you thought your audience might be interested in this research? You'll have a better idea about how to focus your message. What is the broadcast or publication frequency? Less frequency—weekly versus daily—often means more in-depth reporting.

You should also ask if the specific story for which you are being interviewed will be produced in the same way. If your story will be handled differently from the outlet's typical approach, you should ask why. News outlets may deviate from their normal presentation when they are rushing to cover controversial news, expect to be the first to offer a highly compelling story, or seek to create a public debate. You may want to consider whether you are comfortable with the role you will play when deciding whether to participate in these interviews.

You can also ask the reporter about his or her approach. What's the theme of the story, or in what direction does the reporter think the story is moving? What information is the reporter looking to you to provide? If you are not offered a copy of the questions for the interview, it doesn't hurt to ask if the reporter could share the questions he or she believes might be asked so you can do your best to prepare answers that will be helpful. However, if you do receive such a list, don't assume that the interview will be limited to it. If the reporter says, "I'm really just beginning to talk to some people about this," it's a golden opportunity for you. It may require a bit more time on your part, but it's a chance to educate the reporter and therefore have more influence on the story than any other news source, mainly by sharing background information. The Web sites many researchers have created to describe their research can be an excellent background source.

Who else has the reporter spoken to or planned to speak to? This information can often give you a clue as to the direction or possible bias of the story. The reporter may ask you to suggest other experts who might provide useful information. This service helps you as well as the reporter. By giving the names of some researchers who will support your views and some who will offer alternative viewpoints, you will be able to anticipate the supports and the criticisms the reporter will use to create the story, helping you to prepare to elaborate on the supporting material or speak to the counterarguments that are likely to appear.

If you're being asked to appear on a broadcast show, pay extra attention to the show's format. You may want to avoid an interview if what is being set up is actually a heated debate. The usual tip-off that a heated

debate is in the offering is the choice of the other interviewee. Ask the show's producer who else will be interviewed as part of the broadcast and ask about their position on the issues or your research. It can also be helpful to do Internet searches on the other guests to determine their positions. If you believe that another guest will be unfairly hostile or will seek to misinform the audience, you may decline to be a part of the interview or be prepared for battle.

After you have asked these questions and gotten answers, it is time to decide if you are the right person to do the interview. If the answer is yes, agree on a time that the reporter can call you back or come to your office to do the interview. Keep in mind the reporter's time pressures. The earlier in the process the reporter gets your information and point of view, the better he or she can synthesize the information into the story and put it in appropriate context. Remember at this point in the process, you also have the right to set some ground rules as to where the interview will take place and how long the interview will last. Being generous with your time in helping a reporter learn about and understand the subject area makes sense, but spending hours educating does not. A good length of time for a typical phone interview is 15 to 20 minutes; for an in-person interview, approximately 45 minutes.

There are also times when declining an interview is the right decision. For example, if the reporter is asking about a topic that is outside the range of your knowledge, seems intent on pursuing a story line that you know is not supported by the data, or is seeking to create a debate where little or none exists, you may prefer to say no to the interview request.

A special word of caution should go to those researchers working on topics that are controversial or easily sensationalized. If your research is on the effects of abortion on mental health, sexual orientation, or birth order and its effect on intelligence, for example, you will have an even steeper challenge steering the reporter away from stories that are sensationalized or biased by a political orientation. When a researcher is faced with these types of interviews, it is critical to prepare succinct talking points and stick to them by using techniques such as bridging (discussed in the next section) in order to keep the interview on track. When dealing with the most volatile subjects, some interviewees chose to respond to a reporter's questions via e-mail rather than in a traditional interview.

PREPARING FOR THE INTERVIEW

The answers you received in the preinterview phase will help you prepare for the interview. Having learned the objective and tone of the interview and having gained some idea about the approach and the kind of information the reporter is seeking, you are in a better position to define your own goal for the interview. Having a goal and knowing the words and phrases you will use to express your knowledge and point of view is critical to success. Preparing brief summaries of your research not only is a good way to help you frame your message, but it also gives you a valuable overview you can share with reporters to help them prepare, too.

Approach your interview preparation very differently than getting ready to write a journal article. When writing for a journal, the methodology is somewhere at the top of the article, and the conclusions or findings are held until the end. In the middle is lots and lots of information. When approaching an interview, you have to reverse that thinking. That is, start with the conclusion—what were your most important results—and then briefly relay other information about the research and findings, such as the basics of the procedure and other potentially interesting results.

Before the interview begins, create the three most important message points you want to communicate. Write them out. Practice them. Are they credible, simple without being simplistic, brief, and true to your expertise and the research literature? It is also important to give some thought to the questions you will likely be asked about them and, of course, what your answers will be. But don't assume that every question the reporter asks is the right question. Some will be the wrong questions because the reporter lacks an understanding of the subject or is fishing for controversy. It is important to acknowledge a reporter's question but also to correct it if it is based on a false premise by telling him or her so and explaining why. Take, for example, a case in which the reporter mischaracterizes your finding.

Reporter's question: I know that your research has shown that x always equals y. If that is true then. . . .

Your response: Actually, my research does not suggest that x always equals y—let me explain. What my research shows is that. . . .

As in the example above, the researcher has corrected the misinformation and then used a bridge, "let me explain," to move into a discussion of what his or her research actually shows. Bridges help lead the way to messages that you want to deliver.

Examples of "bridge" phases are the following:

- "The real issue is. . . ."
- "What's important to remember is. . . ."
- "I don't know the answer to that question, but what I do know is. . . ."
- "The main point here is . . ." or "The bottom line here is. . . ."
- "We need to do more research, but I can give you my hypothesis. . . ."

Then use a flag, a simple phrase that directly signals to the reporter what is most important about the topic, such as, "What's really important about this new finding is. . . ."

DURING THE INTERVIEW

It is possible to control the tempo and pace of the interview by keeping your answers brief and avoiding the temptation to fill all the time with your voice. Always remember that long, rambling answers greatly increase the possibility that you will be misquoted. Concise responses, in language that the reporter understands, decrease that possibility. Silence between questions should not make you nervous; it gives both you and the reporter time to think. Don't let the reporter rush you. Taking time to think before responding to a question is a good idea.

Reporters can be fond of asking a few questions at one time and are known to interrupt frequently. When faced with multiple questions and an aggressive reporter, it is important to keep your cool. Break down multipronged questions and deal with one issue at a time. When stuck about how to respond or where to go next, remember the message points that you crafted and want to deliver.

Returning to your message points will help you get back on track if you feel an interview is going awry. As the interview progresses, continue to use flags and bridges to signal what is most important and to move away from a question that is not germane to the subject or to the information you want to deliver—your talking points. Think of a reporter's question as if it was a diving board. A diving board gets you into the pool; used properly, it can even add a great deal of style to the way you enter the pool, but once in the water, you still have to swim.

Table 11.1   Interview Tips

Before You Are Interviewed
- Assess the reporter's need for background information.
- Craft your message points; anticipate key questions.
- Prepare key answers; include quotable phrases.
- Prepare and fine-tune your three message points.

During the Interview, Your Rights Are
- to determine the approximate length of the interview.
- to select where you want to be interviewed.
- to ask in advance for the topics to be covered during the interview.
- to set your own pace in answering questions.
- to correct false premises and challenge questionable assertions or assumptions.

During the Interview
- Deliver your message points in brief, understandable, quotable language.
- Speak in plain English and avoid jargon.
- Speak within the range of your knowledge, and don't be afraid to say, "I don't know."
- Be positive, not defensive.
- Use bridges to move away from topics you do not want to talk about and stick to your message points and use flags to signal what is important.
- Don't let the reporter put words in your mouth or create controversy when none exists.

AFTER THE INTERVIEW

Evaluating Your Performance. We are often our own worst critics, especially when it comes to seeing our image on television or hearing our voice on the radio. However, the best way to evaluate your performance is to ask yourself, "Did I deliver my three message points, and did they get into the story in an appropriate context?" The only issue that should concern you with respect to how you looked or sounded is whether your appearance, body language, or voice got in the way of the audience hearing your message. Such questions as, "Did I mumble or speak too rapidly?" "Did I look disinterested or nervous?" or "Was my loud tie a distraction?" are all appropriate.

What to Do When You Are Unhappy With a Story

Very rarely is a news report everything you would have wanted it to be if you had written it yourself. The most important concern is the big picture. What broad theme or message is being received by the reader or viewer? Remember that it takes many, many impressions over time to influence public awareness or opinion. Consider your interview one small piece of that larger effort.

One good rule of thumb for deciding when a correction is necessary is to try gauging how the reporting will be understood by the lay audience. If you are unhappy with a news story, consider sharing it with a nonscientist, a family member perhaps, and ask that person to give you a couple of sentences summarizing what he or she learned from the story. If that "takeaway" message reflects an appropriate degree of understanding for the lay audience (not your research colleagues), then it's possible that the reporter's choice of language achieved the goal of sufficiently informing the news consumer.

Occasionally, news sources believe they were misquoted by a reporter and want to demand a correction. There are times when it is appropriate to ask for such a correction but also times when making such a request can backfire. When a factual error appears in a news story, it is fair and appropriate to ask for a correction. Do so respectfully. Remember that journalists (and their editors) are people, too, and therefore subject to the same issues of ego and anger as everyone else. What's different, however, is that news people have the final say about what will be reported on tomorrow. You do not. Don't go to war or burn a bridge with someone who in part controls what will be reported in tomorrow's news. It will also be important to make the correction in future interviews on the subject. Reporters often use old news clips as a way to brief themselves on a topic.

Although you may feel that the story for which you were a news source has missed a particular context or nuance, this is not necessarily the time to demand a correction. One concern is that you put yourself and your organization at risk of being perceived by the editor or reporter as "protesting too much," and that can beget an embarrassing second-day news story or a less than friendly reporter the next time you are involved in a news event.

CLOSING THOUGHTS

"The American public is overfed on information and starved for understanding" (Giorgianni, 2004). Behavioral science can help fill the void by helping to make decisions, solve problems, and provide new insights in people's daily lives. The importance of communicating this information through mass media has become even more apparent as science and government try to meet the challenge of giving essential technical and practical information to the public to help protect them, for example, from terrorism incidents and the potential outbreak of avian flu.

The U.S. Department of Health and Human Services (2002) advises the following:

> The Tragedies of September 11, 2001 and the emerging threat of bioterrorism have reemphasized the need for public officials to communicate effectively with the public and the media to deliver messages that inform without frightening and educate without provoking alarm. (p. 1)

According to the U.S. Public Health Service (U.S. Department of Health and Human Services, 2002), researchers in risk communications have determined that the most credible experts in a crisis are the scientists themselves. The research community must be ready to interact with a range of professional communicators to fulfill this critical role.

Whether on a daily basis or in times of crisis, the news media are a vital means by which behavioral scientists inform the public and convey the value of their work. As long as the marketplace and public opinion influence the amount of money available for behavioral research, enlightening the public through the news media will continue to be a critical public relations and public education tool. News media and behavioral scientists need each other, and media interviews are the primary means by which behavioral science news is gathered. Researchers interested in working with the news media should avail themselves of media training workshops and seminars offered by the American Psychological Association and other entities because news media relations should be approached not only with a degree of caution but also with a lot of preparation.[1]

NOTE

1. For information about the American Psychological Association's media referral service or media training opportunities, contact the APA Public Affairs Office at (202) 336-5700; e-mail: public.affairs@apa.org.

REFERENCES

Foundation for American Communications. (1990). *Media resource guide: How to tell your story* (5th ed.). Los Angeles: Foundation for American Communications.

Giorgianni, S. J. (Ed.). (2004). The story of science: Health care and the media. *Pfizer Journal*.

Levick, R. S., & Smith, L. (2005). 365 *marketing mediations: Daily lessons for marketing & communications specialists.* Washington, DC: Watershed Press.

Rafe, S. C., & Pfister, W. J. (1983, August). The art of the interview. *VideoPro*, pp. 54–58.

U.S. Department of Health and Human Services. (2002). *Communicating in a crisis: Risk communication guidelines for public officials.* Washington, DC: Author.

CHAPTER 12

From the Lab to the Living Room

Stories That Talk the Talk and Walk the Walk

KATHY HIRSH-PASEK AND ROBERTA GOLINKOFF

Once upon a time, experimental and theoretical psychology was deeply invested in issues of practical application. James's (1890) functional psychology knitted together discussions of stream of thought, memory, and self in an effort to understand individual action and the human capital that created civilization. Dewey (see Viney & King, 1998), who chaired the first psychology department at the University of Chicago, followed in James's footsteps in recognizing the value of psychology for education. Even Watson (1913), the father of behaviorism, was convinced that if people followed the dictates of his field, "the educator, the physician, the jurist and the businessman could utilize our data in a practical way" (p. 169). Psychology was a science that had *relevance* to the problems of the day. Psychology studied problems that affected people's daily lives, from family, to emotions, to the workplace.

Somewhere in its adolescence, the field of theoretical and experimental psychology came to downplay the role of relevance.

Ironically, as our methodological skills improved, relevance went out the window. Predictability, control, and measurement occupied center stage. As philosophical positivism took hold, even fields such as social and clinical psychology changed in character. Morawski (2000) notes that in this shift that occurred early in the 1900s, "the experiment and its conclusion presented no visible theoretical appreciation of the social or of the relation of the individual to the social or society" (p. 429). Many years later, Ulrich Neisser, one of the fathers of cognitive psychology, would echo the same concerns about the lack of ecological validity of lab-based cognitive studies. In 1976, he wrote, "The study of information processing . . . has not yet committed itself to any conception of human nature that could apply beyond the confines of the laboratory" (p. 6). Professor Urie Bronfenbrenner of Cornell University joined the chorus of those hoping to put relevance back into psychology. He argued that somehow the tables had turned and that science needed

AUTHORS' NOTE: This research was supported by NSF grants SBR9601306 and SBR9615391 to the authors. We thank Stanley and Debby Lefkowitz for their support of our research and Maryanne Bowers for her tireless work on our behalf. Our lab coordinators, Meredith Jones and Becca Seston, made concentrating on this chapter possible.

social policy to provide it with two elements it lacked: vitality and validity. Laboratory experiments failed to understand children in their natural ecology; it failed to examine behavior within the larger social systems of child care, school, and neighborhood in which people actually knew each other and participated in roles and relationships (Bronfenbrenner, 1979). In this era, however, psychologists were largely unconcerned about practical matters. With a jargonized vocabulary of operational definitions and a narrow set of hypotheses, they went about building scientific cathedrals that were largely inaccessible to the public.

Today we return to days of old, once again asking how theoretical and experimental psychology might offer evidence-based information to address some of the concerns of our time. Renewed in part by Urie Bronfenbrenner's plea (1979; Bronfenbrenner & Morris, 1998), research psychologists are investigating everything from the criminal justice system (Steinberg & Scott, 2003) to child care (NICHD Early Child Care Research Network, 2005a) to optimal standards for the burgeoning universal preschool movement (Zigler & Bishop-Josef, 2004). Psychology has become not only a science seeking to explore the depths of human behavior but also one that can speak to social and public policy (Foster & Kalil, 2005). As we move back to the future, however, we must relearn how to *talk the talk* of the media writer, the layperson, and the policy maker. How do we make what we do accessible to different audiences? We must also have the courage to *walk the walk* by stepping out of the lab so that we can appreciate how our findings might bear on questions that are somewhat tangential to those we research directly. In what follows, we share our experience in this journey with stories that helped us learn to talk and to walk in foreign lands outside the laboratory and the classroom.

TALKING THE TALK

The Printed Venue

Laaadies, I read your book proposal yesterday. The first page was exciting. I wanted to learn more about how babies talk. By the second page, I was still with you, but I was losing interest. By the third page, I was dyyyyyying! Ladies, you *really* have to learn how to write (said in a deep New York accent).

These words uttered by our agent hit us like a head-on collision. As academicians, we were never trained to write in inviting language so that intelligent college-educated adults could read our work. We were even told that stepping out of the closed system of academic scholarship was frowned upon. In fact, one of us was told disparagingly in graduate school by one of her professors that she had a "Sunday supplement style." Nonetheless, we mustered the courage to write an overview piece on language development for the *World Book Encyclopedia*. We had also given what we thought were clear and coherent interviews to reporters from parenting magazines and national news outlets (e.g., *US News; Newsweek*). The bold next step in our progression was writing a popular press book that shared the fruits of the research community with parents, teachers, and policy makers. We *thought* we had written an interesting and exciting review of the literature that brought science into the hands of consumers. We envisioned our book, *How Babies Talk* (Golinkoff & Hirsh-Pasek, 1999), as representing years of scientific research from laboratories around the globe. Unfortunately, our first attempt at conveying this enthusiasm failed. Our honest agent was "dyyyyiiing" of boredom as she read our dense review.

It soon became clear that writing for lay audiences was completely different than writing cogently and coherently for academic peers or even for encyclopedias. A glance at the *New Yorker* reveals some of the secrets of good writing. *Real* writers start with an anecdote and then lead the reader from the particular to the general. As Jay Belsky taught one of us, writing is about socializing readers and holding their hand as you take them through the mystery of the science. If you've done your work well, by the end of the book, readers are engaged with the writer and often come to the same conclusions.

To understand what we mean, take a minute to review the following two abstracts: one for scientists and one meant to speak to a general audience. The difference in writing style is obvious.

Example 1: Sciencespeak

A core task in language acquisition is mapping words onto objects, actions, and events. Two studies investigate how children first learn to map novel labels onto novel objects. In Study 1, we investigate whether 10-month-olds are able to use both perceptual and social cues to learn a word. Study 2 assessed whether the mapping of word to referent is a product of infants' pairing the label in training with a particular spatial location. Results across both studies showed that 10-month-olds could learn a new label and do so by relying on perceptual salience of the object instead of social cues provided by a speaker. This approach is in direct contrast to the way in which older children (12-, 18-, and 24-month-olds) map and extend new object names. (Pruden, Hirsh-Pasek, Golinkoff, & Hennon, 2006, p. 266)

Example 2: Down Home

Ten-month-old Marissa sits on the living floor rolling her toy car. Marissa's mother is talking on the phone in the same room, "Wow, you got a new dress for the party? What kind of dress?" she says as she looks towards the kitchen.

How do children learn their first words? Much language is used around them and so many objects and actions are present simultaneously. Does "dress" refer to the car Marissa is playing with? To the door? To the kitchen? Or to something completely different? A new study examined how 10-month-old infants learn the names of objects. The authors found that even at this tender age, babies *are* listening to what we have to say. But at 10 months, babies link words to objects in a way that is totally different than their older brothers and sisters or even adults. Like Marissa, 10-month-olds assume that the word "dress" must refer to the car, even though the mother is paying little attention to Marissa or to what she is doing. In just 8 more months, however, Marissa will be keenly aware of her mother's gestures and whether her mother looks at her while speaking. By a year-and-a-half, Marissa will only "glue" a name to her toy car if her mother is looking at the car or gesturing to it. By that time, Marissa will only learn a word when her mother makes the connection clear between what she is talking about and what she is looking at. Once infants can use these correlations, they can learn the name for what the *adult* has in mind rather than what *they* have in mind.

Example 3: Educated Layman

There is power in language. It can start wars or ruin marriages. Readers of these words barely remember a time when they did not have language. But every word you know had to be learned. Imagine bending over your car engine with your mechanic and being told, "Your zorch is shot." You follow your mechanic's eyes and body orientation to the part he is examining. That rusty metal protrusion must be the zorch. How do we learn the mapping between words and the objects and events they represent? (Golinkoff & Hirsh-Pasek, 2006)

Two scientists have made inroads into this question by asking whether the process that word learning involves changes over the course of development. Do 10-month-olds, for example, learn a new word in the same way that an 18-month-old or a 24-month-old does? It turns out that 10-month-old babies learn words for new objects based on how interested they are in the object, whereas older babies attach more importance to whether the speaker is interested in the object. These findings suggest that parents might want to talk more about what their babies are interested in rather than what they, the parents, are interested in.

Somewhere in graduate school, even good writers learn to write in cryptic language and to adopt a concise style. Much of this stems from the premium on journal space. In game-like fashion, we see how many words we can edit out to make our paper seem "tight" and terse and still comprehensible to others in our field. Background for the problem we study is often minimized; why be expansive in reviewing the prior work when the reader can look it up? Scientific writing, while quite exact, is filled with the passive voice. A core task in language acquisition is mapping words onto objects, actions, and events. Good scientific papers always examine alternative explanations for their results and leave the reader with hedges rather than confirmations. For example, one formula for casting doubt on what you just wrote goes something like this: "While these results seem to show X and Y, we have yet to test Z as a possible explanation for these findings. . . ." And these sentences usually come in the final two or three paragraphs of a paper, just before one that says, "Despite these limitations. . . ."

In stark contrast, down home language uses a cute example as illustrative and then unpacks the lessons we can learn from the example. The writing is in an active voice, often fails to acknowledge alternative explanations, and rarely suggests caution in interpretation. Educated layman writing is also active and also makes less use of examples.

The difference between these two styles is that an educated layman stance invites the reader into the intellectual problem that the findings are about and treats the reader more as an intellectual equal who might have considered these issues on his or her own.

What had we done so wrong in our first proposal? First, while we thought we had stripped the writing of scientific jargon, we hadn't completely done so. What seems like often used, easy to understand terms for two psychologists is still jargon to lay readers. We learned to catch each other when we tripped up and replaced a technical word with a lay word. For this reason, it is useful to have an agent or some layperson who knows nothing about your field read your popular press writing. For example, when we were tempted to talk about "processing information" or "linguistic capability," one of us would catch it and transform these phrases into English, as in "learning" or "language skill," respectively. The second way in which we missed the boat was the quality of the writing. Although we mostly used lay terms, we were still far from the active, enticing, and colorful writing that takes a story beyond the facts to the journey and mystery of language development. As David Marcus, a Pulitzer Prize–winning journalist and author once told us, when you write or speak for a more general audience, you want to invite them into the excitement of your field. Make them feel special to be a witness to the information you are sharing. Keep them on the edge of their seat. They will soon see that you can be their private guide into the unknown world that helps us understand children and their growth.

Finally, our writing still too much resembled a textbook in the way that we described people's research. We needed to adapt the way citations are done in popular press writing. Although we had been taught since college that not making attribution to someone's work by name was plagiarism, our agent told us time and again to remove the citations. (As she colorfully put it, "No one cares who did the work! They just want to know what they found!") What works for a textbook does not work for a popular press book. While we occasionally recognized the authors of various research projects by name in the text, we had to become comfortable with having a bibliography for each chapter where the eager reader could find the actual citations and the researchers' names.

We are clearly not ready for the Columbia School of Journalism, but we did revise that proposal, and *How Babies Talk* was released by Dutton/Penguin Press in 1999. Our foray into the world of trade books also taught us a number of lessons. First, few of us will ever write like Stephen Pinker or Stephen Jay Gould or Carl Sagan, but learning to write for more general audiences and to show the spark and passion that we share for our work is an important goal to which we should all aspire. It is one of the reasons that many of us enjoy teaching. In fact, teaching an introductory class in our specialty is a good model to use for how to approach popular press writing. Consider the factors that fuel us to keep improving our offerings and returning to the classroom. The rewards of awakening a class's amazement at the latest findings (e.g., 8-month-old babies are like little statisticians, computing the frequency of the syllables they hear in speech! [Saffran, Aslin, & Newport, 1996]), watching the wheels turn as students offer alternative explanations or additional tests of the hypothesis under discussion (e.g., but if babies do babble on their hands, shouldn't blind babies fail to do so? [Pettito & Marentette, 1991]), and having students blurt out their surprise (e.g., but babies can't do that!) all go a long way toward making us want to communicate the science we treasure. If we feel the excitement, we can find a way to explain it so others will too—without their having a PhD. Just as in teaching, using

examples and analogies the reader can relate to are crucial for getting the point across. And just as it takes time when we begin to teach to appreciate the level of our students, it also takes time to find the right level to write popular press materials.

Anyone interested in doing this who is already an academic will have a leg up, having had to translate complicated concepts into lay language. Importantly, however, popular press writing might be best reserved for after an individual has achieved tenure. This is for several reasons. One is that it takes time to learn the best way to present material in teaching, let alone writing that speaks to broader audiences. Another reason is that it is necessary to establish one's expertise in the field before touting one's credentials as an expert. Finally, budding researchers need to be careful to establish that they are bona fide to their colleagues by conducting excellent independent research before they go in the popular press direction (see Chapter 6, this volume, for related discussion).

Learning to write for more general audiences offered us a second lesson. It added a crispness and timeliness that improves our scientific writing. Learning how to communicate and to communicate well should not be considered "on the side" of what scientists do. Once you have entered the popular arena, you are no longer happy with sentences that contain strings of gobbledygook. We inadvertently continue to produce such sentences, but our commitment to clarity and communication has hopefully decreased their frequency. Third, it is important to be able to write and speak so your grandmother can understand what you are saying and why. Your grandmother represents the taxpayers who support our research and who should also reap the benefits of what we do. It is all about taking the perspective of the reader. If we think a finding is important, we should be able to explain it in a way that communicates this and why; what practical relevance might these findings have? Being forced to explain ourselves (in writing or teaching) often requires that we take the work to the next level, considering the implications that might have passed us by as we worried over the details of a study's design. Looking beyond the design for the big picture can be extremely heuristic for our research programs.

How Babies Talk was an overview of scientific research in the field of language development and was dotted throughout with examples. Each chapter contained boxes called "Try This!" where readers were urged to perform their own mini-experiments in their living rooms in search of the phenomenon we had just described. In a section that ended each chapter, called "Scientific Sleuthing Pays Off," we helped readers to "mine the scientific knowledge base to make informed decisions about everyday issues" (Golinkoff & Hirsh-Pasek, 1999, p. 9). Because we both taught language development at our universities (indeed, that is an understatement: We ate and breathed language development), once we found our voice, we actually enjoyed writing this book and sharing our enthusiasm for our field. Another thing that popular press writing allowed us was to be who we are. No journal article or book chapter allows humor to creep into its somber pages. In a popular press book, we could have a field day kibbitizing with the reader to help bring home our points. If we made each other laugh, we knew that at least some readers would be amused.

In our second and more widely read manuscript, *Einstein Never Used Flashcards: How Children Really Learn and Why They Need to Play More and Memorize Less* (Hirsh-Pasek & Golinkoff, 2003), we pushed the agenda even further. Here we not only reviewed research across the field of child development, but we chose to organize that literature in a way that supported the issue that PLAY = LEARNING. Two factors coalesced to bring forth this book. The first

factor was the inspiration we received from presentations at the meetings of the International Society for Infant Studies. In back-to-back talks, both Professor Andrew Meltzoff of the University of Washington and Professor Rachel Clifton, then president of the organization, asked a pointed question, "Why is developmental psychology so misunderstood?" Our society was being barraged with claims that seemed to reflect developmental science. For example, the word was out that brain development stopped after the first 3 years of life (but see Bruer, 1999, for a critique of this view); that babies could add, subtract, multiply, and divide (but see Wynn, 1998, for a more reasoned view); and that unless parents purchased "educational" toys to introduce their babies to foreign languages, they would never speak like a native (but see Kuhl, Tsao, & Liu, 2003). All these claims in the context of a changing, global economy had the effect of making parents anxious and concerned, an effect that we were observing firsthand in the parents who visited our labs. We wished to reassure parents that the childhoods they experienced were good enough for their own children and that they did not need to invest in "educational" toys, adult-structured classes, or packets of flash cards to have intelligent and well-adjusted children.

The second factor that prompted the book was an offshoot of the first. Due to these "empirical" claims, policy makers were reinventing preschools and schools so that there was more work and little play. Yet 30 years of developmental science suggest that play is the work of childhood, the context in which children learn about the world around them (Hirsh-Pasek, Golinkoff, Singer, & Berk, 2007). We wrote *Einstein*, as we affectionately called it, to share the real research in the field with parents so that they could have something more than the hype in the media and on the toy boxes. We envisioned *Einstein* as an approachable, accessible, and straightforward review of the developmental research that parents and policy makers might learn from. As such, we saw it as an antidote to the current trends to treat childhood like a disease, to be gotten over as quickly as possible. Childhood is not a rehearsal; time in childhood is precious for building memories and learning about the physical and the social world.

Offering an overview of everything from brain research to numeracy and literacy development to social development, we drove home the conclusion that children learn from play. In a world flooded with unfounded developmental claims (Abram & Dowling, 1979) that seem to support the use of didactic learning for young children, this was news. *Einstein* became the voice of balance, and teachers and administrators tell us that they now have something to show parents who are demanding worksheets in the preschool. Written in a way that reviewed the science, it contains sections called "Discovering Hidden Skills" that continued the tradition we began in *How Babies Talk* by showing the reader how they could see their child's capabilities right at home. In "Teachable Moments," we showed readers how to capitalize on everyday situations to guide learning naturally and without "educational" expenditures. Finally, sections called "Bringing the Lessons Home" that ended each chapter offered concrete suggestions from research about what readers could do to promote their children's intellectual, social, and emotional development. *Einstein* reinforced David Elkind's (1981) message that children are not just little adults. It did more, however, than cry wolf. It offered evidence-based descriptions of how children really learn and what works best for helping children become happy, well adjusted, and capable individuals.

Einstein talked the talk but also took us into two other related arenas: that of public speaking and op-ed writing. Each of these is critical to supporting the message that we were trying to give with our writing. Each of these is critical to taking science out of the laboratory and placing it into the public's hands.

The Public Speaking Venue

We are not alone. When you do research in child development, you are vaguely aware that what you discover may influence parents, teachers, and policy makers. But the world is larger than that. Even before *Einstein* hit Amazon.com and the shelves of Borders, the ripples began. Early on, we heard from Ellen Galinsky, founder and president of the Family and Work Institute as well as author and advocate for children and families. She was convening a conference in Washington, D.C., that would be jointly sponsored by the American Library Association, the Association of Children's Museums, media for children (PBS), her group, and the Civil Society, among others. All of these groups were invested in young children. All were deeply troubled by the misuse of science resulting in misleading and confusing information for parents, preschool education, and policy makers. The conference was designed to spark a new conversation supported by real data on children—to change the current agenda now and into the future so that childhood could again be viewed as a journey and not a race.

There were fellow travelers at that conference, including Professor T. Berry Brazelton, a pediatrician, author, and longtime, trusted public advocate for children, and Professor Alison Gopnik from the University of California at Berkeley, who authored the well-received trade book, *The Scientist in the Crib* (Gopnik, Meltzoff, & Kuhl, 1999). The visionary committee wanted us to set forth the data in a way that compellingly and forcefully made the case for balance in early education—that separated the real data from the fiction. Of course, we faced a challenge. How to give a talk that was both substantive and entertaining; a talk that was memorable and that did not drown the diverse audience in facts; a talk that would be seen as relevant for media, schools, and museums?

As in the parallel task of creating print for nonacademic audiences, there was much to learn. The key, and one that is taught in media training classes, is to center your talk on three points and to reinforce them repeatedly but in varying ways. Good politicians do this all of the time. In fact, politicians often twist the question asked to make certain that the three points they are interested in making get heard. For us, the three points were as laid out in *Einstein*: (1) How you learn is as important as what you learn, (2) EQ (emotional intelligence) is as important as IQ, and (3) it takes a village (or the importance of learning in context and with community). *PLAY = LEARNING was the mantra that pervaded each of these messages.* This headline had immediate appeal in libraries, museums, and schools and preschools, where informal learning coupled with more didactic learning helps children reach their potential.

We also learned about the importance of iconography for that first talk. Showing a picture of the 21st-century toddler at a computer says more about today's world than a picture of a child in a stroller. Showing parents on the phone and Blackberry while their children are being ignored says more about today's world than a picture of parents and children reading. And using people in our slides who our audiences know and can relate to—such as Mr. Rogers and Mr. Spock—captures their interest and allows us to say less with more pictures. We have learned the simple fact that too many words on our slides put audiences to sleep. Instead, we have fewer words and pictures on each slide but use a larger number of slides than we would ever use for the same amount of time if we were giving an academic talk.

One public speaking event begat another, and before we knew it, we were invited to share our message with states that wanted to increase children's achievement but not follow national trends slavishly. These venues sometimes resembled prayer meetings, as members of the audience who shared our views practically said "amen" as we presented our points. For many who invited us, the *Einstein* message gave people who worked with children a research-based justification for what they knew was best for children. For example, infusing the new preschool accountability movement with the importance of social development was a welcome message.

Children's museums around the country resonated completely with our message about the importance of play for learning. Libraries that wanted to reach parents with the message that reading was more than just recognizing letters and barking memorized words were thrilled to hear us argue that literacy opportunities are pervasive and, when playful, can readily lead to learning. The interactive venue of speaking also offered us a platform for addressing more localized questions and concerns. For example, as we traveled the country speaking to schools and parents, people shared their concerns with us about the practice of eliminating recess. We were eager to share the work of colleagues in the field such as Pellegrini (2005) or the practices used in Finnish schools to document the importance of recess and breaks for learning.

We also learned much from our audiences. One woman coined the term *plearning* to capture how play = learning. Another told us that she discovered her inner life when left alone by parents who did not endeavor to keep her every childhood moment occupied and managed. And we also learned about things happening around the country that startled us but were important to learn. Preschool teachers in some states, for example, are given a script they must follow for how and what they are to teach their children each day. In their attempts to comply with the No Child Left Behind Act, some schools have required that reading be taught in tightly prescribed ways without regard to the fact that children may speak a dialect different than the texts they are reading.

Through both print and speaking, we were trying to offer our readers and listeners a new lens for development that was informed by research. If parents, teachers, and policy makers could begin to see the rich opportunities in everyday experiences, their definition of learning would more closely parallel that of the developmental scientist. In the real world, few understand that a supermarket is a rich context for learning about literacy and numeracy. This message, however, would need to come from an army of researchers in the field, and our field was just beginning to assemble the foot soldiers. Throughout our history, leaders such as Berry Brazelton and David Elkind spoke to broader audiences. If we are to combat the current misinterpretations and misapplications of the field, however, there need to be more of us trained to speak with groups invested in children and more of us willing to work on applied issues that flow naturally from our work.

Speaking to lay audiences more than pays back the effort. For local venues, it reminds people of the importance of participating in research with their children and, more broadly, how scientific inquiry informs us all. Getting these messages across is crucial to the survival of science in this country. For more national venues, it allows us to become familiar with the issues the particular group we are speaking with faces. We also interview the individual who tendered our invitation to discern the group's concerns beforehand. When our talks are couched in terms of a group's current concerns, they can appreciate what we are saying and, when appropriate, bring their problem-solving skills to the fore as we speak.

The Newspaper
Opinion Editorial Venue

Finally, we can *talk the talk* by addressing specific issues in pieces. Researchers can write pieces at any point during their career.

Once we finish our PhDs, we have the credentials and the knowledge base to call attention to issues relevant to children's lives. We can write a piece critical of some current practice, or on a more positive note, we can inform readers about some aspect of human development they might not have noticed. One of us, for example, wrote a local editorial titled, "They're Taking Away the Blocks!" to remind policy makers and the public that the advent of all-day kindergarten should not mean children in rows at desks doing worksheets. An overheard conversation at a party was the source of the title. A follow-up conversation highlighted the urgent need to make sure this perspective was heard. It has been interesting how often that editorial is cited as evidence for a position. Op-eds can be powerful.

We have also made our voices heard in op-ed pieces about children's toys. Every year, the toy industry announces the new "educational" toys for young children. The educational toy market has grown exponentially in the past 5 years with profits that measure in the billions of dollars. Around the holiday season, parents are barraged with advertisements that make unsupported developmental claims. Among our favorites are those that promise brain growth—separate tapes that feed the right and left brain—and those that sport increases in "newborn IQ"—whatever that is. In 2005, a Kaiser Foundation report exposed the bogus scientific claims printed on the packages. Even before its report was complete, however, it was clear that something needed to be done. Those trained in developmental and child psychology could offer informed opinion about the toys, refute some of the claims made, and herald the advantages of more common toys such as rubber balls, play dough, and construction toys. And the press was ready to listen to our views. For 2 years running, *USA Today* published separate op-ed pieces that spoke to the issue under the following titles: "Bah, Humbug: Whatever Happened to Children's

Toys?" and "Retro Toys: Back to the Future." The rules we follow for producing an op-ed piece are the same rules we use for writing a talk addressed to laymen: Invite the reader in by identifying the problem, make at most three clear points, use examples, discuss what we have learned from research, and avoid jargon.

Lessons From Talking the Talk

It Is Critical to Talk With Rather Than to Talk at Our Audience. As professors and researchers, we tend to lecture and indeed to pontificate, thinking that learning is uni-directional. It is not. There are many lessons to be learned in the field and later translated into research. President Bush authorized No Child Left Behind in 2001. That same year, Head Start Reauthorization required the testing of young children several times per year in the areas of language, numeracy, and literacy. There was a national outcry from teachers and from psychologists on at least three counts. First, professionals of various stripes were worried that teachers would teach to the test, narrowing the curriculum to just those skills to be tested. As *The New York Times* reported, schools are indeed cutting back on class time for subjects other than reading and math since only these areas must meet state testing requirements (Dillon, 2006). Second, the emphasis on academic learning was to be examined in the new regime to the exclusion of the mastery of social skills. In the wake of the ensuing chaos, it became clear that our field had not yet created really good, comprehensive assessments to examine early social skills and that even our tests in language and literacy were somewhat lacking (Hirsh-Pasek, Kochanoff, Newcombe, & deVilliers, 2005). Nonetheless, the research clearly shows that social skills are critical for children's success in school (Konold & Pianta, 2005; Raver, 2003).

Concern from outside of academe helped spark conversation, debate, and then the generation of a request for proposals from the National Institutes of Health (NIH) to fund further research on assessment. Speaking *with* others—especially those outside of our field—often exposes areas where future research is desperately needed. This research feeds not only the theoretical and experimental agenda but also practical concerns.

On a more general note, it is often the case that audiences ask us a question that we then turn back to the crowd. For example, one of us spoke at the Atlanta Speech School recently. A question from the audience focused on why parents feel it is necessary to drive their children to attain a high degree of academic achievement. Asking the audience to respond to this question led to a rich and vibrant discussion about the factors that influence the current zeitgeist. While we may have steered the discussion and underlined key points with support from the research (it's just another form of teaching after all!), the audience gained a great deal by having members of their community own the issues and speak to the solutions themselves.

One Size Does Not Fit All. As is probably obvious, op-eds and books are written for different audiences, and the language used and examples presented have to be relevant for those audiences. When we give talks about play and learning, the talk for educators includes much more data than does the talk for parents. The message must be tailored to the reader or the listener. For example, when we give talks to parents, we begin by asking them to take the STRS test (a test we made up to be able to use the acronym), allowing them to reveal, by a show of hands, how many feel that they are not doing enough for their children. Other, related questions on the STRS test (also answered by a show of hands) help parents realize immediately that they are not alone;

others face the same issues. It also tells parents that this talk will be for them, as it addresses their concerns and their lives.

When we speak to professional preschool or teacher groups, for example, we have used a picture of a seesaw to accompany our assertion that we must find more balance in education between memorization and real learning. We also try to have our graphics complement the message we are giving. Graphics—even cartoons and jokes—often give the message better than our words. For some of our cartoons, we say nothing as the audience laughs, generating the point all by themselves.

There Is Something to Be Said for Informed Opinion. We are used to waiting a long time for research to deliver some answers to our questions. And even then, our research opens new questions and new vistas without being definitive. After all, there is still a .05 possibility that our result happened by chance. While we are content to wait, museum directors building an exhibit, preschool coordinators working on curricula, and parents who want to do best for their children need direction now. In a classic article, Shonkoff (2000) writes of "Science, Policy and Practice: Three Cultures in Search of a Shared Mission." He noted, "When all of the answers are not in, the scientist's job is to design the next study. The service provider, in contrast, does not have the option of waiting for more data" (p. 182). Thus, when we talk the talk, we must recognize the different needs of different consumers.

We must come to understand that opinion informed by research is better than editorial opinion alone and that this at least brings science into the public arena. Scientists who work with research on a daily basis understand the import of findings and their likely limitations. Therefore, it is crucial for scientists to interpret the research for media outlets and for the public directly. This does not mean that we offer unqualified information, although popular venues generally only want the news and not the caveats. For example, when a study came out on how watching television was associated with attention-deficit hyperactivity disorder (ADHD) several years later (Christakis, Zimmerman, Di Giuseppe, & McCarty, 2004), we included this study in our talks. However, we also used this opportunity to explain how correlations are not necessarily causal and suggested some other hidden factors that might be responsible for the association.

The science that we share typically comes from the best, most rigorous journals and has stood up to the test that we cannot point to obvious artifacts that caused the effects. Of course, some of the science we offer may turn out to be incorrect with further research. For this reason, for us to talk about a finding publicly or in print, the particular finding needs to fit with a history of related findings and to make sense given what is already known. But sometimes there is a fine line between discussing the science as if it is the *truth* and helping the media or our audiences recognize that sometimes truth is what we believe. Examples, of course, include the *facts* that the world is flat and that ulcers are caused by stress. That facts sometimes get overturned does not mean that we can wait until it is all sorted out to speak to the press or give a talk about what we have learned. To do so would be to deny the public much useful information that will not be overturned.

Talking the talk is a critical component that will bring scientists in closer contact with practitioners—be they policy makers, journalists, or parents. But talking the talk is only part of our mission. If we are to be truly relevant, we must also walk the walk out of the halls of ivy and into the toy companies, schools, child care centers, and parenting centers, among others. Those in child development, for example, have laboratories that invite parents to visit as they participate in research. But how much do we, as researchers, really know about the world of parents and families today? What toys are available in the toy stores? What are the television shows that capture parents' eyes, and what are they being told about child development? Without doing some homespun anthropological observations of our own and about families of today, our talk—even if accessible—may be off the mark.

Walking the Walk

Adventures in the Toy Store. It was mid-December 2002 when we got the call from ABC News. Peter Jennings's assistant wanted to know if a simple trip through a toy store would reveal the remarkable and extreme claims made by educational toy vendors. We were certain that the shelves would abound with inappropriate material and outrageous developmental claims. Though we did not want to single out any particular company to critique, the zeitgeist was apparent in the industry at large. Touting brain development and early skill learning fed the anxiety of new parents. No parent wants children who will fall behind their peers. If toys can help children acquire the ABCs and 1,2,3s—then why not use them?

One of us went to the toy store, and ABC News followed with a camera in hand. We did not have to travel far down the aisle before noting how many of the toys boasted brain development and learning. One toy company offered parents a report card for brain growth. Another suggested that the electronic gadgetry would teach toddlers social skills. Yet a third toy suggested that babies as young as 6 months of age could learn six languages! These so-called educational toys were offering "brains in a box" (Hirsh-Pasek & Golinkoff, 2006). The television piece that resulted added a dose of reality to the fantastic claims.

Though we were busy being outraged, we were soon to learn how much we did not

know. One of us was invited to leave the lab and journey to Aurora, New York, outside of Buffalo to join the Play and Learn Council for Fisher-Price. The executives at Fisher-Price explained that after 75 years in the toy business, they felt the twin pressures to both do what was right for children and to ensure that their toys were well represented at the nation's two leading stores: Target and Walmart. Buyers from the large chain stores wanted to meet parental demands for educational toys that would prepare preschool children for kindergarten. Thus, toys for preschoolers that were not "educational" were unlikely to be featured. Could we help them work within these constraints and take small steps to turn the market around? Impressively, Fisher-Price even funded a survey of over 1,000 parents and 100 psychologists to learn more about the role of play in learning. Survey results suggested that while parents thought young children should play, they were worried that play would not be as good as more didactic learning for their children. Furthermore, the lower the social class of the parental respondents, the more they believed "educational" toys were important for their children. Developmental psychologists overwhelmingly noted the value of playful learning.

Scientists soon became an integral part of the toy development strategies as the designers considered and tweaked new products for the coming years. In fact, the award-winning *Play and Learn* toys were developed after watching real children play with everyday objects such as lights switches and mailboxes. Fisher-Price also sponsored a major conference that we ran with Dorothy Singer at Yale University in the spring of 2005. Entitled "PLAY = LEARNING," the conference hosted more than 150 guests and had a waiting list of over 500. We were shocked to learn the extent to which teachers of young children needed the support of experts for arguing that play is good for children. This was the message of the conference. The scholars present, including those in media for children, the toy industry, and writers, heard researchers put forth the scientific evidence that was collected for an edited book: *PLAY = LEARNING: How Play Motivates and Enhances Children's Cognitive and Social-Emotional Growth* (Singer, Golinkoff, & Hirsh-Pasek, 2007).

The synergy that took place when we agreed to walk the walk into the toy industry had far-reaching consequences that brought toy makers and scientists into the same conversation. It also gave us a better understanding of the constraints facing the industry and the reaction of parents who will hear our message. By learning about the toy industry, we not only forged a partnership but have a better understanding of how to tailor messages so that they can be heard. If the science of development is to be relevant to children, the toy industry is an important ally because more people buy toys than read books or op-ed columns.

Preschool Tutoring

The *Today* show was among many that were clamoring for developmental scientists who would address the new demand for preschool tutoring. Just a month earlier, in July 2005, National Public Radio (NPR) ran a story reporting on the tutoring fad among upper- and middle-class preschoolers. Now a multimillion-dollar business and growing, Junior Kumon, a branch of Kaplan tutoring, reports that tutoring for the younger set now accounts for over 20% of their business. Driven by many of the same forces that put educational toys on the market, parents of preschoolers can now sign up for lessons in reading and math at the local tutoring center. Though most conduct the sessions in a playful way, children are passively learning the subject matter and practicing at home.

Is this trend good for young children? An inquisitive public wants to know. As in the toy industry, there are little data to suggest that having the alphabet on your toddler rocking chair will hurt you. So, too, there is no research to our knowledge that infant tutoring will hurt, and it might help, say its supporters. Developmental psychologists and other professionals who work with children by and large disagree. While the evidence is sparse, going out to see these programs leaves the researcher with the sense that preschool tutoring is another case of learning devoid of context, of passive learning. For those who embrace a Piagetian approach to development and who are sensitive to Zigler and Bishop-Josef's (2004) argument for the importance of the whole child, these tutoring programs are big business with promissory notes for increased intelligence. Even without direct research in the area, educated guesses might suggest to the press that these programs are less about learning and more about feeding public anxiety.

Getting Parents Involved: An Open Question for Museums, Media, Libraries, and Schools

Finally, there is the overarching question that has been raised by so many venues that it is a burning question of our time. As Bronfenbrenner once said (quoted in Wozniak, 1991), "Development, it turns out, occurs through this process of progressively more complex exchanges between a child and somebody else—especially somebody who's crazy about that child" (p. 4). With so many parents working and with a blurred line between work and home, the time parents and children spend engaged in these increasingly complex exchanges continues to shrink. Furthermore, no child—especially among the affluent (Luthar & Latendresse, 2005)—is immune from isolation from parents. Many institutions wonder how they can promote parents' and children's engagement in joint activity.

Museum staff members note that parents sit with friends on the periphery of an exhibit while children play. Libraries ask how one can encourage more reading between parent and child. Indeed, a number of state initiatives and even United Way (Born Learning With CIVITAS) are addressing this question. Finally, high-quality and trusted media outlets such as PBS and Sesame Street Workshop want to know how to create responsible programming for infants and toddlers that promote better communication between parents and children. Despite a firm recommendation from the American Academy of Pediatrics that children under 2 should not view television, 74% of parents allow children to watch the tube. In fact, 25% of young children up to age 2 years have a television in their bedroom, and these children are watching an average of 2 hours a day of electronic media (Rideout, Vandewater, & Wartella, 2003). Can parents be a part of this process? A recent study for PBS conducted by Mathematica (Boller et al., 2004) found that Herculean efforts on the part of PBS in the form of educational material, coviewing opportunities, and a 90-minute workshop on parent-child interaction around the television screen left barely a mark on parent involvement in children's television viewing and had no affect on child outcomes.

The question of how to get busy parents more involved with their children is an overwhelming one. Few families are eating together, and yet research shows how crucial this is for children's development (Center on Substance Abuse & Addiction, 2002). Even Kentucky Fried Chicken has joined the movement, noting that parents rarely have meals with their children. The company uses this fact as a basis for its recent advertisement campaign that families should have fried chicken together. Perhaps we can walk the walk with museums, libraries, and media developers and jointly ask how to enrich

parenting and child development by supporting more child-parent interaction. The research is clear that children do best when they have sensitive and responsive parenting (Shonkoff & Phillips, 2000). Perhaps the social organizations in our communities can partner with us to put science into practice. We can, in turn, study whether the implementations bear any fruit in parent education and action as well as in child outcome.

Taking the walk is a critical piece of turning talk into action. We must become aware of the many organizations that have wide-reaching appeal and are seriously committed to the issues we study. By meeting these groups halfway, we not only increase the influence of our work but also learn about new and sometimes obvious questions that can further our research agenda.

Talking the Talk, Walking the Walk, and Coming Back to the Lab

There are many good studies in early literacy (e.g., Dickinson & Tabors, 2001; NICHD Early Child Care Research Network, 2005b; Senechal & LeFevre, 2002; Storch & Whitehurst, 2002). It might even be fair to say that early reading is among the few areas in which research has penetrated policy and practice. Those creating state standards for preschools are keenly aware that the development of print skills, phonics, and letter-to-sound correspondence is among the factors central to later reading success.

Yet, even with this remarkable synergy between research and practice, large holes exist. By way of example, electronic books now account for an apparently growing percentage of the book market for young children. Unlike traditional paper books, these books are nested into an electronic base and are accompanied by buttons, sounds, and gizmos. Given that these books read to the child, they signal a reading experience that appears to be more solitary. What happens when children pick up these books? Are parents likely to be involved in the reading experience? Do children engage in the kind of dialogical reading with adults that allow them to ask questions and to go beyond the words in the text? Surprisingly, we know little about the interactions that these books stimulate and even less about what children might learn from these experiences. Very few studies have examined these questions. For the few studies that are available, there are relatively mixed findings with respect to the value of electronic literature (Chera & Wood, 2003; Medwell, 1998; Ricci & Beal, 2002; Wartella, Caplovitz, & Lee, 2004).

Given the paucity of evidence especially with young children and the high use of e-books in homes and preschools (Chen, Ferdig, & Wood, 2003), a research question was born. Partnering with Fisher-Price and the children's museums in Philadelphia and Chicago, we are now investigating two questions. First, do parents and children prefer real books or e-books? Second, is the nature of the parent-child interaction different with e-books and matched regular books? Here, developments in the real world inspired research questions and hypotheses that can inform basic research as well as practice. Doing research that lies at the cusp of basic science and practice promotes a better understanding of basic processes while also offering clues to questions that are central to the well-being of the participants in our study.

CONCLUSIONS

The times are changing. In 2002, the National Science Foundation (NSF) announced that all grants would have to meet the criteria of applicability to be considered for funding. The notion of *translational* science has become part of the vernacular in recent years.

Indeed, *Child Development* now requires an abstract for lay audiences that can be shared with the public. Job announcements also reflect the change. Finally, the Society for Research in Child Development is launching a new journal called *Child Development Perspectives,* whose mission is to

> provide *accessible,* reports that summarize emerging trends or conclusions within various domains of developmental research . . . [for] research consumers (e.g., policy-makers, instructors, and professionals who work with children in clinical or intervention settings) who need access to succinct and accessible scientific summaries of developmental research. (www.srcd.org)

We italicize *accessible* to highlight that the communication of science is seen as a primary mission of the main professional society of developmental psychologists. Communication has become so key that an entire journal is being launched to do what we have been arguing for in this chapter: to make research useful to various constituencies that can profit from our findings. Once a new journal arrives with a mission that calls for the ability to describe science to professionals in related fields, perhaps we will even see some graduate programs starting to train their doctoral students to be able to think and write in this way. Surely this volume is a step in that direction as well, as it provides readers with rationales and strategies for how and why to communicate their scientific findings to the person on the street.

Having struggled to talk the talk and walk the walk in our own professional development, we think that behavioral science can and will be advanced as theory and practice begin to talk to each other. If our ultimate goal is to improve human lives, neither theory nor practice can stand alone. Instead, the field seems to be moving toward a marriage of theory and practice, a marriage based on equality and mutual respect that requires (as any good marriage) communication. The tools required for communicating science take some practice to acquire, but the rewards are great for all concerned. It is time to enter that union and to retool ourselves and our students to ensure that we can talk the talk and walk the walk.

REFERENCES

Abram, M. J., & Dowling, W. D. (1979). How readable are parenting books? *The Family Coordinator, 28,* 365–368.

Boller, K., Vogel, C., Johnson, A., Novak, T., James-Burdumy, S., Crozier, L., et al. (2004). *Using television as a teaching tool: The impacts of* Ready to Learn *workshops on parents, educators, and the children in their care* (No. PR04-63). Princeton, NJ: Mathematica Policy Research, Inc.

Bronfenbrenner, U. (1979). *The ecology of human behavior: Experiments by nature and design.* Cambridge, MA: Harvard University Press.

Bronfenbrenner, U., & Morris, P. A. (1998). The ecology of developmental processes. In R. M. Lerner (Ed.), *Theoretical models of human development* (5th ed., Vol. 1, pp. 357–414). New York: John Wiley.

Bruer, J. (1999). *The myth of the first three years: A new understanding of early brain development and lifelong learning.* New York: Free Press.

Center on Substance Abuse and Addiction. (2002). *Family dinners protect kids from substance abuse.* New York: National Center on Addiction and Substance Abuse at Columbia University. Retrieved from http://www.casacolumbia.org/absolut enm/templates/PressReleases.asp?articleid=330&zoneid=47

Chen, M., Ferdig, R., & Wood, A. (2003). Understanding technology-enhanced storybooks and their roles in teaching and learning: An investigation of electronic storybooks in education. *Journal of Literacy and Technology, 3,* 1–15.

Chera, P., & Wood, C. (2003). Animated multimedia "talking books" can promote phonological awareness in children beginning to read. *Learning and Instruction, 11,* 33–52.

Christakis, D. A., Zimmerman, F. J., Di Giuseppe, D. L., & McCarty, C. A. (2004). Early television exposure and subsequent attentional problems in children. *Child Care, Health and Development, 30,* 559–560.

Dickinson, D., & Tabors, P. O. (Eds.). (2001). *Beginning literacy with language: Young children learning at home and school.* Baltimore: Paul H. Brookes.

Dillon, S. (2006, March 26). Schools cut back subjects to push reading and math. *New York Times.*

Elkind, D. (1981). *The hurried child.* Reading, MA: Addison-Wesley.

Foster, E. M., & Kalil, A. (2005). Developmental psychology and public policy: Progress and prospects. *Developmental Psychology, 41,* 827–833.

Golinkoff, R., & Hirsh-Pasek, K. (1999). *How babies talk: The magic and mystery of language acquisition.* New York: Dutton/Penguin.

Golinkoff, R. M., & Hirsh-Pasek, K. (2006). Baby wordsmith: From associationist to social sophisticate. *Current Directions in Psychological Science, 15,* 30–33.

Gopnik, A., Meltzoff, A. N., & Kuhl, P. K. (1999). *The scientist in the crib: Minds, brains and how children learn.* New York: HarperCollins.

Hirsh-Pasek, K., & Golinkoff, R. (2003). *Einstein never used flashcards: How our children really learn and why they need to play more and memorize less.* Emmaus, PA: Rodale Press.

Hirsh-Pasek, K., & Golinkoff, R. M. (2006). Brains in a box: Do new age toys deliver on the promise? In R. Harwood (Ed.), *Child development in a changing society.* Hoboken, NJ: John Wiley.

Hirsh-Pasek, K., Golinkoff, R. M., Singer, D., & Berk, L. (2007). *All work and no play: A call for evidence-based preschool education.* Manuscript submitted for publication.

Hirsh-Pasek, K., Kochanoff, A., Newcombe, N., & deVilliers, J. (2005). *Using scientific knowledge to inform preschoolers: Making the case for "empirical validity"* (Social Policy Report, XIX). Ann Arbor, MI: Society for Research in Child Development.

James, W. (1890). *The principles of psychology.* New York: Holt.

Kaiser Foundation. (2005, December). *A teacher in the living room: Educational media for infants, toddlers and preschoolers.* Menlo Park, CA: Author.

Konold, T. R., & Pianta, R. C. (2005). Empirically-derived, person-oriented patterns of school readiness in typically-developing children: Description and prediction to first-grade achievement. *Applied Developmental Science, 9,* 174–187.

Kuhl, P. K., Tsao, F. M., & Liu, H. M. (2003). Foreign-language experience in infancy: Effects of short-term exposure and social interaction on phonetic learning. *Proceedings of the National Academy of Sciences, 100,* 9096–9101.

Luthar, S., & Latendresse, S. (2005). Children of the affluent: Challenges in well-being. *Current Directions in Psychological Science, 14,* 49–53.

Medwell, J. (1998). The talking books project: Some further insights into the use of talking books to develop reading. *Reading, 32,* 3–8.

Morawski, J. (2000). Social psychology a century ago. *American Psychologist, 55,* 427–430.

Neisser, U. (1976). *Cognition and reality.* San Francisco: Freeman.

NICHD Early Child Care Research Network. (2005a). Early child care and children's development in the primary grades: Follow-up results from the NICHD Study of Early Child Care. *American Educational Research Journal, 42,* 537–557.

NICHD Early Child Care Research Network. (2005b). Pathways to reading: The role of oral language in the transition to reading. *Developmental Psychology, 41,* 428–442.

Pellegrini, A. D. (2005). *Recess: Its role in development and education.* Mahwah, NJ: Lawrence Erlbaum.

Pettito, L. A., & Marentette, P. (1991). Babbling in the manual mode: Evidence for the ontogeny of language. *Science, 251,* 1483–1496.

Pruden, S., Hirsh-Pasek, K., Golinkoff, R., & Hennon, E. (2006). The birth of words: Ten-month-olds learn words through perceptual salience. *Child Development, 77,* 266–281.

Raver, C. C. (2003). *Emotions matter: Making the case for the role of young children's emotional development for early school readiness* (Social policy report). Ann Arbor, MI: Society for Research in Child Development.

Ricci, C. M., & Beal, C. R. (2002). The effect of interactive media on children's story memory. *Journal of Educational Psychology, 94,* 138–144.

Rideout, V. J., Vandewater, E. A., & Wartella, E. A. (2003). *Zero to six: Electronic media in the lives of infants, toddlers and preschoolers.* Menlo Park, CA: Kaiser Family Foundation.

Saffran, J., Aslin, R., & Newport, E. (1996). Statistical learning by 8-month-old infants. *Science, 274*, 1926–1928.

Senechal, M., & LeFevre, J. (2002). Parental involvement in the development of children's reading skill: A five-year longitudinal study. *Child Development, 73*, 445–460.

Shonkoff, J. (2000). Science, policy and practice: Three cultures in search of a shared mission. *Child Development, 71*, 181–187.

Shonkoff, J., & Phillips, D. (Eds.). (2000). *From neurons to neighborhood.* Washington, DC: National Academy Press.

Singer, D., Golinkoff, R. M., & Hirsh-Pasek, K. (Eds.). (2007). *PLAY = LEARNING: How play motivates and enhances children's cognitive and social-emotional growth.* New York: Oxford University Press.

Steinberg, L., & Scott, E. (2003). Less guilty by reason of adolescence: Developmental immaturity, diminished responsibility, and the juvenile death penalty. *American Psychologist, 58*, 1009–1018.

Storch, S., & Whitehurst, G. (2002). Oral language and code-related precursors to reading: Evidence from a longitudinal structural model. *Developmental Psychology, 38*, 934–948.

Viney, W., & King, D. B. (1998). *A history of psychology* (2nd ed.). Boston: Allyn & Bacon.

Wartella, E., Caplovitz, A. G., & Lee, J. (2004). From baby Einstein to Leapfrog, from Doom to the Sims, from instant messaging to Internet chat rooms. *Social Policy Report, 18*, 3–19.

Watson, J. B. (1913). Psychology as the behaviorist views it. *Psychological Review, 20*, 158–177.

Wozniak, R. H. (1991). *Childhood: Viewer's guide.* New York: WNET.

Wynn, K. (1998). Psychological foundations in number: Numerical competence in human infants. *Trends in Cognitive Science, 2*, 296–303.

Zigler, E., & Bishop-Josef, S. J. (2004). Play under siege: A historical overview. In E. Zigler, D. Singer, & S. Bishop-Josef (Eds.), *Children's play: The roots of reading* (pp. 1–15). Washington, DC: Zero to Three Press.

CHAPTER 13

Working With Science Information Specialists

Earle M. Holland

"Pay no attention to the man behind the curtain," booms the ominous voice of the all-powerful Oz, wizard of the Emerald City. Dorothy's inquisitive pet has pulled aside the cloth, unveiling the sideshow charlatan whose knobs, levers, belching fire, and smoke have bamboozled the citizenry into blissful and idyllic security.

As an adult, every time I've watched that scene from Victor Fleming's 1939 classic film, *The Wizard of Oz,* I've been struck by its parallel to the role public information officers play in the communication of research to the masses. Not the charlatan part, to be sure, but the idea that there is an unseen player in the process who is essential to its success. That's where the linkage resides in my mind.

Most people gleefully maintain an infantile belief in the machinery by which research findings routinely flow out among the masses. They envision a "eureka moment" on the part of a researcher, after which that new knowledge osmotically wafts from laboratory into the populace. Comforting though that might be, I've never seen it happen in real life in more than three decades of covering research. In truth, this middleman—this bridge between scholars and the public—is the oft-ignored figure at most research institutions who is most responsible for the transfer of scientific knowledge.

What follows is a look into the process, the people, and the problems surrounding the interaction of behavioral and social scientists and the news media, as well as the bridge that science information specialists become in linking the two. Scholars who've been interviewed before may see this as old hat and be tempted to skip this offering. I urge them not to since most researchers I have encountered in my 33 years of covering science consistently fail to "study" the media and how they inform the public. Younger scholars who've never faced a reporter should pay close attention. Explaining one's work before the unblinking eye of a television camera, a radio reporter's microphone, or the edgy questions of a newspaper journalist is guaranteed to cause a weakening of the knees. Navigating this strange and unfamiliar territory has abundant rewards to the scholar, but like any other discipline, it takes work and study to lead one to knowledge. Consider this a handy primer to keep you safe.

WHO ARE THESE PEOPLE?

Their profession bears many names: public information, public relations, public affairs, communications, science communications, outreach, and even marketing, in some cases. They can work at universities and colleges, at federal agencies or foundations, in businesses and industry, and various other venues. And while the names can denote significantly different approaches, philosophies, and tactics, the core similarity rests with their role in translating research findings and presenting them in a context appealing to varying audiences. Without these practitioners, most research advances would remain hidden inside academic disciplines forever. And yet few researchers are ever instructed to seek out these *aides de camp* in the ongoing battle for academic recognition by the news media and the public.

In many cases, these people are former reporters or editors who have had experience working as daily journalists. In other circumstances, they may be graduates of public relations programs at journalism schools with a goal of best representing the institution they work for. Still others—currently a minority—have come through specialized science writing programs that focused intently on the different challenges that reporting on research demands. In all cases, they tend to have a strong knowledge of the needs, behaviors, values, and stimuli that guide working journalists to report on science.

Just as they come from differing backgrounds, the jobs they hold may also differ widely. Some will work for an institution's public relations or public affairs office and be specifically assigned to certain "beats"—life sciences or clinical sciences or physical sciences, for example. In these cases, they will provide communications support for an array of needs, not just research. Consequently, these individuals tend to be more generalists than specialists when it comes to

science writing. In other cases, they may be responsible only for reporting on research, leaving other communications/PR tasks to colleagues.

Likewise, their reporting line is a variable. Those in the public relations/public affairs offices are responsible first for representing the institution as a whole. Others may report through an office of research and therefore only attend to research interests. Still others may report to the heads of smaller units within an organization and subsequently have a narrower focus.

For behavioral and social science researchers, these distinctions can offer clues to how supportive they can expect these communicators to be. In the best situations, these professionals will acknowledge their own chain of command but will concentrate on the needs of the individual researcher. In their minds, the larger institution can take care of itself. When the needs of researchers are supported, the entire institution will benefit.

In previous chapters of this volume, other experts have focused on the mass media, both the similarities threading through various forms—newspapers, broadcast, magazines, and so on—and the distinctive differences characterizing each one, presenting both advantages and disadvantages for journalists and sources alike. But fundamentally, they all depend on a simple prerequisite—that is, that the information they disseminate be "news."

Even within the diverse field of journalism, people struggle with clear definitions of news. In many ways, an almost indistinct and amorphous mechanism sifts news from nonnews—we know it when we see it. Such sixth-sense analyses won't work for the rest of the world, however, and a better standard is needed. I've always argued that "news" is something that would be "new" to the readership, listenership, viewership, or audience to which it is directed. But that's not quite enough either. For something to be "news," it must be important as well, not just important to the experts but valuable for most others, a data point that is enriching in some essential, everyday way, a context.

News is the coin of the realm with the mass media; therefore, it is the gold sought out by science communicators. And this is a key point for academics to remember: That truly reaching the lay public is often impossible, but reaching the gatekeepers who determine what is news, and how much of it flows to the public, is an attainable goal.

Another chapter of this book that covers scientists using the Internet mentions that some researchers may avoid the middleman of the news media and point their message directly to the public through Web sites (see Chapter 14). That is, of course, a choice open to all researchers, but with it comes a host of caveats and constraints. First, an individual Web site usually lacks the imprimatur of a larger organization and, therefore, that organization's credibility. Also, many organizations will limit a researchers' content on an individual Web site to a curriculum vitae (CV), a list of specialties and publications, and perhaps a picture. The intent here is to humanize the organization by showing the people behind it. What the organization does not want is hundreds of researcher Web sites doling out information unconstrained.

In these cases, the public information officer (PIO) will probably not be an ally if the researcher wants to exceed the institutional norm. But if scholars want to operate within institutional constraints, the PIOs can provide links to stories they have done on the scholar's work, helping readers to better understand the science behind the studies.

My career has mostly been spent at large public research universities, but the rules that govern science communications on such campuses usually apply quite well to other venues. These locales are populated mainly by research faculty whose charge it is to both teach the next generation of scholars the best

science available at the time and also to create new science and discovery. The latter of those duties is the mine from which the science communicators seek nuggets and gems.

Most major research institutions have specific staff hired to explain and, in many cases, publicize, that science. Those who do it well understand that theirs is a true balancing act. On one hand, it is critical to be precise and accurate, to convey exactly what a scientific advance actually is, without exaggeration and with all appropriate caveats. On the other hand, it has to be news, and that means a translation that flushes all jargon, downplays the caveats, and emphasizes the future potential importance of the work. Living up to both standards is no small feat, but both are essential in gaining and maintaining the respect of researcher and reporter alike.

HOW THE SYSTEM WORKS

The usual scenario goes something like this: Realizing his or her work has yielded important findings, the researcher(s) writes a paper and submits it to a prominent journal in the field. (The same holds true for major papers presented at national meetings as well.) Once the journal accepts the paper, the researcher usually pats himself or herself on the back and may perhaps inform the department chair before returning to the next phase of research.

And herein lies the problem. For effective communication of the science, someone must inform the science communicator.

In the best situations, the researcher contacts the PIO, explains that the paper was accepted, and offers to send a copy of the manuscript (or galleys, if available) to the PIO for a review to determine potential news value. If that is positive, an interview is set up, the conversation takes place, and a news release is drafted. At most institutions, the policy requires the researcher to review that release.

This review is sometimes a minefield for both parties. Scholars are accustomed to having near-total control over the content of their papers. This means not only the technical specifics of the research but also its presentation, style, and order. The review of these research releases should not offer scholars that level of authority. Instead, they are asked to review the content to ensure that it is "essentially" correct. I say "essentially" rather than "precisely" on purpose since the intent of the release is to offer a general understanding of the scholarship, not a detailed one.

The reason for this is simple: Most audiences don't want—or need—a detailed explanation. They're content with a general understanding. For that reason, the PIO will often reserve the right of editorial presentation, that is, how the story is told. This ensures that readers will be drawn toward the research findings, instead of being mired in the detail. Scholars need to accept the expertise of the PIOs in the realm of storytelling, just as the PIOs accept the expertise of the scholar in his or her discipline.

In the end, the scholar ensures that the science is "correct" at a level of a general audience, and the PIO ensures the story will be read.

It is essential, however, that the researcher remember that the audience for the release includes journalists—whose job it is to be surrogates for the public—not other scientists, so the review is solely to ensure that the content is generally accurate. Once it is reviewed, the PIO then distributes it to members of the news media for their consideration.

So the take-home message for researchers is to inform their science communications officer about an accepted journal article—or meeting presentation—early, that is, either before the publication date or the scheduled presentation. Most practitioners ask for at least a week's notice but would gladly accept more if possible.

Depending on the nature of the research, the editorial quality of the news release, the extent of distribution to the news media, the other competing "news of the day," and a half-dozen other variables, the story could lead to coverage ranging from a brief mention in the local weekly newspaper to a story in major national media such as the *Washington Post* or National Public Radio. Part of the PIO's role is to advise researchers on the reasonable expectations for media coverage of their work. It may be less or more than what scholars would think.

WHAT CAN GO WRONG?

Ideally, the process proceeds normally. The release interests reporters who do their own interviews. Their stories appear in print or over the airwaves. The researcher has a generally positive experience and, in turn, remembers that his or her work may be newsworthy in the future and that he or she should keep the PIO regularly informed of advances. Would that it were always so. In truth, wrenches can fall into the machinery at any point, either killing the potential story or shifting its emphasis away from the true nature of the research. For example:

• A release saying that varying the stress on laboratory animals during experiments can alter their susceptibility to cholesterol buildup can suddenly become a story saying that hugging your spouse more often can help save him or her from a potential coronary.

• A release reporting on the true pattern of sexual interactions among teens and how that affects public health planning can rapidly grow to a controversy over the propriety of public university scientists studying adolescent sex.

• A project centering on a potential new mechanism for DNA analysis that focuses on mitochondria gets converted into an exposé on institutional researchers' supposed work to identify Bigfoot or Sasquatch.

Each of these scenarios played out at my institution, as have hundreds of others, leading us to constantly emphasize to researchers the inherent unpredictability of communicating their work to the news media. That leads more than a few to ask, "Why bother?" Answers abound. The public has a right to know. Science coverage is important for public policy. In many instances, findings can improve health or quality of life. And sharing the researchers' passion for wonder helps the public support science. All of these are true, but at the end of the day, researchers need to remember that an essential part of science is the sharing of knowledge.

GETTING DOWN TO BUSINESS

So far, we've discussed news, the media, types of PIOs, the process of releasing news, potential minefields, and justifications for science communications. It's time to dig deeper into the first essential step—the interaction between the PIO and researcher, how to enhance that dialogue, and what is reasonable to expect and why. In many ways, it can be like an adolescent's first dance—whom shall I ask, who leads, will I seem foolish, what if the music slows. . . .

Much of the success depends on the actual dynamics of this relationship: How do the players interact, how do they see their respective roles, how closely aligned are their individual goals, and do they see themselves as partners? This last point is potentially problematic. Researchers usually hold a reasonably prominent place in an organization. They tend to see others as members of their team, though lesser in stature. And those individuals not on their team quite often are seen as even more subservient. But scientists who view these science PIOs as support staff or functionaries risk offending the very same professionals who might help raise their research to public prominence.

As I explained above, in successful interactions, the researcher and PIO see each other as equals, experts in their respective fields who seek to combine their talents to reach a point unattainable to either working alone. It is the same logic governing scientific collaborations between disciplines. Unfortunately, it can quickly devolve into a power struggle over control of the message and specifics of the content. Many researchers, assured by their own editorial experience from publishing in journals, assume a mantle of expertise in communications as well as their own field. But if that were actually true, there would be no need for PIOs—and clearly, the numbers of these individuals at research institutions have been growing rapidly for the past decade.

The PIO's main task is to translate the researcher's discoveries into a language readily understandable to the public and to the journalists who serve it. But that's not all. They also must present those discoveries in a way so that both public and journalist will easily recognize the significance of the work. It isn't enough for the scientist to affirm that the new work is important—the reader must be able to deduce that quickly from the story. How the story is actually told, what aspects are included or rejected, the context and potential—that is the purview of the PIO.

I used to shock students and researchers alike by saying that "success is a reporter getting the story 70% right." The researchers—most of them teaching faculty as well—quickly responded that 70% warranted a low C, if not a D, in their world. And students saw that benchmark as an easily attainable goal, not one requiring much diligence. Both groups were wrong. The public didn't sign up for a course; they didn't pay tuition and therefore have invested nothing but their curiosity into understanding such stories. Making them work too hard is a sure way to convince them to shift their reading from science to sports. Conversely, if interested in the topic or the news, they will devote whatever energy necessary to understanding the text.

WHAT DRIVES COMMUNICATION?

Motivation is the key in all effective communications. I've argued often that anything can be communicated assuming two criteria are met. First, you must be a good storyteller. And second, you must have an audience open to a good story. Applying that to research is actually easier than many might think. At its core, all research is a mystery story. What happened? How? Why? What did it affect? Who's to blame? How did it work? What would happen if...? People inherently love mysteries and will follow one for chapters on end. Science mystery stories in the news media—if told well—are much shorter and appealing to most readers, listeners, or viewers.

The PIO's task is to figure out, with each project he or she covers, what the elements of that mystery story actually are, how they should be presented and explained, and why the nameless masses of the public should care about that work. The researcher's role is to understand that this is a culture somewhat outside his or her own, with its own rules and paths, and through which the PIO should help guide the reader.

Consider the following as an example: Most academic papers, or presentations, for that matter, emulate the Bible's first chapter: "In the beginning, there was...." This Genesis-like approach brings the reader up to date with scholarship to understand the new discovery. Research stories—be they stories by the news media or research releases by institutions—solve the mystery at the beginning. They tell the reader what is new and why it is important. Then they backtrack to fill in the blanks. This approach ensures that the reader knows why he or she is investing the time to read the story.

If a researcher mandates his or her way of storytelling over that of the PIO, chances are readers will ignore the research altogether. In some cases, the PIO will simply refuse to do the story and move on to interesting work done by the other researchers who are more understanding. Giving up that control is a difficult challenge for many researchers, but unless they do, they will never effectively work with skilled communicators.

TRANSLATING THE BEHAVIORAL AND SOCIAL SCIENCES

In the broad field of research communications, differences between disciplines are often minimal. While the scholarship varies between the physical sciences, the clinical sciences, the biological sciences, or the social sciences, the process is essentially the same.

It always begins with research questions. Hypotheses follow as does experimental design. Data are uncovered and analyzed until conclusions can be drawn, and from these, researchers can extrapolate their findings to a larger context. The basic scientific method applies regardless of discipline. But there are significant differences at play here, and for research communicators, the behavioral and social sciences often present the greatest challenges.

Young science writers see cosmology, molecular biology, and genetics as the most daunting fields they must cover. They see it that way based mainly on their own weaknesses in understanding the basics of such subjects. Quantum physics is deemed complex because it isn't perceived as a part of our day-to-day existence. Psychology, sociology, or anthropology, however, is all about our daily lives and therefore seems more familiar, less difficult. That is the stereotype the behavioral and social sciences have borne for decades—they are easier, not really science. Pity the science writers who believe that. They forget that the rules governing most of those "elder" sciences have long been written. Those governing the behavioral and social sciences are, in some cases, still works in progress.

Add to this problem the dilemma of public perception. Since the behavioral and social sciences involve our daily lives, they are familiar and readily applicable. They lack the sometimes "foreign" status of the natural sciences, giving most readers a perceived comfort level with the issues that they don't feel with geology or astronomy.

In practice, this represents a huge obstacle in research communications surrounding the behavioral and social sciences. Often the news media fail to recognize the research as such and assign feature writers instead of science writers to handle the coverage. This means that the reporting is done by journalists, at best, only vaguely familiar with the scientific method and, at worst, totally oblivious about how research is done.

The "Duh!" Effect

Moreover, there is the "duh!" effect. Consider these examples from actual behavioral and social science research we reported at my institution:

- When it comes to living together with a man, daughters often follow the lead of their mothers. Research showed that young adult women whose mothers reported cohabitation were 57% more likely than other women to report cohabitation themselves.

- Children of divorced parents can benefit when they split time between their parents' homes—but the positive impact can be offset by ongoing conflict between the parents. Without parental conflict, children in physical joint-custody arrangements showed fewer behavioral problems than children under the custody of a single parent.

- Children who grow up with one or more siblings get along better with their classmates in kindergarten than do only children, new research shows. Teachers rated students who had at least one sibling as

better able to form and maintain friendships, get along with people who are different, comfort and help other children, express feelings in a positive way, and show sensitivity to the feelings of others.

Hearing about these studies for the first time, the average person on the street is likely to respond with a "Well, duh!" signifying the obvious nature of that information based on his or her own life experiences. Simply put, the findings seem to make perfectly good sense, so why would anyone waste their time doing research to discover that? Sadly, that response permeates the news media, reinforcing the perception that behavioral and social science is a poor sister to the other seemingly more sophisticated fields of research.

In actuality, the news media seldom realize that much of which is considered "common sense" has never been tested scientifically, and frankly, that portion that has undergone the scrutiny of researchers is often proved wrong or, at least, misunderstood. Reporters need to be reminded that behavioral and social science scholars have to apply solid scientific methods to these seemingly obvious questions if the field is ever to lose its perception of being a lesser science. And if the translation of those studies remains with scientifically naive feature writers, who knows where there stories will lead—thus the need for the scholar-science writer partnership.

Knowing that the "duh effect" might apply to their work, behavioral and social researchers should decide in advance how to head off that reaction, perhaps offering the reason why "people" believed something to be true and why their beliefs might be wrong or at least ill directed. The scholar who does this well demonstrates both to the reader and the news media that he or she retains the "common sense" of the masses and therefore deserves their attention.

It is a simple additional effort but one that will pay off enormously in communicating about the science.

Where Behavioral and Social Science Stories Are Born

As said before, most important behavioral and social science stories in the news media derive from reports in journals or presentations at major meetings. Both venues provide the end results of studies and the necessary "news hook" for reporters. Knowing that, good public information officers will monitor the contents of dozens of such journals and the programs of major meetings, looking first for presentations by "their" scholars and, from among those, selecting which ones seem immediately translatable. The exercise of this "news judgment" is perhaps the most valuable action a public information officer can take.

Public affairs offices on campuses mimic, to a certain extent, conventional media newsrooms in that while some staffers cover the waterfront, most focus on specific areas, or "beats," which limits their responsibilities and allows them to enhance their understanding of particular fields. Campus PIOs are likewise categorized. At Ohio State University, there are four of us covering all research, and of those, one specific staffer follows the social sciences. At smaller institutions with only one science writer, he or she may cover all scholarship. The key point is, however, that each of these professionals brings to the table a substantive understanding of research and a specific expertise with the academic disciplines involved. That should allow behavioral and social science researchers a greater comfort level in partnering with PIOs to report their findings to the media and the public.

Some stories, however, are not hinged on a journal article or a meeting presentation. They may have a seasonal aspect, for instance.

Recurrent media coverage of so-called winter depression and sunburn prevention are easy examples of this type. Other stories may focus on an emerging issue where researchers may be working but where no clear-cut conclusions have been drawn. And there are always the "reaction-to" stories, where an Ohio reporter might interview a local researcher about another scholar's work reported across the country. These efforts are built on the premise that all readers are "local" and trust local information more than they do distant experts.

At some institutions, a healthy share of the public information work focuses on such reaction-to stories. For one thing, they are easy—every institution has a psychologist who might be willing to comment on the work of an out-of-state colleague—and the return on the PIO's invested effort is media coverage for the institution without having to perform the work. Obvious ethical questions arise, and for my part, we routinely let such opportunities pass. For other PIOs, reaction-to stories are their bread and butter.

For behavioral and social science researchers, it may be worthwhile to peruse their institution's "news" Web site to determine what kinds of stories dominate their coverage. Remember that it is easier for a reporter—and for a PIO—to produce a reaction-to story than it is to report on the results of original work, mainly because there is less to understand. And while this certainly is understandable human nature, it simply isn't good science communications. At institutions where a large fraction of their stories are reaction-to, PIOs are basically acknowledging that their comments on the work of others are more substantive than their own scholars' work. Reporters understand that—scholars should as well.

Let me be clear: There is nothing wrong with reaction-to stories if that is all an institution has to offer. They have a value and certainly deserve a scholar's participation.

But simply put, original scholarship gains more attention and respect from the news media, so that is where the most effort should be concentrated. Given the chance to comment for a reaction-to story, scholars should always say yes. But they shouldn't have this as the focus for their media exposure.

One approach gaining popularity is for researchers to provide "lay abstracts" to accompany their papers or precede their presentations. While well intended, this practice has its drawbacks. As I said before, few researchers excel at writing for the general public, and fewer still have a "nose for news." The lay abstracts that I have seen—and I see many regularly—focus more on length than understanding, and that is their great deficiency. In effect, the first several paragraphs of a good research story are a better abstract for the work than what is routinely offered now. If a researcher partners with a PIO immediately upon acceptance of a journal article or proposed presentation, the PIO's story will provide that abstract-of-sorts.

Abstracts also play a role in attracting media attention when they are requested by professional organizations prior to the meetings where the talks will be delivered. In my experience, when it comes to courting news coverage, most of these groups would treasure a well-written research story from a scholar's institution more than they would a compact scientist-generated abstract.

Working with such professional groups may present additional power struggles for both PIO and scholar. Some associations want to manage all coverage of studies presented at their meetings or in their journals. Some will offer to partner with institutions to do "joint" releases that have been vetted by both entities.

I'm an admitted Neanderthal in this regard: We will not "partner" in that sense with any other entity. The best we will do is provide our own releases and set their release date to coincide with the presentation or publication. While many institutions are much more welcoming of these arrangements, I've always believed that the merging of different institutions' agendas dilutes the strength of the science reporting. My responsibility as a PIO is to my scholars, and I will not trade that off to partner with another institution. Others of my peers disagree.

The Writer-Editor Tug-of-War

Science writers who cover physics or genomics or cosmology seldom experience the kinds of editorial grappling that behavioral and social science writers can with their editors. All editors draw on their own experiences, as well as their journalistic abilities, to oversee the stories of their writers, and few have more than a fleeting knowledge of those fields. Because of that, they can feel less empowered to fiddle with the verbiage for fear of getting the science wrong. But with behavioral and social science stories, editors perceive a broad license to actively participate in the storytelling. After all, editors are all, by definition, acute observers of society, of behavior and human nature. That self-assuredness reinforces their willingness to reach beyond their true knowledge, and the resulting reporting can become downright disastrous.

In truth, I fall into that trap often. Since I have one of the very best social science writers on my staff, Jeff Grabmeier, who covers most of our work in these disciplines, I find myself most often playing that editor's role rather than the reporter's. And this allows me to critique his reporting with actually very little understanding of the particular research involved. Surprisingly, this is not automatically bad, but it certainly is dangerous. In reviewing his stories, which were based on his reading of the journal papers and interviews with researchers, I will look for those opportunities to extrapolate and simplify the findings, usually seeking connections that might not seem readily apparent. When this works, it converts the story into one on a slightly higher plane than might normally be possible, and in doing so, it becomes much more interesting to reporters in the news media and therefore to the public at large.

But the risk here is great. That type of extrapolation—while useful and exciting—most often exceeds the scope of the research. Or, as Jeff so often tells me, "But that isn't what the study was all about," or "The research just didn't look at that."

From the editor's viewpoint, the obvious conclusion or extrapolation is much more important. Moreover, it often meshes with the lay public's perception of the obvious, or near obvious, which enhances the likelihood that readers will take the time to absorb it. But it is still wrong.

This is a chance for the researcher to experiment outside his or her discipline. When the PIO posits a conclusion that overreaches the research, it signals where he or she is headed with the story. A smart scholar can quickly detect that and redirect the PIO along a better path. That incorrect extrapolation carries with it the "thinking" of the PIO and maps a direction both writer and scholar can head. The scholar's role, however, is to navigate, not to halt, the progress of public understanding. PIOs will greatly appreciate this kind of map making.

Good science communications never exceed the conclusions based on the data, no matter how tempting or obvious that next step may be. In our case, I'm smart enough to listen to Jeff's reminders. That's not always the case among the world of PIOs and reporters. Our comfort level with the behavioral and social sciences should not trick us into assuming our own expertise.

If Only They Had Done That Work . . .

The potential pitfalls surrounding behavioral and social science reporting on campus are frightening, assuming the PIO is savvy enough to recognize them, or the researcher is aware of their existence. Both PIOs and journalists see themselves as surrogates of the public, and in that role, their naïveté can be an enormous advantage in selecting the research that will interest the masses. But like the public, they are apt to make assumptions—the greatest of which is that scholars and scientists have done the research "proving" a belief or event or fact. The truth is, however, that in many cases, those proofs have not been done, and researchers are working on assumptions rather than conclusions. This isn't bad, of course, unless the public assumes that the proofs exist.

Assumptions aren't bad—they just need to be acknowledged, and therein lies the frequent problem. Researchers may mistakenly believe that everyone accepts the validity of the assumption because their peers do, but the public will not. Scholars would be wise to point out in detail what is and what is not known in their research. This helps the PIO to build boundaries on the information and define it for the reader. Facts can stand on their own, whereas assumptions need logical arguments and observations to back them up. Also, these elements add a valuable comfort to a story, placing it more in the context of a conversation rather than sterile rhetoric.

Generally speaking, after they have competed formal schooling, readers, viewers, and listeners don't want to be taught—lectures and messages sent in one direction are seldom successful. But "teaching" is different from "learning." The public, when interested, will thirst for information they have decided is important. Our job is to ensure that it is.

Perhaps now is the time to warn against jargon, the vocabulary of a discipline and the problems it raises. A somewhat unique language and lexicon exists in nearly every field of research. It is the shorthand for scholars, expediting their conversations and adding precision to their dialogues. And in particle physics or molecular biology or organic chemistry, such jargon stands out as if it were in scarlet neon lights. But in many of the behavioral and social sciences, their jargon resembles common verbiage and can be taken too lightly outside of the field. Words that fit comfortably into daily conversation may also hold specific—and sometimes unexpected—meaning to researchers but would be misunderstood by reporters or the public. PIOs who cover the behavioral and social sciences usually understand this risk and may subtly correct for the differences in the stories they prepare. When there is a possibility of such dual-meaning terms in research, scholars would be well served to point that out.

When Things Go Wrong

Most of this discussion has centered on the straightforward telling of the research story, the interpretation of publications and presentations, and the novelty of individual studies. These are "good news" stories, and they represent the majority of work facing most science PIOs. But not all of it. Research communications inherently includes the areas of research risk and how to deal with them. These are episodes that involve human subjects, laboratory animals, radiation safety, biosafety, fraud and misconduct in science, computer security, infection control, and other troublesome realms. Those of us in the field may reference these as occasions "when *60 Minutes* is on the phone," but they are a real probability for most research institutions. Prudent PIOs and researchers alike are wise to prepare for it.

In truth, few behavioral and social scientists will face the typical campus problems of radiation safety or biosafety or infection control in their work. And while they certainly use human subjects in their research—and therefore must abide by strict federal regulations—they aren't testing new chemotherapeutic

regimens and risking patient deaths in their studies. So it is understandable that behavioral and social scientists might think they are secure against research risks. It is also unwise. Insightful scholars will remember that the public worries about the "dark side" of research as well.

An entire field of crisis communications has arisen in the past decades, an area of expertise that is called upon at the worst possible times for an organization. And it is a field that surprisingly owes much to the behavioral and social sciences in that it relies on the discipline of risk perception. Hinged closely to the evolution of the environmental movement, the study of perceived risks has helped to explain why the public—often along with the news media—respond to events in the way that they do.

Two rules govern most approaches to crisis communications: Tell the truth, and tell it quickly. The first, while seeming empirically obvious, is often the hardest for organizations—and their researchers—to adopt. The primary roadblock to that is a fear that the public will understandably react negatively if it finds an organization or individual has done wrong. In reality, the opposite is more often true. The public seems inclined to forgive mistakes that are openly acknowledged, especially if accompanied by assurances that those mistakes won't be repeated. It shows the common humanity of institutions and their people and their willingness to learn from their errors. Though the public may not forget infractions, it will often forgive them. And in many cases, the only "problem" at issue is the natural reluctance to admit fault or reveal secrets.

The second rule—"tell it quickly"—has grown more and more important in recent decades with the evolution of the news media. Some three decades ago, communications in the United States was governed mainly by the three main television networks and a handful of national newspapers, each of which had mainly a once-a-day cycle for the release of news. Now, with the number of networks and cable channels reaching into the hundreds, with the Internet's blogs and news Web sites, there is no news cycle—the hunger for news is constant. That means if there is something gone awry that is awaiting discovery, then organizations and individuals are running out of time as they wait.

Once enough information on a negative event or issue is available for initial coverage, then it should be released. An organization that waits to release information on such topics abdicates its option to present it in a fair light and, in effect, elects to be pushed into a defensive role. That places the public and the media in an adversarial role against an organization or its researchers, and such positions are hard ones to defend. In the end, the reputations of the slow-to-tell tend to be harmed much more than those willing to announce their problems and the solutions that they have adopted.

Some Examples

Old Bones. Some years ago, a reporter from a rather obscure West Virginia news media outlet called raising questions about a collection of Native American remains he'd heard were in storage in Ohio State's anthropology department. The remains were stored in hundreds of boxes after having been rescued from being discarded by another university. A grad student decades ago had noticed the boxed remains set aside as trash and asked for them for study. That institution agreed, and the bones were trucked to Ohio State University and stored until researchers could begin a detailed study of the remains.

But as sometimes occurs, study space and funding were scarce, and the remains continued to be stored on campus, slowly slipping from memory. Only the reporter's call decades later brought the "Buffalo 600"—as the remains had become known—back to light.

Several points made this a potential crisis: Where once field researchers could cavalierly harvest Native American remains, this has evolved in recent years into a sensitive cultural issue; claims of ownership of the remains were unclear, as was access to the original site from which they were taken; and the federal Native American Graves Protection and Repatriation Act specifically required the "holder" of the remains to only release them "upon the request of a known lineal descendant of the Native American or of the tribe," and that hadn't occurred.

Faculty were upset, the anthropology chair felt scapegoated, and the institution—while it would love to relinquish its control of the remains—was legally bound to secure them. The media, however—and the public they represented—wondered why things were so complicated.

In the end, the partnership between the anthropology department, the science PIO, and the institution's attorneys melded to provide ample information on both the history of the remains and the constraints binding the institution from releasing them. Coverage could have been a nightmare of accusations against the university, but instead, the stories provided insight into the complexities of honoring the dead.

Bigfoot DNA. That same chair of anthropology was a closet cryptozoologist—that is, a researcher who studies creatures whose existence is uncertain. Years before, he was one of the first Americans allowed into some of the more remote areas of the People's Republic of China to search for the hairy Wildman of local legend there. The researcher was convinced that the beast existed but, rather than being an unknown, that it was the rare golden monkey. And through his negotiations with Chinese scholars, he had encountered one who claimed to have found "Wildman" hairs, the roots of which might provide DNA that could point to the animal's lineage.

At the same time, across campus, a grad student in molecular biology was finishing her master's thesis research and devising a potential new mechanism for DNA analysis, this one focusing on mitochondrial, rather than nuclear, DNA. To test the new assay, she needed both known and unknown samples to analyze. That's where the Wildman hairs came in. And in one of those wonderful collaborative arrangements that universities offer, the hairs were used as the unknowns.

Both the biologists and the anthropologists were aware that a finding pointing to a new species—even one linking of the hairs to a known creature—would be newsworthy, so they swore each other to secrecy until the work was completed. And then the anthropology chair agreed to an interview with a local science reporter on a completely different topic.

Following classic reporter's behavior, the journalist asked the department chair if there was anything else new going on. The chair responded, "Yes, we're trying out a new DNA test to try to identify a possibly mythic beast, but that's all secret and you can't write about it."

In the space of a scant 10 seconds, that naive researcher broke two cardinal rules of interacting with journalists, doomed the project, jeopardized the grad student's research, and transformed the science into a search for Bigfoot! The rules:

• Never expect a journalist or reporter to withhold information you've provided unless he or she has agreed to do just that beforehand.

• And never provide any confidential information to a journalist or reporter that you need to stay secret—even if you have a longstanding relationship with the person.

The front page of the next day's *Columbus Dispatch* newspaper carried the story "DNA Scientists at OSU on a Quest for Bigfoot" that focused on the mythology and totally ignored the science. The anthropologist was surprised that his secret had not been kept. And I began fielding the first of more than 650 calls from reporters around the world wanting access to our scientists. The biologists were furious and broke off all contact with both the anthropology department and those of us fielding media calls. Sadly, the science was completely lost as the frenzy continued for more than 2 weeks with calls coming in from as far away as New Zealand.

An otherwise imminently intelligent anthropologist had fallen into a fairly common trap. The reporter was well known as one who loved "looking under rocks" for stories, and this was a perfect chance for him to grab for the sensational in lieu of the science. Reporters, like other members of society, may have their own select traits and prejudices, and scholars are unwise to ignore such variables.

Had the researcher simply called the institution's science PIO before the interview, he would have been warned. That's the primary reason why scientists and scholars should partner with an institution's public information officers when dealing with the media. And that should be done beforehand to establish the relationship between writer and scholar. When research has a potential for controversy, scientists need to lean on their science communications partners. And that trust must be established before the moment of crisis.

The culture of journalism is vastly different from that of science when behavior is considered. What may be prohibited in science may be allowable in the news media, and only those who understand both cultures can map out a safe path. That's why science communicators are so valuable in these circumstances.

SUMMING UP

Scientist-news media interactions are, at their core, all about control—the control of information and the control of the message. Scholars seek out new knowledge and are obligated to share it. Journalists, on the other hand, want news, and that new knowledge may or may not fit their definition. While information may originate with the researcher, it is ultimately conveyed to the public via the media. The institutional science PIO is the bridge between the two and the glue connecting the two sets of interests. But scientists need to form partnerships with these communicators early in the game and nurture those collaborations. These long-term relationships are the key to ensuring that the scholarship is accurately and fairly conveyed to the world.

CHAPTER 14

The Internet

NANCY MARTLAND AND FRED ROTHBAUM

The Internet provides news and information to a huge and growing audience and so has the potential to be as powerful a resource as broadcast media. By the fall of 2005, the percentage of Americans with home Internet access had risen to 68% (Fox, 2005), up from 55% in the fall of 2000 (Rainie & Packel, 2001). This audience appears to use the Internet as a source of information when making important decisions. According to the Pew Internet & American Life Project, 45% of Internet users (about 60 million Americans) say that "the Internet helped them make big decisions or negotiate their way through major episodes in their lives in the previous two years" (Horrigan & Rainie, 2006). In a survey of Internet consumers of health information, 58% of the participants reported that they would choose the Web the next time they needed such information; 35% said they would choose a medical professional (Fox & Fallows, 2003). Likewise, in a recent survey of policy makers, advocates, and journalists, most respondents (63.3%) said they accessed the Internet for policy information at least once per day, and the overwhelming majority (87.8%) reported accessing it at least once per week (Rothbaum & Martland, 2006).

The audience for online information from science is commensurately large. In its report, *The Internet as a Resource for News and Information About Science,* the same Pew Internet project revealed that 40 million Americans rely on the Internet as their primary source for news and information about science, and 87% of online users have looked for science information online (Horrigan, 2006). *Science News* (http://www .sciencenews.org/) and *Science Daily* (http:// www.sciencenews.org/), two Web sites that deliver science news to the public, each claim 45,000 unique visitors daily ("Advertise With Us," 2006; "Advertising," 2006). EurekAlert!, a science news site from the American Association for the Advancement of Science, claims 200,000 unique visitors per month (AAAS, 2006). The EurekAlert! audience represents some 4,400 journalists as well as members of the interested public.

It seems safe to assume that consumers of behavioral science will turn to the Web in similar numbers. Segments of the public have developed a broad appetite for information from behavioral research, seeking answers to questions about death, divorce, trauma, mental health, child care, sibling rivalry, and so on as they try to cope with everyday life. Parents, for example, frequently go online to find answers to their questions about child rearing (Zero to Three, 2000) and are even more likely to do so as Internet penetration into American households rises. Among Americans with children younger than age

18, 70% were online in 2002 compared to 53% of nonparents (Allen & Rainie, 2002). Also by 2002, 58% of online parents were seeking school-related information (Allen & Rainie, 2002). College students who routinely seek information from the Internet are another large segment of the online audience for behavioral science. Of the top 10 most popular undergraduate majors, psychology is number two ("The Top Ten," 2006), and other majors in the top 10 such as education relate directly to the behavioral sciences.

Clearly, the size and scope of the Internet audience make it a critical vehicle of dissemination. Moreover, unlike traditional media and most other dissemination forums, the Internet makes it possible for behavioral scientists to communicate with their intended audiences easily and directly. The challenge lies in learning to use the Internet to reach their audiences effectively.

In this chapter, we discuss some of the issues involved in using the Internet to disseminate behavioral research. We explore the following: What's so special about the Internet? What dissemination issues and strategies are unique to the Internet? What research is needed to help scientists use the Web more effectively? We conclude by briefly considering linkages between behavioral science and the continuing evolution of the Internet.

WHAT'S SO SPECIAL ABOUT THE INTERNET?

Though the Internet and traditional media have characteristics in common, they differ in at least two major ways. First, because the Internet is an interactive medium, *searching is the most important difference between the Internet and traditional media.* Activity online revolves around individual preferences and searches for information, rather than viewing or listening to scheduled broadcasts or reading what is offered in a magazine or newspaper. The online audience knows what it's looking for and expects to find it quickly.

Users exercise nearly complete control over what they find in the vast repository of Internet content. As a result, the process and dynamics of searching are *key elements* to online dissemination (Martland & Rothbaum, 2006). More and more, Web users are turning to search engines to locate the information they seek. From mid-2004 to mid-2005, the use of search engines on a typical day rose from 30% to 41% of the Internet-using population, according to the Pew Internet Project (Rainie & Shermak, 2005). In other words, on an average day, the use of search engines increased from about 38 million Internet users in June 2004 to about 59 million in September 2005—an increase of about 55% (Rainie & Shermak, 2005). To reach this online audience, behavioral scientists will need Internet-specific strategies that take into account the public's patterns of searching.

The skill with which different users approach searching varies as does the U.S. population's access to the Internet, a problem that has been dubbed "the digital divide." In the late 1990s, the main issue was one of access: Lower income, minority, and older Americans were less likely to be online than other groups (Komar, 2003; Lenhart, 2000; Martin, 2003). Though equal access remains a problem, overall access has increased over time, with minority and older Americans showing the fastest growth in Internet use by 2004 (USC Annenberg School, 2004). As the access gap continues to close, differences in skill use have become increasingly recognized (Hargittai, 2002; Robinson, DiMaggio, & Hargittai, 2003; Van Dijk & Hacker, 2003).

Because Web users must actively search for the information they want, searching skills determine what users will find, skills that not all users possess (Cho, de Zuniga,

Rojas, & Shah, 2003; "The New Divides," 2001; Van Dijk, 2002). For example, in one study, the completion of Internet searching tasks was found to vary with educational level, with the most educated having the most success (Hargittai, 2002). Basic searching skills that tend to be lacking include selecting a good search engine (Google seems to be the most effective at present), limiting the searched domain (e.g., instructing search engine to only search .edu or .gov domains), using a very specific search that increases the likelihood of relevant results, and refining or rephrasing the search terms to get even better results (Martland & Rothbaum, 2006).

A recent study examined the relationship between socioeconomic status (SES) and parents' Internet skills more closely (Rothbaum, Martland, & Jannsen, in press). A sample of 120 parents was observed while searching for information on topics of their choosing. Parents were asked to comment on their searches and on the results as they searched for and viewed Internet sites. The parents also answered questions about their Internet use. Parents with high SES were more likely than those with middle or low SES to exhibit sophisticated searching skills, such as changing keywords to improve search results. Parents with high SES were also more likely to consider the site's sponsoring organization in judging the trustworthiness of the information on the site. These findings suggest that reaching audiences at all SES levels will require behavioral scientists to use strategies that make their material accessible to users with a wide range of searching skill.

A second major difference between the Internet and traditional media is the lack of a middleman or gatekeeper. The openness of the Web means that no middleman comes between the generators of information and their audience. Opportunities for posting credible information from behavioral science are available on sites maintained by universities,

research centers, and professional or advocacy organizations, among others. Government sites are an important source of posted research relating to health, education, economic, and other societal concerns. Direct posting obviates the need to convince reporters or editors to cover a story. Because research findings don't need to be pitched, issues such as reporting angles and news hooks can become less relevant.

Direct posting affords total control of the content presented, and it allows tailoring information to the needs of different target audiences. By posting articles on the Internet, scientists can capitalize on Web-specific capacities that allow using a range of communication styles and approaches to meet the needs of a highly varied audience. Link networking, for example, can be used to supply links to simpler or more complex text, to graphics or to other forms of information most useful to particular audiences. Offering materials for audiences with different reading levels, sophistication with the topic, preferences for complexity, and so on is essential to reaching a diverse public.

But the incredible ease of simply posting material online, especially compared with placing it in the traditional news media, may lead scientists to be complacent in their methods of presenting information. Avoiding the middleman in traditional media—the university public information officer, the magazine editor, the newspaper reporter—comes with a downside. These middlemen can increase the likelihood that scientific information is repackaged into forms that the public can access and digest, a task that can be very difficult for behavioral scientists. For example, what is unique about the Internet, and a potential strength, is that users search for information in their own words, not using categories defined by researchers. So, it is important to use a variety of keywords because the public, with its diverse levels of searching skill, may use either simple, lay search terms (*sadness*), academic or technical search terms (e.g., *depression, bipolar disorder*), or a combination of the two. Anticipating the keywords that users may enter can be difficult. Behavioral scientists committed to directly disseminating research online must make an effort to understand their target audience and to secure essential resources and tools, such as those for identifying the search terms the Internet audience is likely to use.

The lack of a middleman can also exacerbate the problem of the public receiving information of uneven quality because the average Internet user is often not equipped to judge the quality of the information appearing online (Fallows, 2005). Personal Web sites often appear professional and trustworthy, yet many of them supply inaccurate information. Viewers can believe that what appears on the screen is credible when it is not (Wyman, 1997). The Practice Directorate of the American Psychological Association (APA) was so concerned about this issue in the context of health-related sites that it developed materials especially to help consumers evaluate mental health information provided on the Web (APA, 2005). Yet, not much is known about the public's use of such educational resources.

Behavioral scientists who directly post information online can help to address the quality issue by increasing the amount of trustworthy information on the Web. Research with a variety of audiences, including undergraduates, library scientists, child development experts, and other scholars, consistently indicates that the credibility or authority of the information source is a major criterion relied on when evaluating Web sites (Liu, 2004; Martland, 2001; Rieh, 2002; Tate & Alexander, 1996). Treise, Walsh-Childers, Weigold, and Friedman (2003) found that audiences identified some domains, such as .edu and .gov, as more credible than others (e.g., .com) and that an individual author's

identification with a recognized scientific institution, such as NASA, was also viewed as a positive indicator of trustworthiness. Other criteria used to determine the overall credibility of a Web site include references and citations that support the statements made on the Web site, the consistency of the content with viewers' beliefs, the layout and appearance of the site, the format of the material, and the usefulness or relevance of the information (Liu, 2004; Rieh & Belkin, 1998).

Behavioral scientists interested in clarifying the trustworthiness of their online postings should take pains to prominently display their institutional affiliations. In the name of the site, on the homepage banner, in the interior pages, and elsewhere, it is helpful to emphasize one's affiliation with a government or academic institution, for example. Even when material is aimed at a general audience, the names of the authors should be given for all the material, preferably with links to the authors' qualifications. Supporting references should be included in some form; links at the end of an article can help to avoid an overly academic appearance.

Why does the posting of information that is clearly trustworthy matter? Evidence shows that the Internet audience for behavioral science is likely to encounter questionable sites when searching. For example, a recent simple search of *spanking* on Google (December 13, 2006) produced a hit list of more than 919,000 sites. Of the first 10, 7 had to do with sexual practices; one was a religious site that said it gives a balanced view on corporal punishment and that cited research; one was a site opposed to the spanking of children and that also cited research; and one was a Wikipedia entry on corporal punishment. Later screens returned sites that encourage and support corporal punishment. These search results are alarming because

- behavioral research consistently indicates that spanking is harmful;
- most of the top 10 (and top 20) sites returned are of no use to parents who are looking for help with this issue.

Moreover, sites providing either irrelevant or suspect information increase the risk that parents will develop unrealistic expectations or understandings of children's behavior. Research has repeatedly suggested that parents' unrealistic expectations and lack of understanding of children can be a risk factor for abuse and neglect (Goldman, Salus, Wolcott, & Kennedy, 2003).

We have argued thus far that the interactive nature of the Internet and the lack of a middleman are two features of the Web that make it a unique medium and that present excellent opportunities for researchers to directly disseminate behavioral science. But realizing this potential requires developing Internet-specific strategies for dissemination.

WHAT DISSEMINATION ISSUES AND STRATEGIES ARE UNIQUE TO THE INTERNET?

Behavioral scientists seeking to directly disseminate their work and the field's accumulated knowledge using the Internet will need to consider how to (1) proactively attract visitors to their site; (2) deliver useful, up-to-date content that site visitors find appealing and can easily understand and retain; and (3) take advantage of the Internet's strengths that include *the diverse audience, speed, direct bidirectional communications, networking,* and *layering.*

Attracting Visitors to a Site

Because searching is the primary means of locating information online, behavioral scientists who want to attract visitors *must* understand how search engines work. When a user enters a word or phrase into a search engine, the search engine scans the Internet and returns a list of sites based on rank (the number of sites linking to the site in question) and relevance (the terms associated with the site). Associated terms include not only those internal to the site. Terms in the title of the site and in any links to the site are even more important because they are prioritized by search engines. Sites that rank highest (the ones that come closest to the top of a search return list) will attract more traffic. The field of search engine optimization (SEO) focuses on maximizing the results using these and other criteria. For more information on how search engines work, visit SearchEngineWatch (http://searchenginewatch.com).

All searching revolves around the use of keywords (or search terms). The most useful terms for attracting visitors are those popular key phrases that the public commonly uses to refer to behavioral science and to find information relating to behavioral research. Wordtracker.com, a subscription service, is a research tool that can retrieve the words Internet users are entering and how many times each key phrase is searched. The *WebGuide Thesaurus of Common Keywords*, which we created and made available free of charge as part of the Tufts University Child & Family WebGuide (www.cfw.tufts.edu), is a list of the most commonly used keywords that relate to child development. It also contains an extensive selection of common keywords related to behavioral science.

After commonly used search terms have been identified, they should be embedded within a site's content. For each page of a site, select two to three key phrases related to the page's content, and repeat them several times throughout the page, taking care to not to repeat the key phrases too often and to otherwise maintain user friendliness and readability. The key phrases should be located strategically on the page. In addition to dispersing them throughout the main text, they should be placed in the page title and main heading of the page and in the text of links to the site because these locations are heavily weighted by search engines. Only ethical search engine optimization should be used. That is, sites should not be "packed" with keywords that are not relevant to the material just to achieve the desired search engine result. Also, sites should be kept updated because the popularity of key phrases and topics changes frequently. Pages may need to be refreshed to sustain the maximum number of visitors.

Finally, each site should have a well-developed linking system. Along with scanning a site's content, search engines scan a site's internal links and inbound links (i.e., from other Web sites) to judge how relevant a page is to the term being searched. A site that has more relevant linked pages and more key terms embedded in the link text will elevate the target's page position in a search return. Because it is easy to control a site's internal linking structure, link text is a good place to begin optimizing. Ultimately, the number and quality of inbound links to the page is of even greater value for optimizing search engine results.

Delivering Useful Content

Presenting content electronically raises a number of issues related to learning from an electronic medium: How do the content's overall visual appearance on the screen, use of hyperlinks, graphics, the content organization, and other features affect the user's ability to learn from the presentation? What has been perceived by many as Internet strengths—the ability to link to related material and to present graphics, animated illustrations, and video or audio—seems to have corresponding weaknesses in the way users absorb, comprehend, and retain information.

The added functions enabled by the electronic format can place additional demands on the user's ability to process all of the information (known as increasing the user's cognitive load) and can have negative effects on retention (Macedo-Rouet, Rouet, Epstein, & Favard, 2003). Few clear answers are available from research to help address this concern.

One in-depth study of users of the science information site the Why Files indicated that users spent a great deal of time "orienting" to the site—that is, understanding how the site was organized, how to navigate it, and what content was available. Such orienting time detracted from the time spent viewing and processing the content, regardless of the user's level of Web experience (Dunwoody, 2001). In other research, a number of on-screen features have been shown to affect legibility. Reading is slowed, for example, by much clicking and scrolling, small font, and screens dense with content. Flash animation and informational graphics are especially challenging for users (Dillon, 1994; Macedo-Rouet et al., 2003).

The hyperlinking opportunities offered by the Web allow for "nonlinear" structure, which involves breaking text with links to related material such as supplementary content, attractive but nonessential graphics, and other ancillary information. This approach differs from the "linear" structure used to present information in traditional media that encourages, for example, reading a newspaper story from start to finish. Though the effects of nonlinear structure are not fully understood, initial research studies suggest different learning outcomes for each structural style. A linear presentation seems to result in better recall of an article's facts, whereas a nonlinear style seems to result in better connection of bits of related information (Eveland, Cortese, Park, & Dunwoody, 2004; Tremayne & Dunwoody, 2001). One explanation for this finding may be that users of linear material are more likely to view all of the article's content, whereas users of nonlinear material are more likely to view the information offered to deepen and expand the topic but are not as likely to read the entire main article (Eveland et al., 2004). The nonlinear style also more often produces disorientation in its users (Tremayne & Dunwoody, 2001).

More research on these and other issues of presentation would be helpful for advancing Web design, but addressing some of the issues that research has already revealed is relatively straightforward. All audiences can benefit from clearer presentation in the form of high-contrast, large-font, clean screens with limited content and an extremely well-organized site with a simple, clear structure and a prominent navigation system. Clarity of presentation especially helps with orienting to the site. To adapt to the slower reading inherent in online presentations, text should be shortened and streamlined to highlight main ideas and avoid density.

Choosing between a linear and a nonlinear presentation is less straightforward. Eveland et al. (2004) note that the choice should depend on the intended audience and the goals for learning one has for the site. If the intended outcome is simply factual recall, then a more linear style might work best; if the intended outcome is a deeper, more highly developed understanding of a topic, a nonlinear style might work better. A compromise might be to provide links to complementary material but to include all essential material in the main body of the text. To avoid disorientation, links could be placed in a sidebar or at the end of article, rather than within the text.

Unlike a printed journal article, one cannot post an article online and forget about it. Presenting content effectively online requires continuous monitoring of Web pages to be sure all links are working, graphics are loading, and contact information is correct and functional. The digital world is very fast paced, change is constant, and so a successful site must also improve its presentation and upgrade regularly to be attractive to visitors.

Taking Full Advantage of the Internet's Strengths

Besides optimizing a site to increase its rank in a search, a site should be designed to maximize five other strengths of the Internet: its diverse audience, speed, opportunity for direct and bidirectional communications, networking, and layering.

The Internet's Diverse Audience. The Internet has the potential to attract a wide range of visitors because online activity is not limited to information gathering. People go online for all kinds of purposes—to communicate via e-mail, for commerce (e.g., shopping or travel planning), for entertainment (e.g., online games or gambling)—as well as for information. After they're online, they may use the Web to seek information as well. Moreover, all segments of the varied behavioral science audience (e.g., policy makers, parents, students, parent educators, health care providers, commercial businesses, journalists) use the same mechanisms to find information. As a result, online material intended for one audience has the potential to easily find its way to other audiences that might also have an interest in the subject covered, unlike traditional media such as printed trade journals or magazines that target specific audiences with particular outlets. One outcome of this crossover is the potential to reach journalists seeking stories for the traditional media. For example, in a survey we conducted in 2005, 73% of journalist respondents (who covered child policy issues) reported that they used the Internet at least once per day to "look for or access research, studies or reports" related to their work (Rothbaum & Martland, 2006). The option of searching directly for information has the potential to move journalists "beyond the rolodex" if behavioral scientists are savvy about how they post their research.

Perhaps the greatest challenge for behavioral scientists is finding out how to capitalize on the Internet's large and highly varied audience. Successful dissemination depends largely on the way the material is posted. The variability in the keywords used by different audiences, for example, makes SEO problematic. Carefully identifying and defining one's target audience is essential. If the target is parents, simpler and more vernacular, idiomatic keywords will probably work best and should be used to optimize the site's pages. If the target is policy makers, keywords that are more technical might work better. In the case of multiple intended audiences, prioritizing is recommended because of the difficulties associated with optimizing for multiple keywords. Presentation style and layering of content also should be tailored to meet the needs of one's target audience, as discussed in a later section.

Speed. Web material is readily available to any audience at any time and can meet the immediate needs for information easily (as compared with a scheduled TV program, for example, or a newspaper or magazine story that may be more difficult to find). Searching for information from behavioral science involves many possible search terms that can overlap or vary from vernacular to technical, and the speed of the Internet helps a searcher sift quickly through any irrelevant material. Speed is especially attractive to members of the policy audience such as legislative aides, policy advocates, and journalists (Rothbaum & Martland, unpublished interviews, 2002).

Sites can capitalize on and enhance the Internet's speed by employing a transparent, functional, and well-organized design. If material is intended for multiple audiences, for example, then create separate, well-marked sections on the site so that each audience can find its section immediately. Large sites especially need transparency. Users will not spend much time looking around a site in which the information they want is buried beneath layers of subsections and search pages. Highlight the best and most important material on every page of the site; many visitors do not enter through the homepage and so have no opportunity to view an introduction or navigation items posted on the homepage. All essential internal links should be included in a sidebar so that the site is quickly navigated and the desired content quickly found. Slow-loading graphics should be avoided on the main pages of a site. If they are important, place them on a separate page and offer a link to them for the interested viewer, or offer a "skip" option. Viewers in search of fast information don't want to spend time watching graphics load—they can easily move on to another, faster site. Take advantage of layering options (discussed fully below) to make browsing faster using, for example, very brief abstracts with links to full-text articles and reports.

EurekAlert! (www.eurekalert.org), a site from the American Association for the Advancement of Science, presents summaries of current research across the sciences and is an excellent example of crisp, transparent site organization that allows the user to navigate easily through a large volume of material. Its homepage offers a prominent list of science categories that is clearly labeled "News by Subject." A click on one of these categories, "Social and Behavior," for example, brings the user directly to a page that lists the newest releases with links to text and supplies a search box at the top of the page that allows for browsing subtopics. The sought-after content is one or two clicks from the homepage, the design is clean and clear, and the site does an admirable job presenting complex information.

Direct, Bidirectional Communications. Unlike traditional media, the Internet allows communications from source to audience and from audience to source. This direct connection makes it very easy for behavioral scientists to offer full-text reports and articles that describe research findings or practical research applications, material that only rarely appears in traditional popular media. A wide audience not only has the potential to find this material, but it can also connect with experts in ways that normally would not occur, allowing Internet users and researchers to ask questions and give one another feedback through e-mail or discussion boards.

On their Web site, behavioral scientists may wish to invite communications with those viewing their work. Visitors to a site are often eager to ask a direct question of an expert; journalists are frequently interested in interviewing an expert for a story; policy makers may want help interpreting a set of research findings in light of a pressing policy issue; students may have questions about the findings and the methods used in the research. From these contacts, scientists can learn about issues of concern to each of these audiences, which can inform both research and practice.

To make the most of this potential for direct communications between source and audience, behavioral scientists should first identify the target audience(s) for their work and then tailor the material for that audience. For example, if the target audience is parents, material should clearly be marked as such and should be presented in a form and style that parents will find useful. Information from journal articles, though of interest to any audience, is best presented in succinct, jargon-free summaries with links to the full text. About Our Kids (www.aboutourkids.org) from the New York University Child Study Center does an excellent job of creating articles of short and medium length that speak to the concerns of parents with simple, appealing, and fast-loading graphics and textual markers that chunk the content for easier reading, all done without sacrificing markers of quality such as author information and references.

The Web also offers the ability to present nontextual materials such as video, pictures, and audio, which greatly appeals to the public and can be very effective for conveying information from behavioral science. Zero to Three (www.zerotothree.org), a highly respected national organization dedicated to meeting the needs of infants and toddlers, currently offers audio clips and streaming video, an option that is becoming increasingly common. The public likes interactive opportunities such as blogs, and behavioral scientists could benefit from expanding their presence on these sites. Blogs are a popular means of enabling individuals to express their opinions, recount their activities, and exchange ideas—they can function in a manner similar to a column or op-ed style piece. The WhyFiles.org, a science information site from the University of Wisconsin, features a blog-like column that recently debunked the science in a popular Hollywood production. An earlier, similar effort by the Johns Hopkins School of Hygiene and Public Health produced brief TV spots to be shown following episodes of the medical drama *ER*. The spots explained the medicine behind the episode. Creative behavioral scientists could use the blog format to comment on issues of public interest, bringing to bear the best scientific knowledge.

Networking. Site creators can take advantage of the many different sources online through linking to other sites, thus creating an information network—a true "Web" of information sources. Networking is in effect an alternate form of searching. After the user finds a site that provides relevant, useful information, external links from it to other sites serve as pathways to more detailed information or to information that extends a specific topic and allows the user to move to these related areas. Care must be taken, however, to avoid overloading and disorienting the viewer. Placement of links outside the text (perhaps in a sidebar or at the end) and a small, well-chosen set of useful links are recommended. As mentioned earlier, for some purposes and audiences, a linear approach to presenting links may be more effective than a nonlinear one.

Networking is especially well suited to the varied needs the public has for information from behavioral science. For example, users are often interested in background, diagnostic, intervention, outcome, policy, and advocacy information. *Your Child*, from the University of Michigan Health Care System (http://www.med.umich.edu/11ibr/yourchild), is an excellent example of networking. It provides highly credible information on a variety of topics and excellent external links to other trustworthy sites. Each *Your Child* report embeds links to trustworthy sites at points in the text where additional information might be useful. For example, in a report on obesity, links take the user to *KidsHealth* for information about healthy weights, to an American Heart Association article on overweight in children, and to the National Institutes of Health for a pamphlet on how to help an overweight child.

To be a full player on the Web, sites must participate in the interconnectedness of the Web. A site posting a scientific article or report on early language development, for example, should seek out and take advantage of reciprocal links with other sites that offer information on different age groups, on educational considerations, on parenting practices that foster healthy development, or on stages of brain development that are relevant to the growth of language. The reciprocity of links is an important means of multiplying the effect of online postings. Those responsible for managing sites should proactively arrange exchanges of links to expand the information possibilities for their users.

Layering. One of the Web's most valuable assets is its inherent ability to support varied presentation formats to reach audiences with diverse interests and levels of sophistication with a topic. In this medium, the user can jump from screen to screen instantly and at will, and site designers can nest various types of content within a site, all connected by internal links. So, for example, layering allows easy dissemination of behavioral science to audiences that range from the parent concerned about social development to the journalist writing a piece on depression to the legislative aide gathering data on early brain development and learning effects. Zero to Three posts a site that provides an excellent example of layering. The organization offers brief materials aimed at parents, such as short articles and downloadable pamphlets, as well as FAQs and parenting tips, while offering longer and more practice-oriented articles and reports for professionals and policy makers. All of this material is available from a single homepage, and it is nested on pages within the main site so that the full site content is available to anyone who visits the site.

Layering of material within a site involves more than just internal links. The site's organizational structure should be extremely clear and easy to navigate, and care must be taken not to overload the viewer with options. Knowledge of the target audience(s) is essential. For an audience interested mainly in scientific reports and other kinds of research findings, efficiency and appeal can be enhanced simply by providing succinct abstracts that then link to full text, appendices, charts, statistics, references, and so on. If a lay audience such as parents or the general public is the target, the task is a bit more difficult because the material will need to be rewritten and reformatted to remove the scientific trappings and to be more readily accessible to diverse users. Layering for the public can involve shortened texts, graphics, chunked text with headings, and links to additional material on the site, such as fact sheets, brochures, or FAQs, that will extend the information presented. The policy audience also has specific needs and interests, such as outcome data for interventions and the implications of such data as for public policy.

WHAT RESEARCH IS NEEDED?

The Internet is at an early stage of development, and behavioral scientists have much to learn about using this new medium to disseminate research to their varied constituencies. Indeed, developing a deeper understanding of the primary audiences for behavioral science would be an excellent place to start. We need to know more, for example, about audience preferences for information—who wants basic research findings, information about professional applications, advice about particular life problems, details about research-based interventions and their outcomes, theoretical background and other scientific context, and so on, and how should this information be presented depending on the audience? Studies are needed to determine who benefits most from particular formats that vary, for example, in level of topic sophistication, complexity of language, site organization and navigation, and opportunities for direct contact with an expert. Though a substantial beginning already has been made, a deeper understanding of the effects of linear versus nonlinear presentations would help advance approaches to site design.

The problem of the digital divide continues to warrant research. In the not too distant future, nearly every home will be online,

just as nearly every home currently has access to TV. Studies are needed to better understand the information needs, searching behaviors, and relatively less sophisticated searching skills of Web users with lower SES, as well as the factors that contribute to these users' heightened vulnerability to information of poor quality. A better understanding of this audience could help to create sites that increase its odds of locating quality information suited to its needs. This research could build on the early and substantial work of academic librarians on essential Web skills (e.g., Tate & Alexander, 1996, 1999).

Behavioral scientists have historically been interested in communicating their knowledge to policy audiences (e.g., Fowler, 1999, 2000; Sherrod, 1998), which already use the Internet frequently to gather information. But we understand little about this audience's preferred search behaviors, preferred formats, and needs for online information relating to behavioral research. As with all of the behavioral scientist's intended audiences, studies of policy makers' habits and preferences for seeking, receiving, and processing information online would undoubtedly help researchers understand how to appeal to them using the Internet.

In closing, we wish to consider the next frontier for searching and how it could apply to the Internet audience for behavioral science. A promising direction for research could be to create and evaluate a process to unite searching efficiency with search result credibility—the two currently dominant Web issues. A recent Google product, released in fall 2006, enables custom search design and so may offer a glimpse into the future. It allows placing a Google search on a nonprofit organization's sites and designating a limited set of sites to be searched (as compared with the entire Web as in the standard Google search). The Child & Family WebGuide (www.cfw.tufts.edu) has implemented this option by creating a search set of only those sites that already have been evaluated and rated highly by WebGuide staff. Questions raised by this search option include how to create a search set of sites, how best to classify and group or mark sites (e.g., by topic, by level of difficulty, by type of information), and how to tailor limited searches to target audiences (e.g., for those seeking searches only of policy sites or only of sites listing practical advice for coping with a particular problem).

The Web is an ever-changing medium. New alternatives in searching will certainly emerge. For example, the semantic Web, a version of Web programming and design that relies on machine-readable information and metadata, is expected to change the way searching is accomplished (Lombardi, 2006) by moving beyond the search of text. This tool will change a good deal of what we now know about SEO, for example. It is essential that behavioral scientists stay abreast of such new developments so that they can both advance the dissemination of their own research and contribute to scientific discoveries about how Internet technologies can help to meet the information needs of a diverse and growing Internet audience.

REFERENCES

Advertise with us. (2006). *Science News*. Retrieved December 11, 2006, from http://www.sciencenews.org/pages/mediakit.asp

Advertising. (2006). *Science Daily*. Retrieved December 11, 2006, from http://www.sciencedaily.com/advertise/

Allen, K., & Rainie, L. (2002, November). *Parents online* (Pew Internet & American Life Project). Retrieved December 12, 2006, from http://www.pewInternet.org/PPF/r/75/report_display.asp

American Association for the Advancement of Science (AAAS). (2006). *AAAS news & notes*. Retrieved December 11, 2006, from http://www.aaas.org/news/newsandnotes/inside95.shtml

American Psychological Association (APA). (2005). *American Psychological Association helps consumers guard privacy, assess mental health information online* [Press release]. Retrieved December 12, 2006, from http://www.apa.org practice/dotcom.html

Cho, J., Gil de Zuniga, H., Rojas, H., & Shah, D.V. (2003). Beyond access: The digital divide and Internet uses and gratifications. *IT & Society, 1*(4), 46–72. Retrieved December 12, 2006, from http://www.stanford.edu/group/siqss/itandsociety/v01i04/v01i04a04.pdf

Dillon, A. (1994). *Designing usable electronic text: Ergonomics aspects of human information usage*. London: Taylor & Francis.

Dunwoody, S. (2001). Studying users of the Why Files. *Science Communication, 22*(3), 274–282.

Eveland, W., Cortese, J., Park, H., & Dunwoody, S. (2004). How Web site organization influences free recall, factual knowledge, and knowledge structure density. *Human Communication Research, 30*(2), 208–223.

Fallows, D. (2005, January). *Search engine users: Internet searchers are confident, satisfied and trusting—but they are also unaware and naïve* (Pew Internet & American Life Project). Retrieved December 12, 2006, from http://www.pewInternet.org/pdfs/PIP_Searchengine_users.pdf

Fowler, R. D. (1999, May). Giving psychology away. *APA Monitor*, p. 3.

Fowler, R. D. (2000). The Internet: Changing the work we do. *Monitor on Psychology, 31*, 4.

Fox, S. (2005, July). *Pew Internet Project report*. Retrieved April 19, 2007, from http://www.pewinternet.org/PPF/r/165/report_display.asp

Fox, S., & Fallows, D. (2003). *Internet health resources: Health searches and email have become more commonplace, but there is room for improvement in searches and overall Internet success* (Pew Internet & American Life Project). Retrieved December 12, 2006, from http://www.pewInternet.org/pdfs/PIP_Health_Report_July_2003.pdf

Goldman, J., Salus, M., Wolcott, D., & Kennedy, K. (2003). *A coordinated response to child abuse and neglect: The foundation for practice* (National Clearinghouse on Child Abuse and Neglect Information). Retrieved December 12, 2006, from http://www.childwelfare.gov/pubs/usermanuals/foundation/index.cfm

Hargittai, E. (2002). Second-level digital divide: Differences in people's online skills. *First Monday, 7*(4). Retrieved December 12, 2006, from http://www.first monday.org/issues/issue7_4/hargittai/index.html

Horrigan, J. B. (2006). *The Internet as a resource for news and information about science* (Pew Internet & American Life Project). Retrieved December 1, 2006, from http://www.pewInternet.org/pdfs/PIP_Exploratorium_Science.pdf

Horrigan, J. B., & Rainie, L. (2006). *When facing a tough decision, 60 million Americans now seek the Internet's help* (Pew Internet & American Life Project). Retrieved December 12, 2006, from http://pewresearch.org/obdeck/?Ob DeckID=19

Komar, B. (2003). Race, poverty and the digital divide. *Poverty & Race*. Retrieved December 12, 2006, from http://www.prrac.org/full_text.php?text_id=775& item_id=7804&newsletter_id=66&header=Education

Lenhart, A. (2000). *Who's not online: 57% of those without Internet access say they do not plan to log on* (Pew Internet & American Life Project). Retrieved December 12, 2006, from http://www.pewInternet.org/PPF/r/21/report_display.asp

Liu, Z. (2004). Perceptions of credibility of scholarly information on the Web. *Information Processing and Management, 40*, 1027–1038.

Lombardi, V. (2006). *Noise between stations*. Retrieved December 13, 2006, from http://www.noisebetweenstations.com/personal/essays/metadata_glossary/meta data_glossary.html

Macedo-Rouet, M., Rouet, J.-F., Epstein, I., & Favard, P. (2003). Effects of online reading on popular science comprehension. *Science Communication, 25*(2), 99–128.

Martin, S. P. (2003). Is the digital divide really closing? A critique of inequality measurement in *A nation online. IT & Society, 1*(4), 1–13. Retrieved December 12, 2006, from http://www.stanford.edu/group/siqss/itandsociety/v01i04/v01i04a01 .pdf

Martland, N. (2001). *Expert criteria for evaluating the quality of Web-based child development information*. Doctoral dissertation, Tufts University.

Martland, N., & Rothbaum, F. (2006). Thinking critically about the Web: Suggestions for practitioners. *Child Welfare, 85*(5), 837–852.

The new divides. (2001, May 10). *Education Week, 20*(35), 10–11.

Rainie, L., & Packel, D. (2001). *More online, doing more* (Pew Internet & American Life Project). Retrieved December 12, 2006, from http://www.pewInternet.org/ PPF/r/30/report_display.asp

Rainie, L., & Shermak, J. (2005). *Search engine use November 2005* (Pew Internet and American Life Project). Retrieved December 12, 2006, from http://www.pew Internet.org/pdfs/PIP_SearchData_1105.pdf

Rieh, S. Y. (2002). Judgment of information quality and cognitive authority on the Web. *Journal of the American Society for Information Science and Technology, 53*(2), 145–161.

Rieh, S. Y., & Belkin, N. J. (1998). Understanding judgment of information quality and cognitive authority in the WWW. In C. M. Preston (Ed.), *Proceedings of the 61st ASIS annual meeting* (pp. 279–289). Silver Spring, MD: American Society for Information Science.

Robinson, J. P., DiMaggio, P., & Hargittai, E. (2003). New social survey perspectives on the digital divide. *IT & Society, 1*(5), 1–22. Retrieved December 12, 2006, from http://www.stanford.edu/group/siqss/itandsociety/v01i05/v01i05a01.pdf

Rothbaum, F., & Martland, N. (2006). *Effective online abstracts for a policy audience* (Annual program report for the William T. Grant Foundation). Unpublished document, Tufts University.

Rothbaum, F., Martland, N., & Jannsen, J. (in press). Parents' reliance on the Web to find information about children and families: Socio-economic differences in use, skills and satisfaction. *Journal of Applied Developmental Psychology.*

Sherrod, L. (1998). Report from the committee on child development, public policy, and public information. *Society for Research in Child Development Newsletter, 41*(1), 3–7.

Tate, M. A., & Alexander, J. E. (1996, November/December). Teaching critical evaluation skills for World Wide Web resources. *Computers in Libraries, 16*, 49–55.

Tate, M. A., & Alexander, J. E. (1999). *Web wisdom.* Mahwah, NJ: Lawrence Erlbaum.

The top ten most popular majors. (2006). *Princeton Review.* Retrieved December 11, 2006, from http://www.princetonreview.com/college/research/articles/majors/popular.asp

Tremayne, M., & Dunwoody, S. (2001). Interactivity, information processing, and learning on the World Wide Web. *Science Communication, 23*(2), 111–134.

Triese, D., Walsh-Childers, K., Weigold, M., & Friedman, M. (2003). Cultivating the science Internet audience. *Science Communication, 24*(3), 309–332.

USC Annenberg School Center for the Digital Future. (2004, September). *The digital future report: Surveying the digital future.* Retrieved December 12, 2006, from http://www.digitalcenter.org/downloads/DigitalFutureReport-Year4-2004.pdf

Van Dijk, J. (2002). A framework for digital research. *Communication Institute for Online Scholarship, 12*(1–2). Retrieved November 1, 2005, from http://cios.org

Van Dijk, J., & Hacker, K. (2003). The digital divide as a complex and dynamic phenomenon. *The Information Society, 19*, 315–326.

Wyman, S. K. (1997). *User and system-based quality criteria for evaluating information resources and services available from federal websites: Final report.* Dublin, OH: OCLC Online Computer Library Center, Inc. (ERIC Document Reproduction Service No. ED 409 020)

Zero to Three. (2000). *Survey reveals child development knowledge gap among adults.* Retrieved November 1, 2005, from http://www.zerotothree.org/pr-survey.html

Part IV

COMMUNICATING
WITH POLICY MAKERS

A *Knowledge Utilization Framework for Making Behavioral Science Useful to Policy Makers*

ROBERT F. RICH

It may seem obvious and premature to talk in terms of a new or even well-developed field of study (such as knowledge transfer or utilization). But, as a result of a climate of thinking about how human values and scientific programs interact, I see the creation, dissemination, and utilization of knowledge moving clearly from peripheral functions at the edge of society to a major role in the more central activities of planned social change. I believe that there is a need to foster and enrich these developments.

—Editor, *Knowledge: Creation, Diffusion, Utilization*
inaugural issue, September 1979

A social system learns whenever it acquires new capacity for behavior . . . but government as a learning system carries with it the idea of public *learning, a special way of acquiring new capacity for behavior, in which government learns for society as a whole. In public learning, government undertakes a continuing, directed inquiry into the nature, causes and resolution of our problems.*

If government is to solve new public problems, it must also learn to create the systems for doing so and to discard the structure and mechanisms grown up around old problems. . . .

—Donald Schön (1973, p. 109)

AUTHOR'S NOTE: I am very grateful for the suggestions and editing assistance provided by Melissa Welch-Ross and Lauren G. Fasig. The assistance of Kelly Merrick of the University of Illinois is also gratefully acknowledged.

As indicated in the quotations cited above, the use and utility of information from the behavioral sciences for the policy-making process has been a topic of longstanding concern. Adapting knowledge[1] to the needs of society dates back to the Greeks and is a theme that runs through much of Western thought (Rich, 1979). Within the past 30 years, the role of information in policy development and decision making—both individual and organizational—has been given increased attention in the social science literature. This trend was reflected in 1979 with the establishment of the new journal, *Knowledge: Creation, Diffusion, Utilization* (which is now known as *Science Communication*). Despite a tremendous growth of attention to the importance of knowledge in the policy-making process, past studies generally indicate that decision makers make little use of knowledge (see Caplan, Morrison, & Stambaugh, 1975; Ciarlo, 1980; Dickinson, 2003; Estabrooks, Wallin, & Milner, 2003; Florio & DeMartini, 1993; Hutchison, 1995; Lester, 1993; Oh & Rich, 1996; Rich, 2001; Rich & Oh, 1994; Webber, 1987). Research studies have been directed toward discovering ways to improve knowledge utilization in a number of policy areas. However, the extant research provides little support for claims that particular variables affect the use of knowledge in decisive ways (Landry, Amara, & Lamari, 2001; Lavis, Ross, & Hurley, 2002; Lester, 1993). In other words, explaining patterns of "use" remains more of an art than a science.

But past research may have overlooked how information actually gets used. Policy makers tend to approach the acquisition, dissemination, and use of information with a basic set of assumptions that may be rather different than those made by the research community:

- Information is collected for a variety of reasons and not necessarily for purposes of use; information may be collected simply for building inventory or building capacity.
- There may be negative, unintended consequences of using information.
- It may be fully rational to ignore available information or to actively reject it.
- Intended nonutilization is different from misutilization of information.

In other words, policy development and decision making occur in an organizational or institutional context that is central to our understanding of what the role of information actually is—a role that may be substantially different from the scientific community's ideas about what the role of information is or should be.

> As valuable as information is, information by itself is meaningless. Information only takes on meaning in the context of the social practices of the communities that give it life. . . . Why is it, then, that we always think of learning in individualistic terms of acquisition of information. . . ? (Wenger, 1991, p. 7)

This chapter, which provides a knowledge utilization framework for applying science to policy making, is organized into six parts: (a) part one presents a general model for understanding knowledge utilization and how it is measured; (b) in the second part, alternative theories of knowledge utilization and its impact are examined; (c) given the model and alternative theories, the next part focuses on distinguishing between types of knowledge and information; (d) part four, then, examines different cases of knowledge utilization in policy making, ranging from high utilization and high impact to deliberate nonutilization; (e) in part five, core findings from the empirical literature on knowledge utilization and policy making are presented; and (f) part six concludes by briefly discussing implications of the scholarship and themes presented in this chapter.

A GENERAL MODEL OF UTILIZATION: THE "KNOWLEDGE CYCLE"

Over the past 30 years, some of the research issues that have received considerable attention in this growing literature on knowledge utilization include information overload (e.g., strategies for dealing with "overload problems," access to information, and the "processing" of information by individuals and organizations, including questions of "processing errors," "biases," and information symmetries and asymmetries), management of information, the impacts of information technology (e.g., e-mail and the World Wide Web), the integral role of information in "rational" decision-making processes, the role of information in organizational and public learning and in developing "organizational intelligence" capacity, the "political" role of information in the public policy-making process (including the role of government in limiting the distribution of information and the increasing importance attached to public opinion data), and the use and abuse of information by individuals and organizations.

Looking at this body of literature, which consists of empirical research, testimonials, and think-pieces, one quickly arrives at the conclusion that most past studies lack a comprehensive conceptual framework that addresses how information is acquired, disseminated, and used or what might be characterized as the knowledge inquiry process One useful way to conceptualize these processes is through a basic conceptual model: "the knowledge cycle" (Rich, 1981a). The term *cycle* is used to suggest that information use is not a discrete event in isolation; instead, it is one stage in an interrelated set of stages or phases (Rich, 1981a; van Lohuizen, 1986; Wingens, 1990). Researchers have tended to select one aspect or stage of knowledge processing in policy making with little

consideration of the interrelated stages. The term *cycle* is also used to suggest that these interrelated sets of stages should not be thought about or depicted as a linear process where one stage automatically follows—step by step—from the previous one.

There are several interrelated stages or components in the process of obtaining, disseminating, and using information for policy making: (a) search or acquisition, (b) diffusion or dissemination, (c) use or utilization, and (d) impact. While each "stage" of the knowledge inquiry system can be studied as distinctive agendas for research and practice, it is important to analyze how the stages are interrelated and what the critical issues are for each component of the "cycle."

The information search phase (or the information acquisition stage) is understood as a task in which a policy maker seeks information about problems or policy issues on his or her agenda. After information is acquired, the next logical question becomes, What is done with it? One option is to disseminate it within the organization, to other organizations or agencies, or to the public a whole. Another option is not to share the information with others. An important part of this "dissemination" phase is the way in which information flows or does not flow through formal (organizational structure) or informal (interpersonal communications) channels.

Once information is received and processed, it may or may not be used. "Use" is implicitly a choice or decision about whether to apply information in a policy maker's work. It is an intentional action. Use may simply mean, however, that information has been received and read; it does not necessarily mean that it is being applied for a particular purpose.

- *Use* is also not a universal concept that has the same meaning to everyone; there is no commonly agreed on definition. In this chapter, two assumptions are made. First, use is different from acquiring information and from disseminating it. Dissemination simply means that some channel of transmission has been used to send data or information from one source to one or more other sources. Second, use can be distinguished from utility, influence, and impact:

• *Use* may simply mean, as mentioned earlier, that information has been received and read; it does not necessarily imply that information has been understood; it also does not imply that some action has been taken after the information was received and read or that, if action is taken, information contributed to the action.

• *Utility* refers to some user's judgment that the information could be relevant or of value for some purpose that has not been identified as of yet. It also does not imply that some action has been taken.

• *Influence* means that information has contributed to policy development, an action, or to a way of thinking about a problem; in this case, the user believes that by using information, he or she was aided in a decision of action.

• *Impact* is more directly action oriented. In this case, information has been received, understood, and has led directly to some concrete decision or action, even if that action is to ultimately reject the information (also see Leviton & Hughes, 1981). Consequently, the final "stage" is the "impact phase." In this phase, the question is, What effect has the information had on the individual or institution in the policy-making process?

As the field of knowledge utilization has matured, increasing attention has been given to the impact phase. Ultimately, one can think of impact as a form of learning. Public learning is a process in which citizens *become engaged* in a continuing search for "appropriate" responses to problematic issues or situations. Such learning is a social phenomenon—involving interaction with government agencies and with other stakeholders both to formulate or—using Schön's (1973) terms—to frame the problem and also to participate in the design of learning systems for achieving a practical, achievable process of change. Public learning is a process in which the attitudes, beliefs, and *behavior* of the civil society are changed in the search for new "solutions"—new ways of coping with currently perceived problems that affect the public interest (Rich & Alpert, 2004). From the perspective of the public,

> It is very important . . . to be able to say that we are learning, to be able to admit that we are acting to learn, because it is very difficult to learn if one is required at the same time to pretend to be certain. (Schön, 1973, p. 12)

Policy making can be seen as a learning activity based on information gathering and analysis. Schön and others have noted that we tend to view social problem-solving processes, including policy making, as being "rational." From this perspective, government decision makers or policy makers represent "rational actors." "It is not so much the content of ideas that counts, but their role as information in reducing uncertainty or maximizing utility" (Bhatia & Coleman, 2003, p. 727). According to these theories, information helps to reduce uncertainty, increase rationality, and, in turn, maximize the effectiveness of the policy-making process (Rich & Oh, 2000).

All rational actor theories call for canvassing of alternative courses of action, the systematic analysis of the consequences of each alternative in terms of the values and goals one wants to maximize and for the ultimate choice to be guided by this analysis.

Indeed, the "rationalist dream" is that knowledge will "emancipate us individually and collectively from scarcity, ignorance, and errors. . . . Currently, in the context of the knowledge society, we are being enticed, cajoled, and otherwise encouraged to increase and improve the transfer and utilization of research knowledge" because this will help to promote rationality (Dickinson, 2003, p. 42).

THEORIES OF KNOWLEDGE UTILIZATION

The "knowledge cycle" is a model that describes the flow of information—how information is acquired, processed, and used in organizations or agencies. Given these processes, what social science theories account for how the knowledge inquiry system works? In this section, we will examine three alternative theories.

Rational Choice Theories

In the 1970s and 1980s, knowledge utilization studies appeared to be preoccupied with what was perceived (primarily by researchers) as a gap between the production of valuable social science knowledge and its under- or nonutilization by policy makers. Some researchers argued that underutilization is counterintuitive (DeMartini & Whitbeck, 1986). Indeed, social science researchers believed that this underutilization can be explained by "irrational" behavior on the part of policy makers in government. Studies that focus on the knowledge cycle or some component of it have been dominated by a "rationalistic" bias. This "bias" is expressed in terms of the *belief* that the act of acquiring information will automatically lead to its utilization, which, in turn, will automatically lead to improved or high-quality policies or decisions (Rich & Oh, 2000).

Rational choice theories posit that information is an essential part of rational decision making but do not explicitly deal with how individuals process information. The major underlying assumptions of the rational choice theories with respect to information acquisition, dissemination, and use/impact are as follows:

1. The human mind is capable of processing all sources of available information (March & Simon, 1958).

2. All relevant sources of available information will be searched for and should be applied to a given problem (Rich & Oh, 2000).

3. Once information is acquired, it will be widely disseminated to all who "have a need to know" (Rich, 2001; Rich & Oh, 2000).

4. When the information is collected and disseminated, it will be used if it is sensible and scientifically valid (Huberman, 1987; March, 1988).

5. Use of information will lead to a choice among a set of competing alternatives (March, 1988); hence, the information will have an impact.

The model accounts for the fact that information is not simply acquired (or produced) and used for instrumental purposes. It is also acquired for building databases, investing in research for "research's sake," and other functions (March, 1988; Quadrell & Rich, 1989; Rich 1981b). It also allows that policy making is not simply the application of information. There are many other legitimate and appropriate inputs into policy development, including politics, ideology, past traditions, and expert judgment. Still, the model assumes that despite these competing influences, information will have an impact.

The Input/Output Model

Other conceptual or theoretical perspectives in the area of knowledge utilization studies are closely associated with the rational choice models. Those who have studied how knowledge—especially research-based knowledge—affects policy making and other types of outputs and outcomes have tended to focus on the following kinds of questions:

1. What are the specific uses of information in policy making?

2. What types of information are preferred over others? Are there some types that are selectively passed over or ignored (Rich & Oh, 1994)?

3. To what extent do policy makers and other decision makers take research into account in their work (Weiss & Bucuvalas, 1980)?

4. From the time that information/knowledge enters into an organization (through some channel), what happens to it—what are the diffusion/dissemination patterns (see Bardach, 1984)?

5. What patterns does information follow as it flows through an organization or through a specific decision-making hierarchy (Rich & Oh, 1994)?

6. To what extent does information confirm or legitimate policy decisions that are already made or about to be made (Feldman & March, 1981)? To what extent does research influence change from a position that a decision maker is already inclined toward (Knorr, 1977; Zaltman, 1979)?

7. What is the rate of adoption of new information sources that are made available to policy makers (Weiss & Bucuvalas, 1980)?

8. What are the characteristics of social science research that make it useful for policy making (Weiss & Bucuvalas, 1980; Webber, 1987)?

9. To what extent does information benefit the decision maker or the decision-making process (Landry et al., 2001; Lavis et al., 2002)?

10. To what extent can one document levels of premature utilization, deliberate nonutilization, and/or selective utilization of information (T. D. Cook, Levinson-Rose, & Pollard, 1980; Rich, 1975, 1981b)?

The critical assumption behind many of these questions is that many specific policy decisions can be attributed to (or are "caused by") the use of specific bits of data. In this context, a key question becomes, How does one document the use of information or its impact? In answering this question, researchers seem to have had an input/output model in mind. Within this framework, it is thought that (a) one can trace the flow of information from the time it enters an organization to the time that some action is taken (predicated on or influenced by the new information), (b) impact or influence can be measured relative to a single piece or cluster of discrete information that enters an organization (or to which an individual is exposed), and (c) it is appropriate and possible to assess the impact or influence of a single piece of information on the problem-solving behavior of an individual. In most corners of the scientific community, there has been a value-based underpinning to these assumptions: The application of scientific information is the most legitimate input into policy development.

In short, for purposes of conceptualization and measurement, researchers/analysts have tended to adopt a deterministic view of how knowledge (especially research-based knowledge) is disseminated and used (Bulmer, 1981; Rein & White, 1977; Weiss, 1981). Respondents in empirical studies are conceived of as being able to identify how discrete bits of information affect specific behaviors, choices, or actions. In this context, it is assumed that the relationship between information processing and decision making is a linear one. For example, it is thought that users can say, "The study recently completed by X led me to take an action that I would not (or probably would not) have taken, if I had not been exposed to the study." Implicitly, it is also being said that the information generated by X is the key element in reaching a policy decision; the work environment, past experience, ideology, beliefs, and educational background of an individual do not affect a particular choice or decision in the same way or to the same extent that the study conducted by X does.

A problem with the input/output approach to conceptualizing and measuring the flow and impact of information is that its assumptions are rarely met, as is apparent in reviewing the empirical literature:

• Knowledge produces effects, not a single effect. If one concentrates on a single effect, one will underestimate the impact that knowledge is having (Mandell & Sauter, 1984).

• Decisions do not generally represent a single event; it is difficult to understand a single decision without examining the series of events that led up to it (Booth, 1990; Pollard, 1987).

• It is almost impossible to predict or to track what knowledge has an effect and at what point in decision-making (Bimber, 1996).

• Problem-solving is affected by many variables other than information (e.g., ideology, work environment, demographics; see Bozeman & Bretschneider, 1986; Lavis et al., 2002; Nelson, Roberts, Maederer, Wertheimer, & Johnson, 1987; Oh, 1992; Pollard, 1987).

However, if one wanted to reject the input/output approach and "advance" beyond it, formidable conceptual and methodological problems need to be overcome. First, because knowledge accumulates and builds in organizational memories, some policy decisions (or outputs) are made that seem to

be independent of any identifiable, discrete inputs. The "process" simply cannot be traced in a step-by-step, linear fashion. For the analyst and potential evaluator, this poses the problem of not being able to identify the universe of inputs for a particular output or decision. It is also true that the universe of inputs related to a policy issue or set of issues has accumulated and grown larger over time. Thus, one is not able to judge levels of utilization and the processes affecting utilization at a certain moment in time.

Second, as noted above, because knowledge produces multiple effects, it is often impossible to trace outputs back to their specific inputs, even if it were possible to identify the universe of information inputs. It seems clear that input/output models are only appropriate when one is able to analyze the mechanical application of knowledge to problem-solving activities. For example, statistic X is needed to justify policy Y. In that case, a "tracing" approach could work out well—outputs can be traced back to specific, discrete inputs. Otherwise, it is difficult to trace the subtler, more naturalistic application of information to the myriad of decision-making channels within organizations.

The Politics of Expertise

The theories discussed to this point focus on communication-related and psychological factors that affect knowledge use. From extensive empirical work, a great deal also has been learned about the aspects of bureaucracies and organizations that affect the use of information, including the role of knowledge inquiry systems in politics and in the public policy-making process (Rich, 1981b, 2001). However, the realities of bureaucratic and organizational politics continue to dominate over rational decision making. The public policy-making system has become quite sophisticated in assigning status and credence to scientific information, technology, and the development of sophisticated and complex information systems, but it has not advanced very much in allowing the outputs of these systems to have a significant impact on the substance of American public policy.

The perception that knowledge is power is pervasive in the literature on organizations and bureaucracies. However, not all knowledge is equally powerful. From the bureaucratic perspective, knowledge that is owned and controlled by a single agency or individual is much more desirable and influential than information that is in the public domain and widely accessible. Control of information is directly correlated with power. In addition, the source of the information being provided is at least as important as its content. When the source is a "trusted aide" (an insider) who reports to the policy maker (i.e., he or she is in the formal organizational hierarchy), the information is of greater value than if it comes from an outside source—known or unknown—who cannot necessarily be trusted. The policy maker receiving new information poses the following questions: Why am I receiving this information? What risks am I taking by using this information? Does the person providing the information understand and appreciate the political constraints that my agency operates under? Whose interests are being served if I use it?

Over the past 20 years, public opinion and survey data also have become increasingly important to politicians and to the policy-making process. Politicians at all levels of government have become very cognizant of the results of opinion polling; it plays a major role in developing voting preferences, campaign/marketing materials, and formal statements and positions. It is commonplace to poll the public after a major presidential address and to regularly monitor approval ratings of presidents, governors, mayors, and

other elected officials. The electronic and print media also prominently display the results of such polling.

Surveys of a random sample of the American public or some specialized segment are also very important in the development and implementation of public policy. The critical use of this type of data was illustrated in the important debates over health care reform in 1993–1994, in the controversy over welfare reform in 1995–1996, in the debates over reimbursement for prescription drug expenses as part of Medicare in 2005, and in the debates over Social Security reform in 2004 and 2005. Survey data are also often used in the formal evaluations, formative and summative, of major policy initiatives.

Organizations make their own investments in information systems (e.g., information technologies such as decision support systems or databases), but these investments will not automatically lead to regular and systematic use of data or knowledge or to the information having an impact. For example, it is common for government organizations to acquire multiple systems and sources of expertise; however, there is not an automatic linkage between acquiring the information and applying it to problem solving. In addition, the acquisition of information technology may be seen as desirable and even considered to be a high-profile or high-status organizational activity; this, by itself, however, does not guarantee that the technology will be appropriately used or that it will become part of a learning organization.

TYPES OF INFORMATION AND KNOWLEDGE

The analysis of policy makers' inquiry systems (methods and infrastructure for using information) may also be sharpened by distinguishing between types of information and knowledge and their functions in the decision-making process.

The term *knowledge* has been defined in many different ways. Fritz Machlup (1980) has provided a classification of five major types of knowledge: practical knowledge, intellectual knowledge, small-talk or pastime knowledge, spiritual knowledge, and unwanted knowledge.

Practical knowledge refers to knowledge that is instrumental or central to one's work or profession, intellectual knowledge satisfies one's "intellectual curiosity," small-talk knowledge satisfies one's "nonintellectual curiosity and one's desire for light entertainment and emotional stimulation," spiritual knowledge is related to one's religious beliefs, and unwanted knowledge is outside of one's interests, "usually accidentally acquired, aimlessly retained" knowledge. For purposes of decision making or policy making, "practical" or "intellectual" knowledge is the primary focus of attention.

Machlup (1980) is going beyond some rather traditional distinctions among data, information, and knowledge (also see Majone, 1989). Traditionally, data refer to the most rudimentary unit of analysis (i.e., raw material, such as professional or scientific observations). Information is more than data; it is thought of as refined data that provides some added value to the user (e.g., professional expert opinion). And knowledge provides added value and has been subjected to some validation or "truth test" (e.g., a conclusion drawn from scientific evidence).

The distinctions one makes among different types of information and knowledge affects how one defines utilization and how one thinks about the range of relevant and appropriate outcomes that are possible in the policy-making or decision-making context. Depending on the circumstance, some types of knowledge can assume more importance than others. Yet, past studies often refer to use as if there are no significant differences in the types of knowledge that might be used (Oh, 1992; Rich, 1991).

CASES OF KNOWLEDGE UTILIZATION

This section presents cases of high utilization, nonutilization, and deliberate nonutilization of information by governmental decision makers and agencies. In each of the three cases, the impact of information on specific policy developments or decision-making processes is examined.[2]

High Utilization—The Antismoking Campaign

A primary recent example of high utilization of scientific information is the very successful antismoking public education campaign. Over the past four decades, there has been a major change in societal attitudes about smoking, including legal suits against the tobacco industry by victims of smoking. Surgeon General C. Everett Koop was the champion of a public education campaign, which led to a significant paradigm shift in U.S. society as a whole and, even to some degree, in other countries. Some of the indicators for this major change include the following:

- the Surgeon General's Committee on Health, which advocated "warnings" on packages of cigarettes (1964);
- widespread dissemination of information that documented the negative effects of smoking on people's health;
- the inclusion of information about smoking in the curricula of health classes taught in middle and secondary schools;
- laws that declare that public places (e.g., airports, restaurants) may designate "nonsmoking" zones;
- court decisions that have held tobacco companies liable for documented health problems of smokers;

- places of work being declared nonsmoking zones so that smokers have to leave the building to smoke;
- major increases in taxes on the sale of cigarettes; and
- a real decrease in the rate of smoking among all demographic groups (except for women between the ages of 18 and 25).

Why were the surgeon general's initiatives so successful? Why was society willing to limit the rights of smokers in public places? What accounts for a general change in the position of society—which had previously been sympathetic to a smoker's assertion that "I have just as many rights as you do!"? A key step in the process was the very convincing scientific evidence—as accepted in legal proceedings—of the negative secondary effects of smoke. Consequently, from the societal perspective, it was difficult to maintain the position that if you choose to harm yourself by smoking, this is your own individual choice. The new evidence showed that aside from smokers hurting themselves, the secondary effects of their smoking could hurt some of those who breathe the surrounding air.

In this case, much of the public appears to have learned from the convincing scientific evidence, which was translated into an effective public education campaign and widely disseminated. This campaign was then translated into vigorously enforced laws and regulations.

Nonutilization—Needle Exchange

Government-sponsored research and evaluation studies have demonstrated that needle exchange programs decrease HIV transmissions and drug use. Yet, voting records of elected officials indicate that lawmakers have continued to ban federal funding of such programs. What is the basis for this seeming contradiction? Why has the convincing scientific evidence not been translated into action?

The empirical research in this area is well understood and widely recognized as being of high quality. The research cannot, however, be directly translated into policy because of political considerations. Elected officials have concluded that there is not sufficient public support for needle exchange programs from a public health perspective. The fear is that support of these programs would be seen as promoting drug use (Des Jarlais, 2000; Wodak, 1994).

Deliberate Nonutilization—Climate Change (Global Warming)

In some high-visibility areas such as climate change, the public policy environment surrounding the question of how scientific research is translated into action is one of conflict and controversy. For many scientists and public policy makers, there is also deep concern that the objectivity and quality of scientific research is being negatively affected. In this context, Russell Train, Environmental Protection Agency (EPA) administrator under Presidents Nixon and Ford, has observed, "How radically we have moved away from regulation based on independent findings and professional analysis of scientific, health and economic data by the responsible agency to regulation controlled by the White House and driven primarily by political considerations" (American Civil Liberties Union, 2005, p. 27).

In its over 100-year history as a scientific issue, climate change has nearly always been controversial, with projections that the globe is warming due to human activity facing strong criticism. However, in a groundbreaking study that addressed the question of the scientific consensus on climate change, *Science* magazine published an article by Naomi Oreskes in 2004, analyzing 928 peer-reviewed scientific papers on global warming published between 1993 and 2003. None of these papers challenged the widely held scientific belief that the Earth's temperature is rising and that such a rise is due to human activity. In fact, "without substantial disagreement, scientists find human activities are heating the Earth's surface." The study concludes, "Many details about climate interactions are not well understood, and there are ample grounds for continued research to provide a better basis for understanding climate dynamics. The question of what to do about climate change in terms of law and public policy is also still open. But there is scientific consensus on the reality of anthropogenic climate change. Climate scientists have repeatedly tried to make this clear. It is time for the rest of us to listen" (Oreske, 2004, p. 1686). Oreske's analysis demonstrates a general consensus in the scientific community on climate change science.

The case of climate change research represents a new chapter in the politics of expertise and how scientific expertise is used within government. Scientific knowledge on the impact of greenhouse gases on climate change has been expanding, and it is widely recognized as an important area for innovative research. Industry has also recognized the validity and importance of the research findings and has translated them, for example, into the development of hybrid cars. The international community has also translated this research into treaties and domestic policies to limit the impact on the environment.

Within American government, past tradition has been to use the best science as measured by peer review and professional standards in the development of policy and on official advisory committees, which have traditionally been relatively independent of strictly partisan politics. Presently, however, politics of climate change has become melded with science to an even greater degree than has existed in the past.

Core Findings in the Knowledge Utilization Literature

Empirical studies of knowledge or research utilization over the past 30 years have produced a core set of findings.

- Though it is true that factors such as format and style of presentation and timeliness of the information are important factors that help lead to utilization, they, by themselves, will not guarantee use (Lavis et al., 2002; Rich, 2001).

- Potential users' needs, values, and interests are critical in understanding knowledge utilization (Florio & DeMartini, 1993; Hultman & Horberg, 1998; Landry et al., 2001; Lester, 1993; Slappendel, 1994; Tyden, 1996).

- Who provides the information (i.e., the source of the information) to a potential user is more important than what the content of the information actually is. Decision makers rely on "trusted aides" for information that is considered to be useful. Trusted aides are the ones who can assess the risk involved with using information and who have the "best interests" of the policy makers and the organization in mind. Thus, information transmitted by a trusted aide will be readily used, even if it is not of the same "scientific quality" as information produced by an individual not known to the decision maker (Rich, 1981b; Rich & Oh, 1994).

- Internal sources of information are more heavily used than information provided by external sources. However, information generated by external sources ultimately has a greater impact on policy making than those provided by internal sources (or trusted aides) (Cousins & Leithwood, 1993; Lester, 1993; Rich, 2001; Rich & Oh, 2000; Slappendel, 1994).

- Knowledge produces effects, not a single effect. If one concentrates on a single effect, one will underestimate the impact that knowledge is having (Mandell & Sauter, 1984).

- It is true, as many studies have demonstrated, that there are the two cultures of science and government; moreover, it is true that the two cultures have a deep distrust for each other (Caplan, 1979; Dunn, 1980; Rich, 2001). However, the existence or nonexistence of the two cultures may not be a significant factor in predicting utilization. In other words, simply documenting that there are two cultures and that they both recognize that a "gap" exists does not necessarily determine whether information will be used (Rich, 2001).

• It is true that understanding the process of information use is very important. It is, however, equally important to understand the processes of misutilization, nonutilization, and deliberate nonutilization of information. Misutilization and deliberate nonutilization are integral parts of policy development and decision making (T. D. Cook et al., 1980). Nonutilization of information may, from the perspective of politics or policy development, be a rational, fully justifiable action.

• It is almost impossible to predict when and where a specific knowledge input is likely to have an effect on a particular policy or decision.

• Policy development and problem solving are legitimately affected by many variables other than information, including scientific information (e.g., ideology, work environment, demographics) (Bozeman & Bretschneider, 1986; Nelson et al., 1987; Oh, 1992; Pollard, 1987).

These core findings illustrate that the literature consists of a series of studies that focus on describing particular factors or sets of factors that affect how and when information is used in the decision-making process. Although the direction of the work has been driven by certain assumptions, theories about policy makers' knowledge use and how to influence it have not been systematically developed or tested. The cumulative

literature thus provides a catalog of "factors affecting utilization" as opposed to evidence for or against a comprehensive theory or model, or particular strategies for influencing knowledge use.

CONCLUSION

Whether or not one believes the use, application, and utility of behavioral and social science research to be important depends on one's conception of the social contract between science and society (Guston, 2000). This social contract evokes the voluntary but mutual responsibilities between government and science, the production of basic research that inherently serves the public good, and the investment in basic research for future prosperity (Guston, 2000, p. 32). These arguments, originally put forth in 1945 by Vannevar Bush, science and technology adviser to President Roosevelt, became a foundation for federal science policy. Scientists, including behavioral and social scientists, believed that government has an obligation to invest heavily in research—especially basic research—and those researchers, in turn, have an obligation to produce high-quality studies of inherent value but that may or may not be useful for addressing a particular social problem or issue.

This conception of the social contract was pretty well accepted by government and by scientists from 1945 through the Great Society years. At that point, government officials began asking some critical questions: What is the return on our investment? What is the utility of the research that is being supported out of public funds? There seemed to be a growing feeling that funded research should, at least to some extent, have utility and that researchers applying for government funding should address this question: How is this information going to be used?

Consequently, some real tension developed between the "scientific community" and its professional associations and some policy makers and other governmental officials. To what extent was this social contract going to be renegotiated?

It seems clear that the contract has changed. Federal and state government agencies are investing more heavily in applied research, evaluation studies, and policy analysis. Basic research is still given a very high priority; it is no longer, however, the only priority. Nevertheless, some tension continues between science and government around the appropriate roles of scientists as the "producers" of research and of policy makers as "users" of it. If government officials are to continue to have confidence in the scientific research enterprise, then issues related to utility and utilization cannot be ignored.

In the future, therefore, the process of knowledge utilization must become better understood. The three cases presented in this chapter illustrated some of the conditions under which high-quality scientific and behavioral science research may be translated (or not translated) into policy. There is no doubt that in all three instances, research has had an impact on the decision-making process, but they differ with respect to how influential the research has been on the development of policy and societal attitude change.

It seems clear, however, from the research and practice reviewed in this chapter that the processes of acquiring, disseminating, and using information or information systems is directly related to the concept of "learning" at the individual and organizational levels. Organizations in the form of government bureaucracies have a need to become efficient learning organizations. Traditionally, they are responsible for implementing policy initiatives and administering programs. They are also responsible for monitoring and evaluating program results, and they

help to fine-tune and redesign policies and programs. Another important function of administrative bureaucracies is to keep policy makers well informed and to make sure that they are not embarrassed or caught by surprise. Consequently, it is natural for officials to collect information and invest in information systems that will help in the dual process of informing and developing policy while at the same time reducing political risk.

Investing in information systems and their use suggests that the organization is a "learning organization." The so-called learning organization (Argyris, Putnam, & Smith, 1985; Chawla & Renesch, 1995; Senge, 1995; Stacey, 1996; Stewart, 1997) is usually concerned with notions of accountability, continuous improvement, and continuous inquiry (Dilworth, 1995). They are open to change and innovation.

But for government organizations, learning may be a problematic or risky activity because it can challenge the *essence* of bureaucratic life. The process of learning may be inconsistent with the day-to-day demands of the bureaucratic environment that is reactive and protective and does not demand innovation, introspection, and self-reflection in its members (Rich & Alpert, 2004; Rich & Oh, 2000; Senge, 1995). In this context, just as individuals can have learning disabilities, the organization can be thought of as having "learning disabilities" to overcome in order to make effective use of knowledge.

Understanding the use of information, including scientific and technical knowledge, continues to be a real challenge. With the changing social contract, the policy-making and scientific communities have increasing interest in developing and understanding how to acquire, disseminate, and use information. The academic disciplines of communications, political science, psychology public administration, and sociology have all devoted increasing attention to issues related to knowledge utilization. But researchers and policy makers will not advance very much further by continuing to rely on the two-cultures metaphor, simple input/output approaches, or the rational actor model. The major challenges of the knowledge utilization field will be to continue to develop comprehensive theories of the knowledge utilization process, to develop more sophisticated approaches to measuring the interrelated stages of the knowledge inquiry system, and to advance the study of organizational and public learning, including the use of individual and organizational systems of knowledge inquiry.

NOTES

1. In this chapter, the term *knowledge* refers to information that has been validated through procedures such as scientific methods. *Information* refers to any information that potentially benefits the user whether or not it has been validated. Issues of definition are discussed further in this chapter.

2. *Deliberate nonutilization* is distinguished from simple *nonutilization* in this section of the chapter. Nonutilization may simply occur as a routine part of the decision-making process (e.g., it is lost in the din of information), or it may result from perceiving applications of the science to be infeasible or irrelevant. In *deliberate nonutilization,* information is rejected and not used even if perceived as feasible and relevant to the policy development process.

REFERENCES

American Civil Liberties Union. (2005). *Science under siege: The Bush administration's assault on academic freedom and scientific inquiry.* New York: Tania Simoncelli & Jay Stanley.

Argyris, C., Putnam, R., & Smith, D. M. (1985). *Action science.* San Francisco: Jossey-Bass.

Bardach, E. (1984). The dissemination of policy research to policymakers. *Knowledge, 6,* 125–145.

Bhatia, V., & Coleman, W. D. (2003). Ideas and discourse: Reform and resistance in the German and Canadian health care systems. *Canadian Journal of Political Science, 36,* 715–740.

Bimber, B. (1996). *The politics of expertise in Congress: The rise and fall of technology assessment.* New York: SUNY Press.

Booth, T. (1990). Researching policy research: Issues of utilization in decision making. *Knowledge, 12,* 80–100.

Bozeman, B., & Bretschneider, S. (1986). Public management information system: Theory and practice. *Public Administration Review, 46,* (special issues), 475–487.

Bulmer, M. (1981). Applied social research: A reformulation of "Applied" and "Enlightment" models. *Knowledge, 3,* 187–209.

Caplan, N. S. (1979). The two community theory and knowledge utilization. *American Behavorial Scientist, 22,* 459–470.

Caplan, N. S., Morrison, A., & Stambaugh, R. J. (1975). *The use of social science knowledge in policy decisions at the national level.* Ann Arbor, MI: Institute for Social Research.

Chawla, S., & Renesch, J. (Eds.). (1995.) *Learning organizations*. Portland, OR: Productivity Press.

Ciarlo, J. A. (1980). *Utilizing evaluation: Concepts and measurement techniques*. Beverly Hills, CA: Sage.

Cook, T. D., Levinson-Rose, J., & Pollard, W. E. (1980). The mis-utilization of evaluation research: Some pitfalls of definition. *Knowledge, 1,* 477–498.

Cousins, J., & Leithwood, K. (1993). Enhancing knowledge utilization as a strategy for school improvement. *Knowledge: Creation, Diffusion, Utilization, 14,* 305–333.

DeMartini, J., & Whitbeck, L. (1986). Knowledge use as knowledge creation. *Knowledge, 7,* 383–396.

Des Jarlais, D. C. (2000). Research, politics, and needle exchange. *American Journal of Public Health, 90,* 1392–1394.

Dickinson, H. D. (2003). The transfer and utilization of social scientific knowledge for policy-making perspectives in sociology. In L. Lemieux-Charles & F. Champagne (Eds.), *Multidisciplinary perspectives on evidence-based decision-making in health care* (pp. 41–70). Toronto: University of Toronto Press.

Dilworth, R. (1995). The DNA of the learning organization. In S. Chawla & J. Renesch (Eds.), *Learning organizations* (pp. 243–256). Portland, OR: Productivity Press.

Dunn, W. (1980). The two communities metaphor and models of knowledge utilization: An exploratory case survey. *Knowledge: Creation Diffusion, Utilization, 1*(4), 515–537.

Estabrooks, C. A., Wallin, L., & Milner, M. (2003). Measuring knowledge utilization in health care. *International Journal of Policy Analysis & Evaluation, 1,* 3–36

Florio, E., & DeMartini, J. (1993). The use of information by policy makers at the local community level. *Knowledge: Creation, Diffusion, Utilization, 15,* 106–123.

Guston, D. H. (2000). *Between politics and science: Assuring the integrity and productivity of research*. Cambridge, UK: Cambridge University Press.

Huberman, M. (1987). Steps toward an integrated model of research utilization. *Knowledge, 8,* 586–611.

Hultman, G., & Horberg, C. R. (1998). Knowledge competition and personal ambition: A theoretical framework. *Science Communication, 19,* 328–348.

Hutchinson, J. R. (1995). A multimethod analysis of knowledge use in social policy. *Science Communication, 17,* 90–106.

Knorr, K. (1977). Policymakers' use of social science knowledge: Symbolic or instrumental? In C. H. Weiss (Ed.), *Using social research in public policy-making*. Lexington, MA: Lexington Books.

Landry, R., Amara, N., & Lamari, M. (2001). Climbing the ladder of research utilization: evidence from social science research. *Science Communication, 22*(4), 396–422.

Lavis, J. N., Ross, S. E., & Hurley, J. E. (2002). Examining the role of health services research in policymaking. *The Milbank Quarterly, 80*(1), 125–154.

Lester, J. (1993). The utilization of policy analysis by state agency officials. *Knowledge: Creation, Diffusion, Utilization, 14,* 267–290.

Leviton, L. C., & Hughes, E. F. X. (1981). Research on the utilization of evaluation. *Evaluation Review, 5,* 525–548.

Machlup, F. (1980). *Knowledge and knowledge production*. Princeton, NJ: Princeton University Press.

Majone, G. (1989). *Evidence, arguments, and persuasion in the policy process*. New Haven, CT: Yale University Press.

Mandell, M. B., & Sauter, V. L. (1984). Approaches to the study of information utilization in public agencies. *Knowledge, 6,* 145–164.

March, J. G. (Ed.). (1988). *Decisions and organizations.* Cambridge, UK: Basil Blackwell.

March, J. G., & Simon, H. (1958). *Organizations.* New York: John Wiley.

Nelson, C. E., Roberts, J., Maederer, C. M., Wertheimer, B., & Johnson, B. (1987). The utilization of social science information by policy makers. *American Behavioral Scientist, 30,* 569–577.

Oh, C. H. (1992, March). *Rationality, organizational interest, and information searching in government bureaucracy.* Paper presented at the annual meeting of the American Society for Public Administration, Chicago.

Oh, C. H., & Rich, R. (1996). Explaining use of information in public policymaking. *Knowledge and Policy, 9,* 3–35.

Oreskes, N. (2004). Beyond the ivory tower: The scientific consensus on climate change. *Science, 306,* 1686.

Pollard, W. (1987). Decisionmaking and the use of evaluation research. *American Behavioral Scientist, 30,* 661–676.

Quadrell, M. J., & Rich, R. F. (1989). Information selection in the House of Representatives. *Knowledge, 11,* 123–154.

Rein, M., & White, S. H. (1977). Policy research: Belief and doubt. *Policy Analysis, 3,* 239–271.

Rich, R. F. (1975). Selective utilization of social science related information by federal policymakers. *Inquiry, 13,* 239–245.

Rich, R. F. (1979). The pursuit of knowledge. *Science Communication, 1,* 6–30.

Rich, R. F. (Ed.). (1981a). *The knowledge cycle.* Beverly Hills, CA: Sage.

Rich, R. F. (1981b). *Social science information and public policy making.* San Francisco: Jossey-Bass.

Rich, R. F. (1991). Knowledge creation, diffusion, and utilization: Perspectives of the founding editor of *Knowledge, Science, and Communication. Knowledge, Science, and Communication, 12*(3), 319–337.

Rich, R. F. (2001). *Social science information and public policy-making (with a new introduction).* New Brunswick, NJ: Transactions Publishers.

Rich, R. F., & Alpert, D. A. (2004). *Public learning: Paradigm shifts in public attitudes, beliefs, and actions.* Working paper, Institute of Government and Public Affairs, University of Illinois, Urbana-Champaign.

Rich, R. F., & Oh, C. H. (1994). Utilization of policy research. In S. Nagel (Ed.), *Encyclopedia of policy studies* (2nd ed., pp. 69–94). New York: Marcel Dekker.

Rich, R. F., & Oh, C. H. (2000). Rationality and use of information in policy decisions: A search for alternatives. *Science Communications, 22*(2), 173–211.

Schön, D. (1973). *Beyond the stable state.* Harmondsworth, UK: Penguin.

Senge, P. M. (1995). *The fifth discipline.* New York: Currency Doubleday.

Slappendel, C. (1994). Knowledge use versus capability development: The case of applying ergonomics to product design. *Science Communication, 16,* 195–205.

Stacey, R. D. (1996). *Complexity and creativity in organizations.* San Francisco: Berrett-Koehler.

Stewart, T. A. (1997). *Intellectual capital.* New York: Currency Doubleday.

Tyden, T. (1996). The contribution of longitudinal studies for understanding science communication and research utilization. *Science Communication, 18,* 29–48.

van Lohuizen, C. W. W. (1986). Knowledge management and policymaking. *Knowledge, 8,* 12–38.

Webber, D. (1987). Legislators' use of policy information. *American Behavioral Scientist, 30,* 612–631.

Weiss, C. (1981). The use of social science research. In H. Stein (Ed.), *Organizations and the human services* (pp. 50–69). Philadelphia: Temple University Press.

Weiss, C. H., & Bucuvalas, M. J. (1980). *Social science research and decision making.* New York: Cambridge University Press.

Wenger, E. (1991, Fall). Communities of practice: Where learning happens. *Benchmark,* pp. 6–8.

Wingens, M. (1990). Toward a general utilization theory. *Knowledge, 12,* 27–42.

Wodak A. (1994). How do communities achieve reductions in alcohol- and drug-related harm? *Addiction, 89,* 147–150.

Zaltman, G. (1979). Knowledge utilization as planned social change. *Knowledge, 1,* 82–105.

CHAPTER 16

Working With the Federal Government

ANGELA L. SHARPE

Contrary to the beliefs of many researchers, science is an important part of the political process. Science and technology touch almost every aspect of modern public policy from economic development, health care, and education to national security, energy, and the environment. Over the past 50 years, scientists have helped to shape America's prestigious science and technology enterprise through their engagement with public policy as government employees, as advisers to the federal government (legislative and executive branches), as researchers, and as individual citizens. In basic terms, federal public policy includes the laws written and programs created and funded by Congress and the rules and regulations established by the executive branch to operate those programs. Social policy is designed primarily to promote human well-being, and it has a long history of being shaped by behavioral and social science (Featherman & Vinovskis, 2001). Science policy preserves and advances the infrastructure and processes of science.

Though more and more behavioral and social scientists appreciate the impact that research can have on public policy, not all scientists are inclined to participate and can be reluctant to interact with the federal government other than as recipients of federal grants. Policy decisions are made every day without input from those who conduct relevant and often federally sponsored research. Among the many reasons for this aversion, scientists can believe that their involvement in "politics" will compromise the integrity of their science and perhaps damage their reputations, or they may perceive that their involvement would be unproductive in an antiscience government. At the same time, other researchers would like to participate but may be unfamiliar with the policy issues, the complex legislative process, and the varied and numerous opportunities to affect science and public policy within Congress and the federal agencies. Because of the many competing factors that go into policy making (discussed later in this chapter) and because policy arguments built around sound science may not always persuade or result in a direct policy outcome, scientists can also underestimate the essential contribution that science makes to public policy.

The first section of the chapter, therefore, takes a brief look back at the relationship between public policy and the social and behavioral sciences and illustrates the value of science using as an example the policy issue of HIV/AIDS. The chapter continues by showing why policy makers must be continually educated about how scientific work is administered and conducted. The following section explains that to engage successfully in policy making scientists, should develop knowledge in three key areas: understanding the structure and function of Congress and the executive branch agencies, how to develop a communications strategy and the skills needed to execute it, and how to establish and maintain relationships with federal policy makers. The chapter concludes by describing the roles of professional societies and associations in supporting scientists' policy-related work.

BEHAVIORAL AND SOCIAL SCIENCE IS ESSENTIAL TO POLICY MAKING

Fostering Human Progress: Social and Behavioral Science Research Contributions to Public Policy, a publication celebrating the 20th anniversary of the Consortium of Social Science Associations (COSSA), observes that the contributions of the social and behavioral sciences are not always noticed because they often come in "ripples, not waves" and so are frequently "taken for granted by legislators and policymakers who use the science to make choices about competing demands for scarce resources" (Consortium of Social Science Associations, 2001, p. 1). *Fostering,* therefore, provides examples of how these sciences have helped to attain the six societal goals of creating a safer world, increasing prosperity, improving health, educating the nation, promoting fairness, and protecting the environment. COSSA, an advocacy group established to promote social and behavioral science research, maintains that policy makers are able to make choices in these six areas as a result of

the "continued presence of social and behavioral scientists in the Executive and Legislatives branches of government and as witnesses before congressional and regulatory bodies" (COSSA, 2001, p. 3). Social and behavioral research has, for example, contributed to major changes in crime prevention and crime-fighting policies by improving our understanding of the causes of criminal behavior and increasing the ability to predict its onset and persistence. As *Fostering* explains, "The major development of the last 25 years has been the recognition of the changing nature of criminal behavior over the course of one's life, the resulting need for multiple theoretical perspectives to explain these changes, and the value of longitudinal studies of crime to test and improve theories at both the individual and collective levels" (COSSA, 2001, p. 18). This case illustrates but one of the many accomplishments achieved since broad federal support for the behavioral and social sciences first began.

A Brief Look Back

The 1960s and President Lyndon Johnson's Great Society programs ushered in a "golden age" for social and behavioral studies (COSSA, 2001). Massive increases in government programs in both the Johnson and Nixon administrations changed the nation's science policy. The social and behavioral sciences "benefited from the need for evaluations of new programs and the desire to complete the unfinished agendas of the New and Fair Deals" (COSSA, 2001, p. 1).

The social and behavioral science fields, however, were vulnerable during the "national malaise" and economic tough times of the 1970s. An amendment was offered on the floor of the House of Representatives aimed at cutting the budget to the National Science Foundation (NSF) Directorate for Biological, Behavioral, and Social Sciences by the precise amount budgeted for social science research. In an acknowledged attack on social science research, the amendment passed the House. "Both the attacks and defenses of social science research were carried on in the absence of any participation by the social [and behavioral] science community" (COSSA, 1982, p. 8).

In the early 1980s, decision makers began to recognize the potential contributions of the social and behavioral sciences to health promotion and disease prevention. The release of the 1982 Institute of Medicine (IOM) report, *Health and Behavior: Frontiers of Biobehavioral Research,* focused national attention on the relationship between health and behavior by documenting the extent to which lifestyle contributed to chronic diseases such as heart disease and cancer.

By the late 1980s, recognition of the role these sciences could play in the making of effective policy began to increase, leading to the creation of the Social, Behavioral, and Economic Sciences Directorate (SBE) at the NSF in 1991. SBE supports research to develop and advance scientific knowledge on human cognition, language, culture, social behavior, geography, and the interactions between human societies and the physical environment through its Behavioral and Cognition Sciences research division. The Social and Economic Sciences Program (SES), SBE's second research division, seeks to enhance the understanding of human, social, and organizational behavior. SES accomplishes these missions by building social science infrastructure and developing disciplinary and interdisciplinary research projects that advance knowledge in the social and economics sciences (Social and Economic Sciences, n.d.).

In the early 1990s, policy makers officially recognized the potential contributions of the social and behavioral sciences to health policy. In 1993, Congress created the National Institutes of Health (NIH) Office of Behavioral and Social Sciences Research (OBSSR). The OBSSR's mission is to "develop

initiatives designed to stimulate research in the behavioral and social sciences arena, integrate a bio-behavioral perspective across the research areas of the NIH, and encourage the study of behavioral and social sciences across NIH's institutes and centers" (OBSSR, n.d.). The mission also requires the OBSSR to "initiate and promote studies to evaluate the contributions of behavioral, social, and lifestyle determinants in the development, course, treatment, and prevention of illness and related public health problems" (OBSSR, n.d.). In 2000, Congress created the NIH National Center for Minority Health and Health Disparities to conduct and support research, to train researchers, and to disseminate information regarding minority health conditions. This legislation resulted from a diverse coalition of scientists, advocates, and individuals who identified gaps in the research and highlighted the lack of adequate government policies surrounding health disparities. Advocates for the legislation, including scientists, lobbied the Congress, engaged in collective letter writing, held congressional briefings, and made telephone calls in support of the legislation.

Though the above examples illustrate an appreciation for the contributions of SBS research to society, COSSA was formed in response to a crisis: the selective assault against the social and behavioral sciences in the early 1980s by the Reagan administration. The president's budget threatened cuts up to 75% in the NSF's social and behavioral science budget and threatened the research supported by other agencies (COSSA, 2001).

An informed and politically active social and behavioral science community opposed the proposed budget cuts to NSF and, led by the newly incorporated COSSA, actively lobbied against them. A memo was sent to more than 4,000 scientists urging them to contact their representatives on the proposed cuts. Each House member was contacted via the postal service, followed by personal visits to their offices. Scientists also met with members in their congressional districts. Representatives who supported the restoration of social and behavioral science research funds were solicited to make oral statements of support for the research on the House floor during the debate. The floor statements were written by COSSA staff and others supporting the effort. The amendment was defeated 264 to 152. This effort significantly increased the social and behavioral science community's visibility and credibility.

While COSSA was critical to providing the overarching strategy in this movement, the efforts of the many social and behavioral scientists who provided testimony, wrote, called, and visited their representatives made the case that the budget cuts for social and behavioral science research were ill advised and unwarranted. The social and behavioral science community demonstrated that its engagement in the public policy process can make a difference, doing so without the ease of the electronic communication that we enjoy today.

The evolution of federal policy regarding HIV/AIDS also illustrates the magnitude of change in public policy that can occur when scientists join with the rest of the public to influence federal policy. HIV/AIDS was first publicized in the popular press in 1981. In the beginning of the epidemic, everyone, including the government, ignored the lethal impact of the illness. This lack of action by the government fueled the AIDS cause, and what emerged is probably one of the most sophisticated movements ever to affect public policy.

Advocacy for HIV/AIDS policy extended from grassroots activists to advocacy organizations, including health educators, journalists, writers, researchers (including social and behavioral scientists), and service providers, and cut across the various communities affected by the HIV/AIDS epidemic. Groups

traditionally not thought to have an extensive amount of political persuasion joined forces with those who often neglected to use their political capital.

Congress and the executive branch responded to this activism by setting a new scientific research agenda and implementing new policies surrounding the treatment of those with HIV/AIDS. Congress responded to the demands of activists that it review NIH's spending on HIV/AIDS research and put into motion a planning process that included the extramural scientific community, the NIH staff, and the affected communities. Activists fought for the right to sit on federal advisory committees and convinced NIH that it was prudent to allow people with HIV/AIDS to participate in designing the clinical trials. Incorporated in the 1993 NIH reauthorization bill, the response dramatically overhauled the way the NIH coordinates and funds HIV/AIDS research. The bill also led to the creation of the NIH Office of AIDS Research (OAR), which was statutorily authorized to develop and coordinate a comprehensive plan for HIV/AIDS research activities. The statute mandated that the plan provide for basic and applied research, including social and behavioral science.

Following this initial success by advocates of AIDS policy, the social and behavioral science community, led by COSSA and it members, explored ways that social and behavioral scientists could continue contributing to a federal response to the many problems associated with HIV/AIDS by, for example, understanding the course of the disease in society, the long-term impact of selective depopulation on society, and the basics of persuasion, deviance, addiction, sexuality, community organization, voluntary and group behavior, and so on, as they relate to HIV/AIDS (COSSA, 1986). Social and behavioral scientists pushed for health promotion, education, and strong evidence-based intervention programs. They also sought to help policy makers understand the need for long-range planning to address the societal impact of the crisis.

In a report about HIV/AIDS to the president and at a press conference, U.S. Surgeon General C. Everett Koop demonstrated that the social and behavioral science community's message had been heard by the federal government. In his press conference statement, Koop discussed a number of areas in which social and behavioral scientists were the leading knowledge sources for strategies involving effective research application.

Soon after, a wide range of programs, including social and behavioral research, demonstration, and evaluation projects, were funded for the first time.

WHY POLICY MAKERS NEED CONTINUAL EDUCATION ABOUT SCIENCE AND SCIENCE POLICY

For the most part, research benefits from strong support from the executive branch, Congress, and the public. Scientific knowledge, however, regardless of the discipline, is not always appreciated. The scientific community expends a tremendous amount of energy defending against the misapplication and lack of understanding of science. Every decade since the 1970s, science itself or its potential contributions to public policy have come under scrutiny by either the administration or Congress or both. The current decade is no exception. Recent years have seen the return of this "uneasy relationship" between science and politics as the current administration has been charged with politicizing science and disregarding scientific evidence when it comes to implementing policy (Union of Concerned Scientists, n.d.).

Congress, unfortunately, has not been above the fray. Recent recurring congressional attacks on areas of scientific research that some in Congress deem not worthy of federal funding have increased the tensions between the federal government and the scientific community. The most recent congressional assault on social and behavioral science research included legislative language by the chair of the Senate committee with jurisdiction over the NSF suggesting that the agency was placing too much emphasis on the social and behavioral sciences. The chair suggested that perhaps support for this research should be removed from the NSF. COSSA again led the response to this charge, working with its allies in the scientific and higher education community to eliminate the threat to NSF's social and behavioral science research.

But recent years have seen the most persistent congressional attacks. The assaults were directed against specific NIH-supported research and, by extension, the NIH peer-review process. In 2003, a member of Congress who was running against a powerful incumbent in the Senate from his own party offered an amendment to the bill that would have rescinded the funding for five research grants awarded by the NIH (COSSA, 2003b). Four of the five grants supported research on sexual behavior and its relation to health. On the House floor, the representative argued that funding this area of research was not as important as funding disease-specific research and therefore should not be part of NIH's portfolio.

The leadership of the Labor, Health, and Human Services (LHHS) Subcommittee and the full Appropriations Committee, however, understood the value of peer review and came to NIH's defense during the floor debate. The chairman of the subcommittee strongly opposed the amendment and explained the peer-review process, while the chairman of the Appropriations Committee also argued in strong opposition to the amendment, calling it "mischievous" (COSSA, 2003a).

The ranking minority members of both the LHHS Subcommittee and the full Appropriations Committee further condemned the amendment, arguing that the House of Representatives should not make political judgments about scientific research. Despite the Appropriations leadership's forceful response on the behalf of peer review and the NIH, the amendment was defeated by only two votes—210 for and 212 against.

The 2003 amendment was followed by subsequent House amendments offered to the annual spending bills in 2004 and 2005 that would have each defunded successfully peer-reviewed mental health grants funded by NIH's National Institute of Mental Health (NIMH) (COSSA, 2005). In 2004, recognizing the need to educate Congress about the peer-review process and to respond to future attacks on peer-reviewed research and the NIH, a diverse group of social, behavioral, and biomedical organizations; patient groups; and women's health organizations, which had worked together to defeat the 2003 amendment, formed the Coalition to Protect Research (CPR).

To prevent passage of the 2004 and 2005 amendments, CPR used a number of strategies. At CPR's request, professional associations and research societies from across the biomedical, behavioral, and social research spectrum, along with community organizations, wrote letters of support for the NIH and its peer-review process, and CPR posted these letters on its Web site. CPR sponsored congressional briefings in which scientists broadly explained the research, discussed the relevance of sexual health and behavior research to NIH's mission, and answered congressional staff's questions about the NIH peer-review process. Individual CPR organizations mobilized their grassroots membership to call members' offices in support of the NIH generally and, in some organizations, specifically requested the support of sexual behavior and health research. CPR also started two electronic petitions in support of NIH's work. More than 5,000 individuals signed both petitions, which were subsequently combined and delivered to members' offices prior to the LHHS bill's consideration on the House floor, providing members with the benefit of feedback on the issue from their constituents.

CPR solicited editorials in scientific and professional journals, along with stories in the popular press, that proved instrumental in engaging the scientific community and the public. CPR gave copies of the editorials to congressional staff. These intellectual resources were also linked to CPR's Web site, providing background information to those interested in the issue.

As part of the proactive effort to guard against the possibility that similar amendments would be offered again, CPR members made numerous visits to individual members' offices to discuss their vote on the 2003 amendment in 2004 and 2005. Coalition organizations also mobilized their members to reach out to members of Congress in their district offices. The visits allowed CPR members to offer the coalition as a source of information about NIH, the research it supports, and the peer-review process. These activities enhanced the knowledge of legislators, policy makers, program managers, the general public, and fellow scientists in the biomedical and behavioral research communities.

Although these efforts did not stop representatives from offering the amendments in 2004 and 2005, the work of CPR contributed to a strategy that resulted in dropping the amendments before the final bill was passed. CPR's work provides an example of a successful strategy for affecting congressional policy making and demonstrates the level of effort required to do so.

KEYS TO SUCCESSFUL ENGAGEMENT IN POLICY MAKING

As the activities engaged in by COSSA, HIV/AIDS advocates, and CPR demonstrate, scientists' successful involvement in the federal policy arena can happen in a variety of ways:

- communicating with individual members of Congress or the executive branch agency staff through letters on topics addressed by that entity;
- assisting in organizing congressional hearings;
- providing testimony at congressional hearings;
- participating in congressional briefings;
- signing on to advocacy groups' and professional societies' joint letters, statements, and petitions;
- calling members of Congress or agency staff to register concerns directly;
- meeting with members and staff in their Washington or district offices;
- meeting with executive agency staff at conferences and workshops;
- building relationships with members of Congress and their staffs and with federal appointed officials; and
- communicating indirectly with the federal government and the public through the media, including op-eds and letters to the editor.

And the list could go on. To embark on the appropriate approach and engage effectively in federal policy making, scientists need knowledge and skills in three main areas: knowledge about the functions of Congress and the executive branch agencies and how decisions in these bodies actually get made, knowledge about how to develop a communication strategy and the communication skills needed to execute the strategy effectively, and an understanding of how to establish and maintain relationships with federal policy makers.

What Are Congress and the Executive Branch, and How Do They Function?

Congress. The first step to working with Congress is becoming familiar with the federal legislative process, and so this section presents a very broad overview. In addition to the many available courses and texts on the legislative process, readers wanting to know more should see the American Association for the Advancement of Science's (AAAS's) *Working With Congress: A Practical Guide for Scientists and Engineers* (Wells, 1996), an excellent guide for scientists and engineers interested in policy activities.

Senators and representatives serve as advocates for their constituencies in Congress and with the federal government. Although Congress regularly considers social policy issues, science and technology topics—such as genes and the environment; nanotechnology; global competitiveness; the ethical, social, and legal implications of genetics research; cyber infrastructure; and so on—increasingly dominate the congressional agenda.

Each year, Congress is expected to cast hundreds of votes on various motions, bills, and amendments. Congress has been entrusted with national taxing and spending powers, as well as the power to create, reform, or abolish agencies and departments. One of its duties is to conduct oversight to ensure that agencies are performing in accordance with their missions. Congress authorizes and oversees federal programs and passes the annual appropriations bills that fund them. These measures, particularly the appropriations bills, affect federal research agencies and programs, thereby shaping research priorities in science policy and courses of action on social policy issues.

No single factor determines a representative's voting behavior. Prior to a major vote, members are often inundated with divergent opinions. They receive statements from expert witnesses testifying before congressional hearings. Professional associations and societies provide research findings. Think tanks and advocacy organizations supply fact sheets. Their colleagues send "Dear Colleague" letters asking them to support or oppose a particular bill. Keenly aware of their responsibility to mirror the viewpoint of the people in their districts, members are also constantly seeking an accurate reading of their constituents' opinions about legislative proposals. Virtually all members of Congress travel back to their home states several times a month to meet with constituents and seek them out at public functions.

Members also must be aware of political considerations when casting votes, particularly on hot-button issues, or subjects being scrutinized by the public or mass media. For some topics, it is not uncommon to see the majority of one party vote one way and the majority of the other party vote the opposite way. The president's position on an issue is considered when votes are cast. Members feel pressure to support a president of the same political party or to block the agenda of a president from the opposing political party. Members' personal beliefs about an issue also, of course, have some bearing on their voting decisions. Against this complex backdrop, those representing the voice of science must learn to recognize opportunities to productively infuse science into a particular policy debate and the constraints against it.

Because members of Congress are in high demand and are extremely busy people, they have staff whose jobs are to provide them with the best possible information on the various issues they consider. Legislative staff, whether in the member's personal office or on a committee, influences congressional decision making. Most congressional staffs are responsible for a wide range of issues. Staffs also act as "gatekeepers," affecting the flow of information to and from members. Generally, most are just out of college and very young, especially when the amount of responsibility they have is considered. It is a mistake, however, to underestimate their influence on the legislative process.

The structure of individual member offices varies in staff size, staff structure, and office procedures. The administrative assistant (AA) or chief of staff is usually in charge of the staff. Whereas some members prefer a hierarchical office structure with only certain staff interacting personally with the member, other members may work directly with all of the staff. Given that the internal functioning of the office may be difficult to ascertain, it is crucial to treat all staff as you would the member. In addition, turnover for some offices can be extensive. Today's receptionist may be tomorrow's legislative director (LD), the individual responsible for coordinating the work of the rest of the staff, also known as the legislative assistant or simply staff assistant. It is the responsibility of the legislative assistants to identify and track issues of interest to their member and his or her legislative positions. Other duties include drafting testimony for hearings, floor statements, and speeches; meeting with constituents; assisting constituents in dealing with the federal agencies; and responding to constituent mail. For most members of Congress, their Washington staff is responsible for budget and legislative issues, and district staff handles constituent services.

Congress uses a committee process to sort through the thousands of bills that are introduced in a session. These committees complete the majority of the work of Congress, conducting hearings, amending proposed legislation, and voting to pass the legislation on to the next level in the committee process. Congressional hearings are a formal method of collecting and analyzing information in the beginning stages of policy making. An official record of the information gathered at the hearing is generated along with the opinions that were expressed. Hearings are often initiated in response to the concerns of the chair, his or her staff, or individual members of the committee or subcommittee.

It is through hearings that most researchers and scientists interact with Congress. Public congressional testimony is not as likely to radically change members' views as a private meeting. Still, it serves vital functions. Congressional hearings provide visibility on the issues at hand. They also offer opportunities for various constituencies to give Congress advice on priorities, opportunities, and challenges. Serving as a witness at a committee hearing is a very effective way to provide input into policy development and to help resolve the problems with which Congress wrestles. It is an opportunity to reach many members at once, to increase exposure to the issue through media coverage of the hearing, and to offer examples and a rationale for legislators inclined to argue for your position.

Though most hearings tend to be bipartisan, it is not uncommon for a hearing to be held for ideological, partisan, or other political reasons. The forum might be used as a tool for promoting an administration's agenda and arguments, or a member might request and be allowed to conduct a hearing, perhaps as a quid pro quo, that enables him or her to appear to "take action" on an issue of special concern in a forum that does little to detract from or otherwise threaten the majority agenda.

Legislation that survives the committee process in the House may be considered by the full chamber and, if passed there, may begin the process anew in the other chamber, the Senate. The process works similarly in both the House and the Senate. After passing both chambers, a conference of members from both chambers meets to resolve differences in the legislation passed by each. Legislation that is approved following this conference is then sent to the president. Although most of the opportunities for scientists to have input occur at the committee level, messages from research can be effectively introduced at all stages of the legislative process.

The Executive Branch. The federal government is the primary sponsor of both basic and applied research, and most behavioral and social scientists are familiar with the federal

agencies from which they receive most of their research support—the NIH within the Department of Health and Human Services (DHHS) and the NSF. Research support also comes from a number of other agencies, including the Department of Agriculture, Department of Commerce, NIH's sister agencies in the Public Health Service (Centers for Disease Control and Prevention, Agency for Healthcare Research and Quality, Health Resources and Services Administration [HRSA], and Substance Abuse and Mental Health Services Administration [SAMHSA]), Department of Homeland Security, Department of Housing and Urban Development, Department of Justice, Department of Defense (DOD), Department of Education (ED), Department of Labor, the Federal Aviation Administration, the Environmental Protection Agency (EPA), and the National Aeronautics and Space Administration (NASA) (American Association for the Advancement of Science, 2005).

Though many formal roles and other informal opportunities exist for interacting directly with federal agencies, most scientists tend to focus all their attention on affecting congressional language, spelling out the intent of Congress in reports that accompany bills, thereby missing chances to affect the direction of science policy as well as the use of research in program operations. Although Congress passes legislation to create and fund public policy, it must cede some of the discretion for executing and implementing policies to the federal regulatory agencies that are empowered to create and enforce rules that carry the full force of law. Thus, the real and enforceable actions behind acts of law passed by Congress happen largely unnoticed in the offices of the federal agencies rather than in the halls of Congress.

The Office of Management and Budget (OMB) is the regulatory agency that establishes the rules for the NIH, NSF, and other nonregulatory agencies that include research in their mission. The rules and regulations relating to science affect the conduct and management of both intramural research (science conducted by government-employed scientists) and extramural research. In addition to science policy issues, rules and regulations for regulatory and nonregulatory agencies deal with social issues surrounding criminal justice, poverty and welfare reform, retirement, disease prevention, cancer and smoking, early childhood learning and teaching, civil rights, national security, environmental regulation, and global change, among many other topics relevant to social and behavioral science. These rules and regulations are published in the *Federal Register*[1] accessible through the Government Printing Office.

Scientists have myriad opportunities to involve themselves in the work of the executive branch agencies. The federal government often asks scientists outside of the agencies to provide independent advice on issues ranging from research funding priorities, to strategic planning of federal investment in research, to funding recommendations on specific research proposals. Nongovernment scientists are also asked to serve as advisers on the hundreds of committees considering policy issues. Other opportunities for engagement include meeting with officials in the federal research and regulatory agencies about their research portfolios or agency priorities, attending the open meetings of federal advisory boards or seeking invitations to sit on such boards, attending or participating in workshops or agency-sponsored conferences on specific science or social policy topics, responding to *Federal Register* notices requesting public comments on particular policies and regulations, serving on grant or cooperative agreement peer-review panels, and testifying before federal agency panels to explain the value of particular research programs.

In some instances, these interactions can assist government scientists in connecting with higher level officials in their own agencies and

with Congress, potentially improving the status, and thereby the resources, of the related research portfolio. Also, federal programs are reorganized and reprioritized regularly, and these changes can affect the way research is conducted and financed. Maintaining direct relationships with federal agency scientists and program personnel provides opportunities for input that may mitigate detrimental changes to research programs. For example, in 1998 and 2004, reorganizations of the NIMH by its new directors were designed to improve the functioning of the institute. This type of change frequently occurs within a federal agency to effect changes in the science it supports. In these cases, although not all of the scientific communities benefited from the reorganizations, both directors worked with their advisory committees, composed of scientists, practitioners, and advocates, to make their final decisions. Organizations that monitor NIMH publicized the process and solicited comments from the scientific community regarding how the proposed changes might affect the science.

Of the available opportunities, serving as an adviser to a federal agency is probably the primary way many scientists contribute to federal policy. Federal advisory boards, panels, committees, and councils of the federal agencies play essential roles in determining research policies. These groups advise agency directors about almost all aspects of the agency's functioning, such as long-term strategic planning, identifying new directions in research, discontinuing lines of research, and providing guidance on many specific science policy issues, including the treatment of human research participants or ownership and sharing of research data. They provide peer review of proposed and completed research, as well as review bodies of scientific literature to offer opinions on the adequacy of the scientific data for drawing particular conclusions or for particular applications. In addition, because these committees are composed to mirror public policy issues of current interest to the federal government and the public, they often take up a range of social, scientific, health, and workplace issues. Advice from such committees serves to enhance the quality and credibility of federal decision making, and they expand the depth and breadth of knowledge and expertise provided by federal employees (Committee on Science, Engineering, and Public Policy, 2005).

Congress has formally recognized the merits of seeking the advice and assistance of our nation's citizens and has placed certain rules and constraints on the composition of such committees through the Federal Advisory Committee Act (FACA). According to a 2004 report of the U.S. General Accounting Office, now known as the Government Accountability Office (GAO), approximately "950 advisory committees perform peer reviews of scientific research; offer advice on policy issues; identify long-range issues; and evaluate grant proposals, among other functions" (General Accounting Office, 2004). Advisory committee members are drawn from various disciplines, occupational and industry groups, and geographical regions of the United States and its territories. FACA requires that committee memberships be fairly balanced in terms of the points of view represented and the functions to be performed; individuals on one side of the issue to be examined by the advisory committee cannot dominate the committee.

Federal agencies are constantly seeking scientists to serve on these committees and publish committee vacancies in the *Federal Register*. The agencies are required to consider for membership any interested parties with professional or personal qualifications or experience. In addition, professional associations and societies are continually searching for individuals to nominate to represent their discipline or science and provide input to the committees.

But to take advantage of the numerous opportunities to engage policy makers in Congress and the executive branch, scientists must determine their individual goals for engaging in the public policy process and construct a plan to reach them.

Developing a Strategy for Engagement

Good policy begins with good ideas. Regardless of whether one is communicating with Congress, the executive branch agencies, or both, the first step is to define the issue's relevance to a current policy topic. Begin developing your strategy by determining the points of connection: How can the research, yours and others, improve current policy? What new ideas or models should the Congress or the federal agency consider that might help them look at an issue in a new way? What do the data say with relative certainty, and what specific research studies or programs of research should be initiated to secure the needed answers? What issues are not currently on "the radar screen" of the federal government that warrant attention according to the science? Which findings might give opposing political viewpoints something to agree on so that some steps forward can be taken in areas paralyzed by deadlock? Framing your interests this way will help you to craft your message and to identify your audience.

Knowing what topics are under Congress's or the agency's purview is essential to correctly identifying your audience. Does addressing the issue take an act of Congress, or could the actions be accomplished through an agency? If Congress is the appropriate audience, consider which committees, subcommittees, and individual members are interested in your issue and might be ready to hear your message. For members of Congress in particular, it is helpful to be informed about the member's district, committee assignments, professional background, stance on various issues including yours, and any issues considered a priority for the member's district. This knowledge will help you to emphasize why your issue is important to the member and his or her district or state. If an executive branch agency is the correct audience, determine the appropriate division and research portfolio, and identify the relevant staff members to contact. Targeted efforts usually yield better results than a one-size-fits-all approach.

Once the audience is identified, define the message. Prepare talking points from the data. The format should reflect the audience's knowledge, interest level, and typical means of receiving information. Members of Congress and their staff are often generalists and meet daily with a number of people on many different issues. So, prepare a one- or two-page bulleted document that highlights your main points. Be clear and concise, and use language that the lay public easily understands. Adding anecdotal examples also helps to communicate the meaning and value of the science. Stories are easier to retain and to repeat to colleagues than a recitation of statistics. Federal agency personnel are usually experts in an issue area and usually have more interest in your published paper, abstract, or brief summary of the relevant research with more technical information. Be prepared to discuss the fit between your work and the larger body of research on the topic, especially how the findings relate to research with which congressional and agency staff may already be familiar.

The timing of your message is critical. You must know where the issue is on the agenda in Congress or within the relevant agencies. Policy makers can be most open to information from science when they are establishing a policy agenda, considering new issues, or otherwise not yet committed to a position (Phillips, 2002). Advocating for an issue after the decisions have been made serves little purpose. Though members of Congress and agency staff do not expect you to be an expert on policy procedures, it is imperative to demonstrate your understanding of the decision-making process within relevant offices, committees, or branches of government.

Evolutions in public policy, whether through legislation or through the promulgation of rules and regulations, happen over time. Years may pass between the introduction of a topic and a vote on relevant legislation or the creation of a related funding stream. In certain parts of the process, however, a short-term effort can result in an immediate and significant change. Consider whether the issue you desire to affect is ripe for immediate change or if a long-term commitment will be required, and plan your efforts accordingly.

After identifying the appropriate audience, crafting your message, and determining the appropriate time to contact your audience, focus on effectively communicating your message. An essential component of the strategy should be developing relationships with your audience.

Establishing and Maintaining Relationships

Promoting the use of research in policy making requires more than just cries for attention by science advocates in times of emergencies. It requires establishing and maintaining personal relationships developed through persistent networking and ongoing interactions. These relationships take time but are a most effective way to influence public policy. Successful relationships are built on mutual respect. They facilitate understanding, help to prevent the misuse of science, and increase the chances of achieving your goals. They are also bidirectional. Understanding the policy makers' needs helps scientists or other messengers tailor their messages appropriately and can help scientists identify gaps in the research and new directions for investigation. Whether an individual scientist or an organization or network, the most credible information sources help policy makers to achieve their goals, even when those goals may not be directly related to the sources' priorities. For example, a researcher may respond to a request from a local member of Congress for information about a topic other than his or her own research by helping the member to contact the appropriate expert. Although these activities do not further one's own research or policy interests, by providing this information, the researcher appears reliable and helpful, thereby strengthening the relationship with the policy maker.

Personal relationships are crucial for getting a representative to consider an issue to be a priority. If possible, relationship building should begin before a specific pressing issue arises. Introduce yourself to the member or staff and explain how you might serve as a resource. Maintain contact by providing additional information such as summaries of new research or notices of media coverage relevant to the issues you have discussed. Letters, e-mails, telephone calls, and personal visits are highly regarded when it comes from constituents who are well known and who have been helpful in the past. Members of Congress represent all of the people in their district, regardless of political party, and so are open to relationships with all constituents.

Between visits, keep abreast of the issues and track how the member has voted or otherwise spoken on an issue. Look for additional opportunities for interacting with the office, such as when legislation has been introduced, hearings scheduled, a vote planned, or the media have covered the issue. Keep in mind, it will most likely take several meetings to influence legislative activity, and although you may have already contacted staff members, the high turnover of congressional staff may require repeated contact and initiation of new relationships as staffs change.

Initiating contact with federal employees is surprisingly simple, whether by telephone, through e-mail, or in person. As with Congress, face-to-face meetings with federal staff continue to be one of the most effective means for initiating and maintaining relationships. Meetings can occur at conferences sponsored by the agency, professional associations, or others. Federal employees regularly reserve time in their conference schedules for such meetings and are not only usually receptive to such meetings but also can appreciate the opportunity to receive input and constructive feedback from the scientific community on issues within their purview. Political appointees who direct the executive agencies, such as the Secretary of Education or the Assistant Secretary for Children and Families, are equally receptive to hearing from their agencies' constituents. These officials ultimately sign off on policy or on the implementation of a rule and execute administration priorities that are within their jurisdiction. Whether by letter or in person, scientists can create opportunities to help these officials become aware of research that might contribute to the policies and programs relevant to their agency. Such meetings can be mutually beneficial: The federal official gains direct access to expert information that might be useful in setting and implementing the agency's agenda, and the scientist learns about the official's main interests and concerns.

SCIENTIFIC AND PROFESSIONAL SOCIETIES

Professional associations, scientific societies, foundations, and think tanks play a critical role in public policy in part by bringing information from research to policy makers (see

Chapter 18, this volume, on the work of think tanks and advocacy organizations). Professional and scientific associations also serve the important function of organizing scientists to achieve policy goals, especially as they relate to science policy. These groups expend great effort to maintain and increase the budgets and portfolios of social and behavioral science research in the federal agencies, and they can provide objective scientific expertise on topics of interest to policy makers. They also strive to protect science from misapplied politics that might inappropriately use research findings to support a particular ideological point of view or question the integrity of the scientific enterprise.

As such, these groups can be a useful resource for the scientist who is interested in participating in policy. They can help you keep up to date on public policy initiatives, become familiar with the history of the issue, help to identify achievable goals, identify who has the authority to make your goal happen, direct you to the appropriate people, help decide when to contact an office, and all other critical aspects.

Scientific and professional societies also provide opportunities to postdoctoral researchers to work as legislative assistants for a member of Congress or congressional committees, give workshops on advocacy training through which members can learn about the legislative process, and help scientists get involved in grassroots activities such as calling, writing, and visiting policy makers regarding a particular issue.

Scientific and professional associations also sponsor or cosponsor congressional briefings and seminars held on Capitol Hill, providing another venue for researchers to share their expertise. The organizations invite individuals with specific expertise to present their research in a user-friendly manner, usually on an issue under consideration by Congress at the time. Briefings and seminars are designed to inform, not to lobby.

Transcripts of these proceeding are sent to all members of Congress, relevant federal agencies, and other interested individuals, at the discretion of the sponsor. The briefings not only highlight a particular issue or area of research, but they also bring recognition to the agency supporting the research or implementing the policy and so are indirectly critical to supporting a scientist's program of research.

CONCLUSION

Public policy affects us all, and policy decisions will be made regardless of whether behavioral and social scientists participate. Almost on a cyclical basis, researchers are called on by policy makers to justify their work and its results. This development alone should be incentive enough for most scientists to learn how to navigate the policy environment. The collective participation of scientists has the potential to answer many of the questions that members of Congress and their staff often have about research findings and the scientific process. And the demand for scientist involvement continues to grow. Despite the competing variables that ultimately influence policy decisions, federal legislators increasingly use scientific input and seek it as a decision-making resource. In the executive branch agencies, scientists outside the government can be essential to shaping and implementing public policy. In these roles, scientists are in the unmatched position of contributing a rational, data-driven perspective to policy development that helps to quell irrational fears and speak to the legitimate questions and concerns policy makers have about how science is conducted and managed and how it relates to social policy issues.

In short, whether operating independently or through professional societies and associations, scientists' participation can serve the public and the national interest, the interests of science, and the scientists' own personal interests and concerns. Participation can buttress Congress's limited understanding of behavioral and social science and its findings, enlightening them not only about the value of particular research objectives and agendas but also the entire scientific enterprise. A choice not to participate, however, leaves these vital science communications solely in the hands of others.

NOTE

1. Federal law requires that regulatory agencies publish all proposed new regulations in the *Federal Register,* the federal government's daily newspaper, 30 days before they take effect, along with the opportunity for interested parties to comment, propose amendments, or oppose the regulations. Proposed rules are new regulations or amendments to existing regulations. Notices of public hearings or requests for comments on proposed rules are also published in the *Federal Register,* as well as on agency Web sites, in newspapers, and in other publications. In addition, nonregulatory agencies issue notices seeking public comment on policy proposals to advance research. Anyone can submit comments to these requests.

REFERENCES

American Association of the Advancement of Science. (2005). *Behavioral and social science research in the Administration's FY2006 Budget, AAAS report XXX: Research and development FY 2006.* Retrieved April 2005 from http://www.aaas.org/spp/rd/

Committee on Science, Engineering, and Public Policy. (2005). *Science and technology in the public interest: Enduring the best presidential and federal advisory committee science and technology appointments.* National Academy of Sciences, National Academy of Engineering, and Institute of Medicine. Washington, DC: National Academies Press.

Consortium of Social Science Associations (COSSA). (1982). *Annual report.* Washington, DC: Author.

Consortium of Social Science Associations (COSSA). (1986). *Annual report.* Washington, DC: Author.

Consortium of Social Science Associations (COSSA). (2001). *Fostering human progress: Social and behavioral science research contributions to public policy.* Washington, DC: Author.

Consortium of Social Science Associations (COSSA). (2003a). *NIH peer review threatened: House barely defeats attempt to stop NIH grants.* Washington, DC: Author.

Consortium of Social Science Associations (COSSA). (2003b, July 14). *The precariousness of peer review: House barely defeats attempt to stop NIH grants.* Washington, DC: Author.

Consortium of Social Science Associations (COSSA). (2005, June 27). *House overturns peer review, accepts grant defunding amendment.* Washington, DC: Author.

Featherman, D. L., & Vinovskis, M. A. (2001). Growth and use of social and behavioral science n the federal government since World War II. In D. L. Featherman & M. A. Vinovskis (Eds.), *Social science and policy-making: A search for relevance in the twentieth century* (pp. 40–82). Ann Arbor: University of Michigan Press.

Government Accounting Office. (2004, April). *Federal advisory committees: Additional guidance could help agencies better endure independence and balance* (GAO-04-328). Retrieved March 23, 2006, from http://www.gao.gov/new .items/d04328.pdf

Institute of Medicine (IOM). (1982). *Health and behavior: Frontiers of biobehavioral research.* Washington, DC: Author.

Office of Behavioral and Social Science Research (OBSSR). (n.d.). About OBSSR. Retrieved December 16, 2006, from http://obssr.od.nih.gov/Content/ About_OBSSR/about.htm

Phillips, D. (2002). Collisions, logrolls, and psychological science. *American Psychologist, 57*(3), 219–221.

Social and Economic Sciences. (n.d.). Behavioral & cognitive sciences (BCS). Retrieved December 16, 2006, from http://www.nsf.gov/sbe/bcs/about.jsp

Union of Concerned Scientists. (n.d.). Restoring scientific integrity in policymaking. Retrieved July 8, 2004, from http://www.ucsusa.org/scientific_integrity/interfer ence/scientists-signon-statement.html

Wells, W. G., Jr. (1996). *Working with Congress: A practical guide for scientists and engineers* (2nd ed.). Washington, DC: American Association for the Advancement of Science.

CHAPTER 17

State Your Case

Working With State Governments

BILL ALBERT AND SARAH S. BROWN

T hose interested in communicating with state government leaders would do well to remember the words of the late Thomas P. "Tip" O'Neill, longtime Speaker of the U.S. House of Representatives. A garrulous, old-school politician from Massachusetts, O'Neill is warmly remembered for the phrase: "all politics are local." Adopting this particular page from the O'Neill playbook seems wise counsel for those wishing to establish, maintain, or strengthen relationships with state-level leaders as well as those looking for a way to effectively communicate research.

Reaching state leaders and their staffs in the executive and legislative branches and paying careful attention to state-level action makes sense for three primary reasons. First, it is easier to reach state-level decision makers than national ones. Second, states play a critical role in determining *what* various projects, issues, and concerns get funded and what *level* of funding each receives. When it comes to spending money, the rubber usually meets the road at the state level. Third, states often serve as the "laboratories" where new and innovative policies are hatched. National welfare reform, for example, was modeled in large part on various state experiments with the welfare process.

This chapter focuses on ways to successfully communicate with those in state executive and legislative offices and how to help ensure that your research reaches these state leaders—whether you are communicating a new set of findings from a research study, communicating what is known from an existing body of research and its relevance to a particular policy issue or question, or anything in between. In particular, the chapter covers four areas: specific advice for working with state-level leaders, ideas for making research relevant to leaders and their staff, thoughts about harnessing the power of the media to your advantage, and advice on how best to make progress with your research agenda in the face of conflict.

WORKING WITH STATE-LEVEL LEADERS

Many of those who have successfully worked with state governments over the years say the basis of their success is—like many things in life—due in large part to establishing relationships. Although this is easier said than done, we offer below a few modest suggestions on ways to turn a stranger into an ally.

Similarities and Differences Between State and Federal Policy Makers

Not surprisingly, there are many similarities to working with state-level leaders and their federal counterparts. Both want research presented to them in a short, easy-to-understand format, for example, with clear policy implications spelled out when possible. And both place great value in hearing "real stories from real people." While data and research are important, it is often the individual story—preferably one from a constituent—that makes a lasting impression. Even so, there are ways that state-level leaders differ from federal leaders. For example, state legislators tend to have fewer staff, so you may end up working directly with the elected official themselves. On the other hand, when working with members of Congress, you are far more likely to interact primarily with their staff. A case could also be made that state legislators may be a bit less buffeted by partisan winds. When presented with a good idea, state policy makers are often able to work with others in their own caucus or across the aisle to get legislation enacted—the bar for federal law is often much higher.

Finessing the "Masters of None" Dilemma

Over the past several years, as part of a cooperative agreement from the Centers for Disease Control and Prevention, the National Campaign to Prevent Teen Pregnancy has been translating research on science-based approaches to preventing teen pregnancy into user-friendly materials for practitioners, policy makers, and advocates. Through this project, the National Campaign worked with Philliber Research Associates in New York on a survey of state policy makers and their staff, practitioners in the field, and others about

science-based approaches to teen pregnancy. One of the more interesting findings of this survey concerned state legislative staff. Of seven different groups surveyed—local teen pregnancy coalitions, program administrators, national organizations, funders, youth programs, and state coalitions—state legislative staff were the *most* likely to report that they were "not very well informed" about science-based approaches to preventing teen pregnancy and were *most* likely to say that a lack of knowledge about science-based approaches to teen pregnancy was the greatest barrier to putting in place science-based programs. State legislative staff reported this lack of knowledge about research-based approaches to preventing teen pregnancy despite the fact that throughout the course of a year, they had regularly been sent materials on this very same topic by the National Campaign. This finding exemplifies both the difficulty in reaching policy makers and the need to do so.

Keep in mind that although some staff may have expertise or interest in particular areas, they are more likely—through sheer necessity—to be successful generalists but masters of no particular area or issue. This is not surprising given that state legislative and executive staffs make public policy decisions every single day and are inundated with information on hundreds of topic areas. A chief of staff or press secretary might be well versed on the hot-button issues of the moment, for example, while a legislative assistant might be tasked with being the staff expert on health care issues. This presents researchers, advocates, and others trying to communicate with state governments with both a challenge and an opportunity. The challenge, of course, is convincing those working in executive and legislative offices to pay attention to your issue or research in the first place. The opportunity is that those making public policy decisions are in constant need of expertise, information, and research on any number of topics, and finding such help is often difficult because of rapid staff turnover, short memories, or an endless search for the latest and best information on a particular topic. A common mistake academic researchers can make is simply to assume that state-level leaders and their staff are already familiar with a particular topic and, consequently, uninterested in the research or information you may have to offer.

Connect *With* Existing *Legislative Priorities*

As your research begins to materialize, think carefully about what state-level policy makers *already* consider to be legislative priorities. Does your research fit into that mix in any way? This strategy has obvious advantages. First, you don't have to do any "cold calling" with your results. That is, you are far more likely to find an eager and attentive welcome if you have data or information germane to issues that are *already* engaging state leaders, policy makers, and staff than if you are trying to convince them about the importance of an issue that is not on the legislative agenda or has captured the public's attention. Consider, for example, speeding up the release of your research—without compromising the integrity of your findings—to coincide with something that may already be on the legislative calendar. Even if your research is not finished, preliminary findings, if acknowledged as such and put into appropriate context, may be of great interest to those shaping public policy on the state level.

Do Your Homework and Establish Relationships

Establishing relationships with key policy makers and staff in a position to support your agenda is critical. Sheri Steisel, federal affairs counsel and senior director of the Human Services Committee for the National Conference of State Legislatures, suggests the very first step in developing these critical relationships is to know your audience before you walk in the door. For example, when working with state legislators, know about the legislative calendar, how long members of the legislature have served, whether their staffs are permanent or temporary for the particular legislative session, who the key personal staff and committee staff are, and, of course, who the champions are on your issue (personal communication, March 29, 2006). Visiting a state legislators' Web site, reading news articles, and talking to others who have met the legislator and his or her staff are all ways to learn about an elected official and the staff prior to meeting with them.

John Wallace, vice president of Development and External Affairs at the widely respected and influential MDRC (Manpower Demonstration Research Corporation), a nonprofit, nonpartisan social policy research organization, suggests that the way to establish, maintain, and strengthen relationships with state leaders is by building relationships with elected officials' staff (personal communication, March 17, 2006). Keep in mind that it is the staff in executive agencies who are often around through successive administrations, and in the legislative branch, this is increasingly the case given the prevalence of legislative term limits. As Wallace notes, "Staff are the officials' trusted liaisons with any number of outside groups and individuals, and the first person who the official will turn to ask, 'Is this valuable to me? Why?'"

Avoid Blindsiding

No one wants to first learn about your new research findings in the morning newspaper, particularly if that person feels that he or she has already invested a fair amount of time and effort in understanding your issue and concerns and feels that he or she has already established a relationship with you. Consider establishing a list of people to contact regularly about the work you are doing. Create a "research" listserv, drop state-level leaders a note, or pick up the phone; do whatever it takes to ensure that your state-level friends stay in the loop. At the very least, think of your research like having a baby—have a plan in place in advance about alerting the people close to you before the blessed event occurs. Keeping your potential research champions well informed allows them to be ready to comment thoughtfully on your findings, prepared for any potential political fallout, and more favorably inclined to your efforts in the future. Consider too that even if you are not conducting the research yourself, it is helpful to make state-level contacts aware of relevant existing research.

Be Accurate and Responsive

Those working with state-level leaders should also pay attention to two very old-fashioned notions: accuracy and responsiveness. As a general matter, researchers are scrupulous about their work and are exceedingly cautious about their findings. Sometimes, however, the *interpretation* of solid research gets lost by those doing the translating. Simply put, always avoid overstating research findings, be careful in reporting what is known and what is not known, distinguish between casual findings and simple associations, and/or be even-handed in evaluating data, programs, or interventions. In addition, as best you can, help those who will use your research to properly interpret the findings.

Being responsive is also critical given that policy makers, in particular, work on very short time lines, which has several implications. First and foremost, if someone involved in state government calls, it is important to return the call within the same day, even if

your response is that it will take you a few days to develop a complete answer to the question posed. If you do not know the answer to a question, you can become a valuable resource by connecting that person to other researchers or sources of information. Second, because conducting top-notch research frequently takes years, it is absolutely essential that you keep state-level leaders abreast of your work *throughout* the research process, not just when you have a final report ready to publish. When feasible, it even makes sense to engage key officials when your research project is in the early conceptual stage and before final research questions have been identified. By doing so, state-level policy makers and staff can help shape the research agenda so that it reflects topics they are interested in and helps answer questions they want answered. Also, consider a concise e-mail written in plain English that documents key milestones in your research as one way to keep interested parties informed or occasional face-to-face visits.

And because some lawmakers won't even be in office by the time your research is completed, consider ways to keep other important individuals with longer life spans—such as nonpolitical appointees in state-level departments—in the loop.

MAKING RESEARCH RELEVANT

Given the importance of reaching state-level leaders, how best to make sure your research reaches state-level policy makers and staff *and* that your research makes a difference? There are, of course, no assurances, but some combination of the following three elements can make a difference: (1) Produce quality research that is easily understandable, localized when appropriate, and that attaches costs when possible; (2) offer human interest anecdotes to help the research come alive; and (3) use a powerful, convincing messenger to deliver the research findings. In short, combine solid, understandable research with powerful personal stories and a convincing messenger. Discussed next are some specific ideas for achieving these three goals.

Make Research Understandable

People will not act on what they do not understand. John Wallace of MDRC encourages researchers to recognize that the "primary audience for research aimed at shaping or informing public policy is *policy makers*— not fellow researchers, academics, think tanks, or public interest advocacy groups." Therefore, it is imperative that your research be understandable to the average layperson. Even if your research is complicated or hard to summarize, the primary findings must be easily understandable to those with whom you are trying to communicate. Try this experiment: Does your research pass the elevator test? That is, can you describe your primary findings in the time that an average elevator ride takes?

Even though we are from Washington— the home of making things wordy and complicated—we strongly urge researchers, advocates, and others trying to communicate with state government leaders to use simple language and avoid jargon at all costs—you know, *stakeholders, prioritizing, dialogue, repurpose, operationalize, feeling ownership, capacity building,* and all the rest. Extra words and unclear words only confuse the reader; and in truth, they also reveal confusion in the mind of the authors! Say it simply. Less is more.

A Word About Caveats

An important part of making your work understandable is to remember that the primary finding of your research simply cannot be "we know less than we would like" or that "more research is needed." More research is *always* needed. Use your research to make a case for what is known, however modest, rather than simply providing a laundry list of what is not known. It may be helpful to think about what journalists call the inverted pyramid. That is, the primary findings of the research should come first followed by a discussion of the importance of the findings and the methodology. Once that is on the table, a full airing of the limitations and caveats of the research is appropriate. Of course, this is *not* to suggest that individuals or advocates go beyond what science suggests or mischaracterize the actual state of knowledge. It is simply a suggestion to lead with your best material.

Consider Tall, Grande, and Venti Versions of Your Research

A critical but often overlooked part of making sure your research agenda gets noticed is to make sure that your research gets read *at all*. To help ensure that this happens, try developing derivative products based on the research findings—a one-page overview, a five-page summary providing more details, and the full report for those few who have the time and desire to read through detailed findings. Consider the amount of material we *all* receive that we never read and then consider the amount of material that crosses the desk of state policy makers and others. There is great power in a well-crafted one-page summary of the research that can be quickly read and understood, one that provides key stats, facts, and findings; assumes no prior knowledge of the topic; and uses graphics to convey the findings when possible. Patricia Quinn, director of Policy at the Massachusetts Alliance on Teen Pregnancy, puts it this way: "brief, bulleted, and no jargon" (personal communication, March 23, 2006).

This task may be a particularly difficult one for those closest to the research or for those who have been working on a certain set of issues for a long time. "The longer you work in any field, the worse you seem to get at providing information that a layperson can understand and use," Quinn notes. She suggests vetting materials with other staffers, board members, and even family members to make sure that what you are trying to communicate makes sense to those unfamiliar with the research. Of course, after reading your brief summary, some will want more meat and some may want the full meal—that is why it makes sense to develop several options for state-level leaders to digest.

Make It Local

National data, trends, and findings are interesting, but nothing tends to resonate as strongly with state-level leaders as research that contains a local component. Two examples of successfully localizing national research—the *What If* project from the National Campaign to Prevent Teen Pregnancy and the Annie E. Casey Foundation's annual *Kids Count* report—are described below.

With generous support from the United-Health Foundation, in 2005 the National Campaign to Prevent Teen Pregnancy released research connecting declining teen birth rates with improved overall child well-being in all 50 states and the District of Columbia. The teen birth rate in the United States has declined by about one third between 1991 and 2002 (Martin et al., 2005). The research released by the National Campaign answered the following direct question: What if teen birth rates in each state had *not* declined? We presented data on several key measures, including the following:

- the number of additional children younger than age 18 who would have been born to teen mothers between 1991 and 2002,

- the additional number and percentage of children younger than age 6 who would have been living in poverty in 2002, and
- the additional number and percentage of children younger than age 6 who would have been living in single-mother households in 2002.

Several days before the release of the *What If* research, the National Campaign conducted a conference call with over 70 interested individuals from 31 states. Participants on the call included state health officials, state and local teen pregnancy prevention leaders, and others representing youth-serving organizations. Before the call, participants were given an embargoed copy of their state fact sheets and tables, along with listings and rankings of key data for all states. On the call, participants learned how and why the data were compiled and heard from peers on concrete ways to use the data with policy makers and with the press. In essence, the research helped the National Campaign and advocates in states across the country convincingly argue that national and state investments in teen pregnancy prevention pay huge dividends. The analysis made a compelling case that preventing teen pregnancy is one of the most direct and effective ways states can reduce poverty and improve overall child well-being.

Reaction to the research was very encouraging. The *What If* data appeared in news reports in 32 states and the District of Columbia; state health departments and organizations—including New Jersey, Mississippi, and Tennessee—developed their own press releases incorporating the research, national organizations such as the National Governors Association provided details of the research to its policy staff, and practitioners and advocates nationwide used the data to argue for continued funding of initiatives to prevent teen pregnancy.

The Annie E. Casey Foundation's annual *Kids Count* research is also illustrative. Each year, the foundation releases a report card of sorts on the well-being of children. And every single year, the research garners significant amounts of media coverage, as well as attention among governors and state legislators, and it is used by advocacy groups throughout the year in statehouses nationwide. *Kids Count* compiles in one volume—and on a user-friendly Web site—such indicators as teen birth rates, the share of children younger than age 18 living in poverty, and infant mortality rates. Most of those who use the Casey *Kids Count* data credit its success to the following three factors: (1) The report is issued on a regular basis. Advocates and others can rely on getting the data on an annual basis and can plan local activities and outreach accordingly. (2) The data are local. In addition to national data, the *Kids Count* report also provides detailed state-by-state data. (3) The data are ranked. The data allow individuals to compare specific data across multiple states so that each state knows how it compares with other states. These rankings may, in fact, exert some political pressure on those who score lowest and reinforce the good work of those who rank higher.

National data are important, but state-level people want state-level data. Strongly consider if there are ways you can localize your own research findings or, perhaps, put a local twist on a larger body of existing research.

Consider What the Neighbors Are Doing

Success stories from other states can also be useful. These examples can convince state-level leaders to act, view things in a new light, or recognize that progress *is* possible on many tough problems. Over the years, the National Campaign has heard from many state-level practitioners about the power of regional comparisons—specifically, highlighting the progress in declining teen pregnancy and

birth rates among neighboring states. As one state-level health official told us, "We couldn't get the issue of teen pregnancy on the radar screen of our governor and state legislature until they heard that declines in teen childbearing in our state paled in comparison to the declines in states surrounding us. All of sudden they wanted to know why 'we're' not doing as well and what can be done to catch up."

A final thought about the use of success stories. John Wallace of MDRC correctly cautions, "The challenge is to be sure that the success stories are (1) truly success stories and not hype or success based on poor or misleading research, (2) documented well enough so that one knows *why* it was a success (for example, the nature of the program intervention, staffing messaging, etc.), and (3) is representative of what happened or could happen, not idiosyncratic."

Personalize Your Research

Coupling your work with anecdotes that help underscore your larger findings can also be a powerful tool. Consider the experience of the National Campaign to Prevent Teen Pregnancy: Teen pregnancy and birth rates in the United States have declined by nearly one third since the early 1990s due to both less sexual activity and better contraceptive use among those who are sexually active. This remarkable progress on an issue many considered intractable is worth noting and celebrating, as is exploring why these declines have taken place and carefully considering why it is still the case that about one third of girls in the United States continue to get pregnant by age 20. Indeed, the National Campaign and many other organizations and researchers have looked at all of these issues in great detail and shared what we have found with policy makers and others nationwide.

Our collective experience in sharing these findings makes clear, however, that nothing is as powerful—nothing serves to make research come alive—as the testimonials of teens themselves and those who work with young people. Hearing directly from a teenager on why he has chosen to delay sexual activity, from a participant in a successful teen pregnancy prevention program, or from a teen who consistently and carefully uses contraception can greatly help the public make the connection between research and real life.

The Massachusetts Alliance on Teen Pregnancy has done this successfully through an annual teen parent lobby day at the state capitol. In 2006, more than 500 teen parents descended on the Springfield state house to share their stories with policy makers and staff. "Connecting policy makers to the 'story' of teens and teen parents in their communities is the most effective way to meet our public policy goals," notes Patricia Quinn of the alliance.

Make the Cost Case

Those about to get married are often counseled that disagreements in a relationship frequently tend to be about money. A similar case can be made for those working with state governments. Few things seem to generate passion and interest quite like the expenditure of public funds. Consequently, attaching costs to research findings can go a long way toward focusing the attention of busy legislators and other state-level leaders. Indeed, counting the costs is probably the closest anyone is likely to get to a sure thing when it comes to attracting the attention of those who hold the state's purse strings.

Consider the example of the National Campaign's By the Numbers project. In October 2006, the National Campaign released new research on the public-sector costs of teen childbearing. The research—conducted by Saul Hoffman, PhD, of the University of Delaware—provided the first update of the national costs of teen childbearing in 10 years and the first ever state-by-state analysis (Hoffman, 2006). The research showed that despite a one-third decline in the teen birth rate since the early 1990s, teen childbearing in the United States cost taxpayers at least $9.1 billion in 2004. The estimated cumulative public costs of teen childbearing between 1991 and 2004 totaled $161 billion, and state costs ranged in 2004 from $1 billion in Texas to $12 million in Vermont. Most of the public-sector costs of teen childbearing are associated with negative consequences for the children of teen mothers, including increased public-sector health care costs, child welfare costs, incarcerations costs, and lost revenue due to lower taxes paid by the children of teen mothers over their own adult lifetimes. The analysis also makes clear that the one-third decline in the teen birth rate between 1991 and 2004 also yielded substantial costs savings. The estimated national savings to taxpayers in 2004 alone due to the one-third decline in the teen birth rate between 1991 and 2004 was $6.7 billion. State advocates have told us that this cost calculation has helped in several important ways, including

- focusing the attention of policy makers and others who are interested in the bottom line but might not otherwise be interested in the issue of adolescent pregnancy and childbearing;
- demonstrating the value of investing in teen pregnancy prevention by making clear the costs savings of lower rates of teen childbearing;
- bringing together various advocates, including those concerned with health care, the justice system, and child welfare; and
- underscoring the value of making continued progress on an issue some have considered "solved" due to the steady progress the nation has made in reducing adolescent pregnancy and childbearing.

What Might Make Your Research Stand Out?

Think carefully about some of the particulars of your research. For example, does your research allow you to answer questions that may be important to a state leader's particular constituencies such as schools or businesses? Does your research shed any light on racial or ethnic differences that might be relevant to a state legislator? Is it even possible to isolate findings from a legislator's district?

Perhaps there is a way to position your research in a nontraditional way. Consider another example from the National Campaign's work. As a general matter, the vast majority of teen pregnancy rates presented in the press and in various reports and articles are based on data collected from teens ages 15 to 19 *regardless* of their sexual experience. Recently, the National Campaign released data examining the risk of pregnancy only among those who have had sex. The data helped underscore that despite improving rates of teen pregnancy, the proportion of sexually experienced teens who get pregnant or cause a pregnancy remains startlingly high.

Messengers Matter

Those trying to reach state government leaders and staff should also carefully consider who is best suited to deliver your research message. Let's be honest, researchers themselves may not be best suited for this particular task. Even the most thorough and compelling research can be buried by a mediocre or ham-handed presentation of the findings. Perhaps a friendly state legislator, the leader of an advocacy group, or simply a respected individual in the community is better suited to be the public face of your research message. In this media-saturated age—when the challenge is often making sense of an abundance of existing information rather than seeking out information—*who* is making the case can make a real difference.

When it comes to presenting research, no matter who makes the presentation, think carefully about how the research is likely to be received. What questions can you anticipate about your findings? What are people most likely to not understand or misinterpret? How do your findings support or refute previous findings? How does the research relate more broadly to what is known in a particular area or issue, and how might that relate to public policy concerns? Thinking of answers to these questions and more ahead of time will likely help strengthen the credibility of the person presenting the research and, in turn, the perceived credibility of the research itself.

HARNESS THE POWER OF THE MEDIA

The media are also a powerful and proven way to shape state public policy priorities. State-level politicians and employees pay scrupulous attention, of course, to what their constituents are reading, watching, and listening to. Researchers who do not at least try to avail themselves of this bully pulpit are missing an important tool for moving research off the shelf and into action.

Moreover, the media's need for interesting research has never been greater. The growth of cable news outlets, news Web sites, blogs, specialized magazines, and talk radio has increased exponentially the amount of time and space these outlets need to fill. This "news hole" is frequently filled with research findings. Scan any newspaper or watch a television newscast; a fair proportion of time is devoted to covering the findings of new research. Here are a few ideas on how best to harness the power of the media.

Simplify Your Message

A common complaint from researchers and others is that the media always get it wrong. But think about why this might be the case. At the state level, beat reporters—those who cover single issues or a general subject area—are an increasingly rare breed. One day a reporter might have to become an expert in the mating habits of the giant panda after the local zoo secures the rights to exhibit one of the rare creatures. The next day, the same reporter might be assigned to cover the county executive's rollout of a new road improvement plan and become an expert on growth versus sprawl. The following day, the same journalist might be asked to get the reaction of a local politician to a Senate vote that day on campaign finance reform. It can be a daunting task, indeed (see Chapters 7 through 10 in this volume for a thorough discussion on working with the news media).

For these reasons and others, it is imperative that your research be simple and understandable. Spend some serious time thinking about how to make sure that your primary findings are clear. If nothing else, consider this activity an act of self-defense—simple messages are less likely to get lost in the translation.

What's Your Water Cooler Moment?

What is it that might make people discuss your research around the water cooler?

- Do you have some counterintuitive information?
- Do you have a local angle on a national story?
- Do you have surprising data?
- Do you have a trend to report or a change from the previous year?

Again—Personalize, Personalize, Personalize

In the book *Making the News: A Guide for Non-Profits and Activists,* author Jason Salzman offers the following bit of helpful advice from the booker of a national television morning news program: "Don't send me your reports, send me your stories" (Salzman, 1998). More than ever, the media seek to put a "face" on issues. It is in your best interest to do all you can to help them in this pursuit. High-minded discussions of complicated social questions don't make good television—dramatic stories that personify important research do.

In no way are we suggesting that research does not matter—it *does* matter a great deal. In fact, as noted above, new research is frequently what opens the door to media coverage in the first place. The point is to underscore *how* the media do their job—they tell stories. Intense discussion of methodology simply doesn't fly in today's fast-paced media market. Coupling a human face to your research can help increase your chances of media coverage and is likely to increase the impact of your findings. *Relationships matter again, too.*

As is the case with state-level employees and politicians, relationships with reporters can make a real difference. If a reporter is familiar with your previous work or has spoken with you in the past, considers you a straight shooter, or has even come to know you over the years, it can make a real difference. Journalists are no different than anyone else; they like to talk with people they feel comfortable with, have a relationship with, and trust.

Remember, too, that if you want the media to pay attention to your research, be certain you are there when *they* need you, not just when *you* need them. Return phone calls promptly, be ready to assist them at a time that may not be convenient for you, and offer suggestions and alternatives that are not self-aggrandizing. It is more desirable to be seen as a helpful source rather than a badgering advocate.

MOVING FORWARD IN THE FACE OF CONFLICT

Can science and compromise peacefully coexist? To overstate things a bit: Researchers can have little tolerance for efforts and policies that are not completely aligned with what they believe research suggests as the best course of action. Similarly, those outside the research world often believe that community preference and individual values and beliefs should take precedence over science. At other times, progress on a particular issue is beset by true differences of opinion about the accurate interpretation of science.

The experience of the National Campaign suggests that there are indeed ways to make progress on difficult issues that both allows for fidelity to research and is respectful of differences of opinion—an approach that is sensitive to the interplay between science and values. Moreover, there is often real value in such strategic compromises. Practically speaking, it may mean that a particularly effective approach that engenders controversy is set aside in favor of a more agreeable alternative that is still supported by science.

A case study of sorts might be illustrative here. As the organizational name implies, the National Campaign to Prevent Teen Pregnancy is focused exclusively on how best to convince young people to delay pregnancy. This is a goal shared by the overwhelming majority of those in the United States (Albert, 2004). Nevertheless, there remain sharp disagreements among men and women of good will about how best to reach that goal. Preventing teen pregnancy has become a mini culture war of sorts. While the American public takes a quite practical and centrist view of how to prevent teen pregnancy—strongly encourage young people to delay sexual activity *and* provide them with information about contraception—many advocacy groups and others passionately argue over abstinence versus contraception, as if they were two competing strategies (Albert, in press; Bleakley, Hennessy, & Fishbein, 2006). Some argue that public funds should be spent only on initiatives designed to convince teens to delay sexual activity; others feel that public money is best spent on efforts that focus more on convincing sexually active young people to use contraception consistently and carefully.

One strategy the National Campaign has used effectively is to concentrate on aspects of our issue that draw people together rather than those that send them to their corners. For example, can agreement about a particular goal be reached while agreeing to disagree about a particular strategy? As noted above, there is widespread support for the goal of reducing teen pregnancy. Where the edges begin to get frayed, however, is in deciding the best strategy for realizing that goal. Rather than continuing an unproductive debate over whether teens should be given a message that stresses abstinence (there is very limited evidence suggesting such interventions are successful, but there is overwhelming public support for encouraging young people to delay sexual activity) or one that suggests young people are better served by interventions that stress the value of delaying sexual activity and contraceptive use (which has more evidence of success and also enjoys strong public support), perhaps there are ways to bridge this divide. For example, sometimes more progress can be made by focusing on the common ground of encouraging parent-child communication about sex, love, and relationships or in the value of after-school programs that do not necessarily focus on sex (both of which have strong evidence of success and strong public support).

Embracing the Broader Context

How an issue and the research related to it are presented—"framed"—can have a big impact on how your messages are received. Carefully take into account how your research might be positioned within a broader framework. In its 2006 publication *This Just In: 10 Lessons From Two Decades of Public Interest Communications,* Fenton Communications (one of the largest public interest communications firms in the country) lists framing the conversation as the number one lesson. Fenton uses the example of the "What Would Jesus Drive" campaign as a successful example of reframing an issue in a broader context: "The drive for stronger fuel-economy standards got a fresh start when the 'What Would Jesus Drive?' campaign urged automakers and consumers to protect God's creation by building and driving fuel-efficient cars. . . . By making national headlines, the campaign helped refuel the debate on climate crisis." Framing research on climate change and fuel efficiency within a new context certainly did not end disagreement about these topics, but it likely elicited new and wider support.

The National Campaign's experience over the past 10 years suggests that there is real value in framing issues in new ways. As noted above, teen pregnancy and birth rates have declined by nearly one third since the early 1990s (Hamilton, Sutton, & Ventura, 2003, Hamilton, Ventura, Martin, & Sutton, 2005; Henshaw, 2004; Martin et al., 2005; Ventura, Mathews, & Hamilton, 2001). The increased commitment to preventing teen pregnancy during this time—both federal, state, and local initiatives—have brought new energy and often new funding to the

issue. Even so, policy makers often do not understand how preventing teen pregnancy connects to other issues. Too often, they see teen pregnancy as being totally in the realm of sex education and contraceptive services (divisive ways of looking at it, for some). A more inclusive framework links reducing teen pregnancy to broader ends, such as educational improvement, workforce development, welfare reform, and improved child and family well-being generally. By positioning teen pregnancy prevention in these terms, we find we can make friends with people and sectors that might have otherwise steered clear of this issue when it is defined in terms of sex, condoms, and sex ed.

Understand the Value and Limitations of Good Research

Strong, impartial research can go a long way toward making progress in the midst of disagreement. In particular, policy makers may find that learning about relevant research offers a good place to start. Even so, it is important to recognize that individual opinions, attitudes, and behavior are not shaped entirely by research and good information. One need look no further than the nation's collective waistline for evidence of this. If we were all so beholden to research and information, we would more likely be a nation of healthy individuals who exercised regularly and ate wisely rather than a nation with high rates of obesity.

SUMMARY

Communicating and disseminating behavioral research to state government leaders and their staff is both manageable for researchers, advocates, and others and beneficial to both "buyer" and "seller." State executive and legislative offices are in constant need of high-quality research to help inform their decisions—good news for all those who want to help shape public policy. Establishing relationships rich in communication and trust, understanding the way public policy is shaped, being sensitive to legislative calendars and timelines, and trying to connect with *existing* legislative priorities all can help ensure that your research gets noticed.

Paying careful attention to *how* your research is presented also can make a real difference when it comes to communicating with state-level leaders. Making sure that your research is easily understandable to a lay audience, provides localized findings and attaches costs whenever possible, and can be coupled with personal stories and a credible messenger are all hallmarks of research that has successfully reached state governments.

Using the power of the media is an obvious way to communicate research findings to state government officials. The explosive growth in the number and type of media outlets means the need has never been greater for information—another real opportunity for those willing to work with the media to get their research noticed.

Finally, working in the public policy arena where public monies are involved almost certainly means that there will be controversy about the particular agenda being offered. Researchers should be sensitive to this reality, and advocates should consider ways to move forward in the face of inevitable conflict, including positioning your research within a broader framework that might widen the circle of those who might care about it and increase the likelihood that the research will stimulate action.

REFERENCES

Albert, B. (2004). *With one voice: America's adults and teens sound off about teen pregnancy*. Washington, DC: National Campaign to Prevent Teen Pregnancy.

Albert, B. (in press). *With one voice 2006: America's adults and teens sound off about teen pregnancy*. Washington, DC: National Campaign to Prevent Teen Pregnancy.

Bleakley, A., Hennessy, M., & Fishbein, M. (2006). Public opinion on sex education in U.S. schools. *Archives of Pediatrics and Adolescent Medicine, 160,* 1151–1156.

Fenton Communications. (2006). *This just in: 10 lessons from two decades of public interest communications*. New York: Author. Retrieved from http://www.fenton .com/pages/5_resources/pdf/ThisJustIn.pdf

Hamilton, B. E., Sutton, P. D., & Ventura, S. J. (2003). Revised birth and fertility rates for the 1990s and new rates for Hispanic populations, 2000 and 2001: United States. *National Vital Statistics Reports, 51*(12), 1–94.

Hamilton, B. E., Ventura, S. J., Martin, J. A., & Sutton, P. D. (2005). Preliminary births for 2004. *Health E-Stats*. National Center for Health Statistics. Retrieved October 28, 2005, from http://www.cdc.gov/nchs/products/ pubs/pubd/hestats/prelim_births/prelim_births04.htm

Henshaw, S. K. (2004). *U.S. teenage pregnancy statistics with comparatives statistics for women aged 20–24*. New York: The Guttmacher Institute.

Hoffman, S. (2006). *By the numbers: The public costs of teen childbearing*. Washington, DC: National Campaign to Prevent Teen Pregnancy.

Martin, J. A., Hamilton, B. E., Sutton, P. D., Ventura, S. J., Menacker, F., & Munson, M. L. (2005). Births: Final data for 2003. *National Vital Statistics Reports, 54*(2), 1–116.

Salzman, J. (1998). *Making the news: A guide for non-profits and activists.* Boulder, CO: Westview.

Ventura, S. J., Mathews, T. J., & Hamilton, B. E. (2001). Births to teenagers in the United States, 1940–2000. *National Vital Statistics Reports, 49*(10), 1–23.

CHAPTER 18

Think Tanks and Advocacy Organizations

KARABELLE PIZZIGATI

B ehavioral scientists have, over recent years, shown increasing interest in connecting science with policy and practice. Many factors are driving this interest. The science has evolved and matured and, as a result, is generating useful information that can help develop new policy and evaluate existing policy. Researchers today also have far more exposure to policy issues and environments than ever before (Huston, 1994, 2005; McCabe, 2005), and with this greater exposure, they have come to understand firsthand the impact policies can have on society—and the need to ensure that the most relevant and valid science gets communicated to policy makers.

Policy makers, for their part, increasingly call on researchers for guidance. More policy makers also keep tabs on the topics studied by behavioral science, a trend that no doubt reflects rising political and public interest in these issues. Policy makers—and Americans in general—want to know how we can improve societal conditions and make services more effective and efficient. Citizens and policy makers together, ever more frequently, are asking about what works—and what behavioral science research can tell us.

This chapter will explore how all this interest in research and policy actually plays out in the contemporary American polity. We will examine the two key institutional players that link social and behavioral science to policy making at the national, state, and local levels. These institutions come at the world from markedly different perspectives and operate in significantly different ways. But think tanks and advocacy organizations conduct their work in the same political environments. They affect each other, as well as policy. To understand them and the context in which they work, we need to examine them together.

Some think tank leaders would rather we not. These think tank professionals see themselves as neutral resources and so would take issue with appearing in the same chapter, much less the same sentence, with advocacy organizations. Some advocacy group professionals feel the same way. But think tanks and advocacy organizations, however large or small, both have influence over policy and seek more of it. They engage the same audiences. They often employ the same or similar strategies.

This chapter describes the political context and functions of think tanks. It draws from policy issues relating to children, youth, and families, which have come to have a higher profile in recent years, to discuss what these organizations do, how they do it, with whom and why, and how they relate to each other and the larger policy and research community. We will take this exploration of the children and family think tank and advocacy world beyond the "usual suspects" that focus solely or mainly on child and family issues to examine the major think tanks and advocacy groups that affect child policy. Why employ this wider lens? We need to look more broadly because, as issues around children and families have gained a higher political profile, organizations that historically have not had programs in these areas have created them. In some cases, these broader organizations show the benefits of connecting a particular policy issue to related policy areas. Some completely new organizations have also emerged, some with broad portfolios, others with a more specialized focus. In this chapter, we will look at them all.

THE POLICY-MAKING CONTEXT

Policy making often gets compared to making sausage. The end product may be wonderful, but the producing can be revolting. Policy decision making can certainly come across as revolting, particularly to professionals trained to value thoughtfulness and open-mindedness, thoroughness, and patience. Policy makers and broader publics, by contrast, often engage in sweeping discussions that boil complex issues down to yes-no propositions, in highly charged and politically partisan environments that value immediate action.

Think tanks and advocacy organizations operate in these environments. Almost all of them define themselves as independent, nonpartisan voices in the policy-making process. Outside observers, be they from the media or politics, seldom let these claims to disinterested independence go unchallenged. Reporters and lawmakers typically refer to

think tanks and advocacy organizations in political terms. They label them conservative or neocon, center or moderate, right or left leaning, and so forth. Think tanks and advocacy groups themselves do sometimes explicitly embrace a political label. Or they may, more commonly, allow a label to be implicitly assumed.

A label may also derive from an organization's funding sources. Most organizations receive support from foundations and other private sources. Some, particularly those that consider themselves "R&D" houses, rely on governmental grants and contracts to carry out research on issues deemed priorities by governmental agencies (Nakamura, 2005). The stronger and more explicit the political orientation of an organization's funder, the more firmly that funder's political orientation will define an organization's political label.

THE FUNCTIONS OF THINK TANKS AND ADVOCACY ORGANIZATIONS

In the United States today, literally thousands of large and small private organizations—from the RAND Corporation and the American Public Health Association to the Citizens' Committee for Children of New York and a wide variety of local community-based organizations—contribute information and perspectives to the policy-making process. Traditional think tanks and advocacy groups make up but two of the organizational categories in this considerable mix. Institutions of higher education and their various departments and research centers sit in their own category, as do research centers without a formal academic home, such as the Center for the Study of Social Policy, and professional groups, such as the American Academy of Pediatrics, that maintain research arms. Private research organizations, such as Mathematica Policy Research and the

American Institutes for Research, also appear in this broad array. All of these organizations engage in varied programs of policy-related research and analysis. They defy neat labels. But neat labels—like *think tank*—have nonetheless emerged.

In theory, a think tank conducts research and analysis and provides information and advice that can be applied to policy making. The *American Heritage Dictionary* (2003) defines think tank as "a group or an institution organized for intensive research and solving of problems, especially in the areas of technology, social or political strategy, or armament." The term originally gained currency in the mid-20th century as a descriptor for research organizations focused largely on military issues, but observers now apply the "think tank" label to a diverse group of organizations. Contemporary think tanks such as the Brookings Institution and the American Enterprise Institute often work in multiple public policy arenas, while others such as the Center on Budget and Policy Priorities concentrate more narrowly.

Advocacy organization, as a term of art, typically refers to an "interest group" defined as "a group of persons working on behalf of or strongly supporting a particular cause, such as an item of legislation, an industry, or special segment of society" (*American Heritage Dictionary*, 2003). Advocacy organizations such as the Children's Defense Fund and Voices for America's Children are about social action. They work to create and build momentum in line with their priorities and points of view.

Organizations with a particular policy advocacy agenda as their first priority do not, of course, have the corner on the advocacy market. Other organizations, such as the Child Welfare League of America, represent networks of institutions (in this case, public and private child welfare agencies) and also consider advocacy an essential part of a broader mission. In effect, organizations

that consider advocacy central to their mission have been around a good deal longer than the designation *advocacy organization.*

Advocacy organizations, think tanks, and related institutions all share a long and rich history—and an honored place—in social policy development and change. Leaders from all levels and sectors have encouraged this engagement. A century ago, for instance, President Theodore Roosevelt addressed a 1909 conference on the "Care of Dependent Children":

> I earnestly hope that each of you will consider not only the interests of his own immediate locality but the interests of the nation as a whole.... The government can do much. But never forget that the government cannot do everything; there must always be help by individuals and associations outside. (*Proceedings,* 1909, pp. 35, 36)

Back in the 19th and 20th centuries, broad social movements helped establish a foundation for present-day advocacy activity. These movements brought to life new social realities that ranged from increased access to public schools and child protection laws to the Social Security Act and childhood immunization programs. Activists in these movements sought to correct systemic ills and improve the conditions that caused them. They marshaled information and went public in the media to raise critical concerns, grab the attention of policy makers, and affect political decisions.

The original think tanks in the United States, starting in the early 20th century, played a role in this process. The president of the Brookings Institution, an organization often referred to as America's first think tank, reflected recently on this history.

> Over the past nine decades, Brookings and like-minded institutions have simultaneously concentrated on informing the public about the major issues of the day and playing

our own part in generating ideas about how our nation might better govern itself and lead the world. . . . In the 1920s, we helped the government learn how to establish a modern accounting and management system; in the '30s, we helped create Social Security; in the '40s we had a significant hand in designing the UN and the Marshall Plan; in the '50s, we worked to improve the presidential transition process and modernize the military; in the '60s, we contributed to the case for deregulation; in the '70s, the design of the Congressional Budget Office; in the '80s, it was tax reform. (Talbott, 2006, p. 437)

In contemporary policy debates, think tanks and many advocacy organizations typically both initiate action and respond to pressing situations. The experts tied to think tanks gather and disseminate information that advances an idea in multiple ways. They may, at times, communicate directly with policy makers, especially where lines of communication and relationships exist. They also use the media, events, and other opportunities to convey their messages.

Disciplines that focus on child and family matters and human development—the behavioral sciences, child and family health, and nutrition, among others—have placed value on connecting research to policy and practice from the earliest days. The Society for Research in Child Development, for example, made the application of research findings one of its founding goals (Hagen, 1997).

Researchers within the developmental science field itself—particularly those who embrace the ecological model of human development—have almost always recognized the importance of a wide-angle view, a perspective that stresses the interdependence of families, schools, peers, community, and society (Bronfenbrenner, 1979). This wide-angle perspective has encouraged outreach to worlds beyond the academy. Understanding child and family development, wide-angle

researchers believe, must go far beyond understanding what happens at the level of the individual child to take into account the social and political environment. Newer research on the brain and early development has reinforced this sense that social and environmental factors deeply matter, further strengthening both researcher interest in policy and public interest in research (Shonkoff & Phillips, 2000).

Within the research community, this growing interest creates both excitement and apprehension, especially as scientists see new research poorly conveyed to broader publics or poorly interpreted by them. Responsible researchers clearly feel a need to pay close attention to how research gets used in policy making. But engagement with policy worlds need not be just a matter of setting the record straight. It can actually help advance the science, by identifying new questions and areas of study, by quickening the development of new and more robust methodologies that can help assess and understand complicated social problems and mobilize effective responses.

THE WORK: SIMILARITIES AND DIFFERENCES

Think tanks and advocacy groups differ in mission, structure, and operation, but the lines of difference can often blur. As we've seen, both seek to influence policy. Each also may conduct basic or applied research that has implications for policy, meta-analyses on a body of existing research, policy research on high-profile topics of interest to decision makers, or policy evaluation at different phases of policy making. All these research approaches contribute, in critical ways, to the policy-making process. Research can support an idea already under consideration, spur development of new policy, or provide periodic assessments of a program that a policy may govern. In conducting this work, think tanks and advocacy organizations may—to help meet particular information demands—seek out and partner with other entities. They may also reach out to policy makers, their community, and, to varying degrees, the general public in an attempt to inform them about the realized or potential benefits and disadvantages of certain programs and policies. This education takes place in many ways, from material publications to in-person meetings.

Advocacy groups, unlike think tanks, do not center their work on research. But successful advocacy depends heavily on making a sound case for action that draws on relevant and valid research. Advocacy organizations, for instance, tap research resources to prepare materials to share with policy makers. Such materials might include fact sheets that describe an issue and summarize available research on relevant conditions, interventions, and their outcomes or research briefs, which are typically longer and more detailed than abstracts but shorter and less technical than research articles in journals.

Organizations billed as advocacy groups usually also conduct a broad range of other activities that think tanks do not. Advocacy groups take explicit positions on specific proposals and often engage in direct or grassroots lobbying, as defined under federal and state laws. These organizations may mount campaigns to affect policies that increase health benefits for children and families, support early childhood education, or improve child protection policies and programs. Take one example. Extensive advocacy efforts over the past decade have helped create and expand the State Children's Health Insurance Program, the federal initiative that helps states insure children. Advocacy will play a large role in upcoming activities surrounding the legislative reauthorization of this popular program. Advocacy group efforts have, similarly, helped shape reforms in the major federal-state child welfare programs authorized under the Adoption and Safe Families Act.

Think tanks, for their part, do often have definite perspectives on policy themes and directions, but they do not usually advocate or oppose particular policy proposals and generally steer clear of any advocacy label. Think tanks deliberately seek to keep the partisan political fray at arm's length. Instead of direct lobbying, most think tanks seek to position research findings and analyses "to speak for themselves." Still, their work, by design and practice, almost always advances a particular point of view. A think tank, for instance, can help build legislative momentum for a particular policy outcome by choosing to release information at a specific time or increase media attention on an issue simply by thrusting a well-known expert into a policy debate. Some think tanks openly acknowledge this reality. The Heritage Foundation, for example, explicitly describes its work as an ongoing effort to "formulate and promote conservative public policies." And so, in the end, on a day-to-day basis, think tanks and advocacy organizations engage the policy-making community via many of the same activities, materials, and strategies.

In Washington, D.C. policy circles, briefings and policy forums constitute two principal vehicles for engaging policy makers, their staffs, and the media. These are events that bring together researchers and other issue experts, including practitioners and consumers of services, to educate policy makers and broader publics about a particular issue and its policy implications. Organizations and coalitions of groups with shared goals regularly convene briefings and forums at a variety of points—when new research becomes available, when policy debates important to them heat up, or when events and occasions such as a National Child Abuse Prevention Month offer an opportunity to spotlight an issue. These information exchanges take place routinely on and off Capitol Hill.

Leaders in this advocacy work understand the importance of building strategic relationships. Without good working relationships with policy makers and their staffs, ideas from the think tank and advocacy world simply do not get a meaningful hearing. Many operatives in the policy world would argue that building a good relationship—getting to know the policy maker, the staff, their interest and expertise on key issues—is absolutely essential to becoming a resource. Advocates have learned that establishing those connections demands honesty, courtesy, and diplomacy.

Professionals in think tanks and advocacy groups also understand that their work, to be effective, must be credible. They must be seen by policy makers as providers of accurate data and information, as reliable and timely. This time element carries special weight. Information shared before an issue becomes the subject of intense inquiry or controversy, think tanks and advocacy group leaders have come to understand, yields the most productive results.

Leaders in these organizations and institutions also acknowledge the importance of the media and work persistently to gain media attention. A major newspaper article on an organization's issue and work or on the release of new research findings pertinent to an ongoing policy discussion can enlighten and influence policy makers. Issue experts who work with the media with skill and patience come to be called to appear on widely respected news and discussion programs. Similarly, securing media coverage for policy briefings and forums helps to get the information disseminated beyond the audience of policy makers and staff who attend. In any given week while Congress is in session, a number of these types of events occur.

Well-regarded think tanks and advocacy organizations boast highly qualified and well-respected staff based at the organization or at an affiliated institution, such as a university or research center. These scholars and other professionals have strong academic credentials in their disciplines and valued experience gained in policy environments. On a daily basis, researchers in these roles and other professional staff monitor issues and trends relevant to the organization's work. They gather and compile data. They write and disseminate research reports, issue briefs, public testimony, and commentary in accessible nontechnical language. They meet with policy makers and their staffs. They organize and participate in briefings, policy forums, and public hearings. They also disseminate information widely through their own networks. These networks may consist of dues-paying organizational members or interested individual citizens who have contributed financially to the work of an organization or taken some other action that has placed them on the organization's "mailing list."

Many advocacy groups also belong to formal and informal coalitions of like-minded groups. These coalitions provide pipelines for still more information sharing and increasing the voices advocating on particular issues. The Coalition on Human Needs, for example, based in Washington, D.C., brings together national organizations "concerned with the well being of children, women, the elderly and people with disabilities" to share information and work collaboratively and strategically "to promote public policies that address the needs of low-income and other vulnerable populations." Coalitions also target efforts on particular issues and programs.

THE PLAYERS: NATIONAL, STATE, AND LOCAL INSTITUTIONS AND ORGANIZATIONS

Think tanks and advocacy groups working on research and social policy can be found operating at all policy-making levels. These groups situate themselves, for the most part, in Washington, D.C., and state capitals. Some limit their focus to particular topics, such as child and family matters. Others work on child and family issues as part of a broader set of institutional concerns, including general economic policy or health care. The next section highlights several groups focused on children and families to illustrate the range of work under way in these organizations and the growing connections between research and policy in a wide variety of settings.

Putting a Spotlight on Children and Families

A growing number of the research organizations dedicated to children and families have become, among policy makers, respected sources for information and advice. Variously called think tanks, research institutes, and policy centers, they include Child Trends, a resource for data on the conditions of children and key policy issues, and Zero to Three, with a research focus on the earliest years, both based in Washington, D.C. Beyond the beltway, we find the National Center on Children in Poverty in New York, the Chapin Hall Center for Children at the University of Chicago, and The Search Institute in Minneapolis.

Organizations directly dedicated to advocacy on behalf of children have also become more well known and influential in policy-making circles. Among the most prominent is the Children's Defense Fund, founded in 1973. The Children's Defense Fund focuses on children in the greatest need, especially children from poor and minority families and children with disabilities. Advocacy organizations such as this one recognize the weight policy makers today can place on research. They draw on research from multiple sources, everything from original research and data collected by their own research units to public clearinghouses, academia, and other institutions and consortia with related interests and research information.

Some multipurpose organizations on the national scene also have advocacy as a core function. The Child Welfare League of America, a membership organization of agencies that work to protect and serve children who have been abused, neglected, and abandoned, has offered leadership in child welfare practice, research, and advocacy throughout its nearly century-long history. Research has a central role in the Child Welfare League's operations. The organization's National Center for Research and Data actively currently supports both original and secondary research in child welfare.

Widely respected public policy advocacy on behalf of children is also currently coming from Voices for America's Children, a national organization with state and local affiliates. Voices provides research-based information; Internet-based networking tools; contacts for media, congressional, and public outreach; and strategic technical support on policy, advocacy, and organizational matters for its members. Many individual organizations have affiliated with this national group's state and local network. These include many state-based organizations that compile data for KIDS Count, a widely disseminated resource that tracks the status of children in each state.

Advocacy organizations that work on national policy typically base their operations in the nation's capital, but they operate from elsewhere around the country as well. For instance, Children Now, based in Oakland, California, began in 1988 as a research and advocacy organization working to make children a top national public policy priority. Organizations not headquartered in Washington, D.C., often strengthen their national presence by establishing a second office in Washington or by affiliating with individuals or related groups and coalitions that work on similar agendas. Having a base outside of Washington, D.C., serves to broaden the reach of an organization, its work, and its message. This beyond-the-beltway presence creates connections among local communities that are vital for supporting advocacy—and helps to dispel "inside-the-beltway" stereotypes that can limit an organization's effectiveness.

Connecting Child and Family Issues to Broader Organizations and Policies

Established think tanks and advocacy organizations *not* directly focused on children and family issues have also come to affect child and family policy debates. This dynamic has become especially striking on issues of early childhood education and child health, as well as on issues relating to welfare policy spurred by the controversial changes to the federal-state welfare system enacted in the 1990s, which affected children and families. More recently, education reforms under the federal No Child Left Behind Act have generated widespread debate among practitioners, researchers, policy makers, and the public. Public policy issues such as these are currently engaging and connecting researchers, advocates, and policy experts from organizations not traditionally considered child centered, which is not surprising given the growing array of child and family issues and programs and their heightened profiles in state and federal budget and policy discussions.

Several think tanks have established special centers that spotlight children and families. The Brookings Institution, once largely centered on economic and military matters, has established a Center for Public Policy Education. This division, created in the 1980s, now includes a Policy Center on Children and Families, an operation that focuses "on the well-being of America's children and their parents, particularly those in less advantaged families" (The Brookings Institution, 2005). The center works in partnership with Woodrow Wilson School at Princeton University and jointly publishes the journal *The Future of Children,* an important source of research and policy affecting children and families. This journal, launched under the auspices of the David and Lucile Packard Foundation in 1991, had enjoyed a solid reputation in policy-making circles for more than a decade before becoming part of the center's work.

In a similar vein, the RAND Corporation, established in the 1940s with a concentration on national security, now lists child policy and education as two of its core research areas. RAND has a number of research divisions, and several of them contribute to child policy. RAND researchers are currently exploring areas of inquiry that include child care, child health, adolescents, juvenile justice and delinquency, and families and communities.

The Urban Institute has a similarly broad sphere of influence but a different history. Funded first by cabinet agencies after recommendations from a blue-ribbon panel set up by President Lyndon Johnson "to monitor and evaluate the Great Society initiatives that sprang from some 400 laws that had been passed since 1964" (Urban Institute, 2005), the institute now explores a range of children, youth, and family issues, with an emphasis on health, welfare and work, child welfare, child care, education, issues related to aging, and immigration.

Policy makers and advocates frequently cite data and analysis from the Urban Institute's Assessing the New Federalism program, an initiative that began with a focus on welfare reform and now analyzes trends and policies affecting low-income families. The institute's research on the *Cost of Protecting Vulnerable Children* (Scarcella, Bess, Zielewski, & Geen, 2006) has documented and analyzed child welfare spending and financing strategies over multiple years and has become a trusted source for policy makers and advocates working on reframing and reforming children's services and the financing for them.

Some think tanks that do not have specialized centers that focus on children, youth, and families nonetheless often address education and other child and family issues, mainly because these issues now constitute such a major piece of the nation's political agenda. These organizations reflect a variety of missions and points of view. From the right of center, the American Enterprise Institute (AEI), founded in 1943, supports research and analysis on an array of social policy issues as part of its dedication "to preserving and strengthening the foundations of a free society—limited government, competitive private enterprise, vital cultural and political institutions, and vigilant defense" (American Enterprise Institute, 2005, p. 1). AEI is currently working on education and health policy as well as alternative approaches to addressing poverty. From the left of center, the Economic Policy Institute (EPI), established in 1986, has as its mission "to provide high quality research and education in order to promote a prosperous, fair, and sustainable economy" (www.epi.org). EPI addresses the economic conditions of low- and middle-income individuals and families. EPI research focuses on education as one of several main areas, and it has also developed issue guides on family economic circumstances and welfare policy.

Another grouping of private research organizations also carries the think tank label from time to time. These organizations conduct and summarize research relating to public policy issues and, like traditional think tanks, place research findings in the mix of information that policy makers see and on which they have come to rely. The American Institutes for Research, for example, operates as a network with programs of research,

evaluation, and technical assistance on a wide range of education, human development, health, and workforce issues. Westat, an employee-owned research corporation, also conducts similar research, with a concentration on education, health, employment and training, social services, and housing. Mathematica Policy Research, Inc. conducts policy research and analysis in health care, welfare, education, nutrition, employment, early childhood development, and other social policy areas. These organizations are structured and equipped to compete for grants and contracts to conduct research projects directed and supported by government agencies that, with the growing attention to child and family issues, have increased their demand for specialized monitoring, assessment, and other research services.

THE PEOPLE: RESEARCHERS, POLICY EXPERTS, AND TRANSLATORS

Over the past quarter century, psychologists and other scientists have become involved both in conducting research that has policy implications and communicating research findings to support policy formulation, analysis, and evaluation. Over these same years, institutions that focus on the intersection of science and social policy have increased in number, stature, and influence. They provide education, work experiences, and career stepping stones for research scientists with policy interests.

The number of research scientists with some policy experience is continuing to grow, as links between academic and policy settings increase and more scientists experience the policy world through fellowships and other professional development opportunities (Huston, 2005; Susman-Stillman et al., 1996). These opportunities take scientists to work in Congress, federal and state agencies, and private research and policy organizations. Fellowships sponsored by the American Association for the Advancement of Science, the American Psychological Association, and the Society for Research in Child Development have provided such policy opportunities for more than 25 years. Former fellows have gone on to pursue careers and assume leadership positions in academic institutions and policy settings, and sometimes both. A related encouraging development: Applied behavioral science and policy-related studies that rarely appeared on a university campus not too long ago have gained considerable academic traction.

Specific to children and families, research scientists and those who communicate research findings have seen their training and professional opportunities multiply both in and outside of academia. Some widely recognized university-based centers, such as the Bush Center in Child Development and Social Policy at Yale and Cornell University's Family Life Development Center, took initial shape back in the 1960s and 1970s. But many influential centers have emerged that present new opportunities, including the Chapin Hall Center for Children at the University of Chicago and the Brandeis University Institute for Child, Youth and Family Policy. Such new degree programs and specialized centers that focus on children, youth, and families have heightened visibility—and support—for efforts that connect research to policy.

The organizations and groups described throughout this chapter also offer scientists professional development and career options as well as the opportunity to establish valuable working relationships with those directly involved in policy making and with those who convey social science to policy makers. They routinely advertise research-related positions from research assistants to principal investigators and often include information on employment opportunities on their organizational Web sites.

Interested researchers should keep in mind, though, that think tanks and advocacy organizations differ fundamentally from academic institutions, in everything from basic operating assumptions to day-to-day expectations. The training, skills, and judgment that researchers bring from the academic environment certainly make an essential contribution in the think tank and advocacy group environment. Research expertise can help define which data are most adequate and pertinent and which interpretations most appropriate, but academic skills by themselves do not ensure that research will positively affect advocacy and policy.

Researchers need additional skills to be effective—and feel professionally comfortable— in these environments. Effective think tanks and advocacy groups have a structure, as well as a mission clarity, that matches their own organizational needs to professionals with the skills to meet these needs. Individual researchers looking for opportunities in the think tank and advocacy worlds would need to be clear about how their knowledge, skills, and perspectives fit into those workplace environments. Though the same type of personal determination needs to be made when considering any professional opportunity, in this case, researchers would also need to consider factors that may not be relevant to thinking through professional opportunities in academia, including the political positioning of the think tank or advocacy organization.

TIGHTENING THE CONNECTIONS: CHALLENGES FOR THE BEHAVIORAL SCIENCES FIELD

In the years ahead, as connections between behavioral science and social policy continue to grow, scientists will need to more seriously confront basic new questions. One such question: Beyond high-quality graduate research preparation, what additional training, tools, and support would help researchers who work in policy environments and organizations stay true to quality research principles and practices?

Internships and fellowships can certainly give researchers a connected and supervised experience. Mentoring new entrants in these career pathways can also provide important support. But what do we know and what can we learn about navigating highly charged political environments that could help researchers as they explore and work in policy settings? We know that the politics cannot be ignored given the nature of the policy environments. We also have learned that savvy scientists can maintain the integrity of the research and not get swept up by political winds. How can we share this wisdom with newcomers to the policy world?

Networks and associations of researchers with an interest and experience in social policy are emerging to help with questions such as these (Huston, 2005), including networks of alumni from fellowship programs. We need to ask what additional organizational linkages, in academic settings and in private research and advocacy organizations, would help to grow these emergent new learning communities. Building such linkages would benefit researchers in a variety of organizational settings—and the work of the organizations themselves. It would expand and strengthen the institutional infrastructure vital to supporting researchers who venture into the policy world and likely generate new opportunities to advance the knowledge base of the behavioral sciences.

CONCLUSION

As observers have noted (Huston, 1994), for scientists interested in connecting research and policy, these are good times. The policy world is demanding research data and skilled researchers knowledgeable about policy. Think tanks, advocacy organizations, and other institutions have diversified their issue rosters to work much more systematically across a broader range of behavioral science topics. But reasons for caution also abound. Outright bias, data misinterpretations, narrow political agendas, and superficial and shallow issue perspectives can highjack policy debate and steer policy into nonproductive and even dangerous directions. By building a strong and well-connected research presence in institutions that seek to influence public policy, behavioral researchers can help to avoid these dangers—and help our society realize the promise our new century holds.

REFERENCES

American Enterprise Institute for Public Policy Research. (2005). *2005 annual report*. Washington, DC: Author.

American Heritage dictionary of the English language. (2003). Boston: Houghton Mifflin.

Bronfenbrenner, U. (1979). *The ecology of human development: Experiments in nature and by design.* Cambridge, MA: Harvard University Press.

The Brookings Institution. (2005). *2005 annual report*. Washington, DC: Author.

Hagen, J. (1997). The Society for Research in Child Development: Early roots, history and current organization. *SRCD Newsletter, 40,* 3.

Huston, A. C. (1994). Children in poverty: Designing research to affect policy. *Social Policy Report, 8*(2), 1–12.

Huston, A. C. (2005). Connecting the science of child development to public policy. *Social Policy Report, 19*(4), 1–19.

McCabe, M. A. (2005). Dissemination of science and the science of dissemination: SRCD developments. *Newsletter of the Society for Research in Child Development, 48*(4), 2.

Nakamura, M. (2005). *Public funding and think tanks—Asian, EU and US experiences.* Tokyo, Japan: National Institute for Research Advancement.

Proceedings of the conference on the care of dependent children. (1909, January 25–26). Washington, DC: Government Printing Office.

Scarcella, C. A., Bess, R., Zielewski, E. H., & Geen, R. (2006). *The cost of protecting vulnerable children.* Washington, DC: Urban Institute Press.

Shonkoff, J. P., & Phillips, D. A. (2000). *From neurons to neighborhoods: The science of early child development.* Washington, DC: National Academies Press.

Susman-Stillman, A. R., Brown, J. L., Adam, E. K., Blair, C., Gaines, R., Gordon, R. A., et al. (1996). Building research and policy connections: Training and career options for developmental scientists. *Social Policy Report, 10*(4), 1–19.

Talbott, S. (2006, March 28). *Ideas, policy, and politics: The role of independent research in partisan times.* Remarks of the president, The Brookings Institution, at Miller Center of Public Affairs, University of Virginia, Charlottesville. Retrieved from http://www.brookings.edu/views/speeches/talbott/20060328.htm

Urban Institute. (2005). *Annual report 1968–1998.* Washington, DC: Urban Institute Press.

Part V

DISSEMINATING BEHAVIORAL SCIENCE TO SERVICE PROFESSIONS

CHAPTER 19

Disseminating Behavioral Medicine Research to Practitioners

Recommendations for Researchers

KIMBERLEE J. TRUDEAU AND KARINA W. DAVIDSON

Behavioral science—both behavioral medicine research and the broader field of health psychology—is crucial to improving the quality of health care.[1] Behavioral medicine research, the focus of this chapter, assists with issues such as medication adherence, smoking cessation, and management of stress resulting from various chronic conditions. The behavioral practitioners who educate and counsel patients about behavior change are a diverse group of professionals that includes not only psychologists but also nurses, physicians, physical therapists, occupational therapists, social workers, and nutritionists. Most practitioners recognize that finding ways to motivate behavior change is essential to the health of their patients. Still, the dissemination of behavioral practices with evidence to support their use is not yet efficient or routine (e.g., Committee on Quality Health Care in America, 2001; Kerner, Guirguis-Blake, et al., 2005; Kerner, Rimer, & Emmons, 2005). Whereas paths have been forged to move other sciences quickly into medical practice

(e.g., Mosca et al., 2005), behavioral scientists and practitioners in medicine still struggle to implement research findings and to interact in ways that are useful to each other (e.g., Addis & Hatgis, 2000; Montgomery & Ayllon, 1995; Sogg, Read, Bollinger, & Berger, 2001; Spring et al., 2005).

During the course of this chapter, we recommend five steps toward the effective dissemination of behavioral research: (1) produce sound and relevant science, (2) synthesize research in scientifically rigorous and practically meaningful ways, (3) use existing mechanisms that support disseminating behavioral science, (4) advocate for systematic change in education and policy, and (5) conduct dissemination research to discover the best methods of disseminating findings to diverse target populations, mainly practitioners, other researchers, students, consumers, and policy makers.

We begin by reviewing the tools and opportunities that exist to support dissemination and then comment on their strengths and weaknesses. Next, we identify problems

AUTHORS' NOTE: Preparation of this chapter was supported by awards HL-76857 and HC25197.

in disseminating behavioral science and propose some solutions. We conclude by summarizing our specific recommendations to researchers. Although these recommendations stem from our experiences in the field of behavioral medicine, they apply to disseminating behavioral science more generally.

EXISTING TOOLS AND OPPORTUNITIES

Many resources have been developed to help move research to practice, originally in medicine and now in behavioral medicine as well. In this section, we describe existing methods, organizations, and guidelines that can help behavioral researchers to disseminate their findings for practical use.

Creating Evidence

Basic Science. When attempting to translate research into practice, the importance of basic science can be overlooked. "Behavioral medicine's great strength as a field historically has been in basic research that demonstrates the importance of psychosocial factors in physical health" (Spring et al., 2005, p. 131). Such research must be of the highest quality to have solid evidence to disseminate. But that's just the beginning. Davidson and Spring (2006) suggest that one must move through five stages to ultimately implement an intervention program or other research-based practice with the desired efficiency and effectiveness (see Figure 19.1). Basic science inspired by practical need is an essential part of the model. First, an area of need must be defined using qualitative and descriptive methods such as case studies, focus groups, and surveys. Second, an area of inquiry must become standardized for scientific inquiry using methods such as observational studies, epidemiological data, and prospective research. Measures must also be

developed to assess processes of change and outcomes. Third, change mechanisms must be proposed based on theories of behavior and tested using appropriate methods, such as randomized clinical trials. Fourth, interventions must be developed and tested for effectiveness using small-scale and then large-scale randomized trials. Finally, results from effectiveness research may be translated and dissemination research conducted to determine how best to deliver the intervention and associated information to the appropriate target groups (administrators, service providers, policy makers, consumers).

Basic science also can ease barriers to dissemination by providing the necessary evidence to justify exposing participants to experimental behavioral medicine interventions. Moreover, dissemination is strengthened when basic scientists work with systematic reviewers and policy makers to help identify gaps in the research needed to meet medical needs and to help fill these gaps in knowledge (Lavis et al., 2005). For example, developing programs of research using the goals of *Healthy People 2010,* a report issued regularly by the U.S. Department of Health and Human Services (2000), would increase the likelihood that findings from basic science will contribute to understanding problems of vital importance to public health, such as smoking and childhood obesity.

Randomized Clinical Trials and Practical Behavioral Trials. Randomized clinical trials (RCTs) are accepted in the medical and behavioral science fields as the gold standard of research methodologies for evaluating the effectiveness of an intervention (e.g., Sackett, Richardson, Rosenberg, & Haynes, 2000). They reduce risks to internal validity, such as confounding variables and sampling bias (as well as investigator bias if the trials are double blind), and so allow for making cause-effect inferences (see also Friedman, Furberg,

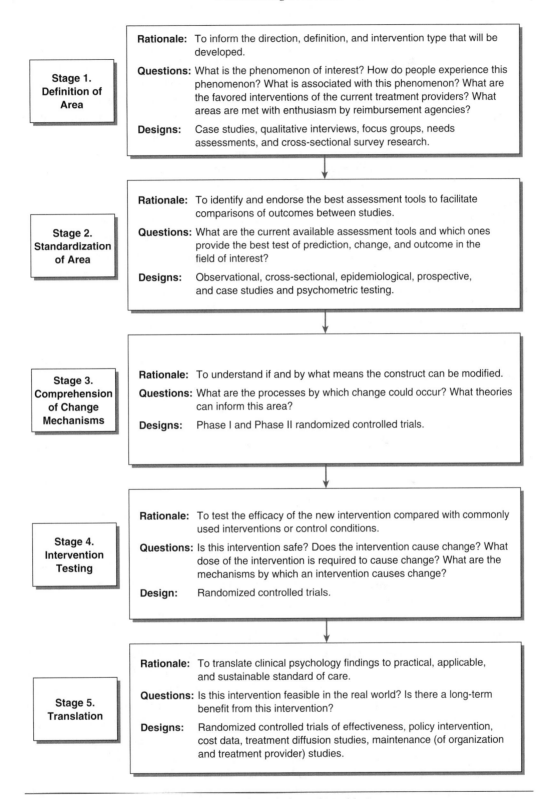

Figure 19.1   The Stages of Evidence-Based Psychological Health Care

& DeMets, 1998). RCTs, therefore, are more likely to be included in systematic reviews of research and so are more likely to influence practice guidelines, policies, and reimbursements that ultimately affect individual patient and public health. (For related resources, see the text *Fundamental Clinical Trials* [Friedman et al., 1998] and information about training opportunities such as the Office of Behavioral and Social Sciences Research [OBSSR] Summer Institute on designing and conducting RCTs involving behavioral interventions, http://obssr.od.nih.gov/Conf_Wkshp/rct/RCT_Info.htm.)

The RCT methodology does have some drawbacks. The trials are sometimes expensive or difficult to conduct (for example, it is not always feasible to randomize schools or communities). Strict inclusion criteria that bolster a study's internal validity limit generalizability and usefulness of the findings. For example, a study of an intervention to reduce depression may exclude those with dual diagnosis of depression and substance abuse because the primary outcome, the Beck Depression Inventory, includes items that are associated with substance use withdrawal. But what if the majority of clients a practitioner sees for depression treatment have co-occurring substance use disorders? According to Glasgow, Davidson, Dobkin, Ockene, and Spring (2006), a behavioral medicine trial that is designed without considering the practical value of the intervention in practice is unlikely to be disseminated.

Consequently, recommendations for practical clinical trials (PCTs) that were originally put forth by Tunis, Stryer, and Clancy (2003) have been adapted and extended by Glasgow and colleagues (2006) for use in behavioral medicine and are known as practical behavioral trials (PBTs). This approach encourages scientists to design experiments, keeping in mind those factors that affect the practical value of the science, such as feasibility, generalizability, and patient concerns, including quality of life. Specific recommendations for conducting PBTs are (1) consider the concerns of key stakeholders such as administrators and other policy makers and, as a result, assess conditions affecting feasibility such as staffing, infrastructure, and intervention cost; (2) compare current clinical practice to the new intervention rather than to a control condition to be more representative of clinic protocol; (3) recruit participants who represent the health condition of interest, including incidence and types of comorbidity; and (4) recruit patients from multiple settings and recruit representative practitioners to conduct the trial. Unique to PBTs is an emphasis on training the intervention provider, patient preferences for treatment, and opportunities to tailor the intervention over the course of the trial to meet individual patient needs. These newer, more client-centered methodologies may reduce practitioner complaints about the incompatibility between interventions conducted in research trials and the needs and conditions of clinical practice (Spring et al., 2005; see Glasgow et al., 2006, for more about PBTs).

Checklists for Reporting Research. To increase the reliability and completeness of the information to be disseminated, reports of individual clinical trials should be incorporated into systematic reviews or meta-analyses (if enough data are available for quantitative analyses) and published in peer-reviewed journals. But published reports of clinical trials are not always detailed enough for recommending an application or for including in a systematic review (e.g., McGrath, Stinson, & Davidson, 2003). The medical community was confronted by this issue as well and developed the CONSORT statement (Consolidated Standards of Reporting Trials; see Altman et al., 2001, for the most recent version). The CONSORT statement is a 22-item checklist designed to help researchers fully present their work in each section of a journal research report. The checklist is intended to help reviewers evaluate submitted studies for publication, help systematic reviewers synthesize findings across studies, and help clinicians judge whether to apply published work to their practice. In addition, it can provide specific guidelines on how to design a research project for those writing grant applications for research funding.

CONSORT checklist items include the following: "How participants were allocated to interventions (e.g., random allocation, randomized, or randomly assigned)"—included in the Title/Abstract; "Method used to implement the random allocation sequence (e.g., numbered containers or central telephone), clarifying whether the sequence was concealed until interventions were assigned"—included in the Methods section; and "All important adverse events or side effects in each intervention group"—included in the Results section (see www.consort-statement.org for the complete list of items and related articles).

Why are these reporting omissions problematic? When authors don't report that the methodology was a randomized clinical trial in the title or the abstract, it is difficult for systematic reviewers to find the trial for inclusion in their reviews. When authors don't describe the randomization or masking strategies, it is difficult for peer reviewers to evaluate the efficacy of the intervention. When authors don't provide a detailed description of potential adverse events, clinicians don't have adequate information for evaluating the risk-to-benefit ratio of employing the intervention in their clinical practice.

The positive impact of CONSORT on transparency in reporting has been quantified by various researchers (Devereaux, Manns, Ghali, Quan, & Guyatt, 2002; Moher, Jones, & Lepage, 2001). The CONSORT statement also has been applied successfully to behavioral medicine trials

(Trudeau & Davidson, 2001–2002; Trudeau, Mostofsky, Stuhr, & Davidson, in press) and incorporated into the review process of many journals in the behavioral medicine field (e.g., *Journal of Consulting and Clinical Psychology, Annals of Behavioral Medicine, Psychosomatic Medicine,* and *Journal of Pediatric Psychology*). Behavioral medicine researchers are advised to include five additional items designed to address behavioral medicine-specific issues in clinical trials (Davidson et al., 2003): training of treatment providers, supervision of treatment providers, patient and provider treatment allegiance (preference), treatment integrity, and treatment adherence. Checklists to improve reports of studies with nonrandomized designs have also been developed to support the appropriate use of this research in both science and practice. Scientists at the Centers for Disease Control and Prevention and editors of journals concerned with poor reporting in public health literature developed the Transparent Reporting of Evaluations with Nonrandomized Designs (TREND) statement (www.trend-statement.org; Des Jarlais, Lyles, Crepaz, & the TREND Group, 2004). Like CONSORT, TREND focuses mainly on issues that affect the internal validity of clinical trials. In response to concerns about the underreporting of conditions that affect external validity, Glasgow, Vogt, and Boles (1999) developed a reporting checklist using the RE-AIM model (www.re-aim.org). The RE-AIM checklist assesses the following: **Reach** (whether the intervention was offered to all individuals who may benefit and not only, for example, to individuals with no comorbidities), **Efficacy** (whether the intervention had an impact on all participants or only on particular subgroups), **Adoption** (whether the intervention was adopted by diverse practice settings and not only the supportive setting of university clinics), **Implementation** (whether the intervention was consistently implemented by staff members as opposed to research staff who leave at the end of the trial), and Maintenance (whether a beneficial intervention was maintained and not perfunctorily terminated at the end of the trial). Reviews of the literature on behavior change intervention research in health care settings (Glasgow, Bull, Gillette, Klesges, & Dzewaltowski, 2002) and in community settings (Dzewaltowski, Estabrooks, Klesges, Bull, & Glasgow, 2004) confirmed that these details have been underreported (see http://www.re-aim.org/2003/ck_ccs.html for RE-AIM checklist items that augment CONSORT).

In addition to checklists to enhance reporting of randomized and nonrandomized clinical trials, there are also checklists designed to help evaluate the quality of published trials—mainly, tests of pharmaceutical interventions (see review by Katrak, Bialocerkowski, Massy-Wstropp, Kumar, & Grimmer, 2004). Behavioral medicine researchers may be most interested in the CLEAR NPT checklist, which was designed to assess study conditions, such as clinician skill and patient adherence that affect the internal validity of nonpharmaceutical trials (Boutron et al., 2005) (see Trudeau et al., in press, for other checklists and more information about the evolution of CONSORT).

Synthesizing Evidence

Historically, journal editors have preferred submissions of original research to summaries of research studies, but the systematic review is now gaining appreciation as an important translational mechanism. Users of the research literature seem to appreciate that summarizing findings across research studies using different settings and populations can provide more reliable and nuanced information about the efficacy and generalizability of an intervention than can a single study. A recent study found that systematic reviews receive more citations than other study designs (Patsopoulos, Analatos, & Ioannidis, 2005). Such trends should result in those journals being rewarded with higher impact factors relative to their peers, perhaps further increasing the value of dissemination to the academic community (see Chapter 7, this volume, for a related discussion of impact factors and dissemination).

Many organizations present opportunities to find, propose, and write reviews. They also allow scientists to contribute research to clinical practical guidelines (i.e., recommendations for best practice). We describe these organizations and opportunities next and conclude with a discussion of how professional societies have contributed to getting the word out about evidence-based medicine.

Finding a Review. Reviews of research relating to health are proposed and disseminated by international organizations such as The Cochrane Collaboration and the International Network of Health Technology Assessment. The Cochrane Collaboration, founded in 1992, has members from over 90 countries (The Cochrane Collaboration, 2005). Thus far, more than 2,800 systematic reviews of medical interventions have been published in *The Cochrane Library.* Abstracts for these reviews are publicly available at www.cochrane.org. In addition, many organizations extract information from *The Cochrane Library* to develop evidence-based resources such as clinical guidelines, electronic databases, topic-specific indices of reviews, and textbooks (The Cochrane Collaboration, 2004).

The International Network of Health Technology Assessment (INHTA), founded in 1993, includes government-sponsored centers from 45 countries that conduct systematic reviews to inform practice (INHTA, 2006). INHTA's primary means of disseminating information is a Web site (www.inahta.org); other methods include presentations and publications, such as briefs (summaries of the agency's published reports) and a newsletter.

A U.S. representative within the INHTA network is the Agency for Healthcare Research and Quality (AHRQ; http://www .ahrq.gov/; Newman, 2000). AHRQ has 13 evidence-based practice centers (EPCs; AHRQ, 2006) that are mandated by the Congressional Healthcare Research and Quality Act of 1999 to summarize and disseminate information about research on health interventions (AHRQ, 2002). EPC reports (http://www.ahrq.gov/clinic/epcix .htm#reports) are organized under three headings: Clinical (e.g., Heart and Vascular Diseases, Mental Health Conditions and Substance Abuse), Health Care Services (e.g., Information Technology, Quality Improvement and Patient Safety), and Technical (i.e., Methodology). Though the AHRQ makes information about behavioral interventions available, it does not focus on them exclusively or distinguish them from other kinds of interventions. Of the 138 completed reports listed on their Web site in April 2006, 37 reports (i.e., 27%) come within the scope of behavioral medicine as defined by the Cochrane Behavioral Medicine Field (Davidson, Trudeau, & Falzon, 2006). These reports are disseminated in many ways that include reports, education programs, practice guidelines, conferences, tool kits, and so on (see Table 1 on p. 1121 in Matchar et al., 2005). As with The Cochrane Collaboration, scientists and other users of the system can propose a review of a missing topic. According to the *EPC Partner's Guide* (AHRQ, 2005b), nominations for reports are requested via a notice in the *Federal Register* but are accepted all year. Those who nominate topics are expected to assist with disseminating the completed reports.

Initiated by the U.S. Public Health Service in 1984, the United States Preventive Services Task Force (USPSTF, 2006) is another systematic review-producing organization sponsored by the AHRQ. USPSTF reviews the evidence compiled by EPCs, evaluates the strength of that evidence ("A" = strongly recommends, "B" = recommends, "C" = no recommendation for or against, "D" = recommends against, "I" = insufficient evidence to recommend for or against), and provides specific health care recommendations. Most of the 63 reports published in the organization's most recent *Guide to Clinical Preventive Services* (AHRQ, 2005c) cover various kinds of health screening. Since 1994, USPSTF also has used the program Putting Prevention Into Practice to disseminate recommendations to consumers about health care interventions based on research reviews (AHRQ, 2005a). (For a detailed description of the USPSTF process, including the use of analytic frameworks to define areas for review, please see Harris et al., 2001.)

Writing a Review. Because systematic reviews are so important in assessing the efficacy of interventions, the new "Evidence-Based Treatment Review" series has been initiated in *Health Psychology* (Davidson, Trudeau, & Smith, 2006), under former Editor Arthur Stone and with continuing support from current Editor Robert Kaplan. The series was modeled on the *Journal of the American Medical Association*'s Clinician's Corner, in which articles are "to provide clinically relevant information that will be immediately useful in clinical practice" (DeAngelis & Fontanarosa, 2002, p. 104; e.g., Nunes & Levin, 2004, on "Treatment of Depression in Patients With Alcohol or Other Drug Dependence"). The new *Health Psychology* series strives to accomplish this same objective by including in a single issue one evidence-based treatment review relating to a specific behavioral medicine interventions (e.g., insomnia; Irwin, Cole, & Nicassio, 2006) and an accompanying clinician comment (e.g., Smith & Perlis, 2006). The new

Health Psychology series incorporated some Cochrane Collaboration methodology such as submitting a priori review protocols (outlines of planned reviews) for peer review.

One can also propose to write a review through The Cochrane Collaboration. Reviews are written by international volunteers (researchers, practitioners, and consumers) who value the importance of evidence-based medicine. Cochrane has compiled various resources for reviewers, such as *The Cochrane Handbook for Systematic Reviews of Interventions* (a manual describing the review process), the Cochrane Central Register of Controlled Trials (a searchable database of trials for possible inclusion in a review), and Review Manager (free statistical software for conducting meta-analyses). (For information on writing a systematic review or peer reviewing see http://www.cochrane.org/docs/involve.htm.)

Check the Clinical Practice Guidelines. Perusing existing clinical practice guidelines helps scientists evaluate whether their own work or other relevant work is being made available to intended users. The National Guideline Clearinghouse (NGC) of the AHRQ disseminates clinical practice guidelines, including 184 guidelines for "Behavioral Disciplines and Activities" (National Guideline Clearinghouse, 2006b), on topics such as Mental Health Services (73 guidelines) and Psychological Techniques (7 guidelines) (National Guideline Clearinghouse, 2006a). *The Guide to Community Preventive Services* (http://www.thecommunityguide.org/about/), produced by the Centers for Disease Control and Prevention's nonfederal Community Task Force, also includes updated information from systematic reviews on health topics in diverse formats suitable for policy makers, practitioners, managed care administrators, academic researchers, and community members (Briss, Brownson, Fielding, & Zaz, 2004; Truman

et al., 2000). The *Guide* includes a systematic review of the research literature with research-based recommendations from a panel of experts with detailed information about the populations studied so that *Guide* users can determine applicability to their questions and needs (Truman et al., 2000). *Guide* topics were identified by reviewing the objectives of *Healthy People 2000* (U.S. Department of Health and Human Services, 1990) and include ones relevant to behavioral science such as tobacco use, nutrition, and physical activity as well as the topic of sociocultural environment as it relates to health (Zaza et al., 2000). Because it is updated regularly, the *Guide* is an opportunity for behavioral medicine researchers to provide feedback that may be incorporated in future analyses. In reviewing the current edition, researchers may find that relevant research, including their own, has been overlooked, or they may discover areas for future research that could contribute to subsequent volumes. (For more information about the *Guide*, see the January 2000 supplement of the *American Journal of Preventive Medicine.*)

Getting the Word Out. Some professional societies (e.g., Society of Behavioral Medicine) and associations (e.g., American Diabetes Association) collate the dissemination resources discussed above (checklists, *The Cochrane Library*, practice guidelines, and so on) to make them available to their membership. These organizations provide forums for researcher-practitioner discussion via conferences, newsletters, and listservs, as well as opportunities for CME courses at which training in evidence-based behavioral medicine interventions could be offered.

Division 12 of the American Psychological Association (APA), for example, charged its Task Force on Promotion and Dissemination of Psychological Procedures (1995) to develop a list of empirically supported treatments

(ESTs) and commissioned an interdisciplinary *Guide to Treatments That Work,* now in its second edition (Nathan & Gorman, 2002). This text includes a few chapters of potential interest to behavioral medicine community members, such as "Psychosocial Treatments for Alcohol Use Disorders." Despite these efforts, when internship sites were asked if one or more Well Established Treatments (for a minimum of 15 hours) of the ESTs were included in their training programs for professional psychologists, only 28% responded in the affirmative; reasons given for lack of training in ESTs included that sites were not accountable to managed care and that client needs were not addressed by ESTs (Hays et al., 2002).

More recently, an APA Presidential Task Force on Evidence-Based Practice (EBP) completed a report that was approved by the Council of Representatives of APA. The objectives of this task force were to consider how diverse types of research evidence (e.g., controlled effectiveness studies, public health research, health services research) should be integrated and applied to inform the development of EBP for use in health services, comment on the role of clinical expertise in EBP, and specify how to include patient values in EBP. In this report, EBP was defined as "to promote effective psychological practice and enhance public health by applying empirically supported principles of psychological assessment, case formulation, therapeutic relationship, and intervention" (http://www.apa.org/practice/ebp.html). The task force decided that the use of a clinician's judgment alone does not constitute EBP, but it did not elaborate on the specific supports clinicians would need to integrate clinical observations and judgment with scientific research.

The behavioral medicine community joined the evidence-based movement in 2000. The Society of Behavioral Medicine acquired funding from the Office of Behavioral and Social Sciences Research of the National Institutes of Health to form an intersocietal committee including representatives from American Psychosomatic Society, Division 38 (Health Psychology), of the American Psychological Association. Founded and coordinated by the two authors of this chapter, the goal of the Evidence-Based Behavioral Medicine (EBBM) Committee was to develop a system of evidence review informed by an analysis of existing models (e.g., Davidson, Trudeau, Ockene, Orleans, & Kaplan, 2004), to educate behavioral medicine professionals about evidence-based behavioral medicine (e.g., Spring et al., 2005), and to increase the quality of reported evidence (e.g., CONSORT; Davidson et al., 2003). (For past publications and current activities of this committee, please see www.sbm.org/ebbm/.)

The work of the EBBM Committee indicated that behavioral medicine research and practice would benefit from developing an evidence base of trials on behavioral medicine interventions (Davidson et al., 2004). Consequently, in August 2004, an ad hoc international group of behavioral medicine scholars recommended that behavioral medicine join The Cochrane Collaboration (www.cochrane.org) as a Cochrane Behavioral Medicine Field. Officially registered in February 2006, the new Cochrane Behavioral Medicine Field will increase and improve access to evidence-based behavioral medicine interventions through fostering collaborations between behavioral medicine society affiliates and Cochrane Review Groups. In addition, the Cochrane Behavioral Medicine Field will benefit behavioral medicine by compiling a trial register and advocating for reviews of behavioral medicine interventions. (See www.cochranebehavmed.org for resources on conducting systematic reviews, such as Pai et al., 2004, and Lipsey & Wilson, 2001, and for ways to contribute to the Cochrane Behavioral Medicine Field.)

Commentary on Existing Tools and Opportunities

As we've described, multiple tools exist for creating and advocating for dissemination-worthy evidence, and many organizations have taken on the important work of synthesizing, evaluating, and disseminating the available evidence through guides, Web sites, and clinical practice guidelines. Existing approaches, however, have certain strengths and weaknesses.

As previously mentioned, randomized clinical trials are the gold standard for identifying the efficacy of an intervention, but the methodology has required some adapting to be applicable to behavioral medicine research questions (e.g., practical behavioral trials; Glasgow et al., 2006), and more work remains to be done to increase the practical value of randomized trials. Moreover, quality reporting of studies facilitates comprehensive systematic reviews. For example, the *Health Psychology* Evidence-Based Treatment Review series helps fortify the link between quality research and effective dissemination in behavioral medicine by drawing from an existing medical publication model (i.e., the inclusion of a clinical commentary on a simultaneously published systematic review—*JAMA*'s Clinician's Corner), as well as from elements of The Cochrane Collaboration process (e.g., a priori protocol submission).

Though the practice guideline has potential as a useful dissemination tool, there are too many, and the content is not coordinated across guidelines. Often, the guidelines also are not evaluated against the available evidence. One known exception is national smoking cessation guidelines, which were derived from literature reviews and meta-analyses (Silagy, Stead, & Lancaster, 2001). Still, research shows that although Cochrane systematic reviews could have informed between 39% and 73% of recommendations included in the smoking guidelines, and reviews were only used in

0% to 36% of them (Silagy et al., 2001). In addition, Cochrane reviews were used to develop guidelines less often in the United States than the United Kingdom. The study authors speculated that relevant Cochrane reviews may not have been used because they were not available in 1996 when the U.S. guidelines were developed; however, the United States replicated several Cochrane reviews to inform its 2000 guidelines, suggesting a lack of international cooperation and coordination of efforts. Perhaps guidelines will more often be evaluated using all available evidence now that criteria for developing and evaluating practice guidelines (American Psychological Association [APA], 2002b) and treatment guidelines (APA, 2002a) have been commissioned by the APA Board of Professional Affairs and made available. The extent of their use at this time is unknown.

All of the important resources available from organizations such as the APA, The Cochrane Collaboration, and federal agencies cost money both for production (e.g., pages in journals) and advertising. Scientists have a responsibility, therefore, to inform professional social networks (e.g., via listservs) about these existing dissemination activities and to contribute to the scientific literature through research, peer review, and commentary as health care consumers. Such professional social networks exist in the form of societies (e.g., Society of Behavioral Medicine, which is linked to the International Society of Behavioral Medicine). Participating in these networks helps reach scientists and professionals with information about EBBM interventions, but the agenda of these networks may change. Society boards are transient, and so commitment to maintaining attention on disseminating evidence-based practice may also ebb in time. As society members, we can continue to advocate for the personal, social, and fiscal resources essential to sustained action and for weaving evidence-based practice into the fabric of each professional society.

Government agencies have resources and the ability to attract expertise to dissemination, and researchers in behavioral medicine are fortunate that they have made dissemination a priority. But, unfortunately, it is not clear that their work, although accessible online, is well known to consumers and researchers, raising questions about the effectiveness of their dissemination methods. For example, although the Agency for Healthcare Research and Quality places the Evidence Practice Center reports on its Web site, it does not submit abstracts of these reports to PubMed (a database of medical research citations available at www.pubmed.gov), which would make them more likely to be included in registers of reviews and used. Last, the many available federal (e.g., AHRQ) and private (e.g., The Cochrane Collaboration) dissemination opportunities that exist may help get research included in systematic reviews and practice guidelines, but how can researchers ensure that these secondary-level resources reach their target audience?

FROM PROBLEMS TO SOLUTIONS IN DISSEMINATION: FUTURE DIRECTIONS

Though barriers to efficient and effective dissemination always exist, the number and complexity of barriers to disseminating information from behavioral science and behavioral interventions seem particularly daunting. As we discuss next, education and policy barriers must first be tackled to improve the dissemination of effective behavioral medicine practices, and programmatic research must be undertaken to develop and test the effectiveness of dissemination mechanisms.

Education

Consumers. In today's Internet age, consumers are actively seeking answers to their health questions (Stolz, 2006), but are they finding the answers they need? In fact, what *are* their needs? Who *are* the consumers of behavioral medicine interventions? Smokers who try to quit without using pills or patches? Support group members attempting to cope with their chronic medical conditions? People who work with personal trainers to enhance their exercise routines or who visit nutritionists for advice? Yes, all of these! How can the needs of such a diverse consumer community be met?

Behavioral medicine practitioners can help meet individual consumer needs by educating their clients about evidence-based behavioral medicine interventions (Eckel, 2006) and directing them to resources produced by experts in the field. Scientists also can educate behavioral medicine consumers through existing consumer networks and then capitalize on the snowball effect that comes from many consumers talking about their care. Scientists could also work more closely with existing networks in major consumer societies such as the American Cancer Society and the Arthritis Foundation as well as organizations devoted to disseminating information to consumers such as Active for Life, funded by the Robert Wood Johnson Foundation (http://www.activeforlife.info/default.aspx).

Involving consumers in systematic reviews also may increase the effectiveness of dissemination by promoting consumer awareness of evidence-based medicine and producing information that can better meet consumer needs. Consumers seem to appreciate learning how to generate, evaluate, and disseminate behavioral medicine evidence through The Cochrane Collaboration structure: Cochrane Reviews Groups have been involving consumers in identifying research questions, reviewing a priori review protocols and review drafts, and disseminating review content (e.g., the Pregnancy and Childbirth Group [Sakala, Gyte, Henderson, Neilson, & Horey, 2001]; the Musculoskeletal Group [Shea et al.,

2005]). The "Consumers in Cochrane" Web page of the Cochrane Consumer Network suggests ways of recruiting, using, and maintaining consumer involvement to promote evidence-based health care (The Cochrane Collaboration, 2006).

But as we explain in more detail later, reaching practitioners and consumers with information about behavioral interventions remains difficult because, whereas the Food and Drug Administration (FDA) disseminates information and regulates claims about the risks and benefits of food or drugs, no authoritative body educates, regulates, and disseminates information about useful, useless, or harmful behavioral medicine practices. Without some such system or process for behavioral interventions, effective dissemination seems a very distant goal.

Students. Many graduate and professional schools training our next generation of behavioral medicine practitioners and scientists do not disseminate evidence on effective behavioral interventions, nor do they explain the research methodologies critical to evaluating the interventions and dissemination efforts. Such education exists (e.g., Carpenter, Nieva, Albaghal, & Sorra, 2005), but it is not standard practice for most professionals (i.e., scientists *and* practitioners) who study behavior. Mandatory curriculum changes are needed for both researchers and clinicians regarding empirically supported treatments and the research methods required to test behavioral interventions and to effectively disseminate them (see, e.g., Baldwin et al., 2005, a position paper by the American Academy of Health Behavior Work Group on doctoral research training). Professional development events, such as the OBSSR Randomized Clinical Trials Summer Institute, are trying to address curriculum deficits in order to support creating quality evidence on the effectiveness of behavioral interventions, but training programs have a responsibility

to teach the full range of skills that behavioral medicine scientists and practitioners will need to be competitive in an increasingly evidence-based health care market.

Aspiring practitioners could also benefit from being taught how to locate the behavioral medicine practices likely to help their patients in regularly published practice guidelines and repositories of treatment manuals with evidence to support their use. But these systems would first need to be developed. Moreover, new students should demand training in empirically based treatments (Persons, 1995) and quality research methods. Unless the next generation is trained to participate in evidence-based practice and appreciate the viability and effectiveness of dissemination, behavioral medicine is doomed to another generation of interesting studies that have little to no impact on public health.

Ongoing Education for Practitioners. A system is also needed to efficiently and effectively disseminate new behavioral medicine practices to the existing practitioner community and to support their use. This system would also need to provide essential training because, unlike applying recommendations for using new pharmaceutical formulas, quality control on the delivery of behavioral change interventions requires more complex and sustained interactions between the trainer and the professional.

In the medical world, a train-the-trainer model is used to facilitate adherence to practice guidelines. Advances to this model are required, however, that would develop research-based practice guidelines, create mechanisms for disseminating guidelines to practice settings, and support the implementation of guidelines with the support of on-site directors. But gaining the support and resources needed to improve training may require policy changes.

Policy

Regulation by a Government Body. As mentioned earlier, a regulatory body such as the FDA does not regulate behavioral interventions or disseminate information about them to the public. The FDA serves an important role in ensuring that drugs are tested through clinical trials in a four-phase system: a new drug is tested on 20 to 80 healthy participants to assess its metabolic and pharmacologic effects (Phase I), then the new drug is tested on several hundred participants to assess effectiveness and side effects (Phase II), next the drug is tested on several hundred to several thousand participants to assess its effectiveness and safety (Phase III), and finally, the drug is monitored in demonstration projects or when in use in the population to determine if unexpected adverse events occur (Phase IV) (U.S. Food and Drug Administration, 2006).

People often mistakenly believe that behavioral medicine interventions are not potent enough to do harm or have benefits significant enough to justify regulating them for widespread use. To help refute this belief, we argue that a regulatory body for behavioral medicine interventions is needed that would similarly require multiple phases of trials to assess the safety and efficacy, as well as the effectiveness, of a proposed intervention. Interventions that survive this approval process would then be attractive to reimbursement entities such as insurance companies, and so ultimately to practitioners. Reimbursement for deploying an intervention is one of the most effective mechanisms for ensuring dissemination. When a drug, medical device, or medical service appears to be effective, it is disseminated to the public because someone pays for it. Currently, few behavioral medicine practices are routinely reimbursed, and the number is not likely to grow rapidly in the current health care environment.

Although the FDA process has received some criticism relating to conflicts of interest, inattention to safety and effectiveness (Deyo, 2004), and disregard of dissenting opinions (Kaufman & Masters, 2004), behavioral medicine may be able to avoid such critiques. Behavioral medicine, unlike drug companies with conflicts of interest, does not have funds to pay user fees to speed up the process of review, even if it were so motivated. Second, registering trials ensures that all data are available, allowing more complete and accurate information to be provided about how consumers might or might not benefit. Overall, the advantages both to the field of behavioral science and the practice of behavioral medicine seem likely to outweigh the potential risks. Without such a body to provide oversight and systemization, behavioral medicine practices will always move very slowly toward dissemination.

Develop, Disseminate, and Mandate Practice Guidelines. Professional groups can contribute to developing the market for evidence-based health care by volunteering to create practice guidelines specific to behavioral medicine. For example, though guidelines exist for physical health (e.g., cardiovascular disease [CVD]) and for mental health (e.g., depression), guidelines are lacking for treating the comorbid conditions treated by behavioral medicine practitioners (e.g., CVD plus depression).

A new, more collaborative approach also is needed for developing practice guidelines. Traditionally, guidelines are written by committees, not communities. Instead, all stakeholders—clinicians, researchers, consumers, politicians, and insurers—should be invited to discuss the evidence together and to submit a joint report for public commentary. The APA Presidential Task Force on Evidence-Based Practice, for example, invited comments on a preliminary draft of their report from all community members and then reviewed and incorporated many of these comments into their final report. Including the community in reviewing practice guidelines may also increase awareness about evidence-based practices and motivate the subsequent application of such guidelines—a hypothesis that requires research attention. Insurance companies could help cover the costs associated with this more inclusive guideline development process because they, like consumers and health care settings, are motivated to identify beneficial and cost-effective health care methods.

Research on Dissemination Mechanisms

We've described many resources and approaches for disseminating research-based information and practices via training and various print and electronic tools intended to reach practitioners, consumers, policy makers, and other stakeholders. But we've also noted that some of these resources do not appear to be well known to target audiences. And even if the information and training reaches the intended users, do they affect the quality of health care and how might dissemination approaches be improved? To answer these questions, sustained programs of research must be undertaken. In addition to rectifying education and policy, therefore, behavioral medicine needs models of how to effectively disseminate behavioral science that are informed by theory, experience, and *research*.

Some research has tested various methods of disseminating evidence-based interventions to health care practitioners, as well as consumers and policy makers.[2] For example, a comprehensive review of 41 systematic reviews on disseminating interventions to *practitioners* (Grimshaw et al., 2001) concluded that passive outreach is not effective, but educational outreach or reminders is effective. The systematic limitations to this body of work included methodologically poor designs and no discussion of cost evaluation (Grimshaw et al., 2001; see also Bero et al., 1998).

Dissemination research specific to behavioral medicine must become more programmatic and guided by a comprehensive conceptual model of the dissemination process. Lessons can be learned from attempts to disseminate findings from other sciences that have improved the quality of health care. The model proposed by Davidson and Spring (2006) described at the beginning of this chapter (see Figure 19.1) presents one promising approach. As mentioned earlier, these researchers outlined a five-stage continuum between research and practice gleaned from their historical analysis of the work done to assess the effect of cholesterol components on cardiovascular risk.

First, the area of study required definition of high-density lipoproteins (HDL) and low-density lipoproteins (LDL). The area was standardized by a consensus conference held by the National Heart, Blood, and Lung Institute in 1970 on the diagnostics of lipoproteins. Research was conducted to look at how coronary disease is affected by hyperlipidemia and modifying factors associated with total lipid levels (e.g., diet) to identify potential mechanisms of change. Evaluation of interventions of diets, medication, and lifestyle factors on LDL followed the discovery of a simple equation to determine LDL. Translation was eventually achieved through public education (i.e., the National Cholesterol Education Program) and practice guidelines for practitioners on cholesterol management by using networks of organizations and agencies. Patients with hyperlipidemia then had improved patient outcomes, and reimbursement was available for health providers for using evidence-based lipid treatments; this type of process of moving from basic science to dissemination serves as an example of the way many behavioral interventions could be formed, tested, and disseminated to improve public health.

The behavioral medicine community needs a similar process for dissemination: definition, standardization, research, evaluation of proposed dissemination interventions, and then translation. However, there are many barriers to overcome before such a process of research to dissemination can be implemented for behavioral interventions. For example, are all practitioners interested in evidence-based behavioral medicine? Unfortunately, they are not. Anecdotal evidence suggests that clinicians are concerned that adopting EBBM will lead to cookbook care and practice restriction, or they believe that developing systems to support EBBM is unnecessary because providers currently practice evidence-based care (Spring et al., 2005). Clinicians also are concerned about the lack of applicable scientific evidence and the lack of time in their practices to review evidence for quality and applicability to their clients (Straus & McAlister, 2000). Encouraging EBBM therefore will require studying the best methods of marketing the approach to intended users and researching the most effective and efficient ways of helping practitioners integrate scientific evidence with clinical judgment.

Another approach for increasing motivation may be to apply and test strategies known to motivate clients toward positive behavior change, such as those following from the *stages of change* model (Prochaska, DiClemente, & Norcross, 1992). These methods may help to change practitioners' attitudes, too (Persons, 1995). For example, according to the stages of change model, clinicians who are not motivated to embrace evidence-based practice would be considered in the precontemplation stage. The field might focus first, therefore, on those in the contemplation stage who are more motivated to consider adopting evidence-based practices. Reviewing the pros and cons of evidence-based practice may help to move those in the contemplation stage into the stage of preparation; individuals in this stage state their willingness to make a change in the near future. Offering practitioners a specific plan for implementing the practice may then move them toward action.

Once motivated, how do interested clinicians get information, and what are the most preferred and beneficial ways to receive it (e.g., e-mail summaries of journal articles; Arfken, Agius, & Dickson, 2005)? Survey studies would help to answer these questions. As with all surveys, particular attention must be paid to sampling to reduce the influence of potential biases (e.g., selection bias—only those who are interested in evidence-based practice participate).

Research is also needed to promote uptake of research-based information and practices and to evaluate whether they result in desired outcomes. For example, almost 10 years ago, treatment manuals were proposed to help enhance application of research to practice (Addis, 1997; Morgenstern, Morgan, McCrady, Keller, & Carroll, 2001), yet no research has tested this hypothesis (Addis & Waltz, 2002). Such research must be conducted to advance training, especially studies that can identify the components of training manuals and ongoing support necessary for producing the desired behavior changes in both practitioners and patients. Effective dissemination is not a one-time process, and so research is also needed to identify the conditions that affect sustained use of research-based information and practices over time—for example, research on practitioners' perceptions of the cost/benefit of using evidence in clinical care, consumer interest in and experience with receiving evidence-based care, and organizational support for evidence-based practice.

OVERVIEW AND CONCLUSION

Jonathan Lomas (1993), an international leader in dissemination at the Canadian Health Services Research Foundation, wrote that diffusion (e.g., journal articles) changes nothing, dissemination (e.g., practice guidelines) changes attitudes, and implementation (e.g., training and policies) changes behavior. In his parlance, our review has shown that the behavioral medicine research community has much diffusion (e.g., journal reports of clinical trials), is just starting on dissemination (e.g., systematic reviews and clinical practice guidelines), and has not yet tackled implementation (e.g., regulations and education).

Table 19.1 summarizes our key themes and specific recommendations for the future. Behavioral science can serve behavioral medicine by using and strengthening existing research tools and dissemination opportunities, supporting changes in education and

Table 19.1   Disseminating Behavioral Research: Specific Recommendations for Researchers

Existing Tools and Opportunities

To Create Evidence

1. Conduct basic science research to address public health-specific needs.
2. Use the gold-standard method of testing the efficacy and effectiveness of interventions—that is, randomized clinical trials.
3. Adapt trial methods to increase their practical value.
4. Use checklists for transparent reporting of randomized and nonrandomized trials.

To Synthesize Evidence

5. Use existing reviews in your work, propose reviews in your topic area, and write reviews to answer clinical questions.
6. Contribute to developing clinical practice guidelines from research evidence and review existing guidelines for citations to your relevant work.
7. Advocate for evidence-based practice and dissemination in your professional societies.

From Problems to Solutions in Dissemination: Future Directions

Education

8. Involve consumers in generating review topics and disseminating review findings.
9. Teach students in the behavioral sciences how to create evidence (e.g., conduct randomized clinical trials), locate evidence (e.g., *The Cochrane Library*), evaluate evidence (e.g., CONSORT checklist), and use evidence.
10. Advocate for mandatory ongoing training of evidence-based treatments in the disciplines that employ behavioral interventions.

Policy

11. Propose and support government regulation of behavioral treatments.
12. Develop, disseminate, and mandate practice guidelines.
13. Propose and support reimbursement for evidence-based treatments.

Research

14. Review past research on dissemination methods across fields and disciplines.
15. Conduct new dissemination research specific to behavioral medicine in areas such as practitioner motivation to apply evidence-based practices, practitioner access to and uptake of evidence, and maintenance of information and practices available through various dissemination mechanisms.

policy, and conducting programmatic dissemination research. Of course, making advances in our approaches to disseminating research-based information and practices takes funding. Many sources already exist at the National Center for Injury Prevention and Control, the National Center for the Dissemination of Disability Research, the Substance Abuse and Mental Health Services Administration (SAMHSA), and the Dissemination and Implementation Research Program at the National Institutes of Health, to name a few. We hope to see the number of funding options continue to increase as private and government organizations, as well as the scientific community, grow to appreciate not only the need for evidence-based practices but also the complexities of disseminating them.

NOTES

1. Health psychology and behavioral medicine are complementary; the behavioral medicine community includes many health psychologists. Behavioral medicine is the use of behavior therapy to promote health, whereas health psychology is applying psychological theory and methods (including behavior therapy) to promote health.

2. This chapter focuses mainly on *practitioners,* but there are several reviews on dissemination to policy makers and consumers that may be of interest. See Innvaer, Vist, Trommald, and Oxman (2002) for a comprehensive review of interview studies with *policy makers.* See Choi et al. (2005) for additional insights on the difficulties of disseminating research to policy makers (e.g., disparate goals, languages, attitudes toward information). See Brehaut and Juzwishin (2005) for a proposed method (i.e., STEEPLE) of bridging the evidence to policy gap. See Fox (2005) for a case study of how systematic reviews about pharmaceuticals are used by policy makers. See Owen, Glanz, Sallis, and Kelder (2006) for a description of successful methods for disseminating behavioral physical health programs to *consumers.*

REFERENCES

Addis, M. E. (1997). Evaluating the treatment manual as a means of disseminating empirically validated psychotherapies. *Clinical Psychology: Science and Practice, 4*(1), 1–11.

Addis, M. E., & Hatgis, C. (2000). Values, practices, and the utilization of empirical critiques in the clinical trial. *Clinical Psychology: Science and Practice, 7*(1), 120–124.

Addis, M. E., & Waltz, J. (2002). Implicit and untested assumptions about the role of psychotherapy treatment manuals in evidence-based mental health practice: Commentary. *Clinical Psychology: Science and Practice, 9*(4), 421–424.

Agency for Healthcare Research and Quality. (2002, April). *Systems to rate the strength of scientific evidence* (AHRQ Pub. No. 02-P0022). Rockville, MD: Author. Retrieved from http://www.ahrq.gov/clinic/epcsums/strenfact.htm

Agency for Healthcare Research and Quality. (2005a, November). *About PPIP.* Rockville, MD: Author. Retrieved from http://www.ahrq.gov/ppip/ppipabou .htm

Agency for Healthcare Research and Quality. (2005b, January). *EPC partner's guide*. Rockville, MD: Author. Retrieved from http://www.ahrq.gov/clinic/epc partner/

Agency for Healthcare Research and Quality. (2005c, June). *Guide to clinical preventive services, 2005* (AHRQ Pub. No. 05–0570). Rockville, MD: Author. Retrieved from http://www.ahrq.gov/clinic/pocketgd.htm

Agency for Healthcare Research and Quality. (2006, February). *Evidence-based practice centers overview*. Rockville, MD: Author. Retrieved from http://www.ahrq.gov/clinic/epc/

Altman, D. G., Schulz, K. F., Moher, D., Egger, M., Davidoff, F., Elbourne, D., et al., for the CONSORT Group. (2001). The revised CONSORT statement for reporting randomized trials: Explanation and elaboration. *Annals of Internal Medicine, 134,* 663–694.

American Psychological Association (APA). (2002a). Criteria for evaluating treatment guidelines. *American Psychologist, 57,* 1052–1059.

American Psychological Association (APA). (2002b). Criteria for practice guidelines development and evaluation. *American Psychologist, 57,* 1048–1051.

Arfken, C. L., Agius, E., & Dickson, M. W. (2005). Clinicians' information sources for new substance abuse treatment. *Addictive Behaviors, 30*(8), 1592–1596.

Baldwin, J., Beck, K. H., Black, D. R., Blue, C. L., Colwell, B., Gold, R. S., et al. (2005). A vision for doctoral research training in health behavior: A position paper from the American Academy of Health Behavior. *American Journal of Health Behavior, 29*(6), 542–556.

Bero, L. A., Brilli, R., Grimshaw, J. M., Harvey, E., Oxman, A. D., & Thomson, M. A., on behalf of the Cochrane Effective Practice and Organisation of Care Review Group. (1998). Closing the gap between research and practice: An overview of systematic reviews of interventions to promote the implementation of research findings. *British Medical Journal, 317,* 465–468.

Boutron, I., Moher, D., Tugwell, P., Giraudeau, B., Poiraudeau, S., Nizard, R. M., et al. (2005). A checklist to evaluate a report of a nonpharmacological trial (CLEAR NPT) was developed using consensus. *Journal of Clinical Epidemiology, 58,* 1233–1240.

Brehaut, J. D., & Juzwishin, D. (2005). *Bridging the gap: The use of research evidence in policy development* (No. 18). Edmonton, Canada: Health Technology Assessment Unit, Alberta Heritage Foundation for Medical Research.

Briss, P. A., Brownson, R. C., Fielding, J. E., & Zaz, S. (2004). Developing and using the Guide to Community Preventive Services. *Annual Review of Public Health, 25,* 281–302.

Carpenter, D., Nieva, V., Albaghal, T., & Sorra, J. (2005). Development of a planning tool to guide research dissemination. *Advances in Patient Safety, 4,* 83–91.

Choi, B. C. K., Pang, R., Linn, V., Puska, P., Sherman, G., Goddard, M., et al. (2005). Can scientists and policy makers work together? *Journal of Epidemiology and Community Health, 59,* 632–637.

The Cochrane Collaboration. (2004). *The dissemination of Cochrane evidence: An inventory of resources that use Cochrane reviews*. Retrieved March 28, 2005, from http://www.cochrane.org/reviews/impact/dissemination.htm

The Cochrane Collaboration. (2005). *Newcomer's guide*. Retrieved August 3, 2006, from http://www.cochrane.org/docs/newcomersguide.htm#organisation

The Cochrane Collaboration. (2006). *For Cochrane review groups and fields*. Retrieved July 28, 2006, from http://www.cochrane.org/consumers/cinc.htm# forcochrane

Committee on Quality Health Care in America. (2001). *Crossing the quality chasm: A new health system for the 21st century.* Washington, DC: National Academy Press.

Davidson, K. W., Goldstein, M., Kaplan, R. M., Kaufmann, P. G., Knatterud, G. L., Orleans, C. T., et al. (2003). Evidence-based behavioral medicine: What is it, and how do we achieve it? *Annals of Behavioral Medicine, 26*(3), 161–171.

Davidson, K. W., & Spring, B. (2006). Developing an evidence base in psychology. *Journal of Clinical Psychology, 62*(3), 259–271.

Davidson, K. W., Trudeau, K. J., & Falzon, L. (2006). Behavioral medicine. *About The Cochrane Collaboration (Cochrane Fields),* Issue 2.

Davidson, K. W., Trudeau, K. J., Ockene, J. K., Orleans, C. T., & Kaplan, R. M. (2004). A primer on current evidence-based review systems and their implications for behavioral medicine. *Annals of Behavioral Medicine, 28,* 226–238.

Davidson, K. W., Trudeau, K. J., & Smith, T. W. (2006). Introducing the new Health Psychology series "Evidence-Based Treatment Reviews": Progress not perfection. *Health Psychology, 25*(1), 1–2.

DeAngelis, C. D., & Fontanarosa, P. B. (2002). Welcome to the "Clinician's Corner." *Journal of the American Medical Association, 287,* 104.

Des Jarlais, D. C., Lyles, C., Crepaz, N., & the TREND Group. (2004). Improving the reporting quality of nonrandomized evaluations of behavioral and public health interventions: The TREND statement. *American Journal of Public Health, 94*(3), 361–366.

Devereaux, P. J., Manns, B. J., Ghali, W. A., Quan, H., & Guyatt, G. H. (2002). The reporting of methodological factors in randomized controlled trials and the association with a journal policy to promote adherence to the Consolidated Standards of Reporting Trials (CONSORT) checklist. *Controlled Clinical Trials, 23,* 380–388.

Deyo, R. A. (2004). Gaps, tensions, and conflicts in the FDA approval process: Implications for clinical practice. *Journal for the American Board of Family Practice, 17*(2), 142–149.

Dzewaltowski, D. A., Estabrooks, P. A., Klesges, L. M., Bull, S. S., & Glasgow, R. E. (2004). Behavior change intervention research in community settings: How generalizable are the results? *Health Promotion International, 19*(2), 235–245.

Eckel, R. H. (2006). Preventive cardiology by lifestyle intervention: Opportunity and/or challenge? *Circulation, 113,* 2657–2661.

Fox, D. M. (2005). Evidence of evidence-based health policy: The politics of systematic reviews in coverage decisions. *Health Affairs, 24*(1), 114–122.

Friedman, L., Furberg, C. D., & DeMets, D. L. (1998). *Fundamentals of clinical trials* (3rd ed.). New York: Springer-Verlag.

Glasgow, R. E., Bull, S. S., Gillette, C., Klesges, L. M., & Dzewaltowski, D. A. (2002). Behavior change intervention research in healthcare settings: A review of recent reports with emphasis on external validity. *American Journal of Preventive Medicine, 23*(1), 62–69.

Glasgow, R. E., Davidson, K. W., Dobkin, P. L., Ockene, J., & Spring, B. (2006). Practical behavioral trials to advance evidence-based behavioral medicine. *Annals of Behavioral Medicine, 31*(1), 5–13.

Glasgow, R. E., Vogt, T. M., & Boles, S. M. (1999). Evaluating the public health impact of health promotion interventions: The RE-AIM framework. *American Journal of Public Health, 89*(9), 1322–1327.

Grimshaw, J. M., Shirran, L., Thomas, R., Mowatt, G., Fraser, C., Bero, L., et al. (2001). Changing provider behavior: An overview of systematic reviews of interventions. *Medical Care, 39*(8), II-2–II-45.

Harris, R. P., Helfand, M., Woolf, S. H., Lohr, K. N., Mulrow, C., Teautsch, S. M., et al. (2001). Current methods of the U.S. Preventive Services Task Force: A review of the process. *American Journal of Preventive Medicine, 20*(3S), 21–35.

Hays, K. A., Rardin, D. K., Jarvis, P. A., Taylor, N. M., Moorman, A. S., & Armstead, C. D. (2002). An exploratory survey on empirically supported treatments: Implications for internship training. *Professional Psychology: Research and Practice, 33*, 207–211.

Innvaer, S., Vist, G., Trommald, M., & Oxman, A. (2002). Health policy-makers' perceptions of their use of evidence: A systematic review. *Journal of Health Services Research Policy, 7*(4), 239–244.

International Network of Health Technology Assessment (INHTA). (2006). About INHTA. Retrieved August 3, 2006, from http://www.inahta.org/inahta_web/index.asp?gotoPage=400&catId=9

Irwin, M. R., Cole, J. C., & Nicassio, P. M. (2006). Comparative meta-analysis of behavioral interventions for insomnia and their efficacy in middle-aged adults and in older adults 55+ years of age. *Health Psychology, 25*(1), 3–14.

Katrak, P., Bialocerkowski, A. E., Massy-Wstropp, N., Kumar, V. S. S., & Grimmer, K. A. (2004). A systematic review of the content of critical appraisal tools. *BMC Medical Research Methodology, 4*, 22.

Kaufman, M., & Masters, B. A. (2004, November 6). After criticism, FDA will strengthen drug safety checks. *Washington Post*, p. A12.

Kerner, J. F., Guirguis-Blake, J., Hennessy, K. D., Brounstein, P. J., Vinson, C., Schwartz, R. H., et al. (2005). Translating research into improved outcomes in comprehensive cancer control. *Cancer Causes and Control, 16*(Suppl. 1), 27–40.

Kerner, J., Rimer, R., & Emmons, K. (2005). Introduction to the special section on dissemination: Dissemination research and research dissemination: How can we close the gap?" *Health Psychology, 24*(5), 443–446.

Lavis, J., Davies, H., Oxman, A., Denis, J.-L., Golden-Biddle, K., & Ferlie, E. (2005). Towards systematic reviews that inform health care management and policy-making. *Journal of Health Services Research and Policy, 10*(Suppl. 1), 35–48.

Lipsey, M. W., & Wilson, D. B. (2001). *Practical meta-analysis*. Thousand Oaks, CA: Sage.

Lomas, J. (1993). Diffusion, dissemination, and implementation: Who should do what? *Annals of the New York Academy of Sciences, 703*, 226–235.

Matchar, D. B., Westermann-Clark, E. V., McCrory, D. C., Patwarhan, M., Samsa, G., Kulasingam, S., et al. (2005). Dissemination of evidence-based practice center reports. *Annals of Internal Medicine, 142*(12, Pt. 2), 1120–1125.

McGrath, P. J., Stinson, J., & Davidson, K. (2003). Commentary: The *Journal of Pediatric Psychology* should adopt the CONSORT statement as a way of improving the evidence base in pediatric psychology. *Journal of Pediatric Psychology, 28*, 169–171.

Moher, D., Jones, A., & Lepage, L., for the CONSORT Group. (2001). Use of the CONSORT statement and quality of reports of randomized trials: A comparative before-and-after evaluation. *Journal of the American Medical Association, 285*(15), 1992–1995.

Montgomery, R. W., & Ayllon, T. (1995). Matching verbal repertoires: Understanding the contingencies of practice in order to functionally communicate with clinicians. *Journal of Behavior Therapy and Experimental Psychiatry, 26*(2), 99–105.

Morgenstern, J., Morgan, T. J., McCrady, B. S., Keller, D. S., & Carroll, K. M. (2001). Manual-guided cognitive-behavioral therapy training: a promising method for disseminating empirically supported substance abuse treatments to the practice community. *Psychology of Addictive Behaviors, 15*(2), 83–88.

Mosca, L., Linfante, A. H., Benjamin, E. J., Berra, K., Hayes, S. N., Walsh, B. W., et al. (2005). National study of physician awareness and adherence to cardiovascular disease prevention guidelines. *Circulation, 111*(4), 499–510.

Nathan, P. E., & Gorman, J. M. (2002). *A guide to treatments that work* (2nd ed.). New York: Oxford University Press.

National Guideline Clearinghouse. (2006a). *About NCG.* Retrieved March 23, 2006, from http://www.guideline.gov/about/about.aspx

National Guideline Clearinghouse. (2006b). *Treatment/intervention results.* Retrieved March 23, 2006, from http://www.guideline.gov/browse/browse mode.aspx?node=7542&type=2

Newman, L. (2000). AHRQ's evidence-based practice centers prove viable. *The Lancet, 356,* 1990.

Nunes, E. V., & Levin, F. R. (2004). Treatment of depression in patients with alcohol or other drug dependence: A meta-analysis. *Journal of the American Medical Association, 291,* 1887–1896.

Owen, N., Glanz, K., Sallis, J. F., & Kelder, S. H. (2006). Evidence-based approaches to dissemination and diffusion of physical activity interventions. *American Journal of Preventive Medicine, 31*(4S), S35–S44.

Pai, M., McCulloch, M., Gorman, J. D., Pai, N., Enahoria, W., Kennedy, G, et al. (2004). Systematic reviews and meta-analyses: An illustrated, step-by-step guide. *National Medical Journal of India, 17*(2), 86–95.

Patsopoulos, N. A., Analatos, A. A., & Ioannidis, J. P. A. (2005). Relative citation impact of various study designs in the health sciences. *Journal of the American Medical Association, 293,* 2362–2366.

Persons, J. B. (1995). Why practicing psychologists are slow to adopt empirically-validated treatments. In S. C. Hayes, V. M. Follette, R. M. Dawes, & K. E. Grady (Eds.), *Scientific standards of psychological practice: Issues and recommendations* (pp. 141–161). Reno, NV: Context Press.

Prochaska, J. O., DiClemente, C. C., & Norcross, J. C. (1992). In search of how people change: Applications to addictive behaviors. *American Psychologist, 47*(9), 1102–1114.

Sackett, D. L., Richardson, W. S., Rosenberg, W., & Haynes, R. B. (2000). *Evidence-based medicine: How to practice and teach EBM.* London: Churchill Livingstone.

Sakala, C., Gyte, G., Henderson, S., Neilson, J. P., & Horey, D. (2001). Consumer-professional partnership to improve research: The experience of the Cochrane Collaboration's Pregnancy and Childbirth Group. *Birth, 28*(2), 133–137.

Shea, B., Santesso, N., Qualman, A., Heilberg, T., Leong, A., Judd, M., et al. (2005). Consumer-driven health care: Building partnerships in research. *Health Expectations, 8,* 352–359.

Silagy, C. A., Stead, L. F., & Lancaster, T. (2001). Use of systematic reviews in clinical practice guidelines: Case study of smoking cessation. *British Medical Journal, 323,* 833–836.

Smith, M. T., & Perlis, M. L. (2006). Who is a candidate for cognitive-behavioral therapy for insomnia? *Health Psychology, 25*(1), 15–19.

Sogg, S., Read, J., Bollinger, A., & Berger, J. (2001). Clinical sensibilities and research practicalities: Meeting at the crossroads. *Behavior Therapist, 24*(6), 122–126, 133.

Spring, B., Pagoto, S., Kaufmann, P. G., Whitlock, E. P., Glasgow, R. E., Smith, T. W., et al. (2005). Invitation to a dialogue between researchers and clinicians about evidence-based behavioral medicine. *Annals of Behavioral Medicine, 30*(2), 125–137.

Stolz, C. (2006). *A 10-year checkup: A decade into the E-health era, online medical resources pass a real-life test.* Retrieved July 31, 2006, from http://www.wahsingtonpost.com/wp-dyn/content/article/2006/07/31/AR2006073100893_pf.html

Straus, S. E., & McAlister, F. A. (2000). Evidence-based medicine: A commentary on common criticisms. *Canadian Medical Association Journal, 163*(7), 837–841.

Task Force on Promotion and Dissemination of Psychological Procedures. (1995). Training in and dissemination of empirically-validated psychological treatments. *Clinical Psychologist, 48,* 3–23.

Trudeau, K. J., & Davidson, K., for the Evidence-based Behavioral Medicine Committee. (2001–2002, Winter). A CONSORT primer. *Outlook: A Quarterly Newsletter of the Society of Behavioral Medicine,* pp. 5–8.

Trudeau, K. J., Mostofsky, E., Stuhr, J., & Davidson, K. W. (In press). Explanation of the CONSORT statement with application to psychosocial interventions. In A. M. Nezu & C. M. Nezu (Eds.), *Evidence-based outcome research: A practical guide to conducting randomized clinical trials for psychosocial interventions.* New York: Oxford University Press.

Truman, B. I., Smith-Akin, C. K., Hinman, A. R., Gebbie, K. M., Brownson, R., Novick, L. F., et al. (2000). Developing the *Guide to community preventive services*—Overview and rationale. *American Journal of Preventative Medicine, 18*(Suppl. 1), 18–26.

Tunis, S. R., Stryer, D. B., & Clancy, C. M. (2003). Practical clinical trials: Increasing the value of clinical research for decision making in clinical and health policy. *Journal of the American Medical Association, 290,* 1624–1632.

U.S. Department of Health and Human Services. (1990). *Healthy People 2000: National health promotion and disease prevention objectives* (Pub. No. PHS 91–50212). Washington, DC: Government Printing Office.

U.S. Department of Health and Human Services. (2000). *Healthy People 2010: Understanding and improving health* (2nd ed.). Washington, DC: Government Printing Office.

U.S. Food and Drug Administration. (2006). *New drug development process: Steps from test tube to new drug application review.* Washington, DC: Author. Retrieved from http://www.fda.gov/cder/handbook/

U.S. Preventive Services Task Force (USPSTF). (2006, January). *About USPSTF.* Rockville, MD: Agency for Healthcare Research and Quality. Retrieved from http://www.ahrq.gov/clinic/uspstfab.htm

Zaza, S., Lawrence, R. S., Mahan, C. S., Fullilove, M., Fleming, D., Isham, G. J., et al., and the Task Force on Community Preventive Services. (2000). Scope and organization of the *Guide to community preventive services. American Journal of Preventive Medicine, 18*(Suppl. 1), 27–34.

CHAPTER 20

Advancing Education Through Research

False Starts, Broken Promises, and Light on the Horizon

G. REID LYON AND ELAYNE ESTERLINE

The history of the profession has never been a particularly attractive subject in professional education, and one reason for this is that it is so unrelievedly deplorable a story. For century after century all the way into the remote millennia of its origins, the profession got along by sheer guesswork and the crudest sort empiricism. It is hard to conceive of a less scientific enterprise among human endeavors. Virtually anything that could be thought up for treatment was tried out at one time or another, and once tried, lasted decades or even centuries before giving it up. It was, in retrospect, the most frivolous and irresponsible kind of human experimentation, based on nothing but trial and error, and usually resulting in precisely that sequence.

While this quotation could pertain to the education profession, it actually refers to the field of medicine as it sought to gain its scientific footing over the past century, and the person who said it was the highly respected former president of the Memorial Sloan Kettering Cancer Center, Dr. Lewis Thomas (Thomas, 1983). Though Dr. Thomas's observations on early medicine reflect some of the trial-and-error practices seen in education today, it is encouraging that medicine now is highly regarded in the scientific community for its allegiance to evidence-based practices. The journey from superstition, anecdote, and snake oil to science was a difficult one in medicine, and it was not until the turn of the 20th century that a series of scientific breakthroughs altered the value that both physicians and their patients placed in scientific research. Laboratory and clinical research had exposed ineffective and often harmful outcomes of common medical treatments such as blistering and bleeding and brought evidence-based practices, including antiseptic surgery, vaccination, and public sanitation to the forefront (Beck, 2004).

Despite the advances made in evidence-based medicine, no field can ensure that only the most valid scientific information is disseminated to the public or guarantee that it will be implemented (Cabana et al., 1999; Waddell, 2002). What is clear is that educational decisions must be guided by facts rather than by superstition, anecdote, intuition, and tradition. To achieve this goal, we must develop a clear understanding of the conditions that must be in place so that the field of education is defined by its reliance on evidence-based practices. The need to spread the most trustworthy scientific research findings into schools and classrooms to improve instructional practices is as relevant to education today as it was to medicine in the early 20th century (see Flexner, 1910).

This chapter begins by asking, Why is disseminating research findings from relevant sciences to the field of education essential for improving student learning and achievement? The answer has not always been apparent to educators or to scientists in the education field. Then, we will summarize what has been done both historically and more recently to translate and disseminate research findings in education, discuss the challenges that have been encountered and that remain before us, and suggest what more can be done to increase the spread of proven innovations, programs, and practices into schools and classrooms.

Specifically, we explain that, as educational historians and commentators have noted (e.g., Vinovskis, 2001), the quality of some education research is regarded by academics in other behavioral and social science disciplines as second rate, both conceptually and methodologically, a perception shared by policy makers. Though this conclusion is debated (see National Research Council, 2002), we see ample evidence to support it and so do not find it surprising that the dissemination of research findings has not had a discernable or productive effect on educational practices and policies.[1] We go on to explain some of the philosophical underpinnings that appear to have contributed to the misuse of science in education. Because changing policy can be an effective way to encourage the use of science in practice, and because federal legislation has become a greater force in education in recent years, we discuss how developers of recent federal legislation attempted to infuse science into the education process to help improve educational outcomes for students.

Throughout the chapter, we refer to education as a field rather than a discipline because many disciplines contribute their particular traditions, methods, and values to the study of education. These include, but are not limited to, psychology, philosophy, history, anthropology, sociology, linguistics, and, more recently, cognitive and developmental neuroscience. As we will discuss, the contributions from each of these disciplines can be advantageous when knowledge is derived from systematic and well-coordinated multidisciplinary studies but can be less helpful when there is little planned interaction and collaboration among the scientists involved, as has been the case in education research. Likewise, scientists have been isolated from the culture and other realities of the school and classroom environment. This disconnection between scientists and educators has stymied the dissemination of research findings.

In the final section of the chapter, we suggest steps that will be critical for disseminating trustworthy and useful science that has greater potential to help students learn and achieve. Given the state of the science in education, most of the chapter focuses on the need to produce more sound and useful science in the first place. Before one can effectively disseminate research to guide educational practices, one must have something worthy of disseminating. However, in concluding, we also suggest how individuals and organizations in the education field might work to strengthen dissemination strategies and dissemination science.

WHY SCIENCE SHOULD GUIDE EDUCATION PRACTICES

Keith Stanovich recently articulated a useful analogy that underscores the importance of scientific evidence in guiding educational practice:

> When you go to your family physician with a medical complaint, you expect that the recommended treatment has proven to be effective with many other patients who have had the same symptoms. You may even ask why a particular medication is being recommended for you. The doctor may summarize the background knowledge that led to that recommendation and very likely will cite summary evidence from the drug's many clinical trials and perhaps even give you an overview of the theory behind the drug's success in treating symptoms like yours. (Stanovich & Stanovich, 2003, p. 3)

While Stanovich acknowledges the oversimplification of the analogy, he argues correctly that the doctor has provided you with *data* to support a *theory* about your complaint and its treatment. This is the essence of applying the scientific method to a clinical practice including education.

In this chapter, we take the position that something not done well is not worthy of dissemination. And, we argue that doing something well in education—improving teaching and student learning and achievement, for example—requires that curricular

and instructional decisions are based on the most compelling and replicated scientific evidence available. We fully recognize that this position tends not to be accepted by many in the educational community for reasons we will explain. Unlike health care, welfare reform, defense, agriculture, engineering, or industry, education has undervalued and underused scientific research in developing, evaluating, and improving programs and policies (National Research Council, 2002). Educational programs and practices have historically been driven by values, traditions, philosophies, superstitions, and anecdotes rather than scientific evidence of effectiveness (Reyna, 2004). Until recently, the major policy input to both state and federal education departments has been provided by politicians and special interest groups rather than educational scientists (Lyon, 2005).

The limited utilization of scientific evidence in education is harmful to the field and to the public that it serves. Education, like other sectors that serve the public, must have reliable information about what works and why and how it works (see Reyna, 2005; Stanovich, 2000) for excellent discussions of this position). One could argue that scientific research and dissemination of reliable information to the educational community is nonnegotiable given that all sectors of a productive society depend on an educated workforce. Moreover, because of the rapidly changing demographics in schools and the heterogeneity of students in classrooms today, it is even more imperative to design, evaluate, disseminate, and implement programs that have a proven track record with a wide range of students from different cultural and socioeconomic backgrounds and academic preparation. In short, our view is that we have a responsibility to provide a free and *effective* education to all students in public schools. As Valerie Reyna (2004) so eloquently put it,

Research evidence is essential for identifying effective educational practice. Research—when it is based on sound scientific observations and analyses—provides reliable information about what works and how it works. This information is essential to designing effective instruction and to demonstrating that it is, in fact, effective. Responsible decisions about what is good for students, therefore, require scientific evidence. (p. 47)

WHAT DO WE MEAN BY SCIENTIFIC RESEARCH?

Within the field of education, the conventional wisdom holds that applying the scientific method to questions of teaching and student learning is not productive. The argument frequently offered to support this perspective is that schools and classrooms are too complex to be examined empirically—the contextual variables and extraneous factors that influence student learning and achievement are simply too numerous and confounded to account for (see Lagemann & Shulman, 1999). In our view, this "conventional wisdom" is neither conventional nor wise. Indeed, the National Research Council (NRC) within the National Academy of Sciences recently concluded that the core principles of scientific inquiry are as relevant for education as they are for the physical sciences, the life sciences, the social sciences, and the behavioral sciences (NRC, 2002). But what qualities must research have to be sound and therefore potentially useful to education?

In its 2002 report titled *Scientific Research in Education,* the NRC stated that all scientific endeavors must (a) pose significant questions that can be investigated empirically, (b) link research to theory, (c) use methods that permit directly investigating the question, (d) provide a coherent and explicit chain of reasoning, (e) replicate and generalize across

studies, and (f) disclose research data and methods to encourage professional scrutiny and critique. In essence, as Fletcher and Francis (2004) point out, scientific research is a process of reasoning based on the interaction between theories, methods, and results.

These principles are not new and have been guiding scientific inquiry for centuries (Kuhn, 1962). However, they typically have not been applied in education, despite their successful application to the study of human learning (Reyna, 2005; Schwartz & Reisberg, 1991) and despite repeated appeals to educational researchers to enhance the credibility and impact of their work (Levin & O'Donnell, 1999; Reyna, 2005). If research is so critical to continually improving practice in other fields relevant to the health and welfare of children, then why do some of those on the front lines of education, such as teachers and administrators, frequently view research in education as trivial or irrelevant? And even when a scientific breakthrough has occurred (e.g., the discovery that phonemic awareness is essential to reading development), what is it about the field of education that makes translating, disseminating, and implementing the findings so difficult?

CHALLENGES TO DISSEMINATING EDUCATION RESEARCH

Here we focus on what we see as three of the most significant impediments to disseminating education research: the antiscientific sentiment that has characterized education for well over a century, limitations in the quality of educational research, and the combined effect of an antiscientific culture and limited research quality on the demand in the educational marketplace for trustworthy research findings. (Space limitations preclude analyzing the challenges to disseminating education research in exhaustive detail. For additional discussion, see Berends, Kirby, Naftel, &

McKelvey, 2001; Constas & Sternberg, 2006; Elmore, 1996; Fullen, 2000; Ramey & Ramey, 1998; Slavin & Madden, 1996.)

The Antiscientific Culture in Education

A decidedly antiscientific spirit has had a pervasive influence on the perceived value of research throughout the history of education (see Adams & Bruck, 1995; Lagemann, 2000; Lagemann & Shulman, 1999) and increasingly in the past two decades (Adams & Bruck, 1995; Lyon, Shaywitz, Shaywitz, & Chhabra, 2005). Academic resistance to even the thought that education could be a research-driven field was present in universities as early as the mid-1800s (Lagemann, 1999; National Research Council, 2002). Lagemann (1999) explains that a prevailing early view of teaching was that it was "women's work"—implying a low-status vocation—requiring the ability to nurture rather than impart instruction via sophisticated and technical teaching skills deemed essential by researchers. Teaching was viewed as more akin to a genetically endowed affective ability than a learned intellectual skill to be developed through scientific methods. Thus, few were interested in applying scientific principles in education to develop and enhance teachers' competencies.

Today, although few would argue that particular temperaments and dispositions make some teachers particularly effective, it is encouraging that irrelevant and invalid gender issues no longer enter the argument and that many scientists and educators understand that these qualities can be developed along with other essential knowledge and skills. Still, the role of scientific research in education is debated ad nauseam. Why might this be the case?

The most current cycle of education's reluctance to use scientific evidence stemmed from the philosophy of postmodernism, which in its most dramatic form states that truth is in the eye of the beholder. It is relative and framed only by one's own experience and culture (Ellis & Fouts, 1997; Gross, Levitt, & Lewis, 1997; Lyon et al., 2005; McKenna, Stahl, & Reinking, 1994). Research methods, such as ethnography, that are appropriate for collecting in-depth information about an individual teaching or learning experience became favored over those that would allow for establishing cause-effect principles about teaching and learning that could be generalized. The most hard-line version of postmodernism claimed that because such general cause-effect principles do not exist in the world, scientific methods that seek to identify them are not useful for education decision making and practice. Thus, over the past two decades, data were often not accumulated or disseminated that could dispel assertions about student learning and achievement that arose from philosophical, ideological, and political beliefs. As a result, untested claims have often trumped facts from science (Lyon et al., 2005; Stanovich, 2000). Moreover, many professional development programs that prepare teachers and education administrators view research through this postmodern lens; consequently, many prospective and veteran administrators and teachers are often unfamiliar with the value that scientific research can bring to their professional life or, worse, have been taught to discount scientific research in guiding practices and school policies.

It does not help when, as in the application of any behavioral science, many citizens, no matter their profession or background, believe they are already experts on human behavior and, in this case, on education. Most Americans have attended school and have widely different views on that experience. Whatever its nature and quality, many think the experience provided sufficient background for speaking authoritatively on how to improve education (Kaestle, 1993).

Who needs scientific research to guide policies and practices when you have the necessary expertise in your own house? Indeed, it is fascinating that a substantial number of educators and noneducators who see the value of scientific research in fields such as health care and industry fail to see the contributions it can make to education. Some of this distrust for research and what it can contribute to the educational enterprise is related to the quality, or lack thereof, of education research.

Research Quality

Historically, the dissemination of research has not been successful or even a high priority in education partly because of the limited quality of the science. What do we mean by quality? Carnine (1997) proposes that research quality be judged on the basis of its trustworthiness, usability, and accessibility. Trustworthiness, defined by technical considerations of methodology and analysis, refers to the confidence practitioners can have in research findings. Usability addresses the likelihood that the research will be used by those responsible for making decisions that affect students, teachers, and other relevant educators. Accessibility reflects the ease and rapidity with which practitioners can obtain research findings, extract them, and understand them. To be sure, outstanding scientists from numerous disciplines have contributed and continue to contribute trustworthy, usable, and accessible findings that have led to effective educational innovations and practices (see, e.g., Constas & Sternberg, 2006; Fletcher, Foorman, Denton, & Vaughn, 2006; Lyon, Fletcher, Fuchs, & Chhabra, 2006; Marzano, Pickering, & Pollock, 2001; National Reading Panel, 2000; National Research Council, 2002; Schoenfeld, 2006). However, much of the research published in education journals, books, and other outlets is viewed by both scientists and educators as superficial, lacking in rigor, emphasizing breadth over depth, or as being abstruse (Levine, 2005, 2006). In the past 20 years in particular, the field has largely, for the philosophical reasons explained earlier, overrelied on qualitative methodologies, such as ethnographic data with doubtful reliability and validity, survey research, and case studies (Levine, 2005; Lyon, 2001; Lyon & Chhabra, 2004; Stanovich, 2000).

Indeed, as long as educational research has been published, it has been the target of criticism (Kaestle, 1993; Lagemann, 2000; Lagemann & Shulman, 1999; Levine, 2005, 2006; National Research Council, 2002; Vinovskis, 2001). And the criticism has not been confined to commentators in the United States (see Australian Research Council, 1992; Beveridge, 1998; Grace, 1990/1991). In 1974, for example, J. Nesbitt, the first president of the British Educational Research Association, complained that much educational research was "badly done, amateurish, gimmicky, . . . [and] often simply wrong" (Nesbitt, 1974, p. 4). Similarly, more recently, Labaree (1998) noted that "the broadly confirmed general perception of both the research and instructional programs of education schools in Britain is that they remain weak" (p. 8).

The reasons for the uneven quality of education research are too numerous to review comprehensively here. What we can conclude from reviews of the relevant literature (e.g., see Fletcher & Francis, 2004; Levin & O'Donnell, 1999; Levine, 2005; Mosteller & Boruch, 2002; National Research Council, 2002) is that educational research has been poorly funded (National Research Council, 2002; Vinovskis, 2001), frequently politicized (National Research Council, 2002; Vinovskis, 2001), and guided more by philosophy and ideology than by scientific principles (Lyon, 2005; McDaniel, Sims, & Miskel, 2001; Stanovich, 2000). It is important to note here that the scientific method also stems from philosophy. Indeed, few would refute that the methods that have materialized from philosophical perspectives have spawned trustworthy knowledge that has enhanced human health and well-being and otherwise made human progress possible (for historical and current discussions of this issue, see Ginev, 2005; Kuhn, 1962; Magnusson & Palincsar, 2006; Morrison, 2006; Popper, 1959). Nonetheless, what complicates this situation even further and makes change toward a more scientifically based culture even more difficult is that many colleges of education do not offer their undergraduate and graduate students, and especially doctorial candidates, sufficient training in the philosophical underpinnings, principles, and methods of scientific inquiry. In 2004, David Cohen, a highly respected educational scientist and professor at the University of Michigan, lamented that schools of education "chronically" allow graduate students to matriculate with very weak research skills—"It seems that any student who persists long enough can get a degree as [an educational] researcher" (Viadero, 2004). But, as yet, the academy has been refractory in its willingness to change research training priorities and practices. Cohen (2004) continued to lament at a meeting organized by the National research Council, "I haven't seen any movement in our field to deal with it. . . . It troubles me deeply that so few of my colleagues seem to be taking it seriously" (p. 1).

Largely missing from today's research studies are two major elements of science that contribute to trustworthiness: (a) the suitability of the proposed research design and methodology to address the specific research question(s) posed by the investigator(s) and (b) the scientific rigor of the methodology itself (Fletcher & Francis, 2004; Lyon, 2005; National Research Council, 2002). The frequent mismatch between the research question and the appropriate design and methodology in education research is exemplified in the persistent debates on the relative value of quantitative *or* qualitative research methods in identifying whether an instructional program is effective.

Not only are these debates time-consuming, but they are irrelevant and thus detract from the conversations essential to moving the field forward. That is, obviously we must use both types of designs and methods if we are to develop the most comprehensive understanding of whether educational programs and policies have any genuine impact on critical educational outcomes. The type of research design and method to be used depends on the question under study. Qualitative research simply cannot test and confirm that an instructional approach, for example, causes improvements in student learning and academic achievement—only well-designed randomized controlled experiments (or, to a lesser extent, quasi-experimental studies) can determine what works and what does not. Likewise, the types of designs and methods used to establish cause-effect principles do not allow in-depth understanding of individual experiences of the teacher or student or reveal characteristics of the context that might help or hinder the intervention's effectiveness. But integrating methods in a thoughtful and competent manner demands that researchers, and especially doctorial education students, are sufficiently trained to use both quantitative and qualitative methods, including understanding the assumptions underlying them and the purposes for which they are best suited.

As we have argued before (Lyon, 1999b), we believe educational research is at a crossroads. If the field neglects modern scientific methods, it risks isolating itself from the mainstream of scientific thought and progress. To develop the most effective instructional approaches and interventions for dissemination, we must support the education field in developing the knowledge and skills needed to clearly define which interventions work and the conditions under which they are effective. Educating the field about recent advances in statistical methods—for example, hierarchical linear modeling—can help educational leaders and teachers have confidence that science can objectively identify effective approaches to teaching despite the complexity of the educational environment. These tools can help sort out the range of complex school, teacher, student, and family factors, such as a student's socioeconomic status, a student's previous teachers, and the demographics of schools and families, that also can influence student achievement and the success of program implementation and sustainability (Raudenbush & Bryk, 2002).

The Effects of Limited Quality and Relevance on the Marketplace for Educational Research

As we've explained, many schools of education do not typically prepare future teachers to value the use of research to inform their instructional practices or provide them with the knowledge and skills to keep abreast of the scientific literature in their field. In agreement, Debra Viadero, reporting for *Education Week* in 2003, wrote, "Even if teachers have the fortitude to plow through academic journals, chances are their professional training did not include coursework in how to distinguish good research from bad" (p. 1).

Less than one third of the instructional practices used by teachers are based on scientific research findings (Kennedy, 1997). Even when evidence-based practices are used, teachers cannot clearly explain why they have used them (Kennedy, 1997). When asked, many teachers report that educational research is trivial and irrelevant to their teaching, is too theoretical and complex, and communicated in an incomprehensible manner

(Kennedy, 1997; Lyon et al., 2005). School principals and school administrators trained at the doctoral level are equally reluctant to use research to guide their leadership efforts and infuse research-based practices in their districts and schools. Levine (2005) reported that only 56% of principals, for example, found that the research courses they took in their degree programs were valuable to their jobs. A major reason cited was the courses were too abstract, emphasizing mechanistic aspects of research designs and methods without clear examples of how research can be applied to inform practice in schools and classrooms. In short, the courses emphasized form over function without integrating the two.

Moreover, teachers and educational administrators are frequently buffeted by unpredictable pendulum swings, such as fads in instructional practices. This situation is highly demoralizing to teachers and schools. Many teachers find themselves attempting to implement the latest highly touted instructional "magic bullet" only to learn, after it fails, that the research on which it was based was seriously flawed. Even more frustrating for educational consumers is that the majority of such programs, methods, and educational products today claim to be "research based" despite having little or no scientifically sound evidence of effectiveness. Until educational practitioners are properly trained to ensure that they can discriminate between rigorous and valid research and research that was poorly designed, frustration will increase, and the market for even the best research will continue to decrease (Blaunstein & Lyon, 2006).

Given the historical limitations in the quality and relevance of educational research and the constant sale and labor-intensive implementation of ineffective "research-based" programs, it is not surprising that school leaders and teachers have little respect for or confidence in research. However, we are optimistic that this situation can change and that education can be transformed into an evidence-based field that values reliable research, encourages the use of scientifically based methods, and appreciates the dissemination of trustworthy research. No doubt, it is unrealistic in the near future to guarantee that all educators can or want to develop a common knowledge base to become more effective consumers of educational research. In the meantime, it is our view that the results of science will not translate effectively into practice unless at least three conditions are met.

First, as we discussed previously, scientists must give the education community valid and useful information, and the education community must be provided the necessary background to evaluate and use that information. Although teachers and school administrators need not be researchers themselves, they must know how to access findings from science and be familiar with how research is done. They must possess a basic understanding of the differences among research designs, why a researcher chooses one design over the other, and why a study does or does not yield valid information (McCardle & Chhabra, 2004). In essence, teachers and administrators must become educated consumers of research. Without this basic knowledge, those expected to implement new programs will not be able to evaluate the veracity of the claims of effectiveness made by publishers and vendors of various educational curricula.

Second, in addition to producing scientifically sound research, those who design dissemination strategies must appreciate the conditions essential to implementing findings from research with fidelity in the complex world of schools and classrooms (Sternberg et al., 2006). These conditions include (a) ensuring that teachers and administrators implementing the program have realistic expectations of the time involved in successful upscaling, (b) ensuring that the implementation strategy provides sufficient scaffolding so that teachers can clearly understand the steps in the implementation process, (c) providing teachers with sufficient professional development to be comfortable with the content and the implementation strategy, and, very important, (d) ensuring that those implementing the program are committed to both the form and function of the innovation. This is not a trivial matter. Elmore (1996) and others (Sternberg et al., 2006) have reported that even during highly visible reform efforts, as little as 25% of teachers are interested in implementing the program or innovation.

Third, teachers must be explicitly supported by the school system and its culture, as well as by a capable technical assistance system to sustain the effective use of scientific innovations. For example, Cooper, Madden, and Slavin (1998) found in their examination of factors related to the successful implementation of the Success for All Program (Slavin & Madden, 1996) that the quality of instructional leadership within the school was critical, as was teacher acceptance and commitment. Success for All provided professional development to school building-level administrators, such as principals, to assist them in providing a supportive culture for change and strategies to overcome resistance to change. Moreover, building-level leaders demonstrated a strong commitment to the program and fostered implementation and sustainability by hiring facilitators to support teachers over the change process.

FALSE STARTS AND BROKEN PROMISES: THE DISSEMINATION OF UNPROVEN PRACTICES

There has been no shortage of well-meaning efforts, particularly at the federal level, to provide educators with information from research. The growth of knowledge dissemination and utilization in education began with large-scale efforts to improve the nation's schools in the 1950s and 1960s. By the 1970s, the U.S. Department of Education expanded its dissemination efforts with two major programs: the Educational Resources Information Center (ERIC) and the National Diffusion Network (NDN) (U.S. Department of Education). The two programs shared a number of goals, one of which was the dissemination of "promising practices"[2] and innovations to the educational community.

The NDN was chartered to create a national mechanism for disseminating curricula and other instructional products that would assist public and private educational institutions in sharing exemplary programs, products, and processes. Before a program could be disseminated through the NDN program, it had to be approved by a Program Effectiveness Panel, which examined data provided by the program developers.

The ERIC initiative was designed to give educators and the public access to a wide-ranging body of literature related to education. It was developed in response to the widespread belief that the inaccessibility of research was partly to blame for the infrequent use of research in education. Unfortunately, the quality of the research was not emphasized nearly as much as its availability. As noted, ERIC's strategy for identifying material for its clearinghouses was and continues to be to identify "promising practices." For example, the ERIC Clearing House for Science, Mathematics, and Environmental Education contacts state, county, and local coordinators and curriculum specialists for nominations of programs and materials they consider promising and exemplary.

Given the previous discussion about the limited quality and relevance of educational research, it is not surprising that much of what has been historically disseminated through both NDN and ERIC may not be the result of sound science. Indeed, the process of identifying "promising practices" on the basis of nominations from researchers and practitioners has not required an external evaluation and validation of the practice. Moreover, neither NDN nor ERIC adopted a set of common criteria for evaluating the quality of evidence submitted as proof that a practice was effective. Information on programs and curricula that are accessed through both NDN and ERIC is frequently contained in non-peer-reviewed journals and other information outlets that are not scrutinized for scientific quality. In short, both NDN and ERIC, despite the best of intentions, have disseminated a significant amount of information on "promising practices" that may not have been worth disseminating.

In addition to receiving information about many untested curricula and programs, potential NDN and ERIC users could be overwhelmed easily by the sheer volume of available information. Consider that between 1991 and 2001, there were 334,647 abstracts entered into the ERIC database. Though only some of the abstracts summarized research findings relevant to promising practices, the consumer would have had to read them all to distinguish research from nonresearch information. As we previously pointed out, the typical NDN and ERIC consumer would most likely not have the formal training and background to determine whether a study is valid. Thus, the utility of these dissemination engines was compromised not only by sheer volume but by the lack of a systematic process for ensuring quality control. As to evidence, the bar was set so low that the word itself almost did not apply. In short, this was a case of "let the buyer beware."

Why Policy Had to Drive Research in Education Rather Than the Other Way Around

As the field of education continued to debate the value and utility of scientific research in guiding practice and policy through the 1990s, a substantial amount of converging scientific evidence from basic and applied multidisciplinary research had emerged that helped to answer practical questions about teaching and learning in the nation's schools and classrooms, not just in the laboratory. Much of the work was being led and funded by the National Institute of Child Health and Human Development (NICHD) within the National Institutes of Health (NIH) through its research program in child development and behavior. Within this program, a major focus was on the study of reading development, reading difficulties, and reading instruction and, more recently, the study of early childhood education, mathematics, and science.

The NICHD had supported scientists studying reading development and reading difficulties since 1964 and had made substantial progress in identifying the environmental, instructional, neurobiological, and genetic correlates of reading difficulties. During the 1990s, NICHD scientists had identified, through several experimental studies, the essential elements of reading instruction and several effective instructional strategies that prevent and remediate reading disabilities. The NICHD research was multidisciplinary and longitudinal in nature with teams of scientists from education, psychology, linguistics, neurology, radiology, genetics, anthropology, and sociology studying more than 44,000 children and adults, some for as many as 25 years. The importance of reading proficiency to the education and health of the nation's children, combined with the agency's experience in studying a complex academic skill from a rigorous and practically useful scientific perspective, led Congress to identify the NICHD as the lead federal research arm on many educational topics.

As data from the 44 NICHD reading research sites began to converge in the mid-1990s on how best to prevent and remediate reading difficulties, more than one third of the nation's fourth-grade students were unable to read and understand simple children's books, and an increasing number of adults were unable to read a bus schedule (Sweet, 2004). The NICHD research was not typically viewed as important by the reading community, however, because the quantitative and experimental research methods (though frequently combined with descriptive and qualitative methods) used were at odds with the postmodern view of evidence prevalent at that time. Yet, the national mood was beginning to reflect a significant concern about the prevalence and consequences of reading failure.

By 1996, the extent of reading failure across the country began to get the attention of many congressional members and policy makers as well as President Clinton. In his 1996 State of the Union Address, the president announced that almost 40% of the nation's fourth graders could not read at grade level and subsequently proposed the America Reads Initiative. Simultaneously, the House Education and Work Force Committee, under the leadership of Chairman William Goodling, and the Senate Health, Education, Labor, and Pensions Committee, chaired by Senator James Jeffords, were holding hearings on the national reading deficit. It was within these House and Senate hearings that the first author gave what was to be the first of eight testimonies over the next 8 years on how scientific research could dramatically reduce reading failure in the United States. In essence, the NICHD data, derived from translational prevention and intervention studies carried out in many inner-city public schools, clearly indicated to the congressional members that there were effective approaches and programs that could prevent and remediate reading failure while many others could not. Unfortunately, far too many children in our nation's classrooms were being taught with the ineffective ones.

During the late 1990s, both House and Senate education committees were given data on the gap between scientific evidence and how children were being taught (McDaniel et al., 2001; Song, Coggshall, & Miskell, 2004; Sweet, 2004). Their question was, Why did the gap exist? The basic answer included the complexities discussed in this chapter. Namely, the field of education did not typically base curricular and instructional practices on scientific research. If research information was used, it was communicated in a manner that frequently confused the educational consumer and did not take into account the complexity of the school culture and environment. Neither school administrators nor teachers had been prepared in their training to be knowledgeable consumers of research and to distinguish between the bad and the good. Because of this, schools were inundated with educational fads that invariably failed.

A second question to the first author from congressional members and staff was whether the educational community could begin to integrate the scientific research into their instructional practices. Our conclusion at that time was that forging an evidence-based culture in education would be extremely difficult, particularly if one expected the field to take the initiative on its own (see Lyon, 1997, 1998, 1999a, 2000, 2001, 2002, 2005; Walsh, 2006). Despite the overwhelming scientific evidence on how best to teach reading, the majority of colleges of education institutions were reluctant to adequately prepare prospective teachers for the classroom with information about valid, evidence-based instructional programs (see Levine, 2006, for a review of current teacher preparation limitations). There was no perception of urgency about the need to reduce reading failure, and the antiscientific barriers within the academy and in the professional development sector were simply too formidable to expect meaningful progress. Clearly, these same barriers existed in other education domains beyond reading (see Levine, 2006).

Given this cultural landscape, a number of activities undertaken by several legislators, legislative staff, and scientists, including the first author, were conducted to develop legislation toward establishing scientific standards for the federal funding of educational products and programs available to the schools (McDaniel et al., 2001; Song et al., 2004; Sweet, 2004). In essence, the purpose of these efforts was to make federal funding for educational programs contingent on documenting that the products, as well as professional development associated with the products, were based on scientifically based reading research (SBRR). This strategy is consistent with the notion that a highly effective and desirable way of disseminating findings from science is to attempt to incorporate them directly into the policies that govern the operation of practices and programs.

To ensure that a valid scientific foundation existed on which to base educational policy, Congress charged the director of NICHD (Dr. Duane Alexander), in consultation with the U.S. Secretary of Education (Richard W. Riley), with convening a National Reading Panel (NRP) that was composed of researchers, members of higher education institutions, teachers, and parents. The goal of the NRP was to assess the state of reading research and to identify scientifically based interventions found to be effective with well-defined subgroups of students (NRP, 2000; Song et al., 2004). The NRP was the first federally convened panel to examine the effectiveness of different instructional approaches on specific skills required for proficient reading using established objective review criteria and statistical meta-analyses. The findings of the NRP, combined with the results documented in the National Research Council consensus report, *Preventing Reading Difficulties in Young Children* (*PRD;* NRC, 1998), and frequent presentations of scientific data on reading to House and Senate congressional committees, subsequently informed the development of the Reading Excellence Act (PL 105–277) and the Reading First and Early Reading First programs within the No Child Left Behind Act (NCLB) of 2001. The Reading First Legislation significantly increased the federal investment in scientifically based reading instruction in the early grades and stressed accounting for results and systematic monitoring and evaluation to ensure that approved programs were implemented with fidelity.

The major contributions of these pieces of legislation were to infuse legislative language into NCLB and Reading First that explicitly called for evidentiary standards to guide the use of federal education funds. However, making this change in how federal funds should be used to support effective instruction was not without difficulty, and the resulting legislation did not fully achieve the initial intent of those developing Reading First. Specifically, the first author was convinced that the legislation should only provide funding for those programs that had been found to be effective through the most rigorous research possible. If this strict criterion was not in place, it was anticipated that vendors and publishers of programs would claim that their products were research based without having to provide the published data demonstrating the genuine benefits of their specific program. However, there were very few programs

that met the more stringent effectiveness criteria at that time. As such, Congress made the decision to soften the criteria and allow funding for those programs that were based on *principles* of scientific evidence rather than based on evidence of program-specific effectiveness. This decision had both political and practical foundations.

Politically, vendors without the highest level of scientific evidence would have placed (and did place) significant pressure on Congress if their programs could not be considered. Practically, with so few programs eligible for funding, implementation of the Reading First program would have been difficult. As was expected, given the softening of the eligibility criteria, several programs without sufficient evidence of effectiveness in their own right were purchased and implemented using federal funds. In the first author's opinion, this reduced the capability of the Reading First legislation to reach its potential in establishing policies that held publishers and vendors accountable for the effectiveness of their programs, but this example illustrates the importance of compromise and the need to be practical (and often incremental) when attempting to move complex systems toward evidence-based approaches.

Nevertheless, the Reading First legislation, though not as stringent as it could have been, did require states to review and identify educational programs that were based on principles of instruction that had been demonstrated to be effective through rigorous scientific research. This level of accountability was clearly a first in the history of federal educational funding. To ensure that the educational community developed a clear understanding of what constitutes SBRR and how to implement it in schools and classrooms, two major dissemination programs were launched as a second step of the strategy. These programs were developed and implemented for two major reasons. First, the bulk of peer-reviewed scientific research relevant to classroom instruction and student learning and achievement was in the area of reading. Far less scientific evidence had been obtained in early childhood education, mathematics, and science. Second, as discussed previously, the existing federal programs that disseminated education research—ERIC and NDN—were not designed and implemented to ensure that information accessed by the public was in fact evidence based.

To overcome these hurdles, substantial input from the first author and others on research capacity in education was provided through testimony and one-to-one meetings with congressional members. Robert Sweet, a professional staff member with the House Committee on Education and the Workforce, and Grover Whitehurst, at that time director of the Office of Educational Research and Improvement (OERI), spearheaded these efforts, which ultimately contributed to the passage of the Education Sciences Reform Act of 2002 (ESRA). The specific purpose and rationale for the passage of the ESRA was articulated by the act's sponsor, Michael Castle (2002), chair of the House Education Reform Subcommittee:

> This bill transforms the Office of Educational Research and Improvement into a streamlined more independent "Institute of Education Sciences." Essentially this legislation attempts to address, what I have come to know as, serious shortcomings in the field of education research.

Grover Whitehurst, a developmental and clinical psychologist and a highly respected researcher, became the first director of the Institute of Education Sciences.

The contributions of the ESRA to the slow but steady culture change toward evidence-based practices in education are many, but three stand out for the purposes of this chapter. First, to build scientific capacity across all educational domains, the ESRA required

that federally funded research meet high standards of quality based on the definition of "scientifically based research standards" set forth in NCLB. Second, research applications submitted to the Institute for Educational Sciences must, for the first time, be evaluated against the rigorous peer-review standards similar to those in place at the National Institutes of Health. Third, the ESRA, like the NCLB, provided legislative language to develop dissemination programs that, through rigorous scientific review, could evaluate the effectiveness of different programs, products, and strategies intended to enhance academic achievement and other important educational. These dissemination resources are described in the next section.

Light on the Horizon

Because of the recalcitrance of the educational research community to improve the quality of research from within the field, as well as the foreseeable lack of progress predicted for the future, federal legislation was written, in part, to help the educational community progress from making instructional decisions on the basis of untested assumptions and beliefs to decision making based on converging evidence. We also had no reason to believe that consumers of education would increase their demand for research of quality and relevance unless federal funding was made contingent on the use of scientifically based programs and instructional strategies. Why? As the Coalition for Evidence Based Policy noted,

> Federal, state, and local governments spend more than $330 billion per year on public elementary and secondary education, and religious and independent schools spend an additional $30 billion. This vast enterprise encompasses thousands of educational interventions (curricula, strategies, practices, etc.), the vast majority of which have been implemented without a basis in

rigorous evidence. (*Bringing Evidence-Driven Progress*, 2002, pp. 1–2)

But creating an interest in using scientifically based research in educational practice and policy is one thing—providing educators with access to the best research and helping them understand it is another. Within this context, several dissemination programs were established through the NCLB and ESRA to give the educational community the most current and accurate scientific information relevant to instruction, student learning, and achievement.

In the NCLB legislation (2001), Congress established an important role for the National Institute of Literacy (NIFL). The law directed NIFL, the U.S. Department of Education, NIH, and NICHD to

1. Disseminate information on scientifically based reading research pertaining to children, youth, and adults

2. Identify and disseminate information about schools, local educational agencies, and state educational agencies that have effectively developed and implemented classroom reading programs that meet the requirements of the Reading First legislation

3. Support the continued identification and dissemination of information on reading programs that contain the essential components of reading instruction supported by scientifically based research that can lead to improved reading outcomes for children, youth, and adults

In addition, within the scope of the NCLB and Reading First legislation, the Department of Education established the National Center for Reading First Technical Assistance in 2004 (Sweet, 2004). The major functions of the center include giving educators and the public at large high-quality resources on SBRR; identifying scientifically based instructional assessments, programs, and materials; helping states and local districts build capacity to establish reading programs and accountability systems based on scientific research, such as teacher education academies and training for administrators in SBRR; providing technical assistance to states on curriculum and program selection; and supporting states in working with institutions of higher education to evaluate and improve preservice teacher education programs.

In 2002, under the aegis of the Education Sciences Reform Act, the Department of Education also established the Institute for Educational Sciences (IES). That same year, the IES began a partnership with the Council for Excellence in Government's Coalition for Evidence-Based Policy, whose mission is to promote government policy making on the basis of rigorous evidence of program effectiveness. The coalition initiative continues to promote rigorous evaluation of education programs and strategies and plays a major role in ensuring that program funds support educational activities that research shows to be effective. The initiative draws on successful precedents for evidence-based approaches and their dissemination from medicine and welfare policy, where rigorous evaluation has played a major role in policy and funding decisions.

As part of its charter, the IES established the What Works Clearing House (WWC) (www.whatworks.ed.gov) to summarize evidence on existing programs across all areas of education and to make the summaries available to educational consumers. Within this context, the WWC reviews the research base underlying educational programs or innovations to evaluate, among many other factors, the methodological quality of the research, the degree to which the research was conducted with representative samples and subgroups for whom the program was intended, the appropriateness of the measures used to assess response to the program, and the fidelity of implementation of the program. Moreover, by virtue of its availability to the public, the WWC serves as a reference to enable researchers and consumers of research to better understand the scientific criteria against which educational programs and interventions are evaluated.

It remains to be seen whether the federal legislation and initiatives we've described will make a genuine and long-lasting impact on the learning and achievement of students in the United States. Initial reports show very positive results (Government Accounting Office, 2007; Jennings, 2006). While some imperfections in the legislative initiatives are apparent, they stem from inadequate implementation safeguards and the need for more relevant outcome measures such as authentic performance measures that more accurately represent the actual content that is being learned rather than a narrow set of skills assessed via standardized testing (see Reyna, 2005, for discussion), although others disagree (see Carlson & Levin, 2005, for a range of opinions). Not surprisingly, the federal requirement for evidence-based practices has led some in the educational community to characterize both NCLB and ESRA as examples of government interference in the marketplace of research ideas and practices (Lyon, 2005). These opinions may reflect philosophical, ideological, and turf issues or genuine concern about the role of the federal government in setting any policies that affect localities, even if done to help improve research quality and dissemination. Still, it must be reiterated that the NCLB and the ESRA were not conceptualized in a vacuum. The legislation was driven by a concern that the future of our nation's children was being compromised by a failure to apply what scientific research had indicated was effective, particularly in the area of reading. Although much work remains to be done, we believe that NCLB and ESRA represent a new day in education—a day in which the scientific method has greater potential to supersede tradition, anecdote, ideology, and political persuasion in guiding educational practices and policies in schools and classroom across the country.

SUMMARY AND RECOMMENDATIONS

The consequences of disseminating research information of questionable quality and relevance to schools, teachers, parents, and policy makers are devastating. In this chapter, we have focused on the need to develop information that is worth disseminating. This emphasis is a reflection of where the education field is in thinking about how to advance the dissemination of science. But increasing the quality, relevance, and trustworthiness of research is only part of the challenge. The educational community must now take on the complex task of identifying the conditions under which research-based innovations and programs can be implemented and sustained in districts, schools, and classrooms. But the community does not have to start from scratch. In 1997, Gersten, Vaughn, Deschler, and Schiller reviewed the literature relevant to the implementation and sustainability of interventions and identified six factors essential for success:

1. The intervention must be practical, concrete, and specific, accounting for the realities of schools.

2. The intervention must have a scope and purpose that is neither vague nor narrow.

3. The intervention must be accompanied by collegial support networks within the school and between the school and the implementers of change.

4. Teachers must be given many different opportunities for not only implementing new

procedures but also for receiving feedback from the implementers.

5. The implementers must emphasize the professionalism of teachers by involving them in problem solving and emphasizing the connection between everyday classroom practice and research.

6. Teachers must see the results of their efforts in improved student outcomes.

More recently, a number of educational scientists, working collaboratively with practitioners, have begun to use these principles along with implementation factors identified more recently in developing models and strategies for translating research into practice at a statewide level. For example, Fletcher et al. (2006), Schoenfeld (2006), and Calfee, Miller, Norman, Wilson, and Trainin (2006) have argued for programmatic research that begins with rigorous experimental investigations that proceed from small-scale research through large-scale curricular implementation, accompanied by explicit strategies to ensure sustainability. Within this context, Fletcher et al. describe how the Texas Reading Initiative (TRI) exemplifies this process. The TRI was built on more than two decades of basic scientific research designed to answer three focused questions: How do children learn to read? Why do some children have difficulty learning to read? Which instructional approaches, methods, and strategies have the highest probability of success in improving reading skills? This research was instrumental in the development of assessment instruments to identify children at risk for reading failure through ongoing screening of all students in Texas from kindergarten through the second grade. The research also led to the development of preventative and remedial strategies to increase the probability that all children would be reading proficiently by the third grade. Successful small-scale implementation

efforts were carried out by the NICHD using this same research in Washington, D.C., Atlanta, Georgia, Tallahassee, Florida, Seattle, Washington, Albany, New York, and Toronto, Canada.

However, the implementation of these research-based practices in the TRI required a number of additional initiatives and collaborations to ensure uptake and sustainability. For example, the business community in Texas played a critical role in reinforcing the need for the state, districts, and schools to base all reading practices on the best science available and to build accountability systems to continuously measure whether programs were having beneficial effects. The business community was also instrumental in articulating the need for increased funding to support the reading initiative. Second, during the development of the TRI, partnerships were forged with universities that included researchers in the area of reading. These partnerships were essential because the research-based reading interventions had to be implemented by teachers who were well prepared to do so. The university partners developed statewide reading academies to ensure that teachers received the most current information and also provided continuous support to teachers to reinforce their practices in the classroom. Third, partnerships were developed with large urban districts throughout the state. By demonstrating that the implementation of research-based reading programs could foster significant improvements in student learning and achievement in challenging urban environments, a clear message was sent to all districts and schools that prevention and early intervention programs were indeed scalable and could lead to positive outcomes.

The TRI example demonstrates that solid research is simply not enough. Implementation and sustainability rely on a confluence of factors that includes support from stakeholders outside of the educational enterprise, strong collaborations with universities and committed school districts, and extensive teacher professional development. But the implementation of the TRI, as well as programs such as Success for All, has certainly not been easy, and much remains to be learned to close the gap between research and practice in the educational environment. Indeed, there are many more questions than answers at this juncture. And this means that new research must be undertaken to address a host of complex questions.

Consider that even in fields thought to be more advanced in their approaches to dissemination, studies have documented difficulties in applying new research findings in clinical practice, although the findings are packaged and ready to use in the form of guidelines (Cabana et al., 1999; Lomas, 1997). Within education, research and practice communities must gain a much better understanding of how, when, by whom, and under what circumstances research evidence spreads through colleges of education, federal and state departments of education, school districts, schools, and classrooms. For optimal uptake and sustainability, we must study options for creating the incentive systems that will be critical to helping educators at all levels of practice develop the attitudes, knowledge, and skills needed for incorporating new concepts into their practices. We must identify the amount of time and resources required to enhance learning and adaptability in teachers, administrators, and other decision makers in education so that dissemination efforts reach motivated consumers. We must understand more about how to educate the public that rigorous scientific research is our best hope of helping consumers of education distinguish which educational practices work and which do not and, in that process, help to eliminate the continuous disagreements that characterize the field.

Very importantly, we must learn how to give teachers the basic knowledge and skills needed to translate research into effective classroom practices. Specifically, teachers must have sufficient preservice training to know the subject they are teaching, to guide instruction on the basis of student performance, and to recognize and tailor their approaches to meet the needs of individual students. Without this scientifically based foundation in content knowledge and pedagogy, advances in dissemination, implementation, and sustainability will not be realized. Beyond this, however, the role of teachers in getting research to practice must be redefined. Instead of treating teachers as empty vessels into which research information is poured, teachers must become partners and given opportunities to work collaboratively with scientists in designing and conducting the research that is expected to influence their instructional practices in the classroom. Realizing this goal will require substantial changes in the current training of both teachers and educational researchers.

In summary, the time has come to more systematically (a) identify strategies that motivate the adoption and use of knowledge and practices developed with scientifically sound education research, (b) carry out longitudinal studies to assess the long-term impact of dissemination and the conditions that help sustain improvements in teaching practices and student progress, and (c) support and conduct experimental studies to test the relative effectiveness of different strategies for educating various consumer subgroups about the value of evidence-based practices, such as administrators, teachers, researchers, and policy makers concerned with education in particular environments (urban, rural, suburban, and so on) from college to preschool.

Moving knowledge to practice is a complex challenge. And, to be sure, it will take time to see the effects of distributing new knowledge on everyday practices in the education profession and even more time to see improved student learning and achievement.

In the impatient world of education, the lack of immediate observable results can be frustrating and often leads to fragmented and ineffective implementation. In the end, no matter how robust the educational research enterprise becomes and no matter how stellar the research conducted, it will mean little if sustained efforts are not undertaken to help ensure that the research is infused into practice.

NOTES

1. We define dissemination of research in education as the systematic spreading and implementation of these proven resources, programs, strategies, tools, and policies. Dissemination research is the study of the processes that lead to the improved spread of these effective innovations. Essentially, dissemination research addresses the ways in which research knowledge becomes practice knowledge and with the transformations occurring during such a process (Huberman, 1990).

2. "Promising practices" initiatives were developed as a system for validating effective programs and promising practices for dissemination through the National Diffusion Network (NDN). Such practices were often developed based on theory or some research. "Promising practices" were typically supported by a sufficient amount of original data to determine whether a particular program or practice is effective in improving educational outcomes. Practices in this category are frequently perceived as effective, although studies bearing on this perception were not adequately designed to determine effectiveness. For example, in reviewing a practice studied using a weak design (e.g., one-group pretest posttest), the NDN categorized the practice as promising. If original data have been collected and a strong design has been used but the study uses a sample based on a different student population, NDN would note this and consider the practice promising with the special education population but also that these practices need systematic study with other students with disabilities.

REFERENCES

Adams, M., & Bruck, M. (1995). Resolving the "great debate." *American Educator, 19,* 10–20.

Australian Research Council (ARC). (1992). *Educational research in Australia.* Canberra: Australian Government Publishing Service.

Beck, A. (2004). The Flexner Report and the standardization of American medicine. *Journal of the American Medical Association, 291,* 2139–2140.

Berends, M., Kirby, S., Naftel, S., & McKelvey, R. (2001). *Implementation and performance in new American schools: Three years into scale-up.* Santa Monica, CA: RAND Education.

Beveridge, M. (1998). Improving the quality of educational research. In J. Rudduck & D. McCintyre (Eds.), *Challenges for educational research* (pp. 189–214). London: PCP/Sage.

Blaunstein, P., & Lyon, G. R. (2006). *Why kids can't read: Challenging the status quo in education.* New York: Rowman & Littlefield.

Bringing evidence-driven progress to education: A recommended strategy for the U.S. Department of Education: Report of the Coalition for Evidence-Based Policy. (2002, November). Retrieved June 15, 2006, from http://excelgov.org/usermedia/images/uploads/PDFs/coalitionFin Rpt.pdf

Cabana, M., Rand, C., Powe, N., Wu, A., Wilson, M., Paul-Andre, C., et al. (1999). Why don't physicians follow clinical practice guidelines? A framework for improvement. *Journal of the American Medical Association, 282,* 1458–1465.

Calfee, R., Miller, R., Norman, K., Wilson, K., & Trainin, G. (2006). Learning to do educational research. In M. Constas & R. Sternberg (Eds.), *Translating theory and research into educational practice* (pp. 77–104). Mahwah, NJ: Lawrence Erlbaum.

Carlson, J., & Levin, J. (2005). *The No Child Left Behind legislation: Educational research and federal funding.* Greenwich, CT: Information Publishing.

Carnine, D. (1997). Bridging the gap between the research-to-practice gap. *Exceptional Children, 63,* 513–521.

Castle, M. (2002). *Institute of Educational Sciences* [Press release]. Washington, DC: U.S. House of Representatives Committee on Education and the Work Force.

Constas, M., & Sternberg, R. (Eds.). (2006). *Translating theory and research into educational practice.* Mahwah, NJ: Lawrence Erlbaum.

Cooper, R., Madden, N., & Slavin, R. (1998). Success for All: Improving the quality of whole school reform through the use of a national reform network. *Education and Urban Society, 30,* 385–408.

Ellis, A., & Fouts, J. (1997). *Research on educational innovations* (2nd ed.). Larchmont, NY: Eye on Education.

Elmore, D. (1996). Getting to scale with good educational practices. *Harvard Educational Review, 66,* 1–26.

Fletcher, J., Foorman, B., Denton, C., & Vaughn, S. (2006). Scaling research on beginning reading: Consensus and conflict. In M. Constas & R. Sternberg (Eds.), *Translating theory and research into educational practice* (pp. 53–76). Mahwah, NJ: Lawrence Erlbaum.

Fletcher, J., & Francis, D. (2004). Scientifically based educational research: Questions, designs, and methods. In P. McCardle & V. Chhabra (Eds.), *The voice of evidence in reading research* (pp. 59–80). Baltimore: Paul H. Brookes.

Flexner, A. (1910). *Medical education in the United States and Canada.* New York: Carnegie Foundation.

Fullen, M. (2000). The return of large-scale reform. *Journal of Educational Change, 1,* 1–23.

Gersten, R., Vaughn, S., Deschler, D., & Schiller, E. (1997). What we know about using research findings: Implications for improving special education practice. *Journal of Learning Disabilities, 30,* 466–476.

Ginev, D. (2005). Against the politics of postmodern philosophy of science. *International Studies in the Philosophy of Science, 19,* 191–208.

Government Accounting Office. (2007). *Reading First: States report improvements in reading instruction, but additional procedures would clarify education's role in ensuring proper implementation by states* (DCGAO-07-161). Washington, DC: Government Printing Office.

Grace, G. (1991). The new right and the challenge to educational research. *Cambridge Journal of Education, 21*(3), 265–275. (Original work published 1990)

Gross, P., Levitt, N., & Lewis, M. (1997). *The flight from science and reason.* New York: The New York Academy of Sciences.

Huberman, M. (1990). Linkage between researchers and practitioners: A qualitative study. *American Journal of Educational Research, 27,* 363–391.

Kaestle, C. (1993). The awful reputation of educational research. *Educational Researcher,* 22(1), 22–31.

Jennings, J. (2006). *Keeping watch on Reading First.* Washington, DC: Center on Educational Policy.

Kennedy, M. (1997). The connection between research and practice. *Educational Researcher, 26,* 4–12.

Kuhn, T. (1962). *The structure of scientific revolutions.* Chicago: University of Chicago Press.

Labaree, D. (1998). Educational researchers: Living with a lesser form of knowledge. *Educational Researcher,* 27(8), 4–12.

Lagemann, E. (1999). An auspicious moment for education research. In E. Lagemann & L. Shulman (Eds.), *Issues in education research: Problems and possibilities* (pp. 3–16). San Francisco: Jossey-Bass.

Lagemann, E. (2000). *An elusive science: The troubling history of education research.* Chicago: University of Chicago Press.

Lagemann, E., & Shulman, L. (Eds.). (1999). *Issues in education research: Problems and possibilities.* San Francisco: Jossey-Bass.

Levin, J., & O'Donnell, A. (1999). What to do about educational research's credibility gaps? *Issues in Education: Contributions from Educational Psychology, 5,* 177–229.

Levine, A. (2005, March). *Educating school leaders.* New York: Educational Schools Project, The Wallace Foundation.

Levine, A. (2006, September). *Educating school teachers.* New York: Educational Schools Project, The Wallace Foundation.

Lomas, J. (1997). *Improving research dissemination and uptake in the health sector: Beyond the sounds of one hand clapping.* Hamilton, Ontario: McMaster University Centre for Health Economics and Policy Analysis.

Lyon, G. R. (1997, September). *NICHD research findings in learning disabilities* (U.S. House of Representatives Committee on Education and the Workforce, United States Congress). Washington, DC: Congressional Printing Office.

Lyon, G. R. (1998, April). *Overview of NICHD reading and literacy initiatives* (U.S. Senate Committee on Labor and Human Resources, United States Congress). Washington, DC: Congressional Printing Office.

Lyon, G. R. (1999a, July). *How research can inform the re-authorization of Title I of the Elementary and Secondary Education Act* (Congressional testimony at the U.S. House of Representatives Committee on Education and the Workforce, United States Congress). Washington, DC: Congressional Printing Office.

Lyon, G. R. (1999b). In celebration of science in the study of reading development, reading difficulties, and reading instruction: The NICHD perspective. *Issues in Education: Contributions from Educational Psychology, 5,* 85–115.

Lyon, G. R. (2000, May). *Education research and evaluation and student achievement: Quality counts* (U.S. House of Representatives Committee on Education and the Workforce, United States Congress). Washington, DC: Congressional Printing Office.

Lyon, G. R. (2001, March). *Measuring success: Using assessments and accountability to raise student achievement* (U.S. House of Representatives Committee on Education and the Workforce, United States Congress). Washington, DC: Congressional Printing Office.

Lyon, G. R. (2002, June). *Learning disabilities and early intervention strategies* (U.S. House of Representatives Committee on Education and the Workforce—Subcommittee on Education Reform). Washington, DC: Congressional Printing Office.

Lyon, G. R. (2003, July). *The critical need for evidence-based comprehensive and effective early childhood programs* (U.S. Senate Health, Education, Labor and Pensions Committee). Washington, DC: Congressional Printing Office.

Lyon, G. R. (2005). Why converging scientific evidence must guide educational policies and practices. In J. Carlson & J. Levin (Eds.), *The No Child Left Behind legislation: Educational research and funding* (pp. 77–88). Greenwich, CT: Information Age Publishing.

Lyon, G. R., & Chhabra, V. (2004). Why objective evidence of effectiveness should guide reading instruction. *Educational Leadership, 6,* 12–17.

Lyon, G. R., Fletcher, J. M., Fuchs, L., & Chhabra, V. (2006). Treatment of learning disabilities. In E. Mash & R. Barkley (Eds.), *Treatment of childhood disorders* (2nd ed.). New York: Guilford.

Lyon, G. R., Shaywitz, S. E., Shaywitz, B. A., & Chhabra, V. (2005). *Evidence-based reading policy in the United States: How scientific research informs instructional practices* (pp. 209–250). Washington, DC: Brookings Institute Press.

Magnusson, S., & Palincsar, A. (2006). The application of theory to the design of innovative texts supporting science instruction. In M. Constas & R. Sternberg (Eds.), *Translating theory and research into educational practice* (pp. 31–52). Mahwah, NJ: Lawrence Erlbaum.

Marzano, R., Pickering, D., & Pollock, J. (2001). *Classroom instruction that works.* Saddle River, NJ: Pearson Education.

McCardle, P., & Chhabra, V. (Eds.). (2004). *The voice of evidence in reading research.* Baltimore: Paul H. Brookes.

McDaniel, J., Sims, C., & Miskel, C. (2001). The national reading policy arena: Policy actors and perceived influence. *Educational Policy, 15,* 92–114.

McKenna, M., Stahl, S., & Reinking, D. (1994). A critical commentary on research, politics, and whole language. *Journal of Reading Behavior, 26,* 211–233.

Morrison, M. (2006). Applying science and applied science: What's the difference? *International Studies in the Philosophy of Science, 20,* 81–91.

Mosteller, F., & Boruch, R. (2002). *Evidence matters: Randomized trials in education research.* Washington, DC: Brookings Institution Press.

National Reading Panel (NRP). (2000). *Report of the National Reading Panel: Teaching children to read: An evidence-based assessment of the scientific research literature on reading and its implications for reading instruction* (NIH Pub. No. 00–4754). Washington, DC: Government Printing Office.

National Research Council (NRC). (1998). *Preventing reading difficulties in young children.* Washington, DC: National Academy Press.

National Research Council (NRC). (2002). *Scientific research in education.* Washington, DC: National Academy Press.

Nesbitt, J. (1974, December 4). *Bridging the gap between research and practice.* Paper presented to the National Foundation for Educational Research Conference, London.

Popper, K. (1959). *The logic of scientific discovery.* New York: Basic Books.

Ramey, C., & Ramey, S. (1998). Early intervention and early experience. *American Psychologist, 53,* 109–120.

Raudenbush, S., & Bryk, A. (2002). *Hierarchical linear models: Applications and data analysis* (2nd ed.). Thousand Oaks, CA: Sage.

Reyna, V. (2004). Why scientific research? The importance of evidence in changing educational practice. In P. McCardel & V. Chhabra (Eds.), *The voice of evidence in reading research* (pp. 45–58). Baltimore: Paul H. Brookes.

Reyna, V. (2005). The No Child Left Behind Act and scientific research: A view from Washington, D.C. In J. Carlson & J. Levin (Eds.), *The No Child Left Behind legislation: Educational research and federal funding* (pp. 1–26). Greenwich, CT: Information Age Publishing.

Schoenfeld, A. (2006). Notes on the educational steeplechase: Hurdles and jumps in the development of research-based mathematics instruction. In M. Constas & R. Sternberg (Eds.), *Translating theory and research into educational practice* (pp. 9–30). Mahwah, NJ: Lawrence Erlbaum.

Schwartz, B., & Reisberg, D. (1991). *Learning and memory.* New York: Norton.

Slavin, R., & Madden, N. (1996). *Scaling up: Lessons learned in the dissemination of Success for All.* Retrieved August 15, 2006, from http://www.csos.jhu.edu/crespar/Reports/report06entire.html

Song, M., Coggshall, J., & Miskell, C. (2004). Where does policy usually come from and why should we care? In P. McCardle & V. Chhabra (Eds.), *The voice of evidence in reading research* (pp. 445–462). Baltimore: Paul H. Brookes.

Stanovich, K. (2000). *Progress in understanding reading.* New York: Guilford.

Stanovich, P., & Stanovich, K. (2003). *Using research and reason in education.* Washington, DC: Partnership for Reading (U.S. Department of Education/U.S. Department of Health and Human Services).

Sternberg, R, Birney, D., Kirlik, A., Stemler, S., Jarvin, L., & Grigorenko, E. (2006). From molehill to mountain: The process of scaling up educational interventions (Firsthand experience upscaling the theory of successful intelligence). In M. Constas & R. Sternberg (Eds.), *Translating theory and research into educational practice* (pp. 205–221). Mahwah, NJ: Lawrence Erlbaum.

Sweet, R. (2004). The big picture: Where we are nationally on the reading front and how we got here. In P. McCardle & V. Chhabra (Eds.), *The voice of evidence in reading research* (pp. 13–44). Baltimore: Paul H. Brookes.

Thomas, L. (1983). *The youngest science: Notes of a medicine watcher.* New York: Penguin.

Viadero, D. (2003). Scholars aim to connect studies to school's needs. *Education Week, 22*(27), 1.

Viadero, D. (2004). The skills gap. *Education Week, 23*(16), 30–31.

Vinovskis, M. (2001). *Revitalizing federal education research and development.* Ann Arbor: University of Michigan Press.

Waddell, C. (2002). So much research evidence, so little dissemination uptake: Mixing the useful with the pleasing. *Evidence-Based Nursing, 5,* 38–40.

Walsh, K. (2006). Teacher education: Coming up empty. *FWD: Arresting Insights in Education, 2,* 3–6.

CHAPTER 21

Disseminating Effective Approaches to Drug Use Prevention

MARY ANN PENTZ

T his chapter discusses the history, challenges, and future directions in translating and disseminating drug use prevention research to practice, also known in the field as moving science from bench to bedside. The chapter is divided into six sections. The first section describes the status of translational research and evolutions that have occurred in the translation process from program development through program dissemination. Key terms for the chapter are also defined. The second section focuses in greater depth on dissemination, specifically on the processes used to identify evidence-based prevention programs and the conditions that facilitate or impede the movement of prevention research into practice. The third section reviews current research on dissemination and places it in the context of diffusion of innovation theory, a main theory used to guide dissemination practices and research in the drug use prevention field. The fourth section highlights challenges to disseminating effective programs that must be met with respect to practice, theory development, and changes to the traditional researcher role. The fifth section recommends the use of conceptual frameworks and research methodologies that would help to meet some of these challenges. The

chapter ends with a discussion of recent trends and opportunities in prevention science and their implications for the future dissemination of drug use preventions.

STATUS OF TRANSLATIONAL RESEARCH

Changing Frameworks and Definitions

More than 20 years ago, the National Cancer Institute (NCI) developed a framework by which to categorize research in cancer prevention and control (see Pentz, Jasuja, Rohrbach, Sussman, & Bardo, 2006; Sussman, Valente, Rohrbach, Stacy, & Pentz, 2006). This framework had five stages that were intended to represent the progression of research as the knowledge base grew. The first stage was basic research on the etiology and epidemiology of a specific health-related problem, such as drug use. This stage of research was primarily exploratory. The second stage focused on methods development, during which research designs, measures, and analytical strategies could be formulated, pilot interventions could be developed, and hypotheses about intervention effects could be generated. In the third stage, efficacy trials were conducted. Rigorous experimental studies, usually randomized control trials, or quasi-experimental designs were used to test an intervention on a larger scale, with optimal research support and monitoring to help ensure full implementation. The fourth stage, effectiveness trials, continued the testing of interventions on an even larger scale but under real-world conditions lacking the support for implementation and the controlled conditions of efficacy trials (August et al., 2004). The final stage, referred to as demonstration or technology transfer, involved the "rollout" of intervention to the services sector, similar to a public health model of intervention dissemination. This last stage did not require further research on intervention effectiveness. At best, the coverage of an intervention might be assessed (e.g., the number of intervention settings, providers, and recipients) or administrative records collected on the services that were delivered.

The National Institutes of Health (NIH) has recently reconceptualized the stages of research to reflect the fact that dissemination is not complete when evidence-based programs are made available to potential users in the form of demonstration or technology transfer, previously referred to as translation under the NCI model (Sloboda & Schildhaus, 2002). According to the most recent NIH terminology, *translation* refers to the progression from effectiveness research (Type I research) to program dissemination and dissemination studies (Type II research), and disseminating effective programs after the effectiveness testing phase is now considered a new field of research itself. Thus, Type I includes all stages of research prior to dissemination and usually progresses from animal model research on etiology, to human etiological studies, to human epidemiological studies that yield information on risk and protective factors, to program development, to testing in efficacy trials, which yield evidence-based programs.

Translation to Type II research occurs when evidence-based programs are replicated, adapted, and disseminated to the users. Though movement across these stages appears to be systematic and logical, the progression historically has not been formally planned in the field of drug use prevention, and such linear progression does not always appear in practice.

Table 21.1 lists the original stages of research developed by the NCI, the current NIH Type I and Type II categories of research, and other related terms and definitions used in the chapter. As shown in the table, some terms are used interchangeably in the literature, and some have multiple or overlapping definitions. *Diffusion* is a term used in the drug use prevention field to refer generally to the spreading of programs and, as discussed in more detail later, consists of four stages: program adoption, implementation, sustainability, and dissemination. Thus, although *dissemination* is often used interchangeably with *diffusion,* it is technically considered to be the last stage of diffusion in which programs are delivered beyond the original implementation sites and potentially used on a large scale. Implementation often overlaps with or is considered to be part of dissemination, but in the drug use prevention field, it is also a stage of diffusion that refers specifically to the procedures involved in delivering a practice or program. With respect to translation, this chapter follows the current NIH definition that includes both moving from Type I to Type II research (see Sussman et al., 2006), as well as to adapting a program that has been shown to be effective for use with a particular population, setting, program deliverer, or health behavior or for otherwise improving any stage of diffusion. As in other fields, *translation* refers also in the chapter to applying basic research findings to the development of new practices and programs (i.e., movement within stages of Type I research).

Table 21.1   Definition of Terms Used in This Chapter

	Term				
	Stages of Research (NCI)	Diffusion	Translation	Dissemination	Implementation
Definitions	• Basic research • Methods development • Efficacy trials • Effectiveness trials • Demonstration/ technology transfer	• Spread of a program • Involves four stages: adoption, implementation, sustainability, dissemination	• Type I (etiology, epidemiology, initial program development, and testing) • Type II (beyond initial testing) • Translating from research to practice (synonymous with NCI demonstration) • Translating program from original population, health behavior, or setting to another; to enhance any stage of diffusion	• One stage of diffusion • Synonymous with diffusion	• One stage of diffusion

Translational Research in Drug Use Prevention

To understand the status of translational research in drug use prevention, one needs to consider the goals of prevention (Pentz, 1995), summarized in Figure 21.1. First, developmental periods of drug use are identified, as well as the conditions that contribute to and protect against drug use. Knowledge of these conditions is used to develop drug use prevention programs, which are then tested. Those programs shown to significantly prevent, delay, or reduce early drug use are then identified as "evidence based." Next, as shown on the left side of the figure, one goal is to take evidence-based programs to scale—that is, implement and disseminate them using greater numbers of research participants and research sites and to adapt them to increase their overall effectiveness. Another goal, depicted on the right, is to test variations

of evidence-based programs to determine whether they will work with particular populations or settings or under other conditions that differ from the original test conditions. The programs are adapted to meet particular needs. The final goal is to institutionalize the prevention usually through instigating policy changes that allow for and support the implementation of the program.

Decades of research on the epidemiology and etiology of drug use have led to identifying early adolescence as the first developmental period of risk for drug use and to understanding the risk factors and protective factors (e.g., J. D. Hawkins, Catalano, & Miller, 1992) for drug use during this period. This knowledge was then developed (translated) into counteractive skills and promotive skills (e.g., Pentz et al., 2006) to help ameliorate risk and became the basis for developing prevention program content. The prevention programs were then tested

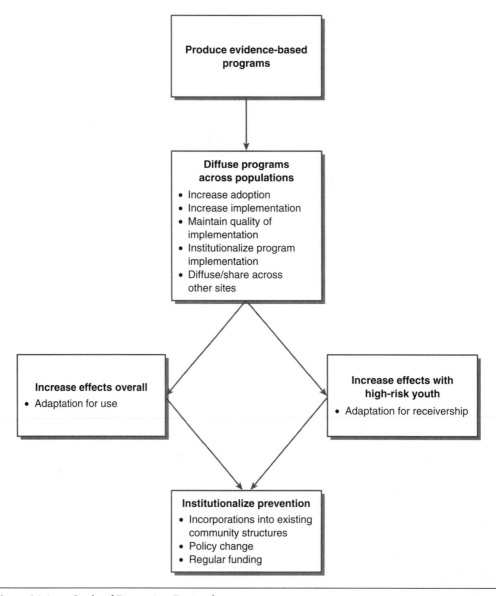

Figure 21.1   Goals of Prevention Research

for their effectiveness in changing the course of drug use behavior that would normally occur during early adolescence without intervention and specifically for their ability to affect counteractive and promotive skills that were the original bases of these programs.

Evolutions in the translation of prevention research, both in the use of research findings to develop prevention programs (Type I research) and in the movement from

effectiveness studies to dissemination and dissemination research (Type II research), can be illustrated with research on sensation seeking and low impulse control (Pentz et al., 2006). In the early 1960s, animal model studies showed the reinforcing effects of novelty seeking on the establishment of neurologic pathways underlying repetitive, impulsive drug use. But little planned progression to human epidemiological studies occurred until the 1970s, first with personality studies that identified sensation seeking as a risk factor for adolescent drug use and then with studies showing correlations between impulse control and conduct problems, delinquency, and drug use. Later epidemiological studies showed the response of high-sensation-seeking adolescents to high-sensation media messages that were either pro- or antidrug use (Pentz et al., 2006). With few exceptions, such as translational research conducted within prevention research centers funded specifically for translational research, it was not until after 2000 that translational research was formally conducted on these risk and protective factors by taking findings from animal research—on the brain, for example—and applying them to studies of humans (Pentz et al., 2006).

Since then, planned translational research has increased both within Type I stages and in moving from Type I to Type II studies. Still, several gaps in translation remain to be addressed. For example, little back or reciprocal translation occurs in which findings from Type II dissemination research that either validate or invalidate previous results from Type I research are used to inform new Type I animal and human studies (Pentz et al., 2006). Much of the reciprocal translation that does exist involves validating genetic and neurobiological contributors to drug use. But other types of reciprocal translation could also be pursued. For example, work is under way to integrate two evidence-based programs (see Center for Substance Abuse and Prevention [CSAP], 2002) that are in the dissemination stage, one for violence prevention (PATHS) and the other for drug prevention (STAR, or the Midwestern Prevention Project), and to translate the findings back to inform the development of a new program for obesity prevention. Translating findings from one health behavior to another shortens the time to develop the new program.

Another gap in translation is the neglect of animal models and human etiological studies in the development of prevention programs (Sussman, 2001). Most of the effective prevention programs used today are considered psychosocial and have their origins in human psychological and sociological theories. They prevent drug use by building skills such as peer pressure resistance and family support. There is no evidence that animal models or human etiological studies have informed the development of these types of programs. Rather, findings are taken from human epidemiological studies that identify cognitive and social risk factors for drug use and embedded into prevention programs to develop the behaviors or social conditions that have been shown to counteract these risks. Translational research would benefit from the relatively shorter time frame required to conduct and interpret animal and human etiology studies.

Consider, for example, the six steps Sussman (2001) has proposed for prevention program development: (a) development of a theoretical model for specifying program content, desired behavior change, and mediational mechanisms for behavior change; (b) pooling of program concepts (i.e., generating a logical set of concepts such as normative expectations and peer pressure resistance, which can then be translated to skill sets); (c) focus group studies on concept receptivity by target audiences (e.g., early adolescents who would receive the program); (d) immediate studies of the impact of potential program components; (e) sequencing of components into a cohesive program; and (f) selection of relevant program mediators and outcomes. Although this sequential strategy for building a prevention program can be logically developed from human drug use epidemiological studies, it does not necessarily build from or otherwise relate to research using animal models or etiological studies. It does not, for example, take into consideration research that has identified an alcohol risk gene in animals or humans, though the results of genetic studies could be used to identify mediators of change for developing program content. And so, in following these steps, such research may not end up being as useful for informing the development of prevention programs.

Another gap in translation occurs in moving from program efficacy trials at the end of Type I research to dissemination trials in Type II research. Instead of planning for dissemination from the beginning of program development, Type II research has been spurred more by fortuitous events—mainly, congressional earmarks to fund the scaling up of effective programs to encourage their more widespread use, anecdotal or process data that revealed barriers researchers had encountered when attempting to implement programs, and a federal initiative to "culturally tailor" prevention programs that was motivated by the absence of data on whether or not such tailoring was needed.

To conclude, the formal process of translating research to practice in health and drug use prevention research is relatively new, and it continues to evolve. Most now recognize that more sustained and programmatic Type I research needs to be undertaken to develop prevention practices and programs, and this work could benefit from more systematically collecting and integrating data across human psychosocial research, epidemiological research, and etiological studies that include humans and animal models. The field has also recognized that dissemination is not complete after a program has been evaluated and found to be effective. Strategic efforts must be applied to moving effective programs into practice through Type II research, and findings from Type II research should be incorporated back into Type I studies to continually refine theories of drug use behavior and prevention.

THE IDENTIFICATION AND DISSEMINATION OF EVIDENCE-BASED PREVENTION PROGRAMS

This section examines more closely how evidence-based programs are identified and disseminated in the field of drug use prevention. As previously defined, evidence-based prevention refers to programs and strategies that have been evaluated using rigorous experimental methods and that have been found to significantly affect drug use. Several federal agencies have established standards for reviewing these programs to create *registries,* or evidence-based lists. Registries of drug use prevention programs have been published by the U.S. Department of Education (1998, 2001), the Centers for Disease Control and Prevention (J. Collins et al., 2002), the Office of Juvenile Justice Programs (Elliott, 1997), the National Institute on Drug Abuse (NIDA, 1997), and the CSAP (2002). In addition, The Cochrane Collaboration database, which has long served as a resource for reviews of randomized controlled trials for treatment programs, recently expanded to include randomized controlled trials on prevention programs (Brown, Berndt, Brinales, Zong, & Bhagwat, 2000; see Chapter 19, this volume, for more detail about trial registries). Most of these registries require a program to be evaluated in one or more studies that have (a) control or comparison groups in either a randomized or quasi-experimental research design; (b) a theoretical hypothesis-driven model by which program mediators are specified and tested; (c) longitudinal measurement of outcomes, such as drug use, (d) measures with sound psychometric properties; and (e) descriptions of procedures, samples, materials, training, analyses, and behavioral outcomes sufficient for supporting replication.

A program that meets these criteria can be further categorized as either *model* or *effective.* Model programs can be readily disseminated. Developers can readily provide the materials and technical assistance to practitioners who want to use the program. Effective programs have characteristics that make them harder to disseminate on a large scale. They are often more complex, perhaps consisting of multiple components that require extensive resources in terms of time, labor, and/or financing. For example, a multicomponent community program that requires extensive involvement and coordination among community leaders, policy makers, school administrators, teachers, and parents is much more difficult to implement than a school-based program that requires only the participation of teachers.

The lack of personnel, infrastructure, or other resources needed for dissemination can also present barriers to being a model program. For example, most prevention programs that are categorized as model or effective were originally developed by researchers at universities. If no structure or support for dissemination activities exists at a university—for example, no facilities are set aside or no personnel are available for training practitioners to deliver the program outside of a supportive research environment—then the program developer must find other means of disseminating the program. The researcher might start a business, partner with another organization that is already structured to disseminate programs, and/or seek additional funding that is specifically earmarked for dissemination, such as state incentive grants or local funds appropriated as part of Drug Free Schools and Communities programs.

Although the program registries were intended to be rigorous, they "opened up the door" to exceptions in the form of programs that were classified as "promising" despite not having been rigorously tested, perhaps because of lack of opportunity or funding. Programs may be labeled promising because of their attractiveness to consumers, ready uptake by implementers or program sites, or because qualitative data suggest positive outcomes. These types of programs can be considered a "skip" or gap in translation because they have progressed to Type II dissemination without the lengthy program development and testing usually associated with Type I studies. To help avoid confusion among practitioners about which programs to select from a registry, as well as to reduce the number of registered programs overall, the CSAP national registry has been recently revised and now requires that program effects be replicated on independent samples, that the program be made available for public dissemination, and that the program have some evidence of being successfully used or adapted for use with populations not included in the original evaluation, especially groups that suffer disproportionately from particular health problems that represent health disparities in our society.

Other factors, such as conditions in the community planning to adopt a program, can also affect dissemination. Here *community* is defined as any social organization that attempts to adopt a prevention program, implement it, sustain it, and disseminate it. So, for example, a city might disseminate a multicomponent prevention program that involves community leaders, a school may seek to integrate a program into the school curriculum, or a parent organization might want a prevention program for adolescents. Research evidence is mounting to indicate that the overall readiness and empowerment of a community to participate in the diffusion of the program are critical for program translation to occur from program developers to practitioners (Chinman et al., 2005; Feinberg, Greenberg, & Osgood, 2004; Wandersman & Florin, 2003).

Readiness does not just refer to the having the resources or infrastructure needed to operate a program. It also includes the public's perception of a program and their preference for using it. For example, communities that still select DARE for a drug prevention program, despite evidence showing its ineffectiveness, can be considered low on readiness, even if they have sufficient funds and resources for operating an evidence-based prevention program. Thus, research on diffusion, described in the next section, may "miss the boat" if strategies to enhance diffusion concentrate only on providing technical assistance, funding, or other types of instrumental support without changing public perceptions about programs that the public believes to be effective but that are in fact not evidence based.

DISSEMINATION AS ONE STAGE OF DIFFUSION: STATUS OF THEORY AND RESEARCH

As previously described, in the field of drug use prevention, dissemination is one stage in the broader process of program diffusion. Diffusion of innovation theory (Rogers, 1995a, 1995b) is one of the main theories that guide the field's efforts to move evidence-based approaches into communities. The theory explains how a new innovation—whether an invention, a procedure, or, in the case of this chapter, a drug prevention program—gets incorporated into practice through four progressive stages: *adoption, implementation, sustainability,* and outward *dissemination.*

Rogers (1995a, 1995b) also proposed that five *factors* predict successful diffusion of a program. The first factor is *trialability,* which refers to the opportunity and ability to try out a new program before it is disseminated widely. *Observability* refers to whether and to what extent the program can be observed to be working as intended. *Relative advantage* is the perceived advantage of using the new program compared to the status quo. *Low complexity* refers to the user-friendliness of the program. *Compatibility* means that the new program can be integrated into or is otherwise consistent with existing programs and values (Pentz, 2003). Only recently were these factors operationalized and tested for predictive validity in a drug use prevention diffusion trial. In that research, a multistate prevention diffusion trial, STEP (Step Towards Effective Prevention), showed that the five factors clustered as three—relative advantage/compatibility, observability/trialability, and low complexity—and each significantly predicted the quality of program implementation by teachers (Pentz, Chou, et al., 2004). The findings support Rogers's theory and also suggest that future research studies should consider including the three factors as covariates in analyses that estimate program effectiveness.

Across the four progressive stages of diffusion, more research has been conducted on barriers to diffusion, especially barriers to adoption and implementation, than on strategies to promote diffusion. The most common barriers include lack of administrator or key stakeholder support for the prevention, lack of administrator or setting support of program implementers, and lack of adequate infrastructure for diffusion (Rohrbach, Ringwalt, Ennett, & Vincus, 2005). More recently, studies have begun to examine the conditions that might promote diffusion—for example, "pretraining" preparation for administrators to improve *adoption* (Parcel et al., 1995); use of participant modeling, refresher, booster, and manualized methods of training to improve *implementation* (Pentz, 2003); and use of indigenous staff, community leader capacity building, and policies that institutionalize prevention programs to promote *sustainability* (Holder, 2001; Pentz, 2003).

Little research has been completed, however, to test speculations about the methods that might support the stage of dissemination.

Several researchers have hypothesized that DARE was so rapidly and widely disseminated throughout the United States because an automatic diffusion structure (policy departments) and communication network (police who could communicate across as well as within departments) was in place for the program (see Backer, 2000). But this hypothesis has not been tested. Similarly, some have hypothesized that dissemination will more readily occur if three conditions are met: funding for drug use prevention is made available, potential program users know about this funding, and potential users can access this funding. For example, the slow increase in the use of evidence-based drug prevention programs appears to follow the level of increase in prevention funding tied to the U.S. Anti-Drug Abuse Act (also referred to as Safe and Drug Free Schools and Communities Act; see Pentz, Chou, et al., 2004), but this relation has not been tested.

Several studies are under way to answer these and other questions about dissemination. For example, Elliott, Mihalic, and colleagues are evaluating the relation between community receipt of state incentive grants and technical assistance and the subsequent quality of implementation of evidence-based drug and violence prevention programs (Elliott, 1997; Mihalic, Fagan, Irwon, Ballard, & Elliott, 2002; Mihalic & Irwin, 2003). Survey research is also suggesting that the presence of a paid prevention coordinator improves the quality of program implementation as well as the amount of resources available for prevention overall and for subsequent dissemination efforts (Ringwalt et al., 2002). In other promising research, Spoth and colleagues (2004) are beginning to evaluate the dissemination of family-based prevention programs in rural communities made available through an existing infrastructure, the agricultural extension services of local land-grant universities. A study of the Community Youth Development Project

also aims to disseminate and evaluate a process for identifying and selecting evidence-based prevention, CTC (Communities That Care), in small communities in several states (D. Hawkins, Catalano, & Arthur, 2005). Though the results are not yet available, a quasi-experimental study of CTC dissemination in Pennsylvania sponsored as a policy initiative through the governor's office suggests that community readiness and community leader empowerment are significant predictors of dissemination (Feinberg et al., 2004).

Finally, the aforementioned STEP project (Pentz, Chou, et al., 2004) has yielded two findings thus far that relate to the dissemination stage of diffusion. First, the presence of a highly structured coalition consisting of community leaders who have a stake in prevention with youth (e.g., law enforcement, schools) and the empowerment of both individual community leaders and community organizations were significant predictors of prevention program dissemination to individual community sites. Second, the use of program implementation methods across trainers within sites and from one site to another in the same community significantly increased adherence to implementation to desirable levels after the training for all types of training methods used—live in-person, interactive televised, and videotape training. Thus, the evidence base is building to identify conditions and strategies that will promote the dissemination of prevention programs.

Though outside of formal diffusion theory, program *extension* is another part of translational research that is critical to effective dissemination. Extension refers to adapting a drug prevention program to tailoring it to local needs or to otherwise increase the program's effectiveness. At least three types of extension have been evaluated thus far in the field of drug use prevention. First, multicomponent and combinational programs have been tested for dissemination in which, for example, a family-based program is implemented with and without an accompanying school-based program to determine the added value of the school-based program to drug use prevention. In general, such combinational programs for drug use prevention yield greater effects than single programs, at least in the context of controlled research studies (Pentz, 2003). When translated to the practice setting, however, participation rates may decrease as a function of the greater logistics involved in coordinating multiple program components or because of the time commitment required of participants. Little research has systematically assessed these declines, with one exception. Programs that require parent participation typically yield significantly lower participation rates than other types of programs. For example, in one study, 20% of parents recruited from agricultural extension services participated in a parent- or family-based program (Spoth, Greenberg, Bierman, & Redmond, 2004), whereas 80% of parents participated when recruited through a school-based program (Pentz, 2003).

The second type of extension adapts programs for use with populations or in settings that differ from those in the original tests of effectiveness. For example, a social skills training program may be extended for use in Boys and Girls Clubs as opposed to schools and for use with minority as opposed to White adolescents (e.g., Botvin, Griffin, Diaz, & Ifill-Williams, 2001; St. Pierre, Kaitreider, Mark, & Alkin, 1992). If successful, information about these types of extension is usually added to national registries of evidence-based programs. However, little is known about how many or which types of programs on registries are likely to be extended successfully and to which kinds of settings.

The third type of extension involves tailoring prevention programs to integrate them with other programs that already exist in the

same setting. For example, programs that build youngsters' social and emotional competencies have been shown to prevent drug use. These programs are typically infused into a regular school educational curriculum rather than being taught as a separate health or prevention program (Bosworth, 1998). There is some evidence that such infusion programs are well adopted by practitioners, particularly by teachers in the school setting. However, more research is needed that compares the adoption of this type of extension with other programs.

CHALLENGES IN DISSEMINATING EFFECTIVE DRUG USE PREVENTION PROGRAMS

The challenge of disseminating effective prevention programs could be summed up as, "You can lead a horse to water, but you can't [necessarily] make it drink." Communities tend not to use evidence-based prevention programs, even after national registries and funding are made available for them. For example, in the early part of this decade, fewer than 30% of schools were using evidence-based programs or practices, despite the availability of registries and funding for at least the previous 5 years (Ennett et al., 2003; Hallfors & Godette, 2002; Ringwalt et al., 2002; Rohrbach et al., 2005). To encourage the use of evidence-based programs, several challenges must be met with respect to practice, theory, and the researcher's role in dissemination.

Practical Challenges. Practical challenges are not static but vary according to secular trends, such as amount and tenure of federal funding for prevention. For the first time since the late 1980s, funding for drug prevention programs is decreasing, and the Office of Drug Control Policy (ONDCP) is instead reverting back to funding more interdiction and other supply reduction approaches to drug control (Pentz, Mares, Schinke, & Rohrbach, 2004). One possible strategy for meeting this challenge is to marshal existing resources designated broadly for community youth development, which would reduce dependency on funds from state incentive grants specifically for drug use prevention and help avoid constraints of school per capita funding allotments for prevention.

Secular shifts in attention away from drug use as a national and local problem toward other problems and initiatives of national and local interest present another practical challenge to dissemination. These shifts are not well understood and cannot be predicted with certainty. They may result from media giving less attention to drug use at any one point in time compared to other problems, or from the amount of funding available for drug use prevention, or simply from the public's need for periodic novelty. Research is needed to better understand these conditions, but communities might also consider implementing and evaluating a dissemination approach that integrates drug use prevention with other pertinent and high-profile health initiatives dealing with problems such as violence, HIV, delinquency prevention, youth development, and even obesity prevention (Pentz et al., 2006; Reynolds & Spruijt-Metz, 2006; Society for Prevention Research, 2005; Solomon, Card, & Malow, 2006). Because these health concerns share some common risk factors, addressing any one is likely to affect the others, and by collaborating and coordinating public awareness efforts, competition for public attention and communication resources may be reduced.

A third practical challenge is to institutionalize drug use prevention in communities. As long as drug use prevention remains a special initiative instead of becoming a routine part of community functioning and individual health decisions, dissemination may be slow or even decline over time. One possible solution is to make drug use prevention part of local governance. Just as cities and communities have departments for water, transportation, safety, and so on, a separate department could oversee drug use prevention. Or perhaps more feasibly, drug use prevention could be infused into the regular functions (and annual budget) of local health departments. Such maneuvers would also eliminate the up-and-down pattern of drug use prevention efforts that often occurs when communities gain and then lose their prevention coordinators or other "champions" (Backer, 2000; Pentz, 2003).

A final practical challenge is to cope with the competition among prevention programs within the same community that tends to occur as communities embrace popular or subjective favorites over evidence-based programs. Communities must be educated about the importance of adopting evidence-based programs and supported in selecting and adapting programs to meet their needs. The revised registry requirements mentioned earlier may help to meet this challenge to the extent that the number of favorite programs appearing on these lists as "promising" can be reduced.

Theoretical Challenges. Most evidence-based drug prevention programs have been developed and tested using psychosocial theories of behavior change, including social learning theory, social development and bonding models, and reasoned action theory, among others (Bartholomew, Parcel, & Kok, 1998; Best et al., 2003; Pentz, 2003). These theories have been instrumental to changing drug use risk and protective factors at the intra- and interpersonal levels. They focus on affecting, for example, individual attitudes and beliefs about drug use and on modifying immediate personal circumstances and relationships in ways that prevent drug use. But these theories do relatively little to help explain or promote change in the person's broader environment, at the level of social organizations and systems, which is where dissemination operates.

In traditional research studies of drug use prevention, only a few attempts were made to develop theories that integrate intrapersonal-, interpersonal-, and environmental-level concepts, mainly in the context of implementing and studying multicomponent community prevention programs and changing related policies (see Best et al., 2003; Pentz, 2003). These theories assumed that the personal characteristics of the potential drug user, his or her social relationships, immediate circumstances, and conditions in the broader environment all affect one another over time to either allow or impede drug use. As comprehensive as these theories were and as useful as they continue to be, they do not typically address issues of diffusion.

A new generation of Type II diffusion research does, however, include theories that are directed toward diffusion "behavior." These theories include persuasion theory to address marketing of prevention programs (Pentz, Chou, et al., 2004), diffusion of innovation theory (Rogers, 1995a, 1995b), and, to a lesser extent, organizational development theories and models to explain and change infrastructure capacity to disseminate prevention programs (Backer & Rogers, 1993; Chinman et al., 2005). With the recent movement toward transdisciplinary research, the field has also begun to incorporate theories and models from other disciplines historically not applied to drug prevention programs, such as political science, policy construction and change, and economics (Pentz, Chou, et al., 2004). Behavioral, diffusion, and policy theories will likely need to be more closely integrated to develop the next generation of prevention programs that effectively target multiple levels of change. An integrated approach would include dissemination "behavior" as part of the behavior change intervention and so seek from the beginning not only to change an individual's ability to avoid drug use but also to modify or work within the organizational, policy, and other conditions of the delivery setting. For a school-based program intended to change drug use norms, these other conditions might include characteristics of the schools, teachers, classrooms, and other students that might affect intervention diffusion and so individual outcomes.

Researcher Challenges. Traditionally, researchers have served as both program developer and program tester, sometimes simultaneously. It has been considered a gold standard in behavioral science that the researcher be objective and separate, if not distant, from program test sites, administrators, and consumers. But translating a program from development and testing into practice can require multiple changes to the traditional researcher role as the program progresses through each stage of diffusion. Researchers whose work involves either effectiveness or diffusion trials may naturally begin to change their traditional roles to enable the research to take place at all. For example, to implement and test a community-level prevention program, the researcher may need to negotiate the terms of conducting the research with a board of community leaders. All of these roles represent a shift in conceptualizing the researcher as being the director of a scientific research program to being a technical assistant (cf. Wandersman & Florin, 2003). Little has been published about the nature of these role changes and how best to undertake them. Yet, if these new roles are not performed well or simply not performed whether due to the researcher's lack of willingness, awareness, or appropriate training, dissemination may fail.

As shown in the Table 21.2, several researchers have proposed that researchers serve at least two important functions at the initial *adoption* stage (Goodman, Tenney,

Smith, & Steckler, 1992; D. Hawkins et al., 2005; McCormick, Steckler, & McLeroy, 1995; Pentz, 2004). First, the researcher can help the community identify and acknowledge its need for prevention. By serving as a process consultant, the researcher can give the community feedback from initial research results on community risk levels and the current capacity of the community to move forward with implementing a prevention program (i.e., provide an assessment of readiness; Chinman et al., 2005). Then, the researcher can provide information to help a community decide which prevention program is likely to fit its needs and resources.

At the *implementation* stage, the researcher can serve as a resource, referral, and service provider for training prospective program implementers in the community. Subsequently, in the *sustainability* stage, the researcher can model how to write a grant proposal to obtain prevention funds or inform the community about how to access prevention funds and training. Finally, in the *dissemination* stage, the researcher can advise the community about any prerequisites for disseminating a program, including the types of organizational structures and collaborations that may be needed to maximize the use of dissemination resources.

Table 21.2   Change in Researcher Role in Prevention by Stage of Diffusion

Stage of Diffusion	Role of Researcher
Adoption	
Identifying need for prevention	Process consultant
Selecting/planning preventive intervention	Information sharer
Implementation	Resource/service provider
Sustainability	Model/adviser
Dissemination	Adviser

Decisions about the changing role of the researcher may appear to be unidirectional, flowing from researcher to practitioner. Increasingly, however, communications are initiated by practitioners who seek evidence-based prevention programs, and these communications become bidirectional over time as the researcher and practitioner build a relationship that involves the mutual exchange of information and expertise that appears to be critical for effective dissemination. Take one example. A prevention coordinator (practitioner) from a community contacts a researcher who has developed a particular drug use prevention program. The practitioner's community has funds to implement

the program, but because the community has identified a particular population at high risk for drug use, the community wants the program delivered to a population that is different from the original test population. The practitioner and researcher can jointly decide on, revise, and plan for this "translated" program and then determine what observed processes and outcomes will constitute success. The 10-step program implementation/process model that was developed by Pentz and used in the Midwestern Prevention Project described earlier (Pentz, 2003; see also Mihalic et al., 2002) required that both the researcher and practitioner agree on each step before the next one was attempted. This process resulted in a productive partnership, but one that was enabled by sufficient funding, longevity, and community prevention "champions" (i.e., the Ewing Kauffman Foundation in Kansas City and the Eli Lilly Foundation in Indianapolis).

Multiple challenges remain to building such a partnership in many communities—most notably, the researcher's inability or lack of time to respond to an individual practitioner's needs (Mihalic & Irwin, 2003), lack of collaboration between the involved schools and community organizations (Greenberg, 2004; Pentz, 2003; Rohrbach, Grana, & Sussman, 2006), inability of the practitioner or community to follow through with an evaluation that may be required by the researcher as part of the partnership agreement, and a community's inability to provide a strong prevention champion, whether a newsworthy individual, well-funded organization, or passionate prevention coordinator (Green & Mercer, 2001). Recent research suggests that communities with a strong community organization structure that includes an effective task force or work committee as well as sufficient funding promote the researcher-practitioner partnership (Greenberg, 2004; Pentz, Chou, et al., 2004; Pentz, Jasuja, Li, McClure, & Chou, 2003). As yet, however, no studies have examined whether the role of the researcher has a measurable effect on either the partnership or prevention program outcomes. Research is needed to address this question and to identify how researchers, by expanding their traditional role in particular ways, can best support dissemination.

NEW METHODS FOR IMPROVING DISSEMINATION

The drug use prevention field could benefit from considering several new methods to help improve dissemination: integrating theory and logic models, using new research and measurement designs, increasing the use and development of new measures, and systematically testing dissemination interventions.

Integration of Theory and Logic Models. Traditionally, programs that have been developed and tested with funding from agencies that take a scientific approach to studying drug use prevention, such as the National Institute on Drug Abuse, require applicants to describe the scientific theory underlying the proposed program. The theory is used to specify how drug use behavior occurs and how the particular program to be implemented and evaluated is expected to prevent drug use. Applicants typically are not required to justify or explain their approach to diffusion or dissemination. In contrast, prevention programs and practices that have been implemented and evaluated with funding by agencies focused on service delivery, such as the Center for Substance Abuse Prevention, typically require that funding applicants present a logic model that outlines the specific steps that will be taken to help ensure that the program gets used as intended and produces the desired results. The logic model is used for practical planning, such as setting specific timelines for each stage of the project, recruiting the appropriate number and type of personnel, securing essential funding for each state of the project, and identifying outcomes and measures that a practitioner may be mandated to report (e.g., number of persons served) or others that those in the practice setting have identified as a priority.

To better support diffusion, program developers might consider how theory and logic models can be integrated to develop more complete conceptual and operational frameworks that better support diffusion. For example, diffusion of innovation theory posits that a set of early adopters (these may be innovators or prevention champions) tends to push for others to adopt and implement it (Rogers, 1995a, 1995b). When adoption and implementation reach about 10% to 11%, they start to spread on their own, spontaneously. In terms of a logic model, this finding could be used to create a logic model step that specifies conducting planning meetings with potential adopters and repeating the meetings until 10% to 11% have been reached and agree to implement the program.

The integration of theory and logic models is already emerging. Current prevention trials such as STEP (Pentz et al., 2003; Pentz, Chou, et al., 2004), PROSPER (Spoth et al., 2004; Spoth & Greenberg, 2005), and Communities That Care (D. Hawkins et al., 2005) have developed integrated models for explaining how evidence-based prevention programs may be diffused by developing community-researcher partnerships, which vary from partnerships with new or existing community coalitions or organizations for prevention, state university extension systems and schools, or boards. Others have articulated theory/logical models to explain the processes by which communities can plan for implementing prevention strategies regardless of the particular programs involved (e.g., Best et al., 2003; Chinman et al., 2005; Wandersman & Florin, 2003). All involve discrete logic steps. All involve or imply several theories at work, including integrative transactional theory (ITT; Pentz, 2003), the social development model (D. Hawkins et al., 2005), and social ecology models (Best et al., 2003), among others.

Research and Measurement Designs. Pentz (2004) has recently reviewed findings from diffusion research, identified gaps in knowledge, and suggested several changes to prevention research designs that could improve diffusion. So far, findings show that using administrator pretraining and pretraining materials expedites the recruitment of sites into research projects and also program

adoption (e.g., Brink et al., 1995; Parcel et al., 1995; Pentz et al., 2003; Rohrbach et al., 2005). Such materials can include brief announcements listing benefits to the site and requirements for involvement in a prevention research project, a commitment letter or contract signed by both the researcher and site administrator that lists "rules of engagement," outlines for sites to use in community presentations about a project, and take-home video or other supplemental materials showing how a prevention skill is taught. Use of national research data on evidence-based programs, local needs assessment, and amount of local prevention coordinator time devoted to a program also increases adoption (Rohrbach et al., 2005). Other research suggests that enabling sites to select evidence-based programs from a menu as opposed to offering only one program, using implementer coaching, and infusing programs into regular educational activities all improve program implementation (e.g., Bartholomew et al., 1998; Bosworth, 1998; D. Hawkins et al., 2005; J. D. Hawkins, Catalano, & Arthur, 2002; Mihalic et al., 2002; Mihalic & Irwin, 2003; Rohrbach, D'Onofrio, Backer, & Montgomery, 1996).

Other research questions have not been evaluated, or at least not as systematically. More programmatic research is needed to identify the essential core components of drug use prevention programs and then to compare the effectiveness of those programs with expanded programs that have added components. Knowing which components are crucial to effectiveness and which supplemental components result in meeting particular additional needs may enable sites to adapt interventions to their local communities without sacrificing the impact (L. Collins, Murphy, & Bierman, 2004). Such designs would also help guide revisions to interventions that are often made to extend their shelf life. Several prevention programs already incorporate planned revisions at specific intervals that may range from 1 to 3 years after a program was originally developed (e.g., Life Skills Training, Botvin et al., 2001; Mihalic et al., 2002; Mihalic & Irwin, 2003). These revisions are made by developers for the purpose of updating content to match secular trends as well as to maintain some novelty for implementers who may want something new to maintain their interest (Backer, 2000). However, relatively little is known about how much revision and what kinds of revisions can be made without sacrificing the program as it was originally tested and found to be effective. Answering this question will require using new designs that can systematically identify core intervention components and identifying the conditions under which particular revisions positively or negatively affect the program results.

Refinements to longitudinal study designs could also advance understanding of diffusion. Although studies often already use longitudinal designs to test the long-term effects of a program, the time points of measurement have not been tied to particular stages of diffusion. In future studies, outcomes might be measured—for example, from baseline to 6-month follow-up to coincide with the adoption stage; a 1-year follow-up could be scheduled to coincide with the early implementation stage, and a 3-year follow-up could occur at the sustainability stage. Moreover, planning to assess successive cohorts receiving the same prevention program would help determine how long the program must be operational and at what levels of adherence to achieve the desired results (Sussman et al., 2006).

Testing Dissemination Interventions. Several practical dissemination strategies could be used now, and their effects on diffusion could be evaluated just as drug use interventions themselves are evaluated through rigorous experimental trials. Examples of these strategies can be categorized by the stage of diffusion they are intended to promote.

Under the adoption stage, studies might test, for example, whether supervisor pretraining should be used more routinely before potential program implementers are even identified. Studies could also test the conditions under which presenting stakeholders in a community with brief information about cost-effectiveness promotes greater buy-in for an effective prevention program. Experiments might show, too, that adoption is enhanced by the use of a flexible contract between the developer and the trainers and other decision makers at an adopting site. These contracts would be similar to those that researchers have used to gain the cooperation of community leaders to conduct prevention research in large community trials. Such contracts spell out the commitment of both parties, in terms of products, timelines to delivery, and any evaluation, but are not legally binding. Finally, developers could explain how the program is expected to change outcomes that have been prioritized by the community—for example, how a drug abuse prevention program may reduce community violence—and studies could identify the most effective ways of presenting this information to facilitate program adoption.

Under the implementation stage, the use of refresher training for implementers might boost adherence to implementation procedures, particularly if a lag has occurred between training and the initial implementation. Contracts with implementers might be useful as well. These contracts would be independent of any flexible contracts with sites relating to the initial adoption and would focus instead on specifying fair and equitable products to be delivered by the program developer (e.g., timely distribution of training manuals or technical assistance) and the implementer/service provider (e.g., guaranteed implementation of a set percentage of program lessons). Arrangement for positive media coverage of the training and/or the initial program implementation might also prove to be reinforcing for implementers and result, for example, in greater adherence to the program. Finally, studies could test whether incorporating particular forms of incentivized brainstorming into practice serves as reinforcement. For example, program implementers could be commissioned to participate in a retreat at the end of an implementation period to give developers specific kinds of feedback and information for revising the program, thereby potentially improving future implementation.

Sustainability might be promoted by at least three means. Incentivized training of trainer models (TOT) could be used for implementers who achieve a "master" implementer ranking (either by program developers or peers) and are given extra compensation to train other new implementers over time. Program developers could also arrange for continuing education (CE) credit for implementers in some fields to help them progress professionally (e.g., CE credit for teachers working toward a master's degree). Resource training could be provided to stakeholders and implementers, such as training in grant-writing skills and in locating potential funding agencies and donors.

Finally, outward dissemination of a prevention program by one site to another might be expedited by several means. Cross-site retreats, for example, that bring community leaders from two cities together to share best program practices may, under some conditions, result in broader use of an evidence-based program. Also, cross-organizational planning may increase program use. For example, a health agency that has implemented a prevention program could enjoin an organization such as the Red Cross or United Way to help disseminate the program to and through other agencies. Dissemination also may be supported through local model implementation sites. These model sites could be identified and supported by program developers in collaboration with national organizations and serve as ongoing "laboratories" that

supply new evidence-based practices and technical assistance for prevention training, program implementation, and program revision for multiple purposes, including dissemination to other sites.

Development and Use of New Measures. Some measures have been developed already that could be used more often to help disseminate evidence-based programs. These measures include the perceived innovativeness or benefit of a program (Pentz et al., 2003; Steckler, Goodman, McLeroy, Davis, & Koch, 1992); measures of community coalition and accountability processes (Wandersman & Florin, 2003); platform measures to assess management information systems needed to plan for, operate, and evaluate the program (CSAP, 2002); and measures of community readiness and prevention planning published by CSAP as part of its Prevention Plus series (CSAP, 2002). All of these measures could help communities gauge their readiness to begin offering drug use prevention services. For example, this author uses an abbreviated form of the CSAP readiness inventory to give feedback to community leaders during an organizational training exercise used to assess community awareness of its need for prevention. If the group has a rating of 3.5 or above out of a possible 9 (higher scores indicate greater community awareness), then the group is considered ready to move forward in mapping specific prevention needs and resources. If the group mean score is less than 3.5, leaders are trained to engage local media to put prevention on the community's public agenda and thereby increase the perceived need for prevention.

Relatively little is known, however, about how routinely communities use these measures on their own and whether communities tend to use the measures appropriately and benefit from their use. Dissemination research is needed to answer these questions and also to determine the best ways of assisting communities in using the measures, given that they currently have little guidance. National registries might consider providing technical assistance in the use of these measures for everyday practice.

Analyses. The field needs to identify more useful methods of analyzing data and informing communities about research results. Improvements in three areas may be especially relevant to communicating research to practitioners and increasing the practical usefulness of scientific data. First, many studies treat poverty status and other characteristics of the populations studied as being fixed, when actually these may vary over time. Treating such characteristics in data analyses as a fixed covariate, as often occurs, can produce misleading results about the effectiveness of a program that has been translated for use with particular subgroups. This issue becomes especially important if producing and communicating data for communities that want to reduce health disparities through prevention practices.

The timing of outcome measurement also needs more careful consideration, especially because of the tangible effects it can have on the dissemination of drug use prevention programs and on communities (L. Collins et al., 2004). For example, communities often must provide outcome evaluations to their state governments to document continued eligibility for state incentive grants for drug use prevention. But scheduling surveys of youth health outcomes often depends on school schedules and on the cooperation of schools. Will the outcomes vary across communities if, as a result, one or more communities assess program outcomes later than the rest? Thus, time of measurement as well as time of implementation should be included in the evaluation of program effects.

Finally, major events surrounding the prevention program can have an impact (usually negative) on dissemination. For example, research on school-based programs shows that the presence of a paid coordinator significantly affects the success of prevention dissemination (Ringwalt et al., 2002). But what happens when the major prevention coordinator in a community moves and is not replaced? Communities and program evaluators can benefit from using measures such as the Community Life Events Scale (CLES) (Pentz et al., unpublished manuscript) to evaluate the potential effects of such events on prevention outcomes and dissemination.

CURRENT TRENDS AND OPPORTUNITIES IN PREVENTION DISSEMINATION

Recent research announcements published by the NIH reflect four emerging trends that may afford opportunities to advance the translation and dissemination of drug use prevention programs: *community capacity building, sustainability, collaborative partnerships between researchers and practitioners,* and *transdisciplinary academic training programs.*

Capacity Building. Several NIH research announcements have required that grantees include community capacity building in their plans to promote prevention practices, especially in health services research. Though capacity-building efforts are needed, two potential problems arise with this particular requirement. First, it implies that developing particular skills in a community organization charged with prevention will translate to improving the diffusion of effective prevention programs. However, most effective prevention programs are still delivered in schools. If a community organization operates independently of the school, which is typically the case, then studies that focus only on building community capacity for prevention may go nowhere, or at least not very far. To use resources wisely, capacity building should focus mainly on strengthening the links and cooperation between the relevant community organization and schools, in addition to training community leaders and school administrators in skills such as assessing prevention needs and resources, using and interpreting data, increasing the efficiency of communication between community organizations and schools, sharing resources, and courting positive local media coverage for prevention, sometimes referred to as media advocacy (Holder, 2001).

Current capacity-building efforts also tend to focus on the organization as a whole (e.g., how an organization creates a mission statement) and, to a lesser extent, on the communication and support among individuals within the organization. Research has shown that either the nonsupportive behaviors or the loss of even one individual within an organization who serves as prevention coordinator, major stakeholder, or prevention champion can impede the progress of prevention. Capacity-building resources should therefore be spent on skills training for community organizations in planning for and training individuals for replacement.

Sustainability. Focusing on the sustainability of the stage of diffusion has become a trend in research initiatives and practice. Communities are increasingly required to demonstrate how they will sustain prevention on their own, without outside research support or funding, which poses a dilemma given that at least some research shows that sustainability is significantly related to a community's ability to gain external funding. Institutionalizing prevention through policy change could help to resolve this problem of fluctuating support for dissemination, but more research is needed on how best to achieve

policy change (see Pentz, 2003; Pentz, Chou, et al., 2004). Questions also remain about whether the recent addition of prevention research trials to The Cochrane Collaboration database registry will influence communities and policy makers to institutionalize prevention because of the credibility a registry carries (Brown et al., 2000; Jett, 2003). Alternatively, the more restrictive criteria that have been proposed for maintaining prevention programs on evidence-based registries may negatively affect institutionalization if the requirements are too time intensive or costly (cf. August et al., 2004; Flay et al., 2005).

Collaborative Partnerships. Collaborative partnerships, also known as participatory community action research, are another recent trend. As discussed earlier, many prevention programs and studies already negotiate these partnerships, usually a necessity in large prevention trials or demonstrations that involve whole communities. However, as yet, no standard operating procedures exist for achieving this partnership. Until such procedures are developed, future dissemination efforts might look to procedures that have already been tested and published as part of a prevention study, such as the 10-step organizational model used in the previously mentioned Midwestern Prevention Project and STEP diffusion trial (Pentz et al., 2003; Pentz, Chou, et al., 2004; see also the summary in Elliott, 1997). According to this model, the researcher (external partner) and community organization (internal partner) together agree on and complete each step of the dissemination before the next step is initiated. For example, the step of needs assessment needed to be concluded before the community organization would identify individuals to be trained as program implementers. Researchers seeking such partnerships should expect that their conventional roles will change in the course of progressing through these steps, as was summarized in Table 21.2.

Transdisciplinary Training. A transdisciplinary approach to prevention science continues to be promoted. This increasing trend is most evident in funding agency calls for new research studies and also in new initiatives that encourage transdisciplinary training for the next generation of prevention scientists. In the field of drug use prevention, transdisciplinary training will be expected to promote greater understanding of neurobiology, neurocognition, and genetics, as well as current knowledge and research on the psychological and social bases of behavior. For example, obesity, violence, and drug use share common risk factors related to emotional regulation, executive cognitive function, and the endocannabinoid system. Understanding these mechanisms from a neurobiological perspective would enable future prevention scientists to incorporate impulse control more effectively into social

cognitive prevention interventions. Scientists could also use training in disciplines such as business to understand prevention program dissemination from a marketing perspective, as well as public policy and planning to better understand communities and practitioners and respond to practical considerations in using prevention programs, such as whether target consumers will like the program. Practitioners may also benefit from transdisciplinary training. This preparation could promote understanding of the main scientific concepts and processes involved in drug use prevention program development, evaluation, and diffusion and so help them collaborate even more productively with the next generation of prevention researchers.

Drug use prevention dissemination research and practice is moving toward identifying the means by which prevention can be made more effective, more efficient, more wide-ranging in effects, and more normative. One day, prevention may be as expected and welcomed in our society as education.

REFERENCES

August, G. J., Winters, K. C., Realmuto, G. M., Tarter, R., Perry, C., & Hektner, J. M. (2004). Moving evidence-based drug abuse prevention programs from basic science to practice: "Bridging the efficacy-effectiveness interface." *Substance Use & Misuse, 39*(10–12), 2017–2053.

Backer, T. E. (2000). The failure of success: challenges of disseminating effective substance abuse prevention programs. *Journal of Community Psychology, 28*(3), 363–373.

Backer, T. E., & Rogers, E. M. (1993). *Organizational aspects of health communication campaigns: What works?* Thousand Oaks, CA: Sage.

Bartholomew, L. K., Parcel, G. S., & Kok, G. (1998). Intervention mapping: A process for developing theory and evidence-based health education programs. *Health Education and Behavior, 25*(5), 545–563.

Best, A., Stokols, D., Green, L. W., Leischow, S., Holmes, B., & Buchholtz, K. (2003). An integrative framework for community partnering to translate theory into effective health promotion strategy. *American Journal of Health Promotion, 18*(2), 168–176.

Bosworth, K. (1998). Assessment of drug abuse prevention curricula developed at the local level. *Journal of Drug Education, 28*(4), 307–325.

Botvin, G. J., Griffin, K.W., Diaz, T., & Ifill-Williams, M. (2001). Drug abuse prevention among minority adolescents: Posttest and one-year follow-up of a school-based preventive intervention. *Prevention Science, 2*(1), 1–13.

Brink, S. G., Basen-Engquist, K. M., O'Hara-Tompkins, N. M., Parcel, G. S., Gottlieb, N. H., & Lovato, C. Y. (1995). Diffusion of an effective tobacco prevention program: Part 1. Evaluation of the dissemination phase. *Health Education Research, 10,* 283–295.

Brown, C. H., Berndt, D., Brinales, J. M., Zong, X., & Bhagwat, D. (2000). Evaluating the evidence of effectiveness for preventive interventions: Using a registry system to influence policy through science. *Addictive Behaviors, 25*(6), 955–964.

Center for Substance Abuse Prevention (CSAP). (2002). *CSAP's prevention portal: Model programs.* Retrieved August 14, 2006, from http://www.modelprograms.samhsa.gov

Chinman, M., Hannah, G., Wandersman, A., Ebener, P., Hunter, S. B., Imm, P., et al. (2005). Developing a community science research agenda for building community capacity for effective preventive interventions. *American Journal of Community Psychology, 35*(3–4), 143–157.

Collins, J., Robin, L., Woole, S., Fenley, D., Hunt, P., Taylor, J., et al. (2002). Programs-that-work: CDC's guide to effective programs that reduce health-risk behavior of youth. *Journal of School Health, 72*(3), 93–99.

Collins, L., Murphy, S. A., & Bierman, K. L. (2004). A conceptual framework for adaptive preventive interventions. *Prevention Science, 5*(3), 185–196.

Elliott, D. S. (Ed.). (1997). *Blueprints for violence prevention.* Boulder: Center for the Study and Prevention of Violence, University of Colorado.

Ennett, S. T., Ringwalt, C. L., Thorne, J., Rohrbach, L. A., Vincus, A., Simons-Rudolph, A., et al. (2003). Comparison of current practice in school-based substance use prevention programs with meta-analysis findings. *Prevention Science, 4*(1), 1–14.

Feinberg, M. E., Greenberg, M. T., & Osgood, D. W. (2004). Readiness, functioning, and perceived effectiveness in community prevention coalitions: A study of Communities That Care. *American Journal of Community Psychology, 33*(3–4), 163–176.

Flay, B. R., Biglan, A., Boruch, R. F., Castro, F. G., Gottredson, D., Kellam, S., et al. (2005). Standards of evidence: Criteria for efficacy, effectiveness, and dissemination. *Prevention Science, 6*(3), 151–175.

Goodman, R. M., Tenney, M., Smith, D. W., & Steckler, A. (1992). The adoption process for health curriculum innovations in schools: a case study. *Journal of Health Education, 23*(4), 215–220.

Green, L., & Mercer, S. (2001). Can public health researchers and agencies reconcile the push from funding bodies and the pull from communities? *American Journal of Public Health, 91*(12), 1926–1929.

Greenberg, M. T. (2004). Current and future challenges in school-based prevention: The researcher perspective. *Prevention Science, 5*(1), 5–13.

Hallfors, D., & Godette, D. (2002). Will the "principles of effectiveness" improve prevention practice? Early findings from a diffusion study. *Health Education Research: Theory and Practice, 17*(4), 461–470.

Hawkins, D., Catalano, R., & Arthur, M. (2005, May 26). *Taking prevention science to scale: The Community Youth Development Study* Paper presented at the Society for Prevention Research Conference program, Washington, DC.

Hawkins, J. D., Catalano, R. F., & Arthur, M. W. (2002). Promoting science-based prevention in communities. *Addictive Behavior, 27*(6), 951–976.

Hawkins, J. D., Catalano, R. F., & Miller, J. Y. (1992). Risk and protective factors for alcohol and other drug problems in adolescence and early adulthood: Implications for substance abuse prevention. *Psychological Bulletin, 112*(1), 64–105.

Holder, H. D. (2001). Community prevention trials: A respectful partnership. *American Journal of Health Behavior, 25*(3), 234–244.

Jett, K. P. (2003). Disseminating substance abuse research findings for policy. *Journal of Psychoactive Drugs, 35*(Suppl. 1), 105.

McCormick, L. K., Steckler, A., & McLeroy, K. R. (1995). Diffusion of innovation in schools: A study of adoption and implementation of school-based tobacco prevention curricula. *American Journal of Health Promotion, 9*, 210–219.

Mihalic, S., Fagan, A., Irwin, K., Ballard, D., & Elliott, D. (2002). *Blueprints for violence prevention replications: Factors for implementation success.* Boulder: University of Colorado, Center for the Study and Prevention of Violence.

Mihalic, S. F., & Irwin, K. (2003). Blueprints for violence prevention: From research to real world settings—factors influencing the successful replication of model programs. *Youth Violence and Juvenile Justice, 1*(4), 307–329.

National Institute on Drug Abuse (NIDA). (1997). *Preventing drug use among children and adolescents: A research-based guide.* Rockville, MD: National Institute on Drug Abuse. Retrieved August 14, 2006, from http://www.drug abuse.gov/Prevention/Prevopen.html

Parcel, G. S., O'Harra-Tompkins, N. M., Harrist, R. B., Bassen-Engquist, K. M., McCormick, L. K., Gottlieb, N. H., et al. (1995). Diffusion of an effective tobacco prevention program: Part II. Evaluation of the adoption phase. *Health Education Research, 10*(3), 297–307.

Pentz, M. A. (1995). Prevention research in multiethnic communities. In G. J. Botvin, S. P. Schinke, & M. A. Orlandi (Eds.), *Drug abuse prevention with multiethnic youth.* Thousand Oaks, CA: Sage.

Pentz, M. A. (2003). Evidence-based prevention: Characteristics, impact, and future direction. *Journal of Psychoactive Drugs, 35*(Suppl.), 143–152.

Pentz, M. A. (2004). Form follows function: designs for prevention effectiveness and diffusion research. *Prevention Science, 5*(1), 23–29.

Pentz, M. A, Chou, C.-P., McClure, M., Bernstein, K., Mann, D., Ross, L., et al. (2004, May). *Adoption and early implementation of STEP: A multi-state teleconference-based prevention diffusion trial.* Paper presented at the 12th annual Society for Prevention Research meeting, Quebec City, Quebec.

Pentz, M. A., Jasuja, G., Li, C., McClure, M., & Chou, C.-P. (2003, June). *Predictors of diffusion of evidence-based prevention programs: Early results of the STEP trial.* Paper presented at the 11th annual meeting of the Society for Prevention Research, Washington, DC.

Pentz, M. A., Jasuja, G. K., Rohrbach, L. A., Sussman, S., & Bardo, M. (2006). Translation in tobacco and drug abuse prevention/cessation research. *Evaluation and the Health Professions, 29*(2), 246–271.

Pentz, M. A., Mares, D., Schinke, S., & Rohrbach, L. A. (2004). Political science, public policy, and drug use prevention. *Substance Use & Misuse, 39*(10–12), 1821–1865.

Reynolds, K. D., & Spruijt-Metz, D. (2006). Translational research in childhood obesity prevention. *Evaluation & Health Professions, 29*(2), 219–245.

Ringwalt, C. L., Ennett, S., Vincus, A., Thorne, J., Rohrbach, L. A., & Simons-Rudolph, A. (2002). The prevalence of effective substance use prevention curricula in U.S. middle schools. *Prevention Science, 3*(4), 257–265.

Rogers, E. M. (1995a). Diffusion of drug abuse prevention programs: Spontaneous diffusion, agenda setting, and reinvention. *NIDA Research Monograph, 155,* 90–105.

Rogers, E. M. (1995b). Elements of diffusion. In E. M. Rogers (Ed.), *Diffusion of innovations* (4th ed., pp. 1–38). New York: Free Press.

Rohrbach, L. A., D'Onofrio, C. N., Backer, T. E., & Montgomery, S. B. (1996). Diffusion of school-based substance abuse prevention programs. *American Behavioral Scientist, 39*(7), 919–934.

Rohrbach, L. A., Grana, R., & Sussman, S. (2006). Type II translation: Transporting prevention interventions from research to real-world settings. *Evaluation & the Health Professions, 29*(3), 302–333.

Rohrbach, L. A., Ringwalt, C. L., Ennett, S. T., & Vincus, A. A. (2005). Factors associated with adoption of evidence-based substance use prevention curricula in U.S. school districts. *Health Education Research: Theory and Practice, 20*(5), 514–526.

Sloboda, Z., & Schildhaus, S. (2002). A discussion of the concept of technology transfer of research-based drug "abuse" prevention and treatment interventions. *Substance Use & Misuse, 37*(8–10), 1079–1087.

Society for Prevention Research (SPR). (2005). *A case for braided prevention research and service funding.* Retrieved August 14, 2006, from http://www.preventionresearch.org/BraidedFunding.pdf

Solomon, J., Card, J. J., & Malow, R. M. (2006). Adapting efficacious interventions: Advancing translational research in HIV prevention. *Evaluation & Health Professions, 29*(2), 162–194.

Spoth, R., Greenberg, M., Bierman, K., & Redmond, C. (2004). PROSPER community-university partnership model for the public education systems: Capacity-building for evidence-based, competence-building prevention. *Prevention Science, 5*(1), 31–39.

Spoth, R. L., & Greenberg, M. T. (2005). Toward a comprehensive strategy for effective practitioner-scientist partnerships and larger-scale community health and well-being. *American Journal of Community Psychology, 35*(3–4), 107–126.

Steckler, A., Goodman, R. M., McLeroy, K. R., Davis, S., & Koch, G. (1992). Measuring the diffusion of innovative health promotion programs. *American Journal of Health Promotion, 6*(3), 214–224.

St. Pierre, T. L., Kaitreider, D. L., Mark, M. M., & Alkin, K. J. (1992). Drug prevention in a community setting: A longitudinal study of the relative effectiveness of a three-year primary prevention program in Boys & Girls Clubs across the nation. *American Journal of Community Psychology, 20*(6), 673–706.

Sussman, S. (Ed.). (2001). *Handbook of program development for health behavior research and practice.* Thousand Oaks, CA: Sage.

Sussman, S., Valente, T. W., Rohrbach, L., Stacy, A. W., & Pentz, M. A. (2006). Translation in health behavior research: Converting science into action. *Evaluation and the Health Professions, 29*(1), 7–32.

U.S. Department of Education (DOE). (1998). Safe and drug-free schools program: Notice of final principles of effectiveness. *Federal Register, 63,* 29901–29906.

U.S. Department of Education (DOE). (2001). *Safe, disciplined and drug-free schools expert panel: Exemplary and promising safe, disciplined, and drug-free schools programs.* Retrieved August 14, 2006, from http://www.ed.gov/offices/OERI/ORAD/KAD/expert_panel/drug-free.html

Wandersman, A., & Florin, P. (2003). Community interventions and effective prevention. *American Psychologist, 58*(6–7), 441–448.

CHAPTER 22

Disseminating and Implementing Evidence-Based Practices for Mental Health

David A. Chambers

Just as health researchers struggle to integrate evidence-based practices into health care, in the field of mental health, we see emerging numbers of efficacious and effective practices that have been tested in clinical trials but that rarely get used in practice (Drake et al., 2001).[1] This disconnection between the practices that have been developed and delivered through intervention studies and the services that are available to the public stems partly from a long-held belief among mental health researchers that their role in research dissemination ends when their scientific work is published in an elite peer-reviewed journal and that supporting the effective and widespread use of the findings must be someone else's responsibility.

More recently, however, mental health researchers have begun to develop the knowledge base underlying the transfer of scientific findings into practice—referred to as "dissemination and implementation" research. Dissemination and implementation research connects behavioral research to clinical practice and to public health by identifying how to effectively deliver research-based information and interventions in specific

public and private health care service settings. In the field of mental health, dissemination usually refers to spreading information from some central source, such as a research publication or treatment manual, to a particular audience that would then be expected to use it. The more intensive process of implementation involves studying the fit between a specific evidence-based intervention and a particular care setting to determine which aspects of the service delivery environment need modifying to support the intervention's use. Implementation research is essential to supporting the use of evidence-based practices primarily because the research designs used in efficacy and effectiveness trials rarely yield the information needed to apply interventions effectively in practice settings, which tend to differ from the ones in which the intervention was developed and tested (National Institutes of Health [NIH], 2006).

Calls for increased attention to dissemination and implementation research have come from across the mental health field. For example, the President's New Freedom Commission on Mental Health (2003) report, the Surgeon General's conference on children's mental health (U.S. Public Health Service, 1999), and the National Institute of Mental Health (NIMH) report, *The Road Ahead* (National Advisory Mental Health Council, 2006), clearly articulate the need to expand the use of evidence-based practices within communities and to conduct research to discover how best to support their use.

This chapter surveys the state of dissemination and implementation research in mental health. Though not an exhaustive account, the chapter highlights major achievements, current initiatives, and remaining challenges. In some cases, literatures outside of mental health are referenced to illustrate lessons to be learned from other fields.

DISSEMINATING EVIDENCE

Disseminating evidence to improve mental health services is a complex process, involving multiple stages and participants. Over time, dissemination has evolved from simplistic diffusion (e.g., presenting research findings in academic journals and conferences) into more strategic approaches that acknowledge the complexities involved in creating sound and relevant evidence, packaging the evidence, delivering it to the field, receiving the evidence, and, ultimately, applying it in care settings to benefit consumers of mental health care. This section briefly summarizes some key findings in each of these areas that are being used to guide dissemination in mental health (for more detailed discussions, see Hornik, 2002; Sechrest, Backer, Rogers, Campbell, & Grady, 1994).

Creating Evidence

In general discussions of how best to disseminate findings from science, a pervasive debate has centered on "what is evidence?" (Tanenbaum, 2005). This topic is comprehensively discussed for mental health

in a recent issue of *Child and Adolescent Psychiatric Clinics of North America* (Drake, McHugo, Leff, & Latimer, 2004). A central issue in the debate is that, with the rise of evidence-based care as a movement, assumptions have been made about the quality of evidence underlying different interventions, usually on the basis of study design, which some scientists and practitioners believe to be questionable. Several research groups have codified a hierarchy of evidence, with the systematic review of randomized clinical trials (RCTs) garnering the highest rating and anecdotal information the lowest (e.g., Guyatt & Rennie, 2002). The assumption behind these rating systems is that, unlike other research methods, RCTs control for biases that allow for making objective, cause-effect inferences about treatment effects that are more reliable and generalizable to diverse practice settings. Some argue, however, that even RCTs are to some degree subjective, and so the results must be interpreted cautiously and put into the appropriate context. For example, researchers must make choices in designing RCTs, such as selection of inclusion and exclusion criteria, site selection, choice of statistical approaches, approach to coping with missing data, time points for patient assessment, and many other decisions that are not always themselves guided by "hard" data but by the scientist's best judgments (Fitzgerald, Ferlie, Wood, & Hawkins, 1999; Huby & Fairhurst, 1998; Westen & Bradley, 2005; Westen, Novotny, & Thompson-Brenner, 2004). As a result, those seeking to apply the results of RCTs must be aware of the choices that were made and the rationales behind them to determine whether the findings might apply to their own clinical practices.

Furthermore, information collected from clinical experience, though observational, can be more objective and reliable than is often recognized. Practitioners acquire knowledge through assessing and treating many patients over time and make many decisions based on an aggregated "data set" of those patients. For example, many clinicians specialize in treating particular kinds of disorders, and as they treat more and more individuals with those disorders, the charting of the results provides a database that links interventions to particular patient outcomes. Reliable patterns can emerge from these data that are useful both for guiding practice and the design of subsequent research using more controlled methods.

Much has been written elsewhere about limitations of the RCT, such as the trading of external validity to achieve greater internal validity. (Controlled studies often create a highly specialized context for conducting research such that the consistency between the study setting and real-world service systems may not be particularly impressive.) The RCT remains the "gold-standard" scientific method, however, because it comes closest to identifying a cause-effect relation between an intervention and the observed outcome (Sackett, Rosenberg, Gray, Haynes, & Richardson, 1996). Still, the RCT requires adapting and supplementing with information obtained from other methods to disseminate the most accurate and complete information and to help ensure the findings are used appropriately (see Chapter 19, this volume, for related discussion). For example, many reviews of evidence in specific areas of mental health have used multiple levels of evidence to form their conclusions, including evidence-based reviews, meta-analyses, and expert consensus statements (e.g., Bartels et al., 2002). It is important that the field continues to draw from multiple forms of evidence, being careful to note the strengths and limitations in all forms of data. Synthesizing evidence from methods typically found in the "lower levels" of the hierarchy is especially important when the evidence base is still developing. Research has not yet determined the pathophysiology

for many disorders (Insel & Scolnick, 2006), and so the field especially needs evidence from practice to identify natural trajectories between treatments and outcomes in actual service settings, information that is not always available from controlled studies.

Ratings also have been applied to research-tested interventions in mental health using such hierarchies of evidence, leading to questions about the usefulness of the ratings for clinical practice. For example, Division 12 (Clinical Psychology) of the American Psychological Association (APA) convened a task force that rated interventions in order to develop a list of empirically validated treatments, which was made available in 1995. In 1996, the federal government's Substance Abuse and Mental Health Services Administration (SAMHSA) created the National Registry of Effective Prevention Programs (later renamed the National Registry of Effective Programs and Practices) to identify evidence-based programs (EBPs) in behavioral health as candidates for implementation (Kerner et al., 2005). State mental health agencies, nonprofit organizations, and academic institutions have also created lists of EBPs (Tanenbaum, 2005). Interventions included in these lists have not always been tested in contexts similar to the practice settings that demand them. Thus, potential users need support for understanding the conditions under which the practices have been evaluated before choosing to adopt them within a particular service setting (see Chapter 19, this volume, for more discussion of these and other EBP lists).

Packaging Evidence

The packaging of evidence also affects whether clinicians ultimately use research findings to change their practices. Framing, for instance, has a profound influence on whether clinicians and other intended beneficiaries respond to the information positively

(Rothman & Salovey, 1997). For example, telling potential users how many lives can be saved by using an intervention is more likely to make a positive impression than saying how many lives will be lost if the intervention is not used (Rothman & Salovey, 1997; see also Wood, Ferlie, & Fitzgerald, 1998).

The packaging of evidence in journals also may dramatically affect how readers make sense of it. Haynes (1990) notes that journals tend to mix rigorous studies with many preliminary investigations, offering a confusing picture of which findings are more certain and which are less so. Systematic reviews of evidence especially can be quite helpful to clinicians who often are unaware of diversity in the quality of evidence (McColl, Smith, White, & Field, 1998), but the evidence should be packaged according to how clinicians themselves assess it (Huby & Fairhurst, 1998). That is, scientists often present evidence in ways they find compelling without considering whether clinicians require more support for interpreting the evidence in the same way (Huby & Fairhurst, 1998). For example, in an article detailing a treatment for depression, scientists may describe treatment effectiveness by saying that it caused a significant reduction in the Hamilton Depression Rating Scale (Nierenberg et al., 2006). However, if the clinician is looking for a treatment that will result in the patient's regained ability to work—a practical goal not included in the outcome measures—she or he may not see the treatment as directly helpful to her or his practice. Thus, information presented by science must be "user-friendly" to the target audience, or it is less likely to be perceived as clinically relevant (Corrigan, 1998). As this example shows, making communications user-friendly goes beyond the need to eliminate jargon from study descriptions after the research is complete; it often requires fundamental changes to how research is conducted, in this case including outcome measures to show that the intervention not only affects the psychological processes of depression but also helps patients achieve practical goals.

As discussed earlier, communicating evidence to practitioners has often occurred with the assumption that scientific evidence, especially evidence from RCTs, is more useful than clinical experience or practice-derived information. This science versus practice debate hinges partly on whether practice can be considered applied science (as in the systematic clinical observations of treatments and outcomes previously described) (Tanenbaum, 2005). It also hinges on the related issue of whether discrepancies between the conclusions derived from local unpublished observations and conclusions of published research should be resolved by prioritizing that which is published. As medical sociologists have long explained, however, the content of knowledge depends on the context in which it was created, and so its value can be interpreted in different ways by different people (Bauchner & Simpson, 1998; Berger & Luckmann, 1966; Fitzgerald et al., 1999; Huby & Fairhurst, 1998; Mannheim, 1936; Mulkay, 1979; Wood et al., 1998). Finding beneficial ways of packaging evidence will require a meeting of minds between scientists and practitioners about the need for both scientific evidence and clinical information, as well as about how these sources of information should be integrated with clinical judgment in meeting the needs of an individual patient. Until scientific evidence is produced and packaged in ways that help clinicians perceive the information as relevant to their particular circumstances, and until strategies are developed to help clinicians understand the value of evidence-based practices and how best to combine them with information derived from practice, the application of scientific evidence will be limited (Hawley & Weisz, 2002; Hoagwood, Burns, Kiser, Ringeisen, & Schoenwald, 2001; McKay, Hibbert, & Hoagwood, 2004;

Schoenwald & Hoagwood, 2001; Weisz, Weersing, & Henggeler, 2005; Weisz, Sandler, & Durlak, 2005).

Transmitting Evidence

Traditionally, scientific findings have been most often disseminated through passive mechanisms, typically through publications in peer-reviewed journals. An implicit assumption among scientists is that published findings are taken up somehow by practitioners. But Balas and Boren (2000) showed in their analysis of the uptake of biomedical research findings that practitioners have used only 14% of published scientific findings, and up to 17 years can pass before this knowledge is used. It is well known that practitioners typically do not read academic journals (Liberman & Eckman, 1989; Prescott et al., 1997), and even if they did, delays in applying the findings would be expected given the time lag between scientific peer review and journal publication, which can be 1 year or more, as well as the additional time needed to make the results available to a broader audience. The recent expansion of online journals has reduced this lag time, but concerns remain that rapid publication, via the Internet, for example, may compromise the accuracy and usefulness of the information being disseminated to potential users of the findings (Bauchner & Simpson, 1998).

In mental health, evidence is usually disseminated broadly to practitioners through continuing education (CE) programs. Licensure for many clinicians requires a certain number of CE credits per year, and so these programs can present a win-win scenario: Assuming the evidence is clinically relevant, a built-in audience can access it in a venue created specifically for that purpose. Systematic reviews of continuing education (e.g., Davis, Thomson, Oxman, & Haynes, 1995) have shown, however, that

these programs rarely result in changes to clinical practice. Some have argued that traditional CE programs are largely passive exercises in which evidence is shared through didactic instruction, and unless clinicians participate more actively, the evidence will likely not get used. For example, in an observational study, clinicians who received standard didactic lectures on research-based recommendations for treating patients with schizophrenia did not change their practices, whereas most clinicians who also received intensive training followed the recommendations (Dixon et al., 1999; see also Backer, Liberman, & Kuehnel, 1986; Liberman & Eckman, 1989).

More recently, several active dissemination strategies have been undertaken that seem to be effective in changing clinical behavior (Bero et al., 1998). These methods have included case conferences (interactive discussions among clinicians about treatment alternatives for an individual patient) and academic detailing (experts in a particular treatment travel to a practice site to present scientific findings on new treatment methods) (Oxman, Thomson, Davis, & Haynes, 1995). As information technologies, including the Internet, have become more accessible to clinicians and other stakeholders and more frequently used, several mental health researchers have begun testing how the Web affects the uptake of information by multiple stakeholders. Donald Steinwachs at Johns Hopkins University, for example, is leading research to test whether access to information about evidence-based practices on the Web for patients with schizophrenia increases consumer demand for evidence-based care. Another research team headed by Armando Rotondi at Western Psychiatric Institute is testing whether participating in a Web-based community for patients with schizophrenia and their primary caregivers results in better clinical outcomes. Other researchers are investigating the potential benefit of tele-psychiatry (delivery of care through telephone and Internet) for reaching patients in rural and other difficult-to-access settings.

Receiving Evidence

Effective dissemination depends on knowing how information is being received and processed by the target audience. As several researchers have noted, different audiences view evidence in different ways, according to their "most valued outcomes" (Allery, Owen, & Robling, 1997; Hatgis et al., 2001; Leeds, 1979). For example, consumers of mental health services might most value positive therapeutic relationships and increased knowledge about health problems, whereas administrators might care more about employee satisfaction and the financial health of their organization (Hatgis et al., 2001). (Of course, as previously discussed, such outcomes must first be incorporated more consistently into study designs to make the information more routinely available to these diverse stakeholders.)

Disseminators must also be aware of barriers to receiving information caused by differences in languages spoken, literacy skills, or access to technology. Many publications require high reading levels for comprehension, and consumers may have insufficient access to online databases such as Medline or even to telephones and the Internet. Practitioners themselves often have insufficient training to understand information from science (Leeds, 1979). For example, few colleges of medicine require medical students to learn statistics as part of their degree, though understanding clinical trials requires familiarity with statistical methods and research design. In addition, a clinic's staff director may not be receptive to dissemination, perhaps because he or she does not see the need for evidence-based approaches or a need to support staff in gaining access to medical journals or other venues for learning

about the latest scientific findings (Backer et al., 1986).

Using Evidence

In mental health, several researchers have specified criteria for judging whether the information to be disseminated is likely to lead to changes in practice. These criteria include relevance, timeliness, clarity, credibility, replicability, and acceptability (for more explanation, see Schoenwald & Henggeler, 2002). Different audiences may act on these concepts differently, but each criterion helps to assess the fit between the evidence and the clinician's practice. In addition, several researchers are working to discover how information systems help to apply evidence in real time. For example, the Texas Medication Algorithm Project, led by Madhukar Trivedi, is evaluating whether a computer-based decision support system encourages real-time use of evidence about medications for depression in the treatment setting. At Western Psychiatric Institute in Pittsburgh, Armando Rotondi is leading a study to assess whether giving schizophrenia patients and their primary caregivers information about the illness, as well as opportunities to discuss their experiences online, can improve patient outcomes. These studies illustrate that promoting the use of scientific evidence ultimately requires that scientists go beyond delivering information in the form of research syntheses, guidelines, and so on and participate in the development of strategies and tools to support the implementation of science-based practices, a more complex, interactive, and ongoing process.

UNDERSTANDING IMPLEMENTATION

Recall that earlier in this chapter, dissemination was defined as communicating information about mental health to multiple stakeholders, whereas implementation refers to the complexities of integrating clinical interventions into practice settings. To effectively implement an intervention, one must thoroughly understand the service settings and other conditions that influence clinical practice, yet these factors have been largely discounted in effectiveness research. Given their critical importance, the next section briefly discusses how characteristics of the individuals, organizations, and systems in the service delivery setting can influence the implementation of interventions in mental health care (for more detailed discussions, see Drake et al., 2001; Ferlie & Shortell, 2003; Griffin, Mathieu, & Jacobs, 2001).

Individual Level

Often, the greatest challenge of integrating an effective mental health treatment or preventive intervention into practice settings is convincing individuals to change their routine. The patient must be willing to try a new treatment, a clinician willing to change the way he or she approaches treatment, the family willing to support a different regimen, the manager willing to make administrative changes to support the practice, or the financer willing to provide coverage for the new intervention. As we describe next, each becomes part of the implementation process and thus influences the eventual outcome.

Patient/Family Members. At the heart of clinical practice is the patient. Interventions must take into account individual characteristics such as race, ethnicity, gender, and age that can moderate the intervention effect (e.g., Westen et al., 2004; Westen & Bradley, 2005). Unfortunately, many clinical trials of mental health interventions have not included diverse populations, especially in the numbers needed to determine whether intervention outcomes differ across subgroups. In some instances, the failure to recruit diverse patients into clinical trials has signaled important barriers to treatment for underserved populations (Drake et al., 2001; King, 2002). Other patient characteristics, such as lack of transportation, competing time demands, lack of a relationship with a provider, and the person's general tendency to seek help can all influence whether patients receive the intervention.

Traditionally, the mental health field has viewed the clinician as a professional expert and autonomous decision maker (e.g., Freidson, 1993) and so has assumed a unidirectional flow of information from expert to patient. Mental health practitioners and researchers are beginning to realize, however, that effective implementation depends on including patients as partners in their own care and understanding the intervention not only from the clinician's point of view but also from the patient's perspective (Howitt & Armstrong, 1999). This more collaborative approach to service delivery is especially helpful to effectively applying scientific evidence in the treatment of an individual patient. That is, clinical trials are designed to test the average effectiveness of an intervention for a study group. Rarely do the clinical trials reveal benefits for every trial participant, nor do they identify potentially harmful effects at the individual level. Likewise, the findings may not benefit the individual patient treated by the practicing clinician and may lead to poor clinical outcomes. Recent discussions about the potential of antipsychotic medications to cause metabolic syndrome in some patients, atypical reactions that may be prevented with effective monitoring, underscores the need to make treatment decisions by integrating individual patient preferences and input with scientific evidence and with clinical experience and judgment (e.g., Lieberman et al., 2005; Newcomer, Nasrallah, & Loebel, 2004).

The burden of mental illness is felt not only by the individual patient but also by the patient's family members. For children, the family plays a particularly strong role both in seeking help for a serious emotional disorder and in the treatment itself (McKay & Bannon, 2004). Furthermore, the fragmentation of the mental health system creates frustration and added burden for family members because they often must interact with multiple providers and ensure appropriate adherence to the patient's course of treatment (Flynn, 2005). Thus, effective implementation strategies must engage key family members at all stages of the treatment process. One ongoing study (principal investigator [PI]: Armando Rotondi) is testing, for example, whether an online support system for primary caregivers (usually a family member) reduces caregiver burden perhaps by improving the level of information that caregivers have along with providing resources where they can get additional help.

Clinician. Frequently, when clinical trials are used to test a novel intervention, the intervention is delivered under ideal conditions. For example, clinicians delivering the intervention have essential training, time, and resources to provide the treatment throughout the life of the study. When broader implementation occurs, however, these supports are often lacking for integrating the intervention into a clinician's usual practice. Barriers to clinician implementation include lack of available evidence about a particular treatment, lack of familiarity with available evidence, difficulty in interpreting statistics from scientific articles in order to understand study conclusions, feared loss of autonomy in their practice as a result of having to deliver a treatment dictated by an administrator or payer, and the perception that tested interventions are too generic and will not meet the particular needs of their patients (Dulcan, 2005).

The success of implementation will be influenced by the clinician's behavior, as well as constraints on the clinician (Corrigan, Steiner, McCracken, Blaser, & Barr, 2001). Several researchers have studied methods to change clinician behavior directly. Robertson, Baker, and Hearnshaw (1996), for example, used a psychological framework to change physicians' practices. They found that self-efficacy, preparedness to change, social influence (such as peers choosing to change their clinical practices), and adverse incidents caused by the mistreatment of a patient all positively influenced clinical practice change. Corrigan et al. (2001) found several barriers to implementing evidence-based treatments that included clinicians' lack of particular knowledge, skills, and attitudes, for example; not knowing the impact of serious psychiatric disabilities on individual patients (e.g., psychiatric symptoms, course of illness) and family members (e.g., stress); the inability to provide interpersonal support to their patients; the inability to set realistic goals for recovery; the inability to understand what additional skills are needed to deliver a novel treatment; and a clinician's tendency to believe that a specific treatment cannot help patients regain a place in the community.

Manager. Management decisions affect all aspects of clinical practice, and so successfully implementing an effective mental health treatment program requires working simultaneously with administrative and clinical personnel (see McFarlane et al., 1993). McFarlane and colleagues (1993) developed an implementation strategy in which managers and clinicians were targeted simultaneously to ensure that clinicians were appropriately skilled to deliver the intervention and that their work was supported at administrative levels. Local administrators were included in decision making from the beginning of implementation. They were consulted about problems related to administering the clinical program and encouraged to participate in all training sessions. As a result, managers were more supportive of the treatment program. Given the importance of managerial support to delivering effective practices, a new generation of studies is testing interventions that target managers of care rather than only clinicians (e.g., PI: Charles Glisson, Patricia Chamberlain).

Financer. The best mental health intervention is useless without the means to pay for it. More and more, financial considerations influence the ability of patients to access mental health treatments. Whether coverage comes from public funding, private insurance, or out of pocket, demonstrating an intervention's cost-effectiveness is crucial to making it widely available. As a result, Drake et al. (2001) argue that successful implementation may require structural, regulatory, and reimbursement changes, as well as identifying new contracting mechanisms to enhance access (see Chapter 19, this volume, for further discussion about the effects of financing and reimbursement on dissemination/ implementation).

Organizational Level

Health care systems commonly have three additional levels of influence beyond the individual clinician (Ferlie & Shortell, 2002): the practice team, the organization, and the broader care system.

Practice Team. Health care is increasingly delivered not by individual providers but by teams of clinicians. For mental health, a number of evidence-based interventions require the joint efforts of multiple providers, often with varying areas of expertise. Assertive community treatment (ACT), for example, combines psychotherapy with additional services (supported employment, vocational rehabilitation, supported housing) and is delivered by a team of providers that includes mental health clinicians and community-based service representatives. Like other complex interventions, ACT requires each member of the team to perform his or her tasks and to communicate effectively with other team members. Medication management also can require working with a team. The psychiatrist or primary care physician who prescribes the medication is often assisted by other health care professionals, such as nurses, physician's assistants, and care managers who follow up with the patient and gather information about whether change in medications or dosages is necessary. Implementing these and other practices requires a fit between the treatment team and the characteristics of the intervention in areas such as professional representation, patterns of clinical practice, and resources. Given the frequent team delivery of mental health care, approaches to implementation that address issues of collaboration may offer more promise than those focusing only on the individual clinician (Timmermans & Mauck, 2005).

Clinic/Hospital/Organization. In recent years, researchers have begun to identify organizational processes as the key to dissemination and implementation, citing the importance of decision-making coalitions for adopting new practices, bodies that determine whether practices are consistent with organizational objectives, and subcultures that develop within the organization to support implementation (Corrigan et al., 2001; Rosenheck, 2001). We now have substantial knowledge of the organizational facilitators and barriers to implementation. Common facilitators include use of opinion leaders, sometimes called "project champions," typically senior clinicians who become advocates for specific treatments that they believe in (Ellrodt et al., 1997; Ferlie, Wood, & Fitzgerald, 1999; Rubenstein, Mittman,

Yano, & Mulrow, 1999; Wood et al., 1998); management and clinician commitment to change (Ferlie et al., 1999; Holloway, Benesch, & Rush, 2000; Mant, Hicks, Dopson, & Hurley, 1997; McFarlane et al., 1993); understanding the culture and climate of the care setting; involving professionally credible "change agents" who are brought in by an organization to consult with clinicians and managers about the benefits of adopting the new practice; and the involvement of professional groups whose members can be encouraged to implement suggested practices (Eve, Golton, & Hodgkin, 1997; Ferlie et al., 1999).

Organizational barriers to implementation include weak leadership; staffing problems such as turnover of personnel or difficulties in recruiting expert clinicians; policies that require a certain number of billable hours of work (Moser, DeLuca, Rollins, & Bond, 2004), which can reduce opportunities for training and collaboration among staff; and inadequate financial resources, which can prohibit training or increasing staff (Bond et al., 2001). In health care, the organizational unit is typically a hospital department, clinic, or private practice. The organization's mission is to provide medical care for patients. In mental health care, a specialty mental health sector does exist. Mental health care is delivered within hospitals and clinics, but treatment and preventive services are also delivered in schools, through the child welfare system, in jails, at the workplace, and so on. As a result, interventions will be implemented in settings whose highest priority is not mental health care, and the argument to support implementation of an evidence-based treatment may likely rest on the intervention's ability to also affect the primary focus of the setting (e.g., academic achievement in schools, reduced recidivism in correctional facilities, increased productivity at work).

Systems. At the level of systems, knowledge of dissemination and implementation is mostly restricted to the anecdotal evidence gained from stories of individual or organizational efforts to introduce a novel clinical practice. Evaluating the potential of this knowledge requires implementing the approaches more broadly across care delivery systems. These broader implementation initiatives are starting to occur in mental health. Several researchers are testing, for example, the statewide implementation of a promising evidence-based practice. Patricia Chamberlain, for instance, is testing an implementation strategy designed to support uptake of a treatment for children with severe emotional disturbances across the California foster care system. Having established the effectiveness of the intervention, the investigator is comparing two different methods of implementation at the county level to optimize the fit between the intervention and the foster care system. In Oklahoma, a study led by Gregory Aarons is asking what system factors predict successful implementation of an evidence-based intervention for parents and children that is designed to reduce child abuse and neglect.

At the system level, well-resourced centers of technical assistance often become necessary for implementation. As many service systems seek to implement a common program, they work with organizations set up to provide technical assistance to help ensure that the program is being delivered as intended. The developers of a number of effective programs have created service organizations (e.g., MST Services, Inc.; TFC Consultants, Inc.) to provide this technical assistance to individual sites. In addition, service systems must ensure that funding for technical assistance is available as part of the standard operating budget to sustain the implemented program; otherwise, the program is likely to be abandoned by the system.

THEORIES AND MODELS OF DISSEMINATION AND IMPLEMENTATION

Investigators bring multiple conceptual frameworks to their research on integrating evidence-based practices into service settings. These include diffusion of innovations theory, complexity theory, and a variety of other models to guide research on how to improve service quality, encourage individuals to adopt new practices, and promote organizational change. The frameworks discussed next, though not an exhaustive list, are used widely and also hold promise because they are strongly grounded in theories of behavioral and organizational science and are empirically based, reproducible approaches to implementation.

Supporting Uptake: Diffusion of Innovations

Diffusion of innovations, a theoretical approach developed by Everett Rogers, has become popular for disseminating and implementing mental health interventions (see Rogers, 1995). Though the early fieldwork for developing the theory was based on approaches used to spread agricultural interventions, it has since been used in many studies of health care interventions. The model specifies factors that affect whether an innovation will be adopted and used by a specific clinician or system, which include its "relative advantage" over existing practices; its "compatibility" with the existing culture and setting; its "complexity," which could affect understanding and use; its "trialability" or amenability to experimentation; and its "observability" or transparency of the positive results to potential adopters.

In addition to being frequently used by researchers in the field as a guiding theoretical basis for intervention, the model has several specific strengths. It emphasizes the need for fit between an intervention and a treatment setting, it considers straightforwardly that a decision to adopt and use the intervention may require stopping an existing practice, and it assumes that the usability of an intervention should be demonstrated as well as the outcomes that result from its use.

The model has several limitations, however, when applied to mental health. First, the model seems to assume that an innovation is always delivered in the same way. Yet, it is known from studies of implementation (Fixsen, Naoom, Blasé, Friedman, & Wallace, 2005) that local adaptations occur, and it is often unclear how many "salient features" of the intervention will be preserved. Second, this model seems to suggest a static view of the adopter and so neglects the constant change typical of the health care landscape. Third, the model is top-down and assumes that interventions can effectively be imposed on clinicians, a process at odds with professional medicine. Despite these limitations, the model holds promise for the future of implementation, particularly as researchers have begun to align the framework with the need to locally adapt effective interventions to fit with the context in which care is provided (Greenhalgh, Robert, MacFarlane, Bate, & Kyriakidou, 2004).

Improving Service Quality

Several researchers are examining the use of quality improvement (QI) approaches as frameworks for implementing evidence-based practices. Within the mental health field, opinions differ about the meaning of QI. Broadly, it refers to an iterative process in which organizational leaders identify a particular problem within the organization that they would like to solve, diagnose its underlying causes, and attempt improvements through changing the type of care that is delivered and/or the methods of delivery (Hermann, Chan, Zazzali, & Lerner, 2006). Models of quality improvement include continuous quality improvement (CQI), total quality management (TQM), and six-sigma (Hermann et al., 2006). Variations of these approaches abound.

The Veterans Affairs' QUERI (Quality Improvement E R Initiative) is a commonly used QI approach. As Fischer et al. (2000) explain, the Mental Health QUERI is an iterative, recursive process that begins by identifying best practices and defining existing practice within the Veterans Affairs (VA) system. The next step is to implement the best practices as needed. After implementation, the QUERI process requires documenting how the best practices actually improved treatment outcomes and that these treatment outcomes in turn improved VA patients' quality of life (Fischer et al., 2000).

McFarlane, McNary, Dixon, Hornby, and Climett (2001) used a QI model derived from a local effort to implement changes in mental health care—the Fairweather Lodge approach—for implementing family psychoeducation, which argues that families can be trained to improve the social environment in which an individual patient lives, which will in turn improve patient outcomes. In this research, implementation began with assessing the needs of communities and collecting their epidemiologic profiles to determine what treatment programs should be implemented. Then, the implementers held an orientation meeting and consensus-building meetings for clinicians, followed by training and intensive on-site consultation. The third stage of the model allowed clinicians to make local adaptations to the family psychoeducation program. In the final stage, clinicians were offered ongoing supervision and consultation. According to research findings, clinicians viewed the model positively, and the model helped treatment sites address resource limitations.

Moreover, implementation required few incentives and was facilitated by minimizing differences between the new and existing treatment methods (McFarlane et al., 2001).

Promoting Organizational Change

Complexity theory attempts to explain organizational change and assumes that rather than being a finite, directed process, change is constantly occurring through the actions of all members of the organization. Under the theory, organizations are considered to be complex systems in which the constituent parts (individuals) work in concert to achieve an optimal result for the organization. Rather than viewing change as a threat to stability, complexity theory argues that change is a natural function of organizations that requires continual adjustments. Implementation strategies based on complexity theory emphasize collaborative relationships among staff.

Complexity theorists use the metaphor of a jazz band (Miller, McDaniel, Crabtree, & Stange, 2001) to explain how individuals within the effective organization perform their own tasks in concert with others in meeting a shared goal. The metaphor depicts each provider as responsible for discrete tasks, but as always "listening" to the other members of the practice team to determine how their own actions can be most compatible with the other parts of the organization. Complexity theorists argue that the resulting "learning organization" is a more flexible, adaptable body and so better equipped to respond to changes in the surrounding environment, which for mental health care means that the active search for better interventions and practices to improve the quality of care becomes a standard operating procedure of the care organization (for more information on complexity theory, see Anderson, 1999; Brown & Eisenhardt, 1997; Miller et al., 2001).

The chronic care model for depression, for example, centers on physicians, nurses, other health specialists, and administrators working together to provide optimal care for the individual patient. Though each professional has a distinct role, care for the patient comes from the consistent adjustments to practice that each professional makes to meet the needs of the patient while coordinating actions with the roles of collaborators. Assessments of quality practice measure both the pieces of care that were delivered and how they related to one another (Nutting et al., 2007). For example, a depressed patient may be prescribed a course of antidepressant medication, along with psychotherapy. High-quality care would require the provider team not only to monitor the specific component of care they are providing (e.g., the physician to check only adherence to medication) but also to determine how medication dosage may be affecting the patient's active and productive engagement in psychotherapy.

Chou and Bloom (2004) have outlined another promising approach to conceptualizing organizational change. It specifies that change is a staged process that begins with perceiving a need for change, followed by awareness that an exemplary practice is available to the organization, a decision to adopt the practice, and finally implementation. After implementation, resources must be devoted by the organization to sustain the practice change, and over time, the practice becomes institutionalized within the organization (Chou & Bloom, 2004). In developing the model, Chou and Bloom found that formalization, coordination, and centralization in decision making were more important to implementation than was the innovativeness of the practice. Moreover, the type of organization influenced likelihood of implementation, with organizations that capitate (i.e., allocate a specific amount of money per patient for services) facilitating more changes in clinical practice than those who pay for each service individually. This could have resulted from the focus on cost allocation for

a patient across the range of services rather than direct reimbursement of all services independently. Cost was particularly important: Implementation increased for cases in which the new practice helped decrease traditional service costs (Chou & Bloom, 2004).

Models for Intervening With Individuals and Organizations

The "train-the-trainer" approach, which targets individual clinicians, is one popular model for implementing mental health interventions. In this model, an expert in the intervention provides ongoing training and consultation to a local clinician, who becomes the internal "expert" responsible for training others (Bartels et al., 2002). This approach has been used to train, for example, clinicians in geriatric mental health (Bartels et al., 2002), treatment for foster care parents (Chamberlain & Smith, 2005), and nurses providing psychosocial interventions to expectant mothers (Olds, Hill, O'Brien, Racine, & Moritz, 2003). The strategy is similar to creating "local opinion leaders," but instead of relying on the trainers only to promote the interventions, the train-the-trainer model gives trainers the expertise to help others integrate the intervention into their own practice. Thus, it may overcome the sometimes questionable impact of opinion leaders (Oxman et al., 1995).

At the organization level, several investigators are developing interventions to enable mental health organizations better implement new treatment and prevention programs. These "organizational" interventions are intended to help change business practices within the organization (e.g., information systems, organizational climate, staff training programs, financing structures) to complement the clinical "evidence-based practices." The ARC (availability, responsiveness, and continuity) organizational intervention, for example, centers on four guiding principles: Decision making should be mission driven, and implementation should be improvement directed, results oriented, and relationship centered, with particular focus on the relationship that the organization has to the environment in which it is set (e.g., Are the values of the surrounding community consistent with the services that the organization provides? Are there other needs that the community may have that are not met by the organization?). The intervention mainly relies on a "boundary spanner," who functions much as an opinion leader, although the purpose is to help the organization, rather than an individual clinician, to change its practices (Glisson, 2002). The boundary spanner helps with a range of issues specific to each stage of the organizational change process and especially facilitates a "fit" between the evidence-based practice and the practice setting. Rather than manipulating the practice to fit the setting, the boundary spanner helps to create a work environment in which the practice can be delivered (Glisson, 2002).

Components of the ARC model include participatory decision making, team building, continuous quality improvement, job redesign, and other positive team communication strategies. The ARC model has been applied successfully to the child welfare and juvenile justice systems, and it is currently being tested in a study implementing multisystemic therapy, an evidence-based mental health practice for adolescents within child welfare and juvenile justice systems across the state of Tennessee (Glisson, 2002).

The community development team (CDT) is an organizational strategy that helps go beyond the "early adopters" in order to encourage resistant organizations to adopt new practices. It is currently being used to help the state of California adopt evidence-based practices within its public mental health system (http://www.apa.org/pi/cyf/california.pdf). Guided by social learning theory, the approach is being used to support multiple sites in reaching common goals, such as the implementation of an EBP. The team blends clinical training and supervision specific to a practice and meets periodically throughout the year to handle all aspects of implementation (e.g., financing, training, leadership, and supervision) (APA, 2006). The CDT also has been used in California to implement functional family therapy, and it is now being evaluated in a randomized trial to test countywide implementation of multidimensional treatment foster care (PI: Patricia Chamberlain).

Individual and Organizational Readiness to Change

As previously mentioned, effective implementation depends on the fit between the particular practice being implemented and characteristics of the organization (Racine, 2006). Because achieving this fit typically requires adaptations at both individual and organizational levels, researchers have investigated "readiness to change" as a predictor of successful implementation.

At the individual level, behavioral health researchers commonly use Prochaska and DiClemente's "stages of change" model to conceptualize the readiness to change practices (Prochaska, DiClemente, & Norcross, 1992). This model, also known as the transtheoretical model of change, specifies five stages of individual change: precontemplation, contemplation, preparation, action, and maintenance. Precontemplation assumes that an individual has not yet identified a particular need to change behavior. Contemplation suggests that the individual has recognized that change might be necessary but has not yet prepared to make a change. The action stage suggests that an individual is ready to make the particular change. The maintenance stage represents individuals who have made a change and are attempting to sustain the new practice over time.

Researchers have begun developing measures to assess the readiness and receptivity of mental health clinicians to implementing and using EBPs in general. Aarons (2004), for example, has developed an Evidence Based Practice Attitude Scale (EBPAS) that measures (a) the appeal of the EBPs to clinicians, (b) the likelihood of the clinician adopting the EBP given the use requirements, (c) the clinician's openness to new practices, and (d) the perceived divergence of the EBP from usual practices. In testing the scale among a diverse group of clinicians, Aarons also found that the majority of clinicians do not have doctoral-level training, a clear difference from the medical care sector that might be expected to influence the uptake of evidence-based approaches (Aarons, 2004).

At the organization level, readiness for change is defined as a comprehensive attitude that is influenced by the content of the change that is desired, the process in which the content is integrated into the organization, and the characteristics of the organization itself and collectively reflects the degree to which an organization is cognitively and emotionally inclined to alter the status quo (Clark, 2003). Though some research has assessed organizational change in mental health (e.g., to develop a readiness measure for use in schools) (PI: Hoagwood), work in this area is just beginning (Computer Retrieval of Information From Scientific Projects [CRISP] database, www.crisp.cit.nih.gov).

CHALLENGES FOR THE MENTAL HEALTH FIELD

Though much progress has been made in disseminating and implementing mental health research, multiple challenges remain that the field must meet to optimize the use of scientific knowledge in clinical practice.

Challenges of Intervention Development

The linear nature of intervention development creates a challenge for implementing interventions in practical settings. Traditionally, intervention development begins with identifying mechanisms that potentially modify particular behavioral or biochemical processes that underlie symptoms of a mental disorder. After these key "mechanisms of action" have been identified, intervention developers test them in a tightly controlled setting with patients who must meet strict criteria in order to participate. This type of efficacy study usually excludes patients with medical or substance abuse problems, and the intervention is delivered by highly skilled clinicians in well-resourced care settings. Assuming positive outcomes from the efficacy study, an effectiveness study is used to test the intervention with a larger and more diverse population. This study can involve multiple sites, with many investigators, and the goal is to provide a definitive answer about the benefit of an intervention relative to some type of "care as usual."

In both efficacy and effectiveness studies, the outcomes studied are individual patient outcomes. Despite the importance of the intervention context for disseminating and implementing effective practices, studies do not typically examine potential contextual influences, such as the capacity of mental health care settings to deliver the intervention, the skill levels of clinicians, or the availability of other essential resources. As a result, mental health professionals rarely have enough information from intervention development and testing to know how well the intervention fits into their routine clinical practice, how they might need to adapt it, or even how to attempt to use it. As others have persuasively argued, the field cannot continue to assume that efficacy tests translate to real-world usefulness (see Hoagwood et al., 2001).

The mental health field can take several steps to better connect intervention research with service systems and practices. First, interventions can be developed taking into consideration the characteristics of practice settings and of the individuals who typically seek care. According to the deployment-based model for intervention development (Weisz et al., 2004), interventions should be developed within the clinical settings in which they ultimately will be used rather than waiting until the efficacy of an intervention is established in a setting that may be atypical of service delivery. Other researchers have integrated principles from the field of marketing to articulate models of intervention development that incorporate "end users" as part of intervention development (Sandler et al., 2005).

To provide effective psychosocial interventions, clinicians need opportunities to become familiar with the particular treatment model and to develop associated skills, such as the ability to provide therapy according to the core components of the intervention. Clinicians must receive detailed information, such as how to deliver therapy sessions of the appropriate frequency and duration, and about which treatments may be appropriate for the populations who visit their clinic.

Second, interventions need to include more information about the sites in which investigators test the interventions, and the effects that these site characteristics have on implementation and treatment outcomes should be studied more systematically. With minimal impact on the study design, investigators can collect data to describe the resources, organizational structure, skills, and abilities of clinicians in the delivery environment. Ultimately, however, unraveling the complexities of setting influences will require experiments that, for example, methodically vary the training models used to prepare interventionists and the settings of delivery to determine if treatment effects differ depending on characteristics of the care setting.

Third, intervention studies can better identify "core components" of complex interventions to help clinicians make decisions about adapting interventions to meet their needs. Many of the evidence-based programs consist of multiple components that have been bundled and tested together. For example, the ACT program covers a range of services, including case management, psychiatric treatment, substance abuse services, family support and education, community integration, and others. Each of these components contains subcomponents. Usually, studies have not been conducted to determine whether all components and subcomponents must be delivered to replicate the treatment effect or whether some are more essential than others and, if so, under which kinds of conditions (Gold et al., 2003). Yet, when programs are implemented in typical care settings, clinicians often adapt them to fit the needs of the local practice, resulting in a program that can differ substantially from the one that was actually tested. Given that science rarely is conducted to identify the "active ingredient" or combination of ingredients that account for treatment effects, science provides little guidance to clinicians about how best to adapt a practice to meet their needs. More studies are needed that disaggregate intervention components in order to test which components either alone or in combination produce the desired effects—and for which populations and under which practice conditions.

Challenges of Research Design

The mental health field would benefit from strengthening existing research measures and methods. First, more studies should include *measures of intervention fidelity*, and better measures are needed to assess it. Researchers have argued (e.g., Falloon et al., 2005; Olds et al., 2003; Salyers et al., 2003) that maintaining fidelity is critical to ensuring that optimal patient outcomes can be achieved. In recent years, many developers of research-tested mental health interventions have created fidelity scales to measure how consistently the implementers of an intervention adhered to its principles. Unfortunately, too few studies show a relation between high fidelity scores and highest achievable outcomes. Questions remain, therefore, about whether the practices were appropriately designed and delivered and whether the measures are capable of identifying the "core ingredients" essential to producing individual outcomes. For example, the Dartmouth Assertive Community Treatment Scale (DACTS) for ACT rates teams along three dimensions (human resources, organizational boundaries, and nature of services) on a scale from 1 (not implemented) to 5 (fully implemented). The items focus mainly on structural components (e.g., small caseload, team approach, staff capacity, frequency of contact) and less on the process of care, which may be as critical or even more critical to outcomes (Salyers et al., 2003). In order to accumulate better guidance for practitioners about how to best deliver interventions, more research is needed to develop fidelity scales, and more intervention studies need to include these measures in their designs.

The field also needs additional *measures of organization readiness* to determine whether an organization is ready to implement new practices and the changes that may be needed at the organizational level to support delivery of the intervention. Other fields such as business, medicine, and education (Clark, 2003) have begun to develop such measures, and so it may be useful to explore the possibility of adapting these for use in mental health care settings in order to improve the fit between interventions and practice settings.

Implementation of mental health practices typically involves individual patients, clinicians, and family members, as well as provider teams, organizations, and even broader systems. Thus, improving research dissemination and implementation will require using study designs and statistical methodologies, such as *hierarchical (multilevel) modeling*, that allow for identifying complex interactions among levels of care that affect treatment outcomes (Ferlie & Shortell, 2002; Hatgis et al., 2001).

Finally, the mental health field needs a *system of measurement* with a core set of variables and associated measures that are appropriate for use in diverse mental health systems in order to assess clinical processes and outcomes of interventions across research studies. Variations in clinical settings, providers, and individuals with mental illness are matched by variation in the research data gathered. As a result, it is often impossible to generalize findings of individual studies to broader service systems. Advancing dissemination and the use of evidence-based practices requires improving the infrastructure of service systems to better determine the impact of treatment on patients and the characteristics of service settings that tend to moderate these outcomes. Whereas some care settings, such as Veterans Affairs, Kaiser Permanente, and Group Health Cooperative, have extensive information systems, many others have little capacity to assess the systematic impact of treatment on their patient populations. Though more systems, including state-level systems, are improving the information technology used to monitor outcomes (Hodges & Wotring, 2004), more data infrastructure is needed so that individual treatment sites are able to determine whether the care they are delivering is improving the outcomes of their consumers. These improvements may require more resources to build information systems, more training of personnel to manage and analyze the data, and an entry system that enables for the collection of data during the practice visit.

MEETING THE CHALLENGES: CURRENT DISSEMINATION AND IMPLEMENTATION INITIATIVES

The National Advisory Mental Health Council (2006) issued a recent report, *The Road Ahead: Research Partnerships to Transform Mental Health Services,* that reinforced the tremendous need to improve the science of implementation in order to take better advantage of the many advances in mental health care. The report recommends that the field "should determine the mechanisms underlying the successful implementation of evidence-based interventions in varying service settings with culturally and ethnically diverse populations" (National Advisory Mental Health Council, 2006, p. 14).

Consistent with this call, both public and private sectors are undertaking efforts to narrow the gap between research and practice. For example, the National Institute of Mental Health has joined the National Cancer Institute and six other institutes of the National Institutes of Health in a research agenda to improve the knowledge base underlying dissemination and implementation research. It calls for research in these areas:

- Analysis of factors that influence the creation, packaging, transmission, and reception of valid mental health research knowledge
- Experimental studies to test the effectiveness of individual, organizational, and systemic dissemination strategies
- Studies of efforts to implement treatments or clinical procedures of demonstrated efficacy into existing care systems
- Studies of the capacity of specific care delivery settings, such as primary care, schools, and community mental health settings, to incorporate dissemination or implementation efforts
- Studies on the fidelity of implementation, including identifying the intervention and implementation components essential for realizing desired outcomes and developing associated fidelity assessments with greater potential to predict the outcomes of implementation
- Studies testing the utility of various dissemination strategies for service delivery systems targeting rural, minority, and other underserved populations (NIH, 2006)

In addition, the Center for Mental Health Services (CMHS), one of the components of Substance Abuse and Mental Health Services Administration of the U.S. Department of Health and Human Services, has launched a $90 million initiative that aims to transform state mental health services through encouraging changes to systems and the implementation of innovations (http://www.samhsa.gov/news/newsreleases/050928_StateIncentive Grants.htm). One major element of each state's comprehensive plan is to implement effective mental health interventions, and consistent with this program, state agencies have embarked on the widespread implementation of evidence-based practices. Many other initiatives have arisen from federal, state, and local public mental health systems, as well as from private service systems and foundations (see Chambers, Ringeisen, & Hickman, 2005, for more detail).

To support adult mental health, the Robert Wood Johnson Foundation and the Center for Mental Health Services, in collaboration with private foundations, initiated the U.S. Evidence-Based Practices Project. This effort began with the selection of six adult evidence-based practices to be implemented over a 5- to 6-year period in three phases: development of implementation packages (referred to as "toolkits"), toolkit pilot testing, and evaluation of toolkits across eight states (Mueser, Torrey, Lynde, Singer, & Drake, 2003). The implementation approach was aimed at multiple stakeholders within the system and was informed by the individual and organizational change literature, focus groups, and researchers with experience in implementation. It focused primarily on facilitators and barriers identified at all levels of the system and on crafting strategies to promote use of the evidence-based practices (Mueser et al., 2003).

Clearly, the opportunity has come for research to lead to significant improvements in health and mental health care practice. The omnipresence of terms such as *evidence-based practice, implementation, technology transfer, diffusion, implementation,* and *dissemination* has raised awareness and motivated research and action agendas that should quicken the path of behavioral science from the laboratory to the local health care setting. The danger remains, however, that the field will move too fast and perhaps assume that it knows how to disseminate and implement evidence-based practices before truly understanding how complex these processes are. The same scientific approaches that have been used to carefully accumulate findings from basic and applied research must now be taken to discover how to systematically disseminate research findings and implement clinical interventions in order to improve the use of evidence-based practices and the quality of mental health care.

NOTE

1. *Efficacy* is defined as the extent to which a specific intervention, procedure, regimen, or service produces a beneficial effect under ideal conditions. *Effectiveness* is defined as the extent to which a specific intervention, procedure, regimen, or service, when deployed in the field, does what it is intended to do for a defined population (Last, 1988).

REFERENCES

Aarons, G. A. (2004). Mental health provider attitudes toward adoption of evidence-based practice: The Evidence-Based Practice Attitude Scale. *Mental Health Services Research, 6*(2), 61–72.

Allery, L. A., Owen, P. A., & Robling, M. R. (1997). Why general practitioners and consultants change their clinical practice: A critical incident study. *British Medical Journal, 314,* 870.

American Psychological Association (APA). (2006). *California's progress adopting evidence-based practices within the public mental health system.* Retrieved July 11, 2006, from http://www.apa.org/pi/cyf/california.pdf

Anderson, P. (1999). Complexity theory and organizational science. *Organization Science, 10*(3), 216–232.

Backer, T. E., Liberman, R. P., & Kuehnel, T. G. (1986). Dissemination and adoption of innovative psychosocial interventions. *Journal of Consulting and Clinical Psychology, 54*(1), 111–118.

Balas, E. A., & Boren, S. A. (2000). *Yearbook of medical informatics.* Amsterdam: Schattauer.

Bartels, S. J., Dums, A. R., Oxman, T. E., Schneider, L. S., Arean, P. A., Alexopoulos, G. S., et al. (2002). Evidence-based practices in geriatric mental health care. *Psychiatric Services, 53*(11), 1419–1431.

Bauchner, H., & Simpson, L. (1998). Specific issues related to developing, disseminating, and implementing pediatric practice guidelines for physicians, patients, families, and other stakeholders. *Health Services Research, 33*(4), 1161–1177.

Berger, P. L., & Luckmann, T. (1966). *The social construction of reality: A treatise in the sociology of knowledge.* Harmondsworth, UK: Penguin.

Bero, L., Grilli, R., Grimshaw, J., Harvey, E., Oxman, A., & Thomson, M. A. (1998). Closing the gap between research and practice: An overview of systematic reviews of interventions to promote implementation of research findings by health professionals. In A. Haines & A. Donald (Eds.), *Getting research findings into practice* (pp. 27–35). London: BMJ Books.

Bond, G. R., Becker, D. R., Drake, R. E., Rapp, C. A., Meisler, N., Lehman, A. F., et al. (2001). Implementing supported employment as an evidence-based practice. *Psychiatric Services, 52*(3), 313–322.

Brown, S. L., & Eisenhardt, K. M. (1997). The art of continuous change: Linking complexity theory and time-paced evolution in relentlessly shifting organizations. *Administrative Science Quarterly, 42*, 1–34.

Chamberlain, P., & Smith, D. K. (2005). Multidimensional treatment foster care: A community solution for boys and girls referred from juvenile justice. In E. D. Hibbs & P. S. Jensen (Eds.), *Psychosocial treatments for child and adolescent disorders: Empirically based strategies for clinical practice* (2nd ed., pp. 557–573). Washington, DC: American Psychological Association.

Chambers, D. A., Ringeisen, H., & Hickman, E. E. (2005). Federal, state, and foundation initiatives around evidence-based practices for child and adolescent mental health. *Child and Adolescent Clinics of North America, 14*(2), 307–327.

Chou, A. F., & Bloom, J. R. (2004, April). *Predictors of decisional participation and implications on treatment selection and health outcomes for women with breast cancer.* Paper presented at the International Conference on Organizational Behaviour in Health Care, Banff, Canada.

Clark, S. W. (2003). *The development of an integrated measure of readiness for change instrument and its application on ASC/PK.* Thesis, Air Force Institute of Technology, Dayton, OH.

Corrigan, P. W. (1998). Building teams and programs for effective rehabilitation. *Psychiatric Quarterly, 69*(3), 193–209.

Corrigan, P. W., Steiner, L., McCracken, S. G., Blaser, B., & Barr, M. (2001). Strategies for disseminating evidence-based practices to staff who treat people with serious mental illness. *Psychiatric Services, 52*, 1598–1606.

Davis, D. A., Thomson, M. A., Oxman, A. D., & Haynes, R. B. (1995). Changing physician performance: A systematic review of the effect of continuing medical education strategies. *Journal of the American Medical Association, 274*(9), 700–705.

Dixon, L., Lyles, A., Scott, J., Lehman, A., Postrado, L., Goldman, H., et al. (1999). Services to families of adults with schizophrenia: From treatment recommendations to dissemination. *Psychiatric Services, 50*, 233–238.

Drake, R. E., Goldman, H. H., Leff, H. S., Lehman, A. F., Dixon, L., Mueser, J. T., et al. (2001). Implementing evidence-based practices in routine mental health service settings. *Psychiatric Services, 52*(2), 179–182.

Drake, R. E., McHugo, G. J., Leff, S., & Latimer, E. (2004). What is evidence? *Child and Adolescent Psychiatric Clinics of North America, 13*(4), 717–728.

Dulcan, M. K. (2005). Practitioner perspectives on evidence-based practice. *Child and Adolescent Psychiatric Clinics of North America, 14*(2), 225–240.

Ellrodt, G., Cook, D. J., Lee, J., Cho, M., Hunt, D., & Weingarten, S. (1997). Evidence-based disease management. *Journal of the American Medical Association, 278*(20), 1687–1692.

Eve, R., Golton, I., & Hodgkin, P. (1997). *Learning from FACTS: Lessons for the Framework for Appropriate Care Throughout Sheffield (FACTS) project.* Sheffield, UK: School of Health and Related Research, University of Sheffield.

Falloon, I. R. H., Economou, M., Palli, A., Malm, U., Mizuno, M., Murakami, M., et al. (2005). The Clinical Strategies Implementation Scale to measure implementation of treatment in mental health services. *Psychiatric Services, 56*(12), 1584–1590.

Ferlie, E., & Shortell, S. (2002). Improving the quality of health care in the UK and USA: A framework for change. *Milbank Quarterly, 79*(2), 281–315.

Ferlie, E., Wood, M., & Fitzgerald, L. (1999). Some limits to evidence-based medicine: A case study from elective orthopedics. *Quality in Health Care, 8*(2), 99–107.

Fischer, E. P., Marder, S. R., Smith, G. R., Owen, R. R., Rubenstein, L., Hedrick, S. C., et al. (2000). Quality enhancement research initiative in mental health. *Medical Care, 38*(6), I-70–I-81.

Fitzgerald, L., Ferlie, E., Wood, M., & Hawkins, C. (1999). Evidence into practice? An exploratory analysis of the interpretation of evidence. In A. Mark & S. Dopson (Eds.), *Organisational behaviour in health care*. London: Macmillan.

Fixsen, D. L., Naoom, S. F., Blasé, K. A., Friedman, R. M., & Wallace, F. (2005). *Implementation research: A synthesis of the literature.* Tampa: University of South Florida.

Flynn, L. (2005). Family perspectives on evidence-based practice. *Child and Adolescent Psychiatric Clinics of North America, 14*(2), 217–224.

Freidson, E. (1993). How dominant are the professions? In F. W. Hafferty & J. B. McKinley (Eds.), *The changing medical profession* (pp. 54–68). New York: Oxford University Press.

Glisson, C. (2002). The organizational context of children's mental health services. *Clinical Child and Family Psychology Review, 5*(4), 233–253.

Gold, P. B., Meiser, N., Santos, A. B., Keleher, J., Becker, D. R., Knoedler, W. H., et al. (2003). The program of assertive community treatment: Implementation and dissemination of an evidence-based model of community-based care for persons with severe and persistent mental illness. *Cognitive and Behavioral Practice, 10*, 290–303.

Greenhalgh, T., Robert, G., MacFarlane, F., Bate, P., & Kyriakidou, O. (2004). Diffusion of innovations in service organizations: Systematic review and recommendations. *The Milbank Quarterly, 82*(4), 581.

Griffin, M. A., Mathieu, J. E., & Jacobs, R. R. (2001). Perceptions of work contexts: Disentangling influences at multiple levels of analysis. *Journal of Occupational and Organizational Psychology, 74*, 563–579.

Guyatt, G., & Rennie, D. (2002). *Users' guide to the medical literature: A manual for evidence-based clinical practice.* Chicago: Evidence-Based Medicine Working Group, American Medical Association, AMA Press.

Hatgis, C., Addis, M. E., Zaslavsky, I., Jacob, K., Krasnow, A. D., DuBois, D., et al. (2001). Cross-fertilization versus transmission: Recommendations for developing a bidirectional approach to psychotherapy dissemination research. *Applied & Preventive Psychology, 10*, 37–49.

Hawley, K. M., & Weisz, J. R. (2002). Increasing the relevance of evidence-based treatment review to practitioners and consumers. *Clinical Psychology: Science and Practice, 9*(2), 225–230.

Haynes, R. B. (1990). Loose connections between peer-reviewed clinical journals and clinical practice. *Annals of Internal Medicine, 113*(9), 724–728.

Hermann, R. C., Chan, J. A., Zazzali, J. L., & Lerner, D. (2006). Aligning measurement-based quality improvement with implementation of evidence-based practices. *Administrative Policy on Mental Health & Mental Health Services Research, 18* (Suppl. 1), 31–38.

Hoagwood, K., Burns, B. J., Kiser, L., Ringeisen, H., & Schoenwald, S. K. (2001). Evidence-based practice in child and adolescent mental health services. *Psychiatric Services, 52*(9), 1179–1189.

Hodges, K., & Wotring, J. (2004). The role of monitoring outcomes in initiating implementation of evidence-based treatments at the state level. *Psychiatric Services, 55*(4), 396–400.

Holloway, R. G., Benesch, C., & Rush, S. R. (2000). Stroke prevention: Narrowing the evidence-practice gap. *Neurology, 54*(10), 1899–1906.

Hornik, R. C. (Ed.). (2002). *Public health communication: Evidence for behavior change.* Mahwah, NJ: Lawrence Erlbaum.

Howitt, A., & Armstrong, D. (1999). Implementing evidence based medicine in general practice: Audit and qualitative study of antithrombotic treatment for atrial fibrillation. *British Medical Journal, 318*(7194), 1324–1327.

Huby, G., & Fairhurst, K. (1998). *How do general practitioners use evidence? A study in the context of Lothian Health policy and practitioners' use of statin drugs: Final report to CSO, August, 1998.* Edinburgh, UK: Primary Care Research Group, Department of General Practice, University of Edinburgh.

Insel, T. I., & Scolnick, E. M. (2006). Cure therapeutics and strategic prevention: Raising the bar for mental health research. *Molecular Psychiatry, 11,* 11–17.

Kerner, J. F., Guirguis-Blake, J., Hennessy, K. D., Brounstein, P. J., Vinson, C., Schwartz, R. H., et al. (2005). Translating research into improved outcomes in comprehensive cancer control. *Cancer Causes and Control, 16*(Suppl. 1), 27–40.

King, T. E. (2002). Racial disparities in clinical trials. *New England Journal of Medicine, 346*(18), 1400–1402.

Last, J. M. (1988). *A dictionary of epidemiology* (2nd ed.). Oxford, England: Oxford University Press.

Leeds, A. A. (1979). The future of communication in psychopharmacology. *Neuro-Psychopharmacology, 3,* 125–131.

Liberman, R. P., & Eckman, T. A. (1989). Dissemination of skills training modules to psychiatric facilities: Overcoming obstacles to the utilisation of a rehabilitation innovation. *British Journal of Psychiatry, 155*(Suppl. 5), 117–122.

Lieberman, J. A., Stroup, T. S., McEvoy, J. P., Swartz, M. S., Rosenheck, R. A., Perkins, D. O., et al. (2005). Effectiveness of antipsychotic drugs in patients with chronic schizophrenia. *New England Journal of Medicine, 353,* 1209–1223.

Mannheim, K. (1936). *Ideology and utopia: An introduction to the sociology of knowledge* (L. Wirth & E. Shils, Trans.). London: Routledge & Kegan Paul.

Mant, J., Hicks, N., Dopson, S., & Hurley, P. (1997) *Uptake of research findings into clinical practice: A controlled study of the impact of a brief external intervention on the use of corticosteroids in pre-term labour.* Oxford, UK: Division of Public Health & Primary Care.

McColl, A., Smith, H., White, P., & Field, J. (1998). General practitioners' perceptions of the route to evidence-based medicine: A questionnaire survey. *British Medical Journal, 316*(7128), 361–365.

McFarlane, W. R., Dunne, E., Lukens, E., Deakens, S., Horen, B., Newmark, M., et al. (1993). From research to clinical practice: Dissemination of New York state's family psychoeducation project. *Hospital of Community Psychiatry, 44,* 265–270.

McFarlane, W. R., McNary, S., Dixon, L., Hornby, H., & Climett, E. (2001). Predictors of dissemination of family psychoeducation in community mental health centers in Maine and Illinois. *Psychiatric Services, 52,* 935–942.

McKay, M. M., & Bannon, W., Jr. (2004). Engaging families in child mental health services. *Child and Adolescent Psychiatric Clinics of North America, 13*(4), 905–922.

McKay, M. M., Hibbert, R., & Hoagwood, K. (2004). Integrating evidence-based engagement interventions into "real world" child mental health settings. *Brief Treatment and Crisis Intervention, 4*(2), 177–186.

Miller, W. L., McDaniel, R. R., Jr., Crabtree, B. F., & Stange, K. C. (2001). Practice jazz: Understanding variation in family practices using complexity science. *Journal of Family Practice, 50*(10), 872–878.

Moser, L. L., DeLuca, N. L., Rollins, A. L., & Bond, G. R. (2004). Implementing evidence based psychosocial practices: Lessons learned from statewide implementation of two practices. *CNS Spectrums, 912,* 926–936, 942.

Mueser, K. T., Torrey, W. C., Lynde, D., Singer, P., & Drake, R. E. (2003). Implementing evidence-based practices for people with severe mental illness. *Behavior Modification, 27*(3), 387–411.

Mulkay, M. J. (1979). *Science and the sociology of knowledge.* London: Allen & Unwin.

National Advisory Mental Health Council, Workgroup on Services Research and Clinical Epidemiology. (2006). *The road ahead: Research partnerships to transform mental health services.* Retrieved November 28, 2006, from http://www.nimh.nih.gov/roadahead.pdf

National Institutes of Health (NIH). (2006). *Program announcement (PAR-07–086): Dissemination and Implementation Research in Health (R01).* Retrieved November 28, 2006, from http://grants.nih.gov/grants/guide/pa-files/PAR-07-086.html

Newcomer, J. W., Nasrallah, H. A., & Loebel, A. D. (2004). The Atypical Antipsychotic Therapy and Metabolic Issues National Survey: Practice patterns and knowledge of psychiatrists: Physician awareness and treatment approaches to metabolic dysregulation with atypical antipsychotics. *Journal of Clinical Psychopharmacology, 24*(Suppl. 1), S1–S6.

Nierenberg, A. A., Fava, M., Trivedi, M. H., Wisniewski, S. T., Thase, M. E., McGrath, P. J., et al. (2006). A comparison of lithium and T3 augmentation following two failed medication treatments for depression: A STAR*D report. *American Journal of Psychiatry, 163,* 1519–1530.

Nutting, P. A., Gallagher, K. M., Riley, K., White, S., Dietrich, A. J., & Dickinson, W. P. (2007). Implementing a depression improvement intervention in five health care organizations: Experience from the RESPECT-Depression trial. *Administration and Policy in Mental Health, 34*(2), 127–137.

Olds, D. L., Hill, P. L., O'Brien, R., Racine, D., & Moritz, P. (2003). Taking preventive intervention to scale: The nurse-family partnership. *Cognitive and Behavioral Practice, 10*(4), 278–290.

Oxman, A. D., Thomson, M. A., Davis, D. A., & Haynes, R. B. (1995). No magic bullets: A systematic review of 102 trials of interventions to improve professional practice. *Canadian Medical Association Journal, 153*, 1423–1431.

Prescott, K., Lloyd, M., Douglas, H. R., Haines, A., Humphrey, C., Rosenthal, J., et al. (1997). Promoting clinically effective practice: General practitioners' awareness of sources of research evidence. *Family Practice, 14*(4), 320–323.

President's New Freedom Commission on Mental Health. (2003). *Achieving the promise: Transforming mental health care in America: Final report* (DHHS Pub. No. SMA-03–3832). Rockville, MD: U.S. Department of Health and Human Services.

Prochaska, J. O., DiClemente, C. C., & Norcross, J. C. (1992). In search of how people change. *American Psychologist, 47*, 1102–1104.

Racine, D. P. (2006). Reliable effectiveness: a theory on sustaining and replicating worthwhile interventions. *Administration and Policy in Mental Health, 33*(3), 356–387.

Robertson, N., Baker, R., & Hearnshaw, H. (1996). Changing the clinical behaviour of doctors: A psychological framework. *Quality in Health Care, 5*, 51–54.

Rogers, E. M. (1995). *Diffusion of innovations* (4th ed.). New York: Free Press.

Rosenheck, R. A. (2001). Organizational process: A missing link between research and practice. *Psychiatric Services, 52*(12), 1607–1612.

Rothman, A. J., & Salovey, P. (1997). Shaping perceptions to motivate healthy behavior: The role of message framing. *Psychological Bulletin, 121*(1), 3–19.

Rubenstein, L. V., Mittman, B. S., Yano, E. M., & Mulrow, C. D. (1999). From understanding health care provider behavior to improving health care: The QUERI framework for quality improvement. *Medical Care, 38*(6), I129–I141.

Sackett, D. L., Rosenberg, W. M. C., Gray, J. A. M., Haynes, R. B., & Richardson, W. S. (1996). Evidence-based medicine: What it is and what it isn't. *British Medical Journal, 312*, 71–72.

Salyers, M. P., Bond, G. R., Teague, G. B., Cox, J. F., Smith, M. E., Hicks, M. L., et al. (2003). Is it ACT yet? Real-world examples of evaluating the degree of implementation for assertive community treatment. *Journal of Behavioral Health Services & Research, 30*(3), 304–320.

Sandler, I. M., Ostrom, A., Binter, M. J., Ayers, T., Wolchik, S., & Smith-Daniels, V. (2005). Developing effective prevention services for the real world: A prevention service development model. *American Journal of Community Psychology, 35*, 127–142.

Schoenwald, S. K., & Henggeler, S. W. (2002). Services research and family based treatment. In H. Liddle, G. Diamond, R. Levant, J. Bray, & D. Santisteban (Eds.), *Family psychology intervention science*. Washington, DC: American Psychological Association.

Schoenwald, S. K., & Hoagwood, K. (2001). Effectiveness, transportability, and dissemination of interventions: What matters when? *Psychiatric Services, 52*(9), 1190–1197.

Sechrest, L., Backer, T. E., Rogers, E. M., Campbell, T. F., & Grady, M. L. (Eds.). (1994). *Effective dissemination of clinical and health information*. Rockville, MD: U.S. Department of Health and Human Services.

Tanenbaum, S. J. (2005). Evidence-based practice as mental health policy: Three controversies and a caveat. *Health Affairs, 24*(1), 163–173.

Timmermans, S., & Mauck, A. (2005). The promises and pitfalls of evidence-based practice. *Health Affairs, 24*(1), 18–28.

U.S. Public Health Service. (1999). *Mental health: A report of the Surgeon General.* Washington, DC: Author.

Weisz, J. R., Sandler, I. N., & Durlak, J. A. (2005). Promoting and protecting youth mental health through evidence-based prevention and treatment. *American Psychologist, 60*(6), 628–648.

Weisz, J. R., Weersing, V. R., & Henggeler, S. W. (2004). Jousting with straw men: Comment on Westen, Novotny, and Thompson-Brenner (2004). *Psychological Bulletin, 131*(3), 418–426.

Westen, D., & Bradley, R. (2005). Empirically supported complexity: Rethinking evidence-based practice in psychotherapy. *Current Directions in Psychological Science, 14*(5), 266–271.

Westen, D., Novotny, C. M., & Thompson-Brenner, H. J. (2004). The empirical status of empirically supported psychotherapies: Assumptions, findings, and reporting in controlled clinical trials. *Psychological Bulletin, 130*(4), 631–663.

Wood, M., Ferlie, E., & Fitzgerald, L. (1998). *Achieving change in clinical practice: Scientific, organisational and behavioural processes.* Warwick, UK: University of Warwick, CCSC.

CHAPTER 23

Behavioral Science in the Military

JANICE H. LAURENCE

Half of the U.S. discretionary budget for 2006, $419 billion, was allocated to the Department of Defense (DoD). Budget authorities for other major agencies pale in comparison. For example, the budget for the Department of Health and Human Services was a distant second at only $69 billion (cf. Office of Management and Budget, 2005). Personnel costs account for over half (55%) of the Defense budget (Department of Defense, 2006b). As of fiscal year (FY) 2006, there were over 2.2 million military members (including members on active duty and those in the Reserves and National Guard) and more than 650,000 civilian employees. This personnel count is modest relative to the troop levels garnered before conscription (i.e., the draft) ended in 1973, but it is impressive nonetheless.

With Defense's reliance on a sizable workforce to accomplish increasingly complex missions, the need for behavioral science looms large. Yet despite this need, the relationship between behavioral science and the military is underdeveloped. This chapter highlights ways in which behavioral science has been and can continue to be of benefit to the military. In addition to describing fruitful applications and other contributions, the chapter presents some of the barriers to effective partnerships between behavioral science and the military along with suggested remedies. Finally, some future challenges faced by Defense are presented with the hope of piquing the interest and talents of behavioral scientists toward their resolution.

THE DEMAND FOR UNDERSTANDING HUMAN BEHAVIOR

The Department of Defense is our nation's largest employer. Defense personnel serve in thousands of locations, at home and abroad, on land and at sea. They engage in or support missions that include warfare, peacekeeping, humanitarian assistance, evacuation, and homeland defense. Enlisted members and officers of the Army, Navy, Marine Corps, and Air Force are organized into teams and

---

AUTHOR'S NOTE: The views and opinions are those of the author and do not represent the Department of Defense, unless otherwise stated.

hierarchical units, not just in the modern infantry and lethal combat specialties but also in hundreds of diverse, technologically sophisticated support and service occupations. Recruiting, training, socializing, assigning, employing, deploying, motivating, rewarding, maintaining, managing, integrating, retaining, and transitioning the Defense workforce relies to no small extent on behavioral science.

Behavioral science is crucial to preparing members of the military workforce for both traditional and irregular warfare. It can support the military in adapting to the evolving challenges of our global, information-age operating environment. What types of people, with what abilities and characteristics, make good soldiers, sailors, Marines, or airmen? What motivates people to enlist, perform their duties, and continue to serve in the military? What training and organizational practices contribute to military effectiveness? Indeed, the military provides fertile ground for behavioral science research and application.

Major Contributions

The behavioral and social sciences, with their emphasis on systematically examining the complexity and intricacies of human behavior, are well suited to tackle the domain of national security (cf. Brandon, 2002). Psychology offered the science of intelligence testing and clinical assessment during World Wars I and II (Society for Military Psychology, 2005a, 2005b). But since those early days, and because of its usefulness in planning for an all-volunteer force (AVF) in 1973, economics has become the lead social science in military policy. Without the power of the draft to legally direct people into military service, economists introduced rational compensation policy to entice people into making this career choice. Human behavior often defies the principles of economics,

however, and so relying on economics alone is not sufficient for understanding and motivating enlistment. What economists see as irrationality may instead be "lawful" if one considers rewards and incentives other than money as responsible for shaping and maintaining behavior. Thus, the perspectives of economists as well as psychologists, sociologists, cultural anthropologists, political scientists, public administrators, and health scientists are often sought to provide the rich, multidisciplinary approaches needed to deal with the complex situations and organizations of the U.S. military. The following section highlights just a few behavioral science contributions.

Personnel Assessment. Psychologists played an important role in World Wars I and II, particularly in advancing the science of aptitude testing and measurement of human performance. Over the years, psychologists have continued their work in areas such as personnel selection, classification, and training. The psychometric advances made in the military setting have also been applied to the wider society (Schratz & Ree, 1989; Wigdor & Green, 1991). Advances in cognitive ability testing and personality assessments and screens have been used to select people for critical positions in such fields as intelligence and special operations. For example, behavioral science has given the military reliable and valid cognitive and noncognitive (e.g., temperament) predictors of job performance as well as job performance criteria (Wise, 1992).

Attitude measurement—the forte of social psychologists—has been invaluable to military recruitment and retention (Laurence, 2006). Attitude measurement in the military also began in World War II. The trailblazing human resource research was published in the four-volume classic, *The American Soldier.*

This is recognition, both by scientists and the military, of the fact not only that social and psychological problems are crucial in modern war, . . . but also that they are now amenable to scientific study. (Stouffer, Suchman, DeVinney, Star, & Williams, 1949, p. 3)

Yet another example of behavioral science's influence comes from the military's strong clinical and health research program. The scientific study of combat stress has led to proactive and effective assessment and treatment following exposure to danger and other traumatic experiences (Lewis, 2006). The study of posttraumatic stress disorder (PTSD) has enabled identifying risk factors and is now leading to the identification of resilience factors (Maguen, Suvak, & Litz, 2006), which will promote better screening and intervention.

Training, Socialization, and Development. From "boot" camp (basic training), to technical training, to operational assignments, the application of behavioral science helps to shape individuals into effective forces. The military has long relied on psychologists for skills training content, techniques, systems, and strategies (Salas, Priest, Wilson, & Burke, 2006). In addition to team and unit interactions, the interactions between humans and technology are studied by human factors scientists. Sophisticated weapon systems, platforms, and equipment offer critical advantage only if they can be mastered. Although armed with state-of-the-art individual combat weapons (e.g., the M16A2 rifle), armor such as Bradley fighting vehicles, attack helicopters, and fighter planes and ships that carry "smart" missiles, human physiological functioning, information processing, cognition, decision making, and so forth remain key ingredients to victory. Even robots and unmanned aerial vehicles need human input and maintenance.

Beyond technical skills, adjustment, comportment, and contextual performance are critical to the military. Behind the indoctrination, socialization, enculturation, and plain old military order and discipline are sound scientific principles. Cohesion, commitment, and morale are fundamental to military readiness and effectiveness. Furthermore, understanding the importance of military culture and traditions as well as adapting to technological change is the purview of behavioral and social scientists. Beginning with Janowitz (1960, 1974), sociologists, psychologists, and cultural anthropologists have come to study, define, and describe the important social systems of the military establishment using methods, perspectives, constructs, and theories of the behavioral and social sciences.

Organizing the vast bureaucracy of the military is also no simple or inconsequential task. The rank structure and hierarchy are not just curiosities or a unique pay band system but are vital to the effective exercise of authority (Janowitz, 1974). Uniforms with their stars, clusters, bars, chevrons, and stripes along with other regalia efficiently signal roles, responsibilities, and relationships. Immersion in military life and lexicon promotes a "warrior" identity and ethos that is effective in garrison and vital on the battlefield. Psychologists have contributed to the content, curricula, and pedagogy of military training and development. Such contributions reach beyond identifying the best techniques for imparting knowledge and skills; they include instilling and reinforcing values, comportment, and teamwork. For example, psychologists and sociologists no doubt "had the ear" of the Chief of Staff of the U.S. Army, which inspired the decision to adopt the symbolic black beret for all soldiers beginning in 2001. Previously, the black beret was reserved for "real warriors" only—the Rangers. With the black beret donned by all soldiers, the Army began reinforcing the notion of the common warrior ethos.

Many things go into military effectiveness, but certainly, unit or primary group cohesion is critical. The power of this latent behavioral construct is exemplified in a fundamental part of war—soldiers tend not to fight against an enemy so much as fight for each other. With the help of psychology, strategies for enhancing cohesion or social solidarity helped transcend racial and gender differences. Despite initial friction, racial integration beginning in 1948, the increasing numbers of women in service, and the removal of assignment barriers for women all have not diminished cohesion and military effectiveness. Of course, the military remains an organization steeped in tradition and reluctant to change its culture. To be sure, equal opportunity must still be monitored, and sexual harassment remains a concern. Furthermore, the stubborn problem of discrimination appears in military policy regarding sexual orientation. Gay men and lesbians are still not welcomed—at least openly—to serve in the armed forces, purportedly because their presence would have negative implications for unit cohesion and privacy (Herek & Belkin, 2006). And so, psychologists, sociologists, and cultural anthropologists continue to promote understanding and offer direction regarding how best to promote diversity.

Leadership, Management, and Quality of Life. Leadership is a complex and elusive construct, but being critical to the military's mission, it continues to be examined by many, including behavioral scientists. In the preface to their edited volume, *Military Leadership,* Taylor and Rosenbach (2005) gave behavioral science top billing for having one of the most informative perspectives on leadership.

> Learning about leadership involves understanding the dynamic relationship between the leader and followers; recognizing the differing contexts and situations of the leadership landscape; and understanding the importance of the behavioral sciences, biography, the classics, economics, history, logic, and related disciplines that provide the perspective so important to leadership effectiveness. (p. 3)

Though theories of leadership continue to be deliberated and tested, most agree that the leader plays a central role in shaping organizational culture (Goleman, 2005; Sashkin & Rosenbach, 2005). So, along with military leader biographies and lore, officer education offers a sprinkling of leadership psychology, mainly from the areas of learning theory, personality, and social influence. Psychologists can be found on the faculties of each service academy. The Army (United States Military Academy) and Air Force (United States Air Force Academy) each has a department of Behavioral Science and Leadership, whereas the Navy (United States Naval Academy) houses its psychology faculty in the Department of Leadership, Ethics, and Law. Psychologists continue to reinforce venerable and unfolding leadership and management principles and lessons throughout officer and noncommissioned officer development. Using information from behavioral science, leadership competencies and development continue to be discussed, debated, and revised within and across the Services.

As previously mentioned, without conscription as a workforce mobilization and channeling tool, the military relies heavily on economics—military pay, benefits, and bonuses—to manage and maintain personnel (Williams, 2004). In the parlance of behavioral psychology, money is contingently scheduled to reinforce job performance. Although it is a powerful reward, money is by no means sufficient for motivating behavior. Intrinsic motivation and intangible rewards are also influential (Stanley-Mitchell, 2004). Job satisfaction, camaraderie, medals and honors, and programs and policies designed to improve quality of life (QOL) for service personnel and their family members all relate to job performance. A number of behavioral and social science disciplines, including psychology, sociology, anthropology, and political science, contribute along with medicine sciences to the military's active program of QOL research and applications (Schwerin, 2006).

Et Cetera. Clearly, the military puts behavioral science to good use. An exhaustive list of contributions is beyond the scope of this chapter. Although examples in such areas as risk analysis, decision making, situation awareness, performance under stress, and others were omitted, they are worthy topics to the military nonetheless.

RESEARCH AND DISSEMINATION FUNDING LEVELS AND PROCESS

R&D Funding

As with the overall federal budget, the Department of Defense has the largest share (54%)[1] of the federal government's research and development (R&D) budget (Koizumi, 2006). Although R&D is budgeted at $74 billion, the allocation for science and technology (S&T) represents only 15% of this sum or $11.2 billion. Further accounting shows $1.4 billion budgeted for basic science and $4.6 billion for applied research (these figures include medical research). Thus, the bulk of Defense R&D spending goes toward advanced technology development, mostly for testing and evaluating weapons systems. Although less than 10% of DoD's R&D budget goes to basic and applied research, the amount is still worthwhile (Silver, Sharpe, Kelly, Kobor, & Wurtz, 2006). Of course, stiff competition for the $6 billion comes from such disciplines as physics, astronomy, atmospheric and earth sciences,

biology, mathematical science, and computing research (American Association for the Advancement of Science [AAAS], 2006).

Inside the military, a modest contingent of uniformed behavioral scientists is flanked by Defense civilians, and together they conduct and manage the basic and applied research that addresses military concerns. These research champions fund, manage, and defend both intramural and extramural human-centered behavioral science. Most work in key military agencies, which are the Army Research Institute for the Behavioral and Social Sciences; Army Research Laboratory—Human Research and Engineering Directorate; Walter Reed Army Institute of Research; Navy Personnel Research, Studies and Technology; Office of Naval Research; Air Force Office of Scientific Research; the Air Force Research Laboratory; and the Defense Advanced Research Projects Agency. In addition, behavioral scientists can be found on the faculties of the military's undergraduate and graduate academic institutions. The above government bodies are joined by legions of research centers, institutes, and consulting firms dedicated in whole or in part to conducting research and analyses under federal government sponsorship—with Defense leading the charge. There are also clusters of researchers who do not conduct or manage research but instead aid policy makers in and around the Pentagon and Service/Defense headquarters and commands and so help communicate and disseminate behavioral research to inform policy.

Just as certain qualities and qualifications are required to serve *in* the military, not all behavioral scientists are prepared to offer their professional services *to* the military. Sadly, civilian colleges and universities are but bit players. Their poor representation is not because intellectual capital is lacking in academe. It is attributable, in part, to academic scientists' inexperience with the military R&D process and to their apprehension about doing business with Defense. These topics are discussed in the next section.

R&D Process

To make funds available for behavioral and social science, government research managers must undertake a complex process to compete for and win a share of the R&D budget by convincing leaders and policy makers of the soundness and value of their research programs. Unlike many large-scale private entities that fund research in the behavioral and social sciences, Defense does not operate mainly as a venture capitalist investing in potentially promising behavioral science research. Rather, Defense defines and scopes its problem and solicits targeted research that is responsive to the problem at hand. Contracts, therefore, are the primary mechanism used to generate new research instead of grants because they give the military more control over the research process and final product.

The government announces its contract activities through "FedBizOpps" published on the Web. Registered prospective bidders may then order the "Request for Proposal" (RFP) and prepare a formal response. This response typically requires preparing a sizable document describing the proposed technical, staffing, and management approach to the "Statement of Work" (SOW). An RFP also requires that bidders describe corporate or organizational experience and qualifications. In addition, a detailed cost proposal must be submitted. After bidding is closed, review and evaluation of proposals according to evaluation criteria as listed in the RFP begin. Proposals are usually evaluated by a committee of government employees with the requisite technical and content expertise in a process that can take many months. To expedite research, "umbrella" contracts may

be awarded with broadly related individual studies and analyses contracted to the successful bidder(s) through a streamlined process. Shortcuts are also possible by contracting with federally funded research and development centers (FFRDCs). FFRDCs are independent, nonprofit organizations funded by the government to achieve long-term objectives in accordance with government needs and FFRDC-stated missions.

Aside from reviewing proposals for scientific merit and applied value, the military has a process for evaluating and vetting scientific research to be disseminated in military settings. First, the Services and DoD assess the research for human subject implications, and if not exempt, the research must be submitted to an institutional review board (IRB) to consider ethics concerns and to otherwise protect human subjects. Once launched, the logistics of conducting research in the military setting must be tackled, and then an arduous process for implementation follows. In the realm of personnel testing, for example, formal advisory committees are assembled to vet the instruments and procedures before an operational test and evaluation of a procedure is even contemplated. For vetted policy changes derived from research—for example, new research-based procedures for promoting officers—Congress must also approve a "demonstration" project to assess procedural fairness and the impact of the project on military structures and readiness.

Relevant research ideas and expertise, even if accompanied by federal contracting savvy, are not enough to compete successfully for Defense R&D funds. Without a proven track record in military research, chances are slim that the proposed investigators and organizations will be awarded a contract. At minimum, researchers must demonstrate understanding of the military's past, present, and future human-centered issues and concerns. Preparing successful research and dissemination proposals requires quite an investment in learning the lingo, structure, functions, and contexts. The military is a complex instrument of national power, and like any profession, the military has its jargon, which is extensive and varies by Service. But beyond the acronyms and unfamiliar lexicon, the structure and systems of the military present a hurdle for many behavioral scientists who seek to design and communicate meaningful research for the military.

As a basic example, the military has four Services, each with Active Duty and Reserve components. Enlisted personnel and commissioned officers (along with a small cadre of warrant officers) are assigned to military occupational specialties (MOS) in the Army and Marine Corps, ratings in the Navy, and Air Force specialty codes (AFSC) in the Air Force. Also, depending on Service, they are organized into branches, communities, or wings with common functions. In addition to function, units are delineated by size. The Army's nomenclature in terms of increasing size is squad, platoon, company, battalion, brigade, division, corps, and army. (In this context, *army* does not refer to *the* U.S. Army but to the First, Third, Fifth, and Eighth Army, which have different responsibilities and regional expertise.) There are two leadership tracks for each of the three military departments,[2] the military chief of staff (a "four-star" general or admiral) and a civilian at the helm in each of the three secretariats. Each of the Services has major commands (MACOMS) with assigned units and facilities. Conducting combined operations falls to the Unified Commands, five of which are Combatant Commands (COCOMS) with geographic responsibility, and four have worldwide, functional responsibility.

Along with such structural complexities come procedural ones. For example, many civilian scientists are familiar with the formal rank structures for enlisted members and officers. But they may not be aware that just doing a good job and earning high efficiency or fitness ratings does not guarantee career progression. Promotion also depends on time in service, history of assignments, achieving progressive levels of command responsibility, slots available in different functional areas, and numeric personnel allowances by grade, as set by Congress. Career progression is mandatory; a so-called "up-or-out" policy requires moving through the ranks in order to continue serving. What's more, the job structures, performance evaluation systems, and personnel policies and practices vary by Service.

Behavioral scientists must know and appreciate the significance of all such cultural, structural, and procedural nuances lest they lead to confounded or contaminated research designs and analyses and wreak havoc with efforts to communicate with military decision makers.

Finally, because politics greatly affects what gets funded in the military, strategic plans for producing and disseminating science may be compromised by limited tenure among both the civilian and military top leadership. That is, the secretary of defense along with his or her deputy, undersecretaries, assistant secretaries, and deputy undersecretaries are politically appointed. Thus, their agendas are tied to the life cycle of the presidential administration. Senior military leaders rotate more often, approximately every 2 years. As a result, much vigilance is needed to protect long-term research and dissemination efforts that are essential to achieving a particular goal, and often such sustained efforts will not be possible in the face of agenda changes. Moreover, with the military's emphasis on command and control, its reverence for tradition, and congressional oversight requirements, moving research into operation is slow and risk averse.

In this political context, behavioral and social scientists both inside and outside the military must be tenacious in helping to make sure that useful science gets produced and used. Despite favorable ratings by the credentialed researchers who assemble to evaluate the technical quality of proposed, in-progress, and completed research studies, no one guarantees the projects will be launched or "go" anywhere other than on a shelf or in a file drawer. And budget crises always exert pressure to pull the plug on "less critical" lines of inquiry. A job of research directors and managers who work inside the military is to champion promising research and convince policy makers of the value of continued funding.

COUNTERING MISUNDERSTANDINGS AND TENSIONS BETWEEN BEHAVIORAL SCIENTISTS AND THE MILITARY

Academic Apprehension About the Military

Despite the time and effort required, there are contingents of military psychologists and sociologists who have embraced the profession of arms. In fact, they have formed formal organizations such as the Society for Military Psychology and the Inter-University Seminar on Armed Forces and Society with their journals, *Military Psychology* and *Armed Forces & Society,* respectively. The first is an eclectic group of psychologists (such as clinical, experimental, industrial/organizational, and social), whereas the second comprises a broader, interdisciplinary group of behavioral scientists (from such fields as sociology, political science, psychology, and public administration).

Outside of these groups, scientists and scholars in the behavioral and social sciences tend to distance themselves from the military and even can be quite antagonistic. Aside from lacking familiarity, reaction to the Vietnam War created a wide rift between the military and academicians (Janowitz, 1974).

Laying the blame for the war at the boots of the military rather than in the hands of politicians, many university-based social scientists turned their backs on the problems of Defense on moral grounds. For example, the Human Resources Research Office,[3] with its staff of psychologists, separated from The George Washington University in response to student protests against Army ties (Ramsberger, 2001). Although the military psychology division of the American Psychological Association (APA) was a charter member, until 2005, APA would not accept employment advertisements from DoD because of the law precluding homosexuals from serving openly in the military. Recently, military psychologists have been falsely accused and unfairly castigated for their purported association with coercive interrogation and other abuses of detainees in connection with the Global War on Terror (GWOT).[4] And although cultural knowledge is vital to countering the non-Western adversaries and irregular warfare that the United States confronts today, such understanding is lacking because of anthropology's retreat from the military as well (McFate, 2005).

Other tensions are less emotionally charged. Anecdotal reports suggest that behavioral science faculty refrain from putting their imprimatur on DoD and consulting firm jobs because they reason that under Defense sponsorship, they forfeit academic freedom and integrity. On a positive note, however, more recent anecdotes suggest that interactions between military college professors and researchers have led their civilian academic colleagues to report more positive attitudes toward working with the military (Morten G. Ender and Michael D. Matthews, personal communication, June 30, 2006). Supporting the military's understanding of human behavior is not tantamount to advocating war. Behavioral science need not loathe entering into partnerships with Defense.

Military Trepidations About Behavioral Science

The lack of understanding between behavioral science and the military is mutual. Military leaders and Defense policy makers do not always appreciate behavioral science and have been known to malign its methods and findings. For example, cadets at the United States Military Academy at West Point refer to cultural anthropology as the study of "nuts and huts" (McFate, 2005). Why does the military hold this negative image?

Recommendations from the hard sciences (e.g., physics, chemistry) and engineering often seem more concrete and definitive to decision makers in the military than the "squishy" topics, inexact theories, and methodological limitations of the behavioral sciences. Typically, behavioral scientists concern themselves with latent constructs such as aptitudes, attitudes, personality, leadership, cohesion, commitment, learning, job performance, and so forth. The behavioral indicators used to measure them, such as test scores and survey item composites, can seem quite removed from the everyday concerns of the military. Moreover, instead of being able to give the military answers to a specific question after conducting one study, research must accumulate over time to test theories about the causes and other influences on the constructs of interest. Military decision makers also tend to be unfamiliar with the array of quantitative and qualitative methods available and do not understand which methods are appropriate depending on the question (Creswell, 2003). Overall, the military is more comfortable with the engineering approach with its direct problem-solving orientation and more familiar calculations, exact measurements, and precise models.

The traditional tool of the behavioral sciences, the carefully controlled randomized experiment, also does not usually yield data that are immediately useful to the military (Campbell & Stanley, 1963). External or ecological validity is a must for the military. Randomized experiments are rare and considered impractical. For example, in studying the impact of deployment on cohesion and commitment, it is not possible to select individuals or units at random for a tour of duty in Iraq. Quasi-experiments with statistical control typically are more appropriate.

Using behavioral science in the military requires stepping outside of our comfortable, controlled conditions and beyond our typical subject pools and conducting and applying research that goes beyond college sophomores and paper people. Experiments must become more ecologically valid, and multiple methods, including qualitative approaches, must be used alongside experimental designs to make realistic and actionable contribution to the military. Currently, however, both scientists and the military often question the rigor, meaning, and usefulness of information from methods such as structured interviews, surveys, focus groups, ethnographies, and the analysis of archival data.

Even if behavioral scientists come to understand military missions, culture, and structure and produce more relevant research, there is still much work to do in conveying the message and the value of the behavioral research in meeting the military's needs. Military leaders and policy makers usually want solid recommendations for action based on empirical evidence and an appreciation for the military's exigencies. Yet, behavioral scientists often hesitate, despite having useful guidance to give military operators in the form of theories, concepts, and data from both basic and applied science. They might instead learn to market their ideas and be bolder in their recommendations for action.

Like the economists who wield greater influence, scientists could not only learn to speak with confidence, but in terms of dollars.

That is, science that enables the military to buy more bullets and beans outweighs science for the sake of "it's nice to know" or even because "it's the right thing to do." Of course, bottom-line research is not at odds with "it's nice to know" or "it's the right thing to do" motivations. Though the military is not a social welfare agency, for example, it was a trailblazer with regard to racial integration because of the rapidly growing need for personnel. Likewise, recruiting demands may bring greater opportunities for women, and concerns about retention may quickly advance quality-of-life and military family initiatives. Still, even when meeting such obvious needs, scientists have an edge whenever they can calculate costs and benefits to the military when recommending a particular course of action.

In communicating, we must also avoid our own jargon. Bombarding DoD sponsors with intricate talk of grounded theory, content coding, regression coefficients, and chi-squares is counterproductive. This entreaty is not to suggest that we hide our methods and measures or engage in shotgun empiricism devoid of theory. Instead, we must document our research in detailed technical reports with supporting theory, tables, and graphs showing coding schemes, measures, and statistics along with recommendations for action. Whereas this report would be welcomed by the military's "in-house" researchers and by technical advisers to policy makers, a corresponding "top-line" executive summary is also recommended. In addition to a clear and concise top-line report, the military is looking for the implications for the "bottom line." That is, the military wants to know about output or effects and costs.

Though no single template exists across DoD for useful summaries and technical reports, perusing the Web sites of key government agencies (such as the Army Research Institute [ARI]; Navy Personnel Research, Studies, and Technology [NPRST]; and Air Force Research Laboratory [AFRL], as mentioned above) and reputable consulting firms can lead to exemplary reports. For example, a recent technical report by Personnel Decisions Research Institutes (PDRI) documents the validation of performance factors implemented as part of the National Security Personnel System (NSPS)—the new performance management system for civilian personnel (O'Leary, Muller-Hanson, LaPolice, & Pulakos, 2005). The RAND Corporation, one of the above-mentioned FFRDCs, makes its research summaries and technical reports available on its Web site (see www.rand.org; for one of the many social science related reports, see Harrell, Thie, Schirmer, & Brancato, 2004). These firms, and a host of others, are adept at communicating behavioral science to the military.

Conclusion

Tensions and misunderstandings between the military and behavioral science are not likely to be eradicated, but they can be eased. If the military is looking for perfect prediction and control from the behavioral and social sciences, it will be disappointed. We will never be able to predict human behavior with absolute certainty—it's too splendidly complex. But we can strive to be practical and do more to persuade decision makers about why they should apply behavioral science—even without 100% reliability and validity. Ultimately, however, to be valued, studies of psychological processes and behavioral science applications must be developed, tested, and evaluated in military contexts using outcomes of importance to the military and not only to academic science.

FUTURE DIRECTIONS AND CHALLENGES

Behavioral science and the military are not strange bedfellows. Their relationship has been mutually beneficial, and strengthening it further would help to solve emerging military problems. Though the military is an institution steeped in tradition, it must now evolve to meet today's demands. The military must tackle the complexity of terrorism and irregular warfare, in a real and virtual global, cyberspace world (Cebrowski, 2004). Behavioral science advances can be brought to bear on old and new challenges.

Given the Department of Defense's increasingly complex and global responsibilities, it is becoming necessary to conduct more and more joint operations across Services, service components (Active Duty and Reserves), federal agencies, and national boundaries (Department of Defense, 2006b). Defense civilian employees and contractors will also continue lending their support. In short, the Services cannot go it alone; interdependence is becoming the norm. Although the Joint-Service concept is not new, present organizational structures and processes do not appear to promote operating jointly. Deficiencies include establishing shared goals and thinking of the "joint" groups as teams. And although the strengths of military culture arguably outweigh its weaknesses, aspects of military culture will surely complicate attempts to transform the organization. Recommendations from the behavioral and social sciences for or against particular actions or approaches should be brought to bear in overcoming resistance and adapting individual Army, Navy, Marine Corps, and Air Force cultures for Joint Service, multinational coalition, and interagency operations. Relevant psychological constructs that will need attention in this military context include teams (Beersma et al., 2003; Cannon-Bowers & Salas, 1997), networks (Provin & Milward, 2001), cooperation (Tjosvold, 1995), and trust (Lewicki & Bunker, 1996).

Changes to reward structures will be among the management issues to consider.

For example, collective rewards are used to support cooperation and individual rewards to promote competition. Yet, the military may need to implement rewards consistent with behavioral science showing that individual responsibility can be retained and even enhanced with collective rewards if the rewarded behaviors are highly visible and if the team holds its members accountable. Rewards at the organizational level may also need restructuring as each Service vies for control of financial, material, and human resources and activities. Finding ways to forge cooperation rather than competition among the Services and to motive true Joint operations is within the purview of behavioral science.

As the technology and conditions of war evolve, so too should we refresh our understanding of the psychological underpinnings of military performance and the conditions that affect quality of life for those who serve. The study of information processing, cognitive limitations, expectations, and perception will continue to aid navigation through the "fog of war." Through efforts to measure the constructs of culture, personality, and social and emotional intelligence, behavioral scientists may enhance cultural awareness and hence international interactions. Sociology, social psychology, and related behavioral and social science subspecialties can be instrumental in understanding, preventing, or mitigating acts of misconduct by military forces brought on by the stress of war. We should, for example, extend our social, psychological, and physiological studies of aggression, impulsivity, obedience, conformity, and resilience to military settings and, in particular, to combat situations.

Though the military could benefit from a closer relationship with behavioral science, several barriers need to be addressed. As this chapter explained, strong ideas for scientific research and dissemination do not guarantee interested behavioral scientists access to military funding. Even if one reads up on the military, without an individual and corporate history of Defense contract research, it's hard to become a recognized contributor. A suggested course of action is to become familiar with the military and those organizations that conduct research and analyses for the military. Read the relevant journals, attend professional meetings (e.g., APA's Division 19—The Society for Military Psychology; the Inter-University Seminar on Armed Forces & Society), and "surf" the Web. Find out *who* is doing *what* Defense research. As with contract opportunities, awards are also listed in FedBizOpps. With a niche or unique expertise, it may be possible and prudent to network and subsequently partner with established military researchers. A quid pro quo may be necessary, such as welcoming military researchers to partner with other sponsors outside their typical sphere of influence. For example, those in academe might include military researchers to partner in National Science Foundation grant proposals or on research contracts sponsored by other federal agencies such as the Department of Education.

To promote mutual understanding and interaction between the military and behavioral and social science, academicians might consider inviting those with military research experience to colloquia and perhaps sabbaticals at institutions with faculty studying social and psychological processes of interest to the military. Furthermore, "seeding" military research agencies and contract research

firms with graduating students may also hold promise. These former students can apply their talents toward noble missions and transmit their growing experience back to their alma maters and mentors.

Though Defense can and does use behavioral science, its missions and operating tempo typically do not lend themselves to wading through the literature in search of general principles that hold promise of transfer to the military. Certainly, good science disseminated via peer-reviewed journals is invaluable to the behavioral scientists employed by DoD and the contractors who assist them in tackling the military's issues and concerns. But for those outside the world of military research who are looking to export their science to Defense decision makers, dissemination must be more direct and deliberate. Behavioral science research also must be conducted, validated, and documented in the military context. Only then can the behavioral scientists on the inside bring the science to the attention of policy makers.

The military is a worthy and fascinating arena for developing and testing behavioral science theories. Behavioral science, in turn, can make worthy contributions to the military. Communicating and disseminating behavioral research requires significant investment in this institution dedicated to "duty, honor, country." The investment is worth the effort. Indeed, with its sizable personnel count and budget—not to mention its sober missions—Uncle Sam needs behavioral science.

NOTES

1. If all Defense R&D is counted, the figure is slightly higher at 57%. The difference is attributable to some R&D conducted outside the Department of Defense, such as in defense programs within the Department of Energy and Department of Homeland Security.

2. The Marine Corps, headed by its commandant, falls under the Department of the Navy.

3. The Human Resources Research Office subsequently became known as the Human Resources Research Organization.

4. Military health care personnel and behavioral science consultants are bound by and uphold established ethical principals and DoD policy that affirms their "duty in all matters affecting the physical and mental health of detainees to perform, encourage, and support, directly and indirectly, actions to uphold the humane treatment of detainees and to ensure that no individual in the custody or under the physical control of the Department of Defense, regardless of nationality or physical location, shall be subject to cruel, inhuman, or degrading treatment or punishment" (Department of Defense, 2006a, p. 2).

REFERENCES

American Association for the Advancement of Science (AAAS). (2006). *AAAS report XXXI: Research and development FY 2007.* Retrieved from http://www.aaas.org/spp/rd/rd07main.htm

Beersma, B., Hollenbeck, J. R., Humphrey, S. E., Moon, H., Conlon, D. E., & Ilgen, D. R. (2003). Cooperation, competition, and team performance: Toward a contingency approach. *Academy of Management Journal, 46*(5), 572–590.

Brandon, S. E. (2002, September). *Combating terrorism: Some responses from the behavioral sciences.* Washington, DC: American Psychological Association.

Campbell, D. T., & Stanley, J. C. (1963). *Experimental and quasi-experimental designs for research.* Chicago: Rand-McNally.

Cannon-Bowers, J. A., & Salas, E. (1997). Teamwork competencies: The interaction of team member knowledge, skills, and attitudes. In H. F. O'Neil, Jr. (Ed.), *Workforce readiness: Competencies and assessment* (pp. 151–174). Mahwah, NJ: Lawrence Erlbaum.

Cebrowski, A. K. (2004, June 17). Transformation and the changing character of war? In *Transformation trends.* Washington, DC: Office of Force Transformation. Retrieved from http://www.oft.osd.mil

Creswell, J. W. (2003). *Research design: Qualitative, quantitative, and mixed methods approaches* (2nd ed.). Thousand Oaks, CA: Sage.

Department of Defense (DoD). (2006a, June 6). *Department of Defense instruction number 2310.08E.* Washington, DC: Author.

Department of Defense (DoD). (2006b, February 6). *Quadrennial defense review report.* Retrieved from http://www.defenselink.mil/qdr/report/Report20060203.pdf

Goleman, D. (2005). What makes a leader? In R. L. Taylor & W. E. Rosenbach (Eds.), *Military leadership* (5th ed., pp. 53–68). Boulder, CO: Perseus.

Harrell, M. C., Thie, H. J., Schirmer, P., & Brancato, K. (2004). *Aligning the stars: Improvements to general and flag officer management.* Santa Monica, CA: RAND.

Herek, G. M., & Belkin, A. (2006). Sexual orientation and military service: Prospects for organizational and individual change in the United States. In T. W. Britt, A. Adler, & C. Castro (Eds.), *Military life: The psychology of serving in peace and combat: Vol. 4. Military culture* (pp. 119–142). Westport, CT: Praeger.

Janowitz, M. (1960). *The professional soldier: A social and political portrait.* Glencoe, IL: Free Press.

Janowitz, M. (1974). *Sociology and the military establishment* (3rd ed.). Beverly Hills, CA: Sage.

Koizumi, K. (2006, April). R&D in the FY 2007 Department of Defense budget. In American Association for the Advancement of Science (Ed.), *AAAS report XXXI: Research and development FY 2007* (Part II, chap. 6). Retrieved from http://www.aaas.org/spp/rd/rd07main.htm

Laurence, J. H. (2006). Poultry and patriotism: Attitudes toward the military. In T. W. Britt, A. Adler, & C. Castro (Eds.), *Military life: The psychology of serving in peace and combat: Vol. 4. Military culture* (pp. 211–228). Westport, CT: Praeger.

Lewicki, R. J., & Bunker, B. B. (1996). Developing and maintaining trust in work relationships. In R. M. Kramer & T. R. Tyler (Eds.), *Trust in organizations: Frontiers of theory and research*. Thousand Oaks, CA: Sage.

Lewis, S. J. (2006). Combat stress control: Putting principle into practice. In A. B. Adler, C. A. Castro, & T. W. Britt (Eds.), *Military life: The psychology of serving in peace and combat: Vol. 2. Operational stress* (pp. 121–140). Westport, CT: Praeger.

Maguen, S., Suvak, M., & Litz, B. T. (2006). Predictors and prevalence of posttraumatic stress disorder among military veterans. In A. B. Adler, C. A. Castro, & T. W. Britt (Eds.), *Military life: The psychology of serving in peace and combat: Vol. 2. Operational stress* (pp. 141–169). Westport, CT: Praeger.

McFate, M. (2005, March/April). Anthropology and counterinsurgency: The strange story of their curious relationship. *Military Review*, pp. 24–38.

Office of Management and Budget. (2005). *The budget for fiscal year 2006*. Washington, DC: Author. Retrieved from http://www.whitehouse.gov/omb/budget/fy2006/pdf/budget/

O'Leary, R. S., Muller-Hanson, R. A., LaPolice, C. C., & Pulakos, E. D. (2005, November). *U.S. Department of Defense: Development and validation of performance factors and benchmark descriptors for the National Security Personnel System (NSPS)* (Institute Report #524). Arlington, VA: Personnel Decisions Research Institutes.

Provin, K. G., & Milward, H. B. (2001). Do networks really work? A framework for evaluating public-sector organizational networks. *Public Administration Review, 61*(4), 414–424.

Ramsberger, P. F. (2001). *HumRRO: The first 50 years*. Alexandria, VA: Human Resources Research Organization.

Salas, E., Priest, H. A., Wilson, K. A., & Burke, C. S. (2006). Scenario-based training: Improving military mission performance and adaptability. In A. B. Adler, C. A. Castro, & T. W. Britt (Eds.), *Military life: The psychology of serving in peace and combat: Vol. 2. Operational stress* (pp. 32–53). Westport, CT: Praeger.

Sashkin, M., & Rosenbach, W. E. (2005). A view of leadership that matters. In R. L. Taylor & W. E. Rosenbach (Eds.), *Military leadership* (5th ed., pp. 39–51). Boulder, CO. Perseus.

Schratz, M. K., & Ree, M. J. (1989). Enlisted selection and classification: Advances in testing. In M. F. Wiskoff & G. M. Rampton (Eds.), *Military personnel measurement: Testing, assignment, evaluation* (pp. 1–40). New York: Praeger.

Schwerin, M .J. (2006). Quality of life and subjective well-being among military personnel: An organizational response to the challenges of military life. In T. W. Britt, A. Adler, & C. Castro (Eds.), *Military life: The psychology of serving in peace and combat: Vol. 4. Military culture* (pp. 145–179). Westport, CT: Praeger.

Silver, H. J., Sharpe, A. L., Kelly, H., Kobor, P., & Wurtz, S. (2006, April). Behavioral and social science research in the administration's FY 2007 budget. In American Association for the Advancement of Science (Ed.), *AAAS report XXXI: Research and development FY 2007* (Part III, chap. 20). Retrieved from http://www.aaas.org/spp/rd/rd07main.htm

Society for Military Psychology. (2005a). *Intelligence testing in the United States military.* Retrieved March 28, 2006, from http://www.historyof militarypsychology.com/index.html

Society for Military Psychology. (2005b). *World War II and the birth of the Division of Military Psychology.* Retrieved March 28, 2006, from http://www.apa.org/divisions/div19/about3divisionhistory.html

Stanley-Mitchell, E. A. (2004). The military profession and intangible rewards for service. In C. Williams (Ed.), *Filling the ranks: Transforming the U.S. military personnel system* (pp. 93–118). Cambridge: MIT Press.

Stouffer, S. A., Suchman, E. A., DeVinney, L. C., Star, S. A., & Williams, R. M., Jr. (1949). *The American soldier: Adjustment during army life* (Vol. 1). Princeton, NJ: Princeton University Press.

Taylor, R. L., & Rosenhach, W. E. (Eds.). (2005). *Military leadership* (5th ed.). Boulder, CO: Perseus.

Tjosvold, D. (1995). Cooperation theory, constructive controversy and effectiveness: Learning from crisis. In R. A. Guzzo & E. Salas (Eds.), *Team effectiveness and decision making in organizations* (pp. 79–112). San Francisco: Jossey-Bass.

Wigdor, A. K., & Green, B. F., Jr. (Eds.). (1991). *Performance assessment for the workplace* (2 vols.).. Washington, DC: National Academy Press.

Williams, C. (2004). Introduction. In C. Williams (Ed.), *Filling the ranks: Transforming the U.S. military personnel system* (pp. 1–28). Cambridge: MIT Press.

Wise, L. L. (1992). The validity of test scores for selecting and classifying enlisted recruits. In B. R. Gifford & L.C. Wing (Eds.), *Test policy in defense: Lessons from the military for education, training, and employment* (pp. 221–259). Boston: Kluwer.

Conclusion

Current Themes and Future Directions

Melissa K. Welch-Ross and Lauren G. Fasig

This book began with two themes. First, disseminating behavioral research requires a strategy that specifies: What innovations and messages from science should be disseminated, depending on the purpose? Who should help to deliver these? Who is the primary audience? By what methods should dissemination occur? What is the effect? Second, it requires understanding the broader context of dissemination—the conditions that affect how and whether dissemination occurs (see Introduction, Figure 1). We now return to these themes to organize our discussion of the volume. Throughout, we highlight suggestions for advancing dissemination research and practice, and we conclude by considering the place of dissemination in the larger scientific enterprise.

WHAT ARE THE GOALS OF DISSEMINATION?

As the contributors to this volume make clear, setting goals is vital for disseminating behavioral science effectively and for evaluating the quality of one's approach, yet dissemination often begins without clearly defined goals and linked communication objectives that are concrete and measurable (e.g., see McCall &Groark, Chapter 1, this volume). The dissemination goals discussed throughout this volume fall into three types. The *central goal* defines why dissemination is taking place—to improve education outcomes, for example. The *strategic goal* refers to the expected outcome of the approach that is used to achieve the central goal. Strategic goals may be to develop or change policies that encourage the use of science-based practices known to affect educational outcomes, to change professional norms around the use of science-based practices, to develop the skill sets required for implementing the practices, and so on. *Communication objectives* are the expected outcomes of each communication method used to reach the strategic goal. They might include educating or informing policy makers, educators, and education consumers about the importance of using science-based practices; identifying and relieving the concerns that each group might have about the use of science-based practices; or garnering the support and commitment of the opinion leaders whose help will be needed to change professional norms, attitudes, and beliefs relating to the use of scientific innovations.

In another example, the central goal may be, as Hirsh-Pasek and Golinkoff (Chapter 12, this volume) have attempted in their popular communications of behavioral science, to help parents make informed choices relating to their children's development. The strategic goal may be to use popular communications to increase public awareness and understanding of basic and applied scientific research on children's early learning, and the communication objective may be to write popular books and speak directly to public audiences, or indirectly through journalists, in order to debunk myths about early learning and replace them with information supported by behavioral science.

Often, dissemination goals are specified too late, leading to reactive postures, missed opportunities, or scientific innovations that end up not being useful, understood, or valued. For example, the scientific community may react to address its discontent about mass media reporting instead of developing a strategy for communicating its message about the research and then, with the priorities and processes of the media in mind, using methods to increase the likelihood that the message is picked up and gets through to the public. Likewise, the dissemination of innovations for service delivery is often considered only after the intervention or tool has been developed and tested. In policy making, goals for disseminating research often occur after opinions on a policy issue have already been formed and come to light. And so authors encouraged setting goals for dissemination when first designing the research whenever it makes sense to do so, and collaborating or consulting with the likely users of the innovation as well as with any other messengers or supporters who will be critical to getting the innovation taken up and used effectively on a wide scale.

When laying out the dissemination plan, several authors emphasized the need to recognize and aim for feasible, short-term accomplishments that will help to achieve long-term goals. Incremental approaches may be called for if, as in the earlier education example, gaps exist in the science base; if the science generally has been of poor quality; if the technical assistance, training, and other resources cannot be secured to support the use of science-based practices; if the most appropriate tools have not yet been developed to help evaluate outcomes; and so on. In such cases, it may not be reasonable to expect that a policy or practice can at a particular point in time meet one's ultimate goal for disseminating the science (see Lyon & Esterline, Chapter 20, this volume, for related discussion). In the interim, researchers can continue working on the relevant scientific and practical issues, laying the groundwork for subsequent policy iterations.

Setting feasible goals requires recognizing how science fits into the broader context. Many legitimate perspectives, sources of information, and competing goals go into the decisions and practices of the service delivery professional, policy maker, and mass media journalist. Scientific research may be used in unforeseen, but not always unpredictable or undesirable ways (see Rich, Chapter 15, this volume; see also Sarewitz, Foladori, Invernizzi, & Garfinkel, 2004). And so, when setting dissemination goals and objectives, it helps to broaden one's ideas about the range of outcomes that may be possible and useful. In mass media, for example, a scientist may provide a journalist with information that increases the accuracy of media coverage by helping the journalist put the research findings into a larger scientific and social context, though the information itself may not appear in the story (see Stocking & Sparks, Chapter 4). Likewise, despite the scientist's belief or hope that decision makers will try to optimize outcomes by taking action that follows directly from the science, such as introducing and passing legislation, scientific research may be used instead to expand, refocus, or reframe a policy debate. When trying to promote the use of research, practical and political constraints must be recognized, and since "negotiation rather than optimization is the apt metaphor for policymaking" (Phillips, 2000), experts often recommend compromising to reach a consensus whenever it becomes necessary for partial success, while looking out for opportunities to achieve the ultimate goal (Albert & Brown, Chapter 17, this volume).

WHAT INNOVATIONS ARE TO BE DELIVERED?

Scientific innovations must be both relevant and trustworthy. Though this imperative may seem obivious, all of the behavioral scientist contributors noted problems around it, and most discussed recent efforts by the field to ensure that whatever is disseminated and communicated comes from relevant and trustworthy research.

Lack of relevance has long plagued the effective dissemination of behavioral science: "Essentially the researcher told the policy maker, practitioner, or general public (perhaps through the media) what to do with little understanding of the concerns, conditions, and needs of the audience. Researchers tended to want to communicate the results of what they had studied, rather than what the audiences needed to know something about. Since there was little contact between researchers and audience, communications were prone to being irrelevant, unrealistic, or inappropriate" (McCall & Groark, Chapter 1, this volume). As mentioned earlier, in service delivery, dissemination tends to be thought about only after an intervention has been identified in randomized trials as being "effective." At that point, questions arise about how to implement the approach outside of the controlled research environment and especially about what tailoring

or adapting the intervention might need to achieve the same results in a different environment—questions not usually answered in effectiveness research.

Often, the essential components of an intervention—ones that are critical to implement without adaptation—have not been identified. Implementation procedures typically have not been sufficiently studied and specified, and the supports needed to achieve implementation often are not known. As McCall and Groark explain in Chapter 1, scientists are then put "in the strange position of having evidence that the 'program' is 'effective' without being certain about what the 'program' is." Thus, all authors speaking to this issue recommended advances to effectiveness trials and to translational research to address these weaknesses and to determine the social, cultural, organizational, and policy conditions that affect uptake and use of an innovation in order to better inform potential users about whether the approach is suitable for meeting their particular needs (see especially Chambers, Chapter 22; Lyon & Esterline, Chapter 20; McCall & Groark, Chapter 1; Pentz, Chapter 21; and Trudeau & Davidson, Chapter 19).

More routinely including measures that key audiences are likely to care about and find meaningful would also facilitate the dissemination of research. For example, service administrators and policy makers want to know about required resources and the costs of implementation that usually are not part of effectiveness studies. Adopters of a depression treatment care about whether improvements in functioning are significant enough for holding a job rather than about statistically significant changes in psychological processes; school administrators will be interested in whether a mental health intervention developed for use in schools affects a range of learning and other school-related outcomes (see Chambers, Chapter 22). Educators care more about whether a teaching practice results in new skills for students than about statistically significant changes in general cognitive abilities. Policy makers responsible for managing government budgets in particular ask whether the research shows a threshold for "good enough" outcomes from certain practices, interventions, services, or policy requirements beyond which additional efforts and resources produce diminishing returns (e.g., see Huston, 2005).

Both basic and applied behavioral research would become more useful if research samples of convenience (e.g., college students, students in university laboratory schools) were replaced with samples from more theoretically and practically relevant segments of the population, if diverse subgroups were included in large enough numbers for studying individual differences in processes and outcomes, and if inclusion criteria for intervention studies matched segments of the population most likely to use the interventions. Then, more would be understood, for example, about how broadly a behavioral theory or intervention could be applied and how they may need to be extended or tailored.

To address the problem of relevance at its root, however, contributors urge both basic and applied scientists to become more knowledgeable about the practical issues and environments that are relevant to their research. Gaining firsthand experiences with the inner workings, concerns, and priorities of the public, industry, policy settings, services fields, and so on can result in greater understanding of psychological and social processes in the contexts in which they occur. It can lead to developing more relevant theories and constructs and to using measures and other procedures that have both scientific validity and practical utility (e.g., see Dovidio & Gaertner, Chapter 5; Hirsh-Pasek & Golinkoff, Chapter 12; Lyon & Esterline, Chapter 20; and Trudeau & Davidson, Chapter 19). Likewise, relevance increases if

potential users of the research participate in the research process: in establishing the overall direction of the research organization; developing specific research objectives and hypotheses; developing research designs, methods, and other plans for executing the research; interpreting the findings; and contributing to the dissemination plan, development of products for dissemination, the dissemination evaluation, and so on (e.g., in this volume, see Hawkins, Halpern, & Tan, Chapter 6; McCall & Groark, Chapter 1; and Pentz, Chapter 21; see also Bogenschneider, Olson, & Linney, 2000; Fantuzzo, McWayne, & Childs, 2006; Jensen, 2003; Lavis et al., 2003). Whether conducting basic or applied science, various formal and informal methods of, as Hirsh-Pasek and Golinkoff (Chapter 12) phrase it, "taking the walk" outside the academy might be used to learn about people's concerns and circumstances, experiences that not only help to shape messages to various audiences but also the direction of research.

To be useful, the science must also be trustworthy. One typical problem is that policy makers, service providers, members of mass media, and the public can latch on to a single recent study or an idiosyncratic selection of studies—often ones that spark their interest or match their personal beliefs and worldviews—instead of routinely considering the quality of the research and its meaning against the entire body of research on the topic. Increasingly, however, both scientists and those who attempt to use scientific research recognize the importance of putting the research into its larger scientific context and that data from across many studies can result in more reliable and nuanced information. As a result, as the demand for information from behavioral science has grown, much effort has gone into producing quantitative syntheses of research on topics of apparent interest and urgency to segments of the public.

A growing practice has been to use synthesized research to develop lists of evidence-based interventions for trial registries and to convene consensus panels that review scientific evidence to make policy recommendations or produce practice guidelines (see especially McCall & Groark, Chapter 1; Trudeau & Davidson, Chapter 19). The intent is to help potential users of these innovations identify which ones have trustworthy evidence that is sufficient to justify their use. Though promising, the approaches are not without problems. For example, different consensus groups can use somewhat different criteria for selecting effective programs, and so as described by McCall and Groark (Chapter 1), some researchers have designed checklists to guide the process. At least one professional society, the Society for Prevention Research, has published standards for judging the quality of the research to be disseminated to help achieve greater consensus (see Flay et al., 2005). In addition, most consensus groups consist mainly of academic researchers who usually do not have the expertise needed to recognize factors that affect dissemination and use of the research, recognize the information and supports that would be helpful for implementing recommended policies or practices, and identify critical areas for future research to improve implementation and dissemination. Research may become more relevant if at the time of synthesis, even more was done to involve segments of the public with practical experience and a stake in the pertinent issues (e.g., see Trudeau & Davidson, Chapter 19; McCall & Groark, Chapter 1).

Formal syntheses, trial registries, and practice guidelines have not yet become a primary concern in many fields, including the military or the judiciary (but see Lamb, 1994), despite the fact that as Laurence explains in this volume (Chapter 23), military staff do not have time to comb through "literature in search of general psychology principles; staff work with contractors to identify relevant studies, measures, theories, knowledge, and procedures usually on short notice." This situation is not unique to the military, and to some extent, it will always exist even for topics in which syntheses are under way. Synthesis takes time, all questions will not have been answered in previous syntheses, and actions will always be taken on the basis of what can be more quickly ascertained from the available science. To the degree that scientists create bodies of literature that are sound and coherent, as well as relevant, experts can more easily draw conclusions, make recommendations, and communicate accumulated knowledge to the mass media, policy makers, service professionals, and the public regardless of whether a formal synthesis exists on the topic.

But contributors noted that behavioral research often is not sufficiently sound or coherent (in this volume, see especially Dovidio & Gaertner, Chapter 5; Laurence, Chapter 23; Lyon & Esterline, Chapter 20; McCall & Groark, Chapter 1; Trudeau & Davidson, Chapter 19). The findings of primary interest and need to our society are those that can ultimately result in innovations or decisions that influence some aspect of human behavior. Producing this type of knowledge requires testing the causes of behavior using randomized experiments combined with other methods that, over a sustained program of research, can help to tease apart the complex combination of forces that affect behavior. Though not perfect, randomized experiments are the best method scientists have for identifying cause-effect relationships, yet they are not used often enough in basic and applied behavioral research. As a result, several authors recommend advances to scientific training to help behavioral researchers become better equipped to produce converging data from studies using a range of methods, including randomized trials, to assess cause-effect relationships, hierarchical linear models to test complex interactions, longitudinal designs, qualitative methods to describe the conditions and processes that may influence behavioral change, statistical methods designed to remove bias and reduce uncertainties about cause-effect relationships in correlational data, and so on (e.g., Dovidio & Gaertner, Chapter 5; Lyon & Esterline, Chapter 20; Trudeau & Davidson, Chapter 19).

The research also suffers from fragmentation because studies are not designed to systematically build on one another to answer applied questions or test theoretical claims. To be most useful, basic research especially must be both programmatic and theoretically driven (Dovidio & Gaertner, Chapter 5). Dovidio and Gaertner explain also that findings from basic research on micro-level processes (e.g., physiological or intrapsychic processes) tend to remain in their reduced forms and not linked to broader macro-level social conditions or connected to relevant behavioral theories that might address practical concerns. Fragmentation is exacerbated by an academic community that encourages scientists to pursue narrow research agendas so that researchers can quickly become recognized experts and compile the record of publications required for academic tenure and promotion review (see Hawkins et al., Chapter 6). These "slivers of knowledge" tend never to be integrated into coherent bodies of work, whether basic or applied. Some journals have taken steps that could be applied more broadly to improve the consistency and transparency of research reports both to support building bodies of research with greater coherency and to enable conducting meta-analyses that can further reduce fragmentation (see Trudeau & Davidson, Chapter 19).

Tightening the connection between basic and applied science would also advance dissemination. Dovidio and Gaertner (Chapter 5) draw from work relating to Fishbein and Ajzen's theory of reasoned action to illustrate the potential of research programs with feedback loops between basic laboratory experiments and field studies. Cause-effect relationships are tested in the laboratory, and the results used to develop interventions that were applied in the field; knowledge gained in the field from small- and large-scale implementations of the interventions are used to continually revise theory through subsequent iterations of experiments. Likewise, Spring and Davidson's stage model of evidence-based behavioral medicine (in Trudeau & Davidson, Chapter 19) describes the process through which the successful discovery of basic mechanisms made its way to the dissemination of scientific innovations that lower cholesterol and reduce cardiovascular disease. Pentz (Chapter 21) also calls for more "reciprocal translation" in which findings from broad dissemination efforts are used to inform basic research on causal mechanisms and applied research on intervention development.

TO WHOM SHOULD THE INNOVATIONS BE DELIVERED?

Throughout the book, authors emphasized the importance of carefully defining and coming to know one's audience both for delivering effective messages and supporting the uptake and effective use of science-based innovations. What individuals and organizations are expected to benefit from the science and in what ways? Which audiences are essential to achieving the dissemination goals? Which of their characteristics affect the ability or willingness to access, understand, or appropriately use the science?

Some dissemination goals may require communicating with only one or two audiences, but to achieve some complex goals, such as changing service systems, a more comprehensive strategy might be needed that involves communicating with the consumers of services, professionals and administrators who deliver the services, policy audiences, various intermediaries such as advocacy groups and issue networks, professional associations, mass media, and so on. Identifying who should be targeted with a particular kind of information can sometimes be difficult, requiring extensive information gathering or consultation with professionals with relevant expertise.

Regardless of how simple or complex the undertaking, key audiences tend to get overlooked or underestimated. In some cases, the audience may be an intermediary who is not as visible as the ultimate decision maker. For example, in policy making, the legislative staff member is just as important an audience as the policy maker himself or herself. Sharpe (Chapter 16) notes also that scientists and their organizations tend to focus mainly on influencing federal legislative language despite the critical role of executive branch officials and staff in developing regulations that carry the weight of law and in designing mechanisms for implementing executive orders and federal legislation. Albert and Brown (Chapter 17) explain that the entire state-level policy maker audience can be passed over as scientists focus on federal policy—even though states serve as laboratories for many innovative policies and programs that eventually end up being implemented in some form at the federal level, state decision makers often determine the content for policies funded under a federal framework, and building relationships with policy makers at the state level may be easier to achieve.

Despite its critical importance, understanding the audience is neglected in both research and practice. Weigold, Treise, and Rausch (Chapter 2) report that "public understanding or attitudes about science have tended to be measured via surveys that seldom assess the kinds of science information people want or how they use it." Throughout the volume, it

becomes clear that systematic research is needed to answer the following: What are the issues of greatest concern or interest to the audience? What content and presentation does the audience need to understand, value, and use the science? What characteristics of the individual affect communication—what motivations, values, and beliefs about the message, about scientific methods, or about behavioral science in particular might affect their willingness to attend to, recall, and use innovations from behavioral science? What conditions in the audience's environments (e.g., professional norms, education, and training) affect their access to the information or innovations, as well as their ability to understand and use the science?

Though not discussed at length in this volume, many nonprofits have begun to invest in strategic communications to better understand their audiences through national polls, targeted surveys, focus groups, and other methods used in marketing and political communications. They focus, for example, on finding the phrases with potential to influence policies and practices relating to public health and well-being by breaking through preconceptions that present barriers to understanding or valuing particular messages. As one senior policy fellow said recently, behavioral scientists with findings to share "need to learn about telling and selling" and to become "comfortable with the tools of marketing" because "strategic communication is the art, *and science,* of directed telling and selling in the service of a goal" (Gruendel, 2003). Chambers (Chapter 22) illustrates the importance of marketing in this volume, citing a study showing that an intervention was more likely to be used if promoted by saying how many lives may be saved if the intervention was used instead of how many lives may be lost if it was not.

Programs of basic audience research could help advance the methods used to communicate science. For instance, though some might believe that simplification can negatively affect understanding and decision making or that detail turns people off and hinders understanding, Stocking and Sparks (Chapter 4) note that we're not yet sure what level of complexity different audiences can handle, will tolerate, or might even desire depending on the need for the information and how best to deliver complex material in particular venues. Only a few studies have begun to explore the effects that particular methods of presenting scientific information have on public understanding and behavior. For example, recent research examines how counterintuitive material can be presented using "transformative explanations" that help audiences recognize and overcome their inaccurate lay theories, thereby encouraging greater understanding, acceptance, and use of information from science (e.g., Rowan, 1999; see Stocking & Sparks, Chapter 4). Systematic studies of audience characteristics such as linguistic skills, and socioeconomic and cultural backgrounds also may help to address barriers that affect meeting one's communication objectives (for example, see Chambers, Chapter 22; Martland & Rothbaum, Chapter 14).

Determining what is newsworthy is a key audience issue in mass media. Siegfried (Chapter 9) asks, Is it new? Is it important? Is it interesting? Journalists and editors have many ideas on the subject, presented in this volume and elsewhere. But as Siegfried notes, judgments about what is newsworthy are made primarily from the perspective of the public rather than the scientist or, more accurately, "through the eyes of an editor's imaginary conception of the average reader."

As early as 1963, journalist and journalism professor Penn T. Kimball suggested that "good editors can use good research" about their audiences. But more than 40 years later, almost no research exists on audience preferences and information needs to guide editors, producers, and journalists in judging the newsworthiness of any topic, much less science or behavioral science. We've found in piloting our own research that editors will continue to question whether scientific audience research would help them to make decisions about what science to cover and how to cover it, driven as they are by the need to increase audience, sales, and revenues. It seems to us, however, that scientific research is needed. For example, in this volume alone, conflicting statements appear about what makes a story newsworthy. Editors are human, and so we can expect the red sports car effect noted in Chapter 10 by Lehrman (i.e., to middle-aged male editors, any story about red sports cars might suddenly become big news) to persist. But behavioral science can encourage the use of more objective criteria by helping to identify what scientific content and messages to communicate, to whom, and under which kinds of conditions in order to meet the public's communication needs. To be convincing and to be used, the research would ultimately need to show that the information helps to meet mass media priorities (a critical part of effectively disseminating scientific research that runs throughout the volume).

A key issue in understanding policy audiences is discerning their perceptions of the various roles behavioral science may play in decision making and the conditions that lead policy makers to choose some roles for the science over others. Behavioral research can, for example, influence policy decisions directly when weighed against other concerns such as constituent opinions, political philosophy, cost-effectiveness, and so on, or wield influence when information is needed to address a well-defined technical issue (see Rich, Chapter 15). Policy makers may also look to science to support a decision already made on another basis. Or, scientific information can frame the boundaries of decision making, encouraging or dissuading consideration of other factors instead of leading directly to a policy decision itself. Though behavioral science perhaps most often serves this last function, it is one of the least understood.

With respect to service professionals, more needs to be understood about how the practical knowledge that practitioners value and deem trustworthy and reliable emerges from their daily observations, of delivering particular treatments and the associated outcomes (e.g., Chambers, Chapter 22), and how to support practitioners in integrating their practical observations and judgment with scientific evidence in order to produce optimal results (see also Trudeau & Davidson, Chapter 19). Relevant studies have begun to emerge in fields such as nursing, but these remain empirical questions that behavioral scientists can help to address.

Contributors emphasize the need to provide education and other supports to professionals in service delivery, mass media, and policy settings, especially to enhance understanding of scientific methods, to promote understanding of relevant behavioral procedures and findings, and to improve the ability to identify trustworthy findings and use them appropriately and effectively in their jobs (see especially Dunwoody, Chapter 3; Jones, Chapter 8; Laurence, Chapter 23; Lyon & Esterline, Chapter 20; Pentz, Chapter 21; Sharpe, Chapter 16; Siegfried, Chapter 9; Trudeau & Davidson, Chapter 19; Stocking & Sparks, Chapter 4). Others point to the need to redress or help prevent negative views that audiences can hold about behavioral science. For example, Laurence (Chapter 23) explains that decision makers in the military can perceive behavioral science to have relatively inexact theories and imprecise methods and measures that are not meaningful to the decisions that must be made. Journalists can hold the same perceptions about behavioral science (see Dunwoody, Chapter 3) as can policy makers (see McCall

& Groark, Chapter 1; Sharpe, Chapter 16). On one hand, negative views signal the need to advance the science in ways already discussed; on the other hand, they show the need to promote better awareness and understanding among particular audiences of behavioral science theories and methods, the kinds of behavioral research methods that are appropriate depending on the purpose, and how the science has led and can lead to new discoveries relevant to the issues or problems at hand.

Still others point to the need to educate scientists about the goals and professional considerations of service professionals, journalists, and policy makers. Behavioral science training does not address how to include such information in hypothesis generation, research design, sampling decisions, and so on or why these factors are important for improving the usefulness of the data.

But how should this education and support be provided? In service delivery fields such as education and behavioral medicine, authors suggested enhancing graduate program curricula by including education about scientific methods, the importance of evidence-based practices, the benefits of using multiple research methods, current methods of synthesizing scientific research, and venues for disseminating information about evidence-based practices. Although some practitioners already receive some science training, it tends to be theoretical and abstract instead of tied tightly to the everyday concerns of professionals. Authors also emphasized the need to improve existing professional development and training mechanisms both to ensure that the content is based on the best available science and that the delivery offers the type of learning experiences and on-site support required to implement and sustain the use of science-based innovations.

For mass media, contributors believed behavioral science may benefit from several models that have been used mainly to advance coverage of other sciences. For example, the Knight Science Journalism Center at MIT offers occasional boot camps so that reporters can strengthen their understanding in certain areas of science; the Environmental Journalism Fellows program brings journalists and scientists together to enhance their relationships and thus journalist and public understanding of the science; the National Institutes of Health (NIH), Dartmouth University, and the Veterans Administration (VA) have together offered workshops on evidence-based medicine for health and medical writers in print and broadcast; the Indiana University's Kinsey Institute along with the School of Journalism designed a workshop for an equal number of sex researchers and journalists with the goal of developing a list of best practices for communicating on the controversial topic of sex research; the Rosalyn Carter Mental Health fellowships pair journalists with mental health scientists and professionals to increase the amount and quality of mental health coverage; the American Association for the Advancement of Science (AAAS) offers mass media fellowships to graduate students who work with journalists in mass media for 1 year to improve relationships and communications between the two fields. The Carnegie Corporation's Carnegie Journalism Initiative provides grants to journalism schools to integrate other university disciplines into journalism education. And so on. To be effective, however, such efforts will need to be more systematic, widespread, and sustained. In addition, evaluations of the efforts would be needed to know whether investments in capacity building had the desired effects (see Stocking & Sparks, Chapter 4).

Providing education to policy makers offers a unique challenge. Legislators and administrators come from a variety of backgrounds and do not participate in any particular level or type of formal training. Thus, no preexisting infrastructure is available to reach them, and the demands of the policy environment do not encourage policy makers to seek out behavioral science. Whatever legislators, administrators, and their staffs understand about behavioral science (or science generally) and about the research relevant to their issues comes mainly from their jobs. Regardless of the method or venue, most educating will need to be done in the context of addressing a pressing issue or problem and so as part of the dissemination itself.

One approach to education, then, is to infuse the working environment with behavioral science. Policy fellowship programs such as the AAAS Science and Technology Policy Fellowships make legislative and administrative staff positions available to scientists and graduate students, introducing behavioral scientists to policy and exposing policy makers to behavioral research. Organizations such as the Consortium of Social Science Associations; the Federation of Behavioral, Psychological and Cognitive Sciences; and the American Psychological Association help to increase understanding through the daily work of their policy staffs who can bring science to bear on policy makers' decisions. These groups also organize science forums, roundtables, briefings, and seminars for federal legislative and administrative policy makers and staff on topics of interest to the policy makers or on emergent science. These events, such as the annual Congressional Exhibits, produced by the Coalition for National Science Funding, showcase scientific advances supported by federal spending and offer opportunities to increase awareness and understanding of behavioral science tied to the topic of the event. More university-based policy centers could consider engaging policy makers at the federal and state level through similar mechanisms, such as the university-based Wisconsin Family Impact Seminars (see Bogenschneider, 2006).

To some extent, promoting understanding and use of behavioral research will require the ongoing education of scientists and science audiences when entering into each new relationship or coping with each new crisis. Sharpe (Chapter 16), for example, illustrates the need to continually educate policy makers about how science is administered and conducted, including the rationale and procedures for the scientific peer review, so that the integrity of the scientific research process will not be compromised. In mass media, diversity in the preparation of mass media journalists for reporting on science and especially behavioral science means that scientists should be prepared to provide within reason any scientific background the journalist might need to understand the quality of the findings and put them into context for the reader. In fact, Stocking and Sparks (Chapter 4) suggest that this ongoing vetting function may be one of the most important of the scientist-journalist relationship.

The need to increase general awareness of behavioral science among those who could benefit from it cuts across audiences. Often, behavioral research is not accessed because mass media editors, policy makers, service providers, and the public are not aware of behavioral science or do not recognize its relevance to an issue that interests them. Here, too, communications will likely need to occur around an immediate concern. One strategy for raising awareness through mass media could be to increase the use of behavioral science as the "side bar" (see Gitow, Chapter 7) or as the interpretive frame (see Dunwoody, Chapter 3), an approach used by Jon Palfreman, who has reported behavioral science discoveries in *Frontline* documentaries on topics such as gangs, drug addition, and mental health (Palfreman, 2002). He credits the unusual support of the show's producer for giving him the opportunity to do this type of public affairs journalism. Encouraging these sorts of media coverage could expand opportunities for behavioral science in the news and perhaps help to make the case for its value.

HOW SHOULD SCIENCE BE DISSEMINATED, BY WHOM, AND TO WHAT EFFECT?

Throughout the volume, authors offered many perspectives on how to create and sustain a context that supports dissemination and on the particular venues, materials, and methods of communicating that tend to be used. More professional wisdom exists than systematic research on which strategies and methods help to achieve particular dissemination goals. Experiments are needed that evaluate various approaches to dissemination and to identify their critical components as would be needed for any other behavioral intervention (see also Biglan, Mrazek, Carnine, & Flay, 2003). As mentioned in the introduction to this volume, evaluations must distinguish between the use of scientific research and their ultimate effects on the intended beneficiary, and whatever the audience and purpose, longitudinal studies will be important for evaluating the conditions that sustain the effective use of innovations. Without this basic level of research sophistication, approaches to dissemination cannot be replicated, and improvements cannot systematically occur.

In the service delivery fields of mental health and drug use, prevention authors point to lessons learned mainly from descriptive methods about the adoption, implementation, and maintenance of an intervention and to directions for future research. For example, it is important to set realistic expectations about outcomes of an intervention, especially in the initial stages of implementation; to support and provide professional development for implementation and sustainability; to get commitments for support and follow-through with key decision makers, administrators, and implementers, including a commitment to create a supportive culture for change and to help overcome resistance; and to identify opinion leaders who can be critical messengers. But more research is needed to understand how to reliably achieve these conditions.

A particularly intractable challenge in service delivery has been to create vehicles such as training and technical assistance centers and other methods of receiving continuing education credits. Dissemination tends to be passive, implementation lacks ongoing onsite support, and the systems fall prey to passing trends. New centers of excellence have been developed in some fields to help move science into practice, but right now it is unclear how many of these function adequately as field laboratories in which approaches to implementation and dissemination are systematically developed and tested using sound scientific methods, as some authors suggest, might more routinely be done to support the dissemination and use of scientific innovations (for related discussion, see Lyon & Esterline, Chapter 20; Pentz, Chapter 21). Questions remain about who should staff such centers— what knowledge and training is required to identify and help to implement evidence-based practices? What are effective methods of providing training and technical assistance, especially the mechanisms and relationships that must be established between service providers and the scientific community to ensure that the most recent research is continually making its way into practice?

Advances to theory would help to accumulate more organized, conceptually coherent, and reliable knowledge about the process of dissemination and the conditions under which effective dissemination occurs. In science communication, for example, Weigold et al. (Chapter 2) note that "with the exception of the deficit model or studies of framing, the research frequently either lacks discussion of underlying theoretical frameworks or offers an assortment of theories and models that have not been systematically tested in sustained programs of research." Likewise, advances are needed

in knowledge utilization theories (Rich, Chapter 15) and diffusion theory and other conceptual models used to guide the dissemination of service delivery practices (see Chambers, Chapter 22; Pentz, Chapter 21).

Measures are needed as well to assess the processes, conditions, and outcomes of dissemination. For example, the Research Roadmap Panel for Public Communication of Science and Technology called for the development of measures to assess which communication strategies change public attitudes, knowledge, and appreciation of information from science and technology, or change behaviors tied to achieving larger communication goals (e.g., aspects of public health). In service delivery, measures that are both theoretically derived and practically useful and, in some cases, tied to community monitoring systems or to existing administrative data will help assess the outcomes of policies and practices when disseminated on a large scale and to identify conditions that influence their effectiveness (in this volume, see Chambers, Chapter 22; Lyon & Esterline, Chapter 20; see also Biglan et al., 2003; Mrazek, Biglan, & Hawkins, 2004).

Advances in descriptive research would help to determine how decision makers in government, service delivery settings, and mass media use information from science and technology. With some notable exceptions (see the Dissemination, Knowledge Transfer, and Knowledge Utilization section of the appendix), much of the existing literature is more than 20 years old (see Rich, Chapter 15; Stocking & Sparks, Chapter 4). In science journalism, theoretically motivated research with more sophisticated coding systems and designs is needed to answer basic questions such as: What is the prevalence of accurate and useful reporting of behavioral science, including handling of the complexities and uncertainties, and under what conditions does it tend to occur? Although much has been written about scientist-journalist relationships (see appendix), little is known about which functions in the system composed of scientists, journalists, and public information officers (PIOs) work well; which could work better; and how the system could be improved (Holland, Chapter 13; Weigold et al., Chapter 2). Likewise, more evidence is needed on the degree to which trial registries of effective interventions and evidence-based guidelines tend to be used, who uses them, in what ways, and with what effect (see Pentz, Chapter 21; Trudeau & Davidson, Chapter 19).

Despite the pervasive need for research, contributors offered practical wisdom, much of it permeated with two main ideas.

If scientists are to be the messengers, they must learn new styles of communicating. Here we highlight three suggestions about the types of communications scientists should use or avoid. First, explanations of science should usually begin with a concise, take-home message that answers, What's the point? The point must relate to the needs and backgrounds of the audience and be stated without equivocation, a particularly difficult barrier for many scientists. Equivocation, Dovidio and Gaertner (Chapter 5) suggest, stems partly from not quite knowing how to convey the research findings derived from inherently uncertain inferential statistics and scientific methods and from producing science that does not quite match the needs of the moment. As a result, scientists can be reluctant to give conclusions or recommendations even when asked. Ignoring the complexities and uncertainties of the science is not the answer because it can lead to inappropriate uses of research (e.g., see Stocking & Sparks, Chapter 4). Instead, boundaries must be put around what is known and what is not known using approaches that do not undercut the main message and that help decision makers take up and appropriately use the science.

Second, technical issues may need to be addressed even for the journalist, editor, service administrator, teacher, implementer of drug use prevention programs, and so on, but at the appropriate level of sophistication. Among the many critical technical issues that may need to be explained are the following: What are the qualities of sound quantitative and qualitative research, what kinds of research questions are each best suited for, and what are the claims that can legitimately be made from different kinds of research methods? What kind of research evidence shows an approach to be effective instead of only promising; why is such evidence not perfect but the best available? What kind of information should one look for in order to understand whether the study applies to them? What are ways of judging the practical significance of a finding as opposed to its theoretical or statistical significance? How does one select measures with appropriate reliability and validity and use them as they were intended to be used?

Third, stories, anecdotes, case studies, and other methods of making the research findings concrete and personal help to communicate messages from scientific data that can otherwise come across as esoteric and abstract. As said in a recent Canadian Health Services Research Foundation (2003) report on using these devices, good stories can show the world in a grain of sand. But research is needed on the elements that make such narratives useful for achieving one's communication objectives, as well as the conditions under which these methods as opposed to others should be used.

Though some scientists will become masterful storytellers, many others will not. Questions arise generally about who should do the disseminating and communicating of behavioral science. In theory, scientists have the greatest potential to be credible messengers given that they produce the relevant knowledge. Within service delivery professions, scientists who are the intervention developers and evaluators already often find themselves expanding their roles to meet technical assistance needs and create the relationships and other conditions for supporting the uptake and effective use of the innovations (see Pentz, Chapter 21, and Biglan & Smolkowski, 2002).

But as many of the authors point out, scientists usually lack the time, skill, or judgment required to communicate effectively beyond their peers, especially in the complex, politically, and emotionally charged environments they are likely to encounter. The individual scientist also may be unable to contact the right audience or a large enough audience to effectively disseminate the research. An assumption of this volume is that promoting the appropriate and effective use of behavioral science requires building a critical mass of scientist-communicators in the academy who are either prepared to perform certain dissemination roles themselves or to engage proactively and productively with various intermediaries. For example, scientists can extend their reach by learning to work with organizations, such as scientific professional societies, policy networks, think tanks, and university-based policy centers, who draw on science in their missions to inform policies and the public, Through such intermediaries, scientists can participate in briefings, forums, workshops, individual meetings with decision makers and their staffs, and various grassroots activities.

Many intermediaries positioned in government, think tanks, and advocacy organizations are themselves trained in academic science and learned their communication skills (or not) on the job, and so more structured opportunities would be beneficial at all career levels to help prepare them. Such positions demand a blend of skills: scientific and technical knowledge, political judgment, communication skill, and so on that is difficult to find and that no one tends to be specifically trained for (Pizzigati, Chapter 18; see also Phillips, 2000).

In the future, graduate and postgraduate preparation training could be enhanced by offering advanced coursework; developing networks and colloquia across disciplines, for example, behavioral science, policy, and journalism graduate training programs; increasing the number of fellowships in policy and mass media for graduate students and professional scientists at all career levels; establishing interdisciplinary short-term training institutes such as those sponsored by the National Institutes of Health, American Psychological Association (APA), and other professional societies; and increasing postdoctoral research training in the dissemination and implementation of interventions.

Dissemination depends on the quality of supporting relationships. Simply presenting research results to relevant audiences or even stating the practical implications tends not to work. Disseminating behavioral science is most effective when a two-way exchange of information occurs in the context of relationships built on coordinated or shared objectives, mutual understanding, and trust. Such relationships may be a primary condition for creating a "research-attuned" culture in organizations that encourages the routine accessing and use of innovations from science and scientific experts (Lavis et al., 2003).

In the complex environments of policy and service delivery, interest is growing in formalizing relationships through issue networks, collaboratives, and consulting arrangements, all vehicles for initiating and strengthening relationships over time between scientists and relevant policy makers, service providers and administrators, consumers, community members, and other various stakeholders. In mass media, developing long-term relationships can result in some level of informality in the exchanges over time, helping the scientist to communicate without academic trappings and helping to ensure that the reporter gets the information, background, and perspective needed to put the research into the appropriate context and report it accurately (see Jones, Chapter 8).

It is unrealistic for the scientist to expect to direct decisions that are outside of the scientist's professional domain and expertise. But sharing information in the context of ongoing, trusting relationships helps audiences to develop a cumulative understanding of the relevant science; helps the scientist to better understand the other person's main concerns, needs, and environment; and thus ultimately helps position both the scientist and the science to shape policy debates, affect media coverage, and meet the needs of service professionals, service consumers, and the greater public whenever critical issues emerge and prime opportunities arise. Authors pointed to the need to systematically study the conditions under which productive formal and informal relationships can be established and maintained, as well as how to remove barriers, including the much-discussed cultural differences that must be bridged between scientific community and professions such as journalism, politics, and human services (e.g., Laurence, Chapter 23; but see Rich, Chapter 15, for a perspective on the limitations of this approach). But experts on all science audiences agreed that the greatest progress can be made if scientists invest in these relationships well before they have some critical message or innovation to deliver.

DISSEMINATION'S PLACE IN THE SCIENTIFIC ENTERPRISE

Many of the authors' suggestions for advancing dissemination have implications for both federal science policy and university culture, two related parts of the larger scientific enterprise. The needs identified throughout this volume match those summarized in a recent review of the organizational factors that influence university-based scientists' involvement in knowledge transfer activities that was undertaken to assess the need for knowledge transfer courses in a university-affiliated health sciences center (Jacobson, Butterill, & Goering, 2004). Five interrelated supports were identified that are essential to, but currently unavailable for, knowledge transfer:

• a knowledge transfer orientation at the university and departmental levels (e.g., tangible and visible commitments to knowledge transfer, emphasizing knowledge transfer in operational plans and mission statements, making knowledge transfer training available to students, recruiting faculty and staff with expertise in knowledge transfer),

• inclusion of knowledge transfer as a priority in promotion and tenure review guidelines,

• the development of methods for documenting the degree and quality of one's involvement in knowledge transfer activities needed for tenure and promotion decisions,

• resources and funding for knowledge transfer activities (e.g., direct costs of convening meetings, networking, skills training, administrative support, production of dissemination plans and communication materials; indirect costs such as coverage for course release time), and

• structures (e.g., organizational structures, such as dedicated units—centers or institutes, offices of knowledge transfer, administrators charged with promoting knowledge transfer, development of knowledge broker positions).

Just as in any other emerging area of inquiry, achieving these conditions requires leading scientists, leaders in universities and academic departments, scientific associations, and leaders in federal science policy and private organizations to work together to identify needs and to provide the resources. Currently, academic departments in the behavioral sciences vary greatly in the range of research and scholarship they value. Still, large grants from federal agencies and private foundations remain the most coveted awards. If interest in both the science and practice of disseminating and communicating science continues to grow among federal agencies and other funding organizations, one might expect the academic community's support to increase. Not only would appreciation for the work of disseminating and communicating science continue to grow, but as researchers acquire external grants and publish their results more routinely in prominent journals, the documentation of one's achievements would appear less alien to tenure and promotion review committees.

But to support the dissemination of behavioral science, changes both great and small will be needed in science policy. A challenging but relatively modest hurdle is to establish appropriate review criteria and expert reviewers for communication/dissemination plans and research. Until recently, agencies that fund research have required little in the way of a full-fledged communication or dissemination plan that convinces reviewers that the approach is feasible, conceptually or empirically justified, and that the methods used will be soundly evaluated to determine their effects.

In service delivery, authors propose integrating scientific research with services programs—for example, conducting studies that merge the implementation of scientifically based interventions with logic models used in service programs that specify steps for dissemination and implementation (see McCall & Groark, Chapter 1; Pentz, Chapter 21). The Society for Research Prevention (2004) has called more specifically for "braided funding" of research and service dollars to more systematically produce

information about the use of scientific innovations that can better support broad dissemination and use, an approach that would likely require changes to the authorizing legislation for research agencies and service programs. Though some collaboration already occurs, policy change may create institutional conditions for ongoing intellectual and financial collaborations for long-range planning of strategic initiatives and greater flexibility to take advantage of emerging opportunities to study the uptake and use of scientific innovations that are being adapted and applied in a new context.

Some have proposed investing in *social technologies,* the capacity of a group of people or an organization to use knowledge effectively, or even more specifically, to turn the outputs of science—knowledge, interventions, tools, and other technology—into positive outcomes for society (Sarewitz et al., 2004). As a basic example, the creation of a vaccine or a new piece of information from research about public health, even if seen as two scientific successes, will become social failures if no one knows, or has the expertise and methods to figure out, how to put together the individual, organizational, political, financial, cultural, and other conditions required to support their dissemination and use. Moving in this direction creates enormous opportunities for the field of social and behavioral science, which specializes in studying the complex combination of contextual and individual influences on behavior in situations such as those surrounding the dissemination and use of science and technology.

The National Cancer Institute (NCI) offers one example of increasing dedication to producing and transferring useful science, including behavioral science—in this case, to promote public health practices and policies. Initiatives range from basic health and biobehavioral research, behavioral and social research, health promotion research, health communications and informatics, and research dissemination and diffusion (see NCI's division of Cancer Control and Population Sciences at http://dccps.cancer.gov/index.html). Behavioral science is called on to help understand influences on health in a program that focuses on conditions from cellular to societal and to merge discoveries and technologies from the field with other disciplines to develop new and innovative methods for promoting public health. Centers of Excellence in Health Communications have been launched, and capacity-building efforts include technical assistance for past and future applicants, grant reviewers, and program staff participating in the Dissemination and Implementation Research program. The institute has dedicated resources to research, research reviews, and other activities aimed at learning how to engage all stakeholders from consumers, to health service providers, to policy makers, to mass media in transferring knowledge for cancer control (for more information see National Cancer Institute, 2004, 2005).

Despite growing interest in dissemination, however, comprehensive and sustained commitments to interdisciplinary, translational, and dissemination research are rare. More widespread efforts will be needed if the dissemination of behavioral science and dissemination research is to be sufficiently guided and supported just as any other vital element of the scientific enterprise would be.

Encouraging broad changes to the scientific enterprise are likely to help behavioral scientists communicate the value of behavioral research. One former assistant director of the National Science Foundation's Social, Behavioral, and Economic Sciences Directorate has lamented the difficulty of explaining the achievements of psychological research to Congress, especially relative to other scientific fields, partly because of the fragmentation

discussed earlier (Bertenthal, 2002). Behavioral scientists are often caught in an awkward position—on one hand, advocating for increased investments in behavioral research while, on the other hand, explaining that the pathway from basic science to trustworthy information and other innovations is long and arduous, inherently unpredictable, emergent, and unmanageable and that the inherent uncertainty of scientific data prevents using many of the findings for decision making (see also Sarewitz, 1996; Sarewitz et al., 2004). Still, as the former assistant director explains, "The perceived value placed on research accomplishments typically has less to do with empirical confirmation and more to do with how well these accomplishments relate to the needs and priorities of the public" (Bertenthal, 2002, p. 217). And so he urges scientists to do more to explain their work to local communities, mass media, and government policy makers and staff and encourages finding new ways to measure, document, and communicate the value of behavioral science discoveries to Congress and the broader citizenry.

But such communications will be effective only if the scientific enterprise actually produces behavioral science innovations—whether basic principles of human behavior, therapeutic interventions, or education practices and tools—that have value to society. Then, the outcomes of behavioral science, as opposed to only outputs such as the number of funded grants or number of journal publications, will need to be measured and communicated (see Garfinkel, Sarewitz, & Porter, 2006, for an example and broader discussion).

Behavioral scientists have a long history of producing and sharing useful information and technologies from their research, and many examples appear throughout the volume. But these accomplishments could have been less challenging and more commonplace if the scientific enterprise had been set up to move behavioral science outside of the academic community. This handbook has underscored that deliberate, coordinated, and sustained action will be needed if behavioral science is to produce innovations that deserve dissemination, advance the strategies and mechanisms it uses to communicate research, discover through scientific inquiry how to improve the dissemination and use of scientific innovations, and groom future generations of scientists to fulfill new roles for which they have been adequately prepared.

REFERENCES

Bertenthal, B. I. (2002). Challenges and opportunities in the psychological sciences. *American Psychologist, 57*(3), 215–218.

Biglan, A., Mrazek, P. J., Carnine, D., & Flay, B. R. (2003). The integration of research and practice in the prevention of youth problem behaviors. *American Psychologist, 58,* 433–440.

Biglan, A., & Smolkowski, K. (2002). The role of the community psychologist in the 21st century. *Prevention & Treatment, 5,* article 2.

Bogenschneider, K. (2006). *Family policy matters: How policymaking affects families and what professionals can do.* Mahwah, NJ: Lawrence Erlbaum.

Bogenschneider, K., Olson, J. R., & Linney, K. D. (2000). Connecting research and policymaking: Implications for theory and practice from the family impact seminars. *Family Relations: Interdisciplinary Journal of Applied Family Studies, 49*(3), 327–339.

Canadian Health Services Research Foundation. (2003, March). *Once upon a time . . . The use and abuse of storytelling and anecdote in the health sector.* Report on the 2003 Annual Invitational CHSRF Workshop, Montreal, Quebec. Retrieved January 28, 2007, from http://www.chsrf.ca/knowledge_transfer/pdf/2003_workshop_report_e.pdf

Fantuzzo, J., McWayne, C., & Childs, S. (2006). Scientist-community collaborations: A dynamic tension between rights and responsibility. In J. Trimble & C. Fisher (Eds.), *Handbook of ethical research with ethnocultural populations and communities* (pp. 27–50). Thousand Oaks, CA: Sage.

Flay, B. R., Biglan, A., Boruch, R. F., Castro, F. G., Gottfredson, D., Kellam, S., et al. (2005). Standards of evidence: Criteria for efficacy, effectiveness and dissemination. *Prevention Science, 6*(3), 151–175.

Garfinkel, M. S., Sarewitz, D., & Porter, A. L. (2006). A societal outcomes map for health research and policy. *American Journal of Public Health, 96*(3), 441–446.

Gruendel, J. M. (2003, Winter). To change policies for children start communicating. *News & Issues.* National Center of Children in Poverty. Retrieved January 28, 2007, from http://www.nccp.org/media/win03-text.pdf

Huston, A. C. (2005). Connecting the science of child development to public policy. *Social Policy Report, 19*(4), 1–20. Ann Arbor, MI: Society for Research in Child Development.

Jacobson, N., Butterill, D., & Goering, P. (2004). Organizational factors that influence university-based researchers' engagement in knowledge transfer activities. *Science Communication, 25*(3), 246–259.

Jenson, P. S. (2003). Commentary: The next generation is overdue. *Journal of the American Academy of Child and Adolescent Psychiatry, 42*(5), 527–530.

Kimball, P. T. (1963). Research: Tool and weapon. How good editors can use good research. *Columbia Journalism Review, 1*(4), 41–43.

Lamb, M. E. (1994). The investigation of child sexual abuse: An interdisciplinary consensus statement. *Journal of Child Sexual Abuse, 3*(4), 93–106.

Lavis, J. N., Robertson, D., Woodside, J. M., McLeod, C. B., Abelson, J., & the Knowledge Transfer Study Group. (2003). How can research organizations more effectively transfer knowledge to decision-makers? *The Milbank Quarterly, 81*(2), 221–248.

Mrazek, P., Biglan, A., & Hawkins, D. (2004). *Community monitoring systems: Tracking and improving the well-being of America's children and adolescents.* The Society for Prevention Research. Retrieved January 28, 2007, from http://www.preventionresearch.org/CMSbook.pdf

National Cancer Institute. (2004). *Facilitating dissemination research and implementation of evidence-based cancer prevention, early detection, and treatment practices.* Retrieved May 4, 2007, from http://cancercontrol.cancer.gov/d4d/dod_summ_nov-dec.pdf

National Cancer Institute. (2005). Dialogue on Dissemination Series: Meeting series summary report. Retrieved January 28, 2007, from http://cancercontrol.cancer.gov/d4d/DialogueSeriesReport.pdf

Palfreman, J. (2002). Bringing science to a television audience. In *Nieman reports: Science journalism* (pp. 32–34). Cambridge, MA: Harvard University Press.

Phillips, D. (2000). Social policy and community psychology. In J. Rappaport & E. Seidman (Eds.), *Handbook of community psychology* (pp. 397–419). New York: Kluwer Academic.

Rowan, K. E. (1999). Effective explanation of uncertain and complex science. In S. M. Friedman, S. Dunwoody, & C. L. Rogers (Eds.), *Communicating uncertainty: Media coverage of new and uncertain science* (pp. 201–223). Mahwah, NJ: Lawrence Erlbaum.

Sarewitz, D. (1996). *Frontiers of illusion: Science, technology, and the politics of progress.* Philadelphia: Temple University Press.

Sarewitz, D., Foladori, G., Invernizzi, I., & Garfinkel, M. (2004). Science policy in its social context. *Philosophy Today, 48* (Suppl.), 67–83.

Society for Prevention Research. (2004). *A case for braided prevention research and service funding.* Retrieved January 28, 2007, from http://www.preventionresearch.org/BraidedFunding.pdf

Appendix of Related Resources

POPULAR SCIENCE, JOURNALISM, AND MASS MEDIA

Blum, D., Knudson, M., & Henig, R. M. (2006). *A field guide for science writers* (2nd ed.). New York: Oxford University Press.

Burnham, J. C. (1987). *How superstition won and science lost: Popularizing science and health in the United States.* New Brunswick, NJ: Rutgers University Press.

Friedman, S. M., Dunwoody, S., & Rogers, C. L. (Eds.). (1986). *Scientists and journalists: Reporting science as news* (American Council on Education/Macmillan Series in Higher Education). Detroit, MI: Free Press.

Friedman, S. M., Dunwoody, S., & Rogers, C. L. (Eds.). (1999). *Communicating uncertainty: Media coverage of new and controversial Science* (LEA's Communication Series). Mahwah, NJ: Lawrence Erlbaum.

Gregory, J., & Miller, S. (1998). *Science in public: Communication, culture and credibility.* Cambridge, MA: Basic Books.

Hamilton, J. T. (2003). *All the news that's fit to sell: How the market transforms information into news.* Princeton, NJ: Princeton University Press.

Miller, J. D., Augenbraum, E., Schulhof, J., & Kimmel, L. G. (2006). Adult science learning from local television newscasts. *Science Communication, 28*(2), 216–242.

Montgomery, S. L. (2003). *The Chicago guide to communicating science.* Dealing with the Press (chap.15). Chicago: University of Chicago Press.

Neiman Reports. (2002, Fall). *Science journalism.* Cambridge, MA: The Neiman Foundation for Journalism, Harvard University.

Nelkin, D. (1995). *Selling science: How the press covers science and technology* (Rev. ed.). New York: W. H. Freeman.

The Pew Charitable Trust. (2004). *The state of the news media 2004.* Retrieved May 22, 2006, from http://www.stateofhtenewsmedia.org

Phillips, D. (2002). Collisions, logrolls, and psychological science. *American Psychologist, 57,* 219–221.

Sommer, R. (2006). Dual dissemination: Writing for colleagues and the public. *American Psychologist, 61*(9), 955–958.

Waddell, C., Lomas, J., Lavis, J. N., Abelson, J., Shepherd, C. A., & Bird-Gayson, T. (2005). Joining the conversation: Newspaper journalists' views on working with researchers. *Healthcare Policy, 1*(1), 123–139.

POLICY MAKING

Bogenschneider, K. (2006). *Family policy matters: How policymaking affects families and what professionals can do.* Mahwah, NJ: Lawrence Erlbaum.

DeLeon, P. H., Loftus, C. W., Ball, V., & Sullivan, M. J. (2006). Navigating politics, policy, and procedure: A firsthand perspective of advocacy on behalf of the profession. *Professional Psychology: Research and Practice, 37*(2), 146–153.

Featherman, D. L., & Vinovskis, M. A. (Eds.). (2001). *Social science and policymaking: A search for relevance in the twentieth century.* Ann Arbor: University of Michigan Press.

Grafton, C., & Permaloff, A. (2005). The behavioral study of political ideology and public policy formulation. *The Social Science Journal, 42,* 201–213.

Gruendel, J., & Aber, J. L. (2007). Bridging the gap between research and child policy change: The role of strategic communications in policy advocacy. In J. L. Aber, S. J. Bishop-Josef, S. Jones, K. T. McLearn, & D. A. Phillips (Eds.), *Child development and social policy: Knowledge for action* (pp. 43–58). Washington, DC: American Psychological Association.

Hilgartner, S. (2000). *Science on stage: Expert advice as public drama.* Stanford, CA: Stanford University Press.

Hoagwood, K., & Johnson, J. (2003). School psychology: A public health framework: I. From evidence-based practices to evidence-based policies. *Journal of School Psychology, 41*(1), 3–21.

Jackson-Elmoore, C. (2005). Informing state policymakers: Opportunities for social workers. *Social Work, 50*(3), 251–261.

Jasanoff, S. (1990). *The fifth branch: Science advisers as policymakers.* Cambridge, MA: Harvard University Press.

Krismsky, S. (2005). The weight of scientific evidence in policy and law. *American Journal of Public Health, 95*(Suppl. 1), 129–136.

Sarewitz, D. (1996). *Frontiers of illusion: Science, technology, and the politics of progress.* Philadelphia: Temple University Press.

Weiss, C. H. (1987). The diffusion of social science research to policymakers: An overview. In G. B. Melton (Ed.), *Reforming the law: Impact of child development research* (pp. 63–85). New York: Guilford.

DISSEMINATION, KNOWLEDGE TRANSFER, AND KNOWLEDGE UTILIZATION

Abrams, D. (2006). Applying transdisciplinary research strategies to understanding and eliminating health disparities. *Health Education & Behavior, 33*(4), 515–531.

Addis, M., Cardemil, E., Duncan, B., & Miller, S. (2005). Does manualization improve therapy outcomes? In J. C. Norcross, L. E. Beutler, & R. F. Levant (Eds.), *Evidence-based practices in mental health: Debate and dialogue on the fundamental questions* (pp. 131–160). Washington, DC: American Psychological Association.

Amodeo, M., Ellis, M., & Samet, J. (2006). Introducing evidence-based practices into substance abuse treatment using organization development methods. *American Journal of Drug and Alcohol Abuse, 32*(4), 555–560.

Barlow, D., Levitt, J., & Bufka, L. (1999). The dissemination of empirically supported treatments: A view to the future. *Behaviour Research and Therapy, 37*(1), 147–162.

Barratt, M. (2003). Organizational support for evidence-based practice within child and family social work: A collaborative study. *Child & Family Social Work, 8*(2), 143–150.

Barton, A., & Welbourne, P. (2005). Context and its significance in identifying "what works" in child protection. *Child Abuse Review, 14*(3), 177–194.

Biglan, A., & Taylor, T. K. (2000). Increasing the use of science to improve child-rearing. *Journal of Primary Prevention, 21*(2), 207–226.

Broner, N., Franczak, M., Dye, C., & McAllister, W. (2001). Knowledge transfer, policymaking and community empowerment: A consensus model approach for providing public mental health and substance abuse services. *Psychiatric Quarterly, 72*(1), 79–102.

Consumer-driven health care: Building partnerships in research. (2005). *Health Expectations: An International Journal of Public Participation in Health Care & Health Policy, 8*(4), 352–359.

Cooke, M. (2000). The dissemination of a smoking cessation program: Predictors of program awareness, adoption and maintenance. *Health Promotion International, 15*(2), 113–124.

Earle, A., Heyman, J., & Lavis, N. (2006). Where do we go from here? Translating research to policy. In J. Heyman, C. Hertzman, M. L. Barer, & R.G. Evans (Eds.), *Healthier societies: From analysis to action* (pp. 381–404). New York: Oxford University Press.

Estabrooks, C. A., Floyd, J. A., Scott-Findlay, S., O'Leary, K. A., & Gushta, M. (2003). Individual determinants of research utilization: A systematic review. *Journal of Advanced Nursing, 43*(5), 506–520.

Flaspohler, P., Anderson-Butcher, D., Paternite, C., Weist, M., & Wandersman, A. (2006). Community science and expanded school mental health: Bridging the research-to-practice gap to promote child well-being and academic success. *Educational and Child Psychology, 23*(1), 27–41.

Glanz, K., Steffen, A., Elliott, T., & O'Riordan, D. (2005). Diffusion of an effective skin cancer prevention program: Design, theoretical foundations, and first-year implementation. *Health Psychology, 24*(5), 477–487.

Greenberg, M. (2004). Current and future challenges in school-based prevention: The researcher perspective. *Prevention Science, 5*(1), 5–13.

Gregrich, R. J. (2003). A note to researchers: Communicating science to policymakers and practitioners. *Journal of Substance Abuse Treatment, 25*, 233–237.

Hemsley-Brown, J. (2004). Facilitating research utilization: A cross-sector review of research evidence. *International Journal of Public Sector Management, 16*(6), 534–552.

Hennink, M., & Stephenson, R. (2005). Using research to inform health policy: Barriers and strategies in developing countries. *Journal of Health Communication, 10*, 163–180.

Hoagwood, K. (2005). The research, policy, and practice context for delivery of evidence-based mental health treatments for adolescents: A systems perspective. In D. L. Evans, E. B. Foa, R. E. Gur, & H. Hendin (Eds.), *Treating and preventing adolescent mental health disorders: What we know and what we don't know: A research agenda for improving the mental health of our youth* (pp. 545–560). New York: Oxford University Press.

Holleman, G., Eliens, A., van Vliet, M., & van Achterberg, T. (2006). Promotion of evidence-based practice by professional nursing

associations: Literature review. *Journal of Advanced Nursing, 53*(6), 702–709.

Hubbard, G., Kidd, L., Donaghy, E., McDonald, C., & Kearney, N. (2007). A review of literature about involving people affected by cancer in research, policy and planning and practice. *Patient Education and Counseling, 65*(1), 21–33.

Kothari, A., Birch, S., & Charles, C. (2005). "Interaction" and research utilisation in health policies and programs: Does it work? *Health Policy, 71*(1), 117–125.

Kramer, D. M., Cole, D. C., & Leithwood, K. (2004). Doing knowledge transfer: Engaging management and labor with research on employee health and safety. *Bulletin of Science, Technology & Society, 24*, 316–330.

Kramer, D. M., & Wells, R. P. (2005). Achieving buy-in: Building networks to facilitate knowledge transfer. *Science Communication, 26*, 428–444.

Lavis, J. N. (2004). Use of research to inform public policymaking. *Lancet, 364*, 1615–1621.

Lavis, J. N. (2006). Moving forward on both systematic reviews and deliberate processes. *Healthcare Policy, 1*(2), 59–63.

Lavis, J. N., Davies, H. T. O., Gruen, R. L., Walshe, K., & Farquhar, C. M. (2006). Working within and beyond the Cochrane Collaboration to make systematic reviews more useful to healthcare managers and policymakers. *Healthcare Policy, 1*(2), 21–33.

Lomas, J. (2000). Using "linkage and exchange" to move research into policy at a Canadian foundation. *Health Affairs, 19*(3), 236–240.

Marlenga, B., Pickett, W., & Berg, R. L. (2002). Evaluation of an enhanced approach to the dissemination of the North American guidelines for children's agricultural tasks: A randomized controlled trial. *Preventive Medicine: An International Journal Devoted to Practice and Theory, 35*(2), 150–159.

Mayer, J., & Davidson, W. (2000). Dissemination of innovation as social change. In J. Rappaport & E. Seidman (Eds.), *Handbook of community psychology* (pp. 421–443). New York: Kluwer Academic.

Ouimet, M., Landry, R., Aamara, N., & Belkhodja, O. (2006). What factors induce health care decision-makers to use clinical guidelines? Evidence from provincial health ministries, regional authorities and hospitals in Canada. *Social Science & Medicine, 62,* 964–976.

Pearson, A. (2004). Getting research into practice. *International Journal of Nursing Practice, 10*(5), 197–198.

Schoenwald, S., & Henggeler, S. (2004). A public health perspective on the transport of evidence-based practices. *Clinical Psychology: Science and Practice, 11*(4), 360–363.

Schrader, M., Weißbach, L., Weikert, S., Schostak, M., & Miller, K. (2006). Paper tigers: Do clinical guidelines improve health care quality in patients with testicular germ cell tumors in Germany? *Health Policy, 75*(3), 338–346.

Seedat, M., & Nascimento, A. (2003). The use of public health research in stimulating violence and injury prevention practices and policies: Reflections from South Africa. *Journal of Prevention & Intervention in the Community, 25*(1), 31–47.

Shorten, A., Wallace, M. C., & Crookes, P. A. (2001). Developing information literacy: A key to evidence-based nursing. *International Nursing Review, 48*(2), 86–92.

Silverman, W. K., Kurtines, W. M., & Hoagwood, K. (2004). Research progress on effectiveness, transportability, and dissemination of empirically supported treatments: Integrating theory and research. *Clinical Psychology: Science & Practice, 11*(3), 295–299.

Small, S., & Uttal, L. (2005). Action-oriented research: Strategies for engaged scholarship. *Journal of Marriage and Family, 67*(4), 936–948.

Tanenbaum, S. (2003). Evidence-based practice in mental health: Practical weaknesses meet political strengths. *Journal of Evaluation in Clinical Practice, 9*(2), 287–301.

van Oostendorp, H., Breure, L., & Dillon, A. (2005). *Creation, use, and deployment of digital information.* Mahwah, NJ: Lawrence Erlbaum.

Weisz, J., Hawley, K., Pilkonis, P., Woody, S., & Follette, W. (2000). Stressing the (other) three Rs in the search for empirically supported treatments: Review procedures, research

quality, relevance to practice and the public interest. *Clinical Psychology: Science and Practice, 7*(3), 243–258.

STRATEGIC COMMUNICATIONS, PUBLIC HEALTH COMMUNICATION, AND SOCIAL MARKETING CAMPAIGNS

Andreasen, A. R. (2005). *Social marketing in the 21st century.* Thousand Oaks, CA: Sage.

Bonk, K., Griggs, H., & Tynes, E. (1999). *The Jossey-Bass guide to strategic communications for nonprofits.* San Francisco: Jossey-Bass.

Earle, R. (2002). *Art of cause marketing: How to use advertising to change personal behavior and public policy.* New York: McGraw-Hill.

Gilliam, F. D., Jr., & Bales, S. N. (2001). Strategic frame analysis: Reframing America's youth. *Social Policy Report, 15*(3), 3–14.

Gruendel, J., & Aber, J. L. (2006). Bridging the gap between research and child policy change: The role of strategic communications in policy advocacy. In J. L. Aber, D. Phillips, S. M. Jones, & K. McLearn (Eds.), *Child development and social policy: Knowledge for action.* Washington, DC: APA Publications.

The Health Information National Trends Survey (HINTS): Development, design, and dissemination. (2004). *Journal of Health Communication, 9*(5), 443–460.

Hornik, R. (Ed.). (2002). *Public health communication: Evidence for behavior change* (LEA's Communication Series). Mahwah, NJ: Laurence Erlbaum.

Kotler, P., Roberto, N., & Lee, N. R. (2002). *Social marketing improving quality of life* (2nd ed.). Thousand Oaks, CA: Sage.

Leff, S., Conley, J., & Hennessy, K. (2006). Marketing behavioral health: Implications of evidence assessments for behavioral health care in the United States. *International Journal of Mental Health, 35*(2), 6–20.

Longo, D. (2005). Understanding health information, communication, and information seeking of patients and consumers: A comprehensive and integrated model. *Health Expectations: An International Journal of Public Participation in Health Care & Health Policy, 8*(3), 189–194.

The Spinworks Project. (2000). *SPIN works! A media guidebook for the rest of us.* San Francisco: Independent Media Institute.

Thompson, T. L., Miller, K., Dorsey, A., & Parrott, R. L. (Eds.). (2003). *Handbook of health communication.* Mahwah, NJ: Lawrence Erlbaum.

WEB SITES

Centre for Community Health Promotion Research, University of Victoria, Canada

http://web.uvic.ca/chpc/resources/knowle dgetrans.htm

An updated bibliography of key works in knowledge translation that includes discussions of topics such as evidence-based practices, evidence-based policy making, developing knowledge systems, collaborative and participatory research, cultural barriers to knowledge transfer, theories and frameworks to study and promote utilization, the role of qualitative research, meta-analyses, qualities of useful program and policy evaluations, the use of systematic reviews, and analysis of current trends in using systematic reviews.

Chair on Knowledge Transfer and Innovation, Laval University, Québec, Canada

http://kuuc.chair.ulaval.ca/english/pdf/bib liographie/sociales.pdf

This program maintains a regularly updated Web site with valuable resources, including a comprehensive bibliography of references of articles up to 2001 on the dissemination and utilization of social sciences research. The chair was initiated to further the scientific understanding of knowledge transfer and innovation in health services, encourage and facilitate the transfer of knowledge, and train graduate students in the field. It began operating in the summer of 2000 with financial support for 10 years as part of a the Capacity for Applied and Developmental Research and Evaluation (CADRE) program, a partnership between the Canadian Health Services Research Foundation and the Canadian Institutes of Health Research.

Frameworks Institute

www.frameworksinstitute.org

This organization helps nonprofits communicate scholarly research to frame public discourse on social problems.

Strategic Communications Resource Library

www.strategiccomm.com

The Jossey-Bass Guide to Strategic Communications for Nonprofits was written by the cofounders of the Communications Consortium Media Center to give step-by-step guidance on how to work with media and use new communications to educate the public and support policy change.

Knowledge Utilization and Policy Implementation Research Program, University of Alberta

http://www.nursing.ualberta.ca/kusp/ Resources/KU%20Resource%20Guide/KU ResourceGuide.pdf

The *Knowledge Utilization Resource Guide* was created in 2004 by an interdisciplinary team of knowledge and information specialists led by Carole Estabrookes. The guide lists introductory and advanced-level resources to promote understanding of the "different ways knowledge can be used, created, measured, transferred, and translated in practice." The resources include bibliographies of classic and cutting-edge academic publications and lists of key journals, special journal issues, key players in the field, relevant centers, research organizations, professional associations and funding agencies, and lists of key search times to support productive literature searchers on this cross-disciplinary topic. Subject areas covered are nursing and health sciences, social sciences and humanities, organization studies, and policy studies. In addition, for a continually updated list of the program's publications on knowledge transfer and utilization,

see http://www.uanursing.ualberta.ca/kusp/
Research_Products.htm.

The Carnegie Corporation's Carnegie Journalism Initiative
http://www.carnegie.org/sub/program/
jour_initiative.html

This site details the initiative's goals of "encouraging experimentation within journalism schools and forging a greater integration with other university disciplines and departments in order to offer students the opportunity to benefit from the resources of the larger university community." The site provides links to the larger Carnegie-Knight Initiative on the Future of Journalism Education and to numerous reports on the state of journalism and a view for the future.

The Project for Excellence in Journalism
http://www.journalism.org/

This organization, affiliated with The Pew Charitable Trust, specializes in using empirical methods to evaluate and study the performance of the press. Its goal is to "help both the journalists who produce the news and the citizens who consume it develop a better understanding of what the press is delivering. The Project has put special emphasis on content analysis in the belief that quantifying what is occurring in the press, rather than merely offering criticism and analysis, is a better approach to understanding." The site includes an archive of all materials produced by the project, a news index, annual reports examining the state of the news media, and journalism resources.

Index

About the Editors

Melissa K. Welch-Ross is affiliated Associate Professor of Psychology at George Mason University. Previously, she served 3 years in the U.S. Department of Health and Human Services as research and policy analyst for the Office of the Assistant Secretary for Planning and Evaluation, Division of Children and Youth Policy. She earlier directed the Early Learning and School Readiness Research Program at the National Institute of Child Health and Human Development at the National Institutes of Health (NIH). In these positions, she worked to stimulate new research to bridge basic and applied science on early learning and development and to apply research to practices and policies, mainly in early childhood education. In 2000, she was Executive Branch Science Policy Fellow at the U.S. Department of Education, sponsored by the Society for Research in Child Development and the American Association for the Advancement of Science. Prior to the fellowship, she was Assistant Professor and Assistant Research Professor at Georgia State University in Atlanta, Georgia, where she conducted NIH-funded research on early memory development. She has served as consulting editor for the flagship journals *Child Development* and *Developmental Psychology*.

Lauren G. Fasig is Associate Director of the Center on Children and Families in the Levin College of Law, and Visiting Assistant Professor of Psychology at the University of Florida. She serves on the Florida Supreme Court's Mental Health Subcommittee on Families and Children in the Court. Previously, she was the founding Director of the Office of Policy and Communications for the Society for Research in Child Development (SRCD). In that position, she conducted the communications and dissemination activities of the Society, including ongoing press relations, media activities, congressional outreach and education, and media and advocacy training for the SRCD membership. She also administered the SRCD Congressional and Executive Branch Fellowships and conducted the federal policy activities of the Society. She has served as editor of the SRCD online newsletter, *Washington Update,* and as consulting editor to *Social Policy Reports* and the *Journal of Youth and Adolescence.* She was James Marshall Public Policy Scholar, awarded by Society for the Psychological Study of Social Issues and the American Psychological Association. As a member of the DC Bar, she participated in the pro bono family law and Guardian ad Litem programs. She's been Program Manager and consultant for the Dependency Mediation Program in the Eighth Judicial Circuit, Florida, where she developed its mediation program, approaches to program measurement, and professional training seminars.

About the Contributors

Bill Albert is Deputy Director of the National Campaign to Prevent Teen Pregnancy. He oversees the organization's communications effort and contributes to writing and editing National Campaign publications. Previously, he spent 12 years working in television news, most recently as the Managing Editor at Fox Television News in Washington, D.C., where he managed the editorial content of two daily news broadcasts.

Sarah S. Brown is the Director of The National Campaign to Prevent Teen Pregnancy, a private and independent nonprofit that she helped set up in 1996. Before helping to found the Campaign, she was a senior study director at the Institute of Medicine, where she directed numerous studies in the broad field of maternal and child health. She has served on advisory boards of many influential national organizations and has received numerous national awards for her work on teen pregnancy and maternal and child health. She speaks frequently on issues of teen sex and pregnancy nationwide and appears regularly in the media.

David A. Chambers has worked at the National Institute of Mental Health (NIMH) since 2001, heading up the Dissemination and Implementation Research Program, part of the Services Research and Clinical Epidemiology Branch. His work has focused on how change occurs in clinical practice, how new practices are introduced into clinical settings, and how health information is disseminated to multiple audiences. He also serves as NIMH Associate Director on Dissemination and Implementation Research and as coordinator of the institute's science and service activities. Previously in Oxford, England, he helped to evaluate several National Health Service initiatives that aimed to translate research findings into clinical practice.

Karina W. Davidson is Co-Director of the Center for Behavioral Cardiovascular Health at Columbia College of Physicians and Surgeons in New York. She researches psychosocial interventions for patients with cardiovascular disease and has conducted randomized controlled trials of anger management and depression treatment for hypertensive and post–myocardial infarction (MI) patients. Her multisite, multiproject study funded by the NIH is exploring the etiology, course, and treatment of depressive symptoms in patients with acute coronary syndromes. She formed and chaired the Evidence-Based Behavioral-Medicine Task Force, charged by seven national and international societies with improving and implementing evidence-based principles in behavioral medicine. She is Convenor of the Cochrane Behavioral Medicine Field, an international effort to synthesize and disseminate evidence for behavioral medicine interventions.

John F. Dovidio is Professor of Psychology at Yale University. He is Editor of the

Journal of Personality and Social Psychology— Interpersonal Relations and Group Processes, and he was previously Editor of *Personality and Social Psychology Bulletin.* His research expertise is in stereotyping, prejudice, and discrimination; social power and nonverbal communication; and altruism and helping. He has served as President of the Society for the Psychological Study of Social Issues and Chair of the Executive Committee of the Society for Experimental Social Psychology, and he is President-Elect of the Society for Personality and Social Psychology.

Sharon Dunwoody is Evjue Bascom Professor of Journalism and Mass Communication at the University of Wisconsin–Madison, where she also serves as associate dean for social studies in the Graduate School and on the governance faculty of the Gaylord Nelson Institute for Environmental Studies. Her doctoral training was in mass communication, and she is a former mass media science writer. She has taught science communication courses and conducted research on a variety of public-understanding-of-science issues at the University of Wisconsin–Madison since 1981. She is a Fellow of both the American Association for the Advancement of Science and the Midwest Association of Public Opinion Research.

Elayne Esterline is a researcher and contributing writer in the research and evaluation department of Higher Ed Holdings. In her research, she identifies national and international education studies relevant to instructional design, assessment, and instructional methodology. Prior to joining Higher Ed Holdings, she served as a contributing writer for the *Texas Observer* and *texasnon profits.org.* She holds graduate degrees in public policy and journalism.

Rhea K. Farberman is the Executive Director for Public and Member Communications at the American Psychological Association. With a graduate background in communications and publications management, she directs the association's media relations program and is often quoted in the national media as the association's lead spokesperson. She is an accredited member of the Public Relations Society of America (PRSA).

Samuel L. Gaertner is Professor of Psychology at the University of Delaware. He received his Ph.D. from the City University of New York, Graduate Center in 1970. His research interests involve intergroup relations with primary focus on reducing prejudice, discrimination, and racism. He has served on the Council of the Society for the Psychological Study of Social Issues (SPSSI) and on the editorial boards of the *Journal of Personality and Social Psychology, Personality and Social Psychology Bulletin,* and *Group Processes and Intergroup Relations.* He and John Dovidio shared SPSSI's Gordon Allport Intergroup Relations Prize in 1985 and 1998 and the Kurt Lewin Award in 2004.

Andrea Gitow is a two-time Emmy award-winning network news producer who spent nearly a decade at NBC News developing, producing, and supervising the production of stories for all of NBC News programs, including *Dateline, The Today Show,* and *Nightly News With Tom Brokaw.* She began her career as a research scientist in the Department of Psychiatry, College of Physicians and Surgeons, Columbia University. She has authored more than 15 academic papers and serves as a featured lecturer at universities.

Roberta Golinkoff is H. Rodney Sharp Chair in the School of Education at the University of Delaware. A recipient of the John Simon Guggenheim Fellowship and James McKeen Cattell Sabbatical award, her research focuses on language development and the benefits of play. She is frequently quoted in newspapers and magazines as a scientific advocate for children. She has appeared on *Good Morning America,* CN8, many regional television morning shows, and hundreds of radio programs across the country. Her book *Einstein Never Used Flash Cards: How Our Children Really Learn and Why They Need to Play More and Memorize Less* (with Kathy Hirsh-Pasek) attempts to liberate caring adults from the cult of overachievement.

Christina J. Groark is Co-Director of the University of Pittsburgh Office of Child Development (OCD) and Associate Professor of Education. She has been the principal investigator for numerous large collaborative programs implementing and evaluating evidence-based service and policy initiatives on behalf of children and families. She is the author of many articles and book chapters on university-community collaborations and implementing and replicating service programs. She was given the University of Pittsburgh Chancellor's Award for Distinguished Contributions to Public Service in 2004.

Diane F. Halpern is Professor of Psychology and Director of the Berger Institute for Work, Family, and Children at Claremont McKenna College. She has published more than 350 articles and many books, including *Thought and Knowledge: An Introduction to Critical Thinking* (4th ed.); *Sex Differences in Cognitive Abilities* (3rd ed.); a special two-volume edited issue of the *American Behavioral Scientist,* titled "Changes at the Intersection of Work and Family" (edited with Heidi R. Riggio, 2006); and *Critical Thinking in Psychology* (edited with Robert J. Sternberg and Henry L. Roediger III, 2007). She was 2004 President of the American Psychological Association.

Stacy Ann Hawkins is project coordinator at the Berger Institute for Work, Family, and Children at Claremont McKenna College and a doctoral student in applied social psychology at Claremont Graduate University. Her research focuses on interpersonal relationships, particularly within families. She won the Grace Berry Award for Women in Graduate Studies in 2006–2007.

Kathryn Hirsh-Pasek is the Lefkowitz Professor in Psychology at Temple University and Director of its Infant Language Laboratory. She has written 9 books and published more than 100 professional articles. She serves as the Associate Editor of *Child Development* and treasurer of the International Society for Infant Studies. She was also an investigator on the NICHD Study of Early Child Care. She is a spokesperson on early development for national magazines and newspapers, radio, and television and an adviser for CIVITAS's Born Learning Series, America's Promise, Sesame Workshop, Fisher Price, The Cartoon Network, and Children's Museums across North America.

Earle M. Holland heads research communications at Ohio State University (OSU). He's served on the boards of the National Association of Science Writers and the Society of Environmental Journalists, as well as on the national advisory committee for EurekAlert!. For 20 years, he taught science reporting at OSU and, for 18 years, wrote a weekly science column for the *Columbus Dispatch.* For 7 years, he wrote the national weekly column, *GeoWeek,* distributed by the New York Times Syndicate. He's a contributor to *A Field Guide for Science Writers,* a primary resource for science writing graduate programs. A former reporter for the *Birmingham* (AL) *News,* his OSU science writing programs have won more than 65 national awards while under his direction.

Rachel Jones is a reporter for National Public Radio (NPR) in Washington, D.C. Since 1998, she has developed stories on issues, including poverty, health, education, and social policy for NPR's Science Desk and National Desk. Previously, she worked for *The Chicago Reporter, The St. Petersburg Times,* and *The Detroit Free Press* and was a national correspondent for Knight Ridder, Inc.'s Washington bureau, reporting on social policy affecting children and families. She served on the advisory board of the University of Maryland's Journalism Fellowships in Child and Family Policy and has joined the Advisory Board for the National Prekindergarten Center at the Frank Porter Graham Child Development Institute at the University of North Carolina–Chapel Hill.

Janice H. Laurence is the Director of Research and Analysis in the Office of the Under Secretary of Defense (Personnel & Readiness). Prior to coming to the Pentagon in 2004, she taught and advised company officers within the Naval Postgraduate School's Leadership Education and Development Program at the U.S. Naval Academy. She has 25 years of experience conducting and managing policy studies and applied research and analysis related to workforce and human capital issues mainly in the military setting. She is the editor of *Military Psychology,* the official journal of the Society for Military Psychology, a division of the American Psychological Association.

Sally Lehrman is an award-winning reporter on medicine and science policy who has written for some of the top names in national print and broadcast media, including *Scientific American, Nature, Health,* Salon. com, and the *DNA Files,* distributed by NPR. Her honors have included the 1995–1996 John S. Knight Fellowship, a shared 2002 Peabody award, the Peabody/Robert Wood Johnson Award for excellence in health and medical programming, and the Columbia/Du Pont Silver Baton (for the *DNA Files*). Before going independent, she worked for the Hearst-owned *San Francisco Examiner* for 13 years. She serves as at-large director and national diversity chair for the Society of Professional Journalists and is a USC Annenberg Institute for Justice and Journalism Expert Fellow.

G. Reid Lyon is Executive Vice President for Research and Evaluation at Best Associates and the Whitney University in Dallas, Texas. Previously, he was research psychologist and Branch Chief at the National Institute of Child Health and Human Development at the NIH. A prolific expert in developmental neuropsychology and special education/learning disorders, he has served as a third-grade teacher and school psychologist and has taught children with learning disabilities. He was adviser to the White House on child development and education and has testified before numerous congressional committees on the role of science in education, reading research and policy, special education, and early child development.

Nancy Martland is Executive Director of the Tufts Child & Family WebGuide. She previously directed Tufts' Child & Family News, an online service that provided child development research to journalists. Her research focuses on the evaluation of Web-based resources and on use of the Web by parents, journalists, practitioners, and policy makers to obtain information on child development. Her work has been published in *Child Welfare, Journal of Applied Developmental Psychology,* and *Applied Developmental Science.*

Robert B. McCall is Co-Director of the University of Pittsburgh Office of Child Development and Professor of Psychology. He has published on infant mental development, age changes in general mental performance, early childhood care and education, science communications through the media, and university-community partnerships. He was a contributing editor, monthly columnist, and feature writer for *Parents* magazine and has received awards for his contributions to research, public service, media, and policy from the American Psychological Association, the Society for Research in Child Development, the American Academy of Pediatrics, the National Council on Family Relations, and the University of Pittsburgh.

Mary Ann Pentz is Professor of Preventive Medicine in the Keck School of Medicine at the University of Southern California, where she has also directed a center for prevention policy research. Her research focuses on multicomponent, community, and policy approaches to the prevention of violence, tobacco, alcohol and drug use, and related problem behaviors, as well as the translation of evidence-based preventions for drug use to other areas, such as obesity prevention. Several of her programs are in the National Registry of Effective Programs. She is one of the founding board members of the Society for Prevention Research and has worked with Congress on the formulation of antidrug abuse legislation.

Karabelle Pizzigati is a policy and leadership development consultant on children and family issues, and president-elect of the National Association of State Boards of Education. She formerly directed public policy for the Washington, D.C.-based Child Welfare League of America (CWLA). Before joining CWLA, she served as staff director of the Select Committee on Children, Youth, and Families of the U.S. House of Representatives. She serves on the Technical Work Group for the National Longitudinal Study of Child and Adolescent Well-Being, the Board of Directors of Parents as Teachers National Center, and the Maryland State Board of Education.

Paula Rausch spent 7 years as a reporter covering government, politics, health, business, and other beats for three Florida newspapers. She began working for the University of Florida in 2000, first as a science/health writer for the College of Medicine and later as a senior science/health writer and editor, overseeing the university's major news release operations. Trained as a nurse and journalist, she is now pursuing a doctorate in mass communication with a focus on public health.

Robert F. Rich is Director of the Institute of Government and Public Affairs and Professor of Law, Political Science, Medical Humanities and Social Sciences, Community Health, and Health Policy and Administration at the University of Illinois. He is the author of 7 books and more than 50 articles. He was the founding editor of *Knowledge: Creation, Diffusion Utilization*, which is now published as *Science Communications*. His book, *Social Science Information and Public Policy-Making*, is in its second edition. His most recent book, *Consumer Choice: Social Welfare and Health Policy*, was published in 2005.

Fred Rothbaum is a Professor in the Eliot-Pearson Department of Child Development and President of the Tufts University Child & Family WebGuide. He has written several publications on disseminating research-based information about child development to a variety of audiences, including parents and policy makers. He has authored more than 40 publications on parent-child relations, perceptions of control, emotion regulation, depression, and cultural variation in development. He is also a licensed clinical psychologist.

Angela L. Sharpe is the Deputy Director for Health Policy for the Consortium of Social Science Associations (COSSA). She lobbies members of Congress and their staff on health and behavior research and represents

COSSA to executive branch agencies, particularly the Department of Health and Human Services. She co-chairs the Coalition for the Advancement of Health Through Behavior and Social Sciences Research and the Coalition to Protect Research, and she is a member of the Ad Hoc Group for Medical Research's Steering Committee. She was legislative assistant to Rep. Carrie P. Meek (D-FL) and to the late Rep. R. Lawrence Coughlin (R-PA).

Tom Siegfried is a freelance science journalist who lives in Los Angeles. From 1985 to 2004, he was science editor of *The Dallas Morning News.* He is the author of *The Bit and the Pendulum, Strange Matters,* and *A Beautiful Math,* and he is a contributor to the National Association of Science Writers's *Field Guide for Science Writers.* He is a recipient of the American Psychiatric Association's Robert T. Morse Writer's Award, and in 2006, he received the American Geophysical Union's Robert C. Cowen Award for Sustained Achievement in Science Journalism.

Johnny V. Sparks is Assistant Professor in the Department of Telecommunications at the University of Alabama, Tuscaloosa. His research specialties are in science communication and cognitive processing and multiple effects of media. He has been a predoctoral research fellow at The Kinsey Institute and research assistant in The Institute for Communication Research at Indiana University. He was editor of *The All State,* his college newspaper, at Austin Peay State University, where he later served as the Director of Student Publications.

S. Holly Stocking is Associate Professor in the School of Journalism at Indiana University, Bloomington, where she teaches a graduate course in science writing. Before becoming an academic, she was a reporter for the *Los Angeles Times,* the *Minneapolis*

Tribune, and the Associated Press and Coordinator of Science Writing Projects for the Boys Town Center for the Study of Youth Development in Omaha, Nebraska. Her research specialty is the public communication of scientific unknowns and uncertainties.

Sherylle J. Tan is a developmental psychologist and the Associate Director of the Berger Institute for Work, Family, and Children at Claremont McKenna College. In her work, she applies developmental theory and methods to understanding the issues of child development, parenting, and work and family. Previously, she was an evaluation consultant for several nonprofit community agencies providing services for children and families in Southern California.

Debbie Treise is a Professor and Associate Dean of Graduate Studies in the College of Journalism and Communications at the University of Florida. She also serves as the graduate coordinator for the Science/Health Communications Track in the college. Trained in mass communications with a specialty in health communication, she has received more than $1.3 million in grants from NASA's Marshall Space Flight Center to study its science communications. Her science communication research appears in *Science Communication* and *Public Understanding of Science.*

Kimberlee J. Trudeau is a Research Scientist at Inflexxion, Inc. in Newton, MA where she designs and tests on-line health interventions. She co-authored this chapter while working at Mount Sinai School of Medicine as Administrator of the Cochrane Behavioral Medicine Field. In that position she applied behavioral science research to the education and professional development of health professionals. She was trained in social psychology specializing in health-related research, especially the promotion of patient empathy as part of nursing education.

Michael Weigold is Professor in the Department of Advertising in the College of Journalism and Communications at the University of Florida. He holds a doctorate in psychology and now conducts research on science and risk communication. He has won several awards for both his teaching and research and is the president of the Association for Marketing and Healthcare Research.